Latin America and Refugee Protection

FORCED MIGRATION

General Editors: Tom Scott-Smith and Kirsten McConnachie

This series, published in association with the Refugees Studies Centre, University of Oxford, reflects the multidisciplinary nature of the field and includes within its scope international law, anthropology, sociology, politics, international relations, geopolitics, social psychology and economics.

Recent volumes:

Volume 41
Latin America and Refugee Protection: Regimes, Logics, and Challenges
Edited by Liliana Lyra Jubilut, Marcia Vera Espinoza and Gabriela Mezzanotti

Volume 40
Un-Settling Middle Eastern Refugees: Regimes of Exclusion and Inclusion in the Middle East, Europe, and North America
Edited by Marcia C. Inhorn and Lucia Volk

Volume 39
Structures of Protection? Rethinking Refugee Shelter
Edited by Tom Scott-Smith and Mark E. Breeze

Volume 38
Refugee Resettlement: Power, Politics, and Humanitarian Governance
Edited by Adèle Garnier, Liliana Lyra Jubilut, and Kristin Bergtora Sandvik

Volume 37
Gender, Violence, Refugees
Edited by Susanne Buckley-Zistel and Ulrike Krause

Volume 36
The Myth of Self-Reliance: Economic Lives Inside a Liberian Refugee Camp
Naohiko Omata

Volume 35
Migration by Boat: Discourses of Trauma, Exclusion and Survival
Lynda Mannik

Volume 34
Making Ubumwe: *Power, State and Camps in Rwanda's Unity-Building Project*
Andrea Purdeková

Volume 33
The Agendas of the Tibetan Refugees: Survival Strategies of a Government-in-Exile in a World of International Organizations
Thomas Kauffmann

Volume 32
The Migration-Displacement Nexus: Patterns, Processes, and Policies
Edited by Khalid Koser and Susan Martin

For a full volume listing, please see the series page on our website:
https//www.berghahnbooks.com/series/forced-migration

Latin America and Refugee Protection

REGIMES, LOGICS, AND CHALLENGES

Edited by
Liliana Lyra Jubilut, Marcia Vera Espinoza
and Gabriela Mezzanotti

berghahn
NEW YORK • OXFORD
www.berghahnbooks.com

First published in 2021 by
Berghahn Books
www.berghahnbooks.com

© 2021 Liliana Lyra Jubilut, Marcia Vera Espinoza and Gabriela Mezzanotti

All rights reserved. Except for the quotation of short passages
for the purposes of criticism and review, no part of this book
may be reproduced in any form or by any means, electronic or
mechanical, including photocopying, recording, or any information
storage and retrieval system now known or to be invented,
without written permission of the publisher.

Library of Congress Cataloging-in-Publication Data

A C.I.P. cataloging record is available from the Library of Congress
Library of Congress Cataloging in Publication Control Number: 2021026261

British Library Cataloguing in Publication Data

A catalogue record for this book is available from the British Library

ISBN 978-1-80073-114-1 hardback
ISBN 978-1-80073-115-8 ebook

To all refugees and other persons in need of protection
in and *from* Latin America

Contents

Illustrations x

Abbreviations xi

Foreword xv
   James C. Hathaway

Introduction. Refugee Protection in Latin America: Logics, Regimes, and Challenges 1
   Liliana Lyra Jubilut, Marcia Vera Espinoza, and Gabriela Mezzanotti

Part I. The Regime of the Cartagena Declaration

1. The 1984 Cartagena Declaration: A Critical Review of Some Aspects of its Emergence and Relevance 31
   José H. Fischel de Andrade

2. The Invisible Majority: Internally Displaced People in Latin America and the San José Declaration 52
   Elizabeth Rushing and Andrés Lizcano Rodriguez

3. The Mixed Legacy of the Mexico Declaration and Plan of Action: Solidarity and Refugee Protection in Latin America 77
   Marcia Vera Espinoza

4. The Brazil Declaration and Plan of Action: A Model for Other Regions 96
   Emily Arnold-Fernández, Karina Sarmiento Torres, and Gabriella Kallas

   Part I Commentary. The Cartagena Declaration Regime of "Refugee" Protection 116
   Susan Kneebone

Part II. The Regime of the Inter-American Human Rights System

5. Against the Current: Protecting Asylum Seekers, Refugees, and Other Persons in Need of International Protection under the Inter-American Human Rights System 125
Álvaro Botero Navarro

6. Refugee Protection and the Inter-American Court of Human Rights 150
Melissa Martins Casagrande

Part II Commentary. The Inter-American Human Rights System and Refugee Protection 169
Deborah E. Anker

Part III. Regional Responses to the International Regime on Refugee Protection

7. From the Brasilia Declaration to the Brazil Plan of Action: How Was the Goal of Eradicating Statelessness in the Americas Forged? 181
Juan Ignacio Mondelli

8. The 100 Points of Brasilia: Latin America's Dialogue with the Global Compact on Refugees 203
Liliana Lyra Jubilut, Gabriela Mezzanotti, and Rachel de Oliveira Lopes

Part III Commentary. Regional Responses to the International Regime on Refugee Protection 228
Jennifer Hyndman

Part IV. Other Forms of Protection Beyond the Regional Refugee Regime

9. The Residence Agreement of MERCOSUR as an Alternative Form of Protection: The Challenges of a Milestone in Regional Migration Governance 237
Leiza Brumat

10. Trends in Latin American Domestic Refugee Law 256
Luisa Feline Freier and Nieves Fernández Rodríguez

11. How Humanitarian Are Humanitarian Visas? An Analysis
 of Theory and Practice in Latin America 276
 Luisa Feline Freier and Marta Luzes

  Part IV Commentary. Other Forms of Protection Beyond
  the Regional Refugee Regime in Latin America 294
  Pablo Ceriani Cernadas

Part V. Current Regional Refugees "Crisis"

12. Responding to Forced Displacement in the North of
 Central America: Progress and Challenges 303
 Suzanna Nelson-Pollard

13. Displacement in Colombia: IDPs, Refugees, and Human Rights
 in the Legal Framework of the 2016 Peace Process 323
 Wellington Pereira Carneiro

14. How the Venezuelan Exodus Challenges a Regional
 Protection Response: "Creative" Solutions to an
 Unprecedented Phenomenon in Colombia and Brazil 346
 *João Carlos Jarochinski Silva, Alexandra Castro Franco,
 and Cyntia Sampaio*

15. No Place for Refugees? The Haitian Flow within
 Latin America and the Challenge of International
 Protection in Disaster Situations 369
 Beatriz Eugenia Sánchez-Mojica

  Part V Commentary. Current Regional Refugees "Crisis" 392
  Leticia Calderón Chelius

Afterword. Driving with the Rearview Mirror? Latin America
 and Refugee Protection 397
 Carolina Moulin

Annex. Legal Frameworks for Refugee Protection in Latin America 403
 Alyssa Marie Kvalvaag

Index 413

Illustrations

Figures

Figure 5.1. Asylum seekers and refugees in OAS States (2008–19), country of origin (created by Álvaro Botero Navarro).   127

Figure 5.2a, b. Asylum seekers and refugees in OAS States (2008–19), country of asylum (created by Álvaro Botero Navarro).   128

Figure 8.1. Structure of the 100 Points of Brasilia (created by Liliana Lyra Jubilut, Gabriela Mezzanotti, and Rachel de Oliveira Lopes).   209

Figure 13.1. Displacement in Colombia 1996–2018 (created by Wellington Carneiro. Data from Victims Unit: www.cifras.uariv.gov.co/home/desplazamiento).   329

Tables

Table 10.1. Migration and Refugee Laws in Latin America (created by Luisa Feline Freier and Nieves Fernández Rodríguez).   258

Table 13.1. Displaced population in Colombia (created by Wellington Carneiro. Data from Victims Unit: http://cifras.unidadvictimas.gov.co/Home/Desplazamiento).   328

Abbreviations

1951 Refugee Convention: 1951 Convention Relating to the Status of Refugees
1954 Convention: 1954 Convention Relating to the Status of Stateless Persons
1961 Convention: 1961 Convention on the Reduction of Statelessness
1967 Protocol: 1967 Protocol Relating to the Status of Refugees
1969 OAU Refugee Convention: 1969 OAU Convention Governing the Specific Aspects of Refugee Problems in Africa
ACHR: American Convention on Human Rights (1969)
ACNUR: Alto Comissariado das Nações Unidas para Refugiados or Alto Comisionado de las Naciones Unidas para los Refugiados (see also UNHCR)
ALBA: Alianza Bolivariana para los Pueblos de Nuestra América (Bolivarian Alliance for the Peoples of Our America)
American Declaration: American Declaration on the Rights and Duties of Man, 1948
ANRLA: Americas Network for Refugees Legal Aid (see also RALRA)
art.: article
BPA: Brazil Declaration and Plan of Action: A Framework for Cooperation and Regional Solidarity to Strengthen the International Protection of Refugees, Displaced and Stateless Persons in Latin America and the Caribbean (2014) (also referred to as Brazil Declaration and Plan of Action)
CAN: Andean Community of Nations
Cartagena Declaration: 1984 Cartagena Declaration on Refugees
CEBAF: Centro Binacional de Atención Fronterizo (Peru) (Frontier Attention Binational Center)
CEDAW: Convention on the Elimination of All Forms of Discrimination against Women
CEU: Council of the European Union
CIJ: Comisión Internacional de Juristas (International Jurists Commission)

CIPPDV: Comisión Interinstitucional para la Protección de Personas Desplazadas por la Violencia (Inter-institutional Commission for the Protection of People Displaced by Violence)
CIREFCA: Conferencia Internacional sobre Refugiados Centroamericanos (International Conference on Central American Refugees)
CJI: Comité Jurídico Interamericano (Inter-American Juridical Committee)
CMC: Consejo Mercado Común (of MERCOSUR) (Common Market Council)
CNIg: Conselho Nacional de Imigração (National Immigration Council) (Brazil)
CNMH: Centro Nacional de Memoria Histórica (Colombia) (National Centre for Historic Memory)
CONARE: Comitê Nacional para Refugiados (National Committee for Refugees)
COVID-19: Coronavirus disease (COVID-19), caused by severe acute respiratory syndrome coronavirus 2 (SARS-CoV-2)
CPDIA: Permanent Consultation on Internal Displacement in the Americas
CRRF: Comprehensive Refugee Response Framework
CSEM: Centro Scalabriano de Estudos Migratórios (Scalabrinian Migration Studies Center)
DP: Defensoria del Pueblo (Colombia) (People's Advocate or Ombudsman Office)
ExCom: UNHCR Executive Committee
FARC: Fuerzas Armadas Revolucionarias de Colombia (Revolutionary Armed Forces of Colombia)
GAR-PAB: Grupo Articulador Regional for the Plan de Acción de Brazil (Regional Working Group of the Brazilian Plan of Action)
GCM: 2018 Global Compact for Safe, Orderly and Regular Migration
GCR: 2018 Global Compact on Refugees
GPC: Global Protection Cluster
Guiding Principles: Guiding Principles on Internal Displacement
HRW: Human Rights Watch
IACmHR: Inter-American Commission on Human Rights
IACtHR: Inter-American Court of Human Rights
IAHRS: Inter-American Human Rights System
IASC: Inter-Agency Standing Committee
ID: identification document
IDMC: Internal Displacement Monitoring Centre
IDPs: internally displaced people or internally displaced persons
IIHL: International Institute of Humanitarian Law
IMF: International Monetary Fund
IOM: International Organization for Migration (see also OIM)

IPPDH: Instituto de Políticas Públicas en Derechos Humanos del MERCOSUR (MERCOSUR Institute of Public Policies on Human Rights)
JIPS: Joint IDP Profiling Service
LGBTI+: lesbian, gay, bisexual, transgender and intersex, plus other sexual and gender orientations and identities
MERCOSUL: Mercado Comum do Sul (Southern Common Market) (see also MERCOSUR)
MERCOSUR: Mercado Común del Sur (Southern Common Market) (see also MERCOSUL)
MIGPROSP: Prospects for International Migration Governance
MIRPS: Marco Integral Regional de Protección y Soluciones (Comprehensive Regional Protection and Solutions Framework)
MPA: 2004 Mexico Declaration and Plan of Action to Strengthen the International Protection of Refugees in Latin America
NCA: North of Central America (El Salvador, Guatemala, and Honduras)
NGO: nongovernmental organization
NRC: Norwegian Refugee Council
NYD: 2016 New York Declaration for Refugees and Migrants
OAS: Organización de los Estados Americanos (Organization of American States) (see also OEA)
OAU: Organization of African Unity
OC: Opinion Consultiva/Opinião Consultiva (Advisory Opinion)
OCHA: Office of Coordination of Humanitarian Affairs
OEA: Organización de los Estados Americanos (Organization of American States) (see also OAS)
OHCHR: United Nations Office of the High Commissioner for Human Rights
OIM: Organização Internacional para as Migrações (International Organization for Migration) (see also IOM)
ONU: Organización de las Naciones Unidas (United Nations) (see also UN)
para.: paragraph
PEP: Permiso Especial de Permanencia (special permit of permanence) (Colombia)
pro persona: in propria persona
PTP: Permiso Temporal de Permanencia (temporary permanence permit) (Peru)
R4V Platform: Plataforma de Coordinación para Refugiados y Migrantes de Venezuela (Coordination Platform for Refugees and Migrants from Venezuela)
RALRA: Red de Apoyo Legal para los Refugiados de las Américas (Americas Network for Refugees Legal Aid) (see also ANRLA)

RAM: Residence Agreement
REDLAC: Risk, Emergency and Disaster Working Group for Latin America and the Caribbean
RSD: refugee status determination
SJD: 1994 San José Declaration on Refugees and Displaced Persons
Superintendencia Nacional: Superintendencia Nacional de Migraciones
UARIV: Unidad para la Atención y Reparación Integral a las Víctimas (victims unit) (Colombia) (The Unit for the Victims Assistance and Reparation)
UN: United Nations (see also ONU)
UNAM: Universidad Nacional Autónoma de México (National Autonomous University of Mexico)
UNASUR: Unión de Naciones Suramericanas (Union of South American Nations)
UNDP: United Nations Development Programme
UNGA: United Nations General Assembly
UNHCR: United Nations High Commissioner for Refugees
UNICEF: United Nations Children's Fund
UNISDR: United Nations International Strategy for Disaster Reduction
UNODC: Oficina de Naciones Unidas contra la Droga y el Delito (United Nations Office on Drugs and Crime)
UNOPS: UN Office for Project Services
UP: Unidad Popular (Colombia) (Popular Unity)
US$: US dollar
WFP: World Food Programme

Foreword

James C. Hathaway

The prognosis for the global refugee protection regime is not good. Wealthy countries are more determined than ever to avoid the arrival of refugees, investing massively in a variety of non-entrée policies to deflect refugees away from their borders. Yet despite the fact that only about 15 percent of the world's refugees reach such states, rich countries spend *four times as much* money to manage and process the refugee claims of the small number of refugees who reach them than to fund the protection of the 85 percent of refugees who remain in the less developed world. Roughly a third of refugees in the global South are still stuck in refugee camps where they can make no contribution to even their own welfare, much less that of the neighboring communities; most refugees able to avoid the hellhole of refugee camps are forced to eke out an existence in equally hellish urban slums. And nearly two-thirds of the world's refugee population are living in protracted refugee situations—waiting on average twenty years for a solution to their plight, with none in sight.

The global response to this dilemma—the much vaunted 2018 Global Compact on Refugees, adopted at the United Nations late that year—avoided even mentioning the deterrent practices of powerful countries. And although it acknowledged in principle the importance of both empowering refugees and engaging in burden and responsibility sharing, it established no obligation to effectuate either of these goals. The Global Compact on Refugees did, however, tip its hand about the future look and feel of refugee protection. It noted, "Past comprehensive responses have ... demonstrated the value of regional cooperation in addressing refugee situations" (GCR: para. 28), and recommended, "Without prejudice to global support, regional and subregional mechanisms or groupings would, as appropriate, actively contribute to resolution of refugee situations in their respective regions, including by playing a key role in Support Platforms, solidarity conferences and other arrangements with the consent of concerned States. Comprehensive responses will also build on existing regional and subregional initiatives for refugee protection and durable solutions where available and appropriate, including regional and subregional resettlement initiatives, to ensure complementarity and avoid duplication" (ibid.: para. 29).

Put simply, the future of refugee protection will in no small measure be predicated on regional—that is, predominantly South-South—cooperation.

The publication of *Latin America and Refugee Protection: Regimes, Logics, and Challenges* by Prof. Jubilut and Drs. Vera Espinoza and Mezzanotti is therefore especially timely. Even as it commemorates the thirty-fifth anniversary of the influential 1984 Cartagena Declaration on Refugees (Cartagena Declaration), the book is fundamentally designed to explain and appraise the protection capacity of the Latin American refugee regime broadly conceived. It wisely pays as much attention to the general human regional human rights system and to migratory and other mechanisms as to the refugee-specific systems in the region, thus neatly positioning us to assess the viability in this part of the world of the regional thrust portended by the Global Compact on Refugees.

In truth, regionalism—at least if properly supported by the broader global community—may stand a better chance of success in Latin America than in other regions of the global South.

To start, the reinvigoration of refugee protection is arguably a less politically marginalized concern there than in many parts of the world, with even the five richest countries in Latin America—Brazil, Mexico, Argentina, Colombia, and Chile—all having both *produced* and *hosted* refugees. There is therefore the basis for a deeper awareness of the importance of making refugee protection work. Latin America also comprises an especially diverse array of national communities, including states well-positioned economically and socially to take on the full range of refugee protection responsibilities—from initial reception, to protection for the duration of risk, to residual resettlement if needed. Equally important, Latin America is home to the global South's most robust regional human rights system, meaning that governments are largely accustomed to taking their cue from nonnational authoritative judicial and other decisions—including in relation to the rights of refugees and other noncitizens.

As the contributions to this volume make clear, however, Latin America also faces some of the same challenges that plague refugee protection in other parts of the world. The region is presently seeing much larger refugee flows than in the recent past, including in particular the exodus of refugees from not only Venezuela, but also the three countries of northern Central America, Colombia, and Haiti. These flows have contributed to the rise of popular xenophobia, leading in some cases to rights-abusive government policies. Compounding the pressure, the United States seems determined to turn Guatemala–and perhaps other states–into its own version of Nauru or Papua New Guinea, forcing refugees into unstable and often fundamentally unsafe conditions in order to avoid its protection responsibilities. The combination of more refugees, decreasing local support for their admission, and no obvious extra-regional exit possibility is cause for concern.

That said, one of the truly valuable attributes of the Latin American refugee regime–thoughtfully explored in detail in this book–is its pragmatic and flexible character. The Cartagena Declaration is merely the foundation for an ongoing norm-setting and implementation process, including a formal reassessment of strategy each decade. The region is committed not only to a broadened understanding of refugee status, but also to complementary pathways for protection and to important general systems to facilitate cross-border movement, especially as pioneered under the Mercado Común del Sur (MERCOSUR; Southern Common Market). Taken in tandem with the strength of the regional human rights regime, there is every reason to see Latin America as having the resilience and institutional capacity needed to cope with refugee movements.

If the future of the refugee protection world is regional–and there is every reason to believe that it will be–then we all owe a huge debt to the contributors to *Latin America and Refugee Protection*. The breadth and thoughtfulness of the analysis presented here position readers not only to understand the realities in one important region, but also and more generally to grapple with the opportunities and challenges of the brave new world in which refugee protection as a global enterprise–while normatively tethered and loosely coordinated–is likely to depend mainly on regional initiatives and institutions.

01 December 2019

James C. Hathaway is the James E. and Sarah A. Degan Professor of Law and Director of the Program in Refugee and Asylum Law at the University of Michigan. He is also Distinguished Visiting Professor of International Refugee Law at the University of Amsterdam. Hathaway's publications include more than one hundred journal articles, book chapters, and studies including *The Law of Refugee Status*, 2nd edition (2014 with M. Foster); *Reconceiving International Refugee Law* (1997); and *The Rights of Refugees under International Law* (2021). He is the founding editor of Cambridge Asylum and Migration Studies.

References

Cartagena Declaration on Refugees. 1984. https://www.oas.org/dil/1984_cartagena_declaration_on_refugees.pdf.
Global Compact on Refugees. 2018. https://www.unhcr.org/gcr/GCR_English.pdf.

INTRODUCTION

Refugee Protection in Latin America

Logics, Regimes, and Challenges

Liliana Lyra Jubilut, Marcia Vera Espinoza, and Gabriela Mezzanotti

Introduction

Refugee protection in Latin America is distinctive, with unique characteristics that range from contextual to conceptual aspects. Contextually, the region has hosted as well as produced refugees, a trend that has generated almost even numbers of refugees from and within the region in the past (Jubilut and Lopes 2018) with a current increase of intraregional refugees (United Nations High Commissioner for Refugees [UNHCR] 2019a: 68, 74). Moreover, Latin America comprises countries of origin, destination, and transit[1] (Jubilut and Lopes 2018). On the conceptual aspects, the region's recognized long-standing commitment to refugee protection has been developed over the past two hundred years (Fischel de Andrade 2014); from the institutionalization of exile since the processes of independence in South America (ibid) and the adoption of the right of asylum in the American Convention on Human Rights in 1969, until the more recent creation of praised mechanisms of responsibility sharing, solidarity, and cooperation (Grandi 2017).

Latin America is also unique due to the coexistence of different protection regimes and systems (Jubilut and Lopes 2018), from the international, regional and national levels. These include (i) the universal regime that stems from the 1951 Convention Relating to the Status of Refugees (1951 Refugee Convention),[2] its 1967 Protocol Relating to the Status of Refugees (1967 Protocol)[3] and the 2018 Global Compact on Refugees,[4] (ii) the dialogue among International Human Rights Law, International Refugee Law and International Humanitarian Law; (iii) the coexistence of political asylum and refuge; (iv) the 1984 Cartagena Declaration on Refugees (Cartagena Declaration)[5] and the regime derived from its review process; (v) the Inter-American Human Rights system within the Organization of American States; and (vi) national legislation either specific to refugees or generally focusing on migrants including refugees; or even complementary protection measures that, albeit targeted to persons outside the protection of International Refugee Law, can, in practice, benefit refugees.

Latin America, thus, presents a complex, and still little known, scenario of refugee protection, that has both positive aspects and shortcomings. The norms and practices that emerged from this multilevel architecture have increased the spaces of refugee protection and have generated some examples of good practices in terms of ascertaining protection and/or implementing access to rights, as well as adopting innovative actions toward refugees and other migrants. However, many challenges remain in terms of implementation and integral protection (meaning the combination of the rights of refugees that steam from this condition and the human rights they are entitled to as human beings; Jubilut and Apolinário 2008; Vera Espinoza 2018a). These are more exposed nowadays given the region is witnessing the massive displacement of Venezuelans, one of the fastest-escalating (Freier and Parent 2018) and largest refugee flows, with close to 5.2 million Venezuelans living abroad as of June 2020, 80 percent of whom are in the region or the Caribbean (Response for Venezuelans [R4V] 2020a). In addition, there is the ongoing displacement of thousands of people from the North of Central America (NCA; comprising El Salvador, Guatemala, and Honduras) (UNHCR 2019b); which has Latin American countries as origin, destination or transit—as some aim to enter the United States. There is also the displacement of Colombians even after the 2016 peace agreement (Casey 2019), of Nicaraguans from April 2018 onward, and of Haitians since the 2010 earthquake, among other groups of both intra- and extraregional refugees. At the same time, the numbers of internally displaced people (IDPs) in the region continue to increase (Internal Displacement Monitoring Centre [IDMC] 2020).

The patterns of displacement have been further shaped by the impacts of COVID-19 in Latin America. Alongside the exacerbated vulnerabilities of displaced populations as a result of the sanitary crisis (Bengochea et al. 2021) and its negative impacts in their process of integration (Jubilut and Jarochinski Silva 2020), there is also emerging migration patterns, such as return and forced immobility, as a result of the unprecedented context of border closures[6] and pandemic mitigation measures (Vera Espinoza, Zapata, and Gandini 2020). All of this context of increased mobility coexists with the difficulties and/or unwillingness of governments to adequately protect refugees (and other migrants), when they are either destination or transit countries.

Despite the enhanced academic, media, and policy interest that these current scenarios have attracted, there is still a scattered understanding of some of the key legal documents, actors, and structures that conform refugee protection in Latin America. A comprehensive approach, able to connect and problematize the different aspects that establish the architecture of refugee protection in the region, is also lacking. This book aims to be a tool in filling this gap. Adopting an interdisciplinary approach, it explores the main regimes and documents of refugee protection (or those that can benefit refugees) in the region and reviews their emergence, development, and effects.

This contribution is particularly timely in light of the Global Compact on Refugees and its strong emphasis on regions,[7] as well as in relation to global debates on fairness in responsibility sharing and cooperation to deal with some of the largest refugee displacements since World War II (Cantor 2019; UNHCR 2019c).

Thus, aiming to contribute to an increased comprehension of the region in terms of refugee protection, as well as to present suggestions on how to improve it, this book orbits around three aspects that together allow for the comprehensive understanding of Latin America's architecture of refugee protection: logics, regimes, and challenges.

About Refugee Protection in Latin America

Logics of Refugee Protection in the Region

The Creation of the "Latin America" Concept

To understand the architecture of refugee protection in Latin America it is relevant to reflect on some of the historic and circumstantial aspects of the region. At least two factors could be raised in that respect: (1) the foundation of the concept of "Latin America" and its development throughout historical circumstances in the second half of the nineteenth century (Mignolo 2005); and (2) the current context of the region vis-à-vis its historic path and going forward. Such notions allow one to better understand the reasons why refugee protection and integration in Latin America are so distinctive.

The forging of the concept "Latin America" can be traced to two main assumptions. The first is the arrival of white Latin Europeans to the region and the construction of a white elite in Latin America (Quijano 2015; Mignolo

2005), even though there is predominance of persons of Indigenous, African, and multiracial descent in the region (Wade 2010; Morrison 2007). That elite has been leading Latin American democracies by "granting" rights to non-whites while at the same time keeping the formal structures of power in their own hands (Acosta 2018; Gobat 2013). A tension between inclusion and exclusion based on race, thus, marked the foundations of Latin America since colonization and may still root current challenges to human rights in general, and refugee protection and integration in particular, in the region (Mignolo 2005).

The second major historical factor around the forging of the Latin America concept is its political drive: toward the second half of the nineteenth century Latin American countries united around the idea of resisting a North American expansionist endeavor toward southern countries in the Americas (Gobat 2013). A white imperialist mind-set prevailed in the leading of this regional initiative, but with an anti-imperialist political purpose against the United States (ibid.). Whereas local struggles for democracy also took place in some countries in Latin America at the time, a treaty designed by Chile, Peru, and Ecuador in 1856 called for an anti–United States alliance for the purpose of preparing to resist any United States–led expansion (ibid.). This coming together of countries can be seen as a constitutional moment for the notion of "Latin America" as representative of a regional sentiment.

This idea of "Latin America" appears to be a consequence of several common grounds that come from centuries and for different purposes, such as colonial backgrounds (related to metropolis with Latin background, i.e. Portugal, Spain, and France), shared cultural traces, geographical location, and/or developing nations status. It also allows for the continental countries of Mexico, Central America, and South America[8] to be referred to as a unity, in the concept of "Latin America". Even though different manners of grouping these States exist, for the purposes of this book Latin America is understood (unless otherwise expressly mentioned) as comprising Argentina, Bolivia, Brazil, Chile, Colombia, Costa Rica, Ecuador, El Salvador, French Guyana,[9] Guatemala, Guyana, Honduras, Mexico, Nicaragua, Panama, Paraguay, Peru, Suriname,[10] Uruguay, and Venezuela.[11]

This unity does not mean homogeneity, given that there are particularities among and within States in the region. However, it is useful to think in terms of refugee protection, both regarding impacts of the States' past that have effects in today's policies and in relation to mutually adopted actions, mainly due to this concept of being part of a collectivity titled "Latin America".

Latin America as a scenario of refugee protection today reflects the region's contrasts, with several different nationalist approaches and initiatives, shaped by ancient racial and social hierarchies that lead to discrimination and unequal distribution of wealth and political power, but also with common grounds in the issue, as well as collective actions being undertaken, that together constitute examples of regional Refugee Law.

Regional Refugee Protection

Regional Refugee Law is relevant to refugees' protection considering it can lead to the expansion of the international framework by being "a *locus* for new norm-creation" (Jubilut and Lopes 2017: 36), as well as by producing specific and tailored responses to more-localized circumstances (Jubilut and Ramos 2014).

Regional law can be said to fall under what is conceptualized as *regionalism*, meaning most formal structures and processes of regional cooperation, including laws promulgated and enforced by established regional bodies (Ramji-Nogales 2019), with clear legal standards and enforcement mechanisms. However, a dual analysis is necessary to capture the "more complex notion" of regionalism associated to refugee protection (Kneebone and Rawlings-Sanaei 2007: 3), by considering the role of different actors and historical processes, and even recognizing that there are limits to what "can be achieved by regional approaches alone" (ibid. 3; Jubilut and Ramos 2014). In this sense, it is necessary to comprehend alongside regionalism the idea of *regionalization*, meaning the more informal processes of exchange, a de facto and manifold process (Grugel and Hout 1999: 10), to understand comprehensively regional approaches to refugee protection (Geddes et al. 2019).

These regional approaches have been identified as a strategic tool to deal with the "increasing scope, scale and complexity of population movements" (Jubilut and Ramos 2014: 66), that many times are not effectively covered by the international legislation or by individual States. At the same time, the greater cohesion of interest and values that countries of the region tend to share would facilitate cooperation and encourage greater regional responsibility sharing (Barichello 2016; Jubilut and Lopes 2017; Schuck 1997). It is relevant, then, to better delineate the concept of region.

Despite cultural similarities, there are no natural regions (Geddes et al. 2019: 5). Instead, "regions are made and re-made" (Grugel and Hout 1999: 9) as they are decided and formed through political negotiation and the interests of different actors. Regions in this context are mostly understood as geographically proximate political constructs made of interrelated units with shared aims of social, political, economic, or organizational cohesiveness (Cantori and Spiegel 1970). Regions "sit between the global and the national" (Geddes et al. 2019: 5), which explains their multilevel reach and scope, as well as the diverse range of actors involved in their processes, including states, regional organizations, international organizations, and civil society, among others. This multileveling of characteristics and associated interdependencies aids in comprehending the multidimensional complexities of Latin America's approach to refugee protection.

First, it is essential to point out the coexistence of regimes for the protection of refugees in Latin America, which occur in the regional-international level, regional-regional level, regional-national level, and national-international level, as will be explored below. This interaction also happens among Refugee Law and other branches of Law, such as International Human Rights and International Humanitarian Law, and within Refugee Law itself. This complexity is relevant given that, as explored in this volume, regional initiatives need to be underpinned by a strong set of norms on refugee protection as well as States' commitments, and these several interactions might contribute to that.

Second, in the region there are more institutionalized approaches and other more informal arrangements that can also influence and shape refugee protection in practice. While this book focuses on more-formal patterns of cooperation, the analyses of many of them also touches on the role of informal processes and of non-state actors. This multilevel analysis is timely since said components gain relevance in a scenario of competing logics in refugee protection such as the one that currently exists in Latin America.

Current Logics at Play in Refugee Protection in Latin America

Latin America has a long tradition in ascertaining the right of asylum (Alto Comisionado de las Naciones Unidas para los Refugiados [ACNUR] n.d.; Fischel de Andrade 2014), which is implemented through either political asylum or refugee status,[12] two forms of protection that coexist in the region. Political asylum has a more discretionary basis, given that it leaves to States the decision of its granting, as well as a more limited scope, as it pertains only to protection in the face of actual political persecution. Refuge, on the other hand, is vested with the nature of a right, and can be implemented only when the normative criteria is met (Jubilut and Lopes 2018, 2019). Moreover, it applies to cases when, "as a result of events occurring before 1 January 1951 and owing to well-founded fear of being persecuted for reasons of race, religion, nationality, membership of a particular social group or political opinion, is outside the country of his nationality and is unable or, owing to such fear, is unwilling to avail himself of the protection of that country ; or who, not having a nationality and being outside the country of his former habitual residence as a result of such events, is unable or, owing to such fear, is unwilling to return to it" (1951 Refugee Convention, Article 1, A, 2).

In the case of Latin America, not only political asylum and refuge coexist, but the latter has also more breadth. This is so given that, in 1984 countries of the region gathered at the Colloquium on the International

Protection of Refugees in Latin America, Mexico and Panama, and adopted the Cartagena Declaration.[13] This nonbinding legal document established other criteria for refugee status determination (RSD) in the region, determining that "the definition or concept of a refugee to be recommended for use in the region is one which, in addition to containing the elements of the 1951 Convention and the 1967 Protocol, includes among refugees persons who have fled their country because their lives, safety or freedom have been threatened by generalized violence, foreign aggression, internal conflicts, massive violation of human rights or other circumstances which have seriously disturbed public order" (Cartagena Declaration on Refugees 1984: 3rd conclusion). In this sense the regional refugee status definition added to the international criteria (that requires individualized well-founded fear of persecution), the possibility of recognition by focusing on the objective situation of the country of origin (Jubilut and Carneiro 2011: 67; Reed-Hurtado 2013, Jubilut 2018), thus expanding the scope of protection.

The Cartagena Declaration, despite its soft law nature, not only enlarged the refugee definition to be applied in Latin America,[14] but also became the cornerstone of the current, and complex, architecture of refugee protection in the region (Jubilut 2018). This is so given that it set up a revisional process with meetings taking place every ten years in order to assess the region's challenges and needs in terms of refugee protection. The resulting products of these meetings have been the 1994 San José Declaration on Refugees and Displaced Persons (SJD),[15] the 2004 Mexico Declaration and Plan of Action to Strengthen the International Protection of Refugees in Latin America (MPA)[16] and the 2014 Brazil Declaration and Plan of Action: a Framework for Cooperation and Regional Solidarity to Strengthen the International Protection of Refugees, Displaced and Stateless Persons in Latin America and the Caribbean (Brazil Declaration and Plan of Action).[17]

The Cartagena Declaration and its revisional process have developed Latin America's tradition toward implementing the right of asylum (Jubilut and Lopes 2018) and have aided the region in adopting a common grammar of refugee protection, one that focuses on solidarity and responsibility sharing (Jubilut, Vera Espinoza, and Mezzanotti 2019).

Mainly due to this, Latin America has been long considered an example of South-South cooperation and solidarity (Harley 2014). Academics and practitioners alike have praised the latter as one of the key characteristics of the Latin American approach to refugee protection (Lavanchy 2006; Maldonado Castillo 2015). In this context, the principle of solidarity has been linked to the "generosity that can be found in the Latin American tradition of asylum" (Barichello 2016: 196) and to the conceptual shift from burden to responsibility sharing in refugee protection (Jubilut and Carneiro 2011). Solidarity, linked to the perception of shared problems and solutions in dealing with refugees' plight, has contributed to norm development in the region

(Cantor and Barichello 2013; Harley 2014). As some authors have pointed out, however, the idea of solidarity is not totally unselfish (Vera Espinoza 2018a), and has facilitated the establishment of the branding of generosity aimed to appeal to States and international donors alike (Kneebone 2016). This dual understanding of solidarity is relevant given that it allows for the exploration of both the utopian ambitions of the region and the limitations of its implementation (Menezes 2016).

Moreover, if, on the one hand, solidarity can be said to be a guiding principle of refugee protection in Latin America, the acknowledgment of its limitations also sheds light on other logics currently at play in the region. First, Latin America has not been exempted from global trends and is experiencing an increase of anti-immigrant sentiment alongside increases in xenophobia and discrimination[18] (Brumat, Acosta, and Vera Espinoza 2018; Jubilut, Vera Espinoza, and Mezzanotti 2019).

Second, interests other than refugee protection seem to be influencing current policies and directly impacting the issue. For instance, the region has not showcased homogeneous behavior but rather a plethora of different approaches within a spectrum that goes from countries accepting to be safe third countries (e.g., Honduras[19]) or being both a safe third country and an offshoring processing center (e.g., Guatemala[20]), to others being pressured but not accepting to being safe third countries albeit changing their national practices (e.g., Mexico[21]); refusing to do so (e.g., Panama[22]), or even having said agreements declared unconstitutional (e.g., Canada in relation to the United States in terms of NCA refugees and other migrants).[23] A scenario of competing logics is, thus, at play in Latin America, and it is important to highlight it so as to prevent refugee protection from being jeopardized.

Third, nationalistic and populist governments that do not positively value migration and have adopted, if not practices, at least a rhetoric against migrants in general[24] (which can directly impact refugee protection) are in power in the region.[25] This has generated a general politicization of migration that has influenced debates and policies around migration and displacement (Brumat, Acosta, and Vera Espinoza 2018; Jubilut, Vera Espinoza, and Mezzanotti 2019)

However, and on the other hand, there are still positive examples in the region, such as the resettling of persons from the NCA to Uruguay[26] and to Brazil[27] as well as national practices of interiorization (i.e., national relocations)[28] in light of large flows of refugees, which are being justified as tools for migration management and for better chances of integration (see Jarochinski Silva, Castro, and Sampaio in this volume).

A fourth aspect in terms of logics at play in the region is the notion, linked to the principle of solidarity, of creative regional responses to deal with refugee protection, particularly in relation to complementary pathways for protection (Jubilut 2017a), such as with humanitarian visas (as in the cases of Brazil (see, e.g., Jubilut, de Andrade, and Madureira 2016) Chile,[29] Peru[30] Argentina[31] and Mexico[32]) (see Freier and Luzes; and Sánchez-Mojica in this volume), and regional instruments deriving from the Mercado Común del Sur (MERCOSUR; Southern Common Market) (see Brumat in this volume). The case of the Venezuelan flow showcases the application of distinct and uneven measures by the countries of the region in terms of protection of refugees (and other migrants) (Freier and Fernández; Jarochinski Silva, Castro, and Sampaio; and the Annex in this volume; Jubilut and Fernandes 2018). At the same time, the ongoing number of arrivals has raised political tensions in some countries, frustration over scarce resources, and fears of xenophobia, all of which demand greater support and involvement of the international community (Betts 2019a), which has been slow to respond (Betts 2019b).

These Latin American responses and their effects need to be analyzed in the long term and in comparison to the reception of other refugee groups as well as to Refugee Law, which, in the regional context, takes the form of several regimes.

Regimes of Refugee Protection in Latin America

The concept of regimes designating "intervening variables standing between basic characteristics of world politics such as power, capabilities, and state behaviours" (Yoshimatsu 1998: 6) was introduced in 1975 by John Ruggie (ibid.: 5). Regimes are also understood as the different sets of rules norms and principles, and decision-making processes (Krasner 1982) and "can facilitate informal contact and communication among officials, and permit governments to attain objectives that would otherwise be difficult or impossible" (Yoshimatsu 1998: 7), and, in this sense be a "causal or constitutive variable that may be useful in explaining cooperation" (Haggard and Simmons 1987: 495), given that they are "*examples* of cooperative behavior, and *facilitate* cooperation" (ibid.: 495; emphasis in the original).

Given that regimes can be understood as "multilateral agreements among states which aim to regulate national actions within an issue area" (ibid.: 495), they can be international or regional, or even subregional, in nature; and multiple regimes can coexist in the same issue area.

This coexistence has become increasingly complex over time. It is generally accepted that the aftermath of World War II generated a common global space of interactions at the global level (Betts 2013), with several institutions mandated to act with clear scopes and little overlapping (ibid.). Further developments in the international arena led to the rising of new institutions and the permanent oscillation in the scope and purpose of existing ones (Betts 2013; Blokker and Schermers 2000). Overlaps in scope and purpose have become more and more frequent and have generated the need for a methodological approach that literature convened to name as "regime complexity" (Betts 2013: 69).

Regime complexity derives from the plurality of institutions with overlapping scopes and purposes, which results in some of these institutions becoming challenged and others becoming reinforced (Henning 2019). Such a scenario defines regime complexity "as a set of international institutions that operate in a common issue area and the (formal and informal) mechanisms that coordinate them" (ibid.: 26). These institutions can be constituted as organizations at the bilateral, plurilateral, regional, or global levels, as well as less formal arrangements that operate in common areas with coordinating mechanisms. Whereas regime complexity has been criticized for undermining international cooperation and leading to the inconsistency of rules and obligations, it has been advocated for allowing decentralization, flexibility, and adaptability (ibid.).

Regime complexity in refugee protection is anchored, from a normative perspective, in the 1951 Convention and its 1967 Protocol. Institutionally, its traditional foundation is the UNHCR[33] (Betts 2013, 2015), created in 1950.[34] The regime complexity is based on the assumption that, with time, refugee protection has started to coexist with several areas and international organizations that have implications to refugee protection, such as humanitarianism, human rights, migration, peacebuilding, and so on (Betts 2013). Some of these areas overlap with refugee protection regime in scope, others in purpose, while still others are complementary (ibid.). The latest example of this overlap is the coexistence of the UNHCR and the International Organization for Migration (IOM) within the UN system, even before the IOM joined the UN as a related organization in 2016[35] The IOM has a broad mandate based on "an extensive definition of 'migrants'" (Pécoud 2018: 1625), therefore including refugees considering that they are forced migrants (Jubilut and Casagrande 2019). Although the IOM and the UNHCR have had a complex relationship, they have cooperated on several occasions (Pécoud 2018). What the inclusion of the IOM into the UN system means for refugee protection in terms of budgeting, resource allocation, and norm setting has yet to be seen, but it already reinforces the regime complexity in refugee governance.

This amalgam of different sets of regimes, rules, and institutions that complement each other, sometimes overlapping, and shape States' responses in terms of refugee protection is the refugee regime complexity in its initial form. It is, however, possible to expand this theoretical scheme to even better understand the complexity of the current refugee regime, especially in Latin America. Whereas refugee regime complexity deals with the complementary and overlap of Refugee Law with other branches of Law and/or other issues, it is also relevant to bear in mind that within Refugee Law there are several regimes at play simultaneously.

Within Refugee Law there is the coexistence of (i) international-regional regimes, which have as its most developed examples the African Refugee Regime[36] and the protection of refugees in Latin America; (ii) international-national regimes; (iii) regional-national regimes, which would allow for the comprehension of the implementation of Refugee Law in the national level; and also (iv) regional-regional regimes. All of these are essential to understanding refugee protection in Latin America.

This book assumes that several regimes of refugee protection are at play in Latin America: (1) the Regime of the Cartagena Declaration: the Cartagena Declaration and its revision process (see chapters by Fischel de Andrade, Rushing, and Lizcano Rodriguez; Vera Espinoza; and Arnold-Fernández, Sarmiento Torres, and Kallas in this volume); (2) the Regime of the Inter-American Human Rights System: deriving from Inter-American Commission on Human Rights' (IACmHR) decisions and documents and the rulings of the Inter-American Court of Human Rights (IACtHR) (see Botero; Casagrande in this volume); (3) the regional dialogues with the international regime on refugee protection and other pertinent international documents (see Mondelli; Jubilut, Mezzanotti and Lopes in this volume); and (4) national responses and legislation rooted in the region's tradition toward displacement (see Brumat in this volume; Freier and Fernández in this volume). There is, thus, a coexistence within a regime complexity that challenges consistency, but delivers flexibility and adaptability in the protection of refugees (and other migrants).

In order to review this complexity in a comprehensive way, this book often uses the term "architecture," aiming to explore the overall framework where those different regimes coexist. This complex architecture of refugee protection in Latin America has expanded spaces of protection and produced relevant examples of good practice, and, at the same time, has seen the increase of actors, processes, and interests that have resulted in some implementation challenges. The overall regional architecture has been successful (Acosta and Oehler 2019), but it is not immune to political change, lack of willingness by States to follow commitments and or traditions, and competition for limited resources, leaving several challenges to be faced.

Challenges of Refugee Protection in Latin America

Four key current set of challenges can be explored in an assessment of some of the contradictions in the region, as well as in identifying areas to consider when outlining suggestions for improvement: (1) contextual challenges stemming from the current "crisis" of displacement, (2) traditional protection challenges, (3) political challenges, and (4) challenges in terms of integral protection.

1. Contextual Challenges Stemming from the Current "Crisis" of Displacement

Of the world's 79.5 million displaced persons due to conflict, persecution violence, or human rights violations (UNHCR 2020: 2), at the end of 2019 Latin America hosted 14,138,901 persons of concern according to the UNHCR (ibid.: 76), and was experiencing relevant intraregional displacement flows that demand actions to ascertain protection.

The largest of these flows—in fact the largest in the history of Latin America—is the displacement from Venezuela (UNHCR 2019c) (see Jarochinski Silva, Castro, and Sampaio in this volume). With officially 5,563,687 Venezuelans displaced by 5 March 2021 (R4V 2020a) and an estimated more than 6.5 million displaced by the end of 2020[37] Latin American countries have taken in an estimate of 80 percent of those displaced (ibid.). This displacement has been met both by ad hoc national (Jubilut and Fernandes 2018; Acosta, Blouin, and Freier 2019) and regional initiatives, with the adoption, in November 2019, of the Regional Response for Refugees and Migrants from Venezuela for 2020[38] encompassing both protection and integration concerns.

A second flow to be mentioned is the displacement from the NCA (El Salvador, Guatemala, and Honduras) (see Nelson-Pollard in this volume) resulting from those fleeing from gang-related and gender-based violence (Anker and Palmer 2014; Cantor 2014; Ziff 2019), and mainly heading toward the United States through Mexico (Vera Espinoza 2019). This displacement has been described as "soaring" (UNHCR n.d.) and has reached 470,000 in 2020 (Ibid), a total that included relevant numbers of unaccompanied or separated children (Jones and Podkul 2012; Musalo, Frydman, and Ceriani Cernadas 2015).[39]

The same subregion has started to experience a new displacement flow from Nicaragua due to a crisis that began in April 2018 following protests against a social security reform (MigraMundo 2019), and that escalated to severe violations of human rights (UNHCR 2019d). Even though this movement is too recent for analysis, it is estimated that more than 102,000 have already fled internationally, with Costa Rica being the main destination country (UNHCR n.d.). This displacement flow has started to be assessed together with the mentioned NCA displacement under the Comprehensive Regional Protection and Solutions Framework (MIRPS, from the acronym in Spanish for *Marco Integral Regional de Protección y Soluciones*), adopted in 2017 as a framework for shared responsibility.[40] Alongside this increased regional mobility, new displacements resulting from the social and political strifes of 2019 might also occur in the region (including internal displacement), for instance in Bolivia (IDMC 2020: 58), and migrants deciding to move to other countries as a result of political instability and rising xenophobia, for instance in Chile (Noticias ONU 2019) and Ecuador (R4V 2020b: 115), whereas new mobility flows have started to occur as a result of the COVID-19 pandemic (Vera Espinoza, Zapata, and Gandini 2020).

Apart from these more recent flows, Latin America also experiences the continuation of older displacements, as in the cases of Cubans[41] but more especially in the voluminous cases of Colombians (see Carneiro in this volume) and Haitians (see Sánchez-Mojica in this volume). Regarding the former, estimates state that during the sixty-year-old conflict more than 7 million persons were displaced (Miroff 2016). Although the 2016 Peace Agreement brought hopes of changing this scenario, the reality is that forced displacement has continued (Casey 2019; see Carneiro in this volume). In relation to the latter, and even though it can be argued that Haitians would better fit the description of environmentally displaced persons (see Sánchez-Mojica in this volume), it is relevant to point out their displacement in a refugee-related book in Latin America, given that, even if Haiti is considered to be outside Latin America and instead part of the Caribbean, Haitians' displacement has turned into a large and continuous migratory flow in the region and gave rise to several humanitarian initiatives of protection based on the refugee regimes, as well as due to the fact that they could be recognized as refugees themselves under the Cartagena Declaration (Jubilut, Madureira, and Levy 2018).

Latin America also receives extra-regional refugees and other migrants, with continued flows from Africa (Yates 2019), new displacements from Asia (ibid.), and the arrival of smaller groups of refugees from Syria (Rodríguez Camejo 2017). In the case of the first two groups, the numbers are said to be growing; most migration is through regular pathways and Latin America can be both a destination and a transit region (Yates 2019).

Some of these patterns of displacement are not new and have already shaped the architecture of refugee protection in the region (see Fischel de Andrade and Vera Espinoza in this volume). Previous displacement crises such as the 1980s refugee situation in Central America prompted the emergence of the Cartagena Declaration, whereas the displacement of Colombians as a result of the internal conflict was the background of the Mexico Plan of Action and Declaration. In this sense, it is relevant to note how practical challenges shape Latin America's refugee protection, as well as to analyze the current challenges in this area to explore whether the region will continue with this tradition.

2. Traditional Protection Challenges

A second setting of challenges being witnessed in Latin America regarding refugee protection relates to traditional protection aspects, which have a more normative nature. In this regard, the challenges do not pertain to lack of legal structures (given that all States in the region, apart from Guyana, are party to the 1951 Refugee Convention and/or its 1967 Protocol, and have developed regional regimes of protection), but rather violation of existing norms.

These violations can occur in relation to (i) safe access to territories, which can lead to rights violations and/or fatalities;[42] (ii) access to safe territories, linked to the cornerstone *non-refoulement* principle of Refugee Law, (iii) access to RSD procedures, (iv) adequate RSD procedures, (v) as well access to rights during RSD procedures, such as the right to not to be subject to torture or detention and family protection; and (vi) respect of rights peculiar to specific groups, such as women, children, the elderly, persons with disabilities, and LGBTI+ (lesbian, gay, bisexual, transgender, and intersex, plus other sexual and gender orientations and identities) refugees (Jubilut 2017b). These violations can occur directly or be camouflaged and therefore be more difficult to be perceived, as for instance, although a ban on *non-refoulement* has not been implemented, the imposition of limits or requirements for entry (such as valid passports) might render protection impossible.[43] Another example is the creation of complementary protection alternatives, not to increase the humanitarian space of protection by benefiting forced migrants other than refugees but as a way to minimize protection under Refugee Law. In light of the COVID-19 pandemic, all of these challenges seem to be reinforced, both in Latin America (Vera Espinoza, Zapata, and Gandini 2020; Bengochea et al. 2021) and globally (Jubilut 2020).

In terms of the current scenario in Latin America, which is different from scenarios in other regions, these traditional protection violations seem to be more on specific rather than systemic bases, but nonetheless impose challenges for protection.

3. Political Challenges

Alongside the challenges imposed by current displacement flows and violations to rights pertaining to traditional refugee protection, there are political challenges in the protection of refugees in Latin America.

Some of these challenges have already been mentioned, but it is relevant to recap, particularly with relation to (i) the lack of political will toward improving access and conditions for refugees and other migrants, (ii) the rise of populist governments, (iii) the rise of anti-immigrant sentiments and the adoption of anti-immigrants rhetoric, (iv) the rise of xenophobia and racism, (v) the politicization of migration, and (vi) the externalization of asylum (Brumat 2019; Vera Espinoza 2019; Jubilut 2017b; Jubilut, Vera Espinoza, and Mezzanotti 2019). All of these contribute to the creation of an environment that may put the regional architecture of protection in jeopardy, and create a contrasting scenario with Latin America's traditions of refugee protection.

Moreover, political choices might impact access to rights, such as the use of detention as a deterrent against migration. Such use of detention has been impacted by COVID-19, and has led the IACtHR to render a resolution granting provisional measures to guarantee rights for detained migrants during the pandemic.[44] This also relates to integral protection.

4. Challenges in Terms of Integral Protection

The last set of challenges to be explored relate to the ascertaining of refugees' human rights. These rights should be respected alongside the rights deriving from their status as refugees, such as the above-noted integral protection, which are particularly relevant in a developing region.

Even if, and maybe due to the fact that, as noted, the challenges in traditional protection topics in Latin America do not seem to be systemic, there is scope to move beyond them and to foster integral protection as a core principle of the regional approach. Although safe access and adequate procedures for status determination are key for refugees' protection in the region, less emphasis has been placed on the need to enhance access to rights (especially economic, social, and cultural rights) and services. Integral protection results in protection that guarantees both access to the country and to RSD, as well as a holistic approach to integration (Jarochinski Silva and Jubilut 2018; Jubilut and Apolinário 2018; Vera Espinoza 2018a, 2018b).

The four challenges outlined here, together with the refugee regime complexity in Latin America and the current contrasting logics that underpin the refugee architecture in the region discussed above, demonstrate the importance of understanding the logics, regimes, and challenges in refugee protection in Latin America as a way to facing the current scenario in seeking integral protection for refugees in the region. This book contributes toward this goal.

About the Book

The book analyzes the frameworks, current state, and challenges of refugee protection in Latin America. Adopting an interdisciplinary approach, the book unpacks the main documents and processes that compose the refugee protection regimes in the region, as well as national practices stemming from the dialogues with the international and regional regimes, together with other forms of (complementary) protection that can benefit refugees, reviewing their emergence, development, and effects. While the book is comprehensive in scope, and explores a large number of key documents and processes, it is regional in its focus.

It aims to bring attention to, and information on, this insufficiently well-known region and its practices in refugee protection. The characteristics of refugee protection in Latin America need to be divulged not only as a way of thinking about better practices and solutions within the region *in se*, but also as a way to compare with other regions regarding good (and also inadequate) practices.

Overview of the Book

The book gathers a diverse group of leading scholars and practitioners from Latin America, with authors from/or established in Argentina, Brazil, Chile, Colombia, Costa Rica, Ecuador, Panama, and Peru, and commentators from within the region (Argentina and Mexico) and outside it (Australia, Canada, and the United States). Some of those authors from Latin America are established elsewhere such as in Spain, Norway, Switzerland, and the United Kingdom. Authors of the foreword (Hathaway) and conclusion (Moulin) are respectively American-Canadian and Brazilian, and the annex was researched and written by an American author based in Norway.

The book draws from a diverse range of theoretical and methodological approaches, both from academics and from practitioners. These different perspectives contribute to an interdisciplinary analysis, description, and assessment of regional approaches to refugee protection and the complex architecture of laws, policies, actors, and policies that make up the refugee regimes in Latin America.

Presentation of Chapters

The book has seventeen chapters (including this introduction and the afterword). Most chapters have a normative base, but the analyses are interdisciplinary, considering that each of them also addresses geopolitical, social, and economic impacts, and aims to describe the existing scenarios and to present assessments seeking the betterment of the regional regimes and of refugees' integral protection.

The book is divided into five parts:

Part I. The Regime of the Cartagena Declaration: encompassing chapters on the Cartagena Declaration (Fischel de Andrade), San José Declaration on Refugees and Displaced Persons (Rushing and Lizcano Rodriguez), Mexico Declaration and Plan of Action (Vera Espinoza) and the Brazil Declaration and Plan of Action (Arnold-Fernández, Sarmiento Torres, and Kallas);

Part II. The Regime of the Inter-American Human Rights System: with a chapter focusing on the main aspects of the system as well as on the IACmHR (Botero) and the other on assessing the rulings of the IACtHR (Casagrande);

Part III. Regional responses to the international regime on refugee protection: focusing on documents adopted by the region that are related to international documents, such as the Brasilia Declaration, related to the 1951 Refugee Convention[45] and the Statelessness Conventions (Mondelli), and the 100 points of Brasilia, related to the Global Compact on Refugees (Jubilut, Mezzanotti, and Lopes);

Part IV. Other forms of protection beyond the regional refugee regime: focusing on national initiatives and practices such as those stemming from MERCOSUR's norms (Brumat), humanitarian visas (Freier and Luzes) and national migration laws–in an assessment of how they can directly or indirectly benefit refugees (Freier and Fernández); and

Part V. Current Regional Refugees "Crisis": including the displacement of Venezuelans (Jarochinski Silva, Castro, and Sampaio), Central Americans (Nelson-Pollard), Colombians (Carneiro) and Haitians (Sánchez-Mojica).

Each of the three first parts are dedicated to a specific Latin America regime of regional protection of refugees; the fourth brings together examples of national regimes in the region and the fifth examples of current displacement "crisis" and regional and/or national responses to them (within the logics, regimes and traditions of Latin American). This effort in "compartmentalization" aims to clarify the architecture in play in the region. Each part of the book ends with a short commentary chapter (by Kneebone for part I, Anker for part II, Hyndman for part III, Ceriani for part IV, and Calderón for part V), as a way to creating dialogues from the standpoints of each of the regimes and case-studies.

To round up the book an annex is presented (with an extended version available online), highlighting the main documents in the Regime of the Cartagena Declaration and the Regime of the Inter-American Human Rights System, as well as good practices in play in Latin America regarding refugee protection. Said practices were considered as "good" as they increase refugee protection, adopt a human-rights approach and/or set Latin America apart as a region in refugee protection in a positive way.

With this, the book aims to be a useful analytical, descriptive and assessment tool in understanding the architecture of refugee protection in Latin America, through its regimes, logics, and challenges.

Liliana Lyra Jubilut holds a PhD and a Master's degree in Law from Universidade de São Paulo and a LL.M in International Legal Studies from

New York University. She is a Professor at Universidade Católica de Santos. She was Visiting Scholar at Columbia Law School and Visiting Fellow at the Refugee Law Initiative. She is an IOM Migration Research and Publishing High Level Adviser and a member of IOM's Migration Research Leaders Syndicate. She is also part of the Global Academic Interdisciplinary Network (GAIN), from the Global Compact on Refugees, and of the Academic Council on the Global Compact for Migration.

Marcia Vera Espinoza is a Lecturer in Human Geography at Queen Mary University of London. She holds a PhD in Geography and a Master's degree in International Studies from the University of Sheffield. She is a researcher at the group Comparative Analysis on International Migration and Displacement in the Americas (CAMINAR), and was an Associate Researcher in the ERC funded Prospects for International Migration Governance (MIGPROSP)project. Marcia is member of the international advisory board of *Forced Migration Review*. She has recently published in *Frontiers in Human Dynamics, Migration and Society, Geopolitics*, and *Global Policy*, among others. Her coedited book *The Dynamics of Regional Migration Governance* was published by Edward Elgar Publishing in 2019.

Gabriela Mezzanotti is Associate Professor at the University of South-Eastern Norway. She is a member of the research group in Human Rights and Diversities (HRDUSN) and a member of the Human Rights and Reconciliation in a Post-conflict, Multicultural Society project (NORPART). She holds a PhD in Social Sciences. She is a lawyer who has coordinated Unisinos UNHCR Sergio Vieira de Mello Chair from 2011 until 2018. Her research addresses critical discourse studies, International Human Rights Law, migration, and Refugee Law.

Notes

1. Another dimension that can be mentioned is the one relating to return. Countries in Latin America—such as Mexico and Colombia—have started to experience being countries of return and to face the challenges regarding this dimension of migration governance. This affects forced migration in general, and probably also refugees (in what can be seen as a violation of *non-refoulement* if the return is not voluntary); however current aggregated data (for Mexico) does not separate in the different legal categories of forced migrants (Vera Espinoza 2019).
2. Available at https://www.refworld.org/docid/3be01b964.html.
3. Available at https://www.refworld.org/docid/3ae6b3ae4.html.
4. Available at https://www.unhcr.org/gcr/GCR_English.pdf.
5. Available at https://www.refworld.org/docid/3ae6b36ec.html.

6. Information about border closure in the region is available at https://www.inmo vilidadamericas.org/cierre-fronteras.
7. See the Global Compact on Refugees (UN 2018: 6, paras. 28, 29).
8. Latin America is often said also to include the Caribbean States, which share either an Iberian-led or French-led colonial past. For the purposes of this book, the more restricted definition is applied, given that its focus is on refugee protection and this is the model used by UNHCR (2019b). In this sense, when the Caribbean States are included, this is spelled out with reference to "Latin America and the Caribbean".
9. French Guyana is an exception to the Iberian metropolis having been colonized by the French, and also in terms of independence given that it is still connected to France.
10. Suriname is an exception to the Iberian metropolis having been colonized by the Dutch.
11. The list including the independent Caribbean states would add Cuba, Dominican Republic, Haiti, and Trinidad and Tobago. Puerto Rico could be added to the list, although it has a peculiar standing in International Law. To complete the list of independent Caribbean states, albeit not connected to Latin America, one would add Anguilla, Antigua and Barbuda, Aruba, Barbados, Bahamas, Bonaire, Cayman Islands, Curaçao, Dominica, Grenada, Jamaica, Saint Kitts and Nevis, Saint Lucia, Saint Martin, Saint Vincent and the Grenadines, Trinidad and Tobago, and Turks and Caicos. Even though Haiti would be outside the realm of Latin America adopted by this book, Haitian displacement is included in the analysis since it is one of the major flows both in recent years and ongoing in the region, as well as due to the connections it shares with neighbouring Dominican Republic and the rest of the continent.
12. For more on these different institutes see Jubilut and Lopes (2019).
13. The Cartagena Declaration also creates the spirit of Cartagena that inspires refugee protection in the region. For more on that, see Jubilut, Vera Espinoza, and Mezzanotti (2019).
14. The Cartagena Declaration suggests a definition of a refugee that includes persons who "have fled their country because their lives, safety or freedom have been threatened by generalized violence, foreign aggression, internal conflicts, mass violations of human rights, and other situations that have seriously disturbed public order."
15. Available at https://www.refworld.org/docid/4a54bc3fd.html.
16. Available at https://www.refworld.org/docid/424bf6914.html.
17. Available at https://www.refworld.org/docid/5487065b4.html.
18. See, e.g., https://www.nbcnews.com/news/latino/latin-america-fears-rising-discrimination-xenophobia-against-venezuelan-migrants-n1068536.
19. See, e.g., https://www.reviewjournal.com/news/politics-and-government/us-asylum-pact-with-honduras-seals-northern-triangle-1856857/ and https://www.bbc.com/news/world-us-canada-49834644?mc_cid=e34d386373&mc_eid=847 14ec347.
20. See, e.g., https://www.telesurenglish.net/news/Guatemala-Social-Organizations-Reject-Safe-Third-Country-Deal-20190727-0002.html, https://www.justsecurity

.org/65967/offshore-processing-in-guatemala-a-deeper-look-at-the-u-s-asylum-deal/, and, https://cnnespanol.cnn.com/2019/09/10/alerta-el-gobierno-de-guatemala-si-podran-negociar-con-ee-uu-el-ser-tercer-pais-seguro-resuelve-la-corte-de-constitucionalidad/.
21. See, e.g., https://noticias.uol.com.br/ultimas-noticias/afp/2019/09/06/mexico-afirma-que-reduziu-em-56-o-fluxo-migratorio-para-os-eua.htm, and https://www.reuters.com/article/us-mexico-usa-immigration-exclusive/exclusive-mexico-opposes-u-s-plan-to-make-it-take-asylum-seekers-document-source-idUSKBN1K23BA.
22. See, e.g., https://www.telesurenglish.net/news/Panama-to-US-We-Wont-be-Your-Safe-Third-Country-20190822-0014.html?mc_cid=dae983f22a&mc_eid=8%E2%80%A6.
23. On the other hand, it has been reported that Panama has adopted restrictive policies toward extra-regional refugees (https://africatimes.com/2019/08/30/for-african-migrants-will-panama-become-the-new-libya/).
24. See, e.g., https://blogs.eui.eu/migrationpolicycentre/migration-rise-right-south-america-increasing-anti-immigration-sentiment-southern-cone/.
25. See, e.g., https://voxeu.org/article/deep-recessions-large-immigration-waves-and-rise-populism.
26. See, e.g., https://www.acnur.org/portugues/2017/12/04/refugiados-da-america-central-chegam-no-uruguai/.
27. See, e.g., https://www.iom.int/news/brazil-iom-unhcr-partner-support-resettlement-refugees-central-america-0.
28. See, e.g., https://www.unhcr.org/news/briefing/2019/3/5c8b6cd44/5000-venezuelans-find-new-homes-brazils-internal-relocation-programme.html.
29. In 2018 the Chilean government announced that it will issue up to ten thousand humanitarian visas a year to Haitians who already have relatives in Chile. More information can be found at https://www.economist.com/the-americas/2018/04/12/chile-gives-immigrants-a-wary-welcome. In August 2019 the government published Resolution no. 3.042 that provides permits to Venezuelan migrants without passport to allow family reunification or for humanitarian reasons. See https://www.leychile.cl/Navegar?idNorma=1135162.
30. See, e.g., https://reliefweb.int/sites/reliefweb.int/files/resources/Venezuela%20IOM%20Regional%20Response%20Overview.pdf.
31. See https://www.unhcr.org/uk/news/stories/2017/11/5a0586774/syrian-refugees-reap-benefits-argentinas-new-visa-rules.html.
32. See, e.g., https://www.nytimes.com/2019/01/25/world/americas/migrant-caravan-honduras-mexico.html and https://www.bbc.com/mundo/noticias-america-latina-45898633.
33. UNHCR's Statute was adopted by the United Nations General Assembly Resolution 428 (V) of 14 December 1950and is available at https://www.unhcr.org/4d944e589.pdf.
34. The UNHCR was created as a subsidiary organ of the UNGA, thus technically differing from specialized agencies that are independent international organizations created by specific treaties, and therefore with specific members and budgets. However, recently the UNHCR has been presenting itself as the UN

refugee agency. To respect its interdisciplinary nature, this book did not interfere with the authors' choice in calling the UNHCR an agency or not.
35. See https://news.un.org/en/story/2016/07/535282-general-assembly-decision-makes-international-organization-migration-part-un#:~:targetText=The%20United%20Nations%20General%20Assembly,its%20social%20and%20economic%20dynamics.
36. Which has in the 1969 OUA Convention Governing the Specific Aspects of Refugee Problems in Africa its cornerstone. Available at https://www.refworld.org/docid/3ae6b36018.html.
37. Available at https://r4v.info/es/documents/details/72315. For more on responses to the Venezuelan displacement see Baeninger and Jarochinski Silva 2018; and Gandini, Lozano Ascencio, and Prieto 2019.
38. Available at https://r4v.info/es/documents/details/72315. For more on responses to the Venezuelan displacement see Baeninger and Jarochinski Silva 2018; and Gandini, Lozano Ascencio, and Prieto 2019.
39. Moreover, there are high number of IDPs in the NCA, with figures estimated at more than 943,000 in 2019 (IDMC 2020), as well as drought-related displacements and displacements due to food insecurity that affect 3.3 million persons in Guatemala alone (Centro Scalabriano de Estudos Migratórios [CSEM] 2019), characterizing migration from the region as a mixed migratory flow.
40. See https://www.unhcr.org/news/press/2019/11/5dc6849c4/unhcr-welcomes-commitment-central-american-states-mexico-address-forced.html?mc_cid%E2%80%A6.
41. See, e.g., https://www.migrationpolicy.org/article/cuban-migration-postrevolution-exodus-ebbs-and-flows; https://www.theguardian.com/world/2019/sep/03/more-cubans-seek-asylum-in-mexico-amid-clampdown-on-legal-path-to-us and https://www.radiotelevisionmarti.com/a/bajo-riesgos-continuos-migrantes-cubanos-por-latinoam%C3%A9rica-/231832.html.
42. According to the IOM, at least 514 migrants have lost their lives in the Americas in 2019 (https://www.iom.int/news/americas-migratory-routes-reach-grim-milestone-over-500-deaths-so-far-2019-3).
43. For more on this in the case of Venezuelans see https://www.unhcr.org/news/press/2019/8/5d67c6e94/situation-venezuelan-refugees-migrants-needs-greater-global-attention.html.
44. The ruling was rendered in the *Velez Loor* case, and is a resolution by the President of the Court. The resolution is available in Spanish at https://www.corteidh.or.cr/docs/medidas/velez_se_01.pdf.
45. As the cornerstone of Refugee Law the 1951 Convention does not appear only in one part or chapter but rather is a transversal topic throughout the book.

References

Alto Comisionado de las Naciones Unidas para los Refugiados (ACNUR). n.d. *Protección de Refugiados en América Latina: Buenas Prácticas Legislativas*. San José, Costa Rica: Unidad Legal Regional del ACNUR.

Acosta, Diego. 2018. *The National versus the Foreigner in South America. 200 Years of Migration and Citizenship Law*. Cambridge, UK: Cambridge University Press.
Acosta, Diego, and Monica Oehler. 2019. The Global Compact for Refugees as a Soft Law Instrument: Lessons from the application of the Cartagena Declaration on Refugees in Mexico. *RLI Blog on Refugee Law and Forced Migration*. https://rli.blogs.sas.ac.uk/2019/03/01/the-global-compact-for-refugees-as-a-soft-law-instrument-lessons-from-the-application-of-the-cartagena-declaration-on-refugees-in-mexico/.
Acosta, Diego, Cécile Blouin, and Luisa Feline Freier. 2019. *La emigración venezolana: respuestas latinoamericanas*. Working Paper Series, Fundación Carolina, 3/2019 https://www.fundacioncarolina.es/wpcontent/uploads/2019/04/DT_FC_03.pdf.
American Convention on Human Rights. 1969. http://www.cidh.org/Basicos/English/Basic3.American%20Convention.htm.
Anker, Deborah, and Lawrence Palmer. 2014. "'Third Generation' Gangs Warfare in Central America, and Refugees' Law Political Opinion Ground." 14–10 *Immigration Briefings*.
Baeninger, Rosana, and João Carlos Jarochinski Silva, eds. 2018. *Migrações Venezuelanas*. Campinas: Unicamp Nepo. https://www.nepo.unicamp.br/publicacoes/livros/mig_venezuelanas/migracoes_venezuelanas.pdf.
Barichello, Stefania E. 2016. "Refugee protection and responsibility sharing in Latin America: solidarity programmes and the Mexico Plan of Action." *International Journal of Human Rights*, 20:2, 191–207, DOI: 10.1080/13642987.2015.1079025.
Bengochea, Julieta, Gabriela Cabezas, Luciana Gandini, Gioconda Herrera, Marta Luzes, Camila Montiel, Victoria Prieto, Marcia Vera Espinoza, and Gisela P. Zapata. 2021. "COVID-19 y población migrante y refugiada. Análisis de las respuestas político-institucionales en ciudades receptoras de seis países de América Latina." In *Inmigrando: Comprender Ciudades en Transición*, edited by Felipe Vera, Verónica Adler, and Fernando Toro, vol. 3: 749–82. Buenos Aires: BID.
Betts, Alexander. 2013. "Regime Complexity and International Organizations: UNHCR as a Challenged Institution." *Global Governance*, 19 (1), 69–81.
———. 2015. "The Normative Terrain of the Global Refugee Regime." *Ethics and International Affairs*, 29 (4), 363–75. doi:10.1017/S0892679415000350.
———. 2019a. "Nowhere to Go: How Governments in the Americas Are Bungling the Migration Crisis." *Foreign Affairs*. https://www.foreignaffairs.com/articles/americas/2019-10-15/nowhere-go.
———. 2019b. Why Venezuelan migrants need to be regarded as refugees, *IRIN News*. https://www.irinnews.org/opinion/2019/02/27/why-venezuelan-migrants-need-be-regarded-refugees?utm_source=Monthly+News+Update%2C+February+2019&utm_campaign=Monthly+News+Update+February+2019&utm_medium=email.
Blokker, Niels, and Henry G. Schermers. 2000. *Proliferation of International Organizations: Legal Issues*. Leinde: Brill/ | Nijhoff.
Brazil Declaration and Plan of Action: a Framework for Cooperation and Regional Solidarity to Strengthen the International Protection of Refugees, Displaced and Stateless Persons in Latin America and the Caribbean. 2014. https://www.refworld.org/docid/5487065b4.html.

Brumat, Leiza. 2019. "Migration and the "rise of the right" in South America: Is there an increasing anti-immigration sentiment in the Southern Cone?" *MPC EUI Blog*. https://blogs.eui.eu/migrationpolicycentre/migration-rise-right-south-america-increasing-anti-immigration-sentiment-southern-cone/.

Brumat, Leiza, Diego Acosta, and Marcia Vera Espinoza. 2018. Gobernanza migratoria en América del Sur: ¿hacia una nueva oleada restrictiva? In *Anuario de Política Internacional y Política Exterior 2017–2018*, edited by Lincoln Bizzozero Revelez and Wilson Fernández Luzuriaga: 205–11. Tradinco: Ediciones Cruz del Sur.

Cantor, David J. 2014. "The new wave: Forced displacement caused by organized crime in Central America and Mexico." *Refugee Survey Quarterly* 33 (3): 34–68.

———. 2019. "Fairness, Failure, and Future in the Refugee Regime." *International Journal of Refugee Law*: 1–3.

Cantor, David and Stefania Eugenia Barichello. 2013. The Inter-American human rights system: a new model for integrating refugee and complementary protection?. *The International Journal of Human Rights* 17 (5-6): 689–706.

Cantori, Louise J., and Steven L. Spiegel. 1970. *The International Politics of Regions: A Comparative Approach*. Englewood Cliffs, NJ: Prentice Hall.

Cartagena Declaration on Refugees. 1984. https://www.refworld.org/docid/3ae6b36ec.html.

Casey, Nicholas. 2019. Colombia's Peace Deal Promised a New Era. So Why Are These Rebels Rearming? *New York Times*, 17 May 2019. https://www.nytimes.com/2019/05/17/world/americas/colombia-farc-peace-deal.html.

Centro Scalabriano de Estudos Migratórios (CSEM). 2019. Insegurança Alimentar entre as Principais Causas da Migração na América Central. https://www.csem.org.br/noticias/inseguranca-alimentar-entre-as-principais-causas-da-migracao-na-america-central/.

Convention Relating to the Status of Refugees. 1951. https://www.refworld.org/docid/3be01b964.htm.

Fischel de Andrade, José Henrique. 2014. "Forced Migration in South America." In *The Oxford Handbook of Refugee and Forced Migration Studies*, edited by Elena Fiddian-Qasmiyeh et al.: 651–63. Oxford: Oxford University Press.

Freier, Luisa Feline; Parent, Nicolas. 2018 A South American Migration Crisis: Venezuelan Outflows Test Neighbors' Hospitality. *Migration Policy Institute*. https://www.migrationpolicy.org/article/south-american-migration-crisis-venezuelan-outflows-test-neighbors-hospitality.

Gandini, Luciana, Fernando Lozano Ascencio, and Victoria Prieto, eds. 2019. *Crisis y migración de población venezolana: entre la desprotección y la seguridad jurídica en Latinoamérica*. Mexico: National Autonomous University of Mexico.

Geddes, Andrew, Marcia Vera Espinoza, Leila Hadj Abdou, and Leiza Brumat, eds. 2019. *The Dynamics of Regional Migration Governance*. Cheltenham, UK: Edward Elgar.

Global Compact on Refugees. 2018. https://www.unhcr.org/gcr/GCR_English.pdf.

Gobat, Michel. 2013. "The Invention of Latin America: A Transnational History of Anti-Imperialism, Democracy, and Race." *American Historical Review* 118 (5): 1345–375.

Grandi, Filippo. 2017. "Foreword: Regional solidarity and commitment to protection in Latin America and the Caribbean." *Forced Migration Review* 56: 47–49.

Grugel, Jean, and Wil Hout. 1999. "Regions, regionalism and the South." In *Regionalism across the north-south divide. State strategies and globalization*, edited by Jean Grugel and Wil Hout: 3–13. Abingdon and New York: Routledge.

Haggard, Stephan, and Beth A. Simmons. 1987. "Theories of international regimes." *International Organization* 41(3): 491–517.

Harley, Tristan. 2014. "Regional Cooperation and Refugee Protection in Latin America: A "South-South" Approach." *International Journal of Refugee Law* 26 (1): 22–47.

Henning, C. Randal. 2019. "Regime Complexity and the Institutions of Crisis and Development Finance." *Development and Change*, 50 (1): 24–45.

Internal Displacement Monitoring Centre (IDMC). 2020. *Global Report on Internal Displacement*. https://www.internal-displacement.org/global-report/grid2020/.

Jarochinski Silva, João Carlos, and Liliana L. Jubilut. 2018. "Venezuelans in Brazil: Challenges of Protection." *E-International Relations*. https://www.e-ir.info/2018/07/12/venezuelans-in-brazil-challenges-of-protection/.

Jones, Jessica, and Jennifer Podkul. 2012. *Forced from Home: The Lost Boys and Girls of Central America*. Women's Refugee Commission.

Jubilut, Liliana L. 2017a. "Humanitarian Alternative Pathways for Protection for Forced Migrants in Latin America." In *Migration Research Leaders' Syndicate: Ideas to Inform International Cooperation on Safe, Orderly and Regular Migration*, edited by Marie McAuliffe and Michele McAuliffe (Conveners): 117–22. Geneva: IOM. https://publications.iom.int/books/humanitarian-alternative-pathways-protection-forced-migrants-latin-america.

Jubilut, Liliana L. 2017b. Refugees are victims of the crisis, not the creators. *World Economic Forum Agenda Blog*. https://www.weforum.org/agenda/2017/11/the-refugee-crisis-or-a-crisis-for-refugees/.

Jubilut, Liliana L. 2018. *Refugee Protection in Brazil and in Latin America—Selected Essays*. London: Transnational Press London.

Jubilut, Liliana L. 2020. Challenges to refugee protection in the time of COVID-19. Covid-19 Watch. Andrew and Renata Kaldor Centre for International Refugee Law. https://www.kaldorcentre.unsw.edu.au/publication/challenges-refugee-protection-time-covid-19.

Jubilut, Liliana L., Camila M. S. de Andrade, and André de L. Madureira. 2016. "Humanitarian Visas: Brazil's experience as a starting point for discussion." *Forced Migration Review*, 53: 76–78.

Jubilut, Liliana L., and Silvia M. O. S. Apolinário. 2008. "A população refugiada no Brasil: em busca da proteção integral." *Universitas Relações Internacionais*, 6 (2), 2008: 9–38. (A translation is available as Refugee population in Brazil: the quest for integral protection. In Jubilut, Liliana L. *Refugee Protection in Brazil and in Latin America—Selected Essays*: 91–110.

Jubilut, Liliana Lyra, and Wellington P. Carneiro. 2011. "Resettlement in Solidarity: a regional new approach towards a more humane durable solution." *Refugee Survey Quarterly*, 3: 63–86.

Jubilut, Liliana Lyra, and Melissa Martins Casagrande. 2019. "Shortcomings and/or Missed Opportunities of the Global Compacts for the Protection of Forced Migrants." *International Migration*, 57:139–57.

Jubilut, Liliana L., and Ananda P. Fernandes. 2018. "A atual proteção aos deslocados forçados da Venezuela pelos países da América Latina." In *Migrações Venezuelanas*, edited by Rosana Baeninger and João Carlos Jarochinski Silva: 164–77. Campinas: Unicamp Nepto. https://www.nepo.unicamp.br/publicacoes/livros/mig_venezuelanas/migracoes_venezuelanas.pdf.

Jubilut, Liliana L., and João Carlos Jarochinski Silva. 2020. COVID-19 at the Brazil-Venezuela borders: the good, the bad and the ugly. *Open Democracy*. 18 June 2020. https://www.opendemocracy.net/en/pandemic-border/covid-19-brazil-venezuela-borders-good-bad-and-ugly/.

Jubilut, Liliana L., and Rachel de Oliveira Lopes. 2017. "Strategies for the Protection of Migrants through International Law." *Groningen Journal of International Law*, 5 (1): 34–56.

Jubilut, Liliana L., and Rachel de Oliveira Lopes. 2018. "Forced Migration and Latin America: Peculiarities of a Peculiar Region in Refugee Protection." *Archiv des Völkerrechts*, v. 56, no. 2: 131–154. https://doi.org/10.1628/avr-2018-0008.

Jubilut, Liliana L., and Rachel de Oliveira Lopes. 2019. "Refuge and political asylum in Latin America: relevance, characteristics, and normative structure." In *The Routledge Companion to Migration, Communication and Politics*, edited by Stephen M. Croucher, João R. Caetano and Elsa A. Campbell: 65–80. Abingdon and New York: Routledge.

Jubilut, Liliana L., André de L. Madureira, and Rafael V. Levy. 2018. "Proteção Complementar e Deslocados Ambientais: Itinerários, Limites e Possibilidades." In *"Refugiados Ambientais."* edited by Liliana Lyra Jubilut et al.: 292–321, Boa Vista: Editora da Universidade Federal de Roraima.

Jubilut, Liliana L., and Erika Pires Ramos. 2014. "Regionalism: a strategy for dealing with crisis migration." *Forced Migration Review* 45: 66–67.

Jubilut, Liliana L., Marcia Vera Espinoza, and Gabriela Mezzanotti. 2019. "The Cartagena Declaration at 35 and the Grammar of Refugee Protection in Latin America." *E-international relations*, 22 November 2019. https://www.e-ir.info/2019/11/22/the-cartagena-declaration-at-35-and-refugee-protection-in-latin-america/.

Kneebone, Susan. 2016 Comparative regional protection frameworks for refugees: norms and norm entrepreneurs. *The International Journal of Human Rights*, 20, 2: 153–72, DOI: 10.1080/13642987.2016.1141499.

Kneebone, Susan; Rawlings-Sanaei, Felicity. 2007. *New Regionalism and Asylum Seekers—Challenges ahead.* New York and Oxford: Berghahn Books.

Krasner, Stephen D. 1982. "Structural Causes and Regime Consequences: Regimes as Intervening Variables." *International Organization* 36: 185–205.

Lavanchy, P. 2006. "The Mexico Declaration and Plan of Action: Reaffirming Latin America's Generous Tradition of Asylum and Innovative Solutions." *International Journal of Refugee Law*, 18 (2):450–451.

Maldonado Castillo, C. 2015. "The Cartagena process: 30 years of innovation and solidarity." *Forced Migration Review* 89: 89–91.

Menezes, Fabiano L. de. 2016, "Utopia or Reality: Regional Cooperation in Latin America to Enhance the Protection of Refugees." *Refugee Survey Quarterly*, 35 (4): 122–141.

Mexico Declaration and Plan of Action to Strengthen the International Protection of Refugees in Latin America. 2004. https://www.refworld.org/docid/424bf6914.html.

Mignolo, Walter D. 2005. *The Idea of Latin America*. Malden, Oxford, Victoria: Blackwell Publishing.

MigraMundo. 2019. *Nicarágua completa um ano em crise interna e gera refugiados na América Central*. https://migramundo.com/nicaragua-completa-um-ano-em-crise-interna-e-gera-refugiados-na-america-central/.

Miroff, Nick. 2016. Colombia's war has displaced 7 million. With peace, will they go home?. *The Washington Post*. https://www.washingtonpost.com/world/the_americas/colombias-war-has-displaced-7-million-with-peace-will-they-go-home/2016/09/05/538df3c6-6eb8-11e6-993f-73c693a89820_story.html.

Morrison, Judith. 2007. "Race and poverty in Latin America: Addressing the development needs of African descendants. (Racial Discrimination)." *UN Chronicle*, 44 (3): 44–45.

Murillo, Juan Carlos. 2015 apud Luisa Feline Freier. A Liberal Paradigm Shift?: A Critical Appraisal of recent Trends in Latin America Asylum Legislation. In *Exploring the Boundaries of Refugee Law: current protection challenges*, edited by Jean-Pierre Gauci, Mariagiulia Giuffré and Evangelia (Lilian) Tsourdi: 118–48. Leinde: Brill/ | Nijhoff.

Musalo, Karen, Lisa Frydman, and Pablo Ceriani Cernadas, eds. 2015. *Childhood and Migration in Central and North America: Causes, Policies, Practices and Challenges*. https://cgrs.uchastings.edu/sites/default/files/Childhood_Migration_Human Rights_English_1.pdf.

Noticias ONU. 2019. Protestas en Chile, Migrantes irregulares y el discurso del odio en internet. 18 Octubre 2019 https://news.un.org/es/audio/2019/10/1464111.

Pécoud, Antoine. 2018. "What do we know about the International Organization for Migration?." *Journal of Ethnic and Migration Studies*, 44 (10): 1621–38.

Protocol Relating to the Status of Refugees (1967 Protocol). 1967. https://www.refworld.org/docid/3ae6b3ae4.html.

Quijano, Anibal. 2015. "Colonialidad del Poder y Clasi? cacion Social." *Journal of World-Systems Research*, 6 (2), 342–86.

Response for Venezuelans (R4V). 2020a. Situation Report: April–June 2020. Coordination Platform for Refugees and Migrants from Venezuela. https://r4v.info/en/situations/platform.

Response for Venezuelans (R4V). 2020b. Refugee and Migrant Response Plan 2020. January–December 2020.

Ramji-Nogales, Jaya. 2019. The Role of the "Regional": Shoring Up Refugee Rights?. *RLI Refugee Law and Forced Migration Blog*. https://rli.blogs.sas.ac.uk/2019/05/07/the-role-of-the-regional-shoring-up-refugee-rights/.

Reed-Hurtado, Michael. 2013. *The Cartagena Declaration on Refugees and the Protection of People Fleeing Armed Conflict and Other Situations of Violence in Latin America*. UNHCR Legal and Protection Policy Research Series. https://www

.unhcr.org/protection/globalconsult/51c800fe9/32-cartagena-declaration-refu gees-protection-people-fleeing-armed-conflict.html.
Rodríguez Camejo, Raquel. 2017. "Syrian Refugees in Uruguay: An Uncomfortable Topic." *Forced Migration Review*, 56 (1): 54–55.
San José Declaration on Refugees and Displaced Persons (San Jose Declaration). 1994. https://www.refworld.org/docid/4a54bc3fd.html.
Schuck, Peter H. 1997. "Refugee Burden-Sharing: A Modest Proposal." *Yale Journal of International Law* 22: 243–49.
United Nations High Commissioner for Refugees (UNHCR). 2019a. *Global Trends – Forced Displacement in 2018*. https://www.unhcr.org/statistics/unhcrstats/5d 08d7ee7/unhcr-global-trends-2018.html.
———. 2019b. *Expanding Operations in Central America 2019*. https://reliefweb.int/sites/ reliefweb.int/files/resources/2019%20Expanding%20Operations%20in%20Ce ntral%20America%20%28February%202019%29.pdf.
———. 2019c. *Venezuela: the largest exodus of Latin America*. https://www.unhcr.org/ ph/15558-april-e-newsletter-venezuela.html.
———. 2019d. *One year into Nicaragua crisis, more than 60,000 forced to flee their country*. https://www.unhcr.org/news/briefing/2019/4/5cb58bd74/year-nicaragua-crisis-60000-forced-flee-country.html.
———. 2020. *Global Trends–Forced Displacement in 2019*. https://www.unhcr.org/glob altrends2019/.
———. n.d. *Displacement in Central America*. https://www.unhcr.org/displacement-in-central-america.html.
Vera Espinoza, Marcia. 2018a. "The Limits and Opportunities of Regional Solidarity: Exploring Refugee Resettlement in Brazil and Chile." *Global Policy*, 9 (1): 85–94.
Vera Espinoza, Marcia. 2018b. "The Politics of Resettlement: Expectations and unfulfilled promises in Chile and Brazil." In *Refugee Resettlement: Power, Politics and Humanitarian Governance*, edited by Adéle Garnier, Jubilut, Liliana L. Jubilut and Kristin B. Sandvik: 223–43. New York and Oxford: Berghahn Books.
Vera Espinoza, Marcia. 2019. "Between depoliticisation and path dependence: The role of Mexico in Regional Migration Governance in North America." In *The Dynamics of Regional Migration Governance*, edited by Andrew Geddes, Marcia Vera Espinoza, Leila Hadj-Abdou, and Leiza Brumat: 166–185. Cheltenham: Edward Elgar Publishing.
Vera Espinoza, Marcia, Gisela P. Zapata, and Luciana Gandini. 2020. Mobility in immobility: Latin American migrants trapped amid COVID-19. *Open Democracy*, 26 May 2020. https://www.opendemocracy.net/en/democraciaabierta/ mobility-immobility-latin-american-migrants-trapped-amid-covid-19/.
Wade, Peter. 2010. *Race and Ethnicity in Latin America*. London; New York: Pluto Press.
Yates, Caitlyn. 2019. As More Migrants from Africa and Asia Arrive in Latin America, Governments Seek Orderly and Controlled Pathways. *Migration Policy Institute*. https://www.migrationpolicy.org/article/extracontinental-migrants-lat in-america.
Yoshimatsu, Hidetaka. 1998. *International Regimes, International Society, and Theoretical Relations*. Working Paper Series, vol. 98-10, The International Centre for

the Study of East Asian Development. http://www.agi.or.jp/workingpapers/WP1998-10.pdf.

Ziff, Tamar. 2019. Nowhere to Turn: Gender-Based Violence in the Northern Triangle and its Impact on Migration. *The Dialogue*. https://www.thedialogue.org/analysis/nowhere-to-turn-gender-based-violence-in-the-northern-triangle-and-its-impact-on-migration/.

Part I

The Regime of the Cartagena Declaration

1

The 1984 Cartagena Declaration

A Critical Review of Some Aspects of Its Emergence and Relevance

José H. Fischel de Andrade

Introduction

The decade from 1974 to 1984 saw the world's refugee population rise from 2.9 million to 10.7 million (United Nations High Commissioner for Refugees [UNHCR] 2020). Toward the end of that decade the search for asylum in Africa (Djibouti, Somalia, Sudan), Asia (China, Pakistan, Thailand) and the Americas (Honduras) involved large-scale migration of hundreds of thousands and even millions (UNHCR 1983: para. 25). The asylum seekers forming part of these large-scale influxes included both forced migrants falling within the definition of "refugee" in the 1951 Refugee Convention and forced migrants who did not satisfy international refugee law terminology but were, nevertheless, in dire need of international protection. As direct products of the postwar time and in the absence of both progressive legal interpretation and doctrinal development the 1950 Office of the UNHCR Statute and the 1951 Refugee Convention risked becoming obsolete. The Western countries, no longer in a majority in the United Nations General Assembly (UNGA) and not directly affected by the large-scale influxes, were unwilling to revisit the 1950 UNHCR Statute or progressively develop the international conventional law of refugees, by and large seeing their interests served by a continuation of the status quo (Coles 1990: 383).

The humanitarian, political, and legal conundrum that the large-scale forced migrations represented allowed the UNHCR to successfully make widespread use of diplomatic channels, to offer its good offices as arbitrator, and to be a go-between in relations between governments with different interests so that it could ensure that its persons of concern were protected (Sanness 1997: 14), a role that resulted in its being awarded in 1981 its second Nobel Peace Prize. From a position of high credibility and legitimacy, the UNHCR pursued twofold action through global and regional initiatives that aimed both at changing the refugee regime and addressing more effectively the phenomenon of the massive influx of asylum seekers.

A successful initiative undertaken by the UNHCR at the global level led to a series of events that culminated in the adoption of the 1984 Cartagena Declaration, which is heralded as one of the greatest accomplishments in the development of the refugee protection regime in Latin America (Reed-Hurtado 2017: 141).[1] Plenty of literature has been written on several interesting aspects of the 1984 Cartagena Declaration, ranging from comparison with large-scale refugee influxes (Tirado 1990: 131–37) and the 1969 Organization of African Unity (OAU) Refugee Convention (Arboleda 1991: 185–207; Arboleda 1995: 87–101), to evaluations of its relevance both as a source (Gros Espiell 1995: 453–70) and to the development of international refugee law in Latin America (Franco and Santistevan 2005: 61–119), to legal analyzes regarding its broader refugee definition (Fortín 2005: 255–90), and to its legal nature and historical importance (Ruiz de Santiago 2005: 291–314).

This chapter, therefore, does not aim to introduce or analyze the main features of the 1984 Cartagena Declaration or simply review or regurgitate the existing literature. Rather, it critically revisits some aspects of its emergence and relevance by answering the following questions: Why was there a need for a change of regime in Central America? What was the drafting process that culminated in the 1984 Cartagena Declaration definition of "refugee" and how important was the UNHCR's role in it? What is the Cartagena Declaration, and what is it not?

Finally, this chapter focuses predominantly on the regional broad definition of "refugee" that the 1984 Cartagena Declaration recommends, rather than the various other important protection aspects that it covers.

The Need for a Change of Regime in Central America

As a result of the forced migration movements in the late 1970s and early 1980s in Central America, all its eight countries[2] were affected by the massive forced migration.[3] Those countries had inadequate, ambivalent, and contradictory policies toward Central Americans asylum seekers (Yundt 1987–88: 137), however. Even though they had (more often than not) a protection-sensitive approach to those seeking asylum, in consonance with the long-established Latin American asylum tradition, some countries including Mexico and Costa Rica moved toward more restrictive policies as a consequence of economic difficulties and increasingly moderate governments (Ferris 1984: 360).

In addition to the political and economic effects resulting from the forced migrant influxes, there was a major legal problem: even though there was both an almost consensual decision to protect those seeking asylum and an international human rights law obligation—captured inter alia in Article 22(8) of the 1969 American Convention on Human Rights and in customary international law—not to deport or return those whose life or personal freedom was in danger of violation, there was a legal void as to the legal instruments applicable when it came to what legal status should be granted to forced migrants seeking asylum.

This was not the first time Latin American countries faced the problem resulting from the inadequacy of their political asylee sub-regime. In fact, since 1959, when the mass exodus of Cubans began and was followed by influxes from countries such as Haiti, Paraguay, Bolivia, the Dominican Republic, Nicaragua, and Honduras, it became evident that few countries in the Latin American region had sufficient resources to provide protection and care to asylum seekers, and that their capacity for absorption was rather limited. Nor had many countries developed institutions and adopted adequate legislation to handle asylum seekers in accordance with the social and legal challenges presented by their sudden and massive influx (Inter-American Commission on Human Rights [IACmHR] 1965: 75–76).

In the mid-1960s the IACmHR had already identified, among the main challenges faced by the region, the lack of domestic legislation that adequately recognized and defined the situation of "political refugees," the non-existence of an Inter-American convention that contemplated and regulated the situation of "political refugees," and the lack of an organization in the Inter-American human rights system, empowered to coordinate the protection and assistance of "political refugees."[4] Notwithstanding the recommendations of the IACmHR and as a result of lack of political will, domestic legislation was not adopted, no organization was set up or charged with the task of coordinating protection and assistance works,[5] and the 1966 Draft Convention on Refugees proposed by the Comité Jurídico Interamericano (CJI; Inter-American Juridical Committee 1966: 47) was stillborn.

Until the mid-1970s the countries in the region did not feel the combination of moral and material pressure that normally leads to change and were mostly satisfied with the then prevailing political asylee sub-regime. As a result of the political situation in Chile and Argentina, advocacy was undertaken mostly with a view to ensuring ratification or accession to the 1954 Caracas Conventions on Territorial and Diplomatic Asylum and the

1951 Refugee Convention, the respect of *non-refoulement*, and resettlement to those whose protection situation justified it (Comisión Internacional de Juristas [CIJ] 1975: 51). In the late 1970s and early 1980s, however, forced migration in Central America became, from the factual point of view, the driving force that triggered recognition–initially by countries of the subregion–of the need for regime change.

The need for a regime change was not missed by the UNHCR. It was in those days that it started playing a significant and decisive role in the region as a norm entrepreneur.[6] At that time the sole asylum regime that existed in the subregion was the political asylee sub-regime based on seven regional conventions that dealt, exclusively or otherwise, with the regulation of asylum and to which there were varying degrees of adhesion.[7] The UNHCR set out initially to bring Central American countries into the refugee sub-regime. As an immediate result of successful diplomatic efforts and accession advocacy, Costa Rica and Panama (both in 1978), Nicaragua (1980), and El Salvador and Guatemala (both in 1983) became parties to the 1951 Refugee Convention.[8]

Despite the progress made, the great majority of Central American forced migrants qualified neither as political asylees in accordance with the political asylee sub-regime, nor as refugees in accordance with the definition of "refugee" adopted in the 1951 Refugee Convention. In consequence, these forced migrants in most host countries did not have a clearly defined legal status and were generally not allowed to work (UNHCR 1981c: para. 199). This result was due to the fact that the very reason for their flight from their countries of origin–massive human rights violations resulting from the widespread consequences of civil war, such as the spiral of violence, indiscriminate bombing, armed confrontation, and terrorist assault–was neither contemplated as a convention ground in any of the instruments of the asylum regime, nor interpreted in such a way as to be included in one of the convention grounds. Therefore there was a need for a change *of* regime–in other words, there was a need for a change in the normative structure of the embryonic refugee sub-regime.[9]

The major change the normative structure needed concerned the very definition of the word "refugee," or, in other words, of the grounds that would justify their refugeehood. The definition used by the UNHCR for recognizing asylum seekers as refugees, adopted in paragraphs 6 and 7 of the 1950 UNHCR Statute, had already been broadened by several UNGA resolutions.[10] In fact the widening of the definition had enabled the UNHCR to make an objective assessment of refugee situations and to extend protection to groups of persons who might not be able to invoke a well-founded fear of persecution according to the traditional criteria. This normative development–a true change of refugee regime at the international global level–had enhanced the UNHCR's protection response in refugee situations involving large-scale influxes (UNHCR 1981b: para. 18). Even though the UNHCR was already using its own broad definition in Central America, it was anxious to promote the use of that definition by countries in the region of a wider definition that would be better adapted to large-scale group situations (Jackson 1999: 395). In this way the forced migrants who were seeking asylum could at least be initially recognized as refugees, and ultimately be granted refugee status by those states. The definition used by the few states that were (and were becoming) parties to the 1951 Refugee Convention was not straightforward in encompassing the vast majority of those who were fleeing the Central American countries. One needed, therefore, a definition that would include those forced migrants, by referring to the reasons of their flight from their countries of origin, so that they could enjoy asylum as—legally speaking—refugees.[11]

The Drafting Process that Culminated in the 1984 Cartagena Declaration Definition of "Refugee"

The drafting of the broad definition adopted in the Cartagena Declaration started well before 1984. In fact, it began in 1981 as a result of a decision made in October 1980 by the UNHCR Executive Committee (ExCom) in its Conclusion No. 19 (XXXI), "to request the High Commissioner to convene as soon as possible a representative group of experts to examine temporary refuge in all its aspects within the framework of the problems raised by large-scale influx" (UNHCR 2014). The group of experts met in Geneva in April 1981 and the report of their four-day gathering concluded, "The refugee problem has become particularly acute due to the increasing number of large-scale influx situations in different areas of the world. The asylum-seekers forming part of these large-scale influxes *include* persons who are refugees within the meaning of the 1951 United Nations Convention and the 1967 Protocol relating to the Status of Refugees or who, *owing to external, aggression, occupation, foreign domination or events seriously disturbing public order in either part or the whole of their country of origin or nationality* are compelled to seek refuge outside that country" (UNHCR 1981a: para. 37; emphasis added).

A few weeks later, in May 1981, the Mexican Diplomatic Academy, Instituto Matías Romero, organized, with the cooperation of the Universidad Nacional Autónoma de México (UNAM; National Autonomous University of Mexico) and under the auspices of the UNHCR, a five-day colloquium on "Asylum and International Protection of Refugees in Latin America." The UNHCR was well represented: the then-High Commissioner, Poul Hartling, opened the colloquium and other high-ranking UNHCR staff also attended. Presentations were made inter alia by members of the Inter-American Court of Human Rights (IACtHR), the IACmHR, and the Organization of American States' (OAS) secretariat for legal affairs. In addition to the UNHCR and other international organization participants and observers, the general attendants were mostly Mexican. At the end of the colloquium its participants adopted nine conclusions and eight recommendations. The fourth conclusion reads, "It is *necessary to broaden* in Latin America the protection that the universal and Latin American instruments grant to refugees and asylees, to all those persons that flee their country as a result of *aggression, foreign occupation or domination, massive human rights violations, or events that seriously disturb public order, in either part or the whole of the territory of the country of origin*" (Coloquio de México 1982: 206; translation by the author; emphasis added).

Some points merit comment here. First, three participants attended both the April 1981 Expert Group meeting in Geneva and the May 1981 Mexico Colloquium: the UNHCR's Director of International Protection, Michel Moussalli; the UNHCR's Chief of General Legal Section, Frank Krenz; and the Brazilian law professor and member of the IACmHR, Carlos A. Dunshee de Abranches. It is more than likely that these three participants significantly influenced the wording of the Mexico Colloquium's fourth conclusion, which clearly mirrors paragraph 37 of the April 1981 Report of the Expert Group (see above).[12]

Second, there are two differences between these two broad definitions of "refugee." The first is that the Mexico Colloquium's fourth conclusion adds "massive human rights violations" as a reason for persons to flee their countries. The second—and equally important—difference is that, although the April 1981 Report of the Expert Group's broad definitions is framed as a description, the May 1981 Mexico Colloquium speaks of the "necess[ity] to broaden in Latin America the protection that the universal and Latin American instruments grant to refugees and asylees" who meet the criteria it lists. Both this nondescriptive but rather propositive wording and the addition of "massive human rights violations" as grounds for refugeehood were adopted by the successive regional attempts to expand the definition (see below).

Third, at the regional level there was a particular interest at the time in exploring the potential role that the Inter-American human rights system could play on behalf of refugees (Dunshee de Abranches 1982: 207–8). The message was well copied by the regional human rights mechanisms and the IACmHR in its 1981–82 annual report, which for the first (and only) time devoted an entire subchapter to "Refugees and the Inter-American System."[13] In its annual report, the IACmHR not only refers to the 1981 Mexico Colloquium and its "recommendations," but also proposes to the OAS General Assembly that the definition of "refugee" in the region be broadened to encompass the grounds mentioned in the colloquium (IACmHR 1982,

Chapter VI, B, 11, d). The OAS General Assembly, however, in exemplary diplomatic language, merely "1. note[d] with interest the annual report and the recommendations of the IACmHR and express[ed] appreciation for the serious and important work it carries out in the area of protecting and promoting human rights" and "10. request[ed] that body to present a report to the General Assembly on the Commission's recommendations contained in Chapter VI of its report" (OAS 1982: 62–63).

Finally, at the international global level, the UNHCR continued its advocacy of a broader definition by recalling that "the Colloquium on Asylum and the International Protection of Refugees, held in Mexico in May 1981, recognized the need for inter-American concepts of asylum and refugee status to be coalesced with those adopted at the international level" (UNHCR 1983: para. 67).

In June 1981, some weeks after the May 1981 Mexico Colloquium, an important roundtable on the "Problems Arising from Large Numbers of Asylum Seekers" was organized at the Sanremo-based International Institute of Humanitarian Law (IIHL). The roundtable counted on the participation of several governmental representatives, academics and UNHCR staff (such as Frank Krenz, who had attended both the April 1981 Group of Expert Meeting and the May 1981 Mexico Colloquium) and considered that the definition of "'refugee' . . . *should be interpreted to include* every person who, owing to *external aggression, occupation, foreign domination or events seriously disturbing pubic order in either part or the whole of his country of origin or nationality* was compelled to leave his place of habitual residence in order to seek refuge in another place outside his country of origin or nationality" (IIHL 1981: para. 8; emphasis added). Four months later, in October 1981, the ExCom adopted its Conclusion No. 22 (XXXII) on the Protection of Asylum-Seekers in Situations of Large-Scale Influx, which stated in paragraph I.1 that "asylum seekers forming part of these large-scale influxes *include* persons who are refugees within the meaning of the 1951 United Nations Convention and the 1967 Protocol relating to the Status of Refugees or who, owing to *external aggression, occupation, foreign domination or events seriously disturbing public order in either part of, or the whole of their country of origin or nationality* are compelled to seek refuge outside that country" (UNHCR 2014; emphasis added).

The subsequent UNHCR "Note on International Protection" did not waste time in asserting that the broadened concept of "refugee" that figured in ExCom's Conclusion No. 22 (XXXII) had made it possible for the international community effectively to meet important humanitarian needs in various areas of the world (UNHCR 1982: paras. 17–18). But notwithstanding the relevance of UNHCR advocacy on behalf of a broad definition at the international global level, it was equally (if not more) important to convince the Latin American countries of the benefits of both putting the new definition to use and regarding the region's large-scale asylum seekers as refugees. The UNHCR insisted on a regional approach that had already been successful in Africa, but the Latin American states were still reluctant.

In the face of the standstill, the UNHCR organized a second event in the region in April 1983. This time it was a four-day seminar in La Paz, Bolivia, entitled "Political Asylum and the Refugee Situation" and was organized with the support of the Bolivian Ministry of Foreign Affairs. Participants were mostly UNHCR staff (including Frank Krenz), academics, and Bolivian officials from a variety of ministries. At the seminar's closure seven conclusions and eight recommendations were adopted. The sixth conclusion states, "emphasize[d] the *need to extend* the scope of application of the 1951 Convention and the 1967 Protocol on the status of refugees, as well as the legal norms that are enacted to this end, to all those persons that flee their country as a result of *aggression, foreign occupation or domination or massive human rights violations, or due to events of a political nature that seriously disturb public order in the country of origin or provenance*" (Seminario de La Paz 1983: 116; translation by the author; emphasis added).

With a result almost identical with that of the 1981 Mexico Colloquium the 1983 La Paz Seminar's sixth conclusion reiterated the *need* for a broader definition of "refugee." The regional approach thus differed from its international global counterparts (see above) in the sense that it did not have a merely descriptive but rather propositive wording, in addition to adding "massive human rights violations" as a ground for refugeehood.

The third and final regional event that advocated a broader definition was the four-day "Colloquium on the International Protection of Refugees in Central America, Mexico and Panama: Legal and Humanitarian Problems," held in November 1984 in Cartagena de Indias, Colombia. Also co-organized by the UNHCR, the colloquium was opened once again by the then-High Commissioner, Poul Hartling, and the Colombian president, Belisario Betancour, and was attended by a combination of state and unofficial delegations. This time, however, there were presentations by governmental delegates of six out of eight Central American countries, namely Belize, Costa Rica, El Salvador, Honduras, Mexico, and Nicaragua. As at the previous events, conclusions and recommendations were adopted, seventeen and five, respectively. The third conclusion reads, "the definition or concept of a refugee *recommended* for use in the region is one that, in addition to containing the elements of the 1951 Convention and the 1967 Protocol, also considers refugees persons who have fled their country because their lives, safety or freedom have been threatened by *generalized violence, foreign aggression, internal conflicts, massive violation of human rights or other circumstances which have seriously disturbed public order* (Coloquio de Cartagena 1985: 366; translation by the author; emphasis added).

The conclusion *recommending* the widening of the definition of "refugee" in Central America listed virtually the same grounds as those of the April 1981 Geneva Group of Experts, the May 1981 Mexico Colloquium, the June 1981 Sanremo Roundtable, the October 1981 ExCom Conclusion, and the April 1983 La Paz Seminar. The UNHCR decided robustly to promote and advocate it at the global, regional, and national levels. Somewhat timidly, the 1985 UNHCR Note on International Protection laconically stated that the conclusions adopted by the Colloquium and embodied in the 1984 Cartagena Declaration "will undoubtedly contribute to the further development of refugee law in Latin America" (UNHCR 1985a: para. 51). The ExCom then adopted Conclusion No. 37 (XXXVI) on Central American Refugees and the Cartagena Declaration, which "(c) Noted with interest the Cartagena Declaration " and "(d) welcomed the use of regional approaches in resolving refugee problems of regional scope" (UNHCR 2014). That conclusion was followed, at the regional level, by a 1985 OAS General Assembly resolution on the "Legal Status of Asylees, Refugees and Displaced Persons in the American Hemisphere" that underscored the importance of the 1984 Cartagena Declaration and "*recommend[ed]* to the member states that they apply that Declaration in dealing with the refugees in their territory" (OAS 1986: 33; emphasis added). At the national level UNHCR staff individually met Latin American diplomats and advocated the global and regional support and endorsement of the 1984 Cartagena Declaration by their respective countries.[14]

From a summary of events cited above one can see that, in the early 1980s, the UNHCR directly and proactively influenced, as a norm entrepreneur, the spontaneous transformation of the refugee sub-regime in Central America. In general, the aim was to address the phenomenon of massive influx of asylum seekers in Latin America. In addition, the UNHCR sought a solution to the status of asylum seekers who were left out of the 1951 Refugee Convention definition. The endorsement of the 1984 Cartagena Declaration by the ExCom and by the OAS General Assembly and the ensuing practice of states concerned allowed the legitimacy of the regime change and resulted in the incorporation of the new norms, in particular the *recommended* broad definition of "refugee" (Yundt 1988: 59).

The Cartagena Declaration: A Reality Check

Decades have elapsed since its adoption, yet the 1984 Cartagena Declaration is still hailed by doctrine and practitioners as a relevant instrument. To what extent does this hold true? This section comments on four distinct but overlapping areas of its potential relevance: practical, political, legal and advocacy.

The 1984 Cartagena Declaration's enormous practical relevance has withered with the passing of time. The irony is that its loss of practical relevance is the result of its own success. In the early 1980s the Central American forced migrants who did not qualify as refugees did not have a clearly defined legal status (see above). In other parts of the world there were attempts, since the beginning of the mid-1970s large-scale forced migration movements, to introduce a new legal status, one that would encompass the rights and duties of those benefiting from a so-called "temporary refuge" (Coles 1980: 202–7; Martin 1982: 603–7). These attempts made at the global level resulted in ExCom Conclusions No. 5 (XXVIII) of 1977, No. 14 (XXX) of 1979, and No. 19 (XXXI) of 1980, which referred to "temporary refuge"; and Conclusions No. 11 (XXIX) of 1978 and No. 15 (XXX) of 1979, which referred to "temporary asylum" (UNHCR 2014). In the 1990s the terminology evolved to "temporary protection," which we can see in ExCom Conclusions No. 68 (XLIII) of 1992, No. 71 (XLIV) of 1993, and No. 74 (XLV) of 1994.[15]

The 1984 Cartagena Declaration therefore successfully prevented the introduction of a parallel legal status in Central America by bringing those forced migrants who did not fall under the 1951 Refugee Convention within the purview of a broader definition that accorded them the same rights and duties enjoyed by Convention refugees. This important development—present in both Latin America and Africa—did not materialize in Europe, where legal statuses entailing lower rights and parallel to refugee status had already been introduced (e.g., subsidiary protection and temporary protection).

Another example of the practical relevance of the 1984 Cartagena Declaration is the fact that, in addition to initially changing the practice of most Central American countries, the recommended definition has inspired the domestic refugee legislation and practice of the vast majority of Latin American countries.[16] Although some countries have directly imported the definition contained in the 1984 Cartagena Declaration in their national legislation, others have used different wording, and only a few have not incorporated a broad definition in their domestic law (Reed-Hurtado 2017: 158–61). Given that the majority of the Latin American countries already have in their national statutes a broad definition that complements the 1951 Refugee Convention's definition, the ongoing practical relevance of the 1984 Cartagena Declaration is difficult to sustain. Instead of making an apologia or eulogy of the 1984 Cartagena Declaration and its broad definition, its advocates should see to it that country-tailored interpretive guidelines are given to the various different wordings captured in the region's national legislation broad definitions.[17]

The last reason for the lack of practical relevance of the 1984 Cartagena Declaration is unfortunate: despite having been replicated or having inspired the domestic legislation of the majority of Latin American countries, the broad definition is seldom used, thus having greater application in rhetoric than in practice (Reed-Hurtado 2017: 163–67, 179–80). A long avenue of legal advocacy lies ahead of the UNHCR to revive this particular aspect of the 1984 Cartagena Declaration's practical relevance.[18]

The 1984 Cartagena Declaration was politically relevant in the second half of the 1980s and in the early 1990s. This is no longer the case. The first reason it was relevant is that relations between Central American countries had become strained, which made it harder for them to find a formal solution through legally binding instruments (Ruiz de Santiago 1992: 138). The colloquium in which the 1984 Cartagena Declaration was adopted allowed for an informal agreement, concluded by experts and some government representatives in a sui generis UNHCR-led event much less formal than an international regional conference would have been. The UNHCR played a key role in breaking the political deadlock that existed, in disguising the 1984 Cartagena Declaration's political nature, and in attenuating the highly politically charged context that prevailed.

Another reason why the 1984 Cartagena Declaration was politically relevant was its wording. The conflicts that emerged in Central America in the late 1970s and early 1980s were of an internal nature; however, its dynamics were hugely influenced by the Cold War and the geopolitical interests of other countries. The extent to which the 1984 Cartagena Declaration is a political document is clearly assessed by what is *not* written in its text–in other words, by what was withdrawn from previous versions. For instance, the broad definitions of "refugee" captured in the 1981 Mexico Colloquium, in the 1981 ExCom Conclusion No. 22, and in the 1983 La Paz Seminar all refer to (foreign) occupation or domination, whereas the 1984 Cartagena Declaration omits both terms. The 1984 Cartagena Declaration also avoided the wording of the then recent 1983 La Paz Seminar, which referred to the "political" nature of events disturbing public order. One sees that the wording of the 1984 Cartagena Declaration sanitized the previous versions in order to render it less politically sensitive, and that it was due precisely to the very politically sensitive environment in which it was drafted and its political character. The changes that occurred in Central America and in the world (in particular the end of the Cold War) have made the 1984 Cartagena Declaration lose the political features that were originally imbued in the choices made regarding its wording.

The legal relevance of 1984 Cartagena Declaration has varied over time and is nowadays rather limited. Being the final text of a colloquium that aimed at "studying the legal and humanitarian aspects of the refugee situation in Central America" (Coloquio de Cartagena 1985: 11), it clearly never had the original intention of establishing binding law. However, it has been argued by a renowned scholar and former president of the IACtHR that the 1984 Cartagena Declaration is part of the origin of the creation of a Latin

American and Caribbean regional custom, and that its persuasive force derives from the fact that there was generalized *opinio juris* (i.e., the belief that an action is carried out because it is a legal obligation) when it was formed (Gros Espiell 1995). The progressive rationale offered by Gros Espiell is sound, although it may be subject to criticism; international refugee law scholar Grahl-Madsen, for instance, has argued that in "customary (unwritten) international law there is no such thing as a generally accepted definition of "refugee." It follows that it conveys no meaning to speak of "refugees in the juridical sense" or "*der Begriff des Flüchtlings*' except in the context of a particular legal instrument" (Grahl-Madsen 1966: 73). The 1984 Cartagena was not and has never become a *legal* instrument but rather, as defined by the UNHCR itself, a "conceptual framework for refugee protection policy" (UNHCR 1994: para. 36).

That the 1984 Cartagena Declaration is nonbinding does not mean that it is without any legal significance. It constitutes a recommendation to states to base their legal practice on its principles, and to some extent state practice has fallen in line with the Declaration's specific recommendations or at least with its spirit.[19] The 1984 Cartagena Declaration's legal relevance, therefore, stems both from its acceptance by states as the expression of legal principles and from the crystallization of some of its principles and recommendations in the region's domestic legislation.

Even if one puts Grahl-Madsen's argument aside and considers that the 1984 Cartagena Declaration had far-reaching legal consequences, it is hard to assert that it has become an authoritative expression of customary international law, particularly because it has not been unanimously and harmoniously adopted. The fact that only a fraction of states have adopted domestic legislation that directly imported the definition contained in the 1984 Cartagena Declaration and that some others altered (sometimes drastically) the original wording proposed by the Declaration corroborates the understanding that there is not a consensus as to a regional definition of "refugee" to be used in Latin America. However, that the majority of Latin American states have adopted legislation broadening the definition of the 1951 Refugee Convention is a clear indication of the importance of the 1984 Cartagena Declaration in paving the way to the progressive development of international refugee law in the region—even if that development has significant domestic variations.

The last area on which this section assesses the 1984 Cartagena Declaration's relevance is its role as an instrument in advocacy and an effective advocacy model. The UNHCR had already used events of the sort in the region and acknowledged—for example, when referring to the 1981 Mexico Seminar—that "seminars and colloquia such as th[is] play a recognised role in the promotion and dissemination of the principles of international protection and refugee law" (UNHCR 1981c: para. 76). However, unlike previous seminars and colloquia, the 1984 Cartagena Declaration had an unprecedented impact in Latin America both on policy and legal development, and on the way protection policy advocacy is conducted.

As for policy and legal development, during the late 1980s and the 1990s the 1984 Cartagena Declaration was *the* region's conceptual framework for refugee protection policy, having inspired public policy and domestic legislation in the majority of the region's states. Even if only a fraction of the latter used the exact wording of the definition recommended by the 1984 Cartagena Declaration in their domestic legislation, the spirit of Cartagena prevailed: the adopted definitions led to the granting of refugee status to forced migrants who were in need of protection as a result of the consequences of armed conflict and violence.

The success of the 1984 Cartagena Declaration as a conceptual framework for refugee protection policy led the UNHCR to increase the use of events of this sort as a model in its advocacy work. The multiplying effect resulting from the 1984 Cartagena Declaration's tangible achievements can be seen inter alia in the adoption of the 1994 San José Declaration on Refugees and Displaced Persons, the 2000 Rio de Janeiro Declaration on the Protection of Refugees, the 2004 Mexico Declaration and Plan of Action to Strengthen the International Protection of Refugees in Latin America, the 2010 Brasilia Declaration on the Protection of Refugees and Stateless Persons in the Americas, the 2012 Fortaleza Mercosul Declaration of Principles on the International Protection of Refugees, and the 2014 Brazil Declaration "A Framework for Cooperation and Regional Solidarity to Strengthen the International Protection of Refugees, Displaced and Stateless Persons in Latin America and the Caribbean" and respective plan of action. Hence, inspired both by the accomplishments of the very effective advocacy model resulting from the 1984 Cartagena Declaration and by the region's reluctance in promoting refugee-related legally binding instruments, the advocacy model consolidated by the Cartagena colloquium has been and is still being successfully used to advance refugee protection policy in Latin America.

Conclusion

The 1984 Cartagena Declaration's broad definition of "refugee" is neither innovative nor pragmatic. Its wording does not differ substantially from that of previous regional and global broad definitions and, as shown above, the essence of the 1984 Cartagena Declaration's broad definition had already been drafted in 1981 in an international global framework to address the problem of large-scale forced migration movements that was affecting several continents. While it has an advisory, recommendatory nature, what was truly pragmatic was the successful UNHCR advocacy persuading states both to accept the 1984 Cartagena Declaration as a conceptual framework for refugee protection policy and to use it in a sensible and realistic fashion, based on practical considerations.

The Latin American tradition of asylum was put to a severe test from the mid-1970s to mid-1980s and the regime norms–which as a rule are the result of the interaction of a set of facts with values and interests–had to be changed. The interaction of the reality of hundreds of thousands of asylum seekers who were not regarded as refugees (UNHCR 1984: para. 31) with the protection values defended by the UNHCR and the political interests of Central American states led to a change of the region's regime norms. The trigger to the regime change, however, was not the very adoption of the 1984 Cartagena Declaration. After all, many similar declarations and conclusions had been adopted before. In this case, rather, the way the UNHCR skilfully promoted it defined the period of change.

In this regard the role played by the UNHCR in the "transformation to stardom" of the 1984 Cartagena Declaration makes a good showcase of the interplay of competing theories of international relations. On the one hand, according to realism, the international global and regional asylum regimes remain an artefact of states. On the other, according to constructivism, institutions matter because they constitute and change the identities and preferences of states. The combination of the Central American states' self-serving interests in addressing the geopolitical situation caused by thousands of forced migrants who were in their territories and of the protection values defended by the UNHCR led to a successful and protection-sensitive change of regime. Of paramount importance in that process was the UNHCR's role as a norm-entrepreneur in directly contributing to the creation, endorsement, dissemination, and implementation of the principles and norms enshrined in the 1984 Cartagena Declaration.

The UNHCR's promotion of regional approaches[20] had its advantages and disadvantages. In Latin America it allowed for a practical solution which both avoided the creation of another category of protected persons and broadened the definition of "refugee" to encompass forced migrants fleeing from the consequences of armed conflict and violence. The regional initiative resulting from the promotion of the 1984 Cartagena Declaration, however, also showed its limits. Because the broad definition was only a recommendation, many states in the region ended up having definitions in their domestic legislation that vary significantly. Therefore, there is no common, harmonized regional broad definition of "refugee" adopted and used in Latin America.

Just as the 1951 Refugee Convention was a product of its time, so was the 1984 Cartagena Declaration. With the passage of time and due to its contextual nature, its practical, political, and legal relevance has become obsolete. The 1984 Cartagena Declaration's legacy is most likely to be found both in the broad definitions of "refugee" adopted in most of the region's domestic legislation, and in the advocacy model that uses ad hoc and sui generis UNHCR-led events to advance conceptual frameworks for refugee protection policy. The spirit of Cartagena is still very much alive and palpable in the region's resolve not to be stuck in the past, but rather to face and address both the changing nature of forced migration movements and the protection needs of the movements' victims.

José H. Fischel de Andrade is a UNHCR senior staff member. A University of Cambridge graduate, he is a past CAPES postdoctoral research fellow at The Graduate Institute (HEID, Geneva) and a *diplômé* of both the Academy of European Law (EUI, Florence) and the International Institute of Human Rights (Strasbourg). He lectures at universities in Milano (Statale) and Berlin (Humboldt).

Notes

*The original, longer version of this chapter, which includes sections on 'The Asylum Regime and its Political Asylee and Refugee Sub-Regimes' and 'The Late 1970s and Early 1980s Forced Migration Movements in Central America,' has been originally published by the author as "The 1984 Cartagena Declaration: a critical review of some aspects of its emergence and relevance," *Refugee Survey Quarterly* 38(4), 2019, pp. 341–362.
**The views expressed in this chapter are those of the author and might not reflect those of the UNHCR.
1. For the purpose of this chapter Latin America encompasses twenty countries, namely three Caribbean (Cuba, Dominican Republic, and Haiti), seven Central American (Costa Rica, El Salvador, Guatemala, Honduras, Mexico, Nicaragua, and Panama), and ten South American (Argentina, Bolivia, Brazil, Chile, Colombia, Ecuador, Paraguay, Peru, Uruguay, and Venezuela) countries. Hence this chapter excludes from its scope one non–Latin Central American country (Belize), one non–Latin South American country (Suriname), the overseas department of France in South America (French Guyana), and the remaining Caribbean countries and British, Dutch, and French territories.
2. Belize, Costa Rica, El Salvador, Guatemala, Honduras, Mexico, Nicaragua, and Panama. Even though Belize is not covered in this chapter since it is not a Latin Central American country, and hence part of Latin America (see above), it enacted a Refugees Act (No. 26) in 1991, amended (Chapter 165) in 2001, that contains a broad definition of the term "refugee" that reproduces *ipsis litteris* the extended definition adopted in the 1969 Organization of African Unity (OAU) Refugee Convention. This indicates that even though Belize wanted to distance itself from the 1984 Cartagena Declaration, it was inspired by the spirit of Cartagena (see below).

3. The best narrative of the protection of refugee groups in Central America from 1981 until 1985 is to be found in Jackson 1999, 347–95. See also Fischel de Andrade 2019, 345–48.
4. IACmHR 1965: 76–77. When referring to "political refugees," the IACmHR introduced a misconceived idea, based on a wrong understanding that endured over decades, that refugees, as opposed to political asylees, move in large numbers and are destitute; see IACmHR 1965: 75. *A contrario sensu*, two relevant examples of large-scale granting of political asylee status were when in late 1973 and early 1974 in Chile more than two thousand persons enjoyed diplomatic asylum as political asylees (see CIJ 1975: 149), and when in 1980 more than ten thousand Cubans enjoyed diplomatic asylum in the Peruvian Embassy in Havana. For a further criticism of the pseudo-difference between political asylees and refugees based on the latter's rural origin, limited economic resources, low level of education, and political irrelevance; see Ruiz de Santiago 1997: 1370.
5. The Argentinean member of the Inter-American Juridical Committee, Miguel Angel Espeche Gil, recommended that the IACmHR assume the role of protection and assistance coordination; see CJI 1966, 47.
6. In the theory of international relations literature, "norm entrepreneur" is defined as an individual or organization that sets out to change the behavior of others; see Florini 1996, 375.
7. See the 1889 Montevideo Treaty on International Penal Law (five states parties: Argentina, Bolivia, Paraguay, Peru, and Uruguay), the 1928 Havana Convention on Asylum (sixteen states parties: Brazil, Colombia, Costa Rica, Cuba, Dominican Republic, Ecuador, El Salvador, Guatemala, Haiti, Honduras, Mexico, Nicaragua, Panama, Paraguay, Peru, and Uruguay), the 1933 Montevideo Convention on Political Asylum (fourteen states parties: Brazil, Chile, Colombia, Costa Rica, Cuba, Ecuador, El Salvador, Guatemala, Honduras, Mexico, Nicaragua, Panama, Paraguay, and Peru), the 1939 Montevideo Treaty on Political Asylum and Refuge (one state party: Paraguay), the 1940 Montevideo Treaty on International Penal Law (seven states parties: Argentina, Bolivia, Brazil, Colombia, Paraguay, Peru, Uruguay), the 1954 Caracas Convention on Territorial Asylum (eleven states parties: Brazil, Colombia, Costa Rica, Ecuador, El Salvador, Guatemala, Mexico, Panama, Paraguay, Uruguay, Venezuela), and the 1954 Caracas Convention on Diplomatic Asylum (thirteen states parties: Argentina, Brazil, Costa Rica, Ecuador, El Salvador, Guatemala, Mexico, Panama, Paraguay, Peru, Dominican Republic, Uruguay, Venezuela).
8. Belize (1990), Honduras (1992), and Mexico (2000) followed suit a bit later.
9. According to Kratochwil and Ruggie (1986: 767), a change in the normative structure of a regime produces change *of*—as opposed merely to *within* a—regime.
10. A comprehensive list of UNGA resolutions is presented in UNHCR 1994: fn8.
11. A change of regime at a regional level had already taken place in Africa, where the 1969 OAU Refugee Convention states in Article 1.2 that "the term "refugee" shall also [i.e., in addition to the grounds of the 1951 Refugee Convention] apply to every person who, owing to external aggression, occupation, foreign domination or events seriously disturbing public order in either part or the whole of his country of origin or nationality, is compelled to leave his place of habitual residence in order to seek refuge in another place outside his country of origin or nationality."

12. It should not pass unnoticed that at the end of the 1981 Mexico Colloquium Professor Dunshee de Abranches wrote a set of conclusions and recommendations from which the colloquium's final conclusions and recommendations drew inspiration; see Dunshee de Abranches 1982: 201–3.
13. IACmHR 1982: chap. 6, B. In fact, Professor Dunshee de Abranches of the IACmHR had already mentioned in his Conclusion No. 14, resulting from the 1981 Mexico Colloquium, the IACmHR's competence to write up reports on the situation of asylees and refugees in the Americas; see Dunshee de Abranches 1982: 202.
14. To mention but one example, at a meeting held on 9 August 1985 between Guilherme da Cunha, Head of the UNHCR's Americas Section, and Fernando Lopes, Counsellor at the Brazilian Permanent Mission to the UN in Geneva, they discussed "the possibility of Brazil's support of an endorsement of the Cartagena Declaration, within the framework of UNHCR's efforts to diffuse and promote the Declaration, in the following three main fora: (1) The UNHCR Executive Committee, (2) The General Assembly of the Organization of American States, and (3) (c) The Contadora Group"; see UNHCR 1985b.
15. UNHCR 2014. It should be noted that the term "complementary forms of protection" mentioned in ExCom Conclusions No. 87 (L) of 1999 and No. 89 (LI) of 2000 is not the terminological evolution of temporary refuge, asylum, or protection. In fact, in its Conclusion No. 103 (LVI) of 2005, the ExCom noted "that temporary protection, without formally according refugee status, as a specific provisional protection response to situations of mass influx providing immediate emergency protection from *refoulement*, should be clearly distinguished from other forms of international protection"; see ibid.
16. The widening of the definition proved to be very useful when asylum seekers from other continents, in particular Africans who did not fall under the 1951 Refugee Convention refugee definition, sought asylum in the region; see D'Alotto and Garreton 1991: 500; Fischel de Andrade 2015: 166; Fischel de Andrade 2017: 68; and Kourula 1997: 153.
17. The 1989 "CIREFCA Legal Document" and UNHCR's guidelines on claims for refugee status related to situations of armed conflict and violence only partially address this need since they focus only on the elements of the 1984 Cartagena Declaration and not on the variations that one finds in the different Latin American domestic refugee legislations; see, respectively, Gros Espiell et al. 1990 and UNHCR 2016: 12–16.
18. The actual use in the region of a broad definition already enshrined in domestic legislation is only one of a long list of areas that need improvement and that includes inter alia accelerated procedures that do not comply with internationally established due process guarantees, refugee status determination (RSD) procedures that are not regulated through domestic law, and RSD bodies that still lack training, efficiency, independence, and expertise; see Fischel de Andrade 2014: 661.
19. It is this author's understanding that the spirit of Cartagena was based on the conviction that a progressive change of regime was needed: in other words, a regime change was needed that would embrace as refugees those forced migrants who were in need of protection as a result of the consequences of armed conflict and violence.

20. For the various ExCom conclusions specific to regional approaches, as well as those that refer to regional initiatives and regional instruments, see UNHCR 2014: 462–70. On the regional policy approaches and harmonization in Latin America, see also Fischel de Andrade 1998.

References

Arboleda, Eduardo. 1991. "Refugee Definition in Africa and Latin America: The Lessons of Pragmatism." *International Journal of Refugee Law* 3(2): 185–207.

Arboleda, Eduardo. 1995. "The Cartagena Declaration of 1984 and its Similarities to the 1969 OUA Convention–a Comparative Perspective." *International Journal of Refugee Law* (special issue): 87–101.

Comisión Internacional de Juristas (CIJ). 1975. *Aplicación de las Declaraciones y Convenciones Internacionales referentes al Asilo en América Latina.* Geneva: Comisión Internacional de Juristas.

Comité Jurídico Interamericano (CJI). 1966. "Anteproyecto de Convención Interamericana sobre Refugiados." In *Trabajos Realizados por el Comité Jurídico Interamericano durante su Periodo Extraordinario de Sesiones (Abril 1966)*, 31–47. Doc. OEA/Ser.I VI.2–CIJ-85, Union Panamericana/OEA, Washington.

Coles, Gervase J.L. 1980. "Temporary Refuge and the Large Scale Influx of Refugees." *Australian Year Book of International Law* 8: 189–212.

Coles, Gervase J.L. 1990. "Approaching the Refugee Problem Today." In *Refugees and International Relations*, edited by G. Loescher and L. Monahan, 373–410. Oxford: Claredon Press.

Coloquio de Cartagena 1985. *Coloquio Sobre la Protección Internacional de los Refugiados en América Central, México y Panamá: problemas jurídicos y humanitarios* (Memorias del Coloquio de Cartagena de Indias, 19–22 Noviembre 1984), Bogotá, ACNUR/Centro Regional de Estudios del Tercer Mundo/Universidad Nacional de Colombia.

Coloquio de México 1982. *Asilo y Protección Internacional de Refugiados en América Latina* (Memorias del Coloquio de Ciudad de México, 11–15 mayo 1981). Mexico City, National Autonomous University of Mexico.

D'Alotto, Alberto and Roberto Garreton. 1991. "Developments in Latin America: some further thoughts," *International Journal of Refugee Law* 3 (3): 499–501.

Dunshee de Abranches, Carlos A. 1982. "Conclusiones y Recomendaciones," in *Asilo y Protección Internacional de Refugiados en América Latina* (Memorias del Coloquio de Ciudad de México, 11–15 mayo 1981), Mexico City, National Autonomous University of Mexico, 1982, 201–203.

Ferris, Elizabeth G. 1984. "The Politics of Asylum: Mexico and the Central American Refugees." *Journal of Interamerican Studies and World Affairs* 26 (3): 357–84.

Fischel de Andrade, José H. 1998. "Regional Policy Approaches and Harmonization: a Latin American perspective." *International Journal of Refugee Law* 10 (3): 389–409.

Fischel de Andrade, José H. 2014. "Forced Migration in South America." In E. Fiddian-Qasmiyeh et al. (eds.), *The Oxford Handbook of Refugee and Forced Migration Studies*, Oxford: Oxford University Press, 651–663.

Fischel de Andrade, José H. 2015. "Refugee Protection in Brazil (1921–2014): an analytical narrative of changing policies," in D.J. Cantor et al. (eds), *A Liberal Tide? Immigration and asylum law and policy in Latin America*, London, Institute of Latin American Studies/University of London, 153–183.

Fischel de Andrade, José H. 2017. "Aspectos Históricos da Proteção de Refugiados no Brasil (1951–1997)," in L.L. Jubilut and G.G. de Godoy (eds), *Refúgio no Brasil–Comentários à Lei 9.474/97*, São Paulo, Ed. Quartier Latin, 41–80.

Fischel de Andrade, José H. 2019. "The 1984 Cartagena Declaration: a critical review of some aspects of its emergence and relevance," *Refugee Studies Quarterly*, 38(4), 341–362.

Florini, Ann. 1996. "The Evolution of International Norms," *International Studies Quarterly*, 40, 363–389.

Fortín, Antonio. 2005. "Doctrinal Review of the Broader Refugee Definition Contained in the Cartagena Declaration." In *Memoir of the Twentieth Anniversary of the Cartagena Declaration on Refugees*, edited by UNHCR. San José, Costa Rica: Editorama, 255–290.

Franco, Leonardo and Jorge Santistevan de N. 2005. "Contributions of the Cartagena process to the development of international refugee law in Latin America," in UNHCR, *Memoir of the Twentieth Anniversary of the Cartagena Declaration on Refugees*, San José, Costa Rica, Editorama, 2005, 61–119.

Grahl-Madsen, Atle. 1966. *The Status of Refugees in International Law*, vol. I, Leiden, Sijthoff.

Gros Espiell, Hector, Sonia Picado and Leo Valladares Lanza . 1990. [CIREFCA Legal Document] "Principles and Criteria for the Protection of and Assistance to Central American Refugees, Returnees and Displaced Persons in Latin America," *International Journal of Refugee Law*, 2(1), 1990, 83–117.

Gros Espiell, Hector. 1995. "La Declaración de Cartagena como fuente del derecho internacional de los refugiados en América Latina," in *Memoria del Coloquio International: 10 Años de la Declaración de Cartagena sobre Refugiados* (Coloquio de San José, Costa Rica, 5–7 December 1994), San José, Costa Rica: Inter-American Institute of Human Rights/ACNUR, 453–470.

Inter-American Commission on Human Rights (IACmHR). 1965. *Informe sobre Refugiados Políticos en América*. Doc. OEA/Ser.L/V/II.11, doc.7 rev. 2, 2 noviembre 1965.

———. 1982. *Informe Anual de la Comisión Interamericana de Derechos Humanos 1981–1982*. Doc. OEA/Ser.L/V/II.57, doc. 6 rev.1, 20 septiembre 1982.

International Institute of Humanitarian Law (IIHL). 1981. *Report: Round Table on the Problems Arising from Large Numbers of Asylum Seekers* (Sanremo, 22–25 June 1981), Sanremo, IIHL.

Jackson, Ivor. 1999. *The Refugee Concept in Group Situations*. The Hague, Netherlands: Martinus Nijhoff.

Kourula, Pirkko. 1997. *Broadening the Edges–Refugee definition and international protection revisited*. The Hague, Martinus Nijhoff Publ.

Kratochwil, Friedrich and John G. Ruggie 1986. "International Organization: a state of the art on an art of the state." *International Organization* 40 (4): 753–75.

Martin, David A. 1982. "Large-Scale Migrations of Asylum Seekers," *American Journal of International Law*, 76(3), 598–609.

Organization of American States (OAS). 1982. "AG/Res. 618 (XII-0/82) on Annual Report of the Inter-American Commission on Human Rights" (adopted on 20 November 1982). In *Proceedings–Certified Texts of the Resolutions*, vol. I, Twelfth Regular Session (15–21 November 1982), Doc. OEA/Ser.P/XII.0.2, Washington, DC, 15 December 1982, 61–63.

———. 1986. "AG/Res. 774 (XV-0/85) on Legal Status of Asylees, Refugees, and Displaced Persons in the American Hemisphere" (adopted on 9 December 1985), in *Proceedings–Certified Texts of the Resolutions*, vol. I, Fifteenth Regular Session (5–9 December 1985), Doc. OEA/Ser.P/XV.0.2, Washington (DC), 2 April 1986, 32–33.

Reed-Hurtado, Michael. 2017. "The Cartagena Declaration on Refugees and the Protection of People Fleeing Armed Conflict and Other Situations of Violence in Latin America." in *In Flight from Conflict and Violence–UNHCR's Consultations on Refugee Status and Other Forms of International Protection*, edited by V. Türk et al., 141–80. Cambridge: Cambridge University Press.

Ruiz de Santiago, Jaime. 1992. "O Direito Internacional dos Refugiados: características e desenvolvimento na América Latina." In *A Proteção dos Direitos Humanos nos Planos Nacional e Internacional: perspectivas brasileiras*, edited by A.A. Cançado Trindade, 125–50. Seminário de Brasília, July 1991. San José, Costa Rica: Inter-American Institute of Human Rights / Friedrich-Naumann Stiftung.

Ruiz de Santiago, Jaime. 1997. "Contribución de Héctor Gros Espiell al desarrollo del Derecho Internacional de los Refugiados," in *Héctor Gros Espiell–Amicorum Lieber*, vol. 2, Brussells, Bruylant, 1351–1378.

Ruiz de Santiago, Jaime. 2005. "The Cartagena Declaration: legal nature and historical importance," in UNHCR, *Memoir of the Twentieth Anniversary of the Cartagena Declaration on Refugees*, San José, Costa Rica, Editorama, 291–314.

Sanness, John. 1997. "Presentation: Speech by John Sanness, Chairman of the Norwegian Nobel Committee." In *Peace, 1981–1990*, edited by T. Frängsmyr and I. Abrams, 7–15. Series Nobel Lectures. Singapore: World Scientific.

Seminario de La Paz. 1983. *Asilo Político y Situación del Refugiado* (Memorias del Seminario de La Paz, 19–22 abril 1983), La Paz, Ministerio de Relaciones Exteriores y Culto/ACNUR.

Tirado, Teresa. 1990. "Evolución del Concepto de Refugiado. La Declaración de Cartagena y el Problema de Flujos Masivos de Refugiados," in *La Protección Jurídica Internacional de la Persona Humana y el Problema de los Indocumentados* (Seminario de La Paz, 12–15 noviembre 1990), La Paz, ACNUR/CICR/CJI/CAJ, 131–137.

United Nations High Commissioner for Refugees (UNHCR). 1981a. *Report of the Meeting of the Expert Group on Temporary Refuge in Situations of Large-Scale Influx* (Geneva, 21–24 April 1981), Doc. EC/SCP/16, 3 June 1981.

———. 1981b. *Note on International Protection*, Doc. A/AC.96/593, 31 July 1981.

———. 1981c. *Report of the United Nations High Commissioner for Refugees*, Doc. A/36/12, 28 August 1981.

———. 1982. *Note on International Protection*, Doc. A/AC.96/609/Rev. 1, 26 August 1982.

———. 1983. *Report of the United Nations High Commissioner for Refugees*, Doc. A/38/12, Supplement No. 12, 17 August 1983.

———. 1984. *Note on International Protection*, Doc. A/AC.96/643, 9 August 1984.
———. 1985a. *Note on International Protection*, Doc. A/AC.96/660, 23 July 1985.
———. 1985b. *Note for the File*, drafted by Francisco Galindo Vélez, Geneva, 12 August 1985, UNHCR Archives: 010.BRA Folio 5.
———. 1994. *Note on International Protection*, Doc. A/AC.96/830, 7 September 1994.
———. 2014. *A Thematic Compilation of Executive Committee Conclusions*, 7th ed. Geneva: DIP/UNHCR.
———. 2016. *Guidelines on International Protection No. 12: claims for refugee status related to situations of armed conflict and violence under Article 1A(2) of the 1951 Convention and/or 1967 Protocol relating to the Status of Refugees and the regional refugee definitions*, Doc. HCR/GIP/16/12, 2 December 2016.
———. 2020. *UNHCR Population Statistics Database*, available at http://popstats.unhcr.org (last visited 18 Aug. 2020.
Yundt, Keith W. 1987–1988. "International Law and the Latin American Political Refugee Crisis." *University of Miami Inter-American Law Review* 19, 1987–1988: 137–154.
Yundt, Keith W. 1988. *Latin American States and Political Refugees*. Westport, CT: Praeger.

2

The Invisible Majority
Internally Displaced People in Latin America and the San José Declaration

Elizabeth Rushing and Andrés Lizcano Rodriguez

Introduction

Although refugees represent only a minority of people forcibly displaced around the world, they tend to dominate the attention of the media and international community. A related phenomenon that draws less political clout is the plight of people who have fled the same conflicts, violence, disasters, effects of climate change, or development projects but who have not crossed an international border, known as internally displaced people (IDPs).[1]

Internal displacement is a global phenomenon. There were 33.4 million new displacements associated with disasters and conflict recorded in 2019 across 145 countries and territories (Internal Displacement Monitoring Centre [IDMC] 2019a). For a number of reasons–in large part related to sovereignty, competing humanitarian issues, and coordination–internal displacement has been addressed at a much slower pace than cross-border displacement. This is despite the fact that of the 79.5 million people forcibly displaced around the world, 45.7 million–or nearly six out of ten–are internally displaced (United Nations High Commissioner for Refugees [UNHCR] 2020). It has taken time and effort for internal displacement to find its place within the international community, with regional actors, and even on the agenda of national governments.

In Latin America, the 1984 Cartagena Declaration on Refugees (Cartagena Declaration) (see Fischel de Andrade in this volume) mentions IDPs only once (Colloquium on the International Protection of Refugees in Central America 1984: Conclusion 9), reflecting the weak commitment to addressing the issue at the time. This was to change ten years later at the International Colloquium in Commemoration of the Tenth Anniversary of the Cartagena Declaration on Refugees, held in San José, Costa Rica, during which time the 1994 San José Declaration on Refugees and Displaced Persons (SJD) was adopted as the first of its sort to comprehensively address internal displacement and encourage governments in the region to develop frameworks that prevent displacement, assist and protect IDPs, and support displaced people in their search for durable solutions (International Colloquium in Commemoration of the tenth anniversary of the Cartagena Declaration on Refugees 1994).

This chapter explores the relevance of the SJD for IDPs. It postulates that, although the SJD is nonbinding and its impacts cannot be pinpointed to explicit contributions to policy, law, or jurisprudence, it formed part of the Latin American region's participation in and contribution to the process that put internal displacement on the humanitarian agenda both regionally and globally.[2]

The chapter begins with the historical context and institutional environment that set the scene for the SJD, which went beyond the Cartagena Declaration to include prevention of and response to internal displacement. It places the SJD in context during a moment when internal displacement was gaining attention as a policy issue. It goes on to analyze whether and how the SJD influenced the approaches of governments and regional organizations to addressing internal displacement, and how it fed into the building momentum which eventually led to the 1998 Guiding Principles on Internal Displacement (Guiding Principles).

Finally, the chapter provides an overview of contemporary challenges relating to internal displacement in the region and shows how a lack of official recognition and comprehensive prevention policies are hampering the understanding of the phenomenon and thus an adequate response to it.

As practitioners, the authors undertook a multidisciplinary approach, drawing from legal, historical, and policy analysis in order to explore the emergence of internal displacement as an issue of concern in the Americas, how it came to be included in the SJD, what the impact of this inclusion was, how it relates to other regional instruments and mechanisms available to support IDPs, and what lessons can be drawn for current practice. A historical review of the emergence of internal displacement as an issue on the global agenda was carried out based on the existing literature on the topic. The authors therefore referred to the main literature on internal displacement: from Cohen and Deng (2012) and Newland, Patrick, and Zard (2003) to regional documents[3] and United Nations (UN) resolutions.

A more challenging question, on the impact of the SJD as an instrument of soft law, could not be answered through the existing literature because it is rarely referenced. It was therefore researched first by carrying out a review of laws, policies, and jurisprudence in the region. For this purpose, the authors reached out to Los Andes University's law department, the Consultancy for Human Rights and Displacement, and the Americas Network for Refugees Legal Aid (RALRA)–a network of more than sixty organizations from more than twenty countries in the Americas working on legal support to refugees. RALRA gathered inputs about the impact of the SJD from partners in Argentina, Brazil, Chile, Colombia, Costa Rica, Dominican Republic, Ecuador, El Salvador, Guatemala, Honduras, Mexico, Uruguay, and Venezuela. Although partners made the link between the content of the San José Declaration and that of national policy, laws, and jurisprudence, however, no direct link or reference was provided.[4]

The authors also reviewed Colombian laws (National Congress of Colombia 1997), official policy documents (National Planning Department [DNP] 1995), and constitutional court sentences related to internal displacement (Constitutional Court of Colombia 1997, 2000, 2001, 2002a, 2002b, 2003a, 2003b, 2003c, 2003d, 2003e, 2003f, 2003g, 2004), as well as documents related to the Guatemalan peace agreement. (Guatemala and Colombia were prioritized for being the only two countries in the Americas with a policy on internal displacement in place before the presentation of the Guiding Principles.) This review was thorough and systematic but not exhaustive. The authors also interviewed practitioners who were working on internal displacement in the region during the 1990s,[5] shaping the desk research with examination of individual accounts. Finally, the authors' assessment of lessons for current practice are largely based on their own research and policy work on internal displacement in Central America.

The Long Road to San José

In the decades following World War II, pleas for protection of and assistance to IDPs were sporadic. Internal displacement was not covered by the 1951 Convention Relating to the Status of Refugees or its subsequent 1967 Protocol Relating to the Status of Refugees, nor the two main regional treaties in the Americas: the 1948 American Declaration on the Rights and Duties of Man (Inter-American Commission on Human Rights [IACmHR] 1948) and the 1969 American Convention on Human Rights, or the Pact of San José (Organization of American States [OAS] 1969). No UN agency was specifically mandated responsibility with regards to IDPs.

Despite these omissions, and based on UNHCR's founding statute, the United Nations General Assembly (UNGA) eventually called on UNHCR to provide protection or assistance to groups of refugees who did not fall under its purview. In 1972, together with the United Nations Economic and Social Council, it approved UNHCR operations in Sudan that included assistance to IDPs. IDPs also received sporadic support from other UN agencies such as the United Nations Children's Fund (UNICEF) or the World Food Programme (WFP), whenever the situation fell inside their mandate, and from the International Committee of the Red Cross and National Red Cross and Red Crescent Societies whose mandates implicitly included them (Cohen and Deng 2012; Newland, Patrick, and Zard 2003: 17–18).

These ad hoc responses to internal displacement started taking shape more systematically in the 1980s. In Latin America the signatories of the Cartagena Declaration expressed their "concern at the situation of displaced persons within their own countries" and called on "national authorities and the competent international organizations to offer protection and assistance to those persons and to help relieve the hardship which many of them face" (Cartagena Declaration on Refugees 1984: Ninth conclusion). The rest of the text nonetheless refers exclusively to refugees, as does a 1985 OAS General Assembly resolution on "Legal Status of Asylees, Refugees, and Displaced Persons in the American Hemisphere," despite its title (OAS 1986).

Toward the end of the 1980s, two major conferences addressed the phenomenon of internal displacement. In 1988, the International Conference on the Plight of Refugees, Returnees, and Displaced Persons in Southern Africa was the first UN initiative to "raise the question of institutionalised assistance to internally displaced persons" (UNGA 1988a). One year later, based on a request by the governments in the region seeking a definitive end to a string of civil wars, the UN hosted the International Conference on Central American Refugees (CIREFCA) in 1989 (CIREFCA 1990).

The first half of the 1990s witnessed a stabilization and then decrease in the number of refugees worldwide, while the number of IDPs continued a seemingly upward trend that had begun the early 1980s (Orchard 2010: 282). With this increased level of attention came more available data on displacement flows and trends.

However, ad hoc responses to internal displacement continued to occur during this period, partly due to eased tensions associated with providing assistance to IDPs following the end of the Cold War. UN involvement in internal displacement situations such as Sudan (1989), Iraq (1991), and Somalia (1992) were highly visible and controversial. In general, the perception that the UN had fallen short of an appropriate response when faced with a rapidly unfolding and highly visible humanitarian emergency "generated a new debate on access, intervention and humanitarian assistance at the UN which set the stage for new approaches to internal displacement" (Newland, Patrick, and Zard 2003: 18).

In reaction to these apparent failures, the UNGA assigned the function of coordinating IDP assistance to the resident coordinators. In 1991 the UNGA created the position of the emergency relief coordinator, the Department of Humanitarian Affairs, and the Inter-Agency Standing Committee (IASC) chaired by the emergency relief coordinator and composed of the heads of the organization's main humanitarian and development agencies (UNGA 1991). That same year, the United Nations Commission on Human Rights requested an analytical report on the situation of IDPs from the secretary general (United Nations Commission on Human Rights 1991), and in 1992 it requested the appointment of a representative of the secretary general on the human rights of IDPs (United Nations Commission on Human Rights 1992). The IASC designated the emergency relief coordinator as the UN reference point for internal displacement and created a task force on IDPs which operated until 1997 (Cohen and Deng 2012; IASC 1997; Newland, Patrick, and Zard 2003: 20–21).

Francis M. Deng, a politician and diplomat from South Sudan, was appointed as the first representative of the secretary general on the human rights of IDPs. Together with his team, they organized missions to countries with situations of internal displacement, reported on them, and carried out a review of the state of the norms and institutions related to IDPs. By 1994 this body of work was starting to move toward a normative framework on upholding the rights of people at risk of or affected by internal displacement.

In the Americas, political dynamics relating to displacement reacted to and evolved in tandem with ongoing displacement flows. More than 2 million people were uprooted from their homes due to the conflicts in the 1980s, most of them forced to move across borders (see Fischel de Andrade in this volume). Refugee camps were set up in Costa Rica, Honduras, and Mexico (IACmHR 1994a). Efforts by the Contadora group[6] to broker peace in the region initiated in 1983 and produced the Contadora Act on Peace and Cooperation in Central America in 1986 (Center for International Policy 1986). Although it was not approved by all countries in the region, it eventually led to a series of regional agreements: Esquipulas (1986) (Parlamento Centroamericano 1986) and Esquipulas 2 (1987) (UNGA 1987), by the presidents of Costa Rica, El Salvador, Guatemala, Honduras, and Nicaragua to promote peace in Central America. The Contadora Act, as well as Esquipulas 2, recognized the issue of displacement as intrinsically linked to the achievement of peace. Furthermore, they both explicitly included IDPs as a category of concern.

Against this global and regional backdrop, and in response to a request by the Central American countries and Mexico (CIREFCA 1988), CIREFCA was convened in 1989 by the UN secretary general, and organized by

UNHCR, the United Nations Development Programme (UNDP), and Central American governments. The conference, held in Guatemala City between 29 and 31 May 1989, stressed the need to help reintegrate displaced persons in general, provided a codification and clarification of the existing legal instruments for the response to displacement, and provided a definition of IDPs[7] and recognized them as a category requiring special assistance.

A key feature of the conference–and one that was ahead of its time–was the attempt to bridge the divide between humanitarian and development action. CIREFCA's development component was implemented through the Development Program for Displaced Persons, Refugees, and Returnees in Central America, which was financially supported by the Italian government. It ran from 1989 to 1995 and was administered by UNDP with support from other UN agencies and several nongovernmental organizations (NGOs) (United Nations Office for Project Services [UNOPS] 2015). The CIREFCA action plan (CIREFCA 1989) was also adopted as the provisions on displacement within the UN's wider development initiative, the Special Plan of Economic Cooperation for Central America (UNGA 1988b).

Funding was largely available during the whole process. Unfortunately, most of it ended up supporting refugees and not IDPs (Cohen and Deng 2012: 28). Nevertheless, CIREFCA and the Development Program for Displaced Persons, Refugees, and Returnees in Central America are among the most recognized regional approaches to reintegration of the displaced (Cohen and Sanchez-Garzoli 2001). The conference in fact initiated a larger process with several follow-up meetings that lasted until 1994, catalyzed several initiatives at the national level, and incorporated NGOs into the planning and decision-making of the displacement response (Betts 2006: 15, 30).

Building on progress made by CIREFCA, the issue of internal displacement started gaining more attention and several innovative initiatives were borne in the first half of the decade. In 1992 the Inter-American Institute of Human Rights created the Permanent Consultation on Internal Displacement in the Americas (CPDIA), comprised of representatives from intergovernmental organizations such as UNHCR, UNDP, UNICEF, WFP, the International Organization for Migration (IOM), the IACmHR, and the Inter-American Institute of Human Rights, NGOs such as the World Council of Churches and the Refugee Policy Group, independent experts, and an observer from the International Committee of the Red Cross (Cohen and Sanchez-Garzoli 2001).

The CPDIA, a unique organization, was meant to serve as "a clearinghouse of information on internally displaced persons; to analyze specific country situations and make recommendations for solutions; to provide technical assistance to governments and organizations working with the displaced; to establish a legal framework; and to promote respect for the human rights of displaced populations through meetings, forums and educational and training programs" (Cohen 1997). During the 1990s it conducted missions to Colombia, Guatemala, and Peru, and drafted a body of legal principles that would later be incorporated into national legislation and jurisprudence,[8] and proved helpful for the formulation of the Guiding Principles (Cohen and Sanchez-Garzoli 2001: 18).

The OAS was also crucial in addressing the issue. As early as 1984 its IACmHR had taken a seminal decision on Nicaragua, ruling that the Miskito Indigenous group should be compensated for the damage done to their property during their displacement (IACmHR 1984). This early decision would eventually influence the development of the Guiding Principles provisions on IDP returnees and their access to property (Cohen and Sanchez-Garzoli 2001: 17).

In the first half of the 1990s, the IACmHR reported consistently on the situation of IDPs in the region,[9] and in 1993, instructed by the OAS General Assembly (OAS 1993) it reported on the current state of protection for refugees, displaced persons, and repatriates in the region, hoping in particular "to demonstrate the applicability of existing international law to the growing phenomenon of internally displaced persons and repatriates" (IACmHR 1994a). The IACmHR also promoted the CIREFCA definition of IDPs, called for an OAS early warning system as a requisite for adequate prevention alongside the promotion of human rights and economic and social development, and even suggested a code of conduct to obligate governments to protect IDPs until a legal mechanism could be implemented (IACmHR 1994a).

Non-international armed conflicts were eventually resolved through elections in Nicaragua in 1990 (Uhlig 1990) and national peace agreements in El Salvador in 1992 (UNGA 1992), and Guatemala in 1996 (UNGA 1997). But the 1990s also shone light onto other internal displacement crises in Latin America such as guerrilla-related and drug trafficking–related violence in Bolivia, Colombia, and Peru, and military repression in Haiti after the 1991 coup. In this context, the need to extend the regional protection instruments for refugees to IDPs was finally confronted when countries met for the ten-year anniversary of the Cartagena Declaration, celebrated in San José, Costa Rica, in December 1994, and signed a new declaration marking this extension.

The San José Declaration: Fueling Momentum for IDPs

In 1994, with momentum from these global and regional developments, the government of Costa Rica, the Inter-American Institute of Human Rights, and UNHCR hosted an international colloquium to celebrate the ten-year anniversary of the Cartagena Declaration (Government of Costa Rica, Inter-

American Institute of Human Rights, and UNHCR 1995). Adopted by participants[10] on 7 December 1994, the SJD outlined the major conclusions and recommendations agreed on during the event.

In recognizing "the challenges posed by the new situations of human displacement in Latin America and the Caribbean, including, in particular, the increase in internal displacement and forced migration due to causes other than those provided for in the Cartagena Declaration" (ibid.: Intro I) the SJD reaffirms its precursor and the subsequent CIREFCA documents, stresses "the complementary nature and convergence between the systems of protection to persons established in International Human Rights Law, International Humanitarian Law and International Refugee Law" (ibid.: 3rd conclusion), encourages its harmonious application (ibid.: 4th conclusion), and promotes the mainstreaming of internal displacement issues across programs of the World Bank, International Monetary Fund, and the Inter-American Development Bank, and relevant regional forums (ibid.: Recommendations III).

Whereas the response to internal displacement was not the main objective of the conference, the challenges governments were facing related to IDPs, the recent institutional developments in the region and globally, as well as the participation of two members of Francis Deng's team in the colloquium, led to new and concrete measures, agreements, and language focused on internal displacement and its relationship to refugee protection, organized here along five broad streams of analysis.

First, the document represents a shift in language since the Cartagena Declaration, which focused exclusively on refugees and referred to IDPs only once–to express concern and "call on national authorities and the competent international organizations to offer protection and assistance" (ibid.: 9th conclusion). By systematically referring to "refugees, returnees, and displaced persons" and specifically addressing the issue, it continues and broadens progress made in the 1990s to a wider group of countries and organizations. Thus, the SJD addresses the challenge of the incipient visibility of the issue and the consequent lack of an adequate and systematic response, which was symptomatic of the humanitarian sector at the global and regional levels.

Second, the document addresses the normative vacuum at the time regarding the rights of IDPs and concretely suggests resorting to the Cartagena Declaration in order to find solutions to the new challenges posed by uprootedness (*desarraigo*) in Latin America and the Caribbean (ibid.: 1st conclusion). It also specifically states a number of rights that should be assured for IDPs:

> a. The application of the three bodies of international law: human rights norms and, when applicable, International Humanitarian Law as well as, by analogy, certain relevant principles of Refugee Law.

b. Recognition of the civilian character of displaced populations and of the humanitarian and apolitical nature of the treatment afforded to them

c. Protection and essential assistance as a responsibility of the national authorities and with the support of the international community

d. Attention to those rights which are crucial for their survival, security and dignity, as well as other rights such as adequate documentation, ownership of land and other assets, and freedom of movement, including the voluntary nature of return

e. The possibility of attaining a dignified and safe solution to their displacement (ibid.: 16th conclusion).

Although the SJD is nonbinding, these rights can be traced back to other international legal norms, many of which are considered customary law. Their explicit inclusion in the SJD was built on and contributed to the momentum carving out IDPs as a population category of concern.

Third, the document affirms that "the problem of the internally displaced, albeit the fundamental responsibility of the States of their nationality, is nevertheless of concern to the international community" (ibid.: 16th conclusion). This first reaffirms the well-recognized tenet that because IDPs remain within their country they should, in accordance with established principles of international law, enjoy the protection and assistance of their own governments as would any other person located within the borders. Based on humanitarian and human rights principles, as well as the reality of potential regional instability caused by unaddressed internal displacement, the SJD goes farther to stress international solidarity and concern, implicitly applying gentle pressure to states to handle their sovereignty as a responsibility rather than a shield against interference.

Fourth, the SJD bases the above contribution—that internal displacement is a concern to the international community—on the fact that "it is a human rights issue which can be linked to the prevention of causes which generate refugee flows" (ibid.: 16th conclusion). This is of particular importance because the focus had been on protection, and to some extent on durable solutions, whereas the prevention of conditions that lead to displacement is also crucial in tackling the root causes of cross-border displacement and irregular migration, as discussed below in the section on contemporary challenges.

Finally, the SJD contributes to the burgeoning institutional framework by underpinning certain ongoing efforts: it supports the work of the representative of the secretary general for IDPs, foreshadowing his preparation of the Guiding Principles and recommending an extension to his mandate (ibid.: 17th conclusion), and it notes "with particular interest the efforts initiated by the Permanent Consultative Group on Internally Displaced in the Americas, as a regional inter-agency forum dedicated to the study and consideration of the acute problems faced by the displaced within their own countries for reasons similar to those that result in refugee flows" (ibid.: 18th conclusion).

Despite the ostensibly innovative provisions of the SJD referring to internal displacement, it is in general probably the least known and the least quoted of the regional declarations (Maldonado Castillo 2014). In contrast to its predecessor, which expanded the definition of a refugee and has been incorporated into the national laws and state practices of fourteen countries, the SJD is not known to be referenced in any national law, policy, or jurisprudence in Latin America.[11]

Participants of the Colloquium who were interviewed for this chapter agree that, although it was no catalyst or key milestone, and did not lead to a radical shift in approaches to internal displacement, the SJD was part of and contributed to a process that was already underway to raise the profile of IDPs as a category that required special attention. This process was largely led by the representative of the secretary general and his team, who understood the workings of the international humanitarian system, Geneva-based organizations, and the UN, and who were savvy enough to raise the issue in the right forums and in the right formats, including through visits to Colombia in 1994 and 1997, as mentioned, as well as to El Salvador, Guatemala, and Peru.

Beyond the actions of the representative of the secretary general, however, the OAS reinforced this ongoing progress, referring to situations of internal displacement in several resolutions during the second half of the decade.[12] The IACmHR, which spearheaded the topic in the OAS, also met with the representative of the secretary general during its ninety-first session in 1996 and appointed Robert Kogod Goldman as rapporteur on IDPs (IACmHR 1997). Goldman greatly contributed to the internal displacement content of the SJD and would go on to be among the principal contributors to the formulation of the Guiding Principles. While the position was a voluntary one, with limited capacity and support, it was the first institutional role at the regional level and contributed to an increased visibility of the issue (Cohen 1997).

Eventually, global and regional efforts coincided: the IDP experts present in San José, the special rapporteur on the rights of IDPs in the Americas, and the rest of Francis Deng's team presented the Guiding Principles. These were still not binding, but they gathered a series of provisions from international human rights law, international humanitarian law, and international refugee law, many of which are now considered to be customary law. They were endorsed by the UN without submitting them to a voting process that could have watered them down and have since been integrated into national law and policy in thirty-six countries (Global Protection Cluster [GPC] n.d.).

Contemporary Challenges in Addressing Internal Displacement in Latin America

There has been significant progress in the normative, policy, and operational responses to internal displacement in Latin America since the SJD was adopted in 1994. At the global level, internal displacement has shifted from incipient visibility to commonly referenced, in large part due to the creation and dissemination of the Guiding Principles.

Legal and policy frameworks in Latin America seeking to address displacement have reflected this trend and evolved, notably through the 2004 Mexico Declaration and Plan of Action to Strengthen the International Protection of Refugees in Latin America (see Vera Espinoza in this volume) and the 2014 Brazil Declaration and Plan of Action: A Framework for Cooperation and Regional Solidarity to Strengthen the International Protection of Refugees, Displaced and Stateless Persons in Latin America and the Caribbean (see Arnold-Fernández, Sarmiento Torres, and Kallas in this volume), and more recently the Comprehensive Regional Protection and Solutions Framework (see Nelson-Pollard in this volume). As discussed above, the SJD and its push toward the specific protection needs for IDPs was an important part of this evolving regional framework.

In parallel to these normative developments, some progress has been made on an institutional level aiming to improve prevention and response to internal displacement in Latin America and elsewhere. Unlike for refugees, there is still no specific UN agency mandated to protect IDPs, so a collaborative response is deemed necessary (United Nations Office of the High Commissioner for Human Rights [OHCHR] n.d.b.). UNHCR, UNDP, and the IOM, as well as many NGOs, have essential roles in providing assistance and protection to IDPs in a variety of contexts. Operationally, UNHCR–as the Global Protection Cluster (n.d.) lead–has spearheaded the protection of conflict-affected IDPs and has several operational policies outlining the agency's priorities (UNHCR n.d.).

The United Nations Office of Coordination of Humanitarian Affairs works in close partnership with Security Council bodies, UNHCR, UNDP, protection-related IASC agencies, UN secretariat organizations and the special rapporteur on the human rights of IDPs, whose mandate works to promote the human rights of IDPs within the UN system and whose mandate has made country visits to El Salvador and Honduras since 2015 (OHCHR n.d.a.). IDMC and the Joint IDP Profiling Service (JIPS) also provide data and expertise on situations of internal displacement worldwide.

Despite this normative and institutional progress at the global and regional levels, many of the displacement-related challenges the SJD sought to address in the 1990s persist today in parts of the region. In 2019 alone, IDMC reported 602,000 new internal displacements due to conflict and a further 1.545 million new internal displacements due to disasters in the Americas, representing 6.4 percent of the global total (IDMC 2019a). These were the families documented fleeing a range of causes, from the effects of violence in Colombia to natural hazard–induced disasters in Mexico; due to challenges in collecting timely, reliable, and accurate data, many more fled invisibly and off the record, or were uprooted by large-scale development projects and so were largely unaccounted for (IDMC 2019a).

This section on current challenges in tackling internal displacement will focus on the North of Central America (NCA), a region in Central America made up of El Salvador, Guatemala, and Honduras, where displacement caused by crime and violence has risen to the level of a humanitarian crisis. In El Salvador and Guatemala, IDMC estimates there were at least 489,000 IDPs as of the end of 2019; 454,000 were newly displaced in El Salvador during 2019, many driven from, and within, cities suffering the highest homicide rates in the world and levels of violence comparable with a war zone (IDMC 2019a). Gang activity, structural violence, and generalized insecurity, coupled with heavy-handed state security responses, corruption, and a culture of impunity, have all been identified as key drivers of internal and cross-border displacement in the subregion (IDMC n.d.). Targeted persecution resulting from this, manifesting as homicides, sexual and gender-based violence, extortions, or threats, are key triggers of flight for many. For others, the decision to leave is one of a combination of factors that may include family reunification or stifling levels of poverty.

The sixteenth conclusion of the SJD begins by affirming that "the problem of the internally displaced, albeit the fundamental responsibility of the States of their nationality, is nevertheless of concern to the international community because it is a human rights issue which can be linked to prevention of causes which generate refugee flows." Building on the key internal displacement clauses considered in this chapter's previous section, the current challenges in addressing internal displacement in the NCA are examined in this section along two broad categories implied–both explicitly and implicitly–in the sixteenth conclusion. The first of those categories are shortcomings in the political will of national governments to assume responsibility for addressing internal displacement through official recognition of and dedicated resources to it; and the second are obstacles to preventing the conditions that lead to people being forced to flee or that prevent them from securing durable solutions to displacement.

Recognition

Official acknowledgement is a vital first step toward any government fulfilling its duties, in line with the Guiding Principles, to protect and assist IDPs and uphold their right to ask for and receive support. The purpose of including the rights relevant to IDPs in the SJD, as discussed above, was in part to stress national responsibility for IDPs and therefore foster political will for governments to recognize and address the phenomenon, ostensibly before an internal displacement crisis spilled across a country's borders as a flow of refugees or irregular migrants. This emphasis on sovereignty as responsibility is demonstrated in the sixteenth conclusion, which describes the problems faced by IDPs as "the fundamental responsibility of the States of their nationality."

The governments of the NCA subregion demonstrate uneven levels in acknowledging and committing to address internal displacement. In El Salvador, although reliable and timely data are particularly scarce, insecurity and criminal violence could be forcing tens of thousands of people from their homes every year (IDMC 2019b). For some, particularly those who have been victims of crime or targeted persecution, it is the only or primary reason to flee within or beyond their country's borders (IDMC 2018a). For others, it is one of a combination of factors that may include economic concerns and family reunification. Other factors also emerge, such as violence perpetrated by the security forces, drought, and food shortages.

Despite these trends, the state response has been lacking and it has failed to provide durable solutions for displaced people. Recent developments appear to hold promise, sparked by the IACmHR granting precautionary measures in favor of several families that had been internally displaced, which prompted the constitutional chamber of the Supreme Court of El Salvador (2018) to order protective measures for them. By the start of 2018, the court had accepted six *amparos* (protection petitions) for sixty IDPs in six family groups. On 13 July 2018 the constitutional chamber issued a landmark ruling in one of the six *amparo* cases presented by a group of IDPs with support from civil society organizations and law clinics. The court ordered the government to officially recognize forced displacement in the country, develop appropriate legislation and policies to assist and protect displaced people, allocate a budget for the response, and take action to prevent displacement (Supreme Court of El Salvador 2018).

In its decision, the court considered it well proven that displacement existed in the country and had a cross-border dimension, and that the government's response has been inadequate. Compliance with the ruling was required within six months and was hoped to greatly advance the protection of IDPs and those who filed the *amparo* cases. The justice minister said in July 2018 that he would comply with the ruling faithfully and absolutely (Avelar 2018; Cornejo 2018; Cristosal 2018; Supreme Court of El Salvador 2018). A law was passed in El Salvador's Legislative Assembly and approved by the new president in 2020 (El Salvador 2020).

These developments undoubtedly constitute progress, but the government still needs to do more to identify and assist IDPs and support them in achieving durable solutions so they "no longer have specific assistance and protection needs that are linked to their displacement and such persons can enjoy their human rights without discrimination resulting from their displacement" (IASC 2010). It must assume primary responsibility for preventing displacement by addressing its causes. Full official recognition of the phenomenon would be a vital first step.

In Guatemala violence and displacement have continued despite the country's thirty-six-year civil war coming to an end more than twenty years ago. Assassinations, extrajudicial killings, disappearances, rapes, kidnappings, threats, the forced recruitment of children into fighting forces, intimidation, extortion, and femicide have forced significant but unknown numbers of people to flee across and within the country's borders (IDMC 2018b).

In pursuit of national economic growth, the government and the private sector have implemented large-scale development projects, often referred to as megaprojects, many of them involving power generation, agribusiness, and natural resource extraction. Intended to support the country's overall development to the benefit of all Guatemalans, many such projects have, in fact, had the opposite effect on local people and communities by deepening their poverty and leading to their displacement. There are no data to suggest those projects have led to improved local livelihoods or better local goods and services. On the contrary, there are indications that some have also damaged protected areas and biospheres (IDMC 2018b).

Addressing internal displacement comprehensively and achieving durable solutions, however, remains a challenge the government has yet to recognize officially (IDMC 2018b). This lack of official recognition of forced migration helps to fuel a popular misconception that people who cross the border toward the United States find it a simple and easy way to access "the American dream" on the other side of the Rio Grande, and are eagerly awaiting their chance to move. Patterns of population movement within Guatemala suggest the opposite, with people generally preferring to remain in their home communities and to make substantial efforts to mitigate factors such as violence in an effort to avoid having to leave (IDMC 2018b).

In Honduras, gang warfare and violence, often the result of underlying structural factors including socioeconomic inequality, impunity, and corruption issues, have transformed parts of the country into some of the most dangerous places on earth. As a result, many families have been forced to flee their homes and communities, both within the country and across its borders. The Honduran government officially recognized displacement in 2013 and has since taken some important and promising steps, notably the establishment in 2013 of the Comisión Interinstitucional para la Protección de las Personas Desplazadas por la Violencia (CIPPDV; Inter-institutional Commission for the Protection of Persons Internally Displaced by Violence), tasked with developing policies, promoting the adoption of measures to prevent displacement associated with violence; and providing assistance, protection, and solutions to those affected. The Directorate for the Protection of People Internally Displaced by Violence was also established to define and implement the state's response to protection needs (JIPS 2015).

CIPPDV has provided a platform to coordinate the response to internal displacement, co-led profilings that reported the number, needs and location of displaced people, and developed draft legislation on IDPs that was under review by El Salvador's Legislative Assembly at the time of writing. A protocol for emergency humanitarian assistance has been developed and consultations were underway in late 2018 on specific interventions for women, children and young people, LGBT+ people, and Indigenous groups. Services and protection are best delivered at the municipal level, so CIPPDV has planned for the national response to be implemented locally–this work has already started in San Pedro Sula and Tegucigalpa, which were identified in 2015 as being among the cities with the highest concentration of displacement (JIPS 2019). In line with its commitments under the Comprehensive Regional Protection and Solutions Framework, the government has also developed guidelines for the identification and reception of returnees with protection needs and launched a project to protect abandoned property and land (Comprehensive Refugee Response Framework n.d.).

Concerns have been raised, however, that CIPPDV lacks capacity, which reflects a lack of political will to invest in institutions that address displacement effectively (Immigration and Refugee Board of Canada 2018; JIPS 2015; Representatives of PADF and Cristosal 2018). As in El Salvador and Guatemala, the resulting absence of a state response has left inter-governmental organizations, NGOs, churches, and civil society to try to provide IDPs with assistance.

Prevention

The Guiding Principles were presented to UN member states in 1998 as an alternative to a formal convention. They included norms that–in addition to protection, assistance, and solutions–cover prevention in principle, but in reality this often recedes into the background. The SJD, four years' predecessor to the Guiding Principles, was explicit in its affirmation of the need to prevent displacement flows by addressing its causes (Guiding Principles: Intro I, Sixteenth conclusion).

Across the NCA subregion, there are a number of political, economic, social, environmental, geographical, and development factors that drive insecurity and make people vulnerable to displacement. These include entrenched and increasing poverty, food insecurity and inequality, disasters, extreme weather events and climate change impacts, as well as endemic corruption and impunity, persistent crime and violence, the militarization of the state, and political repression (IDMC 2018a, 2018b; JIPS 2015).

These causes and structural factors may act as standalone drivers or may combine to aggravate and perpetuate each other, triggering displacement. Megaprojects, for example, may cause displacement and they may also increase people's vulnerability to environmental factors and weather events. Corruption and impunity perpetuate criminal violence, and corruption linked to mega-projects may result in campaigns of harassment or violent intimidation and evictions (IDMC 2018a, 2018b).

Up to 47 percent of people in the NCA are currently affected by food insecurity, the highest incidence ever recorded, linked to the prolonged drought and poor socioeconomic conditions in the region. Vulnerability in the Dry Corridor, which stretches across the NCA countries and into Nicaragua, is aggravated by 68 percent unemployment, shifting labor demands, and poor wages. This situation has been worsened by climate change as well as crop disease, which has affected the production of staples such as maize and beans, and export crops such as coffee. There are reported correlations between the prolonged drought and migration all along the voluntary to forced continuum of movement (IDMC 2016; USAID 2017; WFP 2017; WFP, IOM, and LSE 2017).

Poverty and a lack of opportunities also make people vulnerable to becoming involved in criminal activities as a survival strategy. Young people living in poverty may be compelled to join gangs both for protection and for economic reasons. They are also vulnerable to forced recruitment and face threats and violence if they resist. Their vulnerability may be heightened by family breakdown or having parents who are absent because of work or emigration (IDMC 2018a, 2018b).

Because the causes of displacement are less evident and more engrained in the social, political, and economic systems, prevention requires systemic changes like tackling corruption and structural violence, and promoting good governance and socioeconomic development. These changes are challenging and costly to bring about and they take time. For governments, eager to show results, it can be tempting to implement highly visible security policies rather than addressing the drivers and root causes of displacement.

A re-energized shift toward risk reduction and prevention, as advocated for in the SJD, is needed in order to increase awareness of internal displacement as an economic, security, and political priority. Short of this, the state's role and responsibility cannot be fully delineated or a robust prevention strategy developed. Instead, human rights violations and displacement will continue to take place, and the precarious nature of internal displacement across the NCA will continue to expose people to the ongoing insecurity and risk that leads to repeated displacement, restrictions on freedom of movement, and cross-border flight.

Conclusion: The Path to 2024

Looking back to his final report to the UNGA in 1993, Dr. Francis Deng in 2001 reported to that same body, "The crisis of internal displacement is as acute now as it was eight years ago" (Newland, Patrick, and Zard 2003: 18). As the thirty-fifth anniversary of the Cartagena Declaration approaches, the region finds itself once again overwhelmed with displacement crises: People are organizing in caravans to escape targeted and structural violence in the NCA (see Nelson-Pollard in this volume); Nicaraguans are escaping political repression; Colombians continue to flee violence as the different parties of the conflict compete for trafficking routes, territorial control, and power (see Carneiro in this volume); and millions are leaving Venezuela, escaping repression and the consequences of economic mismanagement such as lack of food and medication (see Jarochinski Silva, Castro, and Sampaio in this volume). Each of these crises has an internal component, which requires an adequate national response.

The SJD was signed at the moment when internal displacement was gaining prominence on the international and humanitarian agenda. It contributed to this momentum through raising awareness about the normative vacuum related to the phenomenon, underlining states' sovereignty as a responsibility, providing a forward-looking focus on prevention, and exposing the lack of an international and regional institutional framework. The SJD did not leave a clear trail of its effects, but it was part of a larger process and iterative approach toward a coherent normative response to internal displacement. There was a pivotal process between Francis Deng's work on the Guiding Principles and other initiatives around the world. In San José, this process is illustrated by the active participation of Deng's colleagues in the Colloquium, largely influencing the internal displacement–related contents of the SJD. Those same colleagues also participated in the institutional innovations the region contributed to the internal displacement response over the 1990s. The regional process, first through CIREFCA and later through the CPDIA, paved the way for the inclusion of IDP definitions in national legislation and jurisprudence across the region. Later, and continuing today, larger parts of the Guiding Principles would follow by supporting national legislation as well as arguments in the high courts.

Some of the challenges the SJD outlined have seen progress in the past twenty-five years: the issue of internal displacement is far from invisible today and the Guiding Principles provided a solid normative basis. Nations and regions have built on this foundation through laws and policies on internal displacement, during the process sparked by the Cartagena Declaration that has been followed up regularly every ten years, and within the current regional processes including the Comprehensive Regional Protection and Solutions Framework. In parallel, institutional frameworks have evolved and continue to do so. At the regional level, institutions like the CPDIA and the regional special rapporteur position have disappeared, but the OAS and its IACmHR continue to lead on the issue, among others through the expanded mandate of the Rapporteurship on the Rights of Migrants (formerly Rapporteurship on Migrant Workers and Members of their Families) that includes IDPs since 2012. They also have many more tools and support to draw on than they did twenty-five years ago.

However, there remains work to be done with regards to national responsibility and prevention. As discussed, the nature of the phenomenon in the NCA has changed, as have its drivers and triggers This poses a challenge for governments who are, in some cases, unwilling to take the first step of acknowledging the existence of internal displacement. Recognition is, however, a prerequisite to an adequate response. Focusing on prevention has equally remained a challenge. Protecting IDPs and providing humanitarian assistance continues to be more urgent. The little actions on prevention tend to focus on addressing the triggers, often fighting direct violence with more violence, and sometimes causing displacement of its own. The root causes of displacement must be addressed in any prevention effort. In order to do this, at least in the NCA, more information and a deeper understanding of the issue is necessary. Comprehensive monitoring mechanisms must be put in place. This can be done, at a large scale, only by the state itself, and it requires prior recognition of the existence and the relevance of the phenomenon.

While the international community is providing support across the region, it seems more relevant than ever to call on national governments to assume responsibility by recognizing internal displacement as a prioritized issue and leading efforts to prevent and respond to it. Understanding and addressing the different causes that are driving people from their homes must be a priority and will likely require a genuine refocus at the next commemorative colloquium of the Cartagena Declaration in 2024.

Elizabeth Rushing coordinated research, analysis, and policy work on internal displacement for the Norwegian Refugee Council's IDMC from 2012 to 2019. She has a particular interest in understanding forced migration in the context of violence and armed conflict, and the relationship between internal displacement and cross-border movements of migrants and refugees. Before joining IDMC, she worked with OHCHR, the Joint United Nations Programme on HIV and AIDS, and la Fédération Internationale des Droits de l'Homme. Elizabeth is now the managing editor of the International Committee of the Red Cross's Humanitarian Law and Policy blog. She holds a juris doctorate degree from the American University Washington College of Law and a master's degree in international human rights law from the University of Paris X Nanterre.

Andrés Lizcano Rodriguez is the Acting Head of Field Support and Capacity Development at JIPS, where he currently advises partners in Guatemala, Honduras, Mexico, and Venezuela, as well as other countries across Europe, Asia and Africa.. Before joining JIPS, he monitored internal displacement in Latin America and beyond at IDMC. His research has focused on international trade, economic development, and agriculture. He served the Colombian government as an advisor to the deputy minister of education, and in working for the National Planning Ministry. Andrés is a mathematician and holds master's degrees in international affairs from the Paris Institute of Political Studies (Sciences Po) in Paris and from Columbia University.

Notes

1. The Guiding Principles on Internal Displacement restate and compile human rights and humanitarian law relevant to internally displaced persons (United Nations Economic and Social Council 1998).
2. The authors would like to thank Roberta Cohen, Robert K. Goldman, Andres Celis, Carmen Rosa de Leon, Sindy Hernandez, Marisela Enseñat, Paola Hurtado, José Pablo Vega, Beatriz Eugenia Sanchez, and the Americas Network for Refugees Legal Aid (ANRLA or RALRA, Red de Apoyo Legal para los Refugiados de las Américas) for conversations sharing their insights and providing valuable inputs for this chapter, and Rachel Dodd and José Miguel Barragán for providing editorial and research support.
3. The main documents relevant to internal displacement in the region include OAS General Assembly resolutions, CIREFCA documents, and IACHC publications.
4. In 2018 RALRA sent an email reaching out to all its members and systematized and shared the responses it received with the authors.
5. Interviews included Roberta Cohen and Robert K. Goldman, who attended the San José Conference and who had a role in the broader process that led to the adoption of the Guiding Principles; Carmen Rosa de León, who participated in the peace negotiations in Guatemala and directed the Comisión Especial de Atención a Repatriados; and Andrés Celis, current country director of UNHCR in Honduras who was involved in the response to displacement in Colombia during the 1990s.
6. The Contadora group is Mexico, Colombia, Panama, and Venezuela. It was later supported by Argentina, Brazil, Peru, and Uruguay, as well as by the United Nations Security Council and the UNGA.
7. "Although there is no generally accepted definition, displaced persons have been obliged to abandon their homes or habitual economic activities because their lives, security or liberty have been threatened by generalized violence or prevailing conflict but who have not left their country. Their need for protection and assistance is at times as great as, if not greater than, that of refugees who have left the country" (CIREFCA 1990).

8. For example, see Constitutional Court of Colombia 1997, 2001, 2003a; and National Congress of Colombia 1997; these documents refer to the CPDIA's definition of internal displacement.
9. For example IACmHR (1993a, 1993b, 1995).
10. The participants were Argentina, the Bahamas, Belize, Bolivia, Brazil, Chile, Colombia, Costa Rica, Ecuador, El Salvador, Guatemala, Honduras, Nicaragua, Panama, Peru, Dominican Republic, and Uruguay, as well as experts, special guests, and observers.
11. See the research methodology in the chapter's introduction. An exhaustive review of national legislation and jurisprudence has not been carried out and the authors appreciate any examples that may have been overlooked.
12. For example, see OAS (1995), which actually quotes the SJD; IACmHR (1995); and IACmHR (1994b).

References

Avelar, Bryan. 2018. "Una sentencia obliga al Estado a reconocer el desplazamiento forzado por violencia." *Revista Factum*, 13 July 2018. https://www.revistafactum.com/sala-desplazamientos/.
Betts, Alexander. 2006. "Comprehensive Plans of Action: Insights from CIREFCA and the Indochinese CPA." Evaluation and Policy Analysis Unit, United Nations High Commissioner for Refugees. https://www.unhcr.org/research/working/43eb6a152/comprehensive-plans-action-insights-cirefca-indochinese-cpa-alexander-betts.html.
Cartagena Declaration on Refugees. 1984. https://www.refworld.org/docid/3ae6b36ec.html.
Center for International Policy. 1986. "Contadora Act on Peace and Cooperation in Central America." Central American Resource Center.
Cohen, Roberta. 1997. "The Response of Regional Organisations to Internal Displacement in the Americas." Conference on Regional Response to Forced Migration in Central America and the Caribbean. Organization of American States, 30 September–1 October 1997. http://www.oas.org/juridico/english/cohene.html.
Cohen, Roberta, and Francis M. Deng. 2012. "Masses in Flight: The Global Crisis of Internal Displacement." Brookings Institution Press, 2012.
Cohen, Roberta, and Gimena Sanchez-Garzoli. 2001. "Internal Displacement in the Americas: Some Distinctive Features." The Brookings-CUNY Project on Internal Displacement. Accessed 11 April 2019. https://www.brookings.edu/wp-content/uploads/2016/06/Americas-Report-Final.pdf.
Colloquium on the International Protection of Refugees in Central America, Mexico and Panama. 1984. "Regional Refugee Instruments & Related, Cartagena Declaration on Refugees." Accessed 6 March 2021. https://www.refworld.org/docid/3ae6b36ec.html.
Constitutional Court of Colombia. 1997. T-227. http://www.corteconstitucional.gov.co/relatoria/1997/T-227-97.htm.

———. 2000. SU-1150. http://www.corteconstitucional.gov.co/relatoria/2000/SU1150-00.htm.
———. 2001. T-327. http://www.corteconstitucional.gov.co/relatoria/2001/T-327-01.htm.
———. 2002a. T-098. http://www.corteconstitucional.gov.co/relatoria/2002/t-098-02.htm.
———. 2002b. T-215. http://www.corteconstitucional.gov.co/relatoria/2002/T-215-02.htm.
———. 2003a. T-268. http://www.corteconstitucional.gov.co/relatoria/2003/t-268-03.htm.
———. 2003b. T-419. http://www.corteconstitucional.gov.co/relatoria/2003/T-419-03.htm.
———. 2003c. T-602. http://www.corteconstitucional.gov.co/relatoria/2003/T-602-03.htm.
———. 2003d. T-645. http://www.corteconstitucional.gov.co/relatoria/2003/t-645-03.htm.
———. 2003e. T-669. http://www.corteconstitucional.gov.co/relatoria/2003/t-669-03.htm.
———. 2003f. T-721. http://www.corteconstitucional.gov.co/relatoria/2003/t-721-03.htm.
———. 2003g. T-790. http://www.corteconstitucional.gov.co/relatoria/2003/t-790-03.htm.
———. 2004. T-025. http://www.corteconstitucional.gov.co/relatoria/2004/t-025-04.htm.
Convention Relating to the Status of Refugees. 1951. https://www.refworld.org/docid/3be01b964.html.
Cornejo, Iliana. 2018. "Las críticas del ministro de Seguridad al fallo de la Sala por desplazamiento forzado." *El Mundo*, 23 July 2018. https://elmundo.sv/las-criticas-del-ministro-de-seguridad-al-fallo-de-la-sala-por-desplazamiento-forzado/.
Cristosal. 2018. "El Salvador's Supreme Court orders protection, policies for victims of forced displacement." https://www.cristosal.org/news/2018/7/16/el-salvadors-supreme-court-orders-protection-policies-for-victims-of-forced-displacement.
Comprehensive Refugee Response Framework (CRRF). n.d. "Central America and Mexico: The Comprehensive Regional Protection and Solutions Framework (MIRPS)." Accessed 6 September 2019. https://bit.ly/2IQ7NMP.
National Planning Department (DNP). 1995. "CONPES 2804–National Program for assisting People Displaced By Violence." https://colaboracion.dnp.gov.co/CDT/CONPES/Económicos/2804.pdf.
El Salvador. 2020. "Ley especial para la atención y protección integral de personas en condición de desplazamiento forzado interno." Accessed 5 August 2020. https://www.refworld.org.es/docid/5e691b974.html.
Government of Costa Rica, Inter-American Institute on Human Rights (IIDH), United Nations High Commissioner for Refugees (UNHCR). 1995. *10 Años de la Declaración de Cartagena sobre Refugiados–Declaración de San José sobre Refugiados y Personas Desplazadas*. https://www.iidh.ed.cr/IIDH/media/2040/memoria-coloquio-10anos-declaracion-cartagena-1995.pdf.

Global Protection Cluster (GPC). n.d. "Global database on IDP law and policies." Accessed 6 September 2019. http://www.globalprotectioncluster.org/global-database-on-idp-laws-and-policies/.
Guiding Principles on Internal Displacement. 1998. E/CN.4/1998/53/Add.2. https://undocs.org/E/CN.4/1998/53/Add.2.
Immigration and Refugee Board of Canada. 2018. "Honduras: Information Gathering Mission Report." https://irb-cisr.gc.ca/en/country-information/ndp/Pages/Honduras-2018P1.aspx#h1131.
Inter-Agency Standing Committee (IASC). Working group 8. 1997. "Item 3: Internally Displaced Persons (IDPs)." https://interagencystandingcommittee.org/system/files/legacy_files/WG28_1.pdf.
———. 2010. "Framework on Durable Solutions for Internally Displaced Persons." https://www.unhcr.org/50f94cd49.pdf.
Internal Displacement Monitoring Centre (IDMC). 2016. "Global Report on Internal Displacement." http://bit.ly/GRID-2016.
———. 2018a. "An atomised crisis: Reframing displacement caused by crime and violence in El Salvador." http://www.internal-displacement.org/sites/default/files/inline-files/201809-el-salvador-an-atomised-crisis-en.pdf.
———. 2018b. "Cause or consequence? Reframing violence and displacement in Guatemala." http://www.internal-displacement.org/sites/default/files/inline-files/201809-guatemala-cause-or-consequence-en.pdf.
———. 2019a. "GRID 2020: Global Report on Internal displacement." https://www.internal-displacement.org/global-report/grid2020/.
———. 2019b. "El Salvador: Figure Analysis–Displacement related to conflict and violence." http://www.internal-displacement.org/sites/default/files/2019-05/GRID%202019%20-%20Conflict%20Figure%20Analysis%20-%20EL%20SALVADOR.pdf.
———. n.d. "Crime and displacement in Central America." Accessed 6 September 2019. http://www.internal-displacement.org/research-areas/crime-and-displacement-in-central-america.
Inter-American Commission on Human Rights (IACmHR). 1948. "American Declaration on the Rights and Duties of Man." Accessed 6 March 2021. https://www.refworld.org/docid/3ae6b3710.html.
———. 1984. "Report on the situation of human rights of a segment of the Nicaraguan population of Miskito origin; and, Resolution on the friendly settlement procedure regarding the human rights situation of a segment of the Nicaraguan population of Miskito origin." Washington, DC: General Secretariat, Organization of American States : 1984.
———. 1993a "Fourth Report on the Situation of Human Rights in Guatemala." http://www.cidh.org/countryrep/Guatemala93sp/cap.7.htm.
———. 1993b. *"Report on the Situation of Human Rights in Haiti."* http://www.cidh.org/countryrep/EnHa93/toc.htm.
———. 1994a. "Annual Report of the Inter-American Commission on Human Rights 1993." OEA/Ser.L/V/II.85. https://www.cidh.oas.org/annualrep/93span/indice.htm.
———. 1994b. Press Communique N° 11/94. www.cidh.org/Comunicados/English/1994/Press11-20.htm.

———. 1995. "Report on the Situation of Human Rights in Haiti." http://www.cidh.org/countryrep/EnHa95/EngHaiti.htm.

———. 1997. "Annual Report of the Inter-American Commission on Human Rights 1996." OEA/Ser.L/V/II.95. http://www.cidh.org/annualrep/96eng/chap.2.htm.

International Colloquium in Commemoration of the tenth anniversary of the Cartagena Declaration on Refugees 1994

International Conference on Central American Refugees (CIREFCA). 1988. "San Salvador Communiqué on the Central American Refugees." https://www.refworld.org/docid/4f3d11ab2.html.

———. 1989. "Declaration and Concerted Plan of Action in Favour of Central American Refugees, Returnees and Displaced Persons" 89/13/Rev.1. https://www.refworld.org/docid/3fbb5d094.html.

———. 1990. "Principles and Criteria for the Protection of and Assistance to Central American Refugees, Returnees and Displaced Persons in Latin America." https://www.refworld.org/docid/4370ca8b4.html.

Joint IDP Profiling Service (JIPS). 2015. "Characterisation of internal displacement in Honduras." https://www.jips.org/jips-publication/profiling-report-honduras-2015-en/.

———. 2019. "Using shared evidence for complementary action at national and municipal levels: experiences from San Pedro Sula, Honduras." https//www.jips.org/jips-news/shared-evidence-for-complementary-action-at-national-municipal-levels-san-pedro-sula-honduras/.

Maldonado Castillo, Carlos. 2014. "The Cartagena process: 30 years of innovation and solidarity." Forced Migration Review 49: 89–91. Accessed 11 April 2019. https://www.fmreview.org/climatechange-disasters/maldonadocastillo.

National Congress of Colombia. 1997. Law 387. https://www.unidadvictimas.gov.co/sites/default/files/documentosbiblioteca/ley-387-de-1997.pdf.

Nelson-Pollard, Suzanna. 2017. "Criminal violence in Honduras as a driver of displacement." Forced Migration Review, 56: 14–17. https://www.fmreview.org/latinamerica-caribbean/nelsonpollard.

Newland, Kathleen, Erin Patrick, and Monette Zard. 2003. "No Refuge: The Challenge of Internal Displacement." United Nations. Office for the Coordination of Humanitarian Affairs. Internal Displacement Unit.

United Nations Office of the High Commissioner for Human Rights (OHCHR). n.d.a. "Special Rapporteur on the Human Rights of Internally Displaced Persons." Accessed 11 April 2019. https://www.ohchr.org/en/issues/idpersons/pages/idpersonsindex.aspx.

———. n.d.b. "Questions and Answers about IDPs." Accessed 11 April 2019. https://www.ohchr.org/EN/Issues/IDPersons/Pages/Issues.aspx.

Orchard, Phil. 2010. "Protection of Internally Displaced Persons: Soft Law as a Norm-generating Mechanism." Review of International Studies 36 (2): 281–303. http://www.jstor.org/stable/40783200.

Organization of American States (OAS). 1969. "American Convention on Human Rights, 'Pact of San Jose', Costa Rica." Accessed 6 March 2021. https://www.refworld.org/docid/3ae6b36510.html.

———. 1986. "AG/Res. 774 (XV-0/85) on Legal Status of Asylees, Refugees, and Displaced Persons in the American Hemisphere (adopted on 9 December 1985),

in Proceedings–Certified 30 Texts of the Resolutions, vol. I, Fifteenth Regular Session (5–9 December 1985), Doc. OEA/Ser.P/XV.0.2, Washington (DC), 2 April 1986: 32–33.
———. 1993. "Legal Situation of Refugees, Returnees, and Displaced Persons in the American Hemisphere." General Assembly Resolution AG/RES.1214 (XXIII-O/93). http://www.oas.org/dil/AG-RES_1214_XXIII-O-93_eng.pdf.
———. 1995. "Situation of Refugees, Returnees, and Displaced Persons in the American Hemisphere." General Assembly Resolution AG/RES. 1336 (XXV-O/95). https://www.oas.org/dil/AG-RES_1336_XXV-O-95_eng.pdf.
Parlamento Centroamericano. 1986. "Esquipulas 1" (Declaración de Esquipulas). http://www.parlacen.int/InformaciónGeneral/MarcoPol%C3%ADticoyJur%C3%ADdico/EsquipulasI.aspx.
Protocol Relating to the Status of Refugees. 1967. https://www.refworld.org/docid/3ae6b3ae4.html.
Representatives of PADF and Cristosal. 2018. Interview in Tegucigalpa, November 2018.
San José Declaration on Refugees and Displaced Persons. 1994. https://www.refworld.org/docid/4a54bc3fd.html.
Supreme Court of El Salvador. 2018. "Ruling on forced displacement." Amparo 411-2017. http://www.csj.gob.sv/Comunicaciones/2018/07_JULIO/COMUNICADOS/Amp.%20411-2017%20Sentencia%20desplazamiento_7MZT.pdf.
Uhlig, Mark A. 1990. "Cease-Fire Begins in Nicaragua As the Contras Agree to Disarm." *New York Times*. 12 April 1990. https://www.nytimes.com/1990/04/20/world/cease-fire-begins-in-nicaragua-as-the-contras-agree-to-disarm.html.
United Nations High Commissioner for Refugees (UNHCR). 2020. "Global Trends Forced Displacement in 2019." Accessed 5 August 2020. https://www.unhcr.org/be/wp-content/uploads/sites/46/2020/07/Global-Trends-Report-2019.pdf.
———. n.d. "Internally Displaced People." Accessed 11 April 2019. https://www.unhcr.org/internally-displaced-people.html.
United Nations Commission on Human Rights. 1991. "Internally displaced persons." E/CN.4/RES/1991/25. https://www.refworld.org/docid/3b00f0b1c.html.
———. 1992. "Internally displaced persons." E/CN.4/RES/1992/73. https://www.refworld.org/docid/3b00f0e71c.html.
United Nations Economic and Social Council. 1998. "Human Rights, Mass Exoduses and Displaced Persons, Report of the Representative of the Secretary-General, Mr. Francis M. Deng, submitted pursuant to Commission resolution 1997/39, Addendum: Guiding Principles on Internal Displacement." E/CN.4/1998/53/Add.2.
United Nations General Assembly (UNGA). 1987. "Letter dated 27 August 1987 from the Permanent Representatives of Costa Rica, El Salvador, Guatemala and Nicaragua to the United Nations addressed to the Secretary-General" (Procedure for the establishment of a firm and lasting peace in Central America). A/42/521J S/19085. https://peacemaker.un.org/sites/peacemaker.un.org/files/CR%20HN%20GT%20NI%20SV_870807_EsquipulasII.pdf.
———. 1988a. "International Conference on the Plight of Refugees, Returnees and Displaced Persons in Southern Africa (SARRED): Report of the Secretary-General." A/43/717. https://www.refworld.org/docid/3ae68f410.html.

———. 1988b. "The situation in Central America: Threats to international peace and security and peace initiatives–Special programmes of economic assistance." A/42/949. http://web.undp.org/execbrd/archives/sessions/gc/35th-1988/A-42-949.pdf.

———. 1991. "Strengthening of the coordination of humanitarian emergency assistance of the United Nations." A/RES/46/182. https://www.humanitarianresponse.info/sites/www.humanitarianresponse.info/files/documents/files/GA%20Resolution%2046-182.pdf.

———. 1992. "Letter dated 27 January 1992 from the Permanent Representative of El Salvador to the United Nations addressed to the Secretary General" (The situation in Central America: threats to international peace and security and peace initiatives). A/46/864 S/23501. https://peacemaker.un.org/sites/peacemaker.un.org/files/SV_920116_ChapultepecAgreement.pdf.

———. 1997. "Identical letters dated 5 February 1997 from the Secretary-General addressed to the President of the General Assembly and to the President of the Security Council." (The situation in Central America: procedures for the establishment of a firm and lasting peace and progress in fashioning a region of peace, freedom, democracy, and development). A/51/796 S/1997/114. https://peacemaker.un.org/sites/peacemaker.un.org/files/GT_961229_AgreementOnFirmAndLastingPeace.pdf.

United Nations Office for Project Services (UNOPS). 2015. "PRODERE [Development Program for Displaced Persons, Refugees, and Returnees in Central America]: Reflections on a revolutionary approach to development." https://www.unops.org/news-and-stories/stories/prodere-reflections-on-a-revolutionary-approach-to-development.

US Agency for International Development (USAID). 2017. "Climate change risk profile: Honduras." https://www.climatelinks.org/resources/climate-change-risk-profile-honduras.

World Food Programme (WFP). 2017. "Food Insecurity and Emigration: Why people flee and the impact on family members left behind in El Salvador, Guatemala and Honduras." https://www.wfp.org/publications/2017-food-security-emigration-why-people-flee-salvador-guatemala-honduras.

World Food Programme (WFP), International Organization for Migration (IOM), and London School of Economics (LSE). 2017. "Hunger Without Borders: The hidden links between food insecurity, violence and migration in the northern triangle of Central America." https://environmentalmigration.iom.int/hunger-without-borders-hidden-links-between-food-insecurity-violence-and-migration-northern-triangle.

3

The Mixed Legacy of the Mexico Declaration and Plan of Action

Solidarity and Refugee Protection
in Latin America

Marcia Vera Espinoza

Introduction

The 2004 Mexico Declaration and Plan of Action to Strengthen the International Protection of Refugees in Latin America (MPA) was adopted in 2004 by twenty Latin American countries at the twenty-year anniversary of the 1984 Cartagena Declaration on Refugees (Cartagena Declaration), defining a continent-wide framework of concrete actions aimed to strengthen protection of refugees in the region (Spindler 2005). The MPA comprised two main components—one focused on protection and the second on durable solutions, based on the principles of solidarity, responsibility sharing, and regional cooperation (MPA 2004).

The MPA has been praised as a "sophisticated instrument of refugee protection" (United Nations High Commissioner for Refugees [UNHCR] 2005b), as an example of South-South cooperation (Harley 2014) and as a "step forward in strengthening the protection of human rights" (Barichello 2016: 203). At the same time, the MPA has been criticized for its limited implementation, overdependence on governments' political will, and the exaggerated use of the solidarity rhetoric that did not necessarily translate into effective cooperation (Menezes 2016; Vera Espinoza 2018a).

Seventeen years after its adoption, this chapter explores the legacy of the MPA and reflects on what lessons can be learned from it. The chapter argues that the MPA leaves a mixed legacy behind. On the one hand, this soft law document is a relevant example of regionalism by which countries of the region aimed to set up a concrete set of actions to advance the protection of refugees and internally displaced persons in Latin America, going beyond the limitations of a declaration alone. On the other hand, however, the MPA's uneven implementation and late assessment protocols meant that the document applicability was less effective than anticipated. More importantly, the MPA sheds light onto the nuances to the principles of solidarity and responsibility sharing that underpinned the document.

In order to develop this argument, the chapter explores the main characteristics of the MPA by reviewing the context in which it was developed and adopted, before moving to explore the principle of solidarity on which it is based as well as the aim of responsibility sharing, and examining both of these in the context of regional cooperation. The chapter then focuses on the implementation of different programs and of resettlement in solidarity in particular—as one of the most distinctive and concrete actions proposed by the document—in order to further the analysis of the mixed legacy of the MPA. The chapter ends with a discussion of what to do with this legacy and how the MPA has influenced subsequent regional projects on refugee protection.

The chapter analyzes development, implementation, and legacy of the MPA by drawing from ideas on regionalism, regional migration governance, and cooperation, with roots in international relations and political geography, emphasizing the relevance of different levels, political actors, and knowledge construction that has been produced and disseminated as part of the regional approach to refugee protection. The chapter draws on analyses of secondary data, including UNHCR documents, policy reports, and preparatory meeting records, as well as nongovernmental organizations' (NGOs') reports. The chapter also considers the analysis of data collected as part of a larger research on refugee resettlement in Latin America (e.g., Vera Espinoza 2017a, 2018a, 2018b), particularly data collected through semi-structured interviews with eighty stakeholders (including UNHCR staff, civil servants, NGO staff, and refugees themselves, among others) conducted in Chile and Brazil between 2012 and 2015.[1]

The MPA: Structure, Logics and Actors

With the forty-years-long Colombian conflict on the background and after four preparatory meetings,[2] twenty countries of the region[3] adopted the MPA in Mexico City on 16 November 2004. The twelve-page document consists of both a declaration and a plan of action, dual components that have been identified as one of the unique characteristics of the regional document (Maldonado Castillo 2015: 90). The plan is divided into four chapters in which the situation of refugees in Latin America is analyzed (chapter 1); actions for doctrinal development and institutional capacity building are outlined (chapter 2), pillars of cooperation and action were developed (chapter 3), and mechanisms of evaluation and implementation are identified (chapter 4).

The MPA aimed to set up a regional framework to improve refugee protection and respond to the complex humanitarian crises emerging from forced displacement in the region (UNHCR 2005a), particularly in reference to the protection needs of Colombians in the Andean region whose forced displacement at that time included more than 3 million people inside and outside the country (Gottwald 2004; also see Carneiro in this volume). According to Moulin (2013), one of the important outcomes of the MPA was to incorporate the Colombian displacement in the institutional and legal framework for refugees in the region. The objectives of the MPA are aligned with the principles of the Cartagena Declaration through two main components: the strengthening mechanisms for protection and the search for durable solutions (MPA 2004: preamble; also see Barichello 2016).

When exploring the component on protection, the MPA focuses on three main areas: (1) Strengthening the cooperation and institutional framework for the protection of refugees through the promotion and development of international refugee law. This aim included actions to deepen knowledge of international law in the region as well as a training program on international refugee protection. (2) Strengthening established refugee status determination mechanisms and national refugee commissions through more financial resources and technical advice. And (3) strengthening national and regional protection networks by enhancing civil society's capacities and involvement "in the design of public policies" (MPA 2004: chap. 2).

Chapter 3 of the MPA focuses on the search for durable solutions that emerged from the needs identified in chapter 1 in relation to three coexistent scenarios in the region: (1) states that receive a small number of asylum seekers and refugees as part of regional migratory flows; (2) countries that host a significant number of asylum seekers and refugees; and (3) countries with emerging resettlement programs (ibid.: 5). Within this scenario, and as stated in the notes of the preparatory meetings, the growing number of refugees living in large urban centers in Latin America and the situation of a large number of Colombians displaced across the borders in Ecuador, Panama, and Venezuela, were identified as situations in need of urgent attention (e.g., UNHCR 2005a).

Durable solutions, in this context, were outlined in three pillars, all of them framed under the principle of solidarity and responsibility sharing (e.g., Jubilut and Carneiro 2016; Menezes 2016; Vera Espinoza 2018a), and with the aim of disseminating best practices and promoting South-South cooperation. The first of these pillars is labeled Solidarity Cities, a program focused on self-sufficiency and local integration. This program not only aims to facilitate the economic self-sufficiency of refugees, but it also puts an emphasis on the difficult situation of host communities and the socioeconomic realities of the region. Through a series of pilot urban centers in Latin America, the program proposes fostering employment and establishing micro-credits, facilitating the expedited issuance of documents and the design of integration projects (MPA 2004: 9–10). According to Varoli, Solidarity Cities promotes a different attitude toward the urban context in which "the city is presented as an open space and a place for opportunities to be explored and exploited" (Varoli 2010: 45), by incorporating refugees in the local public agendas. The MPA emphasizes that, whereas the main goal is to provide "effective protection which encompasses the enjoyment of social, economic and cultural rights" (MPA 2004: 10), the Solidarity Cities program also aims to mitigate the so-called "irregular or secondary movements" in the region (ibid.).

The second pillar entitled the Borders of Solidarity program, recognized the unknown magnitude of the Colombian displacement, in terms of numbers as well as the presumed undocumented situation of many displaced persons in need of protection, particularly at the borders with neighboring countries including Ecuador, Panama, and Venezuela. This pillar aimed to address the humanitarian needs of the displaced population, while at the same time dealing with the structural and community services needs of the host communities in border areas (ibid.: 10). The main priority of this durable solution was to formulate a regional strategic plan to "address the protection, basic assistance and integration needs of all the populations in need" (ibid.: 11), by promoting social and economic development of host communities and refugees alike.

Finally, the third pillar, the regional Solidarity Resettlement Programme emerged from the second subregional preparatory meeting where the government of Brazil proposed the creation of a regional resettlement program within the framework of the Mercado Común del Sur (MERCOSUR; Southern Common Market) for Latin American refugees, which "would confirm the fact that Latin America provides protection and is concerned with finding solutions to the problem of its own refugees" (UNHCR 2006b: 274). The program would later be labeled as a tangible manifestation of the principle of international solidarity (UNHCR 2011: 45). Based on the experiences that Brazil and Chile had at that time as emerging resettlement countries, the proposal aimed to establish a framework of principles and eligibility criteria as well as an appeal to the international community to support the initiative in order to replicate it in other countries of the region (MPA 2004: 11).

The final chapter of the MPA briefly outlines some activities that are needed at different levels to implement the plan. At the national level these activities included the preparation of national projects within the framework of the plan of action, assessment of possible beneficiaries, a study of impacts, and regular evaluation and follow-up reports, all of them supported by the technical expertise of the UNHCR. At the regional level it was suggested that at least two meetings per year were needed to facilitate knowledge exchange. At the international level, emphasis was given to an annual meeting with donor countries and financial institutions to present projects and information about implementation and impact (ibid.: 12).

A thematic analysis of the key components of the MPA and its preparatory meetings shows the recognition that facing "the influx of large groups of persons in need of protection" (UNHCR 2006b: 275) may exceed the possibilities of individual states, which not only emphasizes the relevance of regional cooperation, but also the need of political will and the support of the international community. Other relevant aspects of the MPA is the acknowledgment and focus on the role of the civil society as a strong partner to implement the actions proposed in the plan, with recommendations that included training and resources as well as their inclusion in decision-making and in structures of refugee status determination (Barichello 2016; MPA 2004: 8). In this way, the MPA outlines the different actors in regional and local refugee protection, assigning them tasks and responsibilities within the plan. As stated by Philippe Lavanchy in the memoirs of the twentieth anniversary of the Cartagena Declaration, "Both instruments [the declaration and plan of action] represent, in the framework of the *Agenda for Protection*, a common regional understanding of the actions required to strength the capacity of States, international organizations and Civil Society to provide timely and appropriate responses to refugees, IDPs [internally displaced persons] and other persons of concern. These regional efforts are to be enhanced by the resolute commitment and support of the international community to fully come to fruition" (UNHCR 2005a: 8).

Besides the states, regional organizations, international community, and civil society, the document highlights the pivotal role of the UNHCR not only as part of the design of the MPA but also as a key consultative and expert organ that contributes to the development, implementation, and assessment of the plan of action through its technical expertise (MPA 2004: chaps. 2, 3). The explicit outline of key stakeholders shows who the key players are that are negotiating and providing refugee protection in Latin America; at the same time, the MPA is a reflection of how knowledge is produced and disseminated in the regional refugee regime. In this context, the UNHCR plays a pivotal role reinforcing the regionalism of refugee policies as part of a governance strategy that follows logics that are similar to the one applied to migration management more broadly (Cantor, Freier, and Gauci 2015;

Domenech 2013). Throughout the MPA the UNHCR had a key role to play in designing programs, providing technical advice, dealing with international donors, and contributing to assessment and diffusion of good practices, showing how the United Nations agency develops and disseminates values and resources, which is central to the works of the regional approach to refugee governance (Geddes et al. 2019).

A third element to highlight here is that the MPA makes an explicit recognition that the mechanisms of refugee protection demand covering both the needs of refugees as well as those of host communities. This attention to the needs of host communities is stamped in the second pillar of the durable solutions that focuses on promoting the socioeconomic development of those in need of protection and the host populations at border areas (MPA 2004: 11). While this approach seems now well established at the international level as part of one of the guiding principles of the 2018 Global Compact on Refugees (UNHCR 2018), it is relevant to reflect on how the language used in the MPA's key actions are all part of three out of the four objectives of the Global Compact on Refugees: ease the pressures on host countries, enhance refugee self-reliance, and expand access to third-country solutions. All of those three aims were part of the MPA at the regional level back in 2004 (MPA 2004: chap. 3). Although this could be interpreted as part of the innovative approach that has been associated with the Latin America's approach to refugee protection (Lavanchy 2006), it can also emphasize the argument that the UNHCR has been central in developing the transnationalization of the refugee regime agenda where core ideas and language have been developed at local and regional levels to reach consolidation at the global refugee regime (Geddes et al. 2019; Moulin 2009).

Regional Cooperation: Solidarity and Responsibility Sharing

One of the key ideas established through the design and adoption of the MPA has been the consolidation of the principle of solidarity in the regional approach to refugee protection. From the first page, the document emphasizes that solidarity, together with humanism, "are fundamental principles that should continue to guide State policies on refugees in Latin America" (MPA 2004: 1). From then onwards, the word "solidarity" is written in the MPA alongside "responsibility sharing." As Jubilut and Carneiro (2011: 70) have emphasized, this association represents a relevant shift from the concept of burden sharing to the one of responsibility sharing. This semantic change seems to consolidate a move from perceiving refugee protection as a problem to be solved, to recognizing it as a "responsibility for protecting the victims of violations of human rights" (ibid.:70). The notion of responsibility sharing also sheds light into the disparities in the costs and pressures that different states assume when handling refugees and displaced persons (Barichello 2016: 194). In this context, the focus on responsibility sharing is consistent with the MPA focus on supporting refugee and host communities alike. The notion of responsibility sharing is also linked to the MPA's aim of strengthening the cooperation among States in the region (MPA 2004: 7).

As I explore elsewhere (Vera Espinoza 2018a), solidarity in the context of the MPA refers both to a principle as well as to a "common exercise of interest and cooperation between states in the region, but also between the region and the international community" (ibid.: 87). It is argued, particularly in the context of solidarity resettlement, that many of the actions promoted in the MPA responded to strategic interests related to the concern for regional security as a result of the Colombian displacement (Gottwald 2004) and states' goals of increased presence within the international community (Jubilut 2006; Menezes 2016). That is to say, according to Menezes (2016), the actions of Latin American states in relation to refugee protection are based on strategic interests, similar to the actions of states in any other region, but they are framed on the rhetoric of solidarity. Menezes argues that this branding of solidarity as a guiding principle of the MPA has provided a utopian ambition that has not translated into effective implementation of resettlement as a durable solution.

Moulin provides further nuances of the principle by arguing the need to clarify the meanings of solidarity "in order to avoid the reproduction of exclusionary discourses" (Moulin 2009: 51). Exploring the concept and practice of solidarity in relation to the Borders of Solidarity program, Moulin remind us of the limitations of what she calls managerial solidarity at the core of the MPA: managerial solidarity, connected to strategies of control and discipline, aims to provide protection by identifying and quantifying refugees and people of concern in opposition to the citizen and by equating solidarity with development.

Despite the limitations of the principle of solidarity, it has been argued that the rhetoric of solidarity contributes to a branding of generosity that helps with the recognition of the regional nature of refugees' issues, calls for South-South cooperation (Harley 2014: 22) and is an attractive language to encourage donors' support and facilitate norm development (Barichello 2016). Although the history of regional approach to refugee protection in Latin America is long dated and well explored within academic debates (e.g., Cantor 2018; Jubilut 2006; Kneebone 2016; Lavanchy 2006), the idea of regional solidarity or the perception of shared problems and solutions, as stated by Jubilut and Ramos (2014: 67), can enhance a rights-based approach to humanitarian situations, fostering specific momentum to strengthen a regional response.

Exploring regional cooperation in the context of the MPA through the lenses of regionalism provide relevant reflections here. As a more formal structure of regional cooperation in the framework of the Cartagena Declaration, the MPA could be indeed analyzed as an example of regionalism. More fitting, however, can be the understanding of the regional approach branded under the principle of solidarity looking it through the lens of what is called "regionness." According to Riggirozzi, regionness can be understood as "a progression from geographical units to state-like qualities, equating regionness to a unitary sense of actorness [i.e., region-as-actor] (Riggirozzi 2012: 423). In this sense, Hettne and Söderbaum (2000) assert that regionness defines the position, in terms of regional cohesion, of a particular region. Riggirozzi breaks down the notion of regionness and proposes to look at actors, practices, and process not as a unitary actor, but as "spaces or arenas for action" (Riggirozzi 2012: 423). This reading suggests a double level of analysis that considers the region-as-actor and region-as-arenas for action. In this context, it can be argued that the use of the branding of solidarity may have helped to consolidate Latin America as a region-as-actor, useful to create a regional identity recognizable within and outside Latin America. The region, through the MPA, also develops into arenas for action. The effective outcome of these arenas, however, may be more difficult to assess.

As discussed here, as well as in a growing body of scholarship about refugee governance in Latin America (Cantor, Freier, and Gauci 2015), the region has managed to establish a regional approach to refugee protection that has translated in some concrete actions as demonstrated in the MPA (Barichello 2016; Cantor 2017; Harley 2014; Jubilut and Carneiro 2011). Two questions remain when exploring the legacy of the MPA, however: (1) How were these actions implemented in the countries of the region? (2) Did the regional approach translate in effective cooperation among Latin American states in relation to refugee protection?

Both concerns were already reflected in the MPA's preparatory meetings. In the first subregional meeting held in San José, Costa Rica, there was an explicit concern to reduce the gap "between the normative framework and its effective implementation in practice" (UNHCR 2006b: 274). The recommendation of including civil society in both refugee status determination processes and in the adoption and implementation of public policies discussed above, seems to have emerged as a concrete measure to ensure effective implementation. As emphasized in the notes, however, participants of the meeting confirmed that the States are "primarily responsible for respecting, promoting and protecting the rights of the persons under their jurisdiction" (ibid.:273). On the third subregional meeting, held in Cartagena de Indias, Colombia, states also hinted at the limits of political will that can hinder cooperation in the context of the displacement of large groups of persons in need of protection as this often exceeds the possibilities of individual States (ibid.: 275). In the next two sections, I will explore both questions in relation to the implementation of the MPA.

Solidarity in Practice: The Issues of Implementation

Since the MPA was adopted in 2004 there have been several reports and academic texts that explore the significance of the MPA as a framework of regional cooperation that endorses a pragmatic and flexible approach to reach durable solutions (Barichello 2016; Harley 2014; Lavanchy 2006; Maldonado Castillo 2015). There are other studies, however, that have gone beyond the rhetorical analysis of the MPA and that have explored the effective implementation of the plan of action on the ground (e.g., Alto Comisionado de las Naciones Unidas para los Refugiados [ACNUR] 2010; Guglielmelli-White 2012; Ruiz 2015; Varoli 2010; Vera-Espinoza 2018a). The review of these studies, as well as the reports of the UNHCR, sheds light into the actions implemented and the challenges the MPA faced on the ground.

For instance, the UNHCR annual appeal (UNHCR 2006a) reports that, under the Borders of Solidarity program, this United Nations agency supported small projects such as the construction of water supply systems and the repair of school buildings and health-care centers. According to the report, there was also an emphasis, under the Solidarity Cities program, in providing job placements, vocational training, community-based childcare centers and microcredit schemes to refugees (e.g., Spindler 2005). A year after, another UNHCR report specified that during that period the United Nations refugee agency and its partners had developed "1,000 community projects in 350 border communities in which 25–30 percent of the population in need reside," benefiting more than 160,000 people in these bordering regions (UNHCR 2007: 12). Both documents highlight that one of the most notable achievements under the MPA were the signing of agreements with major cities "to ensure that the displaced are granted their basic rights and social benefits, as well as an increase in resettlement opportunities within the region" (UNHCR 2006a: 290).

Indeed, Varoli (2010) states that some municipal governments and the UNHCR committed to a cooperation framework to ensure international protection, local integration, and assistance for asylum seekers (e.g., Thayer Correa, Correa, and Novoa 2014). Focusing on the case of Chile and the implementation of resettlement, Varoli emphasizes the efficacy of these partnerships with reference to the inclusive municipal school programs and the immediate assistance given to women considered to be at risk. In many cases, argues Varoli, the agreements between UNHCR and the municipal authorities under the Solidarity Cities program have been ratified by the municipal council, becoming public policies that "remain in force through any changes in public administration" (Varoli 2010: 44). At the same time, according to Varoli (ibid.: 45) the recognition of the role of the local level trough these partnerships means extending UNHCR's institutional capacity in the cities.

Other specific achievement of the MPA was furthering harmonization of refugee protection norms in the region (Kneebone 2016). According to the UNHCR (2007:1; ACNUR 2010: 7), sixteen of the twenty countries of the region that adopted the declaration and plan of action had included the broader Cartagena Declaration definition in their refugee legislation.[4] Furthermore, within ten years of the MPA adoption, eight Latin American countries had adopted new asylum legislation, including Argentina (Act 26165-2006), Uruguay (Act 18076-2006), Nicaragua (Act 655-2008), Chile (Act 20430-2010), Costa Rica (Regulation 36831-2009), Mexico (Refugees Act, 2011), Bolivia (Act 251-2012) and Colombia (Decree 2840-2013) (for further details, see Freier and Fernández in this volume). Another good practice identified in the region is the recognition of the right to seek asylum in the political constitutions of some countries, such as Bolivia (2009), the Dominican Republic (2010), and Ecuador (2010) (ACNUR 2010).

The professionalization of refugee status determination and the increasing participation of members of the civil society in the national committees to the refugee status determination can be considered among the achievements as well as the increment and diversification of the partners working with the UNHCR in refugee protection, particularly in relation to solidarity cities and resettlement (Fischel de Andrade 2014). Finally, the strategic use of resettlement and its implementation in five countries of the region has been widely recognized: Argentina, Brazil, Chile, Paraguay, and Uruguay, with more than 1,600 refugees resettled in the region since 2004 (Guglielmelli-White 2012; Harley 2014; Jubilut and Carneiro 2011; Marcogliese 2017; Vera Espinoza 2018a).

Despite the concrete actions and programs implemented across Latin America, challenges remain. Already two years after the MPA's adoption, Spindler stated that the implementation of some of the programs was uneven due to insufficient resources and the "practical difficulties to provide effective protection in some situations" Spindler (2005: 65), particularly in the context of the Colombian conflict. In 2010 the need to keep improving mechanisms and procedures of the status of refugee determination was also recognized, particularly in relation to regularization and documentation of asylum seekers and refugees (ACNUR 2010). Although several assessments of the MPA recognized the positive inclusion of gender dynamics in the practices of refugee protection as well as a specific focus on unaccompanied children (UNHCR 2006a), they also reported that indigenous population and afro-descent communities were essentially invisible, particularly in Colombia, Ecuador, Panama, and Venezuela (ACNUR 2010: 19). At the same time, by 2014 issues remained in relation to refugees' social inclusion, access to housing, poverty, lack of naturalization, and income generation, among others (ACNUR 2010; Bijit 2012; Guglielmelli-White 2012; Ruiz 2015; UNHCR 2007; Vera Espinoza 2018a, 2018b). During the ten-year period between the MPA and the 2014 Brazil Declaration and Plan of Action, it was also difficult to keep the regional and international commitment and political will as well as the financial contributions. This translated into an uneven and difficult implementation of programs (Nardone 2019; Spindler 2005), their suspension or delay (Menezes and Kostas 2017), and poor protection practices in some cases (Vera Espinoza 2018a, 2018b). The tensions that have more recently emerged as a result of the Venezuelan displacement, particularly at the border areas, shows some of the limitations of the MPA where the branding of borders of solidarity, for example, has not been enough to implement local policies that benefit both refugee and local communities in order to encourage integration and to prevent recurrent xenophobic acts (Jarochinski Silva and Jubilut 2018).

As can be expected, lack of implementation (or uneven implementation) is not an uncommon issue within refugee and migration governance. As Geddes et al. (2019) have discussed, the issues of implementation can worsen at the regional level where the institutional enforcement mechanisms can be weak and political will can change quickly, together with changing leadership. That is why the failures and achievements of the MPA cannot be taken at face value and they need to be assessed together and in context. That is to say that the MPA was indeed a valuable attempt to translate the regional aspirations of commitment to refugee protection into actions and programs in different countries of the region. However, there are temporal, social, and geopolitical limitations that remind us that the declaration and plan of action do not necessarily mean effective implementation or long-lasting regional cooperation, as explored in the next section.

Durable Solutions and Regional Cooperation: The Case of Resettlement

Solidarity resettlement emerged as one of the most well-known programs of the MPA. Considered a tangible manifestation of regional solidarity, this discretionary measure by states emerged as a proposal to support neighboring countries of Colombia that, at the beginning of the 2000s, were receiving a large influx of displaced population (Guglielmelli-White 2012; Jubilut and Carneiro 2011). Building up from the pioneer experiences of resettlement in Chile and Brazil, the aim was to build a regional program by which different countries in the subregion would design and implement resettlement programs, contributing to the global aim of opening spaces of refugee protection in third countries (Vera Espinoza 2017b). As I argue elsewhere (Vera Espinoza 2018a), by exploring the experience of resettlement, particularly in Brazil and Chile, it is possible to assess to what extent responsibility sharing and intra-state cooperation were accomplished.

If we analyze the program in terms of adherence by states, it could be argued to be successful since five countries in the region—Argentina, Brazil, Chile, Paraguay, and Uruguay—have implemented programs since 2004 (Ruiz 2015). Only four of these countries still continue to take resettlement refugees, however, and all of them, except Brazil, at some point have been suspended or delayed due to financial or political reasons (Menezes and Kostas 2017; Vera Espinoza 2018a)

According to UNHCR staff the main reason why countries in South America adopted programs of resettlement was the commitments made as part of the MPA: "Resettlement was one of the three pillars of the MPA and as the countries of the region adopted the plan of action, they committed to implement it. So the regional UNHCR office promoted the programme in the Southern Cone. It is framed as a durable solution, but also as a process of solidarity towards countries of first asylum that are taking most of the responsibility. There is an attitude of solidarity, of generosity in the region" (Interview with UNHCR staff, Santiago, March 2013). Only UNHCR staff, however—out of the stakeholders interviewed—mentioned the role of the MPA as one of the state's motivations to implement resettlement (Vera Espinoza 2015). Instead, government officials and implementing partners alluded to reciprocity and desires of regional leadership as the main reasons (Jubilut and Zamur 2018; Vera Espinoza 2018a). These motivations and interest are constantly shifting, since government leadership in the countries involved have changed as well. This shifting interest on the program, evidences some of the structural issues holding back the expansion of resettlement in the region, particularly funding. So far, the UNHCR has provided a large part of the funds for resettlement in Latin America (Guglielmelli-White 2012). But the level of support varies depending on the funds the agency gets from its donors, who can specify where they want their contribution to be used. Canada, Norway, and the United States funded initial resettlement efforts in the region and they also supported the extraregional Palestinian program developed in 2007–8 in Brazil and Chile (Jubilut and Carneiro 2011; Vera Espinoza 2017a). The support decreased both globally and for the region after the 2008 financial crisis (Vera Espinoza 2017b). There was also a growing perception among donor countries that high- and middle-income countries in the region that are engaging with resettlement should be able to cover the costs of the program themselves, as expressed by one of my interviewees back in 2013.

Countries of the region do provide relevant resources in the form of indirect contributions such as the documentation that certifies refugees' legal status, as registered in the cases of Argentina, Brazil, Chile, Paraguay, and Uruguay (Ruiz 2015), as well as direct contributions such as housing subsidies, as in the case of Chile and Brazil. Some scholars argue that, in order to ensure the continuity of the program, the governments of Latin America should increase the internal funding they already provide for their own national resettlement programs (Menezes and Kostas 2017). But again, funding also relies on political will and shifting interests.

In terms of capacity and refugees' intake, the region has resettled more than 1,600 refugees since 2004 in partnership with the UNHCR, including both regional and extraregional refugees.[5] Most of them are people fleeing violence nearby, from Colombia or El Salvador. The rest included Afghans, Palestinians, Sri Lankans, Syrians, and people from the former Yugoslavia. With an estimated 1.445 million refugees globally in need of resettlement in 2021 (UNHCR 2020), the numbers of people resettled by South American states seem to be a modest effort. In order to live up to the commitment of solidarity stamped in the MPA, countries of the region need to increase both the program's capacity (intake number) and its scope (countries reached). The issues with the Solidarity Resettlement Programme, however, are not only related to the spaces and the quantity of people resettled, there are also issues with the quality of resettlement.

As I explore in my research (Vera Espinoza 2017a, 2018a, 2018b) as well as in other assessments (Guglielmelli-White 2012; Ruiz 2015; Sampaio 2010), there are issues with the material conditions of reception in some of the host countries; there are weak reception structures and programs as well as uneven accesses to rights. My own research on the experiences of Colombian and Palestinian refugees, resettled in Brazil and Chile between 2005 and 2013, highlighted the tensions that emerged between the refugees and the organizations involved, largely as a result of unfulfilled expectations (Vera Espinoza 2018b; also Moulin 2012). Refugees criticized the lack of clear information about the support they would receive and the opportunities they could find upon arrival. Palestinians refugees also told me about structural and social barriers that prevented them from accessing certain rights, services and naturalization (Vera Espinoza 2017a, 2018a).

Similar issues were raised by the forty-two Syrian refugees resettled in Uruguay in 2014, who held public protests about their living conditions in the country (Rodríguez Camejo 2017). Some of them even asked to be returned to Syria. It is worth noting that, in the three countries mentioned above, some of the refugees' complaints were heard and dealt with by the governments and the organizations running the resettlement programs. Despite some achievements, an evaluation by the UNHCR of resettlement in South America (Ruiz 2015) noticed that, by 2014, at least 22 percent of the total number of refugees resettled in the region had left their host countries and decided to return to their country of origin, returned to their first country of asylum, or traveled elsewhere. Resettlement comes with the idea of permanent residency, but in some cases people were so frustrated that they wanted to go back, even if their lives were put in danger by doing so.

A comprehensive assessment of resettlement in the region that captures both the complexities of the program and the nuances of resettled refugees' experiences goes beyond the aims of this chapter. However, this brief review of resettlement in relation to capacity, scope, and quality sheds lights onto the limits of regional cooperation and responsibility sharing in the context of humanitarian action and refugee protection in the context of the MPA.

Conclusion

This chapter has explored the development, characteristics, and implementation of the MPA, arguing that the document leaves a mixed legacy behind. The analysis of the MPA showed a strong focus on developing a regional pragmatic approach to strength refugee protection in the region by searching durable solutions. All these actions were framed in the principles of solidarity and responsibility sharing as key to develop regional cooperation. The analysis of these principles in practice showed a mixed legacy. On the one hand, the MPA managed to develop an effective rhetoric on regional cooperation and set up concrete pillars of action to search durable solutions in relation to the Borders of Solidarity, the Solidarity Cities program, and the Solidarity Resettlement Programme. It was also shown that the UNHCR had a key role in the development of the MPA and the diffusion of its principles and aims by taking part in the implementation, the provision of technical support and resources. On the other hand, the review of the execution of the plan of action provides an account of uneven implementation across the region. What is more, the analysis of resettlement in South America shows discontinuities in regional engagement, with challenges of capacity building and program continuity "due to fluctuating political interest and financial constrains" (Vera Espinoza 2018a: 92), showing the limits of regional cooperation.

This mixed legacy is not necessarily a bad feature in the afterlife of the MPA. Indeed, the mixed legacy of any soft law document may be expected, but also may be needed for changes to occur within regional refugee governance. In order to enhance the learning from the MPA and to use it as a catalyst for long-lasting change, however, there needs to be an awareness of what this mixed legacy is, and what was and was not accomplished or implemented in a particular political and social context; in addition, there is the need for an assessment of the role and performance of each actor involved. Indeed, the consultations and final text in relation to Cartagena+ 30 draws from, and also suggests, assessments of the MPA (e.g., Ruiz 2015, and see Arnold-Fernández, Sarmiento Torres, and Kallas in this volume). And whereas good practices can provide relevant information, the region also needs to learn from its failures.

Seventeen years after the adoption of the MPA and in a context of large Venezuelan displacement (see Jarochinski Silva, Castro Franco, and Sampaio in this volume) with fluctuant response from the countries of the region (Acosta, Blouin, and Freier 2019), it seems that the principles of solidarity and responsibility sharing have weakened. Analyzing the MPA showed us the possibilities and limitations of the branding of solidarity, nonetheless effective in portraying Latin America as a region-as-actor. But it also provided an account of where and when the MPA, its processes, and its actors also created arenas for action, some of which still remain today. The adoption of the MPA showed us an ambitious regional project in relation to refugee protection. A comprehensive understanding of its mixed legacy can contribute to take back some of the most ambitious ideas of the MPA and put them into practice.

Marcia Vera Espinoza is a Lecturer in Human Geography at Queen Mary University of London. She holds a PhD degree in Geography and a Master's degree in International Studies from the University of Sheffield. She is a researcher at the group Comparative Analysis on International Migration and Displacement in the Americas (CAMINAR), and she was an associate researcher in the European Research Council funded project, Prospects for International Migration Governance (MIGPROSP). Marcia is a member of the international advisory board of *Forced Migration Review*. She has recently published in *Frontiers in Human Dynamics, Migration and Society, Geopolitics and Global Policy,* among others. Her coedited book *The Dynamics of Regional Migration Governance* was published by Edward Elgar Publishing in 2019.

Notes

1. This chapter is informed by research funded by the Chilean National Agency for Research and Development, Doctorado Becas Chile 2010-72110882 and fieldwork grants from the Royal Geographical Society (with IBG) Slawson Award, the Society for Latin American Studies, and the Sheffield Institute for International Development.
2. In 2004 four subregional preparatory meetings were held: in San José, Costa Rica (12–13 August); Brasilia, Brazil (26–27 August); Cartagena de Indias, Colombia (16–17 September); and Bogotá, Colombia (6–7 October) (MPA 2004; see also UNHCR 2006).
3. The MPA was adopted by Argentina, Belize, Bolivia, Brazil, Chile, Colombia, Costa Rica, Ecuador, El Salvador, Guatemala, Guyana, Honduras, Mexico, Nicaragua, Panama, Paraguay, Peru, Suriname, Uruguay, and Venezuela.

4. These countries consider the most recent numbers published by the UNHCR (see https://www.refworld.org.es/docid/59c29a094.html) and not only the countries that adopted the Cartagena Declaration internally within the ten years that followed the MPA. However, at least two-thirds of those countries adopted the Cartagena Declaration during that period (ACNUR 2010: 7).
5. Overall numbers are based on reports such as Ruiz 2015, who states that, between 2005 and 2014, the program resettled a total of 1,151 refugees from the region plus 363 people from outside the region, mostly Palestinians and Syrians. The total also considers information provided informally by governmental officers in the region after 2014.

References

Acosta, Diego, Cécile Blouin, and Luisa Feline Freier. 2019. *La emigración venezolana: respuestas latinoamericanas.* Documento de Trabajo, n° 3 (2ª época), Madrid: Fundación Carolina.

Alto Comisionado de las Naciones Unidas para los Refugiados (ACNUR). 2010. *The Mexico Plan of Action to Strengthen International Protection of Refugees in Latin America Main Achievements and Challenges During the Period 2005-2010.* http://www.pamacnur2010.com/MPAprogressEnglish.pdf.

Barichello, Stefania E. 2016. "Refugee Protection and Responsibility Sharing in Latin America: Solidarity Programmes and the Mexico Plan of Action" *International Journal of Human Rights* 20 (2): 191–207.

Bijit, Karina. 2012. "El Proceso de Integración Social de los Refugiados Palestinos Reasentados en la Región de Valparaíso, Chile." *Si Somos Americanos. Revista de Estudios Transfronterizos* 12 (1):155–180.

Brazil Declaration and Plan of Action. 2014. https://www.acnur.org/fileadmin/Documentos/BDL/2014/9865.pdf.

Cantor, David 2017. Latin America at Forefront of Emerging Trend in Global Displacement. *Refugees Deeply.* 4 October 2017. https://deeply.thenewhumanitarian.org/refugees/community/2017/10/04/latin-america-at-forefront-of-emerging-trend-in-global-displacement

Cantor, David J. 2018. *Responsibility-Sharing in the Refugee Field: Lessons from Latin America.* Policy Brief. November 2018. Pisa: Observatory on European Migration Law.

Cantor, David J., Luisa Feline Freier, Jean-Pierre Gauci, eds. 2015. *A Liberal Tide? Immigration and Asylum Law and Policy in Latin America, Titles in the Studies of the Americas Series.* London: Institute of Latin American Studies, School of Advanced Study, University of London.

Cartagena Declaration on Refugees. 1984. https://www.oas.org/dil/1984_cartagena_declaration_on_refugees.pdf.

Domenech, Eduardo. 2013. "Las migraciones son como el agua": Hacia la instauración de políticas de "control con rostro humano" La gobernabilidad migratoria en la Argentina. *POLIS Revista Latinoamericana* 35: 1–21. http://journals.openedition.org/polis/9280.

Fischel de Andrade, José Henrique. 2014. "Forced Migration in South America." In *The Oxford Handbook of Refugee and Forced Migration Studies*, edited by Elena E. Fiddian-Qasmiyeh, Gil Loescher, Katy Long, and Nando Sigona, 651–663. Oxford: Oxford University Press.

Geddes, Andrew, Marcia Vera Espinoza, Leila Hadj-Abdou, and Leiza Brumat, eds. 2019. *The Dynamics of Regional Migration Governance*. Cheltenham, UK: Edward Elgar.

Gottwald, Martin. 2004. "Protecting Colombian Refugees in the Andean Region: The Fight against Invisibility." *International Journal of Refugee Law* 16 (4): 517–546.

Guglielmelli-White, Ana. 2012. *A Pillar of Protection: Solidarity Resettlement for Refugees in Latin America*. New Issues in Refugee Research, 239: 1–26.

Harley, Tristan. 2014. "Regional Cooperation and Refugee Protection in Latin America: A "South-South" Approach." *International Journal of Refugee Law*, 26 (1) : 22–47.

Hettne, Björn, and Fredrik Söderbaum. 2000. "Theorising the Rise of "Regionness.'" *New Political Economy*, 5 (3): 457–74.

Jarochinski Silva, João Carlos, and Liliana Lyra Jubilut. 2018. "Venezuelans in Brazil: Challenges of Protection." *E-International Relations*. 12 July 2018. https://www.e-ir.info/2018/07/12/venezuelans-in-brazil-challenges-of-protection/.

Jubilut, Liliana L. 2006. "Refugee Law and Protection in Brazil: a Model in South America?." *Journal of Refugee Studies*, 19 (1):22–44.

———. 2010. "Enhancing refugees' integration: new initiatives in Brazil." *Forced Migration Review* (35): 46–47.

Jubilut, Liliana L., and Wellington P. Carneiro. 2011. "Resettlement in Solidarity: A New Regional Approach Towards a More Humane Durable Solution." *Refugee Survey Quarterly*, 30 (3): 63–86.

Jubilut, Liliana L., and André de L. Madureira. 2014. "Os desafios de proteção aos refugiados e migrantes forçados no marco de Cartagena + 30." *REMHU: Revista Interdisciplinar da Mobilidade Humana*, 22 (43): 11–33.

Jubilut, Liliana L., and Érika P. Ramos. 2014. "Regionalism: a strategy for dealing with crisis migration." *Forced Migration Review* (45): 66-67.

Jubilut, Liliana L, and Andrea C. Zamur. 2018. "Brazil's Refugee Resettlement. Power, Humanitarianism, and Regional Leadership." In *Refugee Resettlement: Power, Politics and Humanitarian Governance*, edited by A. Garnier, L. L. Jubilut and K. Bergtora Sandvik: 70–91, New York: Berghahn Books.

Kneebone, Susan. 2016. "Comparative regional protection frameworks for refugees: norms and norm entrepreneurs." *The International Journal of Human Rights*, 20 (2): 153–172.

Lavanchy, Philippe. 2006. "The Mexico Declaration and Plan of Action: Reaffirming Latin America's Generous Tradition of Asylum and Innovative Solutions." *International Journal of Refugee Law*, 18 (2): 450–451.

Maldonado Castillo, Carlos. 2015. "The Cartagena process: 30 years of innovation and solidarity." *Forced Migration Review* (89): 89–91.

Marcogliese, María José. 2017. "The Solidarity Resettlement Programme, and alternatives, in Latin America." *Forced Migration Review*, 54 (1): 54–56.

Menezes, Fabiano L de. 2016 "Utopia or Reality: Regional Cooperation in Latin America to Enhance the Protection of Refugees." *Refugee Survey Quarterly*, 35 (4): 122–141.

Menezes, Thais S., and Stylianos Kostas. 2017 "The future of the Brazilian resettlement programme." *Forced Migration Review*, 56 (1): 51-52.

Mexico Declaration and Plan of Action to Strengthen International Protection of Refugees in Latin America. 2004. http://www.unhcr.org/refworld/docid/424bf6914.html.

Moulin, Carolina. 2009. "Borders of Solidarity: Life in Displacement in the Amazon Tri-Border Region." *Refugee*, 26(2): 41-54.

———. 2012. Ungrateful subjects? Refugee protest and the logic of gratitude. In *Citizenship, Migrant Activism and the Politics of Movement*, edited by P. Nyers and K. Rygiel: 54-72. Abingdon and New York: Routledge.

———. 2013. "Protection and vulnerability in urban contexts: the case of refugees in Rio de Janeiro." Discussion Paper 6, *Humanitarian Action in Situations Other than War*, September 2013.

Nardone, Mariana. 2019. "Inter-Organisational Cooperation in Resettlement Programmes: A Tripartite Approach." *Refugee Survey Quarterly*, Volume 38 (2): 214-244.

Riggirozzi, Pia. 2012. "Region, Regionness and Regionalism in Latin America: Towards a New Synthesis." *New Political Economy*, 17 (4): 421-443.

Rodríguez Camejo, Raquel. 2017. "Syrian refugees in Uruguay: an uncomfortable topic." *Forced Migration Review* (56): 55-56.

Ruiz, Hiram. 2015. *Evaluation of Resettlement Programmes in Argentina, Brazil, Chile, Paraguay and Uruguay*. Geneva: UNHCR.

Sampaio, Cyntia. 2010. "Programa Brasileiro de Reassentamento Solidário: evolução e reflexões para seu fortalecimento," C*aderno de Debates Refugio, Migrações e Cidadania*, 5 (5): 19-39.

Spindler, William. 2005. "The Mexico Plan of Action: Protecting Refugees Through International Solidarity." *Forced Migration Review* 24: 64-65.

Thayer Correa, Luis Eduardoa, Sara Correa, and Tamara Novoa. 2014. *Plan de Acogida y reconocimiento de migrantes y refugiados de la comuna de Quilicura*, Municipalidad de Quilicura.

United Nations High Commissioner for Refugees (UNHCR). 2005a. *Memoir of the Twentieth Anniversary of the Cartagena Declaration on Refugees*, UNHCR, San José, Costa Rica: EDITORAMA.

———. 2005b. Mexico Plan of Action for refugees is world's most sophisticated, UN refugee chief says. United Nations News 7 October 2005.

———. 2006a. "Latin America (Mexico Plan of Action)" in UNHCR Global Appeal 2007.

———. 2006b. Preparatory Sub-Regional Meetings of San José, Brasilia and Cartagena De Indias, *International Journal of Refugee Law*, 18 (1): 271-276.

———. 2007. *Mexico Plan of Action: The impact of regional solidarity*. UNHCR. San José, Costa Rica: Editorama.

———. 2011. *UNHCR Resettlement Handbook*. https://www.refworld.org/pdfid/4ecb973c2.pdf.

———. 2018. *Global Compact on Refugees*. Final draft. 26 June 2018. https://www.unhcr.org/5b3295167.pdf.

———. 2020. *UNHCR Projected Global Resettlement Needs 2021.* https://www.unhcr.org/protection/resettlement/5ef34bfb7/projected-global-resettlement-needs-2021.html

Varoli, Fabio. 2010. "Cities of Solidarity: local integration in Latin America." *Forced Migration Review,* 34: 44–46. https://www.fmreview.org/sites/fmr/files/FMRdownloads/en/urban-displacement/varoli.pdf.

Vera Espinoza, Marcia. 2015. *"Experiences of 'Unsettlement': Exploring the "Integration" of Palestinian and Colombian refugees resettled in Chile and Brazil."* Unpublished PhD Thesis, Department of Geography, University of Sheffield.

———. 2017a. "Extra-regional Refugee Resettlement in South America: The Palestinian Experience." *Forced Migration Review,* 56 (1): 47–49.

———. 2017b. Is Latin America ready to accept more resettled refugees?, *The Conversation.* 11 October 2017. https://theconversation.com/is-latin-america-ready-to-accept-more-resettled-refugees-85292.

———. 2018a. "The Limits and Opportunities of Regional Solidarity: Exploring Refugee Resettlement in Brazil and Chile." *Global Policy,* 9 (1): 85–94.

———. 2018b. "The Politics of Resettlement: Expectations and unfulfilled promises in Chile and Brazil." In *Refugee Resettlement: Power, Politics and Humanitarian Governance,* edited by Adéle Garnier, Jubilut, Liliana L. Jubilut and Kristin B. Sandvik: 223–243. New York: Berghahn Books.

4

The Brazil Declaration and Plan of Action

A Model for Other Regions

Emily Arnold-Fernández, Karina Sarmiento Torres, and Gabriella Kallas

Introduction: What Is the BPA?

Adopted in 2014, the Brazil Declaration and Plan of Action: A Framework for Cooperation and Regional Solidarity to Strengthen the International Protection of Refugees, Displaced and Stateless Persons in Latin America and the Caribbean (BPA) represents the most recent in a series of intergovernmental commitments in Latin America that build on, and consider new ways of implementing, the 1984 Cartagena Declaration on Refugees (Cartagena Declaration) (United Nations High Commissioner for Refugees [UNHCR] 2014a). The Cartagena Declaration set forth a vision for a Latin American response to forced displacement rooted in the political turmoil of the 1970s and 1980s, one that built on the 1951 Convention Relating to the Status of Refugees (1951 Refugee Convention) and its 1967 Protocol Relating to the Status of Refugees (1967 Protocol), while also pushing the boundaries of states' responsibilities to refugees significantly farther (Bradley 2014: 669).

Every ten years since the passage of the Cartagena Declaration, Latin American states have undertaken to review the state of refugee protection and integration in the region. This process of discussion, analysis, and renewal of commitments is a distinctive practice of Latin America, unlike that of any other refugee-hosting region. It has allowed Latin America to develop and reinforce an ongoing consensus that refugee protection and integration are obligations of states and that therefore states bear the primary responsibility for implementation of refugee protection and integration.

The BPA is the latest expression of this consensus. Adopted in December 2014 by twenty-eight countries and three territories across Latin America and the Caribbean, the BPA renews the region's commitment to progress on refugee response by mapping out a ten-year plan, divided into eight chapters and nine thematic programs (BPA). At a historic moment in which rising global trends toward nationalism, xenophobia, and conservative approaches to refugee protection are driving states to ignore or minimize implementation of refugees' human rights, the BPA is one of a small number of contemporary progressive instruments that proposes measures intended to mitigate these trends.

Throughout this chapter we hope to add a practitioner's perspective to the study of Latin American regional efforts on refugee protection. All three authors work as refugee rights advocates, and one was personally involved in the development of the BPA; specifically, she was part of formal and behind-the-scenes discussions with civil society, governments, refugees, and other stakeholders that led to its creation. Our perspective is informed by professional knowledge and practice of human rights law, as well as by experience in turning the promises of human rights instruments into lived reality. Our legal analysis of the BPA and use of secondary literature are thus supplemented by both our experience in the BPA process and by our experience (before and after the BPA) as refugee rights advocates in Latin America and around the world.

In this chapter we argue that, by understanding the BPA's process and content, we can develop a vision of current best practice in refugee protection and integration. To do so, we begin by situating the BPA in context through the analysis of two distinctive elements of refugee protection in Latin America, namely the role of the UNHCR in advancing refugees' human rights regionally, and the Cartagena review process as it played out in the lead-up to December 2014. We then explore the BPA itself in depth, identifying the unique textual and thematic elements that make it effective in advancing refugee response, protection, and solutions. Finally, we consider the BPA's strengths and limitations in Latin America's current climate, as well as the lessons the BPA–both in and of itself and as part of Latin America's legal and practical framework of refugee response–can offer to other regions.

The BPA in Context: Distinctive Elements of Refugee Protection in Latin America

The BPA must first be set in the context of a greater tradition of asylum and refugee protection in Latin America, a tradition often praised by scholars and practitioners alike for its innovative character and distinctiveness (Barichello 2015; Jubilut 2014). Though not without its shortcomings, regionalism has been touted as a uniquely potent form of promoting refugee protection due to the regional nature of refugee crises (Fischel de Andrade 1998), and the possibilities of shared cultural and other values (Harley 2014; Schreuer 1995). In this section, we discuss two components of Latin American regionalism as distinctive elements through which the BPA should be understood: first, the unique role of UNHCR, and second, the Cartagena process of review (or the Cartagena process).

The Unique Role of UNHCR

As practitioners, we recognize the importance of the unique role of UNHCR in Latin America in promoting refugee protection. In Africa and Asia, when states refuse to accept their responsibilities to refugees, UNHCR often serves as a surrogate state (Kagan 2011); essentially, UNHCR replaces the state as the entity conducting refugee status determination (RSD) and also establishes and maintains social services for refugees that should be provided by the state. In these situations, UNHCR assumes the role of humanitarian assistance provider, and often refrains from pushing states to make progress on implementing rights-respecting policies in order to avoid risking humanitarian access (Loescher 2001). In most states in Latin America, however, the state is directly responsible for RSD and integrates refugees to some degree into existing social services such as education, health care, and welfare (Asylum Access 2018). As a result, in Latin America UNHCR can fulfill a technical assistance role with governments and collaborate with civil society in promoting policy implementation, as is the case in spaces such as the Cartagena process.

The Cartagena Process of Review

A number of scholars have taken up the study of the Cartagena process due to its distinctiveness as a long-standing regional practice concerned with the protection of refugees. This process began with the Cartagena Declaration, which strikingly expanded the refugee definition to include those who fled their country as a result of "generalized violence, foreign aggression[,] . . . massive violation of human rights or other circumstances which have seriously disturbed public order(. . .)" (UNHCR 1984). It is not just the extended definition that makes the Cartagena Declaration significant, however: it also created a process of review of refugee protection in the region every ten years. Such a process serves a dual purpose in that it both reflects dynamics of cooperation within the region and promotes continued cooperation through the creation of an ongoing space to reflect on refugee protection regionally (Cantor 2018). Specifically, Cantor notes that the Cartagena process has been successful due to its permanence and stability as an independent space created to promote refugee response and protection, while maintaining flexibility in both membership and outcomes of the process (ibid.). As such, it has been able both to stay relevant and to address novel issues as they arise.

Of course, scholars and practitioners have also articulated critiques regarding the true impact of the Cartagena process. In his 2016 analysis of implementation of Latin American regional agreements on refugees, Fabiano L. de Menezes argues that the distinction between Latin America and other regions is purely discursive (Menezes 2016). While Menezes poses arguments worth considering—above all that many major refugee-hosting countries in the region have not incorporated the Cartagena definition into their domestic legislation—his critique fails to fully acknowledge the relatively greater shortcomings of other regions. For instance, many major refugee-hosting countries around the world have not even ratified the 1951 Refugee Convention, and lack domestic legislative safeguards of refugees' most basic rights, rendering refugees almost entirely unprotected (Asylum Access 2014).

We do concede, however, that it is vital to consider the limitations of Cartagena-related instruments in practice (although in our own analysis we have focused more on the text and creation of the BPA than on its subsequent implementation, which is ongoing). Consequently, in the conclusion we explore the current context in Latin America, and how even strong models of solidarity may falter in the face of crisis.

While scholars have deeply explored the Cartagena Declaration and even the Mexico Declaration and Plan of Action to Strengthen the International Protection of Refugees in Latin America (MPA) (see Vera Espinoza in this volume; see also Harley 2014; Kneebone 2016), the same analytic lens has not been applied to the BPA. It is this gap that we hope to fill with this chapter. By doing so, we continue the work of Harley (2014), Barichello (2015), Cantor (2018), and others who have explored the distinctive characteristics of regional solidarity in Latin America.

Greater Inclusion, Increased Legitimacy: The BPA's Improvements on Past Approaches

By analyzing the processes leading up to the creation of the BPA, we demonstrate that the BPA is more than simply the most recent iteration of Latin America's process of review of state commitments to advancing refugee protection and integration. Rather, it represents a substantial deepening of the modalities by which states and other stakeholders conduct such a process, promoting greater inclusion and legitimacy.

The BPA adopted the innovations made in the MPA process[1] and took them farther through a broader consultative process that positioned organizations closest to refugees as influential actors in recommending regional refugee policy and practice. J.C. Murillo (interview on 28 July 2020) noted that the participation of civil society was qualitatively distinctive leading up to the BPA since civil society organizations were able to present their input and proposals directly to other stakeholders. While one organization (the Norwegian Refugee Council) had a facilitator role, it was not the mouthpiece for all civil society organizations but rather facilitated the ability of all organizations to participate directly in convenings, discussions, and other processes for providing input alongside states and multilaterals. Those participating in the consultations that led to the BPA included state representatives and substantive issue area experts, as well as human rights institutions, academia, officials of municipal and provincial governments, and civil society (Maldonado Castillo 2015). The inclusion of civil society and other non-state representatives gave rise to a much more inclusive debate on principles of protection and implementation. In addition, compared with past Cartagena-related consultations, a significantly greater number of organizations working with refugees or led by refugees had a hand in shaping the ultimate outcome of these consultations. The influence of this inclusion can be seen in the text and thematic focuses of the BPA, discussed in subsequent sections.

Another important improvement of the BPA process was the organization of four thematic consultations as preparatory meetings a year in advance of drafting of the BPA (UNHCR 2014a). Known as the Cartagena+30 Initiative, these formal government-led thematic consultations held across the region brought together representatives from state governments, civil society, and other relevant actors. Through these meetings, government and civil society were able to identify areas of alignment, explore possible solutions to disagreement, and generate a mutual understanding of the perspectives and challenges of participants. As thematic consultations–a variation on the MPA's subregional approach–these convenings allowed for deeper engagement on key regional issues, as opposed to more superficial and repetitive discussions of key themes at a variety of subregional meetings (ibid.).

To support these thematic convenings, various stakeholders organized their own preparatory meetings alongside formal processes. Civil society was particularly active in planning for participation in the formal BPA process, and thus contributed in more-strategic and more-impactful ways. For example, a set of quasi-formal discussions led by the Norwegian Refugee Council at the request of UNHCR brought together civil society organizations to agree on a common agenda and define delegates for the official thematic consultations hosted by states (Egeland 2014). An independent civil society creation, the Cartagena+30 Initiative provided a space for civil society to organize a shared strategy and tactics to advance its common agenda in the formal consultations, with the goal of securing inclusion of its proposals in the final BPA.

The Cartagena +30 Initiative also provided a foundation on which to develop strategies to promote implementation of the BPA following adoption through the formation of the Grupo Articulador Regional del Plan de Acción de Brasil (GAR-PAB; Regional Working Group of the Brazil Plan of Action) (Asylum Access 2014). Since 2014 GAR-PAB has supported national civil society organizations to advocate nationally for state-specific implementation steps, and has fostered the sharing of lessons, experiences, and successes across the region (GAR-PAB). Unfortunately, resource constraints over the past two years have lessened GAR-PAB's earlier power as a convener and technical support provider.

In the end, many recommendations promoted by civil society were included in the final document, such as those related to RSD; progressive incorporation of an age, gender, and diversity approach; and specific protection measures at borders. Some, though, were left out, such as a regional commitment to abstain from migratory detention for all migrants, and not only children (Asylum Access 2014; Egeland 2014).

As might be expected, the legitimacy of the BPA is not without critics. For example, in our own experience and conversations, we have seen that civil society participants–and participants who believed their voices were not fully represented–have noted that civil society's role should continue to grow significantly in the future. Among other improvements, these critics call for stronger participation mechanisms and a greater role for refugee-led civil society organizations. The incomplete inclusion of civil society is clear–for example, when we compare civil society's Cartagena +30 document with the final BPA (Asylum Access 2014; BPA). Although civil society requested to be part of a tripartite commission to review the BPA, the BPA proclaims only states and UNHCR as producing evaluation mechanisms (BPA: 19), demonstrating that civil society, including refugee-led organizations, are not yet seen as equal participants in the process.

Responding in part to these critiques, which occurred even during the development of the BPA, the BPA established an interim review process that included a meeting three years into the BPA's ten-year timeline to assess initial progress (ibid.: 19). This interim meeting was intended to build the legitimacy of the BPA by providing an early opportunity for evaluation and accountability (UNHCR 2017b: 16). While state reports on progress focused primarily on positive developments and exchange of good practices in line with the BPA's goals (ibid.; 100 Points of Brasilia: 100 Points of Brasilia: Inputs from Latin America and the Caribbean to the Global Compact on Refugees [100 Points of Brasilia]), critical voices were also included. For example, the interim review meeting invited the civil society coalition,

GAR-PAB, to present its alternative report articulating civil society's view of states' progress (GAR-PAB). This inclusion both further reinforced the BPA's commitment to participation of independent civil society voices and provided an opportunity for civil society to make recommendations to further strengthen the legitimacy of the BPA and its successors (ibid.).

Thus, the BPA represents important improvements in the Cartagena process. With the shifting of modalities of consultation, the BPA process became far more inclusive. Through thematic consultations, greater inclusion of civil society, and the creation of follow-up mechanisms, the BPA gained legitimacy as a truer representation of the region's needs, intentions, and aspirations.

Unpacking the BPA: Unique Textual and Topical Elements

The BPA was shaped by a set of unique circumstances, including the contemporary political context of the region and the robust participation of civil society and other non-state actors in the BPA's creation. These circumstances gave the BPA notable thematic and textual attributes distinct from other Cartagena-related instruments; specifically, these attributes include the themes of harmonization and attention to subregional crises, and textual attention to RSD, multiply marginalized persons,[2] and integration.

Unique Thematic Elements of the BPA

Thematically, the BPA emphasizes the promotion of harmonization of state practice vis-à-vis refugees, both with international and regional norms and between states in the region. It incorporates international norms such as "the *jus cogens* character of the principles of *non-refoulement*, including non-rejection at borders and indirect *refoulement*," as well as "the integration of due process guarantees in refugee status determination procedures" (BPA: 2). Both norms are critical in ensuring that refugees are able to obtain formal recognition of their legal status as refugees. Legal recognition in turn is important because refugees are legally entitled to a set of unique rights, in addition to the standard range of human rights, that recognize the specific impact of forced displacement across nation-state borders. In short, refugee status is a gateway to accessing other rights.

Calls for harmonization are also visible in the BPA's language connecting state practice with regional doctrinal and jurisprudential developments within the inter-American human rights system (ibid.: 18). Indeed, the BPA explicitly calls for increased alignment of national laws and norms with those of the region (ibid.: 18). The BPA then reinforces this theme through practical commitments by encouraging states to strengthen their national

RSD bodies through the Quality Asylum program, which enables these bodies to effectively implement international and regional norms (ibid.: 4, 9–10). Notably, however, the BPA does not apply such a lens to other state practices, in particular those relating to *non-refoulement*; adequate information about and access to RSD procedures, including appeals; and the avoidance of migratory detention (ibid.).

Finally, the BPA directly calls for harmonization between states through exhortations to states in the region to continue progressively harmonizing their national-level approaches to asylum (ibid.: 4). It also encourages the incorporation of consistent asylum standards across states within mechanisms established to facilitate regional and subregional migration (ibid.: 4).

Overall, the BPA reinforces that states have simultaneous and complementary obligations, explicitly emphasizing the "convergence and complementarity of International Human Rights Law, International Refugee Law and International Humanitarian Law" as a common legal framework setting forth states' responsibilities to refugees (ibid.: 1). Civil society's use of enforcement mechanisms, such as regional and national courts, to hold states accountable for compliance with their human rights obligations to refugees over the decade preceding the BPA opened states' eyes to the risks of failing to harmonize their national, regional, and international obligations.[3] In emphasizing the importance of aligning state law and practice with not only international and regional refugee law specifically, but also with international and regional human rights standards and international humanitarian law (ibid.: 1), the BPA articulates an expectation that states will guarantee, implement, and safeguard the highest level of human rights for people on the move.

The inclusion of the harmonization theme reflects the impact of the more inclusive processes of consultation that marked the BPA process. As those of us participating in the discussions leading to the BPA saw firsthand, academic input offered a deeper understanding of how international and regional principles applied to state practice. Civil society pushed for provisions that held states accountable to their international and regional obligations and commitments regarding human rights and migration. Stakeholders in the Inter-American Human Rights system, such as multilaterals, civil society, and academics, contributed expertise on jurisprudence regarding the application of human rights norms to the context of human mobility, and ensured that such norms informed the development of the BPA. The inclusivity of the BPA process, therefore, had an important impact on the results that emerged.

The BPA also included increased attention to specific subregional challenges. The BPA establishes a common roadmap for all participating states, but paid special attention to the subregions most affected by forced migration at the time of drafting: the Caribbean (ibid.:16) and the so-called

Northern Triangle of Central America (ibid.: 14–15; also known as the North of Central America, or NCA). The chapters focusing on these subregions provide a foundation for supportive action by other states, and direct the region's collective resources toward assisting with challenges that, while affecting all states in the region, have a deeper impact on source and neighboring countries. Through this recognition, the BPA expresses a belief that the region as a whole is collectively responsible for addressing specific subregional situations and environments of immediate concern (ibid.: 14–18).

As with the harmonization theme, the theme of attention to particular displacement situations reflects improved methods of consultation utilized in the process of developing the BPA. The use of thematic consultations allowed the region to more deeply discuss the challenges facing various parts of the region, including the rise of organized crime as a cause of displacement and the need to integrate asylum into migration response at sea (UNHCR 2014a). Civil society efforts also generated greater attention to the needs of specific subregions, in particular the Caribbean subregion, efforts that some civil society organizations say were sidelined in past processes. Civil society efforts also created an infrastructure capable of exerting greater pressure on the state drafters of the BPA to explicitly address subregional needs (e.g., UNHCR 2014b).

Unique Textual Elements of the BPA

The BPA also has several notable textual elements. Its text focuses more strongly than prior documents on a few key areas: the quality and accessibility of RSD procedures, protection for vulnerable or multiply marginalized groups, and integration.

First, the BPA commits states to strengthen the quality and accessibility of critical RSD procedures (BPA: 9–10). Refugee status is a prerequisite for assertion of rights *as a refugee*, and thus has the potential to improve the refugee population's access to a wide range of human rights (Kagan 2008). It is also extremely high stakes: an error in assessing refugee status can lead to the *refoulement* of a person whose life, liberty, or bodily integrity is likely to be at risk as a result (UNHCR 1997). RSD procedures may therefore be considered similar to trials for capital crimes in this regard. Consequently, refugee status adjudications should accord applicants the highest standards of fairness, transparency, and accountability–the hallmarks of due process– given that an erroneously rejected applicant may pay the ultimate price for that incorrect decision (Kagan 2008; UNHCR 1997).

By focusing on due process in RSD procedures, and on the strengthening of national institutions to conduct fair, transparent, and accountable refugee status adjudications, the BPA demonstrates a focus on how states in the region give effect to the promises of international, regional, and national law.

This focus illustrates an important degree of advancement in the Cartagena process: the region was able to move beyond the basics of implementation, such as the MPA's establishment of RSD procedures near borders, to the BPA's precise, technical recommendations to improve the ways in which implementing structures tangibly give effect to rights.

Second, the BPA includes specific commitments to promote protection for vulnerable groups (BPA: 2, 5, 15). The BPA drafters used the term "vulnerable," but we prefer the term "multiply marginalized," since it emphasizes that vulnerability stems from the actions of the state or other actors to marginalize certain groups, as opposed to from the persons or groups themselves (Goodkind and Deacon 2004). Some examples of multiply marginalized groups addressed in the BPA include survivors of sexual- or gender-based violence, survivors of or those at risk of trafficking, children and adolescents, LGBTQ (lesbian, gay, bisexual, transgender, and queer/questioning) persons, indigenous people, people with disabilities, and Afro-descendants, among others (ibid.: 4–5, 8).

While earlier instruments, including the San José Declaration and the MPA, also mentioned some multiply marginalized populations, the BPA is far more specific and detailed. For example, these earlier documents make brief reference to differentiated responses for women refugees, but they do not mention sexual- and gender-based violence or trafficking (UNHCR 1994, 2007). The BPA, in contrast, devotes paragraphs to each of these issues (BPA: 4–5). Such inclusion reflects, among other factors, the input of civil society organizations with experience working directly with multiply marginalized people, as well as the participation of individuals who themselves fall within these groups.

The incorporation of these commitments serves to promote equitable application of human rights laws across various classes of refugees and reflects increasing understanding among the drafters regarding concepts of equity. Early refugee response instruments, such as the 1951 Refugee Convention, approach refugees' human rights through a lens of formal equality (Edwards 2009). Such an approach counterfactually assumes certain types of refugees (adult, male) and certain types of refugee experiences (threatened or perpetrated physical, nonsexual violence) are the norm (ibid.). In reality, 80 percent of refugees are women and children, and threatened or perpetrated sexual violence is a common experience among refugees (UNHCR 2017a). Moreover, an equality lens (rather than an equity lens) ignores the distinct ways in which a multiply marginalized person–for example, a refugee with a disability or a refugee from a minority ethnic group within their own country–may experience the state of being a refugee (Harris 2003; Ratkovic 2013).

Provisions that move state commitments beyond formal equality and toward equity surface in several parts of the BPA. In particular, the BPA calls on states to strengthen "differentiated referral and response mechanisms" for various multiply marginalized groups, including survivors of sexual and gender-based violence, trafficked persons and those at risk of trafficking, women, and children (particularly unaccompanied children) (BPA: 4–5). By recognizing and responding to the ways in which some refugees are marginalized beyond migration status alone, the BPA promotes a modern, equity-based lens on state responses to forced displacement.

Finally, the BPA specifically promotes the local integration of refugees. The BPA insists on the progressive adoption of policies that promote refugee integration, with specific mention of labor rights, issuance of identity documents without indicators of refugee status, local integration via hospitality and nondiscrimination policies, and paths to naturalization (ibid.: 5). All of these proposals clearly indicate the drafters' intentions that refugees become fully integrated within their host countries and communities. Additionally, the BPA explicitly acknowledges states' obligations to make progress on durable solutions inclusive of local integration for displaced persons (ibid.: 3), and even develops a specific local integration program (ibid.: 12).

That the states drafting the BPA repeatedly and in some places explicitly referenced the local integration of refugees represents a radical departure from the global norm. In the 2018 Global Compact on Refugees, states reluctantly agreed to a single paragraph acknowledging that states wishing to locally integrate refugees should be supported in their efforts to do so (Global Compact on Refugees 2018: 19). Nothing in the Global Compact on Refugees promotes local integration by refugee-hosting states, much less acknowledges state obligations (for those that have ratified the 1951 Refugee Convention or other relevant instruments) to progressively realize integration in line with their commitments under such instruments (Arnold-Fernández 2019). Moreover, the BPA not only encourages local integration, but also articulates the concrete actions states should take to remove barriers that impede refugees from forming and deepening ties within their new communities (BPA: 12). These concrete recommendations are illustrative of the BPA's solutions-based approach.

Conclusion: Lessons from the BPA

The BPA, and the larger human rights framework of which it is the most recent iteration, represents an important accomplishment in Latin America that offers vital lessons for other regions. In this chapter we have seen that the BPA has provided a substantial deepening of previous iterations of the Cartagena process through its broader consultation process. As a result of this process, the BPA features important and unique textual elements, such as the themes of harmonization and subregional crises, and focuses on RSD, multiply marginalized people, and integration.

The BPA represents a significant accomplishment, but it has fallen short as recent refugee crises strain political will. The region is now home to more than 4.3 million Venezuelans fleeing economic collapse and another 500,000 Central Americans fleeing their homes in response to gang violence (UNHCR 2020)–displacement figures that are nearly unprecedented in the region. A growing number of countries receiving Venezuelan refugees are placing increasing restrictions on their entry; Peru requires a humanitarian visa that they must acquire before entry, while Chile requires a valid passport and residency visa, both almost impossible in the face of current conditions in Venezuela (Janetsky 2019; see also Jarochinski, Castro, and Sampaio in this volume). At the time of this writing, only Brazil and Mexico are broadly recognizing Venezuelans as refugees, meaning that states are deliberating avoiding the obligations such a designation would entail (Freier 2018).

Such a response to the region's largest displacement situation shows the limitations of instruments like the BPA in the face of widespread crisis, especially without a commensurate increase in available resources. Alexander Betts notes that host countries in the region have not received the assistance needed for such a crisis, and that the international community has been slow to act (Betts 2019). Although it is outside the scope of this chapter, it is vital to ask at what point solidarity breaks down, and what can be done to prevent that from happening. We believe, like Betts, that the presence of resources to support state response to inflows could aid significantly with the breakdown of political will we are seeing. Although Betts focuses on the provision of technical advice to governments, we believe financial resources to shore up the technical systems and institutions that facilitate prompt integration–including asylum and RSD processes, among others–are equally critical. This proposal is particularly pertinent in Latin America, where states have incorporated refugees' procedural and substantive human rights into legislation; those states may need support to carry out legislative promises when implementing systems confront a massive increase in demand, however.

The region struggles with the challenges of putting promises into practice, but the BPA remains a significant document. As the de jure pinnacle of the progressive Cartagena refugee regime, it illustrates the possibilities for regional commitments that advance the rights of all refugees, even as those commitments today are honored mainly in the breach. In addition, it shows what can be accomplished, at least on paper, when a wide array of representative voices are involved in the development of shared norms. At the same time, the dire circumstances of many refugees across Latin America and the Caribbean are horrific evidence that political and economic realities often trump normative frameworks, particularly when those affected by state failure to comply with regional norms have already been disenfranchised by virtue of their displacement.

Moreover, the BPA is significant as the most recent agreement within the body of agreements that make up the Cartagena regime, which is a set of accords with features that remain unique and intriguing. No other region, with the possible exception of Europe, has developed regional accords similar to this body of agreements. We do not mean to imply that other regions have failed to consider protection of refugees: on the contrary, around the world, regional approaches give governments with common contexts an important setting to share their insights on how to effectively react to forced displacement (e.g., United Nations General Assembly [UNGA] 1981, 1984). Some unique characteristics of Latin America's refugee protection mechanisms that we find compelling, however, include the absence of a cessation mechanism, the discussion of shared responsibility, and the involvement of other regional platforms in advancing refugees' human rights. These characteristics underpin some of the lessons for other regions that we draw later in this section.

The Cartagena regime's absence of a cessation mechanism, and its discussion of shared responsibility, are notable. The 1969 Organization of African Unity (OAU) Convention Governing the Specific Aspects of Refugee Problems in Africa (1969 OAU Refugee Convention), for example, lists several reasons why persons might be subject to cessation (i.e., cease being entitled to refugee status), an act that can be used to remove from an individual the protections of the 1969 OAU Refugee Convention and 1951 Refugee Convention (OAU 1969). On the other hand, the Cartagena Declaration does not follow the 1951 Refugee Convention in providing for cessation of refugee status if certain circumstances occur (UNHCR 1984). Additionally, as this chapter is being written, the international debate regarding how to reallocate responsibilities for refugee protection and inclusion has grown significantly in importance (e.g., Global Compact on Refugees 2018; UNGA 2016). Latin America, however, has been explicitly engaged in regional responsibility sharing since the 1980s (BPA; UNHCR 1984, 1994, 2004), including innovative practices to enable mandatory coordination between authorities in cross-border initiatives (UNHCR 2017b).

The Cartagena regime also signals the region's commitment to include displacement issues in the work of regional platforms that enable intergovernmental discussions, such as the Community of Latin American and Caribbean States, the Mercado Común del Sur (MERCOSUR; Southern Common Market), and the Andean Community (BPA: 18). Furthermore, the region is demonstrably taking into consideration the evolving refugee rights jurisprudence shaped by regional organizations such as the IACtHR and the Inter-American Commission on Human Rights (ibid.: 2, 18) (see Casagrande in this volume). These links between Cartagena mechanisms and other parts of the regional intergovernmental apparatus have allowed the region to maintain a progressive understanding of asylum, refugee protection, and the human rights of people on the move (see Jubilut, Vera Espinoza, and Mezzanotti in this volume).

Here and throughout the chapter, we have noted Latin America's success in maintaining and advancing a progressive refugee human rights regime, while we recognize recent regression in implementation of regional norms. With this in mind, and in particular considering the recent experiences of the BPA's drafting and implementation, what lessons can we draw for other regions? What have we learned from implementation of the BPA five years on?

The first key lesson is the importance of a strong governance framework for human rights, particularly human rights of people on the move. Comprising both legal instruments that express the region's consensus on state obligations vis-à-vis refugees and others on the move, and the human rights enforcement bodies that serve to hold states accountable to their commitments (these enforcement bodies in turn generate political will to make progress on implementation of these commitments), Latin America's human rights governance framework laid the groundwork on which the successes of the BPA were built.

In Asia and the Middle East, applying the lessons of the BPA might start with the development of regional legal instruments and bodies. Alternatively, a less ambitious approach of simply agreeing on shared principles relating to the human rights of refugees and other forced migrants might still yield positive results, particularly in conjunction with a process for regular review and recommitment (the second lesson from the BPA). In Africa there are some elements of a similar framework (including the 1969 OAU Refugee Convention and the African Charter and Court of Human and Peoples' Rights).

The second lesson is the importance of a process for regular renewal of political will to make progress on refugee human rights commitments. The Cartagena Declaration would be far less powerful as a norm-setting instrument absent the accompanying mechanism and practice for regularly convening states and other stakeholders to celebrate progress, identify gaps, define fixed-term goals for improvement, and design action plans to meet those goals.

Africa could implement such a process to regularly review progress against the norms set forth in the 1969 OAU Refugee Convention, the African Charter, and other regional and widely ratified international instruments. Just as jurisprudence from the Inter-American human rights system feeds into the Cartagena process, so too could the decisions of the African Court on Human and Peoples' Rights inform this goal-setting. Asia and the Middle East could, if they agreed on shared principles of refugee human rights at a regional or subregional level, convene regularly to evaluate their own progress toward implementation of these principles as a start toward bringing these areas in line with other refugee-hosting regions.

The third and fourth lessons Latin America can offer to other regions relate to the design and inclusiveness of the Cartagena process: The third lesson is the importance of civil society in maintaining the pressure that maintains and promotes political will. Civil society's involvement in the development, drafting, and implementation of the BPA enhanced the progressive nature of the instrument and ultimately increased the legitimacy with which it is viewed. If other regions are developing similar processes, inviting the participation of civil society will both provide valuable independent assessment and correspondingly enhance the legitimacy with which any final assessment of progress and gaps is viewed. Moreover, when civil society participation includes organizations led by refugees or those directly representing refugees as members or constituents, states will benefit from direct feedback from those most immediately affected.

Relatedly, the fourth lesson is the impact of including, rather than segregating, refugees from the economies, societies, and civic spaces of their host communities. Participation in the BPA process by organizations whose members, constituencies, or leaders are refugees did not happen by accident. Latin America's treatment of refugees was a key factor in enabling refugee participation–specifically, the region's rejection of refugee internment camps, which serve to keep refugees segregated and unable to build relationships or to organize collectively with non-refugees. By permitting refugees to live in the location of their choosing, Latin America fostered a society in which refugees and locals could make common cause. This in turn has led to greater refugee engagement with civil society as a whole, positioning refugees to become a part of civil society advocacy on human rights and migration. It also may have generated greater interest among civil society in addressing the challenges faced by refugees. As states in other regions move toward enabling greater refugee freedom of movement and camps become a last resort under UNHCR policy (UNHCR 2014c), such actions will facilitate refugee inclusion and participation in the development of solutions.

Finally, a fifth lesson is that any refugee human rights regime, even one developed through an inclusive process, is vulnerable to the deterioration of political will. With regional displacement in Latin America at a historic high–although the social, economic, and political costs of such displacement are not adequately shared–political will has eroded rapidly in Latin America since the BPA's inception. In the absence of the large-scale displacement crises rocking Latin America today, however, the BPA was arguably well-positioned to advance refugee protection in the region. Thus, its other lessons should not be overlooked.

The BPA offers, on paper, a groundbreaking path forward in the implementation of refugees' human rights. As the result of a shared commitment between states that has prevailed since 1984, the BPA has much to recommend it as a model: particularly, a commitment to respecting, protecting, and promoting refugees' human rights, and a recognition that doing so is not optional but rather a requirement of states that claim to uphold the modern human rights regime. While articulating key principles of refugee response, international cooperation, and human rights, it also sets forth specific, actionable measures to be taken by states in concrete furtherance of refugees' human rights. Together, these aspects represent a notable departure from other regional and global intergovernmental instruments addressing refugee response. They should become not a departure, but a roadmap.

Emily Arnold-Fernández, a human rights lawyer and scholar, serves as President and CEO of leading refugee human rights organization Asylum Access. Asylum Access has advocated nationally and regionally in Latin America, working in-depth in Ecuador and Mexico, and leading regional civil society initiatives. Emily also has authored journal articles and book chapters on topics in forced migration, human rights, and social entrepreneurship. She has taught at Stanford University, University of London, University of San Francisco, and Pomona College.

Karina Sarmiento Torres is a human rights, refugee and migrants' rights advocate with more than fifteen years of experience. She was director at Asylum Access in Ecuador and Latin America from 2008 to 2018, and worked closely with refugees to promote systems, laws, and policies that help them to build a new life. She led the establishment of the Regional Working Group of the Brazil Plan of Action (GAR-PAB). She holds a Master of Laws degree from the University of Teramo and a Bachelor of Arts with honors from Sussex University.

Gabriella Kallas, a refugee rights advocate and migration policy scholar, works as a Policy Officer at Asylum Access in Mexico City, where they provide support for local, regional, and global advocacy. They have worked with immigrant and refugee populations in Mexico City, New York City, rural Colorado, and in Athens, Greece. They hold a Master's degree with distinction in international migration and public policy from the London School of Economics, and a Bachelor of Arts with honors in American studies with a concentration in Latino/a studies from Williams College.

Notes

1. The process of developing the MPA included three new subregional preparatory meetings, which pushed states to identify and develop draft commitments in advance of the regional convening (UNHCR 2004: 4). The subregional convenings also increased the participation of other stakeholders, who pressed states

for deeper commitments and stronger national and local protection frameworks (Barichello 2015: 165–66).
2   Multiply marginalized people are people who belong to more than one marginalized group. For example, an Afro-descendant woman refugee may be marginalized for her migration status, gender, and race.
3. Examples are the case *Pacheco Tieno Family v. Plurinational State of Bolivia* (2013); Asylum Access's challenge to Executive Decree 1182 in Ecuador; and Inter-American Commission on Human Rights hearings on the situation of asylum seekers and refugees in the Americas, and in Ecuador specifically.

References

100 Points of Brasilia. Inputs from Latin America and the Caribbean to the Global Compact on Refugees. https://www.globalcrrf.org/wp-content/uploads/2018/04/The-100-Points-of-Brasilia-20-02-2018-ENGLISH.pdf.
Arnold-Fernández, Emily. 2019. "National Governance Frameworks in the Global Compact: Dangers and Opportunities." *International Migration* 57 (6): pp. 188–207. doi:10.1111/imig.12643.
Asylum Access. 2014. *Iniciativa Cartagena +30: La proteccion internacional y la effectiva integración*. https://asylumaccess.org/wp-content/uploads/2014/07/cartagena_Completo_2803_resized.pdf.
——. 2018. *El Derecho Al Trabajo de las Personas Solicitantes de Asilo y Refugiadas en América Latina y el Caribe*. https://asylumaccess.org/wp-content/uploads/2019/07/Derechos-Laborales-Refugiadas-en-America-Latina-y-el-Caribe-final-ESP.pdf.
Barichello, Stefania E. 2015. "The Evolving System of Refugees' Protection in Latin America." In Gauci, Giuffré, and Tsourdi, *Exploring the Boundaries of Refugee Law*, 149–171.
——. 2019. "Why Venezuelan migrants need to be recognized as refugees." *The New Humanitarian*. 27 February. https://foreignpolicy.com/2019/01/14/heres-why-colombia-opened-its-arms-to-venezuelan-migrants-until-now/.
Bradley, Megan. 2014. "Forced Migration in Central America and the Caribbean: Cooperation and Challenges." In Fiddian-Qasmiyeh et al., *The Oxford Handbook of Refugee and Forced Migration Studies*, 664–76.
Brazil Declaration: A Framework for Cooperation and Regional Solidarity to Strengthen the International Protection of Refugees, Displaced and Stateless Persons in Latin America and the Caribbean. 2014. https://www.acnur.org/t3/fileadmin/Documentos/BDL/2014/9865.pdf.
Cantor, David J. 2018. "Cooperation on refugees in Latin America and the Caribbean: the "Cartagena process' and South-South approaches" In Fiddian-Qasmiyeh et al., *The Oxford Handbook of Refugee and Forced Migration Studies*, 282–95.
Cartagena Declaration on Refugees. 1984. https://www.oas.org/dil/1984_cartagena_declaration_on_refugees.pdf.
Convention Governing the Specific Aspects of Refugee Problems in Africa. 1969. http://www.achpr.org/files/instruments/refugee-convention/achpr_instr_conv_refug_eng.pdf.

Edwards, Alice. 2009. "Age and gender dimensions in international law." In *Refugee Protection in International Law*, edited by Erika Feller, Volker Türk, and Frances Nicholson, 46–80. Cambridge: Cambridge University Press.

Egeland, Jan. 2014. "A shared burden, a shared responsibility." *Displacement in the Wake of Violence in Latin America*: 3. Oslo: Norwegian Refugee Council. http://www.felixmedia.no/wp-content/uploads/2011/04/Thematic-Report-Cartagena-30.pdf.

Fiddian-Qasmiyeh, Elena, Gil Loescher, Katy Long, and Nando Sigona, eds. 2014. *The Oxford Handbook of Refugee and Forced Migration Studies*. Oxford: Oxford University Press.

Fischel de Andrade, José Henrique. 1998. "Regional Policy Approaches and Harmonization: A Latin American Perspective." *International Journal of Refugee Law* 10 (3): 389-409. doi:10.1093/ijrl/10.3.389.

———. 2018. "Why Latin America Should Recognize Venezuelans as Refugees." *Refugees Deeply*. 28 October. https://foreignpolicy.com/2019/01/14/heres-why-colombia-opened-its-arms-to-venezuelan-migrants-until-now/.

GAR-PAB. 2018. Plan de Acción de Brasil: Evaluación del Grupo Articulador Regional del Plan de Acción de Brasil, 2014–2017. https://www.refworld.org.es/pdfid/5ad10bfd4.pdf.

Gauci, Jean-Pierre, Mariagiulia Giuffré, and Evangelia (Lilian) Tsourdi, eds. *Exploring the Boundaries of Refugee Law*. Leiden, The Netherlands: Koninklijke Brill. doi:10.1163/9789004265585_007.

Global Compact on Refugees. 2018. A/73/12. https://www.unhcr.org/gcr/GCR_English.pdf.

Goodkind, Jessica R., and Z. Deacon. 2004. "Methodological issues in conducting research with refugee women: Principles for recognizing and re-centering the multiply marginalized." *Journal of Community Psychology* 32 (6): 721–739. doi:10.002/jcop.20029.

Harley, Tristan. 2014. "Regional Cooperation and Refugee Protection in Latin America: A "South-South" Approach." *International Journal of Refugee Law* 26 (1): 22–47. doi:10.1093/ijrl/eeu004.

Harris, Jennifer. 2003. "All doors are closed to us: a social model analysis of the experience of disabled refugees and asylum seekers in Britain." *Disability and Society* 18 (40): 395-410. doi:10.1080/0968759032000080968.

Janetsky, Megan. 2019. "Here's Why Colombia Opened Its Arms to Venezuelan Migrants–Until Now." *Foreign Policy*. 14 January. https://foreignpolicy.com/2019/01/14/heres-why-colombia-opened-its-arms-to-venezuelan-migrants-until-now/.

Jubilut, Lilian L. 2014. "Fora and Programmes for Refugees in Latin America." In *Regional Approaches to the Protection of Asylum Seekers: An International Legal Perspective*, edited by Ademola Abass and Francesca Ippolito: 245–266. Surrey, England: Ashgate.

Kagan, Michael. 2008. *No Margin for Error*. San Francisco, CA: Asylum Access. https://rsdwatch.files.wordpress.com/2010/03/nomarginforerror2007.pdf.

———. 2011. "*We live in a country of UNHCR': The UN Surrogate State and Refugee Policy in the Middle East.*" The United Nations Refugee Agency: Policy Development and Evaluation Service Research Paper No. 201.

Kneebone, Susan. 2016. "Comparative regional protection frameworks for refugees: norms and norm entrepreneurs." *The International Journal of Human Rights* 20 (2): 153–172., doi:10.1080/13642987.2016.1141499.

Loescher, Gill. 2001. *The UNHCR and World Politics: A Perilous Path*. Oxford: Oxford University Press.

Maldonado Castillo, Carlos. 2015. "The Cartagena process: 30 years of innovation and solidarity." *Forced Migration Review* 49: 89-91. https://www.fmreview.org/climatechange-disasters/maldonadocastillo.

Menezes, Fabiano L. de. 2016. "Utopia or Reality: Regional Cooperation in Latin America to Enhance the Protection of Refugees." *Refugee Survey Quarterly* 35: 122–141. doi:10.1093/rsq/hdw014.

Mexico Declaration and Plan of Action to Strengthen the International Protection of Refugees in Latin America. https://www.refworld.org/docid/424bf6914.html.

New York Declaration for Refugees and Migrants. 2016. https://www.un.org/en/development/desa/population/migration/generalassembly/docs/globalcompact/A_RES_71_1.pdf.

Ratkovic, Snezana. 2013. "The location of refugee female teachers in the Canadian context: 'Not just a refugee woman!'" *Refuge* 29 (1): 103–114. https://refuge.journals.yorku.ca/index.php/refuge/article/view/37522/34050.

San José Declaration on Refugees and Displaced Persons. 1994. https://www.refworld.org/docid/4a54bc3fd.html.

Schreuer, Cristoph. 1995. "Regionalism v. Universalism." *European Journal of International Law* 6 (3): 477–499. doi:10.1093/oxfordjournals.ejil.a035932.

United Nations General Assembly (UNGA). 1981. *First International Conference on Assistance to Refugees in Africa (ICARA I)*. 11 June, A/36/316. https://www.refworld.org/docid/3ae68f3f8.html.

——. 1984. *Second International Conference on Assistance to Refugees in Africa (ICARA II)*. 22 August, A/39/402. https://www.refworld.org/docid/3ae68f3e8.html.

——. 2016. *New York Declaration for Refugees and Migrants*. 19 September, A/71/1.

United Nations High Commissioner for Refugees (UNHCR). 1984. *Cartagena Declaration on Refugees*. https://www.unhcr.org/about-us/background/45dc19084/cartagena-declaration-refugees-adopted-colloquium-international-protection.html.

——. 1994. *San Jose Declaration on Cartagena Declaration on Refugees.* https://www.unhcr.org/about-us/background/45dc19084/cartagena-declaration-refugees-adopted-colloquium-international-protection.html. *Refugees and Displaced Persons.* https://www.refworld.org/docid/4a54bc3fd.html.

——. 1997. *UNHCR Note on the Principle of Non-Refoulement.* https://www.refworld.org/docid/438c6d972.html.

——. 2004. *Mexico Declaration and Plan of Action to Strengthen the International Protection of Refugees in Latin America.* https://www.refworld.org/docid/424bf6914.html.

——. 2005. *Memoir of the Twentieth Anniversary of the Cartagena Declaration on Refugees.* San José, Costa Rica: Editorama. https://www.acnur.org/fileadmin/Documentos/archivo/3868.pdf.

——. 2007. *Mexico Plan of Action: The Impact of Regional Solidarity*. San José, Costa Rica: Editorama. https://www.acnur.org/fileadmin/Documentos/Publicaciones/2007/5483.pdf.

———. 2014a. "*Conmemoración del 30 Aniversario de la Declaración de Cartagena Cartagena +30.*" https://www.acnur.org/fileadmin/Documentos/BDL/2014/9780.pdf.

———. 2014b. "*Consulta Temática Subregional Andina: Resumen de Conclusiones y Recomendaciones.*" https://www.acnur.org/fileadmin/Documentos/BDL/2014/9768.pdf.

———. 2014c. *UNHCR Policy on Alternatives to Camps.* https://www.unhcr.org/protection/statelessness/5422b8f09/unhcr-policy-alternatives-camps.html.

———. 2017a. *Global Trends, Forced Displacement in 2017.* https://www.unhcr.org/en-us/statistics/unhcrstats/5b27be547/unhcr-global-trends-2017.html.

———. 2017b. *Brazil Plan of Action First Triennial Progress Report: 2015-2017.* https://www.acnur.org/5c89774e4.pdf.

———. 2020. *Venezuelan Situation.* https://reporting.unhcr.org/sites/default/files/UNHCR_Venezuela%20Situation_25%20May%202020.pdf.

PART I COMMENTARY

The Cartagena Declaration Regime of "Refugee" Protection

Susan Kneebone

Introduction: Regimes, Regionalism, and Regionness

Through four instruments, namely the 1984 Cartagena Declaration on Refugees (Cartagena Declaration), the 1994 San José Declaration on Refugees and Displaced Persons (SJD), the 2004 Mexico Declaration and Plan of Action to Strengthen the International Protection of Refugees in Latin America (MPA), and the 2014 Brazil Declaration and Plan of Action: A Framework for Cooperation and Regional Solidarity to Strengthen the International Protection of Refugees, Displaced and Stateless Persons in Latin America and the Caribbean (BPA), the Cartagena regime has responded to local needs and to gaps in the international refugee protection regime, and has developed a rich set of norms on regional refugee protection. In contrast to other regions such as Southeast Asia (Jones 2014), the United Nations High Commissioner for Refugees (UNHCR) is regarded as a successful norm broker and entrepreneur and, indeed, a pivotal actor (Vera Espinoza in this volume). The chapters in part I attest to the constructive role that UNHCR has been able to play in promoting and consolidating the Cartagena regime.

The interesting feature of this book is the focus on regimes rather than on regionalism as a framework of analysis. The notion of regime implies an authoritative system and the exercise of power, so it is therefore no surprise that it has been defined in relation to states (Betts 2009: 8–9). Fischel de Andrade (in this volume) adopts a working definition of regime as "the ensemble of norms and practices that are used by states and other relevant actors in the cooperation and/or coordination of the international and/or national actions aimed at regulating an issue area."[1] The use of the concept of regimes in this book exposes both the strengths of states and the limits of their role.

The instruments of the Cartagena regime created at intervals each decade since 1984, "develop and reinforce an ongoing consensus that refugee protection and integration are obligations of states and that therefore states bear the primary responsibility for implementation of such protection and integration" (Arnold-Fernández, Sarmiento Torres, and Kallas in this volume). In the MPA and the BPA, however, a broader range of actors (or norm brokers and entrepreneurs) are envisaged, including civil society (MPA), as well as human rights institutions, academia, and officials of municipal and provincial governments (BPA). The Cartagena regime thus has ample norms (as explained below), norm entrepreneurs, and a shared state role. It appears to be a model regime.

Regional approaches are often advocated to achieve durable solutions for asylum seekers and refugees; it is often assumed that burden sharing and solidarity will result from regional cooperation. Vera Espinoza observes, however, that although the principles of solidarity and responsibility sharing are clearly established under MPA in the Cartagena regime, this does not necessarily translate into effective regional cooperation. Vera Espinoza refers to the views of Riggirozzi, who uses the notion of regionness to describe the "actors, practices and process not as a unitary actor [the region-as-actor] but as 'spaces or arenas for action,'" a distinction I return to in this commentary's conclusion.

In this commentary I explain how the norms of the international refugee protection regime are expanded by the Cartagena regime. Norm creation and acceptance do not necessarily lead to implementation, however. Building on the idea of regionness, I suggest that it a useful concept for focusing on processes leading to consensus and implementation on refugee protection.

What Is the Regime of International Refugee Protection?

According to Betts, the main institutions of the international refugee regime are the 1951 Convention Relating to the Status of Refugees (1951 Refugee Convention), as well as regional refugee protection instruments such as the Cartagena Declaration, and UNHCR's mandate as defined in its Statute[2] (Betts 2009: 9–10). He defines the key norms of the international refugee regime as asylum and burden sharing (ibid.: 11) but points out that there is no binding obligation on states with regard to the latter (ibid.: 12).

Although there is an established international law principle of asylum, it is accepted that it is the sovereign right of states to grant asylum. This paints a bleak picture of the international refugee regime as reliant on state discretion. Notably, Betts turns to international relations principles to solve this dilemma; he conceives it a "global public good" (ibid.: 8, 25).

As a matter of law, where does this leave us? Betts explains that UNHCR's mandate is intended to ensure access to "durable solutions" (ibid.: 10); *non-refoulement* aside, however, the 1951 Refugee Convention is unclear about the status of the three solutions of asylum–integration, voluntary repatriation,[3] and resettlement.[4] However, from the 1951 Refugee Convention and UNHCR's mandate we can distill the two main legal elements of the international refugee regime: protection and durable solutions. These, as Vera Espinoza points out, are the key principles underlying the Cartagena regime.

What Are the Features of the Cartagena Regime of Refugee Protection?

There are four important features of the Cartagena regime that reflect gaps in the international refugee regime and attempt to fill them.

First, the Cartagena Declaration responds to the changing nature of refugee populations and the causes of displacement in Latin America (Kneebone and Rawlings Sanaei 2007: 8–9), and the need not to limit protection to those who satisfy the elements of the 1951 Refugee Convention definition. The expanded definition in the Cartagena Declaration is complementary to the 1951 Refugee Convention and the international regime of refugee law; it is also intended to pick up gaps in the 1969 Organization of African Unity Convention Governing the Specific Aspects of Refugee Problems in Africa, by referring to internal conflicts, and massive violations of human rights as grounds for refugee status. A majority of states have adopted the broadened definition of the Cartagena Declaration even though there are significant national variations; furthermore, many states have adopted new asylum legislation under MPA, with a focus on gender, minority communities, and unaccompanied children (thus further expanding the 1951 Refugee Convention definition).

Second, going beyond the external or international refugee issue, the Cartagena Declaration expresses its "concern at the situation of displaced persons within their own countries" (Cartagena Declaration: para. III(9)). Other than this, however, the Cartagena Declaration did not deal with the problem of internal displacement. As Rushing and Lizcano Rodriguez (in this volume) show, subsequently the Cartagena regime included the problem of internal displacement or internally displaced persons (IDPs). The SJD was linked to the formulation of the 1998 Guiding Principles on Internal Displacement (Guiding Principles). The authors explain, "although the SJD is nonbinding and its impacts cannot be pinpointed to explicit contributions to policy, law, or jurisprudence, it formed part of the Latin American region's participation in and contribution to the process that put internal displacement on the humanitarian agenda both regionally and globally" (Rushing and Lizcano Rodriguez: 69). Furthermore, in combination, the Cartagena Declaration and the SJD recognize the coincidence of three bodies of law: human rights law, international humanitarian law, and the principles of international refugee law (Kneebone 2010).[5] Through these two instruments the Cartagena regime has embraced extending protection to forced migrants.

Third, the regime has been extended through the MPA and the BPA. Arnold-Fernández, Sarmiento Torres, and Kallas (in this volume) explain how the BPA includes actors other than states. Measures to enhance the capacity of civil society were included in the MPA (Vera Espinoza in this volume) as an application of UNHCR's 2004 Agenda for Protection, Goal 3, which focused on sharing burdens and responsibilities more equitably and building capacities to receive and protect refugees. The quintessential role of contracting states in refugee protection is to confer refugee status, following a comprehensive refugee status determination procedure. Under the MPA, civil society is a strong partner with the states on refugee status determination and implements actions in the plan such as training (Vera Espinoza in this volume). In this and in other important ways, the role of the state under the Cartagena regime is shared with other actors.

Furthermore, as Arnold-Fernández, Sarmiento Torres and Kallas point out, the actors in the regime were expanded under the MPA by including subregional convenings; it also increased the participation of other stakeholders, "who pressed states for deeper commitments and stronger national and local protection frameworks" (in this volume: 156). The inclusion of transnational and subregional actors shows a lessening of the focus on national states in the Cartagena regime.

Moreover, as Rushing and Lizcano Rodriguez explain, the SJD with its focus on internally displaced persons extends the scope of state sovereignty (which is implicit in the concept of regime) to impose positive obligations on state parties, and in promoting the responsibility of the international community as a principle of international law.

Fourth, in comparison to the international refugee regime, the nonbinding norm of burden (or responsibility) sharing is a key feature of the Cartagena regime through the MPA. This plan is based on three pillars of solidarity: borders, cities, and resettlement, which together committed states to engage in specific actions to ensure regional consistency in application of human rights norms.

In summary, the chapters in part I demonstrate how the Cartagena regime has filled gaps in legal principles in the international refugee regime through an expanded definition of refugee; support for the process in formulating the Guiding Principles and thus implicitly recognizing the coincidence of human rights, international humanitarian law, and refugee law; and extending the idea of state responsibility to shared situations as well as to transnational and subregional actors and the international community. Finally, the norm of responsibility sharing is articulated in MPA.

Assessing and Enhancing the Success of the Cartagena Regime

Using the trichotomy that Finnemore and Sikkink (1998: 891) develop (i.e., emergence, acceptance, and internalization), the obvious question is the effect of the Cartagena regime on refugee protection. Although there appears to be a high level of norm emergence and acceptance (on a formal level), the level of implementation suggests a lower level of norm internalization. For example, while fifteen out of twenty Latin American countries adopted the MPA, Vera Espinoza concludes that the results are a mixed legacy. In the case of resettlement, Vera Espinoza says that, although the results are good, underlying political will is shaky: the results suggest strategic responses rather than solidarity or responsibility sharing. Regionalism as defined above does not appear to be a driving factor in shaping regional solutions.

This brings us back to Riggirozzi's proposal for a double level of analysis through considering both the region-as-actor and the region-as-arenas for action. Vera Espinoza suggests that, in the case of Latin America, the branding of solidarity may have helped to consolidate it as a region-as-actor (unsuccessfully, as noted above). The Cartagena regime suggests that the region contains arenas for action rather than representing a region-as-actor.

Vera Espinoza and other authors point to the predominance of soft law and the lack of implementing instruments such as plans of action as obstacles to implementation. On the other hand, Arnold-Fernández, Sarmiento Torres, and Kallas point out that the inclusion of civil society and other non-state representatives has given rise to a much more inclusive debate on principles of protection and implementation. Yet soft law can be used in arenas of action, with plans of action, for a more inclusive debate to achieve stronger consensus. Jurgen Habermas's concept of discourse linked to communication that is oriented toward reaching a common understanding or consensus (Habermas 1984: 286–87), comes to mind as a relevant description of the discursive processes that are needed. Fischel de Andrade describes the Cartagena Declaration as a conceptual framework, but it is that and more. It and the Cartagena regime are part of a discourse in an ongoing process of internalizing and implementing the norms of refugee protection.

Susan Kneebone is a Professorial Fellow and Senior Associate, Asian Law Centre, Melbourne Law School, University of Melbourne. She is also a Research Affiliate at the Peter McMullin Centre on Statelessness. Susan supervises a number of PhD students on migration issues in Southeast Asia and has written widely on issues around forced migration. She is currently working on two funded projects: "Towards Development of a Legal Framework for Regulation of International Marriage Migration" and "Indonesia's Refugee Policies: Responsibility, Security and Regionalism."

Notes

1. Notably both Betts and Fischel de Andrade rely on the views of Krasner (1983: 2).
2. Statute of the Office of the United Nations High Commissioner for Refugees (A/RES/428).
3. This is arguably embodied in the 1951 Refugee Convention, art. 1C(4).
4. Note the direct reference to resettled refugees in the 1951 Refugee Convention, article 30.
5. Furthermore, the broader norm of humanitarian protection underlies UNHCR's Statute and its expanded focus on "persons in need of protection" (Kneebone, Stevens, and Baldassar 2014: 8).

References

Betts, Alexander. 2009. *Protection by Persuasion: International Cooperation in the Refugee Regime*: Cornell University Press

Brazil Declaration and Plan of Action: a Framework for Cooperation and Regional Solidarity to Strengthen the International Protection of Refugees, Displaced and Stateless Persons in Latin America and the Caribbean (BPA). 2014. https://www.refworld.org/docid/5487065b4.html.

Cartagena Declaration on Refugees. 1984. https://www.refworld.org/docid/3ae6b36ec.html.

Convention Governing the Specific Aspects of Refugee Problems in Africa. 1969. https://www.refworld.org/docid/3ae6b36018.html.

Convention Relating to the Status of Refugees (1951 Refugee Convention). 1951. https://www.refworld.org/docid/3be01b964.html.

Finnemore, Martha, and Kathryn Sikkink. 1998. "International Norm Dynamics and Political Change," *International Organization* 52 (4): 887–917.

Guiding Principles on Internal Displacement (Guiding Principles). 1998. E/CN.4/1998/53/Add.2. https://undocs.org/E/CN.4/1998/53/Add.2.

Habermas, Jurgen. 1984. *The Theory of Communicative Action: Volume 1*. Cambridge: Polity: 286–287.

Jones, Martin. 2014. "Moving beyond Protection Space: Developing a Law of Asylum in South East Asia." In *Refugee Protection and the Role of Law: Conflicting Identi-*

ties, edited by Susan Kneebone, Dallal Stevens, and Loretta Baldassar: 251–270. London: Routledge.

Kneebone, Susan. 2010. "Refugees and Displaced Persons: The Refugee Definition and "Humanitarian" Protection." In *Research Handbook on International Human Rights Law*, edited by Sarah Joseph and Adam McBeth: 215–40. Cheltenham, UK: Edward Elgar.

Kneebone, Susan, and Felicity Rawlings Sanaei. 2007. *New Regionalism and Asylum Seekers: Challenges Ahead.* Oxford: Berghahn Books.

Kneebone, Susan, Dallal Stevens, and Loretta Baldassar. *Refugee Protection and the Role of Law: Conflicting Identities.* London: Routledge.

Krasner, Stephen D., ed. 1983. *International Regimes.* Ithaca, NY: Cornell University Press.

Mexico Declaration and Plan of Action to Strengthen the International Protection of Refugees in Latin America (MPA). 2004. https://www.refworld.org/docid/424bf6914.html.

San José Declaration on Refugees and Displaced Persons (SJD). 1994. https://www.refworld.org/docid/4a54bc3fd.html.

Part II

The Regime of the Inter-American Human Rights System

5

Against the Current

Protecting Asylum Seekers, Refugees, and Other Persons in Need of International Protection under the Inter-American Human Rights System

Álvaro Botero Navarro

> The important thing is that our case has shown that these things happen quite often and should not happen. Hopefully, our case will help States to understand that they should not commit such violations on the human rights of refugees.
> Rumaldo Juan Pacheco Osco[1]

Introduction

In recent years the Americas have shown a significant increase in mixed migration movements. These are complex and multicausal cross-border movements of persons with varying reasons to migrate, protection profiles, and needs. Different groups of people against whom different legal frameworks are applied under International Law converge on the same routes, using the same transports or means of travel, often in large numbers and in an irregular manner. The recent so-called migrant caravans of Central Americans trying to reach the United States or to a lesser extent to Mexico or the steady migration of Venezuelan, mainly to other Latin American countries, are just two of the most predominant migration dynamics from a region that does not get as much international attention as other regions when it comes to migration "crises."

As in other regions, forced migration[2] in the Americas respond to multiple causes which in many cases intersects between themselves, such as several forms of violence by state actors as well as non-state actors, such as organized crime groups, drug cartels, paramilitary groups, and *maras* (gangs); high levels of poverty and inequality; food insecurity, hunger, and lack of access to medical treatment; the effects of climate change and natural disasters in places like the Corredor Seco (dry corridor) in Central America or in many Caribbean countries; forced evictions and land conflicts; or the persecution and criminalization of indigenous peoples, communities of African descent, peasants, social leaders, environmental and human rights defenders, and journalists (Sandoval 2005: 45).

In addition to the above, the impacts of the lockdowns, quarantines, physical and social distancing measures, restrictions on freedom of movement, and the closings of borders that have been adopted by States in the region to counter the spread of COVID-19 pandemic since March 2020, as well as the direct and indirect effects of the pandemic on the economy and livelihoods, will be a determining factor in the decision to migrate for thousands of people in the near future, in particular for those in situations of vulnerability. Through its on-site visits and other monitoring mechanisms, the Inter-American Commission on Human Rights (IACmHR) has witnessed that many of the main irregular migrant movements in the region are made up of persons in a situation of poverty (IACmHR 2017b: 127, 128).

At the same time, the situation of persons in the context of forced migration in the Americas is an intersectional phenomenon. Internally displaced persons, migrants, refugees, and other persons in need of international protection tend to be affected in an aggravated manner, and also are part of vulnerable and historically discriminated groups, such as women, children, indigenous peoples, persons of African descent, persons with disabilities, and LGBTI (lesbian, gay, bisexual, transgender, and intersex) persons, among others.

Based on the Global Trends reports published annually by the United Nations High Commissioner for Refugees (UNHCR) over the past ten years, an increase in the number of people in need of international protection is seen in the Americas. In 2009 there were 13,952 asylum seekers (UNHCR 2010), whereas only a decade later, in 2019, the number had increased to 1,902,133 people (UNHCR 2020), representing a percentage increase of 13,533 percent. The number of refugees increased from 519,149 to 592,892 people in 2019, representing a percentage increase of 14 percent.

Nonetheless, figures on the recognition of refugee status remain in a steady low level. Thus, in the past ten years, on average, people recognized as refugees did not exceed 500,000 in the Americas (UNHCR 2010, 2011, 2012, 2013, 2014a, 2015, 2016, 2017, 2018, 2019). These figures reveal that, although there have been responses from states such as solidarity resettle-

Year	Refugees	Asylum Seekers
2009	178909	13952
2010	190454	95378
2011	204585	65412
2012	212450	34708
2013	211679	69349
2014	209480	105018
2015	202754	178294
2016	199635	321694
2017	202541	594970
2018	232859	1026314

Figure 5.1. Asylum seekers and refugees in OAS States (2008–19), country of origin (created by Álvaro Botero Navarro).

ment initiatives, complementary protection, temporary protection status and humanitarian visas (Jubilut 2016; see Vera Espinoza; and Freier and Luzes in this volume), those responses have not been enough.

In addition, due to the political, economic, and social crises in Venezuela in recent years, the Americas are facing the largest migration and refugee "crisis" in recent history (see Jarochinski Silva, Castro, and Sampaio in this volume) and the second-largest in the world at this moment, just behind the Syrian refugee crisis. The IACmHR has stated that the impact of the severe food and health-care crisis has particularly impacted groups in situations of exclusion and historical discrimination, such as children and adolescents, women, older persons, indigenous and Afro-descendant peoples, persons with disabilities and those who are ill, and those living in poverty (IACmHR 2018).

Notwithstanding the different situations described above, the binary division between refugees—or, in a broader sense, persons in need of international protection—and economic migrants has been a predominant feature in the way in which many States of the Americas, particularly the United States, have responded nationally, regionally, and internationally to the complex migration movements in the region. In turn, the emphasis placed on addressing these situations as irregular migration for economic reasons has facilitated a situation where many of the responses have been based on an approach of immigration control, through the use of measures such as the externalization of migration control, securitization and militarization of borders, and the criminalization of irregular migration, in particular through the generalized use of immigration detention and arbitrary deportations and

Year	Refugees	Asylum Seekers	Venezuelans displaced abroad
2009	519148	193746	
2010	513,505	128683	
2011	516796	103250	
2012	515379	74213	
2013	514796	130299	
2014	509341	237109	
2015	496384	350697	
2016	471178	654640	
2017	484261	878723	
2018	534498	1311654	
2019	592892	1902133	3582203

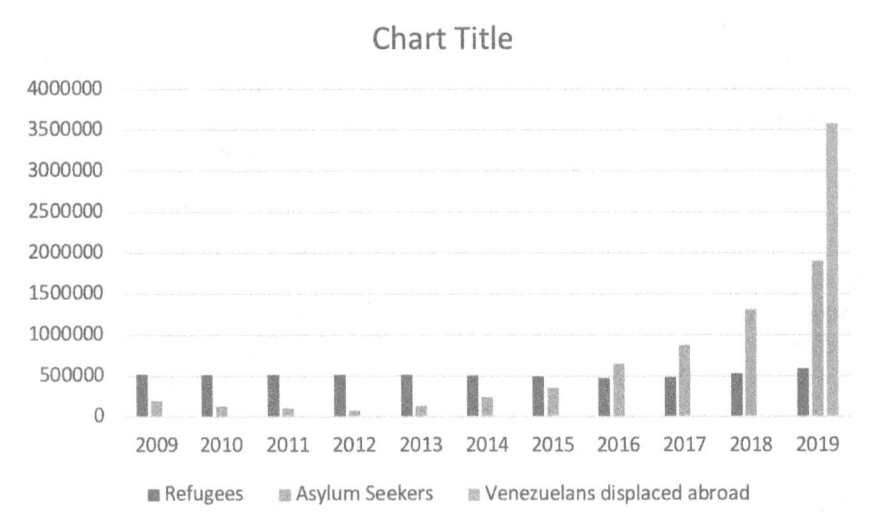

Figure 5.2a, b. Asylum seekers and refugees in OAS States (2008–19), country of asylum (created by Álvaro Botero Navarro).

hence the reduction of international protection to asylum seekers, refugees, and other migrants in need of complementary protection. In the past decades, States have progressively limited access to asylum by introducing extraterritorial controls and increasing their border controls.

Against this background, it is important to review the status of the jurisprudential development of the Inter-American Human Rights System (IAHRS) in relation to the protection of the rights of persons in need of international protection, such as asylum seekers, refugees, persons in need of complementary protection, and stateless persons, in order to analyze the evolving development that the IAHRS bodies have given to international instruments to respond to the needs of persons in need of international protection and the consequent need for their justiciability at the domestic level.

In this regard, from an analytical approach, this chapter will address the scope and content that the bodies of the IAHRS have given to the rights of persons in need of international protection, the reparations granted to victims in need of international protection, the impact at the national level of the decisions of the Inter-American Court of Human Rights (IACtHR) and the IACmHR, and the steps that the IAHRS could take in the future. Likewise, from an empirical approach, this chapter will analyze whether the IAHRS has responded adequately to the changing and urgent challenges that forced migration is placing on the countries of the Americas. For this purpose, the chapter is based on the legal instruments of the IAHRS, as interpreted by the jurisprudence of the IACmHR and the IACtHR in light of developments in International Human Rights Law in general.

This chapter has been developed from the author's professional experience of nearly ten years in the IACmHR, as coordinator and principal specialist of the Rapporteurship on the Rights of Migrants (formerly Rapporteurship on Migrant Workers and Members of their Families), and from his involvement in monitoring situations related to the human rights of migrants, asylum seekers, refugees, stateless persons, and internally displaced persons in several countries of the region, including cases and advisory opinions before the IACtHR.

The IAHRS: A Brief Overview

The IAHRS is made up of two principal bodies: the IACmHR and the IACtHR. The first organ of the IAHRS was the IACmHR, created by a resolution adopted at the Fifth Meeting of Consultation of Ministers of Foreign Affairs in Santiago, Chile, in 1959 with the mandate to promote human rights. Six years later, in 1965, the IACmHR was granted the power to consider individual petitions, and finally, through the Buenos Aires Protocol to the Charter of the Organization of American States (OAS) in 1967, it became a principal organ of the OAS.

Since its first years, the IACmHR has performed a broad role, as a quasi-judicial body, in promoting and protecting human rights in the Americas. It has done so through many different activities entrusted by the statute or established in the IACmHR's rules of procedure, such as preparing studies and reports on specific countries and issues, serving as an advisory body for countries on human rights issues, and drafting human rights instruments. Above all, it has substantively contributed to the protection of human rights through its power to receive individual communications and make recommendations to the OAS member States, as well as through its requests to States to adopt precautionary measures in order to prevent irreparable harm to persons. Also, the IACmHR has the power to carry out on-site visits to OAS member States and to hold public hearings in the framework of its of sessions.

However, there was the need for a normative body aimed at protecting human rights, and, in response, the 1969 American Convention on Human Rights (ACHR) was adopted during the Specialized Conference held in San José, Costa Rica. Unlike the European Covenant on Human Rights, adopted one year after the creation of the Council of Europe, the ACHR emerged from a hostile atmosphere and took more than twenty years to be agreed on and ten more years to be entered into force. It nevertheless created the IACtHR, thus establishing two human rights bodies within the regional system. As Goldman points out, "The entry into force of the American Convention effectively created a dual system for protecting human rights throughout the hemisphere. The American Convention became the primary source of the human rights obligations to state parties thereto, while the American Declaration [of the Rights and Duties of Man] and the OAS Charter continued to define the human rights obligations of those States not parties to the American Convention" (Goldman 2009: 886).

With the entry into force of the ACHR, the IACtRH became the judicial organ of the IAHRS and was given the mandate to ensure the fulfillment of the state parties' obligations. The IACtHR has two different kinds of jurisdiction: adjudicatory and advisory. In the performance of its adjudicatory jurisdiction, the IACtHR is empowered to order remedies and compensation to an injured party if it finds that a violation of the conventional rights has taken place. It can also adopt provisional measures to avoid irreparable damage. As an advisory body, the IACtHR can be consulted by any member state of the OAS (even if not a party to the ACHR) for the interpretation of other human rights treaties in the Americas.

Consequently, the IAHRS has consolidated its contribution through the development of important human rights standards (Banfi and Michelini 2017: 179). Due to the historical context, the first contributions of the IACmHR and the IACtHR were in cases related to serious violations of human rights, such as forced disappearances and extrajudicial executions; however, at present, the IAHRS, is known for its wide range of issues, including the protection of the rights of persons in need of international protection.

The Rights of Persons in Need of International Protection

The IACtHR has understood that the term "international protection" includes the following aspects: (a) the protection received by asylum seekers and refugees on the basis of the international conventions or domestic law, (b) the protection received by asylum seekers and refugees on the basis of the broadened definition of the Cartagena Declaration on Refugees of 1984 (Cartagena Declaration), (c) the protection received by any foreign person based on international human rights obligations, and in particular the principle of *non-refoulement*, as well as complementary protection or other forms of humanitarian protection, and (d) the protection received by stateless persons in accordance with the relevant international instruments (IACtHR 2014b: 15).

Article 22 of the ACHR contains nine paragraphs, which together contemplate four categories of rights and obligations: (1) freedom of movement and residence in the territory of a state, (2) the right to leave a country freely, (3) the right to seek and receive asylum, and (4) guarantees against the expulsion from a territory of both nationals and foreigners (Uprimny and Sánchez 2019: 650). Likewise, Article 27 of the 1948 American Declaration on the Rights and Duties of Man (American Declaration) establishes that "every person has the right, in case of pursuit not resulting from ordinary crimes, to seek and receive asylum in foreign territory, in accordance with the laws of each country and with international agreements."

In fulfilling their mandates, the bodies of the IAHRS have extensively developed the content and scope of the rights of persons in need of international protection. Thus, they have addressed the right to seek and receive asylum; the principle and right of *non-refoulement*; and the right to due process and judicial protection, both during procedures for determining refugee status, complementary protection, and statelessness, as well as procedures that may lead to the expulsion or deportation of a person.

Protecting Asylum Seekers, Refugees, and Other Persons in Need of International Protection

Informing Nature of International Refugee Norms and Standards in the IAHRS

In the 1990s the IACmHR began to interpret Inter-American instruments in light of International Refugee Law. Thus, the IACmHR has affirmed that the norms of International Refugee Law, International Humanitarian Law, and International Human Rights Law complement each other, even taking the standards of protection beyond the provisions of International Refugee Law (see Arlettaz 2016: 199).

In the case of *John Doe v. Canada* in 2011, concerning an alleged policy of indirect *refoulement* by the Canadian government, the IACmHR noted that the American Declaration must be interpreted with due respect for other rules of International Law applicable to member States and, in particular,

International Refugee Law, and "established jurisprudence on the issue of the right to seek asylum and the obligation of *non-refoulement*, under the Refugee Convention, 1967 Protocol relating to the Status of Refugees and the U.N. Convention Against Torture" (IACmmHR 2011b: 17).

Along these lines, the leading case relating to the state's international responsibility for violations of human rights of refugees in the region is the case of *Pacheco Tineo Family v. Plurinational State of Bolivia*. This case relates to the return of a Peruvian family as a result of the rejection of their application for recognition of refugee status in Bolivia. In its judgement, the IACtHR developed the informative nature of International Refugee Law concerning the ACHR in the following terms: "The Court takes into account the significant evolution of the principles and regulation of International Eefugee Law, based also on the directives, criteria and other authorized rulings of agencies such as UNHCR. . . . Thus, by using the sources, principles and criteria of International Refugee Law as a special normative applicable to situations concerning the determination of the refugee status of a person and their corresponding rights in a way that is complementary to the provisions of the Convention, the Court is not assuming a ranking between norms" (IACtHR 2013: 46).

Definition of Refugee

The IACmHR was fundamental to the adoption of an expanded refugee definition at the regional level. In 1982 the IACmHR recommended that OAS member States adopt a broader regional refugee definition to include "persons who have left their countries because their lives have been threatened by violence, foreign aggression and occupation, massive human rights violations, and other circumstances that destroy public order and for which there are no domestic remedies" (IACmHR 1982). This definition was later included in the Cartagena Declaration, which also included the expanded refugee definition proposed by the IACmHR. The same Cartagena Declaration, in Conclusion III, recognizes the doctrine used in the reports of the IACmHR as one of the sources of the expanded refugee definition (see Murillo 2002: 441, 448).

In 2001 the IACmHR used the Cartagena Declaration to argue that the principle of *non-refoulement* "has gradually been broadened to cover persons fleeing from situations of widespread political violence or civil war" (IACmHR 2001). In 2005 the Rapporteurship on the Rights of Migrants of the IACmHR noted that the Cartagena Declaration offered an innovative approach to refugee protection by broadening the definition of a refugee in the Convention Relating to the Status of Refugees (1951 Convention) and its Protocol Relating to the Status of Refugees (1967 Protocol) that should be applied in Latin America at that time.

Likewise, in 2018, in order to respond to the mass migration of Venezuelan people, in the Resolution 2/18 on forced migration of Venezuelans, the IACmHR called on States to "guarantee the recognition of refugee status to Venezuelan people with a well-founded fear of persecution in case of return to Venezuela, or who consider that their life, integrity or personal freedom would be threatened due to the situation of violence, massive violations of human rights, and serious disturbances of public order, under the terms of the Cartagena Declaration on Refugees of 1984" (IACmHR 2018: 1).

By its part, in the Advisory Opinions 21/14 and 25/18, the IACtHR referred to the traditional definition and the expanded regional definition of the Cartagena Declaration, describing the latter as part of the "*corpus iuris* for the protection of human rights of children that are asylum seekers and refugees in the American continent" (IACtHR 2014b: 97). Thus, the IACtHR recommended that States take into account the definition of refugee contained in the Cartagena Declaration as "more inclusive" (ibid.: 32) and that it responds not only to the dynamics of forced displacement that gave rise to it but also meets the protection challenges arising from other patterns of displacement occurring today (IACtHR 2018: 32).

Currently, sixteen States in the Americas have incorporated the expanded refugee definition into their domestic legislation (IACmHR 2015a: 50). According to Juan Ignacio Mondelli, it is also relevant to note that the regional definition has been considered binding for Argentina, Belize, Bolivia, Brazil, Chile, Colombia, Costa Rica, Dominican Republic, Ecuador, El Salvador, Guatemala, Honduras, Mexico, Nicaragua, Panama, Paraguay, Peru, Uruguay, and Venezuela as a rule of particular customary international law–that is, regional custom (Mondelli 2018: 111).

Right to Seek and Receive Asylum

Both the American Declaration and the ACHR recognize the right to seek and receive asylum, in respect of which two obligations arise: on the one hand, the obligation to guarantee that persons have the possibility of seeking asylum, and on the other, the obligation to receive or be granted asylum if conditions so warrant.

For the IACtHR the right to seek and receive asylum within the framework of the IAHRS, is configured as follows: "An individual human right to seek and receive international protection on foreign territory, including with this expression refugee status in accordance with pertinent instruments of the United Nations or corresponding domestic legislation, as well as asylum in accordance with the different inter-American conventions on this matter" (IACtHR 2018: 45).

The IACtHR also understands international protection to mean "the protection that a State offers to a foreign person because, in her or his country of nationality or habitual residence, that individual's human rights are threatened or violated and she or he is unable to obtain due protection there because it is not accessible, available and/or effective" (IACtHR 2014b: 18), which covers not only refugee status, but also other normative frameworks for international protection, as noted above.

In turn, the IACtHR has considered that the right to seek and receive asylum under refugee status imposes specific obligations on States:

1. obligation not to return (*non-refoulement*) and its extraterritorial application;
2. obligation to allow the asylum application and prohibition of rejection at the border;
3. obligation not to penalize or sanction for irregular entry or presence, and obligation of non-detention;
4. obligation to provide effective access to a fair and efficient procedure for the determination of refugee status;
5. obligation to ensure minimum due process guarantees in fair and efficient procedures for determining refugee status;
6. obligation to adapt procedures to the specific needs of children and adolescents;
7. obligation to grant international protection if the refugee definition is met, and to ensure the maintenance and continuity of refugee status;
8. obligation to interpret the exclusion clauses restrictively; and
9. obligation to provide access to rights on equal terms under refugee status (IACtHR 2018: 33).

Right and Principle of Non-Refoulement

The principle of *non-refoulement* arose in the field of International Refugee Law, but today it is a principle of general International Law, where it occupies a central place in the field of International Human Rights Law. The IAHRS has recognized the principle of *non-refoulement* as the cornerstone of the international protection of refugees and asylum seekers (IACtHR 2013: 49) and it is considered to be a customary rule of International Law binding on all States, whether or not they are parties to the 1951 Convention and 1967 Protocol (IACtHR 2018: 58).

The American Declaration does not contain a specific provision that establishes this principle, but the IACmHR has found that other rights such as the right to life, integrity, or security prohibit *refoulement* or expulsion (IACmHR 2011a). Article 22(8) of the ACHR and Article 33(1) of the 1951 Convention, read together, imply that the principle of *non-refoulement* safeguards that "persons cannot be rejected at the border or expelled without an adequate, individualized examination of their claim" (IACmHR 2000).

Also, the IAHRS has a specific treaty, the Inter-American Convention to Prevent and Punish Torture, which sets out the principle of *non-refoulement* in Article 13, complementing the broad protection of the ACHR, and extending it to those persons who have a well-founded presumption that they may be subjected to torture, and other cruel, inhuman, or degrading treatment or that they will be tried by ad hoc emergency courts in the requesting state.

It is important to note that, in the IAHRS, the principle of *non-refoulement* extends to all foreigners and not only to asylum seekers and refugees (IACtHR 2013: 44), offering complementary protection in cases where the foreigner's right to life or freedom is threatened (IACtHR 2014b: 86). This approach is even broader than the 1951 Convention relating to the status of refugees. In particular, the IACmHR has held, "The principle of *non-refoulement* also applies to asylum seekers and refugees whose status has not yet been determined; refugees who have not yet been recognized officially as such; as well as by those who assert their right to seek and receive asylum and who are either on an international border or have crossed it without being admitted officially or legally into the territory of the State" (IACmHR 2015b: 48).

In this regard, Hathaway argues that, since the mid-1980s there has been a development in International Human Rights Law, in particular through the practice of regional human rights protection bodies, that have pushed the threshold of the right of *non-refoulement*–for example, not applying it only to refugees but also to anyone in a situation similar to that of refugees (Hathaway 2010: 503).

The IACmHR has also understood that *non-refoulement* is a mechanism for guaranteeing the most fundamental rights including life, liberty, and personal integrity (IACmHR 2000). Subsequently, the IACtHR developed the relationship between this principle and Article 5 of the ACHR (IACtHR 2015: 40), on the understanding that this principle is the same as the principle of *non-refoulement* (IACtHR 2018: 58).

The IAHRS organs have also referred to indirect *refoulement*. Thus, in the case of *John Doe v. Canada*, the IACmHR indicated, "The right to *non-refoulement* obligates a State not only to prevent the removal of a refugee directly to a country of persecution but also indirectly through a third country (referred to as 'indirect *refoulement*' or 'chain *refoulement*')" (IACmHR 2011b: 23; IACmHR 2015b: 47).

The IACmHR has also understood that the principle of *non-refoulement* applies extraterritorially, insofar as it requires the state to exercise authority or to bring the foreign person under its effective control, irrespective of whether he or she is in the land, river, sea, or air territory. Therefore, the authorities should not send persons back before they reach their state border (IACmHR 2015b: 82); this applies even to persons intercepted at sea (IACmHR 1997a).

Regarding the latter, in the case of *Haitian Boat People (United States,* the IACmHR considered that the return of the petitioners to Haiti exposed them to an authentic and foreseeable danger of death, for which reason the interception policy of the government of the United States clearly violated their right to life, protected by Article I of the American Declaration (IACmHR 1997a). Besides, the IACmHR considered that the action of the United States government to intercept Haitians at sea, transfer them to vessels under its jurisdiction, and return them to Haiti, thus exposing them to acts of brutality in the hands of the Haitian military and its supporters, constituted a violation of the right to security of Haitian refugees (ibid.).

The IACmHR has also held that the right and principle of *non-refoulement* applies to international areas or airport waiting areas within the jurisdiction of States (European Court of Human Rights 1996; IACmHR 2017: 23). In this regard, the IACmHR has expressed concern at the rejection or deportation of asylum seekers and refugees at ports of entry such as international airport areas, despite an asylum application (IACmHR 2015a: 26).

Regarding the relationship between the right to seek and receive asylum, the principle of *non-refoulement*, the right to judicial guarantees, and the right to judicial protection, the IACmHR has held that the protection contemplated in Article 25 of the ACHR also includes the rights established in Articles 22.7 and 22.8 of the same instrument, so that any person who is in the framework of a refugee status determination procedure must have "some level of judicial protection" (IACmHR 2011a: 36). This reasoning would later be taken up by the IACtHR in its advisory opinion on the rights and guarantees of children in the context of migration and/or in need of international protection (IACtHR 2014b: 82).

Finally, in its Advisory Opinion 25, the IACtHR indicated that the principle of *non-refoulement* not only requires that the person not be returned, but also imposes positive obligations, such as a request to the territorial state to issue a safe-conduct, or other obligations under its authority and, in accordance with International Law, to ensure that applicants are guaranteed conventional rights (IACtHR 2018: 63).

The Prohibition of Collective Expulsions

Article 22.9 of the ACHR expressly prohibits collective expulsions. In this regard, the IACtHR has considered that the fundamental parameter for determining the collective character of expulsion is not the number of aliens subject to the expulsion decision, but rather that the decision is not based on an objective analysis of the individual circumstances of each alien (IACtHR 2012a: 48; IACtHR 2014a: 117).

Furthermore, the IACmHR established that the prohibition applies to any measure that has the effect of preventing migrants from reaching the borders of States or pushing them toward another state, including interdiction measures adopted by a state, including in extraterritorial form, to prevent persons from reaching its borders when this has the effect of preventing them from lodging an application for asylum or *non-refoulement* (IACmHR 2015b: 49).

Due Process and Judicial Protection during Refugee Status Determination Procedures

As noted above, the joint reading of the right to seek and receive asylum established in Article 22.7, and Articles 8 and 25 of the ACHR (judicial guarantees and judicial protection), guarantees that the person seeking refugee status has access to due process and judicial protection (IACmHR 2011a: 26).

Along these lines, in the case of *John Doe v. Canada*, the IACmHR ruled on the importance of guaranteeing any person seeking refuge to a hearing that guarantees a proper examination of his or her status. Thus, the IACmHR stated, "The right to seek asylum requires that a person be heard to see if he or she is at risk of persecution—it is the act of hearing the person that implements the most fundamental element of the right to seek asylum" (IACmHR 2011b: 21). Consequently, the IACmHR concluded that Article 27 of the American Declaration, relating to the right to asylum, is the foundation of due process for applicants seeking asylum in a foreign territory.

Also, in its report on merits in the *Pacheco Tineo* case, the IACmHR held that due process guarantees apply to all procedural instances, including procedures for the determination of refugee status and procedures that may culminate in the expulsion or deportation of a person, in the following terms: "The consistent jurisprudence of the organs of the inter-American system indicates that fair trial guarantees are not limited to judicial remedies but apply to all procedural instances, including, of course, any proceeding that could culminate in a person's expulsion or deportation" (IACmHR 2011a: 26). This reasoning was later adopted by the IACtHR in its judgement of 25 November 2013, when it stated that minimum due process must be guaranteed in procedures of a migratory nature, procedures for the determination of refugee status, or procedures that could lead to expulsion or deportation (IACtHR 2013: 53). Regarding due process guarantees within the framework of asylum or refugee status determination procedures, the IACtHR has established the following obligations:

a. They must guarantee the applicant the necessary facilities, including the services of a competent interpreter, as well as, if appropriate, access to legal assistance and representation, in order to submit their request to the authorities. Thus, the applicant must receive the necessary guidance concerning the procedure to be followed, in words and in a way that he can understand and, if appropriate, he should be given the opportunity to contact a UNHCR representative;

b. The request must be examined, objectively, within the framework of the relevant procedure, by a competent and clearly identified authority, and requires a personal interview;
c. The decisions adopted by the competent organs must be duly and expressly founded;
d. In order to protect the rights of applicants who may be in danger, all stages of the asylum procedure must respect the protection of the applicant's personal information and the application, and the principle of confidentiality;
e. If the applicant is denied refugee status, he should be provided with information on how to file an appeal under the prevailing system and granted a reasonable period for this, so that the decision adopted can be formally adopted; and
f. The appeal for review must have suspensive effects and must allow the applicant to remain in the country until the competent authority has adopted the required decision, and even while the decision is being appealed, unless it can be shown that the request is manifestly unfounded (ibid.: 53).

The IACtHR also referred to the power of States to establish accelerated procedures in case of manifestly unfounded and abusive applications for which there is no need for international protection. For this purpose, the IACtHR referred to some guarantees that must be respected, such as "minimum guarantees of a hearing, and determination of the unfounded or abusive nature of the request by the competent authority, and the possibility of a review of the negative decision should be respected before expulsion" (ibid.: 57).

Finally, through its advisory opinions, the IACtHR has referred to the importance of States designing and operating fair and efficient individualized procedures and preventing returns contrary to International Law in order to give useful effect to the right to seek and receive asylum provided for in Article 22.7 of the ACHR and Article 27 of the American Declaration (IACtHR 2014b: 95), as well as the positive obligation to identify those foreign persons who require international protection within their jurisdictions, whether because of refugee status or because of some other type of condition that requires protection (ibid.: 33). Also, the IACtHR has emphasized the importance of using special approaches that take into account the best interests of the child as well as a gender perspective (ibid.: 40).

Detention and the Right to Personal Liberty of Migrants and Persons in Need of International Protection

The IACtHR, in the case of *Velez Loor v. Panama*, addressed the special vulnerability of migrants deprived of their liberty, clarifying "the differences in the possibilities of access to justice and the exercise of judicial remedies suffered by these persons and places at the head of States the obligation to adopt positive measures to mitigate this situation" (Sijniensky 2011: 90). That case was the first in that it is strictly related to the rights of migrants and develops standards relating to personal freedom and integrity in the face of an irregular migratory situation.

In the particular case of refugees or asylum seekers, the IACmHR has considered that the detention of asylum seekers, refugees, applicants for and beneficiaries of complementary protection, and stateless persons should be an exceptional measure of last resort that can be used by authorities only in cases prescribed by national legislation, that should be compatible with the rules and principles of International Human Rights Law, and that should meet the following requirements: (1) necessity, (2) reasonableness, and (3) proportionality (IACmHR 2015a: 186).

The Right to Nationality and the Duty to Prevent and Eradicate Statelessness

The right to nationality is established in Article 20 of the ACHR and Article 19 of the American Declaration. Also, given its vital importance, it is a non-derogable right, in accordance with Article 27.2 of the ACHR. Through the development of the content and scope of the right to nationality, the bodies of the IAHRS have maintained a determining role in the protection of the rights of stateless persons, and the duty of States to prevent and eradicate statelessness.

The jurisprudence of the IACtHR and the practice of the IACmHR have provided a solid legal framework for the protection of the right to a nationality. In this regard, three emblematic cases relating to the right to nationality have been issued: (1) *Ivcher Bronstein v. Peru*, (2) *Yean and Bosico Children v. Dominican Republic*, and (3) *Dominican and Haitian Persons Expelled v. Dominican Republic*. Likewise, in the exercise of the advisory competence of the IACtHR, Advisory Opinion OC-4/84 has been issued related to naturalization.

The IACtHR has defined nationality in the following terms: "political and legal bond that links a person to a given state and binds him to it with ties of loyalty and fidelity, entitling him to diplomatic protection from that state" (IACtHR 2005: 57). Although the bodies of the IAHRS have recognized that the determination of who are nationals of a state has traditionally been their internal competence, they have also considered that this is not an absolute power that can be used arbitrarily: "The classic doctrinal position, which viewed nationality as an attribute granted by the state to its subjects, has gradually evolved to the point that nationality is today perceived as involving the jurisdiction of the state as well as human rights issues" (IACtHR 1984: 9).

With regard to the content of the right to nationality, the IACtHR has understood that, on the one hand, the right to nationality grants the individual a minimum of legal protection in international relations by establishing through his nationality his connection with a given state; and on the other hand, it generates the obligation to protect the individual against the deprivation of his nationality in an arbitrary manner, because in that way he would be deprived of the totality of his political rights and of those civil rights that are based on the nationality of the individual (IACtHR 1999: 35; IACtHR 2001: 42; IACtHR 2011: 46).

The bodies of the IAHRS have also defined the duty to provide individuals with equal and effective protection of the law and without discrimination concerning the exercise of nationality (IACtHR 2005: 58; IACtHR 2014b: 99). This standard was established in the case of the Yean and Bosico children, in which the IACtHR introduced a new prohibited ground of discrimination to the right to a nationality (Van Waas 2008: 110). In particular, the IACtHR has considered that

(a) The migratory status of a person cannot be a condition for the State to grant nationality, because migratory status can never constitute a justification for depriving a person of the right to nationality or the enjoyment and exercise of his rights;
(b) The migratory status of a person is not transmitted to the children, and
(c) The fact that a person has been born on the territory of a State is the only fact that needs to be proved for the acquisition of nationality, in the case of those persons who would not have the right to another nationality if they did not acquire that of the State where they were born. (IACtHR 2005: 62)

With regard to the form of acquisition of nationality, the IACmHR has noted that most States in the region use a mixed system, that is, the combined application of the principles of jus soli for persons born in their territories and jus sanguinis for those born in another country, which has been a factor that has contributed significantly to preventing and reducing statelessness in the region (IACmHR 2015c: 93). The IACmHR has also expressed concern, however, about the persistence of legislative gaps and omissions in state practice at the regional level to prevent statelessness, as well as the enforcement of laws that do not recognize the equal rights of women and men to grant nationality to their children (IACmHR 2015a: 28).

Moreover, the IACmHR has recognized the special situation of vulnerability of stateless persons, since they do not have the protection of any state that recognizes them as its nationals and guarantees them the effective enjoyment of their rights and freedoms (ibid.: 27). Following the concept developed by the Colombian Constitutional Court when referring to the situation of internally displaced persons as an unconstitutional state of affairs in its paradigmatic case T-025-2004, the IACmHR has even considered that the situation of statelessness of people of Haitian descent in the Dominican Republic, due to the magnitude and the prolonged nature of the problem, as well as the repeated and continuous violations of multiple rights, evidences the existence of an unconventional state of affairs (IACmHR 2015c: 131).

To protect stateless persons, the bodies of the IAHRS have established that the States have the duty to prevent and eradicate statelessness, as well as to provide individuals with equal and effective protection of the law and without discrimination. Thus, they have understood that States must (1) refrain from applying laws or practices that result in people being denied access to any nationality (IACtHR 2005: 59), and (2) must not establish requirements or restrictions on obtaining nationality that are not legal, adequate, necessary, and proportionate (IACmHR 2003).

Likewise, Article 20.2 of the ACHR states that every person has the right to the nationality of the state in whose territory he or she was born if he or she does not have the right to another nationality, for no person to become stateless. Also, the IACtHR has established that the observance of state duties concerning the right to nationality and the prevention of statelessness are enforceable from the moment of a person's birth (IACtHR 2014b:100).

Also, an individual assessment must be carried out to determine whether a denial of nationality would cause the person to become stateless (IACmHR 2015c: 118). For this purpose, the state in question must accept that a person is not a national of another state if the authorities of that other state refuse to recognize that person as its national; if there is no certainty, the state where the child was born retains the obligation to automatically grant him or her nationality (ibid.: 118).

In relation to the burden of proof of statelessness, the IACtHR indicated that proof of a person's statelessness comes from considering the person's account combined with information from the country of origin, and must be determined within the framework of their duty to identify, prevent, and eradicate statelessness, as well as to protect the stateless person (IACtHR 2014a: 64).

Furthermore, in order to facilitate access to procedures for the acquisition of nationality, the IACmHR has considered that, even in cases where nationality was acquired on the basis of fraudulent or falsified information or by misrepresentation of facts, the nature or gravity of such conduct should be weighed against the consequences of withdrawal of nationality (IACmHR 2015c: 104).

Finally, on due process guarantees in procedures for conferring nationality, the IACtHR has determined that due process guarantees also apply to administrative procedures dealing with the determination of rights such as nationality (IACtHR 2001: 47). Also, in the case of proceedings that culminate in the loss or deprivation of nationality, the IACmHR has understood that the person in question must have at his or her disposal a review process, where the lodging of the appeal suspends the effects of the decision, as well as corresponding procedural remedies and guarantees so that, in the case of an unlawful or arbitrary decision relating to nationality, nationality is reestablished and access to reparations is guaranteed (IACmHR 2015a: 226).

Integral Reparations

Another element of analysis is the reparations granted to the victims of human rights violations, under an integral reparation approach, which has been developed by the bodies of the IAHRS, in contrast to the European system, not only to erase the traces that the unconventional act has generated, but also to understand the measures to avoid its repetition (Botero 2011). Thus, in its decisions the IACmHR and IACtHR have ordered different measures seeking for the integral reparation of victims of human rights violations, such as *restitutio in integrum* (restitution), compensation, rehabilitation, satisfaction, and guarantees of non-repetition.

In the case of *Velez Loor v. Panama*, the IACtHR ordered, as a guarantee of non-repetition, that the necessary measures should be taken to provide facilities with sufficient capacity to house persons whose detention is necessary and proportionate in the specific case of migration issues, specifically adequate for such purposes, offering material conditions and a suitable regime for migrants, and whose personnel are civilian and duly qualified and trained (IACtHR 2010: 79).

The case of the Dominican Republic is paradigmatic concerning victims in need of international protection. The IACtHR, through its jurisprudence, has ordered structural measures of domestic law relating to the situation of Dominican people of Haitian descent, such as adopting the necessary measures to prevent judgement TC/0168/13 and Law No. 169-14 from continuing to produce legal effects. Likewise, as restitution measures, the IACtHR has ordered the recognition of the nationality of persons who had been arbitrarily deprived of their nationality and the granting of residence permits for persons who were arbitrarily deprived of their nationality.

About guarantees of non-repetition, training measures have been provided for state operators in the area of human rights (IACtHR 2010: 81; IACtHR 2013: 80), for officials of bodies responsible to determine refugee status, authorities responsible for migration policy, and other officials dealing with migrants. They would also cover issues related to the human rights of migrants, due process guarantees and the right to consular assistance, discrimination in immigration detention, and the prohibition of collective expulsions of foreigners, among others.

Impact of IHRS Decisions at the Domestic Level

The long Latin American tradition in the area of asylum has been complemented and strengthened by the progressive development of the bodies of the IAHRS. In this sense, the impact of the decisions of the bodies of the IAHRS at the domestic level has been fundamental for the protection of the rights of persons in need of international protection.

First, through the conventionality control that the authorities must apply in the exercise of their functions, for the domestic legal systems of the States and in the exercise of the judicial function, the decisions of the IAHRS become vitally important (Serrano 2013: 14–20). For example, concerning domestic legislation, Argentina's 2004 immigration law, the first of a series of more progressive texts in the region, was adopted as the result of a friendly settlement reached before the IACmHR in 2003 in the case of Juan Carlos de la Torre (Acosta 2018: 204).

In terms of recent judicial decisions, the Constitutional Court of Ecuador, through case 0014-19-IN, accepted the request for provisional suspension, in the framework of a public action lawsuit of unconstitutionality for the merits, against a set of ministerial agreements that provided Venezuelan migrants and asylum seekers as a prerequisite for entering Ecuadorian territory with a passport valid for a minimum of six months, or, in the absence of a passport, with an identity card, in addition to a criminal record certificate. For this purpose, the Constitutional Court of Ecuador used the jurisprudence of the IACtHR and different statements of the IACmHR such as its 2015 Report on Human Mobility, its Resolution 2/18, and Press Release 47/19 regarding the situation.

Next Steps in the IAHRS for the Protection of Asylum Seekers, Refugees, and Other Persons in Need of International Protection

One of the issues that should be analyzed in subsequent decisions and reports of the IACmHR and the IACtHR is, without a doubt, the strong interrelationship between International Criminal Law, International Refugee Law, and International Human Rights Law; that relationship "is built through universal impunity for severe human rights violations" (Ambos 2004: 86). In this regard, the former judge of the IACtHR, Cançado Trindade, has stated, "Although the Inter-American Court [IACtHR] can only deal with [the international responsibility of the state], there is here a complementarity between the responsibility of the State and that of the individual. There is no way to rely solely on individual responsibility, as is done in the domain of contemporary International Criminal Law" (IACtHR 2004: 40).

The IACtHR has considered it useful to interpret the ACHR, taking into account provisions of International Criminal Law (IACtHR 2009: 41; IACtHR 2011: 37; IACtHR 2016: 13), having regard to its specificity in the matter. Also, both the IACtHR and the IACmHR[3] have resorted to other sources of International Criminal Law in order to nourish their jurisprudence on serious violations of human rights in contexts of crimes against humanity (IACtHR 2006a, 2006b), war crimes (IACmHR 1997b; IACtHR 2012b) or genocide (IACtHR 2016).

In particular, the crimes against humanity of deportation, forcible transfer of population and persecution, regulated by Article 7(1) of the Rome Statute of the International Criminal Court (Moffett 2015: 131–35), are situations that have arisen in the region, although they have not been the object of the greater pronouncement by the organs of the IAHRS. In the absence of criminal investigations against those responsible and a scenario of impunity, International Criminal Law emerges as a response to the victims, and criminal justice measures represent one of the ways in which transitional justice can respond (Andreu-Guzmán 2013).

In this regard, in the recent report "Forced Migration of Nicaraguan People to Costa Rica" (IACmHR 2019b), the IACmHR stated that the Interdisciplinary Group of Independent Experts for Nicaragua determined that during the acts of violence that occurred between 18 April and 30 May 2018 in Nicaragua, they had committed crimes against humanity. The IACmHR also maintained that "the civilian population considered to be opposed to the Nicaraguan government has been forced to move arbitrarily, by force and on a large scale, on the basis that it originates, is a consequence and continuation of a context of repression, persecution, abuses and systematic and generalized violence" (IACmHR 2019b: 73). The evidence and arguments presented by the IACmHR in this report could serve as a basis to consider the possible commission of crimes against humanity such as deportation or forced transfer of population.

Conclusions

Migration in the Americas is characterized by being a multicausal and intersectional phenomenon. In this regard, IAHRS's norms and standards have played a significant role in protecting persons in need of international protection and their rights. Likewise, the decisions and reports of the IACmHR and the IACtHR have led to the development and strengthening of public policies and laws in the areas of asylum, complementary protection, statelessness, and international protection in general in many countries of the Americas.

It is essential, however, that States adopt other measures that have, above all, *effet utile* (effectiveness), such as the training of public servants at all levels, especially those who have first contact with migrants, asylum seekers, and refugees; the training of civil society organizations; or the instruction of migrants, asylum seekers, refugees, and stateless persons in their human rights at the national level as well as those recognized at the international and inter-American levels. Much more needs to be done to take those standards from decisions and reports, and then to implement them in reality. Among the multiple frameworks and norms that regulate international migration in International Law, a very promising development by the IACmHR is the adoption of the Inter-American Principles on the Human Rights of All Migrants, Refugees, Stateless Persons and Victims of Human Trafficking, recently adopted in San Salvador on 6 December 2019. Similarly, in context of widespread state impunity, it is fundamental that the IACmHR and the IACtHR start to build bridges to develop the interrelationship and complementarity between International Human Rights Law, International Refugee Law, and International Criminal Law.

Nine years ago, when there was still no IACtHR sentence on asylum seekers or refugees, Cantor and Barichello noted that "the ability of the two human rights bodies to provide international monitoring and enforcement of these standards will depend on the ultimate impact of the renewed antagonism by certain OAS States towards the Inter-American human rights system" (Cantor and Barichello 2012: 37). Today, with nationalism and populism once again on the rise, and with people also facing the unprecedented challenges of the COVID-19 pandemic, there is no doubt that the decisions of the IAHRS have gone against the current, in a region that despite having been characterized for years as having a strong tradition of asylum, is now progressively limiting the protection of asylum seekers and refugees. How this will end up and what will be the role of the IAHRS is still to be seen, but history tells us that the main conquests in the field of human rights will prevail at the end of the day going against all odds.

Álvaro Botero Navarro is a member and Vice chair of the Committee on the Protection of the Rights of All Migrant Workers and Members of their Families of the United Nations, and Coordinator of the OAS Unit on Refugees and Forced Displacement of the Secretariat for Access to Rights and Equity of OAS. Previously, he worked as Coordinator of the Section of Monitoring of Human Rights and the Rapporteurship on the Rights of Migrants of the Inter-American Commission on Human Rights. He is also

Adjunct Professor of Refugee Law at the Washington College of Law at American University in Washington, DC.

Notes

1. Interview conducted by the author on 25 September 2019, with Rumaldo Juan Pacheco Osco, one of the victims in the case of the *Pacheco Tineo Family v. Plurinational State of Bolivia*, decided by the IACtHR on 25 November 2013.
2. Forced migration encompasses "all those situations in which the individual has been compelled to migrate because his or her life, safety or liberty is in jeopardy, whether because of various forms of persecution based on race, religion, nationality, membership in a given social group or political opinion, armed conflict, generalized violence or human rights violations, or because of other circumstances that have seriously disrupted public order, like disasters–natural and human-made–and other factors. Also, it may imply situations where individuals are physically transported across borders without their consent, as in the case of trafficking" [IACmHR 2015a: 11].
3. On 25 April 2012 the IACmHR and the Office of the Prosecutor of the International Criminal Court signed a memorandum of understanding on cooperation to assist each other in the provision of information on decisions, resolutions, judgements, and reports.

References

Acosta, Diego. 2018. *The National versus the Foreigner in South America. 200 Years of Migration and Citizenship Law.* Cambridge University Press.
Ambos, Kai. 2004. *Derechos humanos y derecho penal internacional*, Diálogo Político, Konrad-Adenauer-Stiftung A. C. Year XXI–N° 3–September: 86.
American Convention on Human Rights. 1969. "Pact of San José." https://www.refworld.org/docid/3ae6b36510.html.
American Declaration on the Rights and Duties of Man. 1948. https://www.oas.org/dil/access_to_information_human_right_American_Declaration_of_the_Rights_and_Duties_of_Man.pdf.
Cartagena Declaration on Refugees. 1984. https://www.refworld.org/docid/3ae6b36ec.html.
Convention Relating to the Status of Refugees (1951 Refugee Convention). 1951. https://www.refworld.org/docid/3be01b964.html.
Andreu-Guzmán, Federico. 2013. "Criminal Justice and Forced Displacement: International and National Perspectives." ICTJ Research Brief. https://www.ictj.org/sites/default/files/ICTJ-Research-Brief-Displacement-Criminal-Justice-Andreu-Guzman.pdf
Arlettaz, Fernando. 2016. "Nature and scope of asylum in the Inter-American System of Human Rights." *Revista Ius et Praxis*, 22(1):187–226.
Banfi, Analía, and Michelini, Felipe. 2017. *Introducción al Derecho Internacional de los Derechos Humanos.* Third Edition. Montevideo: Fundación de Cultura Universitaria.

Botero, Álvaro. 2011. "La reparación de las víctimas en el Derecho Internacional de los Derechos Humanos: Tesina." Universidad Carlos III de Madrid.
Cantor, David, and Stefania Barichello. 2012. "Protection of Asylum-Seekers Under the Inter-American Human Rights System." In *Regional Organizations and the Protection of Asylum Seekers*, ed. Ademola Abass and Francesca Ippolito, 267–94. Surrey: Ashgate
European Court of Human Rights. 1996. Amuur v. France, Case No. 17/1995/523/609.
Hathaway, James C. 2010. "Leveraging Asylum," *Texas International Law Journal* 45(3):503–36.
Inter-American Court of Human Rights (IACtHR).1984. Proposed Amendments of the Naturalization Provisions of the Constitution of Costa Rica. Advisory Opinion OC-4/84. Series A No. 4.
———. 1999. Case of Castillo Petruzzi et al. v. Peru. Merits, Reparations and Costs. Series C No. 52.
———. 2001. "Ivcher Bronstein Case v. Peru. Merits, Reparations and Costs. Judgment of February 6." Series C No. 74.
———. 2004. Case of the Plan de Sánchez Massacre v. Guatemala. Merits. Judgment of 29 April. Series C No. 105. Separate Opinion of Judge A.A. Cançado Trindade.
———. 2005. Case of the Yean and Bosico Children v. Dominican Republic. Preliminary Objections, Merits, Reparations, and Costs. Series C No. 155.
———. 2006a. Case of Almonacid Arellano et al. v. Chile. Preliminary Objections, Merits, Reparations and Costs. Series C No. 154.
———. 2006b. Case of the Miguel Castro Castro Prison v. Peru. Merits, Reparations and Costs. Judgment of 25 November. Series C No. 160.
———. 2009. Case of the Las Dos Erres Massacre v. Guatemala. Preliminary Objection, Merits, Reparations and Costs. Series C No. 211.
———. 2010. Case of Vélez Loor v. Panama. Preliminary Objections, Merits, Reparations, and Costs. Series C No. 218.
———. 2011. Case Gelman v. Uruguay. Merits and Reparations. Series C No. 221.
———. 2012a. Case of Nadege Dorzema et al. v. Dominican Republic. Merits, Reparations and Costs. Series C No. 251.
———. 2012b. Case of the Santo Domingo Massacre v. Colombia. Preliminary Objections, Merits and Reparations. Series No. 259.
———. 2013. Case of the Pacheco Tineo family v. Bolivia. Preliminary Objections, Merits, Reparations and Costs. Series C No. 272.
———. 2014a. Case of expelled Dominicans and Haitians v. Dominican Republic. Preliminary Objections, Merits, Reparations and Costs. Series C No. 282.
———. 2014b. Rights and guarantees of children in the context of migration and/or in need of international protection. Advisory Opinion OC-21/14. Series A No. 21.
———. 2015. Case of Wong Ho Wing v. Peru. Preliminary Objection, Merits, Reparations and Costs. Series C No. 297.
———. 2016. Case of the Members of the Village of Chichupac and neighboring communities of the Municipality of Rabinal v. Guatemala. Preliminary Objections, Merits, Reparations and Costs. Series C No. 328.
———. 2018. The institution of asylum, and its recognition as a human right under the Inter-American System of Protection (interpretation and scope of Articles 5,

22(7) and 22(8) in relation to Article 1(1) of the American Convention on Human Rights). Advisory Opinion OC-25/18. Series A No. 25.

Inter-American Commission on Human Rights (IACmHR). 1982, Annual Report of the Inter-American Commission on Human Rights 1981–1982, OEA/Ser.L/V/II.57 doc. 6 rev.1.

———. 1997a. Merits Report No. 51/96, Case 10.675, Haitian Boat People (United States).

———. 1997b. Report on Merits No. 55/97, Case 11.137, Juan Carlos Abella (Argentina).

———. 2000. Report on the situation of human rights of asylum seekers within the Canadian refugee determination system, OEA/Ser.L/V/II.106, Doc. 40 rev.

———. 2001. Annual Report 2000. OEA/Ser./L/V/II.111 doc. 20 rev.

———. 2003. Complaint before the Inter-American Court of Human Rights, Case of Dilcia Yean and Violeta Bosico Cofi v. Dominican Republic.

———. 2011a. Report on Merits No. 136/11, Case 12.474, Pacheco Tineo Family (Bolivia).

———. 2011b. Report on Merits No. 78/11, Case 12.586, John Doe et al. (Canada).

———. 2015a. Human Rights of Migrants, Refugees, Stateless Persons, Victims of Human Trafficking and Internally Displaced Persons: Norms and Standards of the Inter-American Human Rights System. OEA/Ser.L/V/II. Doc. 46/15.

———. 2015b. Refugees and Migrants in the United States: Families and Unaccompanied Children, OAS/Ser.L/V/II.155.

———. 2015c. Report on the Situation of Human Rights in the Dominican Republic, OEA/Ser.L/V/II. Doc.45/15.

———. 2017a. Observations on the Request for an Advisory Opinion presented by the State of Ecuador. The institution of asylum, and its recognition as a human right under the Inter-American System of Protection (OC-25/18).

———. 2017b. Report on Poverty and Human Rights in the Americas, OEA/Ser.L/V/II.164 Doc. 147.

———. 2018. Resolution 2/18 on forced migration of Venezuelans.

———. 2019b. "Forced migration of Nicaraguan people to Costa Rica," OAS/Ser.L/V/II. Doc. 150.

Jubilut, Liliana. 2016. "Latin-America and Refugees: a panoramic view," *Völkerrechtsblog*, 21.

Moffett, Luke. 2015. "Accountability for Forced Displacement in Democratic Republic of Congo and Uganda before the International Criminal Court." *African Journal of International Criminal Justice*, 2: 129–152.

Mondelli, Juan Ignacio. 2018. *La fuerza vinculante de la definición regional de la Declaración de Cartagena sobre Refugiados (1984)* https://www.refworld.org.es/pdfid/5d03d0b54.pdf.

Murillo González, Juan Carlos. 2002. El fortalecimiento de la protección internacional de los refugiados a través del Sistema Interamericano de Derechos Humanos. https://www.oas.org/dil/esp/14%20-%20murillo1.LR.321-350.pdf.

Goldman, Robert K. 2009. "History and Actions: The Inter-American Human Rights System and the Role of the Inter-American Commission on Human Rights." *Human Rights Quarterly*, 31(4): 856–87.

Sandoval, Clara. 2005. "A Critical View of the Protection of Refugees and IDPs [internally displaced persons] by the Inter-American System of Human Rights:

Re-assessing its Powers and Examining the Challenges for the Future." *International Journal of Refugee Law*, 17(1): 43–66.
Serrano, Silvia. 2013. *El control de convencionalidad en la jurisprudencia de la Corte Interamericana de Derechos Humanos*, Comisión Nacional de los Derechos Humanos, Mexico.
Sijniensky, Romina. 2011. "Limitaciones al uso de medidas privadas de libertad para el control de los flujos migratorios: comentario al caso Vélez Loor Vs. Panamá de la Corte Interamericana de Derechos Humanos," in *Opus Magna*, vol. IV.
United Nations High Commissioner for Refugees (UNHCR). 2010. *Global Trends 2009*. Geneva: United Nations High Commissioner for Refugees.
———. 2011. *Global Trends 2010*. Geneva: United Nations High Commissioner for Refugees.
———. 2012. *Global Trends 2011*. Geneva: United Nations High Commissioner for Refugees.
———. 2013. *Global Trends 2012*. Geneva: United Nations High Commissioner for Refugees.
———. 2014a. *Global Trends 2013*. Geneva: United Nations High Commissioner for Refugees.
———. 2015. *Global Trends 2014*. Geneva: United Nations High Commissioner for Refugees.
———. 2016. *Global Trends 2015*. Geneva: United Nations High Commissioner for Refugees.
———. 2017. *Global Trends 2016*. Geneva: United Nations High Commissioner for Refugees.
———. 2018. *Global Trends 2017*. Geneva: United Nations High Commissioner for Refugees.
———. 2019. *Global Trends 2018*. Geneva: United Nations High Commissioner for Refugees.
———. 2020. *Global Trends 2019*. Geneva: United Nations High Commissioner for Refugees.
Uprimny Yepes, Rodrigo, and Luz María Sánchez Duque. 2019. "Artículo 22. Derecho de Circulación y de Residencia." In *Convención Americana sobre Derechos Humanos: comentada*, edited by Christian Steiner and Patricia Uribe. Mexico: Corte de Justicia de la Nación, Konrad Adenauer Stiftung.
Van Waas, Laura. 2008. *Nationality Matters. Statelessness under International Law*. Cambridge: Intersentia.

6

Refugee Protection and the Inter-American Court of Human Rights

Melissa Martins Casagrande

Introduction

Amidst the international community's concerns with the sharp increase in the number of persons being forced to flee their countries of origin or habitual residence through unsafe routes, the United Nations General Assembly (UNGA) adopted the 2016 New York Declaration for Refugees and Migrants (New York Declaration) in 2016 (United Nations 2016). It could be argued that the New York Declaration is an attempt to address the rise in unsafe and irregular mobility, despite difficulties to quantify irregular migration (Ardittis and Laczko 2017),[1] placing the spotlight on the the human dimension and on United Nations (UN) Member States' obligations to safeguard the human rights of refugees and migrants.

The New York Declaration can, therefore, be perceived as an attempt to set standards as well as to encourage the international community toward an agreement that safeguards human rights and safe human mobility, while simultaneously ensuring international cooperation and responsibility sharing (solidarity) among States. The New York Declaration as well as the negotiated outcomes of the 2018 Global Compact for Safe, Orderly and Regular Migration and the 2018 Global Compact on Refugees, both endorsed as UNGA Resolutions A/RES/73/195 and A/RES/73/151, repeatedly refer to a common approach: the use of regional and subregional protection mechanisms (see also Jubilut, Mezzanotti, and Lopes in this volume).

The 2018 Global Compact on Refugees, for instance, states that "refugee movements often have a significant regional and subregional dimension" and that comprehensive responses to forced migration should "build on existing regional and subregional initiatives for refugee protection" (UN 2018a: 6). The protection provided by regional initiatives can encompass regimes such as the Inter-American Human Rights System (IAHRS) regime (see Jubilut, Vera Espinoza, and Mezzanotti in this volume).

This chapter focuses on one of the two bodies that form the IAHRS regime: the Inter-American Court of Human Rights (IACtHR) (the IACtHr forms the regime alongside the Inter-American Commission on Human Rights [IACmHR]). It aims to present an analysis, from a legal perspective, of the role of the IACtHR as a catalyst and standard-setting body for refugee protection in the Americas, thus investigating what can be achieved with the normative instruments already available,[2] through their evolving interpretation by existing protection structures.

In this chapter it is argued that the IACtHR points to a threefold approach to refugee protection. This approach has been identified through the analysis of the progressive consolidation of refugee protection within the jurisprudence of the IACtHR highlighting and systematizing the significant strides achieved by the IACtHR as protection directives. The jurisprudence framework, which was mapped and critically surveyed, comprises a set of three advisory opinions rendered by the IACtHR in 1999, 2003, and 2014, respectively, on the rights of migrants; applicable, therefore, also to refugees and an advisory opinion rendered in 2018, which assesses the right to asylum. Moreover, it also encompasses the case *Pacheco Tineo Family v. Plurinational State of Bolivia* (2013), which directly tackles human rights and standards for refugee status determination. The breadth of case law used in this chapter does not aim to be an exhaustive analysis of all IACtHR case law regarding any aspect of forced migration. Considering that the object of analysis is a threefold approach to refugee protection, cases regarding internally displaced persons or other migrants, for instance, have not been included.

The first of the threefold approach to refugee protection identified is the right to seek and be granted asylum proper, foreseen in the 1969 American Convention on Human Rights (ACHR) and decisive for its effective implementation. The second approach, which could also be understood as a ramification of the right to seek and be granted asylum, is the right to due process or procedural guarantees when seeking asylum or when appealing a decision by a State not to grant asylum. The third approach is the principle of *non-refoulement*, acknowledged by the IACtHR as jus cogens and applicable not only to refugees and refugee status claimants within the framework of the 1951 Convention Relating to the Status of Refugees (1951 Refugee Convention) but also, in line with the spirit of the 1984 Cartagena

Declaration on Refugees (Cartagena Declaration), which provides an enlarged regional definition of persons requiring international protection, and extends the protection to other persons of concern whose right to life, safety or freedom are threatened if returned to their country of origin.

The chapter argues that the focus on *pro persona* principle furthered by this threefold approach addresses some of the highest concerns in terms of current needs of refugee protection in the region. The IACtHR has constantly upheld a *pro persona* position that focuses on human rights, and, consequently, that focuses on the protection of the asylum claimants themselves rather than on the right of a State to grant asylum (Cançado Trindade 2015: 36; Dembour 2015: 7). This chapter proposes that, by upholding the *pro persona* principle[3] in itself through its advisory opinions, the IACtHR has contributed to refugee protection.

The chapter also adopts the convergence and complementarity approach between International Human Rights Law and International Refugee Law (Cançado Trindade, Ortiz Ahlf, and Ruiz de Santiago 2017) and follows, for the purposes of the analysis proposed, the horizontal approach to international and regional norms applicability found in IACtHR jurisprudence (Filardi 2014: 270–71) by using treaties such as the 1951 Refugee Convention alongside the ACHR to establish potential rights' violations and to propose redress.[4]

The IAHRS and the IACtHR

The IAHRS may be considered the embodiment of what the UNGA Resolution A/32/127, adopted on 16 December 1977, presents as regional machineries for the promotion and protection of human rights (Piovesan 2018: 114; see also Botero in this volume). Regional approaches to human rights have the potential of facilitating consensus both in terms of treaty negotiation as well as implementation of international norms (ibid.: 115).

The Organization of American States (OAS) was established in 1948, and the signing of the 1948 OAS Charter consolidated a process of regional cooperation through the creation of a (regional) international organization that succeeded previous initiatives of regional cooperation that had been in place since 1890. In 2019 the OAS has thirty-five Member States of the Americas and "constitutes the main political, juridical, and social governmental forum in the Hemisphere," using a "four-pronged approach to effectively implement its essential purposes, based on its main pillars: democracy, human rights, security, and development (OAS n.d).

The same OAS Conference that adopted the OAS Charter in 1948 also adopted a nonlegally binding document–the 1948 American Declaration on the Rights and Duties of Man (American Declaration).

The ACHR was later adopted at the Inter-American Specialized Conference on Human Rights in 1969. The ACHR proposed a wealth of civil and political rights and freedoms as well as a compromise that States shall adopt measures toward progressively achieving "the full realization of the rights implicit in the economic, social, educational, scientific and cultural standards set forth in the Charter" (ACHR: art. 26).

The ACHR further detailed the role of the IACmHR by establishing functions and powers for making recommendations, preparing studies, responding to inquiries by Member States on matters relating to human rights, and submitting an annual report to the OAS General Assembly (ACHR: art. 41). The IACmHR, thus, retains the functions of its predecessor determined in 1948 (by the OAS Charter) in addition to those later conferred on it by the ACHR–therefore, making the IACmHR both an OAS Charter organ and a ACHR institution (Buergenthal 1985: 1).

Furthermore, the ACHR enlarged the competence of the IACmHR determining that "any person or group of persons, or any nongovernmental entity legally recognized in one of more Member States of the Organization, may lodge petitions with the Commission containing denunciations or complaints of violation" of the ACHR by a Member State (ACHR: art. 44). The ACHR established the admissibility criteria for the lodging of such petitions (ACHR: arts. 46–47). If the petition is admissible, the ACHR also determines, for instance, that the procedure for the analysis of the claim duly follows the adversarial principle.[5]

Only State parties to the ACHR and the IACmHR have the right to submit a case to the IACtHR. For the case to be submitted, the matter must have been analyzed by the IACmHR and a friendly settlement must not or must have been only partially achieved (ACHR: art. 61). A State party may, upon ratifying or adhering to the ACHR or at any subsequent time, "declare that it recognizes, *ipso facto*, and not requiring special agreement, the jurisdiction of the Court on all matters relating to the interpretation or application of [the ACHR]" (ACHR: art. 62(1)). Still, for the ACHR, "such declaration may be made unconditionally, on the condition of reciprocity, for a specific period, or for specific cases" (ACHR: art. 62(2)) and "the jurisdiction of the Court shall comprise all cases concerning the interpretation and application of [the ACHR] that are submitted to it, provided that the State Parties to the case recognize or have recognized such jurisdiction" (ACHR: art. 62(3)).

Moreover, the ACHR establishes that the IACtHR has a dual jurisdictional role: an adjudicatory role established by Article 63, and an advisory role established by Article 64. It is through the latter role that States call upon the IACtHR to issue advice regarding the interpretation of the ACHR or of other universal and regional human rights treaties.. In fact, it could be argued that this dual jurisdictional role has positively impacted the outreach of the IACtHR with regards to refugee protection.

Regional Asylum Tradition and the Sources of Refugee Law

The history of the right to seek asylum has been a constant within the Americas, most notably, Latin America. An asylum tradition has been recognized within the region (Piovesan and Jubilut 2011), several binding treaties exist[6] prior to the 1951 Refugee Convention and the right to seek asylum has been hailed as regional customary law (Gros Espiell 1995).

Five regional legally binding treaties were adopted on the subject of the right to asylum from 1928 to 1954. The 1928 Havana Convention on Asylum, 1933 Montevideo Convention on Political Asylum, and the 1939 Montevideo Convention on Asylum and Political Refuge, as well as the 1954 Convention on Diplomatic Asylum and the 1954 Convention on Territorial Asylum both concluded in Caracas. These treaties use the terms "asylum" and "refuge" interchangeably and refer to the discretionary right of a State to grant asylum to a person who is persecuted for political reasons. In fact, the Asylum Case, brought before the International Court of Justice, is about the right to political asylum and involves two Latin American countries: Colombia and Peru (International Court of Justice 1951).

It could be argued that the regional tradition of asylum has been reinforced by the formulation of Article 27 of the American Declaration by which "every person has the right, in case of pursuit not resulting from ordinary crimes, to seek and receive asylum in foreign territory, in accordance with the laws of each country and with international agreements." Likewise, the tradition was further reinforced by the formulation of the right to seek and receive asylum brought forth by Article 14(1) of the 1948 Universal Declaration of Human Rights: "Everyone has the right to seek and to enjoy in other countries asylum from persecution."

The compromise of States in the region and of the IAHRS toward the protection of forced migrants and refugees can be ascertained through the progressive ratification of the 1951 Refugee Convention and of the 1967 Protocol Relating to the Status of Refugees (1967 Protocol).[7] In fact, Brazil, Canada, Chile, Colombia, the United States, and Venezuela participated in the *travaux préparatoires* of the 1951 Refugee Convention (United Nations High Commissioner for Refugees [UNHCR] 1990). Furthermore, the 1951 Refugee Convention and its 1967 Protocol add to the evolution of the right to asylum in the Americas, a position later reinforced by IACtHR jurisprudence (i.e., IACtHR 2013: paras. 142–43) to encompass those with a well-founded fear of persecution on the basis of race, nationality, religion, political opinion, or belonging to a social group.

By the time the ACHR was adopted in 1969, it acknowledged the right of every person to seek and be granted asylum in a foreign territory, in accordance with the legislation of the State and international conventions, in the event of being pursued for political offenses or related common crimes (ACHR: art. 22(7)). In 1984 the Cartagena Declaration was adopted with the aim of establishing a compromise between regional stakeholders to address protection challenges that had emerged within the region at the time (see Fischel de Andrade in this volume). The documents that mark its tenth, twentieth, and thirtieth anniversaries also contribute to the identification of obstacles and the proposal of joint solutions toward newly identified protection needs in the region (Maldonado 2015).

The Cartagena Declaration expands the refugee status definition to encompass, in addition to refugee status determination criteria of the 1951 Refugee Convention and its 1967 Protocol, also persons "who have fled their country because their lives, safety and freedom have been threatened by generalized violence, foreign aggression, internal conflicts, massive violation of human rights or other circumstances which have seriously disturbed the public order" (Cartagena Declaration: 3rd Conclusion). The Cartagena Declaration came into existence to address actual forced mobility-related protection needs. As protracted humanitarian crises such as the current situation in Venezuela demand renewed protection solutions, a survey of the IACtHR jurisprudence and its threefold approach to refugee protection could prove instrumental to this endeavor.

IACtHR Refugee Protection: Asylum and *Non-refoulement*

Both the IACmHR and the IACtHR have issued decisions regarding Article 22 of the ACHR—more specifically, 22(7) on the right to seek and be granted asylum and 22(8) on the principle of *non-refoulement*. Moreover, the constant exercise within IACtHR jurisdiction of the complementary use of the three international legal sources of protection—International Human Rights Law, International Refugee Law, and International Humanitarian Law—is argued to provide a renewed approach to refugee protection, distinct from the approach awarded to asylum seekers in cases before other international courts (e.g., Dembour 2015; Olmos 2017).

Article 27 of the American Declaration states that the right to seek and receive asylum in foreign territory will be fulfilled in accordance with the laws of each country and with international agreements. The American Declaration thus implies that the legislation in force in each State as well as in international custom and treaties enacted on the matter, be them regional or global, shall ground the interpretation of the right. The ACHR follows a similar pattern, stating that the right is determined by the legislation of the State (understood here as the State where the right to asylum is sought) and international conventions.

The American Declaration and the ACHR clearly outline the possibility for regional bodies, including the IACtHR, to make use of nearly any norm, domestic or otherwise, applicable to the case under analysis. As stated in Article 22(7) of the ACHR, the right to seek and be granted asylum requires a transsystemic approach between domestic and international (regional and global) provisions (Casagrande 2017) as a paramount condition for the IACtHR to ascertain the right to seek and be granted asylum, as well as other rights derived from that right.

The IACtHR has, therefore, the prerogative to make use of historical asylum treaties still in force, customary law regarding the right to seek and be granted asylum, and the 1951 Refugee Convention and the 1967 Protocol. The IACtHR has stated that the scope and content of Article 27 of the American Declaration and Article 22(7) of the ACHR "relate directly to the norms established by international agreements, and in particular the principle of *non-refoulement* in article 33 of the Refugee Convention" (Harley 2014: 26).

It is noteworthy, that the IACtHR has evolved over the years from being a relatively inactive judicial organ at the beginning of its functions to become an active and innovative judicial body (Olmos 2017: 1479). Furthermore, the flexible approach taken by IACtHR as a whole when applying various methods of interpretation has paved the way for progress, giving judges greater scope to develop Human Rights Law in line with the ACHR going beyond a constrictive interpretation of the ACHR wording (ibid.: 1479). This approach is "also reflected in the implementation of the rights of refugees, asylum seekers, and displaced persons in the region through the actions of the IACmHR and the IACtHR, which have a growing jurisprudence on the topic, including decisions on *non-refoulement*, nationality and the right to life" (Piovesan and Jubilut 2011: 218).

As seen above, another source of refugee protection was negotiated in 1984, when the Cartagena Declaration was adopted with the aim of establishing a compromise between regional stakeholders to address protection challenges that had emerged in the late 1970s and early 1980s within the region, expanding the refugee status definition. The scope of protection brought forth by the Cartagena Declaration, therefore, increases as States within the region progressively adopt such expanded definition in their domestic legislation and practice and the expanded definition of refugee (UNHCR 2017), therefore, becomes applicable legislation by the IACtHR through both the domestic and the international protective norms foreseen by Article 22(7) of the ACHR. Interestingly, as much as the conclusions of the Cartagena Declaration became a resource for the IACtHR, the IACmHR and the IACtHR have, in fact, also influenced the drafting of some of the Cartagena conclusions (Piovesan and Jubilut 2011: 218).

IACtHR Jurisprudence: The Building Blocks of Refugee Protection

Advisory Opinions OC-16/99 and OC-18/03

Advisory Opinion 16, delivered by the IACtHR in 1999, requested by Mexico, concerns the right to information on consular assistance in the framework of guarantees of the due process of law. It relates to the interpretation of Article 36 of the 1963 Vienna Convention on Consular Relations concerning freedom of communication and access to nationals of the sending State by consular officers.

The IACtHR advised that the provision (Vienna Convention on Consular Relations: art. 36) confers rights on detained foreign nationals; among those rights is the right to information on consular assistance; and that such provision is part of the body of International Human Rights Law. Furthermore, the IACtHR stressed that a State's failure to observe a foreign national's right to information is prejudicial to the due process of law having practical effects in concrete cases.

Advisory Opinion 18, delivered by the IACtHR in 2003, was also requested by Mexico. It asked whether a State in the Americas could establish distinct treatment to undocumented migrant workers in its labor legislation, whether an individual's legal residence in the territory of State is a necessary condition for that State to respect and ensure rights and freedoms to those persons under its jurisdiction, and whether the denial of one or more labor rights, on the basis of the undocumented status of the migrant worker, is compatible with the obligation of States to ensure nondiscrimination and the equal protection of rights (IACtHR 2003: para. 52).

The Opinion, unanimously issued by the IACtHR, determined that States have the general obligation to respect and ensure fundamental rights, to avoid taking measures that limit or infringe rights, and to eliminate measures and practices that restrict or violate fundamental rights. Furthermore, it stated that the noncompliance of the State with this general obligation to respect and ensure fundamental rights owing to any discriminatory treatment gives rise to international responsibility. It also stressed in the Opinion that the principle of equality and nondiscrimination is of peremptory nature, entailing *erga omnes* protection obligations that bind all States and generate effects to third parties, and added that labor rights of all workers should be respected and guaranteed, irrespective of status as nationals or nonnationals.

Advisory Opinion OC-21/14: Specific Needs of Protection

Advisory Opinion 21, delivered by the IACtHR in 2014, was requested by Argentina, Brazil, Paraguay, and Uruguay. It addresses the rights and guarantees of children in the context of migration and/or international protection. It requests that the IACtHR issues clear definition and precise standards, principles, and obligations concerning the rights of migrant children and children born to migrant parents. Differently from Advisory Opinions 16 and 18, it directly addresses rights of forced migrants and, it could be argued, overlapping vulnerabilities and specific needs of protection.

Advisory Opinion 21 covers procedures for the determination of the needs for international protection and of special protection measures for migrant children and adolescents through system of guarantees that must be applied to migratory proceedings, such as precautionary measures to uphold the principle of non-detention of migrant children as well as measures of protection of rights that must be applied on a priority basis and that do not entail restrictions on personal liberty; as well as due process guarantees before measures that entail deprivation of liberty of children and adolescents within the framework of migratory proceedings (IACtHR 2014: para. 2).

Furthermore, Advisory Opinion 21 covers the effective implementation of the principle of *non-refoulement* in relation to migrant children, procedures for the identification and treatment of children who may request for asylum or refugee status, and the right to a family life of the children when their parents are removed due to migratory reasons. Advisory Opinion 21 advises States of the prohibition from returning, expelling, deporting, repatriating, rejecting at the border, or not admitting, or in any way transferring or removing a child to a State where the child's life, security, and/or liberty is at risk of violation because of persecution or threat thereof; generalized violence; massive violations of human rights or risk of being submitted to torture or other cruel, inhuman, or degrading treatments; or transferring or removing the child to a third State that might send the child to a State where the child might run such risks (ibid.).

Advisory Opinion OC-25/18: Asylum as a Human Right

Advisory Opinion 25, requested by Ecuador and issued by the IACtHR in 2018, tackles the specific question of the right to asylum as a human right and, more specifically, the interpretation of the right to seek and be granted asylum (ACHR: art. 22(7)) and the principle of *non-refoulement* (ACHR: art. 22(8)); and the right to humane treatment (ACHR: art. 5) in relation to Article 1.1 of the ACHR: the obligation of State parties to ACHR to respect the rights and freedoms contained in it and to ensure to all human beings subject to their jurisdiction the free and full exercise of those rights and freedoms, without any discrimination for reasons of race, color, sex, language, religion, political and other opinion, national or social origin, economic status, birth, or any other social condition.

Advisory Opinion 25 covers the historical developments of the right to asylum, including diplomatic asylum in connection to no extradition for politically motivated crimes as well as the universal regime of refugee protection (IACtHR 2018: paras. 72–163). It reinforces the right to seek and be granted asylum, including diplomatic asylum, on the basis of Article 22(7) of the ACHR and Article 27 of the American Declaration (ibid.). It addresses the mandatory enforceability of the *non-refoulement* principle, stressing that not only does it require that a person not be returned, but also that there are positive obligations imposed on States (ibid.: paras. 194–99).

Case of Pacheco Tineo Family v. Plurinational State of Bolivia (2013)

The case of *Pacheco Tineo* is the first that scrutinizes, per se, a breach of international obligations concerning the right to seek and be granted asylum in light of Article 22(7) of the ACHR as well as the right not be deported or returned to a country, regardless if it is the person's country of origin, if that person's right to life or personal freedom is in danger of being violated in that country because of race, nationality, religion, social status, or political opinions (ACHR: art. 22(8)).

The facts of the case are as follows: Rumaldo Juan Pacheco Osco and Fredesvinda Tineo Godos, a married couple, were indicted and arrested for alleged crimes relating to terrorism in Peru in the early 1990s. After their acquittal in 1995 they entered Bolivia with their two daughters and applied for refugee status, which was later granted. In 1998, after signing a voluntary repatriation declaration, the family left Bolivia and entered Chile, where their refugee status was also determined. In 2001 the family left Chile and reentered Peru–the couple, their two daughters, and a son who had been born in Chile. All five family members then returned to Bolivia with the intention of crossing into Chile, claiming a well-founded fear of persecution, taking into account that, contrary to their belief when they decided to reenter Peru, an earlier judgement convicting them of crimes of terrorism had not been annulled and the case had not been dropped. Bolivian authorities claimed the family had entered the country's territory irregularly and should, thus, be expelled from Bolivia to Peru for violating migratory legislation. Bolivian authorities refused to recognize the family's refugee status even after the intervention of Chilean consular authorities.

The IACtHR declared Bolivia responsible for the violation of the right to seek and receive asylum, of the principle of *non-refoulement* (contained in the right to freedom of movement and residence) and of the rights to judicial guarantees and to judicial protection in relation to all five family members. Furthermore, Bolivia was declared in violation of the right to mental and moral integrity of the five family members. In relation to the three children, Bolivia was found responsible for the violation of the right to protection of children and the family. Bolivia was found not responsible for an alleged violation of the right to physical integrity (IACtHR 2013: para. 299).

The IACtHR established that the judgement per se constituted a form of reparation and, therefore, must have public outreach through the country's official gazette, a national newspaper of widespread circulation, and on an official website, available for one year. Moreover, it determined that permanent training programs for national migratory authorities or other officials who, owing to their functions, are in contact with migrants or those requesting asylum. The judgement also determined the payment of pecuniary and non-pecuniary damage as well as the reimbursement of the Victims' Legal Assistance Fund. As per the ACHR, the IACtHR is mandated to monitor compliance with the judgement (ibid.: para. 299).

Overarching Preemptive Protection: The Dynamics of IACtHR Jurisdiction and the Prevalence of the Pro Persona Principle

The Impact of the Dual Jurisdictional Role of the IACtHR on Refugee Protection

The dual jurisdictional role of the IACtHR has enabled the discussion of several human rights protection issues from actual (in the case of adjudicatory rulings) and hypothetical (in the case of advisory opinions) perspectives. It could be argued that the dual jurisdictional role can impact compliance with refugee protection standards.

One of issues at stake when the dual jurisdictional role of the IACtHR is discussed is the purported nonbinding force of advisory opinions. For Olmos, for instance, "while the IACtHR's judgements may become legal yardsticks for national legal systems, advisory opinions do not carry any binding force" further highlighting, however, that "the IACtHR has asserted the exercise of its advisory jurisdiction as a way to convey a clear message to all OAS Member States, including those who are not parties to the ACHR" (Olmos 2017: 1482).

It could be argued that, although it may be difficult to measure the enforceability impact and levels of implementation of the IACtHR advisory opinions, their positive impact is perceived through the melding of best practices when it comes to migrant rights. These best practices, for instance, are established by the advisory opinions, described above, and rendered by the IACtHR in 1999, 2003, 2014, and 2018,[8] that affirm principles of International Human Rights Law, most of which apply to some extent to the protection of forced migrants. The impact is most strongly felt when the IACtHR itself defends, through the advisory opinions, the jus cogens nature of principles such as nondiscrimination (i.e., IACtHR 1999; IACtHR 2003: paras. 97–111; IACtHR 2018: para. 170), and *non-refoulement* (i.e., IACtHR 2014: para. 225; IACtHR 2018: para. 99).

The Complementarity of International Human Rights Law and International Refugee Law and the Ensuing Prevalence of the Pro Persona Principle

The *pro persona* principle "represents the most relevant interpretive tool put forward in article 29.1 and article 1.1 of the ACHR, whereby legal provisions must be read in the most advantageous manner to protect the human being" (Olmos 2017: 1480). Moreover, the Cartagena process has contributed to anchoring the centrality of the *pro persona* principle within the IAHRS as a whole; more specifically, the Cartagena process has contributed to IACtHR jurisprudence through the need to strengthen the international protection regime for refugees, displaced and stateless persons, and the "convergence and complementarity of International Human Rights Law, International Refugee Law and International Humanitarian Law" (Maldonado 2015: 89).

It could be argued that it is precisely the constant complementary and convergent approach of these three dimensions of international legal protection within IACtHR jurisdiction reinforcing the *pro persona* approach that provide a renewed approach to refugee protection, distinct from the approach awarded to asylum seekers—for instance, in cases before the European Court of Human Rights (Olmos 2017) and the International Court of Justice (1951). While it could be argued the latter courts upheld a State-focused perspective of the right to grant asylum and to decide who has the right to remain in their territories, the IACtHR has defended a *pro persona* position in relation to the right to seek and be granted asylum that focuses on human rights, and consequently, the protection of the asylum claimants themselves (e.g., Dembour 2015: 7; IACtHR 2014: para. 234; IACtHR 2018: para. 149).

Threefold Approach to Protection: The Right to Seek Asylum, Procedural Guarantees, and *Non-refoulement*

The IACtHR and the Right to Seek Asylum and/or Refugee Status

The protection awarded by the American Declaration and subsequently by the ACHR, broadened by the Cartagena Declaration and the ensuing body of international guidelines as well as reiterated state practice, sediment the positioning of the IACtHR that there is a well-established right to seek asylum—understood here in its widest sense.

The IACtHR reinforces the duty to protect a person who had refugee status recognized beyond the borders of any one given State. Once a State "has declared refugee status, this protects the person to whom this has been recognized beyond the borders of that State, so that other States that the said person enters must take into account this status" (IACtHR 2013: para. 150). There is, thus, a guarantee of a duty of special care on the verification of this status and the measures to be adopted.

The IACtHR, furthermore, establishes two protection features that are of special interest: in the *Pacheco Tineo* case the IACtHR expresses that the refugee status cessation clauses—enumerated in the 1951 Refugee Convention must be interpreted restrictively and in tandem with the overarching protection offered by the American Declaration and by the ACHR (ibid.: paras. 142–43) and no other reasons (for cessation) may be adduced by way of analogy to justify the withdrawal of refugee status (Arlettaz 2016).

The Safeguard of Procedural Guarantees in Refugee Status Claims

The IACtHR has not, in any stance, delved into the merit of refugee status determination (RSD) decisions; the right to seek and be granted asylum both from a historical perspective of respect to the right of a State to grant asylum (Jubilut and Lopes 2019) as well as from the fact that a State has purportedly followed the RSD criteria set out in the 1951 Refugee Convention and its 1967 Protocol and ensuing international norms that support its enforcement (Casagrande 2017).

The IACtHR has clearly stated in the *Pacheco Tineo* case that the ACHR does not guarantee a right for the RSD claim to be accepted. It points to the right to have the claim heard. Moreover, any request for RSD application, in line with the protection granted by Article 22(7) of the ACHR, must be processed with the due guarantees (IACtHR 2013: para. 197). The IACtHR decided that, in this particular case, in addition to violating the right to seek and to be granted asylum, the State also violated the rights to judicial guarantees and the right to judicial protection—all foreseen in the IACHR (ibid.: para. 198).

Still within the procedural framework, the ACtHR has reinforced, both in OC-21/2014 (IACtHR 2014) and in the *Pacheco Tineo* case (IACtHR 2013: paras. 211–29) that children are also entitled to the rights established in the ACHR in general, always considering the right to the measures of protection required by his condition as a minor on the part of his family, society, and the State (ACHR: art. 19).

Beyond the 1951 Refugee Convention: The Evolving Implementation of the Principle of Non-refoulement by the IACtHR

The IACtHR has argued for the jus cogens nature of the principle of *non-refoulement* (i.e., IACtHR 2014: para. 225; IACtHR 2018: 99), therefore going beyond the scope of application of *non-refoulement* established in the 1951 Refugee Convention, and thus extending the right to migrants that, within the spirit of the Cartagena Declaration, fall outside the scope of the 1951 Refugee Convention but whose lives and safety are threatened in the event of such return.

Moreover, the IACtHR, in OC-21/14 and in the *Pacheco Tineo* case, expressly mentions that the right to seek and be granted asylum as well as the principle of *non-refoulement* applies to persons under eighteen years of age, and that special attention should be paid to the overlapping vulnerabilities they might face: "Children are entitled to . . . submit applications for recognition of refugee status in their own capacity, whether or not they are accompanied, the elements of the definition should be interpreted taking into account the specific forms that child persecution may adopt, such as recruitment, trafficking, and female genital mutilation, as well as the way in which they may experience these situations" (IACtHR 2014: para. 80).

Furthermore, OC-21/14 calls attention to new safeguards that must be considered in relation to the decision of returning or not returning a person to another territory. The IACtHR states that it is pertinent to be aware of new factors that lead individuals, particularly children, to be forcibly displaced, "among which transnational organized crime and the violence associated with the actions of non-State groups" (ibid.: para. 80).

The IACtHR's understanding of the principle of *non-refoulement* also gains depth when an issue, historically characteristic to the region but fairly new in other jurisdictions, presents itself. The IACtHR follows the positioning of the IACmHR in OC-21/14, and extends the application of the principle of *non-refoulement* to migrants intercepted in international waters "as not to allow their requests to be evaluated in potential host States," understanding that the practice is "contrary to the principle of *non-refoulement*, because it does not permit the evaluation of each person's specific risk factors" (ibid.: para. 220).

Moreover, it should be noted that the States that practice interception of migrants in international waters might be mistakenly taking the migrants' destination for granted, not allowing them to reach out to other States in the area that might be willing to allow entry and, if applicable, to process their RSD claim.

Conclusion

The right to seek and be granted asylum has been rooted in the region through treaties and through State practice; it could be argued, however, that the IACtHR has had a fundamental role in the consolidation of the protection of persons who flee their country of origin or habitual residence due to a well-founded fear of persecution.

First and foremost, the IACtHR has somehow distanced itself from analyzing the merit of RSD decisions, reinforcing the right to seek and be granted asylum both from a historical perspective of respect to the right of a State to grant asylum (determination of asylum as a constitutive right) and from the fact that a State has purportedly followed the RSD criteria set out in the 1951 Refugee Convention and its 1967 Protocol and ensuing international documents that support its enforcement (determination of asylum and/or refugee status as a declaratory right).

Furthermore, the IACtHR has established and reinforced strong parameters for refugee application and recourse procedures, within either the legal or administrative spheres. Within this framework, the IACtHR has reinforced the right to life (ACHR: art. 4), to humane treatment (ibid.: art. 5), to a fair trial (ibid.: art. 8) including the right to prior notification regarding proceedings (ibid.: art. 8(2)(b)), and to judicial protection (ibid.: art. 25). The IACtHR has also strongly reinforced the rights of children, accompanied or not, with regards to protection and family unity, both in OC-21/2014 and in the *Pacheco Tineo* case.

The right of refugees or the refugee status claimants to not be returned to the place where their lives, physical and mental integrity, and safety could be threatened–*non-refoulement*–is perhaps the most prolific contribution of the IACtHR within the realm of protection of those who have fled their places of origin or habitual residence under those circumstances.

In addition to arguing for the jus cogens nature of the principle, the IACtHR has gone beyond the scope of application of *non-refoulement* established in the 1951 Refugee Convention and has extended the right to migrants that, within the spirit of the Cartagena Declaration, might not straightforwardly fit within the protection frameworks of the 1951 Refugee Convention's right to RSD or even the right to asylum established in the American Declaration and the ACHR.

Melissa Martins Casagrande holds a Masters' degree in Public Law and Policy from the Universidade Federal do Paraná (Brazil) and holds a Doctor of Civil Law degree from McGill University (Canada). She is a Postdoctoral Fellow at Universidade Federal do Paraná. She is a member of the research group Direitos Humanos e Vulnerabilidades at Universidade Católica de Santos.

Notes

1. Ardittis and Laczko (2017: 2–3) state that current understanding of the scale and dynamics of irregular migration is quite poor for most regions of the world despite recent efforts to improve the availability and quality of data and estimates. According to data presented by the same authors, more than 1 million migrants and asylum seekers entered Europe irregularly in 2015, compared to fewer than 300,000 in 2014.
2. Provost (2002: 1–2), in the context of massive human rights violations, defends that adding new rules and creating new institutions, even if they are accepted by a large number of states, does not in itself provide relief to individuals. Provost advocates that, in addition to improving the understanding of why violations occur—an analysis primarily undertaken by sociologists and political scientists—what can be achieved with existing available instruments should also be investigated.
3. Ramos (2016: 142) highlights that the *pro persona* principle derives from the international human rights treaties regime and determines that every international obligation regarding human rights cannot be restrictively interpreted pro States and must be interpreted pro individuals, who are the inherent beneficiaries of international human rights protection.
4. There were two decisions in 2020 that concern the rights of migrants that somewhat relate to the analysis undertaken in this chapter. A decision regarding urgent measures within the case *Velez Loor v. Panama* adopted on 26 May 2020 calls for the adoption of appropriate measures to protect the rights of migrants in detention in light of the COVID-19 pandemic. Moreover, the sentencing in the case *Roche Azaña et al. v. Nicaragua*, published on 3 June 2020, acknowledges state responsibility for the death of migrants as well as the violation of the migrants' rights and judicial guarantees.
5. Mrcela (2017: 18) explains that the adversarial principle is often called the principle of contradiction. It consists of the fact that all procedural actions are performed in the presence of both parties who have the right and the possibility to represent their interests and express their position.
6. Those treaties are (1) 6th International Conference of American States, Convention on Asylum, Havana, Cuba, 20 February 1928; (2) 7th International Conference of American States: Convention on Political Asylum, Montevideo, Uruguay, 26 December 1933; (3) Treaty on Asylum and Political Refuge, Montevideo, Uruguay, 4 August 1939; (4) Organization of American States: Convention on Diplomatic Asylum, OAS Treaty Series 18, Caracas, Venezuela, 28 March 1954; (5) Organization of American States: Convention on Territorial Asylum, OAS Treaty Series 19, Caracas, Venezuela, 28 March 1954.
7. According to data gathered by UNHCR in 2015, those States were, in chronological order, Bolivia, Ecuador, Mexico, Belize, Brazil, Guatemala, Paraguay, El Salvador, Peru, Honduras, Argentina, Uruguay, Nicaragua, Chile, and Colombia.
8. IACtHR, Advisory Opinion OC-16/99 of October 1, 1999 requested by the United Mexican States. The Right to Information on Consular Assistance in the Framework of the Guarantees of the Due Process of Law [OC-16/99]. IACtHR,

Advisory Opinion OC-18/03 of September 17, 2003 requested by the United Mexican States. Juridical Condition and Rights of Undocumented Migrants [OC-18/03]. IACtHR, Advisory Opinion OC-21/14 of August 19, 2014 requested by the Argentine Republic, the Federative Republic of Brazil, the Republic of Paraguay and the Oriental Republic of Uruguay. Rights and Guarantees of Children in the context of migration and/or in need of international protection [OC-21/14]. IACtHR, Advisory Opinion OC-25/18 requested by the Republic of Ecuador. The institution of asylum and its recognition as a human right in the Inter-American System of Protection (interpretation and scope of articles 5,22.7 and 22.8 in relation to article 1(1) of the ACHR [OC-25/18].

References

American Convention on Human Rights. 1969. https://www.cidh.oas.org/basicos/english/basic3.american percent20convention.htm.
American Declaration on the Rights and Duties of Man. 1948. https://www.oas.org/dil/access_to_information_human_right_American_Declaration_of_the_Rights_and_Duties_of_Man.pdf.
Ardittis, Solon, and Frank Laczko. 2017, "Measuring irregular migration: Innovative data practices." *Migration Policy Practice* 7 (2).
Arlettaz, Fernando. 2016. "Naturaleza y alcance del asilo en el sistema interamericano de Derechos Humanos." *Revista Ius et Praxis* 22 (1): 187–225.
Buergenthal, Thomas. 1985. "The Advisory Practice of the Inter-American Human Rights Court." *American Journal of International Law* 79 (1): 1–27.
Cançado Trindade, and Antônio Augusto. 2015. *Os Tribunais Internacional e a Realização da Justiça*, Rio de Janeiro: Renovar.
Cançado Trindade, Antônio Augusto, Loretta Ortiz Ahlf, and Jaime Ruiz de Santiago, eds. 2017. *La tres vertientes de la protección internacional de los derechos de la persona humana*. 2nd ed. Mexico City: Editorial Porrúa.
Cartagena Declaration on Refugees. 1984. https://www.refworld.org/docid/3ae6b36ec.html.
Casagrande, Melissa Martins. 2017. "Refugiados: proteção universal sob a perspectiva da aplicação transistêmica do Direito Interno e do Direito Internacional." *Revista Jurídica da Presidência* 19 (117): 125–47.
Convention Relating to the Status of Refugees and its 1967 Protocol, https://refworld.org/docid/4ec4a7f02.html.
Dembour, Marie-Bénédicte. 2015. *When Humans Become Migrants: Study of the European Court of Human Rights with an Inter-American Counterpoint*. Oxford: Oxford University Press.
Filardi, Marcos E. 2014. "Derecho de buscar y recibir asilo. Princípio de no devolución. Garantías judiciales y protección judicial." *Revista Derechos Humanos* 3 (7): 269–89.
Gros Espiell, H. 1995. "La Declaración de Cartagena como fuente del derecho internacional de los refugiados en América Latina," in *Memoria del Coloquio Internacional: 10 Años de la Declaración de Cartagena sobre Refugiados* (Coloquio de San

José, Costa Rica, 5–7 December 1994), San José, Costa Rica: Inter-American Institute of Human Rights/ACNUR, 453–70.

Harley, Tristan. 2014. "Regional Cooperation and Refugee Protection in Latin America: A South-South Approach." *International Journal of Refugee Law* 26 (1): 22–47.

Inter-American Court of Human Rights (IACtHR). 1999. *Advisory Opinion OC-16/99 of October 1, 1999 requested by the United Mexican States. The Right to Information on Consular Assistance in the Framework of the Guarantees of the Due Process of Law.* San José, Costa Rica: Inter-American Court of Human Rights.

——. 2003. *Advisory Opinion OC-18/03 of September 17, 2003 requested by the United Mexican States. Juridical Condition and Rights of Undocumented Migrants.* San José, Costa Rica: Inter-American Court of Human Rights.

——. 2013. *Case of the Pacheco Tineo Family v. Plurinational State of Bolivia. Judgement of 25 November 2013.* San José, Costa Rica: Inter-American Court of Human Rights.

——. 2014. *Advisory Opinion OC-21/14 of August 19, 2014 requested by the Argentine Republic, the Federative Republic of Brazil, the Republic of Paraguay and the Oriental Republic of Uruguay. Rights and Guarantees of Children in the context of migration and/ or in need of international protection.* San José, Costa Rica: Inter-American Court of Human Rights.

——. 2018. *Advisory Opinion OC-25/18 requested by the Republic of Ecuador. The institution of asylum and its recognition as a human right in the Inter-American System of Protection (interpretation and scope of articles 5, 22.7 and 22.8 in relation to article 1(1) of the American Convention on Human Rights.* San José, Costa Rica: Inter-American Court of Human Rights.

——. 2020a. *Case Roche Azaña et al. v. Nicaragua. Judgement of 3 June 2020.* San José, Costa Rica: Inter-American Court of Human Rights.

——. 2020b. *Case of Velez Loor v. Panama, Adopción de Medidas Urgentes de 26 May 2020.* San José, Costa Rica: Inter-American Court of Human Rights.

International Court of Justice. 1951. *Haya de la Torre (Colombia v. Peru).* Judgement 13 June 1951. https://www.icj-cij.org/files/case-related/14/014-19510613-JUD-01-00-EN.pdf.

Jubilut, Liliana Lyra, and Rachel Oliveira Lopes. 2019. "Refuge and Political Asylum in Latin America: relevance, characteristics, and normative structure." In *The Routledge Companion to Migration, Communication, and Politics*, edited by Stephen Croucher; João R. Caetano, and Elsa A. Campbell: 65–80, London: Routledge.

Maldonado Castillo, Carlos. 2015. "The Cartagena process: 30 years of innovation and solidarity" *Forced Migration Review* 49: 89–91.

Mrcela, Marin. 2017. "Adversarial principle, the equality of arms and confrontational right–European Court of Human Rights Jurisprudence." In *Procedural Aspects of EU Law*, edited by Dunja Duic and Tunjica Petrasevic: 15–31. Osijek: Faculty of Law, Josip Juraj Strossmayer University of Osijek.

New York Declaration for Refugees and Migrants. 2016. https://www.un.org/en/ga/search/view_doc.asp?symbol=A/RES/71/1.

Organization of American States (OAS). n.d. Who We Are, online document. http://www.oas.org/en/about/who_we_are.asp.

——. Charter of the Organization of American States (A-41), 30 April 1948. http://www.oas.org/en/sla/dil/docs/inter_american_treaties_A-41_charter_OAS.pdf.

———. Protocol of Buenos Aires, 27 February 1967 http://hrlibrary.umn.edu/oasinstr/buenosaires.html.
Olmos Giupponi, Belen. 2017. "Assessing the evolution of the Inter-American Court of Human Rights in the protection of migrants' rights: past, present and future." *The International Journal of Human Rights* 21 (9): 1477–1503.
Organization of American States (OAS). n.d. *Who We Are*. Online document. http://www.oas.org/en/about/who_we_are.asp.
Piovesan, Flavia. 2018. *Direitos humanos e justiça internacional: um estudo comparativo dos sistemas regionais europeu, interamericano e africano*. 9th ed. São Paulo: Saraiva.
Piovesan, Flavia, and Liliana Lyra Jubilut. 2011. "Americas." In *The 1951 Convention Relating to the Status of Refugees and 1967 Protocol: A Commentary*, edited by Andreas Zimmermman, Felix Machts and Jonas Dörschner: 204–224. Oxford: Oxford University Press.
Provost, René. 2002. *International Human Rights and Humanitarian Law*. Cambridge: Cambridge University Press.
Ramos, André de Carvalho. 2016. *Teoria Geral dos Direitos Humanos na Ordem Internacional*. 6th ed. São Paulo: Saraiva.
United Nations (UN). 1977. *Regional arrangements for the promotion and protection of human rights*. General Assembly Resolution. A/RES/32/127.
———. 2016. *New York Declaration for Refugees and Migrants*. General Assembly Resolution. A/RES/61/1.
———. 2018a. *Global Compact for Safe, Orderly and Regular Migration*. General Assembly Resolution. A/RES/73/195.
———. 2018b. *Global Compact on Refugees*. General Assembly. A/73/12 (Part II).
United Nations High Commissioner for Refugees (UNHCR). 1990. *The Refugee Convention, 1951: travaux preparatoires analysed with a commentary by Dr Paul Weiss*. Geneva: UNHCR.
———. 2016. U*NHCR welcomes "unprecedented force and resonance" of New York Declaration*. https://www.unhcr.org/57dff34f4.
———. 2017. *Cuadro n. 1 Definición de refugiados (Cartagena) Paises de América Latina que han incoporado a sua legislación nacional (por orden cronológico)*. https:acnur.org/fileadmin/Documentos/Proteccion/Buenas_Practicas/9183.pdf.
Universal Declaration of Human Rights. 1948. https://www.un.org/en/universal-declaration-human-rights/.

PART II COMMENTARY

The Inter-American Human Rights System and Refugee Protection

Deborah E. Anker[1]

Introduction

As Botero and Casagrande discuss in the preceding two chapters, the Inter-American Human Rights System (IAHRS) offers, in principle, a robust set of protections for persons seeking asylum in the Americas, including a broader definition of the word "refugee" than is contained in the 1951 Convention Relating to the Status of Refugees, a right to receive asylum, a right to fundamental due process, and protection from unreasonable detention. The instruments and bodies that compose this regime provide for the monitoring and promotion of human rights as well as specific remedies when abuses of these rights take place. In all, as David Cantor and Stefania Barichello have written, the IAHRS provides what is "probably the most expansive and generous framework for the protection of asylum-seekers and refugees to exist within the field of Human Rights Law" (Cantor and Barichello 2013: 700).

But there are also significant limitations that stand in the way of realizing these rights and protections. As is the case in other human rights regimes, domestic politics and the perceived self-interest of states can eclipse the realization of rights as laid out in human rights instruments. These limitations manifest in the Americas where two of the region's most powerful and influential states, Canada and the United States, have not ratified the region's major human rights instrument–the 1969 American Convention on Human Rights–and have not submitted to the jurisdiction of the Inter-American Court of Human Rights (IACtHR).

The Inter-American Commission on Human Rights (IACmHR) maintains that by ratifying the Charter of the Organization of American States (which references the IACmHR in article 106), the United States and Canada are bound, in good faith, to give effect to the IACmHR's rulings. Whereas Canada and the United States generally recognize the IACmHR's authority to process petitions and make recommendations, both states question the obligatory nature of those recommendations. The United States generally treats the rulings of the IACmHR as nonbinding, as does Canada. As some of the examples below illustrate, US and Canadian resistance weakens the human rights system as a whole.

Nongovernmental organizations (NGOs), which have grown in number and stature in recent decades, have played an increasingly important role within the region's refugee protection system. By bringing actions before the IACmHR and by pressing the United States in particular to comply with the IACmHR's rulings, NGOs have been instrumental in upholding the ideals of the IAHRS.[2]

Limitations of the IAHRS

Botero and Casagrande are correct to note that the IACtHR has tracked evolving human rights standards and consolidated the principles of refugee protection to safeguard the rights of, and provide relief to, a more inclusive set of persons in need of international protection. In turn, this has contributed to the "development and strengthening of public policies and laws in the areas of asylum, complementary protection, statelessness, and international protection in general," as Botero explains in this volume.

But the IACtHR's progress has been considerably limited–not because of internal structural shortcomings but because of its lack of jurisdiction over Canada and the United States. As such, a significant number of the refugees in the Americas are beyond the reach of what is arguably the strongest mechanism of enforcement for refugee protection in the region.

As Botero and Casagrande discuss in this volume, though, even those countries outside the jurisdiction of the IACtHR are still subject to the important quasi-adjudicatory process whereby the IACmHR may hear and decide on the merits of petitions by individuals alleging human rights violations by an Organization of American States (OAS) member state. As signatories of the American Declaration, Canada and the United States have an obligation to implement in good faith the IACmHR's recommendations, should the IACmHR find evidence of such violations.

Unfortunately, Canada and the United States, in practice, have not generally complied with these recommendations. The United States, for instance, has faced various allegations of human rights violations with regards to its asylum policies, and the IACmHR has on multiple occasions found the United States to be in violation of the American Declaration. In response, the United States has argued that it retains a sovereign right to develop and enforce its immigration policies.[3] For its part, the IACmHR maintains that "the American Declaration has acquired legally binding force by virtue of U.S. membership in the OAS and ratification of the Charter of the OAS."[4] But while the United States generally acknowledges the standards by which the IACmHR engages in monitoring,[5] the US regards the IACmHR's findings as soft law that does not create binding obligations.[6]

The United States has not been alone in this regard. In a case where Canada was found by the IACmHR to be in violation of an individual's right to seek asylum, Canada made similar statements about the lack of enforceability, arguing that "the Commission's decisions are not binding under International Law."[7]

The rejection of the legal force of the American Declaration and of the IACmHR's decisions has been accompanied by violations of some of the IAHRS's foundational principles. For example, Botero highlights the IACmHR's ruling that the principle of *non-refoulement* applies extraterritorially, and yet this finding, which came as a result of the United States' interception and interdiction of Haitian nationals fleeing the violent and autocratic Duvalier regime, was flatly rejected by the United States.[8] Botero also discusses another important feature of the IAHRS's refugee-protection regime–the principle against unnecessary detention of refugees and asylum seekers. In a case where the so-called Mariel Cubans alleged that they faced indefinite detention in the United States "without adequate evaluation in each individual case of the necessity for their continued imprisonment" and the IACmHR subsequently found the United States to be in violation of multiple articles of the American Declaration, the United States not only rejected the IACmHR's reasoning but also stopped corresponding altogether with the IACmHR, ignoring its recommendations for providing the petitioners relief.[9]

Such a disposition toward the IACmHR's decisions erodes the legitimacy of the IAHRS, resulting in disrespect even for the minimum guarantees it identifies, such as the right to a hearing. In 2019, the Canadian Parliament approved a bill containing a clause that would have stripped this right from asylum seekers who had first passed through a "safe" country in transit to Canada, only removing the clause after facing severe criticism from NGOs and various human rights organizations (Lim 2019).

In all, the relationship between the IAHRS and two of its most influential members casts a shadow over the expansive set of protections described in the preceding two chapters. One of the most blatant examples of the United States' defiance took place in March 2017, when the United States failed to appear at the IACmHR's forum for human rights in the Western Hemisphere (Dakwar 2017).[10] Standing outside the jurisdiction of the IACtHR and at times hostile to the mandate of the IACmHR, the United States and Canada have threatened a human rights system that relies in large part on compliance and legitimation from its member states.

The Role of NGOs

NGOs have been an integral part of the IAHRS, if not an informal member of it, and yet they often receive little recognition in the literature, not excepting Botero's and Casagrande's description and analysis in the preceding chapters. NGOs play a critical role in identifying and exposing human rights abuses, helping victims of these abuses to air their grievances in a public forum, and putting additional pressure on governments to provide protection.

Refugees are among the most vulnerable persons in society. As a result of this vulnerability, it is difficult and often dangerous for them to publicize the abuses they suffer. For this reason, "human rights activists . . . [have] relied on journalists and NGOs to publicize their cause, mobilize support, and secure protection for the displaced" (García 2006: 3).

NGOs have used the institutions of the IAHRS, in particular the IACmHR and the IACtHR, to publicize such abuses. In the early 1990s, for instance, Haitian and US NGOs presented a petition to the IACmHR challenging President Reagan's 1981 Haitian interdiction policy. The result was an IACmHR decision finding the United States in violation of provisions of various human rights instruments. In its ruling, the IACmHR emphasized that a person seeking refuge has a right to a hearing, regardless of whether he or she applies on land or is interdicted at sea.[11] In another case, US and Canadian NGOs worked together to file an IACmHR petition, challenging Canada's informal direct-back policy of returning asylum seekers who presented at its borders to the United States while they awaited assignment of a hearing date in Canada.[12] In 2011, the IACmHR ruled that Canada violated its human rights obligations when it returned refugee claimants to the United States without first providing individualized review of their asylum claims.[13] More recently, US and Canadian NGOs again partnered to file a request for Precautionary Measures against the United States with the IACmHR.[14] That request sought assurances that the United States would not deport detained asylum seekers who had been directed back from Canada due to pandemic-related border closures while they awaited the reopening of the border so their Canadian claims could be processed.

In exposing these abuses, NGOs at times have convinced governing bodies to strengthen and expand the rights at issue and have had some success in shaping public opinion and institutional norms. In the early 1990s, for instance, Haitian women called for a hearing on their de facto government's practice of systematic rape of Haitian women who were known or imputed supporters of the deposed president and opponents of the ruling regime. The IACmHR's subsequent investigation led to its 1995 *Report on the Situation of Human Rights in Haiti*, which contained, among other things, a historic ruling that rape under such circumstances constitutes torture (IACmHR 1995).[15] The IACmHR's ruling advanced the development of gender asylum law, and in following years, NGOs have invoked the 1995 report to support the claim that rape constitutes persecution in the context of refugee claims (Anker 2014: 46, 54). More recently, the US-based NGO Human Rights First, in partnership with five other US and Mexican human rights and nonprofit legal services organizations, called for the IACmHR to hold a thematic hearing on the topics of Mexico's role in cooperating with the United States in the implementation of the Remain in Mexico policy and of Mexico's failure to protect the human rights of persons returned to Mexico pursuant to that policy.[16] Legal clinics at the University of Texas at Austin, the University of Pennsylvania, and Harvard Law School joined in this action; the University of Texas and University of Pennsylvania clinics also issued their own request for a IACmHR in loco visit to the Mexican–US border, to which ninety-six civil society organizations and a hundred and twenty individuals signed on.[17]

Both NGOs and intergovernmental organizations like the IACmHR act to expose human rights abuses and offer recommendations to governments, and both are, practically speaking, at the mercy of governments to follow their recommendations. As James Franklin has noted, however, criticism from NGOs historically has been "more effective than criticism from inter-governmental organizations" (Franklin 2008: 187). The relative success of NGOs is due largely to their name-and-shame strategy, which they have developed since the 1970s and which has since become the "backbone of human rights promotion activities" (Shaver 2010: 667). The legitimacy these organizations have garnered allows them to place reputational sanctions on rights-abusing governments, which may be motivated to reform policies in order to combat the negative publicity these sanctions generate.

Like the IACmHR, the IACtHR, and the other institutions of the IAHRS, NGOs have their own limitations. But NGOs can function in ways that complement the actions of these formal bodies, in particular in securing the protection of refugees in the Americas. At best, each of these entities is able to compensate for the limitations of the others, developing a complex strategy for rights protection. Additionally, these entities can act flexibly and respond to rapidly developing situations. For example, during the coronavirus pandemic, NGOs and the IACtHR responded with recommendations for ensuring the safety of refugees on the United States' southern border, and the latter adopted urgent measures to include the early detection and treatment of COVID-19 as part of the services necessary for protecting the rights to health, life, and personal integrity of individuals found in migrant detention centers.[18]

Botero ends his chapter by stating that "history tells us that the main conquests in the field of human rights will prevail at the end of the day going against all odds." Those odds are greatly improved when NGOs and international organizations work together or at least on parallel tracks to expose human rights abuses and to develop and apply relevant norms.

Deborah E. Anker is Professor of Law and the Founder of the Harvard Law School Immigration and Refugee Clinical Program (HIRC). Author of the leading and annually updated treatise *Law of Asylum in the United States*, Anker has co-drafted groundbreaking Gender Asylum Guidelines and amicus curiae briefs. Professor Anker has received numerous awards, including the Elmer Fried Excellence in Teaching Award from the American Immigration Lawyers' Association (AILA), and the AILA Founder's Award for the Women's Refugee Project. Most recently, she received AILA's Arthur C. Helton Memorial Human Rights Award for HIRC's groundbreaking work.

Notes

1. The author wishes to give special thanks to Logan Seymour for his outstanding research assistance.
2. For other examples of actions by civil society groups, see Cavallaro et al. (2019: 207–12).
3. See, e.g., Andrea Mortlock v. United States, Case 12.534, Inter-Am. Comm'n H.R., Report 63/08, OEA/Ser.L/V/II.134, doc. 5 rev. 1 para. 47 (2008): "The State argues that the Declaration is a nonbinding document that creates no right to health or medical care and acknowledges limits to any purported health right." See also Rafael Ferrer-Mazorra et al. v. United States, Case 9903, Inter-Am. Comm'n H.R., Report 51/01, OEA/Ser.L/V/ II.111, doc. 20 rev. para. 129 (2001): "[A] state has absolute sovereign authority to detain and exclude excludable aliens, which authority is not restricted or otherwise the subject of rights or obligations under the American Declaration."
4. The Haitian Centre for Human Rights et al. v. United States, Case 10.675, Inter-Am. Comm'n H.R., Report 51/96, OEA/Ser.L/V/II.95 doc. 7 rev. para. 66 (1997).

5. See, e.g., Gilman 2013, fn. 166, citing Philip Workman v. United States, Case 12.261, Inter-Am. Comm'n H.R., Report 33/06, OEA/Ser.L/V/II.127 doc. 4 rev. 1 para. 63 (2007) (setting forth the United States' argument that the petition should be rejected "on the basis that it fails to state a violation of the American Declaration"); citing Roach & Pinkerton v. United States, Case 9647, Inter-Am. Comm'n H.R., Report 3/87, OEA/Ser.IJV/II.71, doc. 9 rev. 1 para. 38 (1987) (setting forth the United States' argument that the IACmHR should look to the American Declaration for the relevant standards in analyzing the claim against the United States); citing Henkin, Louis, et al. *Human Rights*, 2nd ed., New York: Foundation Press, (2009), 620 (noting that the United States has somewhat contradictory positions regarding the binding nature of the American Declaration).
6. See, e.g., The Haitian Centre for Human Rights et al. v. United States (n 4) para. 66: "The United States rejects the petitioners' contention that the American Declaration has acquired legally binding force by virtue of US membership in the OAS and ratification of the Charter of the OAS. Because the United States has previously noted, the Declaration is not a treaty and has not acquired binding legal force."
7. See John Doe et al. v. Canada, Case 12.586, Inter-Am. Comm'n H.R., Report 24/11, OEA/Ser.L/V/II.141, doc. 29 para. 120 (2011).
8. See The Haitian Centre for Human Rights et al. v. United States (n 4).
9. See Rafael Ferrer-Mazorra et al. v. United States (n 3).
10. "In the past, when U.S. governments have sought to express displeasure at having their records scrutinized, they have occasionally protested by sending lower-level officials. But today's refusal to engage the commission at all is a deeply troubling indication of its disrespect for human rights norms and the institutions that oversee their protection." Dakwar 2017.
11. See The Haitian Centre for Human Rights et al. v. United States (n 4).
12. For a discussion about the Canada–U.S. Safe Third Country Agreement and the challenges to it, see Paperny 2019; Smith and Hofmann 2019. Most recently, a 2020 Federal Court of Canada decision struck down the Safe Third Country Agreement between the United States and Canada, ruling that the treaty violated Canada's Charter of Rights and Freedoms due to the fact that the United States could not be deemed a safe country for refugees. https://www.nytimes.com/2020/07/22/world/canada/asylum-Safe-Third-Country-Agreement.html.
13. John Doe et al. v. Canada (n 6).
14. Nduwimana et al v. United States, MC-146-21, filed February 4, 2021 by the Harvard Immigration and Refugee Clinic, Freedom House Detroit, the Refugee Law Office of Legal Aid Ontario and the Canadian Council for Refugees (pending as of March 12, 2021).
15. 1995 Report on the Situation of Human Rights in Haiti, Inter-Am. Comm'n H.R., OEA/Ser.L/v/II.88 doc. 10 rev. (1995)
16. For a description of the Remain in Mexico policy, see *The Latin America Working Group*. "All About the 'Remain in Mexico' Policy" (2019). https://www.lawg.org/all-about-the-remain-in-mexico-policy/.

17. For more on the work of one of the leading law school clinics challenging US policies, see University of Texas (2019). For an example of scholarship on this subject, see Gilman (2013).
18. These urgent measures issued by the IACtHR were adopted in connection with the supervision of the implementation of the IACtHR's judgement in the case *Vélez Loor vs. Panama*, originally decided in 2010. See http://www.corteidh.or.cr/docs/medidas/velez_se_01.pdf; the original 2010 decision can be found at http://www.corteidh.or.cr/docs/casos/articulos/seriec_218_ing.pdf. For a legal analysis of this decision, see http://opiniojuris.org/2020/05/30/iachr-decision-in-velez-loor-v-panama-covid-19-and-human-rights-in-the-courts/.

References

Anker, Deborah E. 2014. "Legal Change from the Bottom Up: The Development of Gender Asylum Jurisprudence in the United States." In *Gender in Refugee Law: From the Margins to the Centre*, edited by Efrat Arbel, Catherine Dauvergne, and Jenni Millbank: 46 et seq. New York: Routledge.

Cantor, David James, and Stefania Eugenia Barichello. 2013. "The Inter-American human rights system: a new model for integrating refugee and complementary protection?." *International Journal of Human Rights*, 17 (5–6): 689–706.

Cavallaro, James L., Claret Vargas, Clara Sandoval, and Bernard Duhaime, with Caroline Bettinger-Lopez, Stephanie Erin Brewer, Diana Guzman, and Cecilia Naddeo. 2019. *Doctrine, Practice, and Advocacy in the Inter-American Human Rights System*. New York: Oxford University Press.

Dakwar, Jamil. 2017. "In an Unprecedented No-Show, the U.S. Pulls Out of Planned Human Rights Hearing." *ACLU*. https://www.aclu.org/blog/human-rights/unprecedented-no-show-us-pulls-out-planned-human-rights-hearing.

Franklin, James C. 2008. "Shame on You: The Impact of Human Rights Criticism on Political Repression in Latin America." *International Studies Quarterly*, 52 (1): 187–211.

García, María Cristina. 2006. *Seeking Refuge: Central American Migration to Mexico, the United States, and Canada*. Berkeley: University of California Press.

Gilman, Denise. 2013. "Realizing Liberty: The Use of International Human Rights Law to Realign Immigration Detention in the United States." *Fordham International Law Journal*, 36 (2): 243–333.

Inter-American Commission on Human Rights (IACmHR). 1995. *Report on the Situation of Human Rights in Haiti*. OEA/Ser.L/v/II.88 doc. 10 rev. http://www.cidh.org/countryrep/EnHa95/EngHaiti.htm.

Lim, Jolson. 2019. "House committee adds guaranteed oral pre-removal hearing to asylum changes." *iPolitics*. https://ipolitics.ca/2019/05/27/house-committee-adds-guaranteed-oral-pre-removal-hearing-to-asylum-changes.

Paperny, Anna Mehler. 2019. "Canada Defends Safe Third Country Agreement as Court Challenge Wraps Up." *Global News*. https://globalnews.ca/news/6148781/safe-third-country-agreement-court/.

Shaver, Lea. 2010. "The Inter-American Human Rights System: An Effective Institution for Regional Rights Protection?" *Washington University Global Studies Law Review* 9 (4): 639–676.

Smith, Craig Damian, and Stephanie Hofmann. 2019. "Will Canada Suspend its Safe Third Country Agreement with the United States?." *Foreign Policy.* https://foreignpolicy.com/2019/11/06/canada-suspend-safe-third-country-immigration-united-states/.

University of Texas. 2019. "Experiential Learning: Clinics." University of Texas at Austin School of Law, Austin. https://law.utexas.edu/clinics/immigration/.

Part III

Regional Responses to the International Regime on Refugee Protection

7

From the Brasilia Declaration to the Brazil Plan of Action

How Was the Goal of Eradicating Statelessness in the Americas Forged?

Juan Ignacio Mondelli

Introduction

With the adoption of the 2014 Brazil Declaration and Plan of Action (BPA),[1] twenty-eight Latin American countries and three Caribbean territories[2] committed themselves to eradicate statelessness in America for the first time in their history. This instrument, the BPA, marked the climax of a process initiated several years back with the 2010 Brasilia Declaration on the Protection of Refugees and Stateless Persons in the Americas (Brasilia Declaration).

As discussed in this chapter, after the adoption of the Brasilia Declaration in 2010, the idea that statelessness was a human rights problem that merited greater attention and a coordinated regional response for its eradication was consolidated by OAS General Assembly resolutions on statelessness, voluntary pledges on statelessness the countries assumed in 2011, jurisprudence and advisory opinions of the Inter-American Court of Human Rights (IACtHR), and Inter-American Commission on Human Rights (IACmHR) promotional efforts. The region's countries lacked a strategic framework to guide such efforts, however, and the BPA filled that gap.

As this chapter shows, the regional instruments on refugees adopted in recent years were the engine driving the states' efforts to address the international protection of stateless persons–even if they are not refugees–and the prevention and resolution of cases of statelessness.[3]

Although statelessness is treated rather timidly or modestly in the Brasilia Declaration, over the years the regional instruments on refugees have started to incorporate a more marked language of statelessness and to include the states' specific commitments and best practices. At present, then, a book dedicated to the study of regional instruments on refugee protection in the Americas cannot fail to consider how these instruments have contributed to addressing the problem of statelessness.

This chapter examines the contents on statelessness of the Brasilia Declaration and explores the regional developments that followed it, especially the BPA, up to the 100 Points of Brasilia (United Nations High Commissioner for Refugees [UNHCR] 2018). It seeks to answer the question of whether the actions of the BPA program for eradicating statelessness reflect international obligations for the states, and, if so, on what grounds.

Methodologically, the chapter recaps the regional developments, starting with the Brasilia Declaration that led to adoption of the Eradicating Statelessness program (BPA 2014: 17). It then takes a strictly legal focus to analyze whether the actions provided there are obligatory in nature.

Based on six years of experience as UNHCR statelessness officer for the Americas, and having been involved in the discussion and negotiation of the BPA, I have written this chapter with the aim of providing tools to practitioners and key stakeholders (civil society organizations, e.g.) for strengthening their advocacy work to achieve the Program's goals. An understanding of the humanitarian and political dimensions of the Statelessness Eradication Program by the state authorities responsible for its implementation is certainly important, but of equal importance is an awareness of the legal implications of an eventual failure to implement it, which could be a motivating factor to do so.

The Brasilia Declaration

In November 2010 eighteen Latin American countries[4] adopted the Brasilia Declaration in a gathering to mark the sixtieth anniversary of UNHCR. Their main purpose was to prepare an intergovernmental commemorative event for the sixtieth anniversary of the 1951 Convention Relating to the Status of Refugees (1951 Refugee Convention) and the fiftieth anniversary of the 1961 Convention on the Reduction of Statelessness (1961 Convention), to take place in Geneva in 2011.

The Brasilia Declaration was not connected to the commemoration of the 1984 Cartagena Declaration on Refugees (Cartagena Declaration). Actually, the Brasilia meeting was still reverberating with the ten-point Plan of Action

(UNHCR 2007), where the UNHCR had proposed a way to address the protection of refugees in the context of mixed migration. When the Brasilia Declaration was adopted, the countries were still looking at the conclusions and recommendations of the San José meeting (UNHCR 2009) and their primary concern was extra-regional migration.

The Brasilia Declaration was focused on encouraging application of "the Mexico Plan of Action [2004] as the regional framework to address new challenges related to the identification and protection of refugees in the context of mixed migratory movements" (Brasilia Declaration: Operative para. 3). The question before the countries was how to use the Mexico Declaration and Plan of Action to Strengthen the International Protection of Refugees in Latin America framework to address the challenges posed by mixed movements.

The Brasilia Declaration is perhaps the first regional instrument on refugee protection where the connections between migratory issues and international protection can be seen clearly marked. The countries underscored, for example, the need to consider if migrants and victims of trafficking required international protection as refugees (Brasilia Declaration: Operative para. 6). They also highlighted the importance of providing greater opportunities for regular migration and migratory policies that respect international human right law for preserving the space for refugee protection (Brasilia Declaration: Operative para. 9).

The Brasilia Declaration also emphasizes the importance of using regional migration forums to develop safeguards for the protection of refugees, victims of trafficking, and children who are unaccompanied or have been separated from their families (Brasilia Declaration: Whereas para. 15).

Moreover, the Brasilia Declaration highlighted an approach that UNHCR had promoted with renewed emphasis from the start of the previous decade: the importance of considering *age, gender,* and *diversity* to respond to the *differentiated assistance and protection needs* of men and women, boys and girls, adolescents and older adults (about age sixty-five and above), persons with disabilities, indigenous people, and afro-descendants (Brasilia Declaration: Whereas para. 6).

Although statelessness was not its central theme, the Brasilia Declaration was fundamental for renewing the interest of Latin American countries in statelessness, a theme that was completely absent in the Mexico Declaration and Plan of Action to Strengthen the International Protection of Refugees in Latin America, the 1994 San José Declaration on Refugees and Displaced Persons and the Cartagena Declaration. In this field, the Brasilia Declaration focused on three areas: (1) accession to or ratification of conventions on statelessness, (2) review of national legislation to prevent and reduce statelessness, and (3) strengthening of national mechanisms for ensuring universal birth registration (Brasilia Declaration: para. 7).

Statelessness and refugee protection are issues with a multitude of connections. Statelessness may be a cause of forced displacement of a person who becomes a refugee after crossing an international border, for example. In addition, the arbitrary deprivation of nationality may amount to persecution in the sense of the definition of "refugee" in the 1951 Refugee Convention. In other words, statelessness may lead to the recognition of refugee status in certain cases. Finally, statelessness may prevent voluntary repatriation, in safe and dignified conditions, to the country of origin.

As indicated in the BPA, statelessness implies a violation of the human right to a nationality (BPA: 3). It is a humanitarian problem that affects millions of people the world over and that in the Americas especially affects several Caribbean countries.

The question of protection of refugees who are not considered to be nationals by any state under the operation of its law (stateless refugees) has always been implicit in the regional instruments on refugees. As we know, the definition of "refugee" in Article 1(A) of the 1951 Refugee Convention includes both persecuted persons who are nationals of a country and those who are stateless. The merit of the Brasilia Declaration, however, is that it has made a call to respond to the situation of stateless persons who do not qualify as refugees under the 1951 Refugee Convention or the Cartagena Declaration.

OAS General Assembly Resolutions on Statelessness (2010–2014)

Between 1985 and 2015, after adoption by the countries of the Cartagena Declaration, the OAS General Assembly held thirty-one ordinary meetings and adopted twenty-eight resolutions on refugees.[5] Some of these resolutions included references to the issue of statelessness. Thus, for example, the OAS General Assembly urged accession to the conventions on statelessness in its 1999, 2001, 2002, 2003, 2004, and 2009 resolutions on refugees.[6]

It was not until 2010, however, that the OAS General Assembly approved its first resolution on the Prevention and Reduction of Statelessness and Protection of Stateless Persons in the Americas.[7] The resolution was adopted in June, meaning that it preceded the Brasilia Declaration by several months. The adoption of the two instruments in such a short period of time gave renewed impetus to the topic of statelessness in the region.

Over the years, the contents of the 2010 resolution were expanded through new, special resolutions adopted in 2011, 2013, and 2014.[8] In 2014, for example, the OAS General Assembly adopted its most complete and visionary resolution on statelessness. Taking advantage of the commemoration of the thirtieth anniversary of the Cartagena Declaration (Cartagena+30) and the sixtieth anniversary of the 1954 Convention relating to the Status of Stateless Persons (1954 Convention), the OAS General Assembly invited the states to identify the challenges and actions needed to eradicate statelessness in the Americas. It also called for inclusion of a chapter on statelessness in the future regional strategic framework to be adopted at the conclusion of the commemoration (BPA).

The 2014 resolution instructed the Inter-American Juridical Committee to draft a set of guidelines on the protection of stateless persons. It also proposed that member states should (1) consider ratifying or acceding to the conventions on statelessness, (2) create or strengthen the technical agencies responsible for overseeing their proper implementation, (3) follow up on the commitments assumed at the Ministerial Intergovernmental Event on Refugees and Stateless Persons, (4) amend or adopt domestic laws to comprehensively regulate all matters relating to the identification and protection of stateless persons, and (5) include in their nationality laws appropriate safeguards to prevent new cases of statelessness and to eliminate existing cases.

Voluntary Pledges (2011)

The states' renewed interest in statelessness, reflected in the OAS resolution and the Brasilia Declaration, led various countries in the region to make voluntary pledges on this topic in the Ministerial Intergovernmental Event on Refugees and Stateless Persons held in Geneva in December 2011 (UNHCR 2011).

Argentina, Colombia, and Ecuador pledged accession to the 1961 Convention, while Haiti, Honduras, Paraguay, and Peru pledged to accede to both conventions. All these pledges have now been fulfilled. Argentina acceded on 13 November 2014, Colombia on 15 August 2014, and Ecuador on 24 September 2012. Meanwhile, Haiti acceded to the two conventions on 27 September 2018, Honduras on 1 October 2012 (1954 Convention) and 18 December 2012 (1961 Convention), Paraguay on 6 June 2012 (1961 Convention) and 1 July 2014 (1954 Convention), and Peru on 23 January 2014 (1954 Convention) and 18 December 2014 (1961 Convention).[9]

Brazil,[10] Costa Rica,[11] Peru, the United States, and Uruguay[12] pledged to establish, or take measures to establish, statelessness determination procedures. With the sole exceptions of Peru and the United States, all the countries enacted special stateless person protection laws that created such procedures. In fact, Brazil and Costa Rica went one step farther and became the first countries in the region to facilitate the naturalization of stateless refugees and stateless migrants.

The United States also pledged to address statelessness through foreign policy initiatives. Likewise, the Plurinational State of Bolivia, Mexico, and Panama made general pledges to respect international principles and actions in matters of statelessness (UNHCR 2011: 36–38). All these pledges were fulfilled. In fact, the United States also played a key role in supporting initiatives to eliminate gender discrimination in nationality laws and Panama enacted a protection law–going beyond its initial pledge.

With these voluntary pledges, many of the region's countries remained on board and made steady progress on implementing a statelessness eradication agenda until the Cartagena+30 commemoration opened up a unique opportunity in 2014.

Statelessness in the BPA

Viewed in retrospect, the national and regional developments since 2010, together with the fact that the topic of statelessness had been absent in earlier commemorative events for the Cartagena Declaration, would have made us think that the need to commit to the eradication of statelessness was obvious for the states.

There was no such clarity, however, at the beginning of 2014, when the Cartagena+30 commemorative process was launched. Some countries did not entirely understand the problem of statelessness. Other countries had wrong ideas of its dimensions (e.g., they believed that statelessness was a problem of other regions and that it almost did not exist in the Americas). Finally, some countries were of the idea that acquisition of nationality through jus sanguinis and jus soli was enough for addressing the problem. UNHCR thus had an important role to play in explaining the problem and advocating the inclusion of a special chapter in the BPA (UNHCR 2015b: 58).

Discussion and Negotiation of the Plan

Cartagena +30 was a meeting space where the states, UNHCR, civil society, and other international organizations reflected on the progress and challenges of international protection and the pragmatic way to address them (see Arnold-Fernández, Sarmiento Torres, and Kallas in this volume).

The process included four subregional consultations as follows: in Argentina for the the Mercado Común del Sur (MERCOSUR; Southern Common Market) countries, in Ecuador for the Andean countries, in Nicaragua for the Mesoamerican countries, and, finally, in Grand Cayman for the Caribbean countries and territories. The problem of statelessness was discussed in all the consultations except those in Quito.

The four subregional consultations adopted documents with conclusions and recommendations that served for preparing the drafts of the BPA. These drafts were then discussed and negotiated by the countries in the Group of Latin America and Caribbean Countries in Geneva and, finally, were adopted by acclaim during the final ministerial event held in Brazil (UNHCR 2015a: 12–17).

In the BPA, the states reiterated that every person has the right to a nationality, described statelessness as a violation of that individual right, and reaffirmed that the state's prerogative to regulate nationality in its internal legislation is limited by international law. Furthermore, the states welcomed the UNHCR Global Action Plan to End Statelessness (Global Action Plan) and reaffirmed their commitment to eradicate statelessness (BPA: 2, 5).

In turn, chapter 6 of the BPA proposed to implement, as part of the Eradicating Statelessness program, the following actions for ending this problem, as relevant in each country: (1) accede to the statelessness conventions, (2) harmonize internal legislation and practice on nationality with international standards, (3) facilitate universal birth registration and the issuance of documentation proving nationality, (4) establish statelessness determination procedures, (5) adopt legal frameworks for protecting stateless persons, (6) facilitate naturalization, (7) confirm nationality, and (8) facilitate restoration and recovery of nationality (ibid.: 17–18).

These actions were proposed following the guidelines of the Brasilia Declaration and the resolutions of the OAS General Assembly and, in essence, cover the four thematic areas of the UNHCR's mandate on statelessness: identification, prevention, protection, and reduction of statelessness.

The Eradicating Statelessness program of the BPA is a regional roadmap for reaching the goal of eradication in the Americas. It represents a historic milestone in that never before had Latin American and Caribbean countries come together for a common goal such as this. Since 2014, the program has received the backing of the OAS General Assembly in 2017, 2018, and 2019.

In November 2014 the UNHCR launched the Global Action Plan with the aim of eradicating statelessness in the world within ten years. The Global Action Plan (UNHCR 2014a: 2), which comprises ten actions that should be implemented to eradicate statelessness, was developed simultaneously with the BPA. A fundamental difference, however, is that the Global Action Plan was elaborated by UNHCR in consultation with the states, international organizations, and civil society organizations, whereas the BPA is an instrument that was discussed, negotiated, and adopted by states.

Nonetheless, the BPA is not an initiative unconnected to the Global Action Plan (ibid.: 2); it represents, rather, the Latin America and Caribbean response to UNHCR's call to eradicate statelessness. Hence, the two instruments are complementary and should be read together.

Eradicating Statelessness Program Actions: Obligation or State Prerogative?

Having reviewed the actions proposed by the Eradicating Statelessness program of the BPA, we will now try to determine if they represent merely voluntary commitments or in reality reflect international obligations.

Accession to Statelessness Conventions

From the standpoint of international law, the signing, accession, or ratification of an international treaty by a state is a completely voluntary act. A commitment to accede to the conventions on statelessness cannot be translated as an international obligation for a state.

Colombia, for example, signed the 1954 Convention on 30 December 1954. In 2012 Congress approved it through Law 1588 and the Constitutional Court declared it constitutional in Ruling C-622/13 of 10 September 2013. Until early October 2019, the only pending action was the deposit of the instrument of ratification. The authorities had said that they would not deposit said instrument in order not to recognize the jurisdiction of the International Court of Justice, pursuant to Article 34 of the 1954 Convention. Colombia's support for the Eradicating Statelessness program, or its commitment to consider the possibility of becoming a state party, never entailed an obligation to deposit said instrument of ratification. On 7 October 2019, however, Colombia eventually deposited the instrument at a special treaty event held in Geneva.

Harmonization of Internal Legislation and Practice on Nationality with International Standards

According to general international law, a state cannot allege provisions of its internal law as justification for breaching the obligations arising from the international treaties to which it is a party. For the States Parties to the 1979 Convention on the Elimination of All Forms of Discrimination against Women (CEDAW), for example, this obligation implies that they have to adapt their nationality laws to eliminate discrimination against women in those laws.[13]

Likewise, under the 1969 American Convention on Human Rights (ACHR), the States Parties have the obligation to respect and ensure the rights and freedoms safeguarded in it (ACHR: art. 1.1), including the right to nationality, as well as a general duty to adopt such legislative or other measures as may be needed to give them effect (ibid.: art. 2).

This means that the States Parties must adapt their nationality laws and practices, as necessary, to harmonize them with the standards of the ACHR, in accordance with the way this is interpreted and applied by the IACtHR (see Botero and Casagrande in this volume). In other words, states are internationally obligated to exercise a *control of conventionality* of its laws and practice on nationality to ensure they do not violate the ACHR.

The IACtHR has stated that, although domestic courts and judges are obligated to apply their domestic laws, the fact that the state is a party to the ACHR means they should ensure that the effects of its provisions are not diminished by the application of domestic laws contrary to its object and purpose: "The Judiciary must exercise a sort of 'conventionality control' between the domestic legal provisions which are applied to specific cases and the American Convention on Human Rights. To perform this task, the Judiciary has to take into account not only the treaty, but also the interpretation thereof made by the Inter-American Court, which is the ultimate interpreter of the American Convention." (IACtHR 2006a: para. 124).[14]

The IACtHR repeated this guideline in the case of *La Cantuta v. Peru* (IACtHR 2006c),[15] and then went on to refine the notion of conventionality control, affirming that (1) it implies *verifying the compatibility of domestic laws and practices* with the ACHR, the jurisprudence of the IACtHR, and other inter-American treaties to which the state is a party; (2) it is an *obligation* of *all public authorities*, within the scope of their competencies, and it should even be done ex officio (IACtHR 2006b)[16]; and (3) its purpose is to abolish laws contrary to the ACHR or provide an interpretation or application of the domestic laws in accordance with it (IACtHR 2005).

The IACtHR has made it clear that conventionality control extends even to the guidelines issuing from its advisory opinions.

> Pursuant to international law, when a State is a party to an international treaty, such as the American Convention on Human Rights, such treaty is binding for all its organs, including the Judiciary and the Legislature, so that a violation by any of these organs gives rise to the international responsibility of the State. Accordingly, *the Court considers that the different organs of the State must carry out the corresponding control of conformity with the Convention, based also on the considerations of the Court in exercise of its non-contentious or advisory jurisdiction*, which undeniably shares with its contentious jurisdiction the goal of the inter-American human rights system, which is "the protection of the fundamental rights of the human being. (IACtHR 2014: para. 31; italics added)

In OC-24/17, the IACtHR reiterated that conventionality control includes the guidelines of its advisory opinions.[17]

To sum up, the harmonization of internal legislation and practice on nationality with international standards implies, in reality, an international obligation for the states.

This conclusion is evidenced by the resolution of the National Civil Registry of Colombia, which granted nationality to children of Venezuelan mothers or fathers in situations of statelessness, or at risk of statelessness, who had been born in that country's territory (Colombia 2019). As can be seen from its whereas clauses, the legal basis for this resolution rested, to a large extent, on the international commitments assumed by Colombia on matters of human rights and prevention of statelessness. In particular, the resolution refers to the guidelines of the IACtHR on the right to a nationality and to acquire the nationality of the country where the person was born if he or she has no right to acquire another nationality.[18]

Facilitate Universal Birth Registration and the Issuance of Documentation Proving Nationality

According to Article 7 of the 1989 Convention on the Rights of the Child, the state is obligated to register a child immediately after its birth, and the child has the right from birth to acquire a nationality. The States Parties must ensure the enforcement of these rights in accordance with their national legislation and pertinent international obligations, especially when the child would otherwise be stateless.

Since the state must register all births that take place in its territory, the question is to determine to what extent it is obligated to *facilitate* such registration. Since universal registration of births can be viewed as an obligation, the granting of facilities for registration would be no more than a mechanism for the state to fulfil this obligation, if otherwise the births could not be registered.

Failure to register births can generate risks of statelessness when there are serious legal barriers or practices for proving the fact of the birth (during a late registration, for example). In addition, lack of registration due to discriminatory reasons (national origin, ethnicity, or migratory status of the parents, for example) amounts to an arbitrary denial of nationality that may result in statelessness.

With regard to this point, the IACtHR has said that the requirements demanded by a state to prove birth in the territory should be reasonable and cannot pose an obstacle to acquiring nationality. States should therefore take all necessary measures to ensure that children who need it have access to late registration in conditions of equality and non-discrimination and can exercise and fully enjoy their right to nationality (IACtHR 2005).

The IACtHR indicated that the rejection of late birth registration for discriminatory reasons can equal a denial of nationality and result in statelessness. This in turn implies an impossibility of receiving the state's protection and leads to a well-founded fear of being expelled from the country or separated from family (ibid.: para. 173).

With regard to the requirements set by domestic law for late birth registration, the IACtHR has indicated that they should be coherent with the right to nationality and aimed at accrediting that the birth occurred on the state's territory (ibid.: para. 190). According to the IACtHR, the requirements cannot be an obstacle for enjoying the right to nationality (ibid.: para. 192) nor impose an undue and disproportionate burden of proof for registration of the birth (ibid.: para. 162).

It could be debated to what extent the state should facilitate birth registration. Thus, for example, it could be debated whether a state is obligated to establish late birth registration procedures that allow a person to apply from a foreign country through a consulate or embassy. Likewise, it could be debated whether a state is obligated to implement biometric tools for remotely verifying the identity of a person or the authenticity of the statements and documents needed for starting the process, either from a foreign country or from a remote or almost inaccessible spot in the interior of the country. What cannot be debated is the existence, as such, of the state's obligation to provide facilities according to the needs. This action of the BPA, then, in reality reflects an international obligation of the states.

Establishment of Statelessness Determination Procedures

Since the adoption of the BPA, Argentina (2019), Brazil (2017b), Costa Rica (2016), Ecuador (2017a, 2017b), Uruguay (2018), Panama (2019), and Paraguay (2018) have adopted statelessness determination procedures.

Statelessness determination procedures allow a state to determine when a person is not considered as a national by any state, under the operation of its law. Although the 1954 Convention does not expressly refer to such procedures, the states implicitly have a responsibility to identify stateless persons in order to provide them appropriate treatment according to their standards (UNHCR 2014b: paras. 8, 114). At present, twenty-two countries in the Americas are States Parties to the 1954 Convention[19] and therefore are obligated to establish such procedures, if they have not already done so.

This obligation also exists with respect to member states of the OAS, even if they are not parties to the 1954 Convention or the ACHR. In its Advisory Opinion OC-21/14 (IACtHR 2014), the IACtHR defined "international protection" as the protection received by asylum seekers, refugees, and those who receive complementary protection or other forms of humanitarian protection, as well as the protection received by stateless persons (ibid.: para. 37).

Based on Article 19 of the ACHR and Article VII of the 1948 American Declaration on the Rights and Duties of Man, the IACtHR indicated that border authorities should allow foreign children to enter a state's territory, even if they are not accompanied, and determine their nationality or stateless status (ibid.: para. 86).

The IACtHR sustained, citing UNHCR guidelines, that states should establish or strengthen, depending on the case, procedures for determining statelessness. Such procedures should be fair and efficient and responsive to the needs of age, gender, and diversity (ibid.: fn169).

With regard to the scope of the consultation, Advisory Opinion OC-21/14 limited itself to the situation of migrant children. Nonetheless, since it followed UNHCR guidelines, the IACtHR clearly invoked a broader international obligation regarding the establishment of statelessness procedures as equally applicable to the situation of children. It can therefore be affirmed that the action regarding the establishment of statelessness determination procedures under the Brazil Plan of Action reflects an international obligation of the states.

Adoption of Legal Frameworks for Protecting Stateless Persons

The OAS resolutions on statelessness and human rights have promoted the adoption of domestic laws for the protection of stateless persons. With regard to resolutions on statelessness, the 2010 resolution, for example, promoted "the adoption of institutional mechanisms and procedures" for implementing the conventions on statelessness. In 2011 the resolution urged member states "without prejudice to their ratification of, or accession to, the international instruments on statelessness, to consider adoption of domestic legal provisions to . . . protect stateless persons." In 2014 the resolution called countries "to consider amending or adopting, as applicable, domestic laws to comprehensively regulate all matters relating to the identification and protection of stateless people and their appropriate documentation."[20]

The resolutions on human rights followed along this same line. Thus, for example, the 2017 resolution recommended the states "consider the possibility of including, in their domestic laws, fair and efficient procedures for determining statelessness."[21]

The ACHR recognizes that every person has the right to seek and be granted asylum. It does not expressly contemplate, however, a right to seek and receive protection as a stateless person (non-refugee). At first sight, it would appear that a state would not be obligated to adopt legislative measures to ensure the protection of stateless persons, under Articles 1.1 and 2 of the ACHR. The following reasons could support the opposite argument, however.

In the first place, as state practice demonstrates, the adoption of a legal framework (law, decree, regulation, etc.) is necessary for establishing a statelessness determination procedure, which is, as was seen, a state obligation according to IACtHR guidelines.

In the second place, it is usually necessary for states to adopt legal frameworks to ensure that the human rights of stateless persons are effectively guaranteed in practice. Given the special situation in which stateless persons find themselves in, recognition of their legal personality under Article 3 of the ACHR may require the country to regulate everything regarding their identification, registration, and issuance of identity documentation. In the same way, laws may need to be adopted to regulate the guarantees of due process (right to be heard or right of appeal, for example) in the statelessness determination procedures, under Articles 8 and 25 of the ACHR.

In the third place, in accordance with IACtHR jurisprudence, the restrictions permitted for the enjoyment and exercise of the rights and liberties safeguarded by the ACHR cannot be applied unless they are pursuant to *laws*. The IACtHR has stated that the word "laws" refers to legal norms of a general nature, directed toward the general welfare, passed by constitutionally provided and democratically elected legislatures, and drafted according to the procedure established by the constitutions of the States Parties for the formulation of laws.[22] From this it follows that the human rights of stateless persons can be restricted only pursuant to a law and, as a result, the adoption of a legal framework is usually necessary.

Finally, with regard to the 1954 Convention, although it does not expressly establish an obligation to adopt legal frameworks, their adoption may clearly be necessary to make effective domestically those conventional rights that are not self-executing. Thus, for example, the obligation to provide administrative assistance will usually require a determination of the measures needed to put this assistance into effect.

To sum up, there are good arguments to sustain that the adoption of legal frameworks for protecting stateless persons could be considered obligatory for the States Parties to the ACHR or the 1954 Convention.

Facilitating Naturalization

The acquisition, restoration, and recovery of a nationality is the only way to resolve the problem of statelessness. The problem is that, most of the time, stateless persons cannot meet the requirements that states usually demand of foreigners who have a nationality and are seeking to naturalize; stateless persons by definition cannot present a current, valid national passport. Providing facilities, then, such as making requirements more flexible (e.g., reducing the residency period) or waiving the presentation of certain documents (birth certificate or passport, e.g.), is a necessary condition for these people to be able to naturalize. Otherwise, they will be asked for requirements that are impossible for them to meet.

According to Article 34 of the1951 Refugee Convention, the states should facilitate the naturalization of stateless refugees. Article 32 of the 1954 Convention establishes the same obligation with respect to stateless persons who are not refugees.[23] So what happens with the states that are parties to the

ACHR but not the 1954 Convention? Do they have to facilitate the naturalization of stateless persons?

The jurisprudence of the IACtHR does not expressly resolve this question. Facilitating the naturalization of stateless migrants can be understood as the minimum content of the right to a nationality and therefore an obligation for the state, however (Mondelli 2019).

The right of every individual, including stateless individuals, to a nationality (ACHR: art. 20.1) demands positive discrimination in favor of persons who would otherwise see their right as unachievable. If the focus were otherwise, it would wind up frustrating the purpose of the law, which is to ensure the existence of the bond of nationality and the state protection deriving thereof.

In the Advisory Opinion OC-4/84, the IACtHR addressed, for the first time, the question of the content and scope of Article 20 of the ACHR regarding naturalization (IACtHR 1984). There it said that the *conditions and procedures* for naturalization were matters that depended *primarily* on domestic law. It is the state that should determine to what extent there are conditions to ensure an effective link exists between an applicant for naturalization and the value system and interests of the society to which he or she seeks to belong, and how those conditions should be evaluated. That is, it is up to the state to determine whether to facilitate naturalization to a greater or lesser degree, and it is the state that is able to change, liberalize, or restrict the respective conditions according to circumstances and convenience (ibid.: para. 36).

Putting it this way, it would seem that the state can decide whether or not to facilitate a stateless person's naturalization. Notwithstanding, the IACtHR also sustained, categorically, that nationality is a human right and that the proper interpretation of Article 20 requires harmonious reconciling of the state's prerogative to regulate nationality with the limits imposed by international law to protect human rights (ibid.: para. 38).

Indeed, in the case of the Yean and Bosico girls (IACtHR 2005), the IACtHR affirmed that this state prerogative recognizes two limits: (1) the prohibition of discrimination and the duty of the state to provide equal and effective protection of the law, and (2) the duty to prevent, avoid, and reduce statelessness (IACtHR 2005).

The reduction of statelessness is produced through the *resolution* of existing cases (i.e., naturalization of stateless migrants) and the *prevention* of new cases. As a result, it can be affirmed that, although a state can establish the conditions and procedures it deems most appropriate for naturalization of stateless persons, it should ensure that such requirements (1) help resolve the cases of statelessness (reduction), and (2) do not frustrate the right of stateless persons to a nationality.

The international obligation of facilitating the naturalization of stateless persons, then, can be defended, although it is up to the state to define what that facilitation involves.

Confirming Nationality

The question of *acquisition* of nationality refers to the establishment of the legal link between a person and a specific state. The question of *confirming* nationality is, in turn, linked to proof of the nationality that had already been acquired. A person who faces serious legal barriers or practices to prove his or her nationality will run the risk of not being considered as a national by the authorities, and this could consequently result in statelessness.

Even though the ACHR contemplates the right to a nationality (ACHR: art. 20.1), it does not expressly enshrine the right to obtain documents that can prove it. Notwithstanding, this right can be considered implicit in Articles 3 and 20 of the ACHR. Moreover, the obligation to issue documentation proving individual identity (name, parentage, and nationality) is a way to ensure his or her right to identity.

For the IACtHR, it is possible to determine the existence of the right to identity on the basis of Article 8 of the 1989 Convention on the Rights of the Child, which establishes that it includes, among other things, the right to nationality, name, and family relations. According to the IACtHR, the right to identity may be conceptualized, in general, as the "set of attributes and characteristics that permit individualization of the person in society, and, in that sense, include several other rights depending on the subject of the rights involved and the circumstances of the case" (IACtHR 2005: para. 122)

The IACtHR's jurisprudence has said that a state may violate the right to identity as much by never issuing documentation to the person as by, having done so, not considering such documentation effective. In the case of the expelled Dominicans, the IACtHR found that the actions of the state agents who failed to acknowledge the identity documents accrediting Dominican nationality meant they were not acknowledging their right to identity by not allowing them to identify themselves or not considering their documents (ibid.: para. 274). In the case of the children, the failure to recognize identity also meant a violation of their higher interest.

Thus, making individual identification and confirmation of nationality possible can be viewed as international obligations of the states.

Facilitating the Recovery and Restoration of Nationality

The BPA proposes to "facilitate the restoration or recovery of nationality through legislation or inclusive policies, especially the automatic restoration of nationality as a solution for cases in which the person had been arbitrarily deprived of nationality" (BPA: Action (h)).

Some countries in the region do not allow the renouncing of nationality, whereas others permit it, provided it does not result in statelessness. Where renouncement is admissible, facilitating the reacquisition of the lost or renounced nationality, if the person became stateless, may be viewed as a way to ensure their right to have a nationality (ACHR: art. 20.1). Even though the IACtHR has not had an opportunity to decide if facilitating the recovery of the nationality in these cases is part of the state obligation to reduce the cases of statelessness, it presumably is. Indeed, the IACtHR has said that, even though the states are responsible for determining who their nationals are, this authority should be exercised in line with the standards of international law, particularly with the duty to reduce statelessness (ibid.: para. 274).

Action (h) also refers to the automatic reinstatement (restoration) of nationality as a solution for cases of arbitrary deprivation of nationality. This solution is consistent with international standards on the matter.[24]

Regionally, the IACtHR has said that naturalization is not the appropriate solution in cases of denial or arbitrary deprivation of nationality (IACtHR 2014a: para. 324). Along this same line, the IACHR has said that a state should fully restore nationality, adopting general and automatic measures to guarantee the right to the persons affected by the denial or arbitrary deprivation. The respective mechanisms should be simple, clear, swift, and fair; they cannot be discretional or implemented discriminatorily; and they should be financially affordable (Inter-American Commission on Human Rights 2015: paras. 330, 331.4).

In brief, facilitating the recovery and restoration of nationality, when a person is stateless, can constitute the minimum content of the right to a nationality and therefore entail obligations for the states.

The 100 Points of Brasilia (2018)

Up to this point we have reviewed the regional developments from the Brasilia Declaration to the BPA, and we have paused to establish the obligatoriness of several of the action of this plan, which was intended to consolidate the regional agenda for eradicating statelessness.

In effect, between 2015 and 2017 the countries in the region made significant progress in eradicating this problem, all of which was reported by UNHCR (UNHCR 2018: 72–82). In 2017, as part of the triennial assessment mandated by the states, UNHCR supported a series of subregional thematic consultations that took place in Buenos Aires, Quito, and Nassau.

In culmination of this exercise, various Latin American and Caribbean countries and territories met in Brasilia in February 2018 and adopted the

100 Points of Brasilia document. Reflecting various aspects of the region's progress, as well as best practices in the implementation of the BPA, the document was also prepared to contribute to the discussion of the 2018 Global Compact on Refugees (see Jubilut, Mezzanotti and Lopes in this volume).

In the 100 Points of Brasilia document, the region's countries identified, for the first time, a set of best practices for the prevention and resolution of statelessness and the protection of stateless persons (ibid.: paras. 90–100). The document is important insofar as it evidences the evolution of the state focus on eradication. The countries went from an initial stage, centered on understanding the problem and defining goals and actions, to an intermediate stage, focused on implementing actions, to a stage centered on obtaining specific results and identifying best national and regional practices for achieving the goals.

The 100 Points of Brasilia shows that, in less than ten years, the region passed from renewing an interest in the topic to taking the lead in the global eradication of statelessness. Looking at states' progressive efforts towards achieving this goal, the IACmHR has recently affirmed that every migrant has a non-derogable right to a nationality and not to be stateless (IACmHR 2019).

Conclusion

The humanitarian problem of statelessness was absent in the Cartagena Declaration and, for thirty years, in the commemorative processes that followed. This omission long delayed the possibility of achieving a coordinated state response and putting in place a strategic regional framework on statelessness.

The OAS General Assembly's resolution on statelessness of 2010 and the Brasilia Declaration revitalized the states' interest in the topic. In the following year (2011), the voluntary pledges on statelessness assumed by different countries in the region helped get specific goals onto the national human rights agendas. Then, the OAS General Assembly's successive resolutions on statelessness (2011–14) continued to call the countries' attention to the need for making headway on accessing to the conventions on statelessness, adopting legal protection frameworks, and creating statelessness determination procedures, among other actions.

With the adoption of the Eradicating Statelessness program in the BPA, the consolidation of statelessness on the regional agenda reached its peak. From then on, the countries established clear actions for eradicating statelessness in the Americas before 2024. Many of these actions are, in reality, the reflection of international obligations. Others, on the contrary, are not binding but reflect a strong political commitment by the states to move forward in the same direction.

Finally, the 100 Points of Brasilia shows that countries are no longer debating whether statelessness should be eradicated or what actions are needed to do so. They are now focusing on identifying the best national and regional practices for achieving this goal by 2024.

With the adoption of regional instruments on refugees that included aspects on statelessness, the voluntary commitments undertaken by states in international meetings, and the work of UNHCR and various OAS bodies (OAS General Assembly, IACmHR, and IACtHR) and a human rights approach centered on the realization of the right to a nationality, Latin American and Caribbean countries were able to forge the goal of eradicating statelessness in the Americas.

To continue moving forward toward the effective attainment of this goal, the countries need to maintain the momentum of recent years and their human rights approach to this problem. In line with this, and in the understanding that most of the actions in the BPA reflect international obligations, the states must make this task an imperative.

Juan Ignacio Mondelli is the Senior Regional Protection Officer (refugee status determination) at UNHCR Americas Bureau, based in Panama. Between 2013 and 2018 he was the senior regional officer (statelessness) at UNHCR Regional Legal Unit for the Americas in Costa Rica. He earned his Juris Doctorate degree from the School of Law of the University of Buenos Aires. As a Fulbright-Siderman scholar, he earned Master of Laws degree in human rights and civil liberties from Southwestern Law School, in Los Angeles, California. He also earned a Master's degree in International Relations from the School of Law of the University of Buenos Aires.

Notes

1. In the BPA the countries reaffirmed their "commitment to the eradication of statelessness within the next ten years . . . by resolving existing situations, preventing new cases of statelessness and protecting stateless person" (BPA: 6).
2. Antigua and Barbuda, Argentina, the Bahamas, Barbados, Belize, Bolivia, Brazil, Cayman Islands, Chile, Colombia, Costa Rica, Cuba, Curazao, El Salvador, Ecuador, Guatemala, Guyana, Haiti, Honduras, Jamaica, Mexico, Nicaragua, Panama, Paraguay, Peru, Santa Lucía, Surinam, Trinidad and Tobago, Turks and Caicos Islands, Uruguay, and Venezuela.
3. The opinions expressed in this document represent the author's point of view and are not necessarily shared by the United Nations High Commissioner for Refugees (UNHCR) or by the United Nations (UN). UNHCR documents and guidelines can be consulted at www.acnur.org and www.unhcr.org.

4. Argentina, Bolivia, Brazil, Colombia, Costa Rica, Cuba, Chile, Ecuador, El Salvador, Guatemala, Mexico, Nicaragua, Panama, Paraguay, Peru, Dominican Republic, Uruguay, and Bolivarian Republic of Venezuela.
5. In 2005, 2013, and 2015, the OAS General Assembly did not approve resolutions on refugees, inasmuch as the resolutions on human rights (2016 and 2017) included specific sections on stateless persons and refugees.
6. AG/RES. 2511 (XXXIX-O/09), para. 2; AG/RES. 2047 (XXXIV-O/04), para. 2; AG/RES. 1971 (XXXIII-O/03), para. 2; AG/RES. 1892 (XXXII-O/02), para. 2; AG/RES. 1832 (XXXI-O/01), considerandos; AG/RES. 1762 (XXX-O/00), para. 1; AG/RES. 1693 (XXIX-O/99), para. 1.
7. OAS General Assembly, AG/RES. 2599 (XL-O/10), 8 June 2010.
8. OAS General Assembly, Resolutions AG/RES. 2826 (XLIV-O/14), 4 June 2014, para. 2; AG/RES. 2787 (XLIII-O/13), 3 June 2013, para. 1; AG/RES. 2665 (XLI-O/11), 7 June 2011, para. 2, a; AG/RES. 2599 (XL-O/10), 8 June 2010, para. 2.
9. UN Treaty Series, Vol. 989, p. 175; Vol. 360, p. 117. Status of accessions and ratifications updated at 27 September 2018.
10. Brazil 2017, "Lei de Migração," Pub. L. Law 13.445; Brazil. 2017, "Regulamento da Lei de Migração," Pub. L. No. Decree 9199/17.
11. Costa Rica 2016, "Reglamento Para La Declaratoria de La Condición de Persona Apátrida," Pub. L. No. Decree 39.620.
12. Uruguay 2018, "Reconocimiento y Protección al Apátrida," Pub. L. Law 19.682.
13. According to CEDAW (art. 9.1), the states parties should grant women equal rights with men to acquire, change or retain their nationality. In addition, in accordance with Article 9.2, they should grant women equal rights with men with respect to the nationality of their children.
14. Case of Almonacid-Arellano et al v. Chile. Preliminary Objections, Merits, Reparations and Costs (IACtHR 2006a: para. 124).
15. Case of La Cantuta v. Peru. Merits, Reparations and Costs (IACtHR 2006c).
16. Case of the Dismissed Congressional Employees (Aguado-Alfaro et al.) v. Peru. Preliminary Objections, Merits, Reparations and Costs (IACtHR 2006b).
17. "Identidad de género, e igualdad y no discriminación a parejas del mismo sexo. Obligaciones estatales en relación con el cambio de nombre, la identidad de género, y los derechos derivados de un vínculo entre parejas del mismo sexo (interpretación y alcance de los artículos 1.1, 3, 7, 11.2, 13, 17, 18 y 24, en relación con el artículo 1 de la Convención Americana sobre Derechos Humanos)" (IACtHR 2017).
18. Article 20.2 of the ACHR establishes that "every person has the right to the nationality of the state in whose territory he was born if he does not have the right to any other nationality."
19. Antigua and Barbuda, Argentina, Barbados, Belize, Bolivia, Brazil, Chile, Colombia, Costa Rica, Ecuador, El Salvador, Guatemala, Haiti, Honduras, Mexico, Nicaragua, Panama, Paraguay, Peru, Saint Vincent and the Grenadines, Trinidad and Tobago, and Uruguay.
20. OAS General Assembly. 2014. Resolutions AG/RES. 2826 (XLIV-O/14), 4 June 2014, para. 4; AG/RES. 2787 (XLIII-O/13), 3 June 2013, para. 3; AG/RES. 2665 (XLI-O/11), 7 June 2011, para. 3; AG/RES. 2599 (XL-O/10), 8 June 2010, para. 2.

21. Resolution AG/RES. 2908 (XLVII-O/17), 21 June 2017; Draft Resolution on Promotion and Protection of Human Rights, OAS/Ser.G CP/CAJP-3502/19 rev. 10, June 2019.
22. The word "laws" in the ACHR (art. 30), IACHR, Advisory Opinion OC-6/86, 9 May 1986.
23. The text of the two conventions is identical with regard to facilitating naturalization: "The Contracting States shall as far as possible facilitate the assimilation and naturalization ... They shall in particular make every effort to expedite naturalization proceedings and to reduce as far as possible the charges and costs of such proceedings."
24. The UN Human Rights Council, for example, urged the states to "ensure the access of persons arbitrarily deprived of their nationality to effective remedies, including, but not limited to, the restoration of nationality" (UN Human Rights Council 2012: 3). Likewise, the UN secretary general has indicated that "States should ensure that there is an effective remedy available where a decision on nationality is found to be unlawful or arbitrary. This must include . . . the possibility of restoration of nationality" (UN Secretary-General 2013: 14).

References

American Convention on Human Rights. 1969.
American Declaration on the Rights and Duties of Man. 1948.
Argentina. 2019. Ley 27512, General de reconocimiento y protección de las personas apátridas.
Brasilia Declaration on the Protection of Refugees and Stateless Persons in the Americas. 2010.
Brazil Declaration. 2014. "A Framework for Cooperation and Regional Solidarity to Strengthen the International Protection of Refugees, Displaced and Stateless Persons in Latin America and the Caribbean."
Brazil Plan of Action. 2014. "A Common Roadmap to Strengthen Protection and Promote Sustainable Solutions for Refugees, Displaced and Stateless Persons in Latin America and the Caribbean within a Framework of Cooperation and Solidarity."
Cartagena Declaration on Refugees. 1984. https://www.refworld.org/docid/3ae-6b36ec.html.
Brazil. 2017a. Decreto 9199/17, Regulamento da Lei de Migração.
Brazil. 2017b. Lei 13.445, Lei de Migração.
Colombia. 2019. Registraduría Nacional del Estado Civil. Resolución 8470, Por la cual se adopta una medida administrativa de carácter temporal y excepcional, para incluir de oficio la nota "Valido para demostrar nacionalidad" en el Registro Civil de Nacimiento de niñas y niños nacidos en Colombia, que se encuentran en riesgo de apatridia, hijos de padres venezolanos, que no cumplen con el requisito de domicilio.
Convention on the Elimination of All Forms of Discrimination Against Women. 1979.

Convention on the Rights of the Child. 1989.
Costa Rica. 2016. Reglamento Para La Declaratoria de La Condición de Persona Apátrida, Decreto 39.620.
Ecuador. 2017a. Ley Orgánica de Movilidad Humana.
Ecuador. 2017b. Reglamento a la Ley Orgánica de Movilidad Humana. Decreto 111.
Global Compact on Refugees. 2018.
Inter-American Commission on Human Rights (IACmHR).
———. 2015. Report on the Situation of Human Rights in the Dominican Republic, OAS/Ser.L/V/II, Doc. 45/15, 31 December 2015.
———. 2019. Inter-American Principles on the Human Rights of all Migrants, Refugees, Stateless People, and Victims of Trafficking in Persons, Resolution 04/19, 7 December 2019.
Inter-American Court of Human Rights (IACtHR). 1984. *Proposed Amendments to the Naturalization Provision of the Constitution of Costa Rica*, Advisory Opinion OC-4/84, 19 January 1984, Series A No. 4.
———. 2005. *Case of the Girls Yean and Bosico v. Dominican Republic. Preliminary Objections, Merits, Reparations and Costs. Judgment.* Series C No. 130.
———. 2006a. Case of Almonacid-Arellano et al v. Chile. Preliminary Objections, Merits, Reparations and Costs. 26 September 2006.
———. 2006b. Case of the Dismissed Congressional Employees (Aguado-Alfaro et al.) v. Peru. Preliminary Objections, Merits, Reparations and Costs, 24 November 2006.
———. 2006c. Case of La Cantuta v. Peru. Merits, Reparations and Costs. (Inter-American Court of Human Rights, 29 November 2006.
———. 2014. *Rights and Guarantees of Children in the Context of Migration and/or in Need of International Protection*, Advisory Opinion OC-21/14, 19 August 2014. Series A No. 21.
———. 2017. Gender identity, and equality and non-discrimination with regard to same-sex couples. State obligations in relation to change of name, gender identity, and rights deriving from a relationship between same-sex couples (interpretation and scope of Articles 1(1), 3, 7, 11(2), 13, 17, 18 and 24, in relation to Article 1, of the American Convention on Human Rights). Advisory Opinion OC-24/17, 24 November 2017.
———. 2019. *Cuadernillo de Jurisprudencia de la Inter-American Court of Human Rights No. 7. Conventionality Control 6.*
Mexico Declaration and Plan of Action to Strengthen the International Protection of Refugees in Latin America. 2004.
Mondelli, Juan Ignacio. 2019. "El Derecho Humano a No Ser Apátrida En La Convención Americana Sobre Derechos Humanos." In XLVI Curso de Derecho Internacional (2019), 358. OEA/Ser.Q/V.C-46. Organización de los Estados Americanos (OEA), Secretaría General, Secretaría de Asuntos Jurídicos, Departamento de Derecho Internacional.
Organization of American States (OAS) General Assembly. 2013. *Prevention and reduction of statelessness and protection of stateless persons in the americas*, Reoslution AG/RES. 2787 (XLIII-O/13), Antigua, Guatemala: OAS
———. 2014. *Prevention and Reduction of Statelessness and Protection of Stateless Persons in the Americas*, Resolution AG/RES. 2826 (XLIV-O-14) Asunción, Paraguay: OAS.

———. 2016. *Promotion and Protection of Human Rights, Resolution* AG/RES. 2887 (XL-VI-O/16) Washington D.C: OAS.
———. 2017. *Promotion and Protection of Human Rights, Resolution* AG/RES. 2908 (XL-VII-O/17) Washington D.C: OAS.
OAS Committee of Juridical and Political Affairs. 2019. "*Draft Resolution. Promotion and Protection of Human Rights (Agreed by the Committee of Juridical and Political Affairs on June 14, 2019 for Presentation to the Permanent Council).*"
OAS Inter-American Juridical Committee. 2015. *Guide for the Protection of Stateless Persons. Report.*
Panama. 2019. Reglamenta la Ley 28 de 30 de marzo de 2011, Que Aprueba la Convención Sobre el Estatuto de los Apátridas de 1954 Hecha en Nueva York, el 28 de septiembre de 1954, Decreto Ejecutivo 10.
Paraguay. 2018. Protección y facilidades para la naturalización de las personas apátridas, Ley 6149. h.
San José Declaration on Refugees and Displaced Persons. 1994.
United Nations High Commissioner for Refugees (UNHCR). 2007. *Refugee Protection and Mixed Migration: A 10-Point Plan of Action.* Geneva: United Nations High Commissioner for Refugees.
———. 2009. *Regional Conference on Refugee Protection and International Migration in the Americas–Protection Considerations in the Context of Mixed Migration.* Summarized Report. San José, Costa Rica: United Nations High Commissioner for Refugees.
———. 2011. *Pledges 2011. Ministerial Intergovernmental Event on Refugees and Stateless Persons.* Geneva.
———. 2014a. *Global Action Plan to End Statelessness 2014–2024.* Geneva: United Nations High Commissioner for Refugees.
———. 2014b. *Handbook on Protection of Stateless Persons under the 1954 Convention Relating to the Status of Stateless Persons.* Geneva: United Nations High Commissioner for Refugees.
———. 2015a. "Information Paper, Commemoration of the Thirtieth Anniversary of the Cartagena Declaration 'Cartagena +30.'" In *Memories of the Thirtieth Anniversary of the Cartagena Declaration on Refugees.* Ecuador: United Nations High Commissioner for Refugees.
———. 2015b. "MERCOSUR. Discussion Paper." In *Memories of the Thirtieth Anniversary of the Cartagena Declaration on Refugees.* Ecuador: United Nations High Commissioner for Refugees.
———. 2018. *Brazil Plan of Action. First Triennial Progress Report 2015–2017.* San José, Costa Rica: United Nations High Commissioner for Refugees.
UN Secretary-General. 2013. *Human rights and arbitrary deprivation of nationality, Report of the Secretary General,* A/HRC/25/28, December 19, 2013.
UN Human Rights Council. 2012. *Resolution N° 20/5, Human rights and arbitrary deprivation of nationality,* A/HRC/RES/20/5, 16 July 2012.
Uruguay. 2018. Reconocimiento y protección al apátrida, Ley 19.682.

8

The 100 Points of Brasilia

Latin America's Dialogue with
the Global Compact on Refugees

*Liliana Lyra Jubilut, Gabriela Mezzanotti,
and Rachel de Oliveira Lopes*

Introduction

International Refugee Law is undergoing a norm-creating experience at the universal level, with an aim to enhance existing refugee protection by establishing new legal documents for migration governance in general, and for refugees' protection in particular. This process began with the 2016 New York Declaration for Refugees and Migrants (NYD) and culminated with the 2018 Global Compact on Refugees (GCR).[1]

During the period between the documents, initiatives were in play to aid in the construction of the new architecture of refuge governance. In this context, an example of regional-universal action and dialogue can be found in the 100 Points of Brasilia, a document adopted by Latin American States,[2] who gathered in Brazil in February 2018 to compile their contributions to the GCR. The document uses existing Latin America good practices, normative standards, and principles of refugee protection as bases for a hundred suggestions to the GCR.

In light of the adoption of this document, the aims of this chapter are to (i) introduce the 100 Points of Brasilia to a larger audience, (ii) describe its main characteristics, and (iii) unpack and analyze its practical impact—inquiring about (a) its suitability to the regional regime of refugee protection in Latin America, (b) its subsumption into the GCR, and (c) its adequacy in providing solutions to current challenges in refugee protection. These assessments will draw from a triple analytical lens, appraising the 100 Points of Brasilia in relation to (i) the Latin American context, (ii) the universal system of refugee protection, and (iii) the current challenges of refugee protection. The analyses adopt International Law, International Refugee Law, and Human Rights as its theoretical frameworks while engaging with issues pertaining to International Relations in the descriptions and assessments.

To fulfil its goals, the chapter proceeds as follows: first, it presents the background contexts of both the 100 Points of Brasilia and the GCR; then it describes the way in which Latin America States contributed to the process of creation of the GCR; and, finally, it assesses the 100 Points of Brasilia by presenting the main characteristic of this document as well as of the GCR, taking into consideration, in separate sections, its dialogue with the regional and the universal contexts, and the challenges of refugee protection as a transversal theme in both.

The Common Background Context of the 100 Points of Brasilia and the GCR

The need for new instruments in migration governance and for cooperation toward migrants' protection, both among States and with the United Nations (UN), has been perceived for years (Jubilut, Madureira, and Torres 2019: 22). It was not until 2016, however, that the NYD consolidated migration issues in a single legal framework, expressing "the political will of world leaders to save lives, protect rights and share responsibility on a global scale" (UN 2019) through its approval by all 193 UN Member States (Jubilut, Madureira and Torres 2019: 23).

This was due, at least in part, to the growing numbers of forced displaced persons in the second decade of the twenty-first century, with numbers that increased exponentially from 2012 (United Nations High Commissioner for Refugees [UNHCR] 2019), and which, by 2016, had grown from 33.9 million in 1997 to 65.6 million (ibid.).

At that time most, if not all, of the world's States were already part of migratory itineraries, as countries of origin, transit, or destination (Klein-Solomon 2005). And even though there was some increase in (i) resettlement, (ii) humanitarian solutions, (iii) funding and hosting, and (iv) participation of civil society (United Nations General Assembly [UNGA] 2016: 3), as responses to this scenario, joint action and cooperation among States for equitable responsibility sharing were still less than enough (Maia, Morales, and Cetra 2018). In some cases, in fact, there was cooperation to end or prevent migration, and not to guarantee rights or migrants' protection (ibid.).

Normatively, migration has not yet been regulated in all its (economic, political, historical, sociological, and legal) complexity, dichotomies, and causes

(Jubilut and Lopes 2017: 35–36). So far, and from a subjects of migration standpoint, only refugees can be said to have a structured protection regime, found universally in the 1951 Convention Relating to the Status of Refugees (1951 Refugee Convention) and its 1967 Protocol Relating to the Status of Refugees (1967 Protocol). In turn, the situation of other migrants is addressed by either broad specific norms with few States' commitments (such as the 1990 International Convention on the Protection of Rights of All Migrant Workers and Their Families[3]), soft law instruments (such as the 1998 Guiding Principles on International Displacement), or regional frameworks (such as the 2009 African Union Convention for the Protection and Assistance of Internally Displaced Persons in Africa–the Kampala Convention). In terms of general rights, all migrants (forced or not, refugees or other migrants) are entitled to the protection of International Human Rights Law, as are all other human beings. However, there is still a gap in implementing these rights.

In this scenario, the NYD was the result of an effort to present normative strategies that might assist and guide the protection of all migrants (including refugees) (UNGA 2016). In this context, it is interesting that the NYD was designed during the institutional change that placed the International Organization for Migration within the UN system[4] (Newland 2018), bringing an organization with general mandate on migrants to this system (ibid.).

Even though it is a soft law document, the NYD has considerable weight, since, as mentioned, it consolidates the will of all UN members (UNHCR 2016a). In this sense, it is relevant in that States have made a commitment to share responsibility (NYD: para. 11) for migrants and refugees' protection in more-equitable (ibid.: para. 68) and more-predictable (ibid.: paras. 38, 86) ways. Moreover, it takes human rights (ibid.: para. 22) and whole of society (ibid.: para. 69) approaches, which should also consider the causes of migration, and origin and host countries situations (ibid.: paras. 37, 12), without disregarding "different national realities, capacities and levels of development and respecting national policies and priorities" (ibid.: para. 21).

From the NYD arose the commitment to create two new separate documents: the 2018 Global Compact for Safe, Orderly and Regular Migration, negotiated and drafted in a State-led process; and the GCR, drafted by the UNHCR.

Latin America and the Building Up to the GCR

Latin America's Political Contribution to the GCR: Negotiations and Voting

The GCR highlights the important role that regional (and subregional) mechanisms and cooperation can play in refugee protection (GCR: paras. 28, 29). In this context, Latin America can be regarded as an example considering it has both a long-standing tradition of refugee protection (Alto

Comissariado das Nações Unidas para Refugiados [ACNUR] n.d.) and was actively involved in the process toward the GCR, being present at all stages of this document's construction process, starting from the unanimous approval of the NYD.

As soon as the NYD was adopted, Argentina, Brazil, Costa Rica, Mexico, and Uruguay committed themselves to (i) increasing funding for humanitarian assistance, (ii) and/or expanding admissions, (iii) and/or developing policy changes for greater refugee protection (UNHCR 2016a). In this sense, Argentina pledged to accept three thousand refugees from Syria and/or neighboring countries through humanitarian visas schemes that might lead to permanent resident status (ibid.); Brazil committed to resettle refugees from the North of Central America (NCA; comprising El Salvador, Guatemala, and Honduras) with State funding (ibid.); Costa Rica pledged to continue to support the Protection Transfer Arrangement for the most vulnerable asylum seekers from the NCA, to redesign its refugee identification document (ID) card to be more in line with its national ID card, to reduce the backlog of asylum applications, and to establish processes to more effectively manage increased numbers of applications moving forward (ibid.); Mexico committed to donate $8 million to humanitarian actions, as well as to strengthen and expand its asylum system; and Uruguay also committed to receive refugees from the NCA (UNHCR 2018a).

At the same time, actions were taken by States in the region concerning the Comprehensive Refugee Response Framework (CRRF), established by the NYD, to foster the general goals of ratifying existing commitments under the refugee regime and of extending the scope of shared responsibility (Hansen 2018: 132). The CRRF is presented in Annex I of the NYD and can be considered to be its plan of action. It specifies key elements for effective and protective response to large movement of refugees (NYD), and "include[s] rapid and well-supported reception and admissions; support for immediate and on-going needs; assistance for local and national institutions and communities receiving refugees; and expanded opportunities for solutions" (UNHCR 2016b). Central American countries participated in the CRRF from the start, with Belize, Costa Rica, Guatemala, Honduras, Mexico, and Panama having started to apply "a 'comprehensive regional protection and solutions framework' to address forced displacement issues in the region" (UNHCR 2017a).

Latin American States also gave contributions in thematic discussions in the process toward the GCR; in addition to specific mentions to the International Conference on Central American Refugees and to the 2014 Brazil Declaration and Plan of Action: a Framework for Cooperation and Regional Solidarity to Strengthen the International Protection of Refugees, Displaced and Stateless Persons in Latin America and the Caribbean (BPA) as past and current examples on burden and responsibility sharing for the first thematic discussions for the adoption of the GCR (UNHCR 2017b). Brazil, Ecuador, and Honduras presented statements and written contributions to the GCR.[5]

Moreover, Argentina, Brazil, Chile, Colombia, Costa Rica, Ecuador, El Salvador, Guatemala, Guyana, Honduras, Mexico, Panama, Peru, Uruguay, and Venezuela were present at the Tenth Annual High Commissioner's Dialogue on Protection Challenges (UNHCR 2017c), for progress and thematic discussions of the CRRF (UNHCR 2017a).

Also relevant is the fact that work toward the GCR progressed in parallel with the three-year evaluation of the BPA. The BPA is the latest document of the ongoing revisional process of the 1984 Cartagena Declaration on Refugees (Cartagena Declaration), intended to periodically reassess needs and mechanisms for the protection of refugees and other forced migrants in Latin American (Jubilut and Lopes 2019) and adopt regional documents on refugees' protection. So far, three such documents have been adopted: 1) the 1994 San José Declaration on Refugees and Displaced Persons (SJD) (see Rushing and Lizcano Rodriguez in this volume), 2) the 2004 Mexico Declaration and Plan of Action to Strengthen the International Protection of Refugees in Latin America (MPA) (see Vera Espinoza in this volume), and 3) the BPA (2014) (see Arnold-Fernández, Sarmiento Torres, and Kallas in this volume).

The BPA set out an evaluation of its implementation, three years after its adoption, which took the form of four subregional meetings. The first, organized by UNHCR and the Organization of American States, was held in Honduras and resulted in the 2017 San Pedro Sula Declaration[6]—a subregional contribution to the GCR, focusing on forced displacement from the NCA. The second took place in Argentina,[7] and addressed the Quality of Asylum Programme (know in practice as QAI)—an initiative conceived to improve refugee status determination (RSD) procedures (UNHCR 2018b)— and the eradication of statelessness in the region. The third was held in Ecuador,[8] focusing on comprehensive, complementary, and sustainable solutions, specifically in the MPA-conceived Resettlement in Solidarity and Cities of Solidarity initiatives. The latter was also the issue of the fourth meeting, focusing on the Caribbean region and held in the Bahamas (Brazil. Ministério das Relações Exteriores 2018). Conclusions of the BPA three-year evaluation process were presented at the Consultation Meeting of Latin America and the Caribbean as a Contribution to the GCR, held in Brazil in 2018.

Thus, both the processes toward building the GCR and of the three-year evaluation of the BPA shared the same event in 2018 (Brazil. Ministério das Relações Exteriores 2018), which resulted in the 100 Points of Brasilia (UNHCR 2018b).

Latin America's Substantive Contribution to the GCR: The 100 Points of Brasilia

Since its zero draft, the GCR has mentioned the importance of regional perspectives on migratory issues (UN 2018a). This choice by the GCR is due to several facts. First, most migration occurs at the regional level, with current data showing that 88 percent of those fleeing their homes find protection in bordering countries or in their immediate region (UNHCR 2018a: 19–20), a fact that highlights the importance of identifying regional causes and consequences of migration, and of taking appropriate measures at this level.

Second, since border proximity generally results in regular contact due to security, political, or economic interests, and/or cultural reasons, States usually are more prone to cooperate and solve common problems at the regional level (Anderson 2016). At the same time, regional forums reduce the amount of political will and power issues at play, given that there are fewer actors involved (Jubilut and Lopes 2017: 54–55). Thus, "regional solutions that are tailored to the specific scenarios may be politically more acceptable, and therefore more effective and easy to apply" (Jubilut and Ramos 2014: 66).

Third, regional regimes–principles, norms, rules, and decision-making procedures (Krasner 1982: 186)–can complement global regimes, and, thus, extend protection (Jubilut and Ramos 2014: 66).

Furthermore, history and practice show that cooperation in handling migration issues has, in fact, been more easily established in regional scenarios (Jubilut and Lopes 2017), creating more protective regimes such as regional Refugee Law in Africa and Latin America. The latter, for instance, has extended the concept of "refugee" to allow for the protection of persons fleeing gross and generalized violations of human rights (Cartagena Declaration: 3rd Conclusion) and has advanced human rights–based refugee protection (Grandi 2017; Jubilut, Vera Espinoza, and Mezzanotti 2019).

In compiling regional solutions as contributions to the GCR, the 100 Points of Brasilia might have aggregated new pathways for international forced migration governance that could also be used in the global regime. Considering that it is "rooted in reality" (UNHCR 2018a), the document reaffirms the historic regional solidarity and humanitarian spirit as bases for refugee protection, a foundation that can be replicated globally.

In addition to ratifying a commitment to South-South cooperation (UNHCR 2018c: 1), the 100 Points of Brasilia also reaffirms a communion of values and respect for human rights. It does so by adopting a constructivist approach, insofar as the cooperative processes described therein are based on social constructions and on sharing of identities, beliefs, and practices (Hurd 2008: 299).

The 100 Points of Brasilia is divided into four protection axes: quality of asylum, durable solutions, management of special needs, and statelessness.

The 100 Points of Brasilia | 209

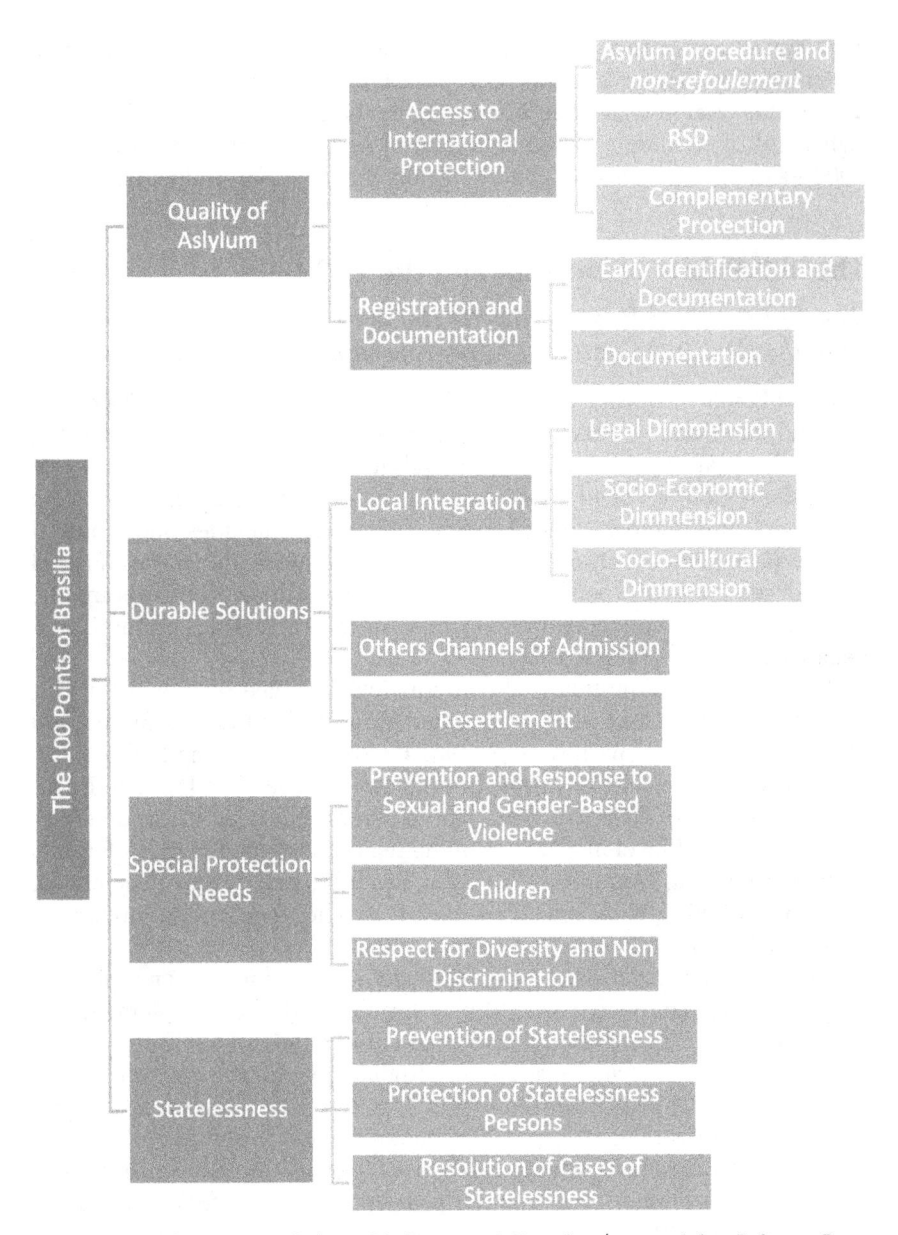

- **The 100 Points of Brasilia**
  - **Quality of Asylum**
    - Access to International Protection
      - Asylum procedure and non-refoulement
      - RSD
      - Complementary Protection
    - Registration and Documentation
      - Early Identification and Documentation
      - Documentation
  - **Durable Solutions**
    - Local Integration
      - Legal Dimmension
      - Socio-Economic Dimmension
      - Socio-Cultural Dimmension
    - Others Channels of Admission
    - Resettlement
  - **Special Protection Needs**
    - Prevention and Response to Sexual and Gender-Based Violence
    - Children
    - Respect for Diversity and Non Discrimination
  - **Statelessness**
    - Prevention of Statelessness
    - Protection of Statelessness Persons
    - Resolution of Cases of Statelessness

Figure 8.1. Structure of the 100 Points of Brasilia (created by Liliana Lyra Jubilut, Gabriela Mezzanotti, and Rachel de Oliveira Lopes).

These axes are, in turn, divided into specific subheadings (figure 8.1) that portray the search for integral protection for refugees—which includes refugee status related-rights and human rights (both sets of civil and political rights and of economic, social and cultural rights) (Jubilut and Apolinário 2008)–as well as respect for gender-age-diversity and for multiculturality.

The 100 Points of Brasilia and the GCR

The 100 Points of Brasilia and Its Dialogue with the Regional Context of Latin America

The 100 Points of Brasilia was created in the context of the region's perception and tradition regarding migration, a setting fraught with contradictions, especially regarding forced migration (Jubilut and Lopes 2018). On the one hand, the region has been praised for its generosity in the application of the right of asylum (Demant 2013; Grandi 2017), which includes both political asylum (a regional tradition dating back to the nineteenth century (Fischel de Andrade 2014)) and refuge (both with the international standards and the above-mentioned conceptual regional expansion carried out by the Cartagena Declaration) (Jubilut 2007).

The region is committed to the international refugee regime given that, "with the exception of Cuba, Guyana and Venezuela, all Latin America and Caribbean States are parties to the 1951 Convention Relating to the Status of Refugees. Venezuela, however, is a signatory to the 1967 Protocol Relating to the Status of Refugees. The right to asylum has been incorporated in the constitutional level in 15 States of the region: Bolivia, Brazil, Colombia, Costa Rica, Cuba, Dominican Republic, Ecuador, El Salvador, Guatemala, Honduras, Mexico, Nicaragua, Paraguay, Peru, and Venezuela" (Jubilut and Lopes 2018: 134–35).

Besides this, it has also been posited that Latin America has an aspiration to protect all migrants (Acosta 2016), considering (i) the complementarity between International Law, International Humanitarian Law, International Refugee law and International Human Rights Law, (ii) the coexistence between them is highlighted in the region (it is seen, for instance, in the protection regime for refugees and other migrants found in the Inter-American Human Rights System) (Jubilut and Lopes 2018; see also Botero and Casagrande in this volume), and (iii) their protection by *non-refoulement* (Cantor and Barrichello 2013).

On the other hand, however, Latin America has witnessed several forced mass displacements from within, such as in Colombia, Haiti, the NCA, Venezuela, and, more recently, in Nicaragua. The figures of forced displaced persons have reached the millions (14,851,194 as of the end of 2019) (UNHCR 2020: 82). And, as the scale of forced displacement continues to grow, anti-migrant sentiments have begun to blossom—with some speaking of a dissipation of the spirit of solidarity (Muggah, Folly, and Abdenur 2018)—and restrictive measures have been imposed (even before the COVID-19 pandemic), including administrative detentions of undocumented migrants, which, in some cases, are backed by internal legislation established under previously ruling dictatorships (Jubilut and Lopes 2018).

Thus, the region presents a contradictory scenario. In light of this, the 100 Points of Brasilia and its proposals are, at the same time, a collection of good practices and a compilation of challenges to be overcome.

The first protection axis addressed in the 100 Points of Brasilia concerns the quality of asylum. Research has shown that asylum seekers do not primarily worry about material needs, but rather about "their security of status, and issues around their identity as refugees" (Norwegian Refugee Council 2018)—in other words, the rights associated with RSD. In this context, the 100 Points of Brasilia includes considerations on the provisions on refuge and/or asylum in the internal legislation of Latin American and Caribbean States (highlighting the regionally expanded definition of "refugee" and the dialogue with human rights), on access to international protection, and on documentation (100 Points of Brasilia: points 1–6).

Still within this framework the 100 Points of Brasilia deals with *non-refoulement*, access to adequate RSD procedures, and complementary protection for persons outside of the refugee regime but who are in need of international protection (100 Points of Brasilia: points 7–18).

In terms of RSD procedures, in most Latin America States there are government bodies vested with the responsibility for them (Demant 2013). In Argentina, Bolivia, Brazil, Chile, Costa Rica, Ecuador, Mexico, Panama, and Peru, these procedures also include the commitment to implementing the already mentioned Quality of Asylum Programme, encompassing quality standards for "registration, interviewing, decision-making and appeal" (UNHCR 2017b).

However, there are backlogs in RSD in the region, explained due to exponential increases in refuge requests not matched by sufficient resources (ibid.). For instance, by the end of 2019, Brazil and Peru were among the top five States with pending asylum claims (UNHCR 2020: 45). This has led the region (and the 100 Points of Brasilia) to start to manifest concern about registration practices, both in terms of logistics and of identification of persons in need of international protection (100 Points of Brasilia: points 19–25).

Regarding documentation (100 Points of Brasilia: points 26–29), there are also standards in domestic systems—for instance, in Brazil (Jubilut, Lopes, and Galdino 2018) and Ecuador (Asylum Access and Refugee Works Right Coalition 2014)—that guarantee immediate access to a provisional document, from which access to basic rights, including the right to work, is guaranteed (see the annex of this volume). Practically, however, this access to rights is still hampered by bureaucracy (Sozansky, Sarmiento, and Reyes 2016) and discrimination (Jubilut et al. 2015).

An issue that could be seen as correlated to the backlogs and bureaucracy, as it pertains to resources, is that of funding. In this regard, although the 100 Points of Brasilia does not take up the matter and does not address issues of investment, it focuses on issues of community inclusion and access to rights and vulnerability, which could be understood in light of the stage of regional development in Latin America and the Caribbean.

The second protection axis in the 100 Points of Brasilia refers to durable solutions (100 Points of Brasilia: points 30–69), with an emphasis on local integration in its legal, socioeconomic, and sociocultural dimensions (Crisp 2004), on alternative legal channels of admission, and on resettlement. This is the largest section of the document.

In the legal dimension of local integration, progressive acquisition of rights and local integration in host States are highlighted; in the economic dimension of local integration self-sufficiency, by the implementation of a sustainable way of life, is emphasized; and in the social dimension of local integration, peaceful and nondiscriminatory coexistence with the local population are the main issues in the text.

Continuing the durable solutions subheading, the 100 Points of Brasilia tackles other legal pathways for humanitarian migration. Considering that recent migration in Latin American is characterized by mixed flows (Ramos 2018), and that not all (forced) migrants that arrive in the region can be protected as refugees (even in the terms of the broader definition of Cartagena), the region has created other legal pathways for humanitarian migration (Jubilut 2017; Jubilut and Lopes 2018: 151). In this regard, humanitarian entry visas to allow refugees to access safer territories (e.g., in Brazil in relation to Haitians and Syrians, and in Argentina in relation to the latter) (Jubilut, Andrade, and Madureira 2016; Jubilut and Lopes 2018); humanitarian residency permits to enable regular stays (in relation to Haitians in Argentina, Brazil, and Mexico, and for victims of human trafficking in Brazil) (Jubilut, Andrade, and Madureira 2016; Jubilut and Lopes 2018: 151); and residency permits for nationals of bordering countries (such as for Venezuelans in Brazil) have been established. Moreover, regional residency permits, in the context of the Mercado Común del Sur (MERCOSUR; Southern Common Market) have also been implemented (see Brumat in this volume).

Regarding resettlement, it is important to note the above-mentioned Resettlement in Solidarity initiative–a regional solidarity- and responsibility-sharing mechanism (Jubilut 2017), that has existed since 2004. This initiative, although having benefited only a small number of refugees so far (Ruiz 2015), might be entering a new implementation phase resulting from the commitments of the NYD (UNHCR 2018c)

The third protection axis of the 100 Points of Brasilia is the management of special protection needs, which includes prevention and response to sexual and gender-based violence (100 Points of Brasilia: points 70–75), protection of children (ibid.: points 76–81), and respect for diversity and nondiscrimination (ibid.: points 82–89).

In International Refugee Law, gender is not a standalone cause for refugee status the way race, religion, nationality, political opinion, and membership of a social group are, so that protection on the basis of gender needs to be subsumed to one of these criteria (Jubilut 2007). In Latin America, however, there are reports of good practices in developing gender as a reason for refugee status, such as the introduction of gender-based crimes and persecution in national laws as grounds for asylum claims (Moloney 2017), and the legalization by Argentina, Colombia, and Uruguay of same-sex marriage (Corrales 2018). There have also been steps to protect women's rights, such as the creation of a specialized court and of a Special Prosecutor's Office for Femicide in Guatemala, and the adoption of a Latin American model protocol[9] to guarantee that investigations are followed through (Arguello and Couch 2018).

These measures are designed to address the regional scenario of high levels of violence against women and LGBTI+ (lesbian, gay, bisexual, transgender and intersex, plus other sexual and gender orientations and identities) persons. Regarding women, statistical data indicate that a death occurs due to femicide every thirty hours in Latin America (Arguello and Couch 2018), and that gender-based violence is the main reason for forced migration of women and girls from the NCA (ibid.). Furthermore, "along some migrant routes, half or more of women surveyed reported experiencing sexual assault during the journey, and many take birth control to avoid becoming pregnant from rape" (Parish 2017).

Regarding LGBTI+ refugees, and even though some progress has been made both in terms of general protection such as in terms of gender identity laws in Argentina (Corrales 2018) and of specific protection relating to mobility, there are still negative trends in the region, such as criminalization, sexualization, stereotyping, the demand for discretion, and disregard of self-identification (Türk 2013). All these trends put this population at risk and jeopardize international protection, especially given that Latin America "experience[s] the highest rates of violence against LGBT individuals in the world" (Steggert n.d.).

Considering age as a vulnerability, there is also violence against children in the region, which, associated with economic conditions, is the main trigger for child migration in Latin America (Clemens and Gough 2018). Youth vulnerability also exists during displacement with separate and unaccompanied migration, trafficking and smuggling, perilous routes, and possible abuse and exploitation among the main issues (United Nations Children's

Fund [UNICEF] 2019). In Latin America remedial actions are in place to support refugee children in Argentina, Costa Rica, El Salvador, Guatemala, Honduras, and Mexico with the involvement of UNICEF (ibid.). These initiatives include training of consular agents on the rights of migrant children, development of alternative models to detention, respect for the principle of family unity, access to legal assistance, access to psychological care, guarantee of safe spaces, and access to education (ibid.).

The 100 Points of Brasilia dedicates an entire subheading of its third axis to the protection of children. On the other hand, elderly refugees and their protection, appear only in mentions in the heading on diversity and nondiscrimination, alongside persons with disabilities (100 Points of Brasilia: points 88–89).

Concerning diversity and nondiscrimination, the 100 Points of Brasilia brings proposals for establishing organs to deal with this issue, awareness campaigns, and confidential and safe access to HIV treatment (100 Points of Brasilia: points 82–89). The document highlights that all of these provisions should apply to both refugees and asylum seekers.

The last protection axis of the 100 Points of Brasilia relates to statelessness. The eradication of statelessness was one of the main targets of the BPA and, although there remain issues of ratification of international documents and on the adoption of internal regulations, it has been said that Latin America has made remarkable progress in tackling the prevention and eradication of statelessness (UNHCR 2018b) (see Mondelli in this volume). Indeed, and even though not all Latin American States are parties to the 1961 Convention on the Reduction of Statelessness (Mondelli 2017), there are widespread internal actions and a will to prevent statelessness and to protect stateless persons, including the establishment of statelessness determination procedures (ibid.) and "projects to verify or review people's birth registration and ensure appropriate registration and access to documentation proving nationality" (ibid.).

In light of the above, one can see that the 100 Points of Brasilia tackles both traditional topics of international refugee protection and integral protection (through durable solutions), as well as highlights the region's concern for the protection of vulnerable refugees in its mentions of women, children, elderly persons, persons of disabilities, LGBTI+ persons, and stateless persons. In this sense, thematically the 100 Points of Brasilia can be said to be a comprehensive document that dialogues with the main regional issues in refugee protection.

The GCR: Characteristics, Developments, and Criticism

Considering that the 100 Points of Brasilia aims at gathering and consolidating Latin America's contribution to the GCR, it is relevant to present the main characteristics and developments of this latter document, so as to see if the former achieved its goal.

Given that the normative basis for the establishment of the GCR is, as mentioned, the NYD, and that this document sets forth the CRRF, also previously mentioned, it can be said that the CRRF guided the structuring of the GCR (UNHCR 2016b). The CRRF was actually incorporated into the GCR (GCR: para. 10), and they share core objectives (CRRF: para. 18; GCR: para. 7), for the purposes of (i) easing the pressures on host countries, (ii) enhancing refugee self-reliance, (iii) expanding access to third countries' solutions, and (iv) supporting conditions in countries of origin for return (Karas 2018)–in other words, repatriation.

In addition to the CRRF, the GCR brings a Programme of Action to facilitate its implementation (GCR: para. 11) in which arrangements for burden- and responsibility sharing are envisaged. These include establishing (i) a Global Refugee Forum intended to foster international cooperation (GCR: paras. 17-19), (ii) instruments to deal with specific refugee situations (ibid.: paras. 20-30), and (iii) tools for effective burden and responsibility sharing (ibid.: para. 31), such as "predictable, flexible, unearmarked, and multiyear funding whenever possible" (ibid.: para. 32), "development assistance in favour of countries of origin to enable conditions for voluntary repatriation" (ibid.), "greater access to financial products and information services for refugees and host communities" (ibid.), and "development of harmonized or interoperable standards for the collection, analysis, and sharing of age, gender, disability, and diversity disaggregated data on refugees and returnees" (ibid.: para. 46). All these measures are part of a multi-stakeholder and partnership approach, to be leveraged by UN system actors and carried out by local authorities, humanitarian organizations, networks of cities, parliaments, civil society organizations, public-private partnerships, faith-based actors, and academic networks (ibid.: paras. 32-43).

The GCR also expresses concern about the (i) reception and admission of refugees, with attention to immediate, safe, and protective entry procedures; (ii) registration and documentation; (iii) specific needs for international protection and support to host communities to make them resilient and sustainable; and (iv) paving of ways for durable solutions (ibid.: paras. 52-63).

The GCR works with the idea of the immediate inclusion of refugees in host communities, and not in parallel systems (such as refugee camps) that keep refugees relegated to the margins of society. In this context, the GCR expresses concern about education, jobs, and livelihoods; health; specific needs of women and girls, children, adolescents, and youth; accommodation and natural resources management; food security and nutrition; civil registry; preventing statelessness; and the need to strengthen social relations for peaceful coexistence (ibid.: paras. 64-84).

Durable solutions, as "any means by which the situation of refugees can be satisfactorily and permanently resolved to enable them to live normal lives" (UNHCR 2005), are also considered in the GCR's Programme of Action (GCR: paras. 85–100). In addition to the aforementioned support to countries of origin for voluntary repatriation (a GCR key objective), the GCR also provides for local integration, as a "dynamic and two-way process, which requires efforts by all parties, including a preparedness on the part of refugees to adapt to the host society, and a corresponding readiness on the part of host communities and public institutions to welcome refugees and to meet the needs of a diverse population" (ibid.: para. 98) and for resettlement as a mechanism for burden- and responsibility sharing and of solidarity (ibid.: para. 90).

At the same time, the GCR recognizes and praises the existence of complementary pathways for admission to third countries (ibid.: paras. 94–95), and highlights the relevance of local solutions, involving States, refugees, and local communities (ibid.: para. 100).

With this basic structure, and after eighteen months of UNHCR-led negotiations, divided into two phases (thematic discussions in 2017 and formal consultations in the first half of 2018) (Karas 2018), the GCR was presented as Part II of the 2018 UNHCR Report to the UNGA. The GCR was then adopted as a nonbinding legal instrument on 17 December 2018, with 181 votes for it, two against (Hungary and the United States), and three abstentions (Eritrea, Libya, and the Dominican Republic) (Rush 2018).

Even though States have massively expressed their support, it should be noted, nonetheless, that the GCR has not been exempt from criticism. A first critique concerns the nonbinding and soft-law natures of the GCR, which might perpetuate dependence on political will (Karas 2018). On the other hand, however, and in terms of the latter, it should not be overlooked that in times of xenophobia and racism, built walls, erected fences, and closed frontiers (Thomas and Yarnell 2018: 1), flexible instruments, such as soft law, may be best suited for resolving the dichotomy between States' sovereignty and their responsibility to protect (Jubilut and Lopes 2017: 50–52).

Second, although the GCR concerns the operationalization of the existing refugee regime, many States have not been willing to move beyond their current obligations (Thomas and Yarnell 2018), and this has resulted in a silence on relevant issues (ibid.), such as on burden-sharing. In this area, it is relevant to note that, although the 1951 Refugee Convention sets out binding and strong commitments toward refugees by formalizing a definition of refugees and defining a catalogue of refugees' rights that were "sensibly oriented to the economic empowerment of refugees, yet flexible enough to take real account of the circumstances of the States to which they flee" (Hathaway 2018: 591), these rights are not present in the GCR.

A third critique is that the GCR has been seen as a rich countries' agreement to keep refugees away from their borders (Karas 2018), in that it emphasizes repatriation (Perry and Schwartz 2019) and, at the same time, seems to bring a reinforcement of funding from traditional host countries, thus maintaining "the old spatial arrangement" and "an unequal international division of labour in refugee protection" (Yaghmaian 2018).

Fourth, the emphasis on economic development in the GCR has been criticized in that, although the importance of job creation in host countries should not be overlooked, economic drivers are not the main triggers in refugees' displacement (Tesfaye 2018). In this sense, it is necessary to emphasize the change of perspective at the GCR–with a turn from the previous focus directed toward humanitarian aid toward development (Jubilut and Casagrande 2019; UN 2018b).

Fifth, the GCR is also said to posit a market-based approach that shifts responsibility for refugee protection from States to the private sector, in a risky slide into privatization (Yaghmaian 2018).

A sixth criticism concerns the lack of a stronger participation of refugees themselves in the GCR (Hathaway 2018), with claims that it is a "cop-out" (ibid.) and a document in which refugees are simply the objects, not the subjects (ibid.).

Despite all these criticisms,[10] it remains that the GCR is a new norm in International Refugee Law, which, at least, sets out a model for joint action, involving many different actors (Karas 2018). Moreover, and even if it has not been a smooth process–with the first round of negotiations underscoring both differences among regions of the world and uncertainty about States' willingness to unify a practical approach to refuge (Maia, Morales, and Cetra 2018), and with mild reactions to the final text given that there was already a previous normative background (Karas 2018), the recognition of the need for cooperation to deal with refuge issues has prevailed (Newland 2018).

The 100 Points of Brasilia and its Dialogue with the Universal Context

In this cooperative spirit, UNHCR's assessment of the 100 Points of Brasilia, as a contribution to the GCR, through comments of its High Commissioner, is of "100 good steps in the direction of managing better what is without any doubt one of the defining challenges of our times" and of a contribution by Latin America to refugee protection (UNHCR 2018a).

Besides, then, being a contribution in itself, the 100 Points of Brasilia reflects good practices from Latin America that could be replicated and translated into the universal arena. Examples of these regional good practices are (i) an expanded concept of "refugee," which could serve as a guideline for conceptual enhancements in, and tailored to, other regions; (ii) the reaffirmation of solidarity as a basis for refugee protection and the consequent shift from burden to responsibility sharing seen in regional programs (such as the MPA initiatives) which could be considered in the implementation of the GCR; (iii) the adoption of concrete alternative pathways for legal migration that could assist the GCR in encouraging States "to expand the number and range of legal pathways available for refugees to be admitted to or resettled in third countries" (GCR: paras. 77–79); and (iv) the adoption of complementarity protection mechanisms, including by the broadening of *non-refoulement*, to allow for the humanitarian protection for forced migrants, and that could help to strengthen a wider framework of protection.

Also of great importance is the regional experience of a follow-up mechanism to review the implementation of commitments in order to identify gaps, new needs, and new challenges, and to consolidate best practices in addressing them. Such continuous assessment and revision initiative seem to be replicated in the GCR, which also designates a follow-up process (ibid.: points 101–107).

An overview of the dialogue between the 100 Points of Brasilia and the GCR denotes that the documents have both points of convergence and points in which they forge parallel but independent paths.

For instance, whereas the 100 Points of Brasilia does not address the issue of funding, which is salient in the GCR, the Latin American and the Caribbean contribution to GCR is consistent with the aforementioned shift in perspective, from humanitarian action to sustainable development, in that it presents suggestions that consider both refugees and host communities (UNHCR 2017b).

Other similarities include the facts that both documents try to encourage cooperation and solidarity and that they are informed by the principles of *non-refoulement* and due process of law; and both highlight the importance of (i) identifying the reasons for forced displacement, (ii) implementing quality of asylum, (iii) providing access to documentation, (iv) establishing mechanisms of complementary protection, and (v) warning of the necessary cross-application of human rights, including to ensure decent living and access to basic services. And, while with a different focus (given that the 100 Points of Brasilia leans more toward local integration and GCR leans toward repatriation) (Perry and Schwartz 2019), both also underscore the importance of durable solutions.

Nevertheless, from an interpretation of its structure, it emerges from the GCR a precedence of the topics of prevention and of identification of root causes, considering that the document deals with them in its foreground, before presenting its Plan of Action. This choice by the GCR may have determined the use of a more aspirational language regarding protection, unlike the 100 Points of Brasilia, which adopts a more practice-oriented phrasing. In this sense, although in the 100 Points of Brasilia each axis is intended for the practical protection of forcibly displaced persons, the GCR highlights some tools of protection but does not advance much on their application.

The lack of advancements in practical terms can be said to be another point of separation between the 100 Points of Brasilia and the GCR, given that, although in the former there are clear proposals for action, the latter remains vague as to the means of implementing its goals. The GCR moves closer to practice by suggesting operational partnerships among relevant actors (GCR: point 12), by establishing the Global Refugee Forum (ibid.: points 17–19), and by addressing the exchange of good practices (ibid.: point 30). More concrete implementation manners are absent, however, such as the indication of means for accessing RSD procedure (such as decentralization of procedures throughout the whole process), unpaid legal advice and counsel, registration systems' management, minimum content for documents, modes of accessing residence permits and of obtaining naturalization, establishment of shelters, prioritization of the most vulnerable migrants, and training of actors. At the same time, although the GCR provides for national arrangements, it does not clarify which arrangements those would be, in terms of either form or content.

The protection logic behind each of the documents also seems to differ. The GCR addresses refugee reception and admission only as a second step (after prevention and preparedness for large flows)–maybe due to a chronological approach to displacement–followed by basic needs' provisions and, then, durable solutions. In a different perspective, the 100 Points of Brasilia adopts a logic of immediate protection This document demands the prompt insertion of displaced persons into international protection schemes, paying attention to durable solutions and diversity after that. The diversity aspect is addressed by the GCR mainly in terms of data collection on age, gender, and disability, thus bypassing the protection proposals for different vulnerabilities made by the 100 Points of Brasilia.

Similarly, the concept of human mobility that could allow for a broadening of the protection space to other migrants, suggested by the 100 Points of Brasilia (100 Points of Brasilia: point 16), was not taken up by the GCR, which remained within the restricted range of the institute of refuge, only briefly mentioning the existence of root causes for other forced displacement (GCR: paras. 8, 12) and of mixed migration flows (ibid.: para. 12).

Moreover, there is no specific reference in the GCR to asylum seekers, even when it comes to registration and documentation, in what could be seem as a shortcoming both in comparison to the 100 Points of Brasilia (which mentions them in its preamble and in dealing with access to international protection, asylum procedures, protection of *non-refoulement*, RSD, registration and documentation, and local integration) and to the current challenges of refugee protection.

It seems that the GCR logic of (i) avoiding displacement, (ii) accepting displaced persons, and only then (iii) protecting refugees, gave rise to a missed opportunity of incorporating the more protective and advanced suggestions of the 100 Point of Brasilia, even though both documents were elaborated against a common backdrop of protection.

Despite this incomplete integration between the documents, nothing prevents the 100 Points of Brasilia from being used as a manner to fill the gaps of the GCR, at least in Latin America, as well as turning from a suggestions document into a materialization guide, and thus enhancing its contribution to the betterment of refugee protection.

Conclusion

A new phase of migration governance has emerged, in which it was made clear that, notwithstanding its connection to issues related to State power (Klein-Solomon 2005), it is understood that the only way forward is through cooperation.

This idea, presented at the NYD, was later ratified by the adoptions of the 2018 Global Compact for Safe, Orderly and Regular Migration and the GCR, which take practical steps toward protecting all migrants, with the latter trying to establish guidelines that will enable the international community to more equitably and predictably share the responsibility to protect refugees (Aleinikoff 2018).

Latin America has contributed to the establishment of the GCR, both by the direct participation of its States in its negotiations and by presenting the 100 Points of Brasilia as a regional propositional document.

The 100 Points of Brasilia reflects the regional advances and adversities relating to the protection of refugees and other forced migrants in Latin America, and intends to encourage "State action within and outside the region, taking into account distinct national and regional realities" (UNHCR 2018c). It is inspired by regional history and the new refugee situations Latin America is facing. It summarizes best regional practices and tries to highlight relevant issues in refugee protection. It displays regional anxieties and desires, which are also global. It also establishes a dialogue for the exchange of initiatives.

In this sense, the 100 Points of Brasilia is a regional document with a global agenda, and it seems in keeping with the challenges of refugee protection in the existing international scenario and to the Latin American landscape, while trying to contribute to the enhancement of the universal system of refugee protection. It has relevant parallels with the GCR, with some of its proposals replicated there. However, it has broader protective structure and commitments. It has regional roots while it tries to contribute to the enhancement of the universal system of refugee protection. Nonetheless, it remains to be seen, if it will be able to impact the GCR's implementation.

Liliana Lyra Jubilut holds a PhD and a Master's degree in Law from Universidade de São Paulo and a LL.M in International Legal Studies from New York University. She is a Professor at Universidade Católica de Santos. She was Visiting Scholar at Columbia Law School and Visiting Fellow at the Refugee Law Initiative. She is an IOM Migration Research and Publishing High Level Adviser and a member of IOM's Migration Research Leaders Syndicate. She is also part of the Global Academic Interdisciplinary Network (GAIN), from the Global Compact on Refugees, and of the Academic Council on the Global Compact for Migration.

Gabriela Mezzanotti is Associate Professor at the University of South-Eastern Norway. She is a member of the research group in Human Rights and Diversities (HRDUSN) and a member of the Human Rights and Reconciliation in a Post-conflict, Multicultural Society project (NORPART). She holds a PhD in Social Sciences. She is a lawyer who has coordinated Unisinos UNHCR Sergio Vieira de Mello Chair from 2011 until 2018. Her research addresses critical discourse studies, International Human Rights Law, migration, and Refugee Law.

Rachel de Oliveira Lopes is a PhD candidate in International Law at Universidade de São Paulo, where she is a member of the study group Direito Comparado. She has a Master's degree in International Law from Universidade Católica de Santos where she is a member of the research group Direitos Humanos e Vulnerabilidades and of the UNHCR Sergio Vieira de Mello Chair. She is a Federal Lawyer, specialized in social security protection and has been researching International Human Rights Law, migration, and Refugee Law.

Notes

1. The Global Compact for Safe, Orderly and Regular Migration is also a part of this process, but it aims to regulate migration in general and not only refugees' issues.
2. In keeping with this book's guidelines, Latin America is understood to comprise Mexico and the continental States below Mexico. When all States of the region are included, reference is made to Latin America and the Caribbean.
3. Which has, as of 28 July 2020, fifty-five States party to it, according to United Nations Human Rights (n.d.).
4. The Agreement between the UN and the International Organization for Migration can be found at https://www.un.org/ga/search/view_doc.asp?symbol=A/70/976.

5. Statements are available at https://www.unhcr.org/towards-a-global-compact-on-refugees-written-contributions.html.
6. Available at http://www.itamaraty.gov.br/images/banners/ReuniaoPactoGlobal Refugiados/Honduras_MIRPS_Declaration_ING.pdf.
7. Report available at http://www.globalcrrf.org/crrf_document/brazil-plan-of-action-thematic-consultations-for-the-elaboration-of-a-triennial-progress-report-programs-on-quality-of-asylum-and-eradication-of-statelessness-2-3-november-2017/.
8. Report available at http://www.globalcrrf.org/crrf_document/regional-discussion-on-the-program-cities-of-solidarity-quito-13-14-november-2017/.
9. The Latin American model protocol for the investigation of gender-related killings of women (femicide/feminicide), edited by UN Women, UN Secretary General Campaign UNITED, and UNHCR is available at https://www2.unwomen.org/-/media/field%20office%20americas/documentos/publicaciones/latinamericanprotocolforinvestigationoffemicide.pdf?la=en&vs=1721.
10. For more on the shortcomings of the GCR, see Jubilut and Casagrande (2019).

References

Acosta, Diego. 2016. "Free Movement in South America: the emergence of an alternative model." *Migration Information Source.* https://www.migrationpolicy.org/article/free-movement-south-america-emergence-alternative-model.

Alto Comissariado das Nações Unidas para Refugiados (ACNUR). n.d. *Protección de Refugiados en América Latina: Buenas Prácticas Legislativas.* https://www.acnur.org/fileadmin/Documentos/Proteccion/Buenas_Practicas/9307.pdf?view=1.

Anderson, Ruben. 2016. "The Global Front Against Migration." *Anthropology of This Century*, 15. http://aotcpress.com/articles/global-front-migration/.

Aleinikoff, Alex. 2018. Some Thoughts on the GCR (and the GCM). *Forced Migration Forum.* https://forcedmigrationforum.com/2018/02/19/thoughts-on-the-gcr-and-the-gcm/.

Arguello, María Fernanda Pérez, and Bryce Couch. 2018. Violence Against Women Driving Migration from the Northern Triangle. *Atlantic Council.* https://www.atlanticcouncil.org/blogs/new-atlanticist/violence-against-women-driving-migration-from-the-northern-triangle/.

Asylum Access and Refugee Works Rights Coalition. 2014. *Global Refugee works rights report. Taking the movement from theory to practice.* https://asylumaccess.org/wp-content/uploads/2014/09/FINAL_Global-Refugee-Work-Rights-Report-2014_Interactive.pdf.

Brazil. Ministério das Relações Exteriores. 2018. *Consultation Meeting of Latin America and the Caribbean as a Regional Contribution to the Global Compact on Refugees: concept note.* https://www.acnur.org/5b58e9d64.pdf.

Brazil Declaration and Plan of Action: A Framework for Cooperation and Regional Solidarity to Strengthen the International Protection of Refugees, Displaced and Stateless Persons in Latin America and the Caribbean (BPA). 2014. https://www.acnur.org/5b5101644.pdf.

Cantor, David James, and Stefania Eugenia Barichello. 2013. "The Inter-American Human Rights System: a new model for integrating refugee and complementary protection." *International Journal of Human Rights* 17: 689–706.
Cartagena Declaration on Refugees. 1984. https://www.oas.org/dil/1984_cartagena_declaration_on_refugees.pdf.
Clemens, Michael; Gough, Kate. 2018. Child Migration from Central America–Just the facts. *Center for Global Development.* https://www.cgdev.org/blog/child-migration-central-america-just-facts.
Convention on the Reduction of Statelessness. 1961. https://www.refworld.org/docid/3ae6b39620.html.
Convention Relating to the Status of Refugees. 1951. https://www.unhcr.org/3b66c2aa10
Corrales, Javier. 2018. "The Gap Between Legal Progress and Daily Realities for LGBT People in Latin America." *World Politics Review.* https://theglobalamericans.org/2018/01/gap-legal-progress-daily-realities-lgbt-people-latin-america/.
Crisp, Jeff. 2004. "The Local Integration and the Local Settlement of Refugees: a conceptual and historical analysis." *New Issues in Refugee Research*, working paper 102. Geneva: United Nations High Commissioner for Refugees.
Demant, Eva. 2013. "30 años de la Declaración de Cartagena sobre Refugiados. Avances y desafíos de la protección de refugiados en Latinoamérica." *Agenda Internacional*, 31: 131–140.
Fischel de Andrade, José Henrique. 2014. "Forced Migration in South America." In *The Oxford Handbook of Refugee and Forced Migration Studies*, edited by Elena Fiddian-Qasmiyeh, Gil Loescher, Katy Long, and Nando Sigona, 651–663. Oxford: Oxford University Press.
Global Compact on Refugees. 2018. https://www.unhcr.org/gcr/GCR_English.pdf.
Global Compact for Safe, Orderly and Regular Migration. 2018. https://www.un.org/en/ga/search/view_doc.asp?symbol=A/RES/73/195.
Guiding Principles on International Displacement. 1993. https://www.unhcr.org/protection/idps/43ce1cff2/guiding-principles-internal-displacement.html.
Grandi, Filippo. 2017. "Foreword: Regional solidarity and commitment to protection in Latin America and the Caribbean." *Forced Migration Review*, 56: 4–5.
Hansen, Randall. 2018. "The Comprehensive Refuge Response Framework: a commentary." *Journal of Refugee Studies* 31 (2): 131–151. https://doi.org/10.1093/jrs/fey020.
Hathaway, James C. 2018. "The Global Cop-Out on Refugees." *International Journal of Refugee Law*, 30: 591-604. https://doi.org/10.1093/ijrl/eey062.
Hurd, Ian. 2008. "Constructivism." In *The Oxford Handbook of International Relations*, edited by Christian Reus Smit and Duncan Snidal: 298–316. Oxford: Oxford University Press. https://doi.org/10.1093/oxfordhb/9780199219322.003.0017.
International Convention on the Protection of Rights of All Migrant Workers and Their Families. 1990. https://www.ohchr.org/EN/ProfessionalInterest/Pages/CMW.aspx.
Jubilut, Liliana Lyra. 2007. *O Direito Internacional dos Refugiados e sua Aplicação no Ordenamento Brasileiro.* São Paulo: Método.
———. 2017. "Humanitarian Alternative Pathways for Protection for Forced Migrants in Latin America?." In *Ideas to Inform International Cooperation on Safe, Orderly*

and Regular Migration, edited by Marie McAuliffe and Michelle Klein-Solomon (Conveners). International Organization for Migration: Geneva.

Jubilut, Liliana Lyra, Camila Sombra Muiños de Andrade, and André de Lima Madureira. 2016. "Humanitarians Visas: building on Brazil's experience." *Forced Migration Review*, 53: 76–78.

Jubilut, Liliana Lyra, and Silvia Menicucci de Oliveira S. Apolinário. 2008. "A população refugiada no Brasil: em busca da proteção integral." *Universitas–Relações Internacionais*, 6 (2): 9–38. https://doi.org/10.5102/uri.v6i2.787.

Jubilut, Liliana Lyra, and Melissa Martins Casagrande. 2019. "Shortcomings and/or Missed Opportunities of the Global Compacts for the Protection of Forced Migrants." *International Migration*, 57: 139–157. https://onlinelibrary.wiley.com/doi/abs/10.1111/imig.12663.

Jubilut, Liliana L., Marcia Vera Espinoza, and Gabriela Mezzanotti. 2019. "The Cartagena Declaration at 35 and the Grammar of Refugee Protection in Latin America." *E-international relations*, 22 November 2019. https://www.e-ir.info/2019/11/22/the-cartagena-declaration-at-35-and-refugee-protection-in-latin-america/.

Jubilut, Liliana Lyra, and Rachel de Oliveira Lopes. 2017. "Strategies for the Protection of Migrants through International Law." *Groningen Journal of International Law*, 5 (1): 34-56. https://doi.org/10.21827/59db699cb49ed.

——. 2018. "Forced Migration and Latin America: peculiarities of a peculiar region in refugee protection." *Archiv des Völkerrechts*, 56 (2): 131–154. https://doi.org/10.1628/avr-2018-0008.

——. 2019. "Refuge and Political Asylum in Latin America: relevance, characteristics, and normative structure." In *The Routledge Companion to Migration, Communication and Politics*, edited by Stephen Croucher, João R. Caetano and Elsa A. Campbell.: 65–80. Abingdon and New York: Routledge.

Jubilut, Liliana Lyra, Rachel de Oliveira Lopes, and Joana Di Angelis Galdino Silva. 2018. "O Acesso ao Direito ao Trabalho para Refugiados no Brasil." In *Direito Internacional dos Refugiados e o Brasil*, edited by Danielle Annoni: 129–159. Curitiba: GEDAI, UFPR.

Jubilut, Liliana Lyra, André de Lima Madureira, and Daniel Bertolucci Torres. 2019. "Current Challenges to the International Protection of Refugees and Other Migrants: the role of and developments from the United Nations 2016 Summit." In *The Routledge Companion to Migration, Communication and Politics*, edited by Stephen Croucher, João R. Caetano and Elsa A. Campbell: 19–33. Abingdon and New York: Routledge.

Jubilut, Liliana Lyra, and Erika Pires Ramos. 2014. "Regionalism: a strategy for dealing with crisis migration." *Forced Migration Review*, 45: 66–67.

Jubilut et al. 2015. Migrantes, apátridas e refugiados: subsídios para o aperfeiçoamento de acesso a serviços, direitos e políticas públicas no Brasil. Brasília: Ministério da Justiça; IPEA.

Kampala Convention. 2009. https://au.int/en/treaties/african-union-convention-protection-and-assistance-internally-displaced-persons-africa.

Karas, Tania. 2018. The New Global Refugee Pact. *IRIN*. https://www.thenewhumanitarian.org/analysis/2018/12/18/briefing-new-global-refugee-pact.

Klein-Solomon, Michelle. 2005. Focus on Regional Consultative Processes on Migration, IOM's [International Organization for Migration] International Dialogue on Migration and the Berne Initiative. *United Nations Expert Group Meeting on International Migration and Development International Migration Management through Inter-State Consultation Mechanisms.*

Krasner, Stephen. 1982. "Structural Causes and Regime Consequences: Regimes as Intervening Variables." *International Organization*, 36 (2): 185–205. https://doi.org/10.1017/S0020818300018920.

Maia, Camila Barreto, Diogo Morales, and Raisa Ortiz Cetra. 2018. Global Compact for Migration: stop the humanity and listen to the Global South. *Open Democracy*. https://www.opendemocracy.net/en/global-compact-for-migration-stop-hypocrisy-an/.

Mexico Declaration and Plan of Action to Strengthen the International Protection of Refugees in Latin America (MPA). 2004. https://www.oas.org/dil/mexico_declaration_plan_of_action_16nov2004.pdf.

Moloney, Anastasia. 2017. Domestic violence pushes Central American women to flee for their lives: UN *Reuters*. https://www.reuters.com/article/us-latam-migrants-refugees/domestic-violence-pushes-central-american-women-to-flee-for-their-lives-u-n-idUSKBN18K2FJ.

Mondelli, Juan Ignacio. 2017. "Eradicating Statelessness in the Americas." *Forced Migration Review*, 56: 45–46.

Muggah, Robert, Maiara Folly, and Adriana Abdenur. 2018. The Stunning Scale of Latin America's Migration Crisis. *Americas Quarterly*. https://www.americasquarterly.org/content/stunning-scale-latin-americas-migration-crisis.

Newland, Kathleen. 2018. Global Compact Lays the Groundwork for International Cooperation on Migration. *Migration Policy Institute*. https://www.migrationpolicy.org/news/global-compact-international-cooperation-migration.

New York Declaration for Refugees and Migrants (NYD). 2016. https://www.un.org/en/ga/search/view_doc.asp?symbol=A/RES/71/1.

Norwegian Refugee Council. 2018. *The Global Compact on Refugees approved with overwhelming support by UN member states bar one, the United States.* https://www.nrc.no/news/2018/november/the-global-compact-on-refugees-approved-with-overwhelming-support-by-un-member-states-bar-one-the-united-states/.

Os 100 Pontos de Brasília. 2018. https://www.globalcrrf.org/wp-content/uploads/2018/04/Os-100-Pontos-de-Bras%C3%ADlia-20-02-2018-PORTUGU%C3%8AS.pdf.

Parish, Anja. 2017. Gender-Based Violence against Women: Both Cause for Migration and Risk along the Journey. *Migration Information Source*. https://www.migrationpolicy.org/article/gender-based-violence-against-women-both-cause-migration-and-risk-along-journey.

Perry, Jocelyn, and Stephanie Schwartz. 2019. The Global Compact on Refugees Misses the Mark on Refugee Return. *Refugee Law Initiative Blog*. https://rli.blogs.sas.ac.uk/2019/02/21/the-global-compact-on-refugees-misses-the-mark-on-refugee-return/.

Protocol Relating to the Status of Refugees. 1967. https://www.refworld.org/docid/3ae6b3ae4.html. https://www.unhcr.org/3b66c2aa10.

Ramos, André de Carvalho. 2018. "Immigration and Human Rights." *Archiv des Völkerrechts*, 56 (2): 156–172. https://doi.org/10.1628/avr-2018-0009.

Ruiz, Hiram. 2015. *Evaluation of Resettlement Programmes in Argentina, Brazil, Chile, Paraguay and Uruguay.* United Nations High Commissioner for Refugees. https://www.unhcr.org/57c983557.pdf.

Rush, Nayla. 2018. Global Compact for Refugees Adopted Today. *Center for Immigration Studies.* https://cis.org/Rush/Global-Compact-Refugees-Adopted-Today.

San José Declaration on Refugees and Displaced Persons. 1994. https://www.refworld.org/docid/4a54bc3fd.html.

San Pedro Sula Declaration as a regional contribution to the Global Compact on Refugees. 2017. https://www.acnur.org/5b58d75a4.pdf.

Steggert, Bobby. n.d. A World Report on the LGBT Immigrant Experience. *Queer Detainee Empowerment Project.* https://www.uua.org/sites/live-new.uua.org/files/world_report_lgbt_immigrant_experience.pdf.

Sozansky, Adeline, Karia Sarmiento, and Carlos Reyes. 2016. "Challenges to the Right to Work in Ecuador." *Forced Migration Review*, 51: 93–94.

Tesfaye, Beza. 2018. Jobs aren't the main reason young people migrate to Europe. *Euronews.* https://www.euronews.com/2018/09/10/jobs-aren-t-the-main-reason-young-people-migrate-to-europe-view.

The 100 points of Brasilia. 2018. https://www.globalcrrf.org/wp-content/uploads/2018/04/The-100-Points-of-Brasilia-20-02-2018-ENGLISH.pdf.

Thomas, Alice, and Mark Yarnell. 2018. Ensuring that the Global Compacts on Refugees and Migration Deliver. *Refugees International.* https://www.refugeesinternational.org/reports/2018/11/19/ensuring-that-the-global-compacts-on-refugees-and-migration-deliver.

Türk, Volker. 2013. "Ensuring Protection to LGBTI Persons of Concern International." *Journal of Refugee Law*, 25 (1): 120–129. https://doi.org/10.1093/ijrl/eet005.

United Nations (UN). 2018a. *The global compact on refugees: zero draft.* https://www.unhcr.org/Zero-Draft.pdf.

———. 2018b. "Global Compact on Refugees: how is this different from the migrants' pact how will it help." *UN News.* https://news.un.org/en/story/2018/12/1028641.

———. 2019. *Refugees and Migrants.* https://refugeesmigrants.un.org/declaration.

United Nations General Assembly (UNGA). 2016. *In safety and dignity: addressing large movements of refugees and migrants.* https://www.un.org/en/ga/search/view_doc.asp?symbol=A/70/59&=E%20.

United Nations High Commissioner for Refugees (UNHCR). 2005. UNHCR Global Report 2005. Glossary. Accessed 10 March 2019. https://www.unhcr.org/449267670.pdf.

———. 2016a. *Summary Overview Document Leaders' Summit on Refugees.* https://data2.unhcr.org/en/documents/download/62658.

———. 2016b. *Comprehensive Refugee Response Framework: from the New York Declaration to a global compact on refugees.* https://www.unhcr.org/584687b57.pdf.

———. 2017a. *Comprehensive Refugee Response Framework: delivering more comprehensive and predictable responses for refugees.* https://www.unhcr.org/comprehensive-refugee-response-framework-crrf.html.

———. 2017b. *Towards a global compact on refugees. Thematic Discussions 1. Past and Current Burden- and Responsibility-sharing arrangements.* Summary Conclusions. https://www.unhcr.org/5971d1b17.

———. 2017c. *High Commissioners Dialogue on Protection Challenges, 2017: towards a global compact on refugees.* https://www.unhcr.org/high-commissioners-dialogue-on-protection-challenges-2017.html.

———. 2018a. *Global Trends: forced displacement in 2017.* https://www.unhcr.org/5b27be547.pdf.

———. 2018b. *The 100 Points of Brasilia: Inputs from Latin America and the Caribbean to the Global Compact on Refugees.* https://www.acnur.org/5b58eb0c4.pdf.

———. 2018c. *UNHCR Welcomes Renewed Commitment to Protect Refugees by Latin America and Caribbean States at Key Meeting.* https://www.unhcr.org/news/press/2018/2/5a8e8e954/unhcr-welcomes-renewed-commitment-protect-refugees-latin-american-caribbean.html.

———. 2019. *Global Trends: forced displacement in 2018.* https://www.unhcr.org/5d08d7ee7.pdf.

———. 2020. *Global Trends: forced displacement in 2019.* https://www.unhcr.org/statistics/unhcrstats/5ee200e37/unhcr-global-trends-2019.html.

United Nations Human Rights (UNHR). n.d. "Status of Ratification Interactive Dashboard." https://indicators.ohchr.org/.

United Nations Children's Fund (UNICEF). 2019. *Migrant and Refugee Children in Latin America and the Caribbean: Support for Migrant and Refugee Children contributes to the Sustainable Development Goals (SDGs).*

Yaghmaian, Behzard. 2018. Global Compact on Refugees—a rich country's model for keeping others out. *Euronews.* https://www.euronews.com/2018/09/19/global-compact-on-refugees-a-rich-countries-model-for-keeping-others-out-view.

PART III COMMENTARY

Regional Responses to the International Regime on Refugee Protection

Jennifer Hyndman

In this brief commentary I wish to foreground the messaging of these two chapters, that Latin American states have made distinct *regional* contributions to the Global Compact on Refugees (GCR), noting that many other world regions have been left off the map of the GCR. The Global Compact for Safe, Orderly and Regular Migration (GCM) is the document that many states in South and Southeast Asia, as well as in the Middle East, rely on for guidance because they are not parties to the 1951 Convention Relating to the Status of Refugees (1951 Refugee Convention) and its 1967 Protocol Relating to the Status of Refugees (1967 Protocol), which is de facto part of the architecture of the GCR. In short, the GCR is 1951 Refugee Convention–centric. This may not be an issue for Central and South American states, but it is for large refugee-hosting countries like Bangladesh, India, Jordan, Lebanon, and Thailand, to name just a few. As Ranabir Samaddar has asked about the New York Declaration and its promised compacts, "Was there any postcolonial voice in this cacophony of anguished statements for humanitarian protection of the victims of forced migration?" (Samaddar 2018). In addition to some brief comments on the chapters, I will provide a response of sorts to this question below.

The two chapters in part III achieve key objectives outlined by the editors for the book: Mondelli analyzes the 2010 Brasilia Declaration on the Protection of Refugees and Stateless Persons in the Americas (Brasilia Declaration) and resulting Plan of Action to address statelessness in the Americas; and Jubilut, Mezzanotti, and Lopes examine the 100 Points of Brasilia, a 2018 document that consolidates the region's contributions to the GCR. Mondelli aims to provide a range of actors with practical tools to address statelessness, and not simply an overview of the Brasilia Declaration. The latter group of authors show that the 100 Points of Brasilia document addresses four protection axes: (1) quality of asylum, (2) durable solutions, (3) management of special needs, and (4) statelessness.

These chapters fill a major lacuna, in particular, in the recent global discourse on statelessness and refugee protection in the region and at a global scale. A comprehensive overview of protection initiatives in the region reveals that the 1984 Cartagena Declaration on Refugees (Cartagena Declaration) celebrates thirty-five years of influencing protection in the region for asylum seekers, internally displaced persons, and stateless persons throughout decades as with Cartagena +20 and Cartagena +30 (Jubilut and Casagrande 2019). Alternative protection strategies and complementary pathways, such as cities of solidarity and borders of solidarity, show how the region has led the world in its understanding that scales of protection are not always state-centric or legal systems. Indeed, urban areas become de facto spaces of humanitarian support and livelihoods in many cases (Kihato and Landau 2016).

My main point is that the salience of Euro-American legal norms from the international refugee regime and related treaties does not work for all world regions. Equally, the GCR does not "fit" or apply to all displaced persons in all host states. The Kolkata Declaration of 2018 highlights this point, given that so many countries are not included in the 1951 Convention, a Euro-centric post-WWII treaty infused with twentieth-century history of Nazism and Cold War politics in which civil and political rights trumped social, cultural, and economic ones (Mahanirban Calcutta Research Group 2018). The 1951 Refugee Convention refugee definition embodies these human rights, foregrounding *persecution* on one of five grounds as its main rationale. Targeted violence generating displacement related to colonialism, imperialism, narco-trafficking, and the politics of extraction is sorely missing, though in part it is acknowledged in the Cartagena Declaration on Refugees (Cartagena Declaration) and is codified in the 1969 Organization of African Unity (OAU) Convention Governing the Specific Aspects of Refugee Problems in Africa (1969 OAU Refugee Convention) (United Nations High Commissioner for Refugees [UNHCR] 2019).

Early in the 2000s, Teemu Ruskola, a comparative legal scholar, introduced the idea of legal orientialism (Ruskola 2002), a reference to the tacit superiority of Western, particularly American, legal regimes and declared inferiority of non-Western regimes, specifically China's laws (ibid.). Ruskola's argument (2013) is nuanced and legal, but it can be extrapolated to this commentary on the GCR in two ways: first, as Edward Said (1978) argued, Orientalism is the politicized cultural production of the "East" (as inferior) by the "West." It is not necessarily a legal construct at all, but Ruskola persuasively shows how it can be so. Second, the 1951 Refugee Convention definition of "refugee" and that of its 1967 Protocol are indeed Occidental political constructions after World War II. That the GCR focuses primarily on countries that have signed one of these treaties demonstrates its geopolitical antecedents and Cold War architecture, as an expression of "legal orientalism." Again, my point is not to provide a legal analysis of the GCR to prove its Orientalist tendencies, but to show which refugee host countries are left off the global map of protection because of this bias. For example, one might ask why the GCR initially included thirteen countries as case studies for the Comprehensive Refugee Response Framework, but excluded states that are not signatories to the 1951 Convention or its 1967 Protocol.

What has been left out of most discussions of the GCR is the exclusionary geography of protection. Although signatory states are covered by the 1951 Refugee Convention definition, which is sometimes tailored further by individual countries in their national laws, states that host large numbers of refugees are not always signatories to International Refugee Law.

As noted by Jubilut, Mezzanotti, and Lopes as part of their chapter in this volume, the world's most salient refugee protection treaty is the 1951 Refugee Convention and its 1967 Protocol. Yet, as noted, these legal instruments leave a number of world regions off the protection map because they are not parties to the treaties that were penned in the midst of the Cold War, when nonalignment (such as not signing a Western treaty) was an assertion of independence and sovereignty in a polarized, recently postcolonial, geopolitical world after World War II.

To be fair, the authors of the GCR have acknowledged the value of both regional approaches and informal practices of protection beyond the Law. "Since its zero draft, the GCR has mentioned the importance of regional perspectives on migratory issues" (UN 2018). As the United Nations High Commissioner for Refugees (UNHCR) notes and Jubilut, Mezzanotti, and Lopes write here, migration usually occurs at the *regional* level. Some 88 percent of those fleeing their homes find protection in adjacent countries and/or in the immediate region, and yet vast swaths of the global in South Asia, Southeast Asia, and the Middle East and North Africa regions are missing. The informal mechanisms of protection, including international education opportunities for would-be refugees or family reunification abroad, also require regional cooperation to achieve lift off.

The 2016 New York Declaration for Refugees and Migrants consolidated unanimous political will to "do something" about migration issues and generated a process with specified outcomes. The consensus of all 193 member states of the United Nations (UN) was nothing short of miraculous in relation to the fraught politics of migration, though the two compacts promised by the NYD were not to be binding in Law, and thus were easier to support in principle. In terms of general rights, all migrants (forced or not, refugees or other migrants) are entitled to human rights as codified in international laws concerning human rights, yet there is still a gap in implementing these rights. The GCM is in large part an amalgamation of existing human rights instruments along with the UN's Sustainable Development Goals, which were also adopted by all UN member states in 2015. Hence it is more utopic and forwarding-looking, and has been less fraught to finalize than the GCR, in my view.

In this respect, Central and South American states are ahead of the curve. Jubilut, Mezzanotti, and Lopes (in this volume) rehearse Acosta's contention that Latin America aspires to protect *all* migrants (Acosta 2016). They note the complementarity between International Humanitarian Law, Refugee Law, and Human Rights Law. As the scale of forced displacement continues to grow, however, they also observe that anti-migrant sentiments have begun to emerge, possibly undermining the region's unique solidarity as political ethos. The rise of detention among undocumented migrants is one signal of cracks in the protection framework, a global trend where migrants have been securitized and vilified as threats to states and their societies. The protection regime for refugees and other migrants found in the Inter-American Human Rights System that embraces a broad framework of human rights that are applicable to international migrants, including those who are seeking asylum (Jubilut and Lopes 2017), and their protection by *non-refoulement* that coexists in parallel with the specific regional refugee protection regime.

One final point raised by Jubilut, Mezzanotti, and Lopes in this volume is the relevant role of the International Organization for Migration (IOM) in the drafting of the GCM. Such a role dovetails on the back of IOM's entry in 2016 into the network of UN-related organizations (United Nations General Assembly [UNGA] 2016). This debut of IOM must be scrutinized carefully. When IOM was not an official UN affiliate, it was contracted by states to conduct all manner of migration-related work, from accompanying refugees from camps to resettlement destinations, to feeding asylum seekers detained on Indonesian islands who had been refused by Australia for the purpose of claiming asylum, to collecting data and conducting evaluations of migration-related programs. As hard as one might look, the IOM did not have a public mandate, mission statement, or set of guiding principles (Pécoud 2017). Without a protection mandate or an explicit purpose, it remains difficult to understand what the IOM stands for.

The funding of IOM can no longer be at the whim of states who contract the organization to do any number of tasks, and one must ponder how so many of the recommendations of the GCM point to work that IOM has done in the past or currently conducts. Was it a conflict of interest to have the IOM in practice so engaged in the drafting of the GCM, which now suggests all kinds of work to be done by an organization like the IOM? We will see. Scholars and practitioners alike no doubt will continue to scrutinize the organization's new role in due course.

To conclude, the authors of these two chapters highlight key elements in relation to the protection regimes for stateless and displaced persons, specifying the region's contributions specifically through the 100 Points of Brasilia and the Brasilia Declaration, among other instruments. The articulation of such regional perspectives and research is vital to knowledge production that might otherwise be effaced by the legal orientalism of the West in terms of the 1951 Refugee Convention definition of "refugee," and the international treaties that leave out key regions beyond Latin American, North America, and European states that do so much of the protection work in the current moment.

Jennifer Hyndman is Associate Vice-President Research at York University, Toronto, where she is also a Professor and Scholar at the Centre for Refugee Studies which she directed from 2013 to 2019. Her research focuses on the geopolitics of forced migration, humanitarian responses, and refugee resettlement in North America. Her most recent book with Wenona Giles is *Refugees in Extended Exile: Living on the Edge* (Routledge 2017). Hyndman is author of *Dual Disasters: Humanitarian Aid after the 2004 Tsunami* (2011) and *Managing Displacement: Refugees and the Politics of Humanitarianism* (2000), among other coedited books, policy papers, and journal articles.

References

Acosta, Diego. 2016. "Free Movement in South America: the emergence of an alternative model." *Migration Information Source.* https://www.migrationpolicy.org/article/free-movement-south-america-emergence-alternative-model.

Jubilut, Liliana L., and Melissa M. Casagrande. 2019. The Global Compact on Refugees and Latin America. *E-International Relations.* https://www.e-ir.info/2019/12/17/the-global-compact-on-refugees-and-latin-america/.

Jubilut, Liliana L., and Rachel de O. Lopes. 2017. "Strategies for the Protection of Migrants through International Law," *Groningen Journal of International Law,* 5 (1): 34–56.

Kihato, Caroline W., and Loren B. Landau. 2016. "Stealth Humanitarianism: Negotiating Politics, Precarity and Performance in Protecting the Urban Displaced." *Journal of Refugee Studies* 30 (3): 407–425.

Mahanirban Calcutta Research Group. 2018. *Kolkata Declaration–Protection of Refugees and Migrants.* http://www.mcrg.ac.in/RLS_Migration/Kolkata_Declaration_2018.pdf.

Pécoud, Antoine. 2017. "What do we know about the International Organization for Migration?" *Journal of Ethnic and Migration Studies,* 44 (10): 1621–1638.

Ruskola, Teemu. 2002. "Legal Orientalism." *Michigan Law Review,* 101 (1): 179–234.

———. 2013. *Legal Orientalism: China, the United States, and Modern Law.* Cambridge: Harvard University Press.

Said, Edward W. 1978. *Orientalism.* London and Henley: Routledge and Kegan Paul.

Samaddar, Ranabir. 2018. "Promises and Paradoxes of a Global Gaze" [a postcolonial assessment of the GCR]. Available at http://www.mcrg.ac.in/RLS_Migration/Module_Wise/Module_A.asp

United Nations (UN). 2018. The global compact on refugees: zero draft. https://www.unhcr.org/Zero-Draft.pdf.

United Nations General Assembly (UNGA). 2016. Agreement concerning the Relationship between the United Nations and the International Organization for Migration. A/70/976. https://www.un.org/ga/search/view_doc.asp?symbol=A/70/976.

United Nations High Commissioner for Refugees (UNHCR). 2019. 1969 OAU Refugee Convention. https://www.unhcr.org/5cd569744.pdf.

Part IV

Other Forms of Protection Beyond the Regional Refugee Regime

9

The Residence Agreement of MERCOSUR as an Alternative Form of Protection

The Challenges of a Milestone in Regional Migration Governance

Leiza Brumat

Introduction

Latin American regional integration schemes have designed regimes for facilitating the movement of persons within the territory of their member states.[1] The most well-known regional policy in the mobility[2] agenda is the Residence Agreement (RAM)[3] of the Mercado Común del Sur (MERCOSUR; Southern Common Market),[4] which was signed in 2002 and entered into force in 2009. The RAM creates a facilitated regime for residence for all the nationals of the signatory states, independent of whether migration was voluntary or forced. This regime means that the RAM could be used for granting residence rights to refugees. I will argue that, in face of the current Venezuelan exodus, the RAM could be used in the region as a way of facilitating the movement and regularization of Venezuelan citizens, and thus granting them residence rights as an alternative to protection.

MERCOSUR, whose original members are Argentina, Brazil, Paraguay, and Uruguay, is one of the most developed regional organizations in the world after the European Union (Kaltenthaler and Mora 2002; Malamud and Schmitter 2006). The RAM is regarded as a milestone in regional migration governance in South America, and was the regional policy that consolidated MERCOSUR as the leading regional organization on migratory issues in the region. It was originally signed by the four MERCOSUR original member states, Bolivia, and Chile, and was later extended to almost all of South America,[5] creating a regional regime for residence. The RAM stated the freedom of movement of persons as a regional objective to be achieved, while it also created one of the most open residence regimes in the world. The RAM allows a simplified procedure based on nationality and not on economic means or a work contract: nationals of all the signatory states have the right to apply for a two-year residence permit that could be turned into a permanent permit after that period (RAM: arts. 2, 5).

Recently, when emigration from Venezuela increased dramatically,[6] South American countries started to elaborate and debate possible policy tools for managing these flows. Two problems emerged: the first was the status of Venezuelans, since there is no regional consensus on whether they (or at least some of them) should be granted refugee status (on the challenges of refugee protection in Latin America, see Jubilut, Vera Espinoza, and Mezzanotti in this volume), despite the fact that many academics (see below in this chapter) and the United Nations High Commissioner for Refugees (UNHCR) called for the recognition of the majority of Venezuelans as refugees (UNHCR 2019b). The second problem is that Venezuela did not ratify the RAM, which could potentially solve the migratory status of a great number of Venezuelans living in other South American countries. Even though the legal status of Venezuelans and the protection of their basic rights has been discussed in many regional meetings since 2017 (Freier and Parent 2019), South American countries could not agree on the application of a common set of rules to deal with this crisis. As a result, Argentina, Brazil, and Uruguay are the only three countries that decided to unilaterally apply the RAM to Venezuelans, whereas the rest of the countries adopted diverse ad hoc measures (Acosta, Blouin, and Freier 2019).[7] Most of the literature has studied the legal content of the RAM, highlighting its legal and political relevance in the South American context as well as in a global perspective (Acosta 2018; Acosta and Freier 2018; Acosta and Geddes 2014; Modolo 2012), while some studies have also looked at the negotiation processes that led to its adoption (Alfonso 2012; Brumat 2016; Margheritis 2013; Montenegro Braz 2018). Facing one of the worst migratory crises in South America's history, however, and given the fact that South American countries seem to be reluctant to grant Venezuelans refugee status (Brumat 2019), could the RAM be an alternative to protection for Venezuelans? What was the rationale behind the adoption of the RAM? What would be the advantages and shortcomings of using the milestone in regional migration governance for Venezuelan citizens, even if Venezuela did not ratify it? Why do only three South American countries apply the

RAM to Venezuelans? This chapter makes a contribution to the literature on South American regionalism and migration governance from an International Relations perspective by looking at the rationale, the ideas, and the interests held by the policymaking actors that led to the adoption of the most important regional agreement on human mobility in South America. This chapter will help us to better understand both the debates around the application of the RAM to Venezuelan migrants, and the opportunities and challenges of applying it.

I argue that, from a political and governance perspective, the RAM could be applied to Venezuelans because the rationale that guided its adoption was threefold. The RAM sought (1) the elimination of the irregular legal status of many regional migrants in South America, which is the situation that many Venezuelans are currently facing (e.g., Migración Colombia 2018); (2) to guarantee a wide set of rights for regional migrants (RAM: arts. 7, 9); and (3) to enhance regional integration in noncommercial areas. States' decisions on which policy instrument to use for human mobility is part of their migration policy. Migration is by definition an intermestic issue that combines the interaction of domestic and international/regional factors (e.g., Manning 1977). Consequently, the disagreement of South American countries about applying the RAM to Venezuelans is explained by the interaction of domestic and regional factors. First, the power configuration of domestic actors has changed. Since the mid-2010s, securitist actors have increased their power within domestic bureaucracies (Brumat, Vera Espinoza, and Acosta 2019) and many of these powerful actors advocate in favor of reciprocity between countries (which is justified by the fact that Venezuela did not ratify the RAM). At the regional level, the regional integration model also changed. Current South American regionalism no longer prioritizes social and political integration and the promotion of a shared identity. Argentina, Brazil[8] and Uruguay are the only countries that apply the RAM to Venezuelans because (1) Argentina, as the main receiving country of migrants in the region historically (e.g., Brumat 2016), was the leader in promoting the RAM as a way of solving its domestic situation of large numbers of regional immigrants with an irregular status; and (2) Argentina, Brazil, and Uruguay are countries whose history and society were heavily shaped by migration (Acosta 2018; Brumat 2016; Novick 2010), and that adopted three of the most progressive migration laws in the world in the 2000s, providing extensive rights to regional migrants[9] (Acosta 2018).

This chapter adopts a governance perspective to explain the provisions and the progressive character of the RAM. By looking at the negotiation process of the RAM, I analyze the rationale, ideas, and interests that guided the leading actors and that allowed the approval of such a groundbreaking agreement. Then I look into the debates on how to manage the Venezuelan "exodus" that have taken place in diverse South American regional forums and I will discuss, from a political perspective, the opportunities and challenges of applying the RAM to Venezuelans.

This chapter draws on information from more than a hundred in-depth interviews with key government actors from eight South American countries (Argentina, Brazil, Chile, Colombia, Ecuador, Paraguay, Peru, and Uruguay) that took part in the elaboration, adoption, and implementation of regional policies for the movement of persons, including the RAM, conducted between 2012 and 2018 within and outside the framework of the Prospects for International Migration Governance (MIGPROSP) project. The chapter is also based on a qualitative analysis of legislation on migration in the region (particularly the content of the RAM) as well as policy documents (mainly documents of meetings of regional forums and institutions where the RAM was negotiated) and on specialized literature on the subject.

The chapter is divided into four sections. The first section briefly explains the main theoretical concepts that guide the analysis of the RAM and of the negotiations that led to its adoption. The second section describes the main provisions of the RAM and assesses the relevance that it acquired for human mobility in South America. The third section looks into the negotiation process of the RAM to explain the ideas and rationale that guided its adoption. The fourth section looks into the debates on how to manage the Venezuelan "exodus" that have taken place in South American regional institutions that deal with migration issues. The chapter concludes with some thoughts on the opportunities and challenges of applying the RAM to Venezuelans.

Regional Migration Governance and Regional Policies for Human Mobility

I adopt a governance approach to better understand policymaking processes. Following this approach, governance is both a structure that includes "formal and informal institutions" as well as the "dynamics and steering functions" involved in policymaking (Levi-Faur 2012: 7).

I consider that regional policies for the mobility of persons comprise international (bilateral and multilateral) legislation that regulates migration flows (entry, exit, residence, and execution of labor activities) (e.g., Brumat 2016).

The processes leading to the adoption of policies for the intra-regional movement of persons involve discursive acts and interactions in which ideas are exchanged. I consider that ideas matter, particularly in South America where rhetorical regionalism (Jenne, Schenoni, and Urdinez 2017) characterizes regional integration processes. Individual actors' ideas and the predominant regional model of integration have a strong influence on building (and changing) consensus, which are the basis for the formulation (and reformulation) of regional policies (Brumat 2016). In Latin America the regional context is key for understanding policy developments (e.g., Dabène 2012), particularly on intermestic issues. The final adoption of a regional policy depends on the (relative) power of the actor(s) that formulated the policy proposal. Power here is understood as "the perceived capacity of one side to produce an intended effect on another through a move that may involve the use of resources" (Zartman and Rubin 2000: 14). In multilateral negotiations, an agent can have issue power, which refers to the "resources that can be directed towards a particular conflict or concern" (ibid.: 10). A certain agent with more issue power in the migration agenda has the potential to lead regional debates in that agenda and to become a regional paymaster if the agent is willing to provide its resources and pay a disproportionate cost for the adoption of regional policies (Mattli 1999).

The RAM of MERCOSUR: A Milestone in Regional Migration Governance in South America

In December 2002 MERCOSUR member states approved four agreements aimed at facilitating the regularization of the citizens of MERCOSUR member states, Bolivia, and Chile who were residing irregularly in another signing state. These agreements were known as the Brasilia Agreements.[10] The RAM for the citizens of MERCOSUR member states, Bolivia, and Chile became the most important legislation and regional policy in the South American migration agenda.

The vocabulary used in the RAM associates the facilitation of intra-regional mobility and the elimination of the irregular status of the citizens of South American countries with a shared regional identity. Its preamble states that solving "the migratory situation of Member States' nationals throughout the region" is defined as the way of strengthening "the ties uniting the regional community" (MERCOSUR 2002).[11]

The RAM also modified in substantial ways the national migration laws of the signatory countries. The objective of the RAM is that the "Member State nationals who wish to reside in the territory of another Member State will be entitled to obtain legal residency in the latter, according to the terms of this Agreement, by proving their nationality and submitting the required documents set forth in article 4"[12] (RAM: art. 1; MERCOSUR 2002). In this way, the nationality principle was established (RAM: art. 3), meaning that citizenship is the primary condition for obtaining residence and replacing the categories of migrants as defined in the national migration laws of the signatory states, which were, until that moment, the main requirement for issuing residence permits. These categories were linked to the economic activity that the persons performed[13] (Alfonso 2012: 47).

The entry applications can be completed in the consular branches or before the migration authorities of the (potential) host state. The application procedure will be done *regardless of the migratory status* of the individual and "will entail an exemption from paying fines or other burdensome sanctions" (RAM: art. 3; emphasis added), which also modifies national regulations substantially by establishing a limit on states' capacity to punish migrants for not having regularized their migratory status.

The RAM then provides for a right of residence for up to two years (RAM: art. 2). Access to permanent residence depends on the "proof of a lawful source of livelihood allowing the subsistence of the petitioner and his/her family group residing with him/her" (RAM: art. 5). So, *permanent* residence is linked to the economic status of the migrants. The residence permit (both temporary and permanent) guarantees a wide set of rights that could work as an alternative to protection. These rights include equal treatment with the nationals, civil rights equality, family reunification, the right to send remittances, and special rights for children born in one of the member states (including access to education) (RAM: arts. 7, 9).

The elimination of irregularity and illegal employment while protecting and prioritizing migrants' rights was one of the main interests that inspired the RAM. This can be seen in Articles 10 and 11, among others. For instance, Article 10 calls for cooperation among states to prevent the illegal employment of immigrants, sanction of employers who hire immigrants in illegal conditions, and dissemination of awareness campaigns.

Therefore, the RAM not only modifies the signatory states' national legislation, but also creates a regional right to residence while guaranteeing a wide set of rights for regional migrants (see Freier and Fernández in this volume). The adoption of this groundbreaking legislation happened at a moment in which a post-hegemonic/post-neoliberal model of regionalism prevailed. Post-hegemonic/post-neoliberal regionalism prioritized regional integration in the social and political agendas, while giving a secondary importance to the commercial and economic agenda (Grugel and Riggirozzi 2018; Sanahuja 2012). The RAM was the result of a proposal put forward by Argentina's government, which acted as the regional paymaster on the agenda and exercised issue power. At that moment (2001/2002), Argentina prioritized relations with its neighbors, and its domestic and foreign policy was based on the promotion of human rights, as is discussed in the next section.

Negotiation Process of the RAM

The first ideas for solving the situation of the irregularity of regional migrants in MERCOSUR were debated in the meeting of MERCOSUR's ministers of the interior in the late 1990s, but the most substantial proposals were presented in early 2002. In March that year the Argentine delegation presented a blueprint of Agreement for the differential treatment of Mercosur citizens and associated states that want to regularize their migratory status in the territory of a Member State or Associated states, without leaving the territory of such state (translation by the author) to the technical commission of the meeting of the ministers of interior of MERCOSUR. The proposal had been developed in the Office of International Affairs of the National Migration Directorate of the Argentine Ministry of Interior. That office "started to go along with some of the changes in the Mercosur, from being an economic and commercial integration to what is today a citizen, political or social Mercosur" (Official of the Ministry of Interior of Argentina, interview, December 2013). The idea behind it was as follows:

> Our idea arises from our own experience in Argentina. In my personal case, I had already witnessed two amnesties, . . . as a mechanism that was not even effective, because [as soon as] the day following the end of the amnesty we started to generate irregular [immigration] again, because the law was not consistent with the reality of our migrants. . . . We then thought of this MERCOSUR criteria, because, 90 per cent of our migrants came from MERCOSUR. Therefore, if we incorporated it as a permanent admission and regularization criteria, . . . as a regime, then it facilitated [the regularization process], because you were not going to have to prove being a worker or being married or being a student, you only had to prove that you were a national of a MERCOSUR country. We had already thought about it *as an internal matter*, and we were waiting for a moment or an internal situation to present it [to the regional negotiation table]. (Official of the Ministry of Justice of Argentina, interview, April 2015)

The officials of the Office of International Affairs of the Ministry of Interior of Argentina were aware that 85 percent of the migrants that their country receives are nationals of MERCOSUR and Associated member states. And, given the vast territory and varied geography of Argentina, people kept crossing the borders into the country. So these officials developed the RAM's proposal based on Argentina's own experience as a receiving country, which includes vast knowledge of the short-term effects of large regularization programs and managing large numbers of migrants. They considered that regularization, and not restrictiveness, was the easiest and most effective solution to irregularity. These officials neutralized the influence of the securitist actors within the Ministry of Interior of Argentina and in the meeting of the ministers of interior of MERCOSUR by highlighting that regularization improves national authorities' knowledge and capacity to control the population residing in their territory, which then would advance national security. They also highlighted how regularization would reduce the incentives for employing persons illegally. Their position took into consideration that the informal labor market in South American economies is very large. At the same time, as the countries went into a deep recession in 2001–2, emigration was increasing, so the legal status and rights of the member states' own emigrates was also put on the table (Official of the Ministry of Justice of Argentina, interview, October 2014; Official of the Ministry of Interior of Argentina, personal communication, December 2013). Therefore, the main strategy was to create a rights-focused regime while strengthening security at the same time. This dual approach was later embraced by Argentina's regional partners, since they found it useful for getting domestic support from their own constituents, as was indicated by several interviewees from the Ministry of Labor of Uruguay, Ministry of Foreign Affairs of Brazil, Ministry of Foreign Affairs of Ecuador, officials of the Andean Community, and MERCOSUR officials.

The Brazilian delegation acknowledged "the importance of the initiative" and the proposal was established as a priority in the agenda (MERCOSUR 2015: act. 1/02, 22). In July Brazil assumed the pro tempore presidency of MERCOSUR. Brazilian president Fernando Henrique Cardoso was finishing his mandate. In October there would be national elections and MERCOSUR was one of the most salient issues of the electoral campaign. Cardoso wanted to finish his administration leaving a significant measure that would give an impulse to MERCOSUR's integration after the 2001–2 crisis (Alfonso 2012; Montenegro Braz 2018). So, at the end of August 2002, Brazil presented a project for a MERCOSUR migratory amnesty. The project proposed an exceptional regularization process for MERCOSUR citizens that would last for six months (Alfonso 2012: 49). The Brazilian officials that had drafted the proposal considered that it was "a social symbol that will stay imprinted in the history of Mercosur's evolution" (Official of the Ministry of Justice of Argentina, interview, October 2014). In that same meeting, the delegations discussed the proposal and the Argentine delegation suggested changing the word "amnesty" to "regularization," as a way of eliminating the six-month temporal limit. The rest of the delegations agreed with the Argentine suggestion. Then, the Argentine delegation presented again the proposal that it had already presented in March of that same year, now entitled Agreement for the Migratory Regularization in the state of Residence (translation by the author). Half an hour later, the Brazilian delegation decided to retire their proposal and to support the Argentine one instead. During the three days of negotiations that followed the proposal, Argentina and Brazil's delegations, acting jointly, were the two most active advocates for the adoption of the RAM (Brumat 2016). This means that Brazil, the largest and most powerful country, supported Argentina, the country with the most issue power in the migration agenda. The coalition of the two most powerful countries was key for the following approval and for the implementation of the RAM. The profile of the leaders of the Brazilian delegation played a role in this coalition: they were specialists in human rights and migration issues, as we could prove in our fieldwork.

The ministers of interior approved the RAM for the citizens of MERCOSUR, Bolivia, and Chile on 8 November 2002 and presented it to the executive organ of the MERCOSUR, the Common Market Council. Brazil pushed strongly for the RAM to be a highly visible policy and included it in the agenda of the MERCOSUR Presidential Summit (Official of the Ministry of Justice of Argentina, personal communication, October 2014). The RAM was approved at the highest level of the regional organization, the MERCOSUR Presidential Summit, in December 2002.

Given MERCOSUR's policy implementation problems (Caetano, Vázquez, and Ventura 2008), many policymakers' expectation was that the RAM would be a failure (Brumat 2016). These problems add up to criticism by scholars and international organizations who have pointed out the RAM's limitations. The main criticism concerns the lack of a right of entrance to the host state (International Organization for Migration [IOM] 2018a). Acosta and Freier (2015) add that the RAM leaves much room for interpretation and, thus, for a lack of coherence and homogeneity in the implementation across countries.

The RAM turned out to be one of the main successes and longer-term policies in the history of MERCOSUR's regional integration (Mondelli 2017), however. As a report by the IOM shows (IOM 2018) almost 3 million South Americans residing in another signing state have already benefited from the RAM since its entry into force. In addition, the RAM proved to be a crucial instrument for providing equal treatment, rights, and equal work opportunities for migrants by increasing regularity. It also substantially facilitated bureaucratic procedures for obtaining residence permits (IOM 2018a). Finally, many of the main provisions of the RAM were incorporated into the migration laws of several South American countries, thus expanding its approach and consolidating the regional regime (Brumat 2020). Implementation also showed that, over time, most of the countries tended to facilitate the documental requirements (e.g., the health certificate requirement was eliminated by all the countries) and that implementation problems are quite specific (e.g., IOM 2018a).

The success of the RAM is mainly related to the combination of domestic and regional factors in the political and historical moment in which it began to be implemented (Brumat 2016). In the 2000–15 period, post neoliberal/post hegemonic regionalism was the dominating model of regional integration in South America (Grugel and Riggirozzi 2018). During those years, the new regional priorities were the political agenda, social questions, and development. The predominant political discourses rejected open, neoliberal regionalism and American hegemony and influence in South America's affairs. This reflected the foreign policy orientation of the leading countries (Argentina and Brazil), which shared some commonalities: they prioritized relations with neighbors, they sought to increase South America's profile in the international scene, they prioritized autonomy, and they had a strong anti-imperialist and Latin Americanist rhetoric that promoted a regional identity (e.g., Gomes Saraiva 2012; Levitsky and Roberts 2011; Merke and Reynoso 2016).

So, following this ideological orientation, migration and migrants' rights became priorities in the regional agenda, as was expressed by President Lula da Silva and President Néstor Kirchner in a joint declaration in 2003 (Kirchner and Lula da Silva 2003). On that occasion, the two countries agreed to stop deportations of Argentine and Brazilian nationals (with the exceptions of those with criminal records); they also agreed that the free movement of persons would be defined as a way of strengthening regional integration. Argentina started applying the RAM unilaterally in 2006, before its entry into force, with the Patria Grande program (Novick 2010), which was also a political manifestation of the Latin Americanist rhetoric. Argentina and Uruguay are the only two countries that unilaterally apply the RAM to all the signatory states as well as to Guyana, Surinam, and Venezuela. Their action is related with these two countries' very progressive migration laws, with the importance that migration historically had for their societies and national identities (Acosta 2018; Brumat 2016; Novick 2010), as well as because they do not apply reciprocity in this agenda (Official of the Ministry of Foreign Affairs of Uruguay, interview, October 2015; Official of the Ministry of Foreign Affairs of Argentina, interview, December 2013). Consequently, almost thirty-two thousand Venezuelans had obtained residence permits in Argentina and Uruguay in the framework of the RAM by 2018 (IOM 2018a). In the next section, I explore the regional discussions on the Venezuelan exodus and look into the reasons why the RAM has not been applied to Venezuelans by the rest of the signatory states.

The Venezuelan Exodus and the Political Responses in South America

Since 2014 Venezuela has been undergoing a deep social, political, and economic crisis. In 2019, Venezuela experienced a ramping up of hyperinflation (International Monetary Fund [IMF] 2019), malnutrition (Caritas 2019), severe health insecurity (United Nations Children's Fund [UNICEF] 2019), and the one of the highest murder rates in the world (World Bank 2019). This situation sparked an enormous number of protests since 2018 and the largest forced displacement in Latin American history[14] (UNHCR 2019a) (see Jarochinski Silva, Castro, and Sampaio in this volume). It has therefore been argued that Venezuelans should be granted refugee status, following the definition adopted in the 1984 Cartagena Declaration on Refugees (Cartagena Declaration), which was incorporated into domestic legislation by many countries in the region (Acosta, Blouin, and Freier 2019; Freier and Parent 2019; Jubilut and Fernandes 2018, see Jubilut, Vera Espinoza, and Mezzanotti in this volume). Even if asylum applications by Venezuelans in Latin American countries were to increase sharply,[15] many Venezuelans are not aware of their right to apply for asylum and many others choose not to do so since they sense that the refugee status comes with a stigma attached (Freier and Parent 2019: 58).

As the situation in Venezuela has worsened, Latin American countries have tried to coordinate their response to the crisis in several ad hoc multilateral forums that issued several nonbinding declarations.[16] These forums are the Lima Group (which openly criticizes the Maduro government) and the Quito Process, which aims to be more neutral and that issued a Declaration on Human Mobility of Venezuelan Citizens in Latin America in September 2018. In that declaration, the eleven signing states[17] urge the Venezuelan government to issue travel documents to its citizens, agree to accept expired documents from Venezuelan citizens for their migratory procedures, and to exchange information about Venezuelan migrants with the end of bringing humanitarian help and "achieving a safe and orderly migration." Most importantly, the countries "ratify their compromise . . . in accordance with the possibilities of each country" providing access to public health care and education, as well as "opportunities in the labor market" to Venezuelan citizens residing in their territory, without making any reference to their migratory condition (Quito Group 2018). The IOM and the UNHCR have also developed regional plans that complement national programs for the reception of Venezuelan migrants (e.g., Acosta, Blouin, and Freier 2019; Jubilut and Fernandes 2018).

The eleven signing states did not agree on applying Cartagena Declaration to Venezuelans, however.[18] There are several reasons for this. First, the asylum systems of these countries are "too underdeveloped and understaffed" to deal with a sudden influx of asylum seekers (Selee et al. 2019: 10). It has been argued that adopting ad hoc instruments instead of giving refugee status could be a way of speeding up residence procedures while also diminishing states' responsibilities, since the refugee status entails wider duties for the states and more rights for migrants (Jubilut and Fernandes 2018). It has also been pointed that the political cost of giving refugee status to Venezuelans could be high, particularly in the main receiving countries (Colombia, Ecuador, and Peru). These countries have little experience in receiving migration flows, and were already facing considerable pressure in the provision of public services. This pressure is being exacerbated because of this large and unprecedented influx of migrants in a short period, and because the influx also raised xenophobic discourses (Acosta, Blouin, and Freier 2019; Freier and Parent 2019). Other scholars point at the excessive power concentrated in the executive power and particularly in the presidents of Latin American countries (Acosta, Blouin, and Freier 2019).

Because the emigration flows increased dramatically following 2016, the national governments started designing ad hoc instruments to provide Venezuelans with documents. Such instruments are, for example, a visa of democratic responsibility in Chile, a one-year temporary stay permit in Peru, and border mobility cards and temporary stay permits in Colombia.[19] When implementing these policies, several problems such as long wait times, high costs, and lack of coordination between state agencies have been registered (Freier and Parent 2019; Jubilut and Fernandes 2018; Selee et al. 2019). As a result, only half of the Venezuelans residing abroad have a residence permit, according to the UNHCR.[20] And, even if the logic behind these measures is still regularization as a solution to irregularity (Selee et al. 2019) a characteristic that defines the regional migration regime created in the 2000s (Acosta and Freier 2015; Brumat 2020), the juridical guarantees that these policy instruments provide have been criticized for leaving many migrants in a vulnerable situation, since most of the guarantees are temporary measures (Acosta, Blouin, and Freier 2019). The RAM guarantees a much wider set of rights than most of these ad hoc agreements, as has been seen before. And, given that most South American countries are already applying it, they already have the expertise and knowledge to extend the application to Venezuelans.

The explanation for the lack of a regional agreement on the application of the Cartagena Declaration and/or the RAM and the adoption of ad hoc measures at the national level instead relies on both the national and regional levels, and on the interaction between these two levels. First, since the center-right-wing governments took power, the influence of securitizing actors has increased. These actors advocate in favor of more-restrictive migration policies and administrative and bureaucratic measures at the national level (e.g., Brumat, Acosta, and Vera Espinoza 2018). At the same time, the regional integration model changed from multiaxial integration (trying to boost regional integration in the social and political agendas) to uniaxial integration (focused only on economic cooperation) (Comini and Tussie 2016). This shift led to the abandonment of the Latin Americanist rhetoric and the identitarian elements that defined the 2000–15 era, in which the South American mobility regime was developed and the RAM was adopted. Also, the conservative governments' response to Venezuelan emigration is deeply linked to foreign policy considerations (Acosta, Blouin, and Freier 2019), so these ad hoc measures are a foreign policy instrument used to criticize and denounce the Maduro government. The combination of these factors is particularly relevant in the case of Argentina, which used to be the regional leader in the migration agenda (e.g., Brumat 2016); that country is currently not using its issue power actively in regional forums to push for a joint response to Venezuelan emigration and limits its action at the national level by giving Venezuelans residence permits under the RAM. So even if the rationale of the elimination of irregularity and the human rights focus that dominated the early 2000s persists, the ideas and the interests in the migration agenda have changed both at the national and the regional levels.

Conclusion

Venezuelan emigration is proving to be the greatest contemporary challenge for regional migration governance in South America. Crucially, though, this crisis is happening at a time when social and political regional integration is no longer the priority for South American governments and regional integration is viewed only in economic terms. This reality prevents the countries in the region from adopting joint decisions that would strengthen the fraternal bonds (RAM: preamble) between South American states.

The RAM proved to be a groundbreaking legislation that substantially modified national migration laws and became a symbol of regional integration in South America. Analyzing the development and characteristics of the RAM helps us to understand the rationale, ideas, and interests that guided its adoption and its (relatively) successful implementation. When it was negotiated, countries sought to eliminate migrants' irregularity, provide a wide set of rights, and develop a sense of regional identity. This is exactly what Venezuelan emigrants need in this critical moment. South America is facing one the worst migratory crises in its history; at the same time, there are many political reasons that prevent most South American countries from providing refugee status to Venezuelans. In this scenario, the RAM could be a legislative tool that countries are already familiar with and whose implementation they already know well, and that could be used to grant legal protection to Venezuelans. Residency permits and the wide set of rights guaranteed in the RAM could serve as an alternative form of protection. At the same time, applying the RAM could help these countries with the bureaucratic issues raised by large inflows of migrants in a short amount of time. The main limitation of the RAM, though, is that many countries apply it based on reciprocity: because Venezuela did not ratify it, they do not want to apply it to Venezuelan nationals.

Venezuelan migration, if managed strategically at the national and regional levels, could prove to be an opportunity not only for the countries that receive a new influx of young people, eager to develop their lives in a new place, but also for the longer-term objective of creating a South American demos.

Leiza Brumat is a Research Fellow at the Migration Policy Centre of the European University Institute (EUI), Italy. She is an International Relations analyst who was awarded a PhD by Flacso–Argentina. Before joining the EUI she was a Lecturer in International Relations and regional integration, as well as a Research Fellow for the National Council of Scientific and Technical Research (CONICET) of Argentina. Her latest publications include *The Dynamics of Regional Migration Governance* (edited with Andrew Geddes, Marcia Vera Espinoza, and Leila Hadj-Abdou) and *Migration and Mobility in the European Union* (2nd ed.), with Andrew Geddes and Leila Hadj-Abdou.

Notes

1. The findings this research is based on were supported by European Research Council funding for the Prospects for International Migration Governance (MIGPROSP) project agreement no. 340430 awarded to Professor Andrew Geddes.
2. For a discussion on the concept of mobility, see Geddes et al. (2019).
3. The RAM is available at https://www.mercosur.int/documento/acuerdo-resi dencia-nacionales-estados-partes-mercosur-bolivia-chile/ (visited in September 2019).
4. MERCOSUR is a regional organization created by the Treaty of Asunción in 1991. Venezuela joined MERCOSUR in 2012, but its membership was suspended in 2017. As will be seen in this chapter, Venezuela did not ratify the RAM, and that is the reason why some countries (like Chile) do not apply it to Venezuelans. As will be seen, however, other countries (like Argentina and Uruguay) still apply it to Venezuelans, even if Venezuela is suspended from MERCOSUR. Bolivia joined MERCOSUR on 17 July 2015 and the only requirement left for its full membership at the time of writing this chapter in 2018 is the final approval by Brazil's parliament. The remaining six countries in South America are associate states.
5. The RAM was signed first by Argentina, Bolivia, Brazil, Chile, Paraguay, and Uruguay. Ecuador and Peru joined it in 2011 (Consejo Mercado Común [CMC] 2011) and Colombia joined it in 2012 (CMC 2012). Venezuela has not signed it as of this writing.
6. In June 2020 the UNHCR estimated the number of Venezuelan migrants in the rest of the world was around 4.7 million (UNHCR 2020).
7. Because Ecuador grants South Americans the right to enter, reside, and work in Chapter IV of its Organic Law of Human Mobility of 2017, it could be argued that Ecuador indirectly extended the RAM provisions to Venezuelans. The author thanks an anonymous reviewer for this observation.
8. Brazil did so in a temporary manner in 2017 and 2018. See Acosta and Madrid Sartoretto (2020).
9. In Brazil, however, many of the most progressive aspects of the law were vetoed by President Temer (see Brumat, Acosta, and Vera Espinoza 2018).

10. The four agreements that make up the Brasilia Agreements are (1) the Agreement for the Internal Migratory Regularization of MERCOSUR Citizens, (2) the Agreement for the Internal Migratory Regularization of MERCOSUR Citizens, Bolivia, and Chile, (3) the RAM for the citizens of MERCOSUR member states, and (4) the RAM for the citizens of MERCOSUR member states, Bolivia, and Chile (translations by the author).
11. In this chapter I cite the unofficial translation of the RAM that was done by Diego Acosta and Victoria Finn (Acosta and Finn 2018).
12. Article 4 lists the documentation to be submitted in the application, which is simplified and not related to the economic situation of the migrant. These documents are a national document (ID, passport, nationality certificate), birth and civil status certificate, certificate of criminal record, and, if required by national law, a medical certificate. (Note that the medical certificate requirement has been gradually eliminated.) Finally, the application is to be accompanied with payment of service fees, which vary across countries.
13. Typical categories adopted in these laws are employees, students, and religious workers, among others.
14. For more information on the characteristics of these flows and migrants' profiles, see IOM (2018b).
15. The UNHCR calculated that there were 464,229 asylum seekers from Venezuela worldwide in December 2018: 49 percent of them were in Peru, 17.7 percent were in the United States, and 17.5 percent were in Brazil (UNHCR 2019a).
16. Regional organizations such as the OAS, UNASUR (which is currently undergoing a deep crisis), the Andean Community, and MERCOSUR have issued declarations stating their position towards the Venezuelan government and the crisis, but not did not address Venezuelan emigration directly. See Acosta, Blouin, and Freier (2019) and Jubilut and Fernandes (2018).
17. Argentina, Brazil, Chile, Colombia, Costa Rica, Ecuador, Mexico, Panama, Paraguay, Peru, and Uruguay.
18. Mexico and Brazil are the only two countries that recognize Venezuelans as refugees under the Cartagena Declaration. Brazil did so only recently, in December 2019 (see Acosta and Madrid Sartoretto 2020). Despite this change, the main points that are formulated in this chapter are still sustained.
19. Acosta, Blouin, and Freier (2019) classify six groups of countries according to the policy instruments that they adopted in response to Venezuelan migration since 2016. For more details on these policies, see Selee et al. (2019), and Freier and Luzes in this volume.
20. According to the UNHCR, almost 1.5 million Venezuelan migrants worldwide had a residence permit in February 2019 (UNHCR 2019a). The calculation is mine.

References

Acosta, Diego. 2018. *The National versus the Foreigner in South America. 200 Years of Migration and Citizenship Law.* Cambridge: Cambridge University Press.

Acosta, Diego, Cécile Blouin, and Luisa Feline Freier. 2019. "La emigración venezolana: respuestas latinoamericanas." 3 (2a época). Documento de Trabajo. Madrid: Fundación Carolina.

Acosta, Diego, and Luisa Feline Freier. 2015. "Turning the Immigration Policy Paradox Upside Down? Populist Liberalism and Discursive Gaps in South America." *International Migration Review* 49 (3): 659–96. doi:10.1111/imre.12146.

———. 2018. "Regional Governance of Migration in South America." In *Handbook of Migration and Globalisation*, edited by Anna Triandafyllidou: 69–85. Cheltenham, UK: Edward Elgar.

Acosta, Diego, and Victoria Finn. 2018. "*Unofficial English Translation of the MERCOSUR Residence Agreement.*" http://www.diegoacosta.eu/portfolio-items/unofficial-english-translation-of-the-mercosur-residence-agreement/.

Acosta, Diego, and Andrew Geddes. 2014. "Transnational Diffusion or Different Models? Regional Approaches to Migration Governance in the European Union and Mercosur." *European Journal of Migration and Law* 16 (1): 19–44.

Acosta, Diego, and Laura Madrid Sartoretto. 2020. ¿Migrantes o refugiados? La Declaración de Cartagena y los venezolanos en Brasil. *Análisis Carolina* 9/2020: 1–17.

Acuerdo Sobre Residencia Para Nacionales de Los Estados Partes Del Mercosur, Bolivia y Chile. 2002. https://www.mercosur.int/documento/acuerdo-residencia-nacionales-estados-partes-mercosur-bolivia-chile/.

Alfonso, Adriana. 2012. "Integración y migraciones. El tratamiento de la variable migratoria en el MERCOSUR y su incidencia en la política argentina." 3. *Cuadernos Migratorios*. Buenos Aires: International Organization for Migration Regional Office for South America.

Brumat, Leiza. 2016. "*Políticas Migratorias y Libre Circulación En El Mercosur (1991–2012).*" PhD Thesis, Argentina: FLACSO. http://repositorio.flacsoandes.edu.ec/handle/10469/10634#.WjqJNlVKuUk.

———. 2019. Venezuelans are the first nationality of asylum seekers worldwide, but South American countries do not recognise them as refugees. Why? *MPC Blog*. 1 July. https://blogs.eui.eu/migrationpolicycentre/venezuelans-first-nationality-asylum-seekers-worldwide-south-american-countries-not-recognise-refugees/.

———. 2020. "Four Generations of Regional Policies for the (Free) Movement of Persons in South America (1977–2016)." In *Regional Integration and Migration in the Global South*, edited by Katrin Marchand, Glenn Rayp, and Ruyssen Ilse: 153–176. New York: Springer-United Nations University.

Brumat, Leiza, Diego Acosta, and Marcia Vera Espinoza. 2018. "Gobernanza Migratoria En América Del Sur: ¿Hacia Una Nueva Oleada Restrictiva?" In *Anuario de Política Internacional & Política Exterior 2017–2018*: 205–10. Tradinco: Universidad de la República Ediciones Cruz del Sur.

Brumat, Leiza, Marcia Vera Espinoza, and Diego Acosta. 2019. "*The Re-Making of Migration Governance in South America: Analysing Policy Change in Argentina, Brazil and Chile.*" Paper presented at ISA 2019 Annual Convention. Toronto.

Caetano, Gerardo, Mariana Vásquez, and Deisy Venura. 2008. *Reforma Institucional Del Mercosur. Análisis de Un Reto*. Montevideo: Cefir.

Caritas. 2019. "*Venezuela exporta migrantes con malnutrición aguda.*" 12 February. https://www.caritas.org/2019/02/venezuela-exporta-migrantes-con-malnutricion-aguda/?lang=es.

Consejo Mercado Común (CMC): MERCOSUR. 2011. *Adhesión de La República Del Perú al Acuerdo Sobre Residencia Para Nacionales de Los Estados Partes de Del Mercosur, Bolivia y Chile.*
———. 2012. *Adhesión de La República de Colombia al "Acuerdo Sobre Residencia Para Nacionales de Los Estados Parte Del Mercosur, Bolivia y Chile."*
Comini, Nicolás, and Diana Tussie. 2016. "Argentina: Reconfigurando El Regionalismo En La Ola Conservadora." 2. *Informe de Coyuntura ORALC.* Montevideo.
Dabène, Olivier. 2012. "*Explaining Latin America's Fourth Wave of Regionalism. Regional Integration of a Third Kind.*" Paper presented at the Annual Congress of the Latin American Studies Association (LASA). San Francisco.
Freier, Luisa Feline, and Nicolas Parent. 2019. "The Regional Response to the Venezuelan Exodus." *Current History,* February: 56–61.
Geddes, Andrew, Marcia Vera Espinoza, Leila Hadj Abdou, and Leiza Brumat, eds. 2019. "Introduction: The Dynamics of Regional Migration Governance." In *The Dynamics of Regional Migration Governance,* edited by Andrew Geddes et al.: 1–14. Cheltenham, UK: Edward Elgar.
Gomes Saraiva, Miriam. 2012. "La Política Exterior de Dilma Rousseff Hacia América Del Sur: Continuidad En Estrategias y Ajustes En Prioridades." In *El Regionalismo "Post-Liberal" En América Latina y El Caribe: Nuevos Actores, Nuevos Temas, Nuevos Desafíos. Anuario de La Integración,* edited by Andrés Serbin, Laneydi Martínez and Haroldo Ramanzani Júnior: 289–300. 9. Buenos Aires: CRIES.
Grugel, Jean, and Pia Riggirozzi. 2018. "Neoliberal Disruption and Neoliberalism's Afterlife in Latin America: What Is Left of Post-Neoliberalism?" *Critical Social Policy* 38 (3): 547–66. doi:10.1177/0261018318765857.
International Monetary Fund (IMF). 2019. *World Economic Outlook (April 2019)– Inflation Rate, Average Consumer Prices.* https://www.imf.org/external/datamap per/PCPIPCH@WEO.
International Organization for Migration (IOM). 2018a. "Evaluación del Acuerdo de Residencia Del MERCOSUR y su incidencia en el acceso a derechos de los migrantes." 9. *Cuadernos Migratorios.* Buenos Aires.
———. 2018b. "*Análisis: Flujos migratorios de venezolanos en Sudamérica mayo 2018.*" Buenos Aires: IOM Regional Office for South America. https://robuenosaires.iom .int/sites/default/files/Informes/FMS_VEN_jun15_sp.pdf.
Jenne, Nicole, Luis Leandro Schenoni, and Francisco Urdinez. 2017. "Of Words and Deeds: Latin American Declaratory Regionalism, 1994–2014." *Cambridge Review of International Affairs,* 30 (2–3): 195–215. doi:10.1080/09557571.2017.1383358.
Jubilut, Liliana Lyra, and Ananda Pópora Fernandes. 2018. "A Atual Proteção Aos Deslocados Forçados Da Venezuela Pelos Países Da América Latina." In *Migrações Venezuelanas,* edited by Rosana Baeninger and João Carlos Jarochinski Silva: 164–78. Campinas: Universidad de Campinas.
Kaltenthaler, Karl, and Frank O. Mora. 2002. "Explaining Latin American Economic Integration: The Case of Mercosur." *Review of International Political Economy,* 9 (1): 72–97.
Kirchner, Néstor, and Luis Inácio Lula da Silva. 2003. *Declaración Conjunta de Los Señores Presidentes de La República Argentina y de La República Federativa Del Brasil.* http://revista.iil.jursoc.unlp.edu.ar/revista_9/Numero9/material/Htm/doc_ declaracion_conjunta_argentina_brasil.pdf.

Levi-Faur, David. 2012. "From 'Big Government' to 'Big Governance'?" In *The Oxford Handbook of Governance*, edited by David Levi-Faur: 3–18. Oxford: Oxford University Press.
Levitsky, Steven, and Kenneth M. Roberts. 2011. *The Resurgence of the Latin American Left*. Baltimore: Johns Hopkins University.
Malamud, Andres, and Philippe C. Schmitter. 2006. "La experiencia de integración Europea y el potencial de integración del Mercosur." *Desarrollo Económico*, 46 (181): 3–31. doi:10.2307/4151099.
Manning, Bayless. 1977. "The Congress, the Executive and Intermestic Affairs: Three Proposals." *Foreign Affairs*, 55 (2): 306–24. doi:10.2307/20039647.
Margheritis, Ana. 2013. "Piecemeal Regional Integration in the Post-Neoliberal Era: Negotiating Migration Policies within Mercosur." *Review of International Political Economy*, 20 (3): 541–75. doi:10.1080/09692290.2012.678762.
Mattli, Walter. 1999. *The Logic of Regional Integration: Europe and Beyond*. Cambridge: Cambridge University Press.
MERCOSUR. 2002. *Acuerdo sobre Residencia para Nacionales de los Estados Partes del Mercosur, Bolivia y Chile*.
MERCOSUR. 2015. "Foro Especializado Migratorio Del Mercosur y Estados Asociados: Reunión de Ministros Del Interior. Memoria Institucional 1997–2015." http://www.migraciones.gov.ar/foro_migratorio/pdf/memoria_institucional_n.pdf.
Merke, Federico, and Diego Reynoso. 2016. "Dimensiones de política exterior en América Latina según juicio de expertos." *Estudios Internacionales*, 48 (185): 107–31. doi:10.5354/rei.v48i185.44555.
Migración Colombia. 2018. *Todo lo que debe saber sobre la migración venezolana y no le han contado*. Bogotá: Ministerio de Relaciones Exteriores. http://www.migracioncolombia.gov.co/venezuela/Todo%20sobre%20Venezuela.pdf.
Modolo, Vanina. 2012. "Política Migratoria Regional. El Caso de La Residencia MERCOSUR (2002–2011)." *Revista Aportes Para La Integración Latinoamericana* XVIII (26): 40–58.
Mondelli, Marcelo. 2017. "Scaling up Citizenship. The Case of the Statute of MERCOSUR Citizenship." In *Handbook of South American Governance*, edited by Pia Riggirozzi and Christopher Wylde: 426–41. London: Routledge.
Montenegro Braz, Adriana. 2018. "Migration Governance in South America: The Bottom-up Diffusion of the Residence Agreement of MERCOSUR." *Revista de Administração Pública* 52 (2): 303–20. doi:10.1590/0034-761220170069.
Novick, Susana. 2010. "Políticas Migratorias En La Argentina: Experiencias Del Pasado, Reformas Actuales y Perspectivas Futuras." In *Estado Actual y Perspectivas de Las Políticas Migratorias En El Mercosur*, edited by Carolina Zurbriggen and Lenin Mondol: 25–54. Montevideo: Flacso Uruguay.
Quito Group. 2018. *Declaración de Quito Sobre Movilidad Humana de Ciudadanos Venezolanos En La Región*. https://www.cancilleria.gob.ec/declaracion-de-quito-sobre-movilidad-humana-de-ciudadanos-venezolanos-en-la-region/.
Sanahuja, José Antonio. 2012. "Regionalismo Post-Liberal y Multilateralismo En Suramérica: El Caso de UNASUR." In *El Regionalismo "Post-Liberal" En América Latina y El Caribe: Nuevos Actores, Nuevos Temas, Nuevos Desafíos. Anuario de La Integración Regional de América Latina y El Gran Caribe 2012*, edited by Andrés

Serbin, Laneydi Martínez and Haroldo Ramanzani Júnior: 19–71. Buenos Aires: CRIES.
Selee, Andrew, Jessica Bolter, Betilde Muñoz-Pogossian, and Miryam Hazán. 2019. *Creativity amid Crisis: Legal Pathways for Venezuelan Migrants in Latin America.* Policy Brief. Washington, DC: Migration Policy Institute. https://www.migrationpolicy.org/research/legal-pathways-venezuelan-migrants-latin-america.
United Nations High Commissioner for Refugees (UNHCR). 2019a. *Los flujos de venezolanos continúan constantes, alcanzando ahora la cifra de 3,4 millones.* 22 February. https://www.acnur.org/noticias/press/2019/2/5c700eb94/los-flujos-de-venezolanos-continuan-constantes-alcanzando-ahora-la-cifra.html.
———. 2019b. *Majority Fleeing Venezuela in Need of Refugee Protection.* 21 May https://www.unhcr.org/news/briefing/2019/5/5ce3bb734/majority-fleeing-venezuela-need-refugee-protection-unhcr.html.
———. 2020. *Situación en Venezuela.* https://www.acnur.org/situacion-en-venezuela.html.
United Nations Children's Fund (UNICEF). 2019. Venezuela (VEN)–Demographics, Health and Infant Mortality. *UNICEF DATA.* https://data.unicef.org/country/ven/.
World Bank. 2019. *Intentional homicides (per 100,000 people).* https://data.worldbank.org/indicator/vc.ihr.psrc.p5.
Zartman, William, and Jeffrey Rubin. 2000. "The Study of Power and the Practice of Negotiation." In *Power and Negotiation*, edited by William Zartman and Jeffrey Rubin: 3–28. Ann Arbor: University of Michigan Press.

10

Trends in Latin American Domestic Refugee Law

Luisa Feline Freier and Nieves Fernández Rodríguez

Introduction

It has been pointed out that legislative reforms in the area of refugee protection in Latin America, especially in South America, do not mirror the pattern of constricting asylum described in the literature (Aleinikoff 1992; Betts 2011; Chimni 2000; Long 2012; Scalettaris 2009; Shaknove 1993), but rather, at least partially, represent a new avant garde in human rights–based asylum legislation (Freier 2015; Freier and Gauci 2020).

Since the late 1990s, policymakers in the region—who, in their majority, inherited restrictive immigration legislation from the era of military dictatorships in the 1970s and 1980s—became increasingly inclined to protect migrant and refugee rights (Acosta and Freier 2015; Cantor 2015; Domenech 2017; Mármora 2010; Martínez Pizarro 2011; Mejía Ochoa 2015), albeit with significant limitations (Ceriani Cernadas 2011; Freier and Gauci 2020; García 2016). Since 1993, sixteen Latin American countries have reformed their immigration laws,[1] with the same number passing new refugee laws,[2] which, in many cases, established national refugee legislation for the first time. Thirteen countries have included the 1984 Cartagena Declaration on Refugees (Cartagena Declaration) refugee definition, which is the cornerstone of Latin American refugee protection (see Lyra Jubilut, Vera Espinoza, and Mezzanotti in this volume) in their domestic legislation.[3]

Various officials of the United Nations High Commissioner for Refugees (UNHCR) have praised Latin American refugee laws, and even declared that the region had surpassed Europe as a global leader of human rights–based asylum legislation (Freier 2015; Freier and Gauci 2020). Testing out this assessment, Freier and Gauci (2020) analyze the legislative good practices for the protection of human rights identified by the UNHCR in Latin America as a benchmark for comparison between nineteen Latin American countries and the European Union, drawn from refugee and immigration laws, international conventions, treaties, and national decrees. Overall, the authors find that the laws of six Latin American countries–Argentina, Brazil, Costa Rica, Ecuador, Nicaragua, and Mexico–indeed surpass European protection standards based on the UNHCR's good practices.

In this chapter we address the following question: What are common trends in Latin American domestic refugee laws in juxtaposition to the asylum provisions in immigration laws? To address this question, we build on a comprehensive legal analysis of refugee and immigration laws, as well as on their respective regulations, in twenty-one Latin American countries. The chapter does not address regional refugee law, but identifies common regional trends in domestic refugee law, which will likely inform future developments in regional refugee protection.

To provide an overview of regional refugee law developments and protection challenges, we take a look at both refugee and immigration laws for two reasons. First, some countries have not yet passed specific refugee laws, and refugee protection is currently regulated through immigration legislation. Second, in the countries that have passed both immigration and refugee laws, the former often supplements the latter, especially regarding the socioeconomic rights of refugees. In addition, other aspects, such as refugees' resident status, are often regulated in immigration laws. In order to provide a complete analysis of refugee protection in any given country, other legislation regarding public health care and education would also have to be taken into consideration. This chapter thus makes an important contribution to the literature on Latin American refugee and immigration legislation, and on legislative liberalization (see Fernández, Freier, and Hammoud-Gallego 2020 for a recent literature discussion), but is not an exhaustive analysis of the legal norms that regulate refugee protection in the region. Table 10.1 lists the Latin American migration and refugee laws, as well as additional regularizations and legal developments that will be considered in this chapter.

This chapter is divided into three sections, followed by conclusions. First, we provide an overview of the common trends in Latin American refugee laws, focusing on each law's definition of "refugee" and some of the basic principles of refugee protection. Second, we analyze commonalities in the provisions on refugees in the region's immigration laws. Third, we discuss the supplementary nature of the immigration laws regarding refugee protection, focusing on the regulation of the right to work, and access to education and health care, which are all key aspects for the integration of asylum

Table 10.1 Migration and Refugee Laws in Latin America

	Refugee Law	Migration Law, Rank, Identification number and/or year	Regulations and Additional Legal Developments
Argentina	Refugee Recognition and Protection General Act (Act 26,165-2006)	Migration Act (Act 25,871-2004)	*
Belize	Refugees Act (2000)	Immigration Act (2000)	*
Bolivia	Refugees Protection Act (Act 251-2012)	Migration Act (Act 370-2013)	Supreme Decree 1,440-2012, Regulation to the Refugees Protection Act
Brazil	Act that defines mechanisms for the implementation of the 1951 Refugee Statute, and determines other measures (Act 9,474-1997)	Act that establishes the Migration Law (Act 13,445-2017)	*
Chile	Act that establishes provisions on refugee protection (Act 20,430-2010)	Decree-law that establishes norms on foreigners in Chile (Decree-Law 1,049-1975)	Regulation to Act 20,430, which establishes provisions on refugee protection (2010)
Colombia	Decree that establishes the procedure for the recognition of refugee status, rules on the Advisory Commission for the Determination of Refugee Status, and issues other provisions (Decree 2,840-2013)	Decree that establishes provisions on migration matters (Decree 834-2013)	*
Costa Rica	Regulation on Refugees (Decree 36,831-2011)	General Migration and Foreign Act (Act 8,764-2010)	*
Cuba	*	Migration Act (Act 1,312-1976)	*
Ecuador	*	Human Mobility Law (2017)	*
El Salvador	Refugees Status Determination Act (Legislative Decree 918-2002)	Migration Act (Legislative Decree 2,772-1958)	Decree 79-2005. Regulation to the Refugees Status Determination Act

Guatemala	Regulation on the Protection and Determination of the Refugee Statute in the State of Guatemala (Government Agreement 383-2001)	Migration Code (Decree 44-2016)	*
Haiti	*	Migration and Immigration Act (Act 128-1959)	*
Honduras	*	Migration and Foreign Act (Decree 208-2003)	*
Mexico	Refugees, Complementary Protection and Political Asylum Act (2011)	Migration Act (2011)	*
Nicaragua	Refugee Protection Act (Act 655-2008)	General Migration and Foreign Act (Act 761-2011)	*
Panama	Executive Decree that develops Act 5-1997, by which the 1951 Refugee Convention and 1967 Protocol are approved (Decree 5-2018)	Decree-Law that creates the National Migration Service, the Migratory Career, and determines other provisions (Decree Law 5-2008)	
Paraguay	Refugees General Act (Act 1,938-2002)	Migration Act (Act 978-1996)	*
Peru	Refugee Act (Act 27,891-2002)	Migration Act (Legislative Decree 1,350-2017)	Supreme Decree 119-2003-RE. Regulation to the Refugee Act
Dominican Republic	Regulation of the National Commission for Refugees (Decree 2,330-1984)	Migration Act (Act 285-2004)	*
Uruguay	Act on the Right to Refuge and Refugees (Act 18,076-2006)	Migration Act (Act 18,250-2008)	*
Venezuela	Refugees and Asylees Basic Law (2011)	Foreign and Migration Act (Act 37,944-2004)	*

Source: Table created by Luisa Feline Freier and Nieves Fernández Rodríguez.

seekers and refugees in host societies. Finally, in the concluding remarks, we discuss the limits of implementation of these legislative trends and advancements in the context of Central American and Venezuelan forced displacement, specifically in the context of the COVID-19 pandemic, and formulate a number of policy recommendations.

Common Trends in Domestic Refugee Laws

While the majority of countries in the region have historically lacked refugee legislation, at the time of this writing, Cuba, Ecuador, Haiti, and Honduras were the only countries in the region that have not passed specific refugee laws. Cuba has not signed the 1951 Convention Relating to the Status of Refugees (1951 Refugee Convention) and asylum has never been regulated in the country's legislation. Ecuador ratified the 1951 Refugee Convention in 1955 and its 1967 Protocol Relating to the Status of Refugees (1967 Protocol) in 1969, earlier than most other Latin American countries (UNHCR 2001). Ecuador passed a first decree regarding refugee protection only in 2012, however.[4] After the approval of its Human Mobility Law in 2017, a regulation was issued that same year, which specified both immigration and asylum,[5] repealing the 2012 Decree. Haiti and Honduras adhered to the 1951 Refugee Convention and the 1967 Protocol[6] only in 1984 and 1992, respectively (UNHCR 2001), with reservations regarding labor rights and freedom of movement. Since Haiti does not have accurate mechanisms to protect asylum seekers and refugees, a specialized office of the UNHCR conducts refugee status determination in that country (UNHCR 2017). Honduras's migration legislation, on the other hand, develops the basic legal aspects of refugee protection. In the case of the Dominican Republic, the very limited and bureaucratic nature of existing refugee law goes hand in hand with a manifest ineffectiveness of the few existing protection mechanisms for refugees.[7]

It is important to point out that, although the absence of specific refugee legislation tends to imply less protection for asylum seekers and refugees, this is not necessarily the case. According to Freier and Gauci (2020), Colombia, Cuba, the Dominican Republic, and Honduras are the countries with the least protection for refugees in the region. Ecuador, in contrast, ranks as the fourth-most-generous country in refugee protection in the region based on their quantitative coding of the UNHCR's best practices.[8]

In the rest of the region, specific laws on refugee protection have been approved, with different degrees of legal authority and varying scopes of protection. Colombia, Costa Rica, Guatemala, and Panama passed decrees, which are of lower rank than parliamentary laws—in other words, they cannot modify or affect the content of the latter. In Argentina, Bolivia, Brazil,

Chile, El Salvador, Mexico, Nicaragua, Paraguay, Peru, Uruguay, and Venezuela, however, national parliaments approved the current refugee laws after a political debate. Only a few of these refugee laws, such as laws in Bolivia, Chile, and Peru,[9] have been specified through regulating decrees. Argentina draws special attention in this regard. Although the 2006 Refugee Act is the most generous and comprehensive law in the region (Freier and Gauci 2020), it has not been regulated, despite the fact that Article 59 obliged the executive branch to pass the regulation within sixty days after its promulgation. This lack of regulation limits the implementation of refugee laws since the lack of regularization allows for undue discretion by migration and refugee officials.

Refugee laws in Latin America usually encompass the following aspects: the conceptualization and definition of "refugee";[10] the principles applicable to refugee status;[11] the competent administrative bodies for the recognition of refugee status;[12] the procedure for the granting of refugee status;[13] and the exclusion, cessation, and cancellation of refugee status.[14] With regard to the causes of exclusion and cessation, all countries incorporate those listed in Article 1 of the 1951 Refugee Convention.[15]

Some laws, such as those in Chile, El Salvador, Guatemala, Mexico, Nicaragua, Panama, Peru, and Venezuela,[16] also have a section dedicated to the rights and duties of refugees. In most cases, however, these sections are very superficial, and the rights and obligations of refugees are instead stipulated in immigration laws through provisions on all migrants who share the same residence status (temporary or permanent), which also encompasses refugees. Some important exceptions are the refugee laws of Chile, Mexico, and Paraguay,[17] which refer to the residence status of refugees (permanent in the first two cases, and temporary in the third case). The laws of Bolivia, Brazil, Guatemala, and Panama[18] stipulate the nationalization process for refugees.

Most of the refugee laws explicitly include the identity and travel documents granted to refugees in accordance with the provisions of the 1951 Refugee Convention. This is the case of Argentina, Brazil, Bolivia, Chile, El Salvador, Nicaragua, Panama, Paraguay, Peru, and Uruguay.[19] In exceptional cases, identification is regulated in the immigration law.[20] In most cases, a provisional document granted to asylum applicants only legalizes their stay in the country, but is not a proper identity document.[21] Travel outside the country is almost always explicitly forbidden for asylum seekers. Also, the duration of resolution processes is usually discretionary. Here, Mexico's law presents an exception with its legislation establishing a period of forty-five days to resolve an asylum claim.[22]

One of the most noteworthy characteristics of refugee legislation in the region is most countries' adoption of not only the definition of "refugee" found in the 1951 Refugee Convention, but also the one in the Cartagena Declaration,[23] which expands protection to people who flee their country "because their lives, security or freedom have been threatened by generalized violence, foreign aggression, internal conflicts, massive violation of human rights or other circumstances which have seriously disturbed public order" (Cartagena Declaration: 3rd Conclusion; see Fischel de Andrade in this volume). Some countries adopted the Cartagena refugee definition only partially. In the case of Peru, the reference to generalized violence was omitted. This does not modify the spirit of the Cartagena definition, however (Berganza, Blouin, and Freier 2018). The Honduran law does not mention "other circumstances which have seriously disrupted public order," which limits the scope of the Cartagena definition significantly. The Brazilian refugee law—often cited as the pioneer of progressive refugee legislation in the region (International Labour Organization [ILO] 1997)—extends refugee status of the 1951 Refugee Convention only to the individual who, due to the serious and widespread violation of human rights, is forced to leave his country of nationality to seek refuge in another country. With this limited expansion of the refugee definition, it is questionable whether Brazil actually adheres to the concept of refugee of the Cartagena Declaration. The refugee laws of Costa Rica, the Dominican Republic, Panama, and Venezuela do not include the refugee definition of the Cartagena Declaration, but in Costa Rica the Administrative Dispute Tribunal concluded that the Constitutional Court had effectively incorporated that declaration into domestic law.[24]

The basic principles of refugee protection regulated in the region's refugee laws include *non-refoulement*, no sanction for illegal entry, family unity, nondiscrimination, most favorable treatment, inadmissibility of extradition, confidentiality, and free status processing. The principle of *non-refoulement* extends to rejection at the border and extradition as forms of return. Reflecting Article 33 of the 1951 Refugee Convention, Argentina, Bolivia, Chile, Costa Rica, Guatemala, Mexico, Panama, and Uruguay, as well as Brazil in its 2014 Declaration and Plan of Action and Ecuador in Article 41 of its Constitution, explicitly set forth the principle of non-refusal of entry together with the obligation of authorities to guarantee the principle of *non-refoulement*.[25] The Argentine case is especially noteworthy because asylum seekers are protected by the principle of *non-refoulement* from the moment they are subject to the country's authority, without having to be present in the territory. In accordance with Article 31(1) of the 1951 Refugee Convention, Argentina, Brazil, Chile, Costa Rica, Chile, and Uruguay suspend all criminal or administrative procedures pertaining to illegal entry until there has been a refugee status determination.[26]

The laws of Argentina, Bolivia, Brazil, Costa Rica, El Salvador, Guatemala, Mexico, Panama, Paraguay, Peru, and Uruguay grant the right to family reunification.[27] More specifically, the laws of Argentina, Bolivia, Chile, Costa Rica, Mexico, Nicaragua, Paraguay, Peru, and Uruguay encompass extensive understandings of the family.[28] In Bolivia, for example, the refugee condition can be extended to a refugee's spouse or partner; ascendants and descendants; brothers and sisters who economically depend on the refugee; and children, adolescents, and adults under his or her tutelage.[29] In Argentina the law states that, in considering requests for family reunification, the authorities will take into consideration not only the law, but also the needs of the applicant and the cultural values of the applicant's country of origin.[30]

Common Trends in Domestic Immigration Laws

The degree to which the immigration laws and regulations in Latin America stipulate refugee protection varies. The immigration laws of Colombia, Cuba, the Dominican Republic, El Salvador, Guatemala, Nicaragua, and Panama only briefly mention refugee protection, whereas those of Argentina, Brazil, Costa Rica, Peru, and Uruguay are more pronounced, with those from Costa Rica, Ecuador, Honduras, and Peru[31] including sections specifically dedicated to refugee protection; as mentioned earlier, Ecuador and Honduras do not have specific refugee laws. The countries that do not mention refugee protection in their immigration laws at all–Belize, Chile, and Venezuela–have all passed specific refugee laws.

The provisions on refugee protection in immigration laws commonly regulate the following aspects: the need to observe international regulations in the area of human rights and international protection of refugees, the supplementary nature of immigration legislation in relation to that of refugee protection, the residence status of refugees (temporary or permanent), and guarantees or exceptions regarding general rules applied to migrants (such as the requirement for valid travel documentation to access the country). The first of these aspects is contemplated in the laws of Brazil, Costa Rica, and Uruguay.[32]

Even though the second aspect appears explicitly only in the immigration legislation of Argentina, Brazil, and Peru,[33] the principle *lex specialis derogat legis generalis* (special laws trumping general laws) makes refugee law superior to immigration law in all countries that have passed specific refugee acts in the region: Argentina, Bolivia, Brazil, Chile, El Salvador, Mexico, Nicaragua, Paraguay, Peru, Uruguay, and Venezuela.

Regarding the third aspect, all immigration laws that contain provisions on refugee protection regulate the residence status of refugees. Most of the countries–Argentina, Colombia, Costa Rica, Cuba, the Dominican Republic, Ecuador, El Salvador, Guatemala, Honduras, Nicaragua, Panama, Paraguay, and Peru–grant refugees a temporary residence permit. The period of residence varies greatly from one country to another, however.[34] For example, Panama grants refugees a renewable residence permit valid for one year,[35] whereas Colombia provides a temporary visa for a period of five years.[36] Mexico and Uruguay are the only countries in the region where immigration laws grant permanent residence to refugees.[37] This undoubtedly constitutes a very favorable aspect for refugees, and reflects the liberal character of the laws of these two countries (Freier and Gauci 2020).

Finally, many immigration laws also stipulate favorable exceptions for refugees, such as fee exemptions (Costa Rica),[38] and the exoneration of the presentation of valid identity documents to enter the country (Bolivia, the Dominican Republic, Mexico, Peru, and Uruguay).[39] In addition, some immigration laws stipulate specific guarantees to the principle of *non-refoulement*. For example, Argentina requires approval from the National Commission for Refugees[40] before deporting a convicted refugee, and Uruguay provides that the cancellation of residence and expulsion for an offense of intentional nature does not apply to refugees.[41]

The Complementarity of Refugee and Immigration Laws

The above-mentioned analysis highlights the need to examine refugee laws alongside the provisions of refugee protection contained in immigration laws, in order to reach conclusions about the characteristics and scope of refugee protection in different Latin America countries. Relevant provisions or good practices may be present in either law, or even in other specialized laws. This section provides a discussion on refugees' right to work and access to education and health care in the region, which serves to observe the complementarity of refugee and immigration laws, and, in particular, the form in which the latter is applied with a supplementary nature in relation to the former. This section further contributes to our understanding of refugee protection in Latin America, since access to legal work, education, and health care constitute basic rights, and are essential for the integration and well-being of asylum seekers and refugees in host societies.

Right to Work

Article 17 of the 1951 Refugee Convention establishes that States Parties shall accord to refugees "the most favourable treatment accorded to nationals of a foreign country in the same circumstances, as regards the right to engage in wage-earning employment." Furthermore, it adds that any restrictive measures applying to foreigners to protect the labor market shall not apply to refugees.

The refugee laws of Bolivia and Nicaragua[42] grant refugees the same rights and duties their constitutions grant their citizens, among which is the right to employment. The laws of Guatemala and Mexico[43] specifically determine refugees' right to work, and the law of Chile[44] grants this right with the same restrictions that apply to other foreigners. Panama's refugee law also extends the right to employment to refugees, subject to obtaining a work permit, as deduced from Articles 75 and 83. In addition, some refugee laws, such as those of Argentina, Brazil, Costa Rica, Nicaragua, Paraguay, and Venezuela, indirectly establish this right through their documentation.[45]

In the case of the Dominican Republic, which has, as we have seen, one of the most restrictive laws in the region (Freier and Gauci 2020), Article 21 of Regulation 2,330 establishes the right to work for refugees, but conditions it to the authorization of the National Office for Refugees in coordination with the ministry of labor based on the principle of nondisplacement of national labor. This provision is not in accordance with Article 17 of the 1951 Refugee Convention cited above.

Regarding immigration laws, those of Argentina, Brazil, and Uruguay recognize the right to employment in a generic way to all foreigners,[46] among which refugees are implicitly included in the same terms as nationals. Bolivia's law[47] does so with respect to the rights set forth in its constitution, without specifically referring to access to employment. In addition, the immigration laws of Argentina, Ecuador, and Panama recognize the right to employment to foreign residents.[48] Since refugees are granted temporary residence in the three countries, these provisions also apply to them.

Similar to the refugee law of the Dominican Republic, the immigration laws of El Salvador and Peru also establish restrictions on access to employment for migrants, which consequently affect refugees. El Salvador recognizes the right to work for migrants, and therefore refugees, provided that Salvadorans with similar occupations are not displaced.[49] Via Article 9 of Legislative Decree 1,350, Peru recognizes constitutional rights to foreigners subject to the limitations established by the law.[50] Since all three countries have ratified the 1951 Refugee Convention, these restrictions should not be applied to refugees.

In the immigration law of Honduras, a country that included a reservation to Article 17 of the 1951 Refugee Convention, the access to employment of foreign legal residents is conditioned to a formal job offer formulated by an employer.[51] As such, Honduras is the country with the most restrictive legislation in the region in terms of access to employment.

Overall, our analysis shows the importance of considering both refugee and immigration legislation in order to understand refugees' right to employment. To reach a comprehensive, nuanced understanding of this issue, however, it would be necessary to observe the labor legislation of different countries, and to verify what further rights, or limitations, are included in such laws. For instance, the case of Panama is striking. Although access to employment is granted to refugees by law, its labor legislation prohibits them, as foreigners, to practice many professions such as those in the health-care sector, and certain fields of engineering, law, education, or social assistance.[52]

Access to Education and Health Care

Article 22 of the 1951 Refugee Convention obliges States Parties to grant refugees the same treatment as nationals with regard to elementary education, and the most favorable treatment possible—and in no case less favorable—compared to other foreigners, with respect to further education. Although the 1951 Refugee Convention does not contain an explicit regulation of the right to health care, it requires states to grant refugees the same treatment as nationals in public assistance and relief (1951 Refugee Convention: art. 23) and in social insurance (ibid.: art. 24).

As in the case of access to work, some refugee laws, such as those of Bolivia, El Salvador, Nicaragua and Venezuela, implicitly grant the right to education and health care through constitutional and social rights granted to refugees in the same terms as to national citizens.[53] Moreover, the Venezuelan law expressly grants the right to education to refugee minors.[54] Other laws, such as those of Chile, Mexico, and Panama, guarantee access to education and health care, although the Chilean law applies the same limitations as to other foreigners.[55] The refugee laws of Argentina, Nicaragua, and Paraguay indirectly grant social rights, including access to education and health care, or access to education and social insurance (in the case of Paraguay), by establishing that possession of the identity card will grant such rights.[56]

On the other hand, in Argentina, Brazil, Guatemala, and Uruguay the immigration laws guarantee foreigners, including refugees, the right to education and health care in the same terms as nationals.[57] The laws of Costa Rica and Venezuela extend this right by guaranteeing constitutional rights to foreigners, and the law of Peru specifically includes access to health care and education. The above-mentioned laws all introduce the possibility of establishing restrictions, however.[58] The immigration law of Ecuador guarantees the right to health care to foreigners in accordance with international treaties, and requires health-care services to provide emergency services to foreigners.[59] The Ecuadorian law does not contain any provision in relation to the right to education, however. The right to education is regulated by Ministerial Agreement 337/2008, which guarantees access to elementary education to refugees, in the same terms as nationals, and to nonelementary education in the most favorable terms possible.

The cases of Colombia, the Dominican Republic, and Honduras deserve special attention, since none of their laws contain provisions on the rights to education and health care. In some cases, sectorial laws include provisions in this regard. For example, Article 8 of Honduras's Fundamental Law on Education guarantees access for all people to compulsory elementary and secondary education, without excluding foreigners. The same applies to Cuba, which, as has been reiterated, is not a signatory state of the 1951 Refugee Convention.

Conclusion

In the past two decades, Latin America's refugee and immigration laws have shown a clear trend toward liberalization (Cantor 2015; Freier 2015). More specifically, some Latin American countries can be considered international leaders in some areas of refugee protection, for example regarding the scope of protection, as well as in the area of refugee integration (Freier and Gauci 2020).

In this chapter, we have provided a comparative legal analysis of refugee and—given their supplementary nature—immigration laws and regulations in twenty-one Latin American countries. We conclude that most of the countries in the region have passed specific laws on refugee protection, with different degrees of legal authority. Some laws stand out with regards to their scope of protection, including extensive understandings of the family, such as Argentina. Other countries grant the same socioeconomic rights to both foreigners—including refugees—and citizens; examples are Bolivia, El Salvador, and Nicaragua.

At the same time, protection challenges in the region persist. More specifically, Cuba, Ecuador, Haiti, and Honduras still lack specific refugee laws; refugee protection is regulated through immigration laws in the cases of Ecuador and Honduras. Although all other countries in the region have passed specific laws on refugee protection, it is noteworthy that only three countries—Bolivia, Chile, and Peru—specified their refugee laws through regulations. This general lack of regularization, especially when legally required, allows for undue discretion by officials in the application of the law.

As we have shown in this chapter, in order to reach any conclusions about regional trends in refugee protection in Latin America, not only an analysis of the rights stipulated in refugee laws, but also those enshrined in domestic immigration legislation is essential. Specific laws in the fields of labor, education, or health care can also determine the rights granted to refugees.

As we conclude this chapter, it is essential to briefly discuss refugee policy implementation, and specifically application challenges of the Cartagena refugee definition. Latin America is currently facing three major displacement crises: one originating in Venezuela, another from the North of Central America—El Salvador, Honduras, and Guatemala—toward Mexico and the United States, and a third from Nicaragua toward Costa Rica and North

America. As previously discussed, the domestic legislation of fifteen countries includes expanded refugee definitions that go back to the Cartagena Declaration, which has been considered the cornerstone (see Lyra Jubilut, Vera Espinoza, and Mezzanotti in this volume) or flagship instrument of Latin American refugee protection (Freier 2015; Freier and Gauci 2020).

When applying generalized violence, massive violation of human rights, and other circumstances that have seriously disturbed public order, as criteria for refugee status, most Latin American countries ought to recognize Venezuelan citizens as refugees (Berganza, Blouin, and Freier 2020; Freier, Berganza, and Blouin 2020). Governments across the region, however–with the important exception of Brazil and Mexico–, have recognized only few Venezuelan asylum applicants, mostly under the refugee definition of the 1951 Refugee Convention. In addition, the duration of resolution processes is usually discretionary and its prolongation is widespread, due to its lack of state capacity and/or political will (Freier 2019).

In Mexico, on the other hand, Sánchez (2018) finds a differentiated treatment that seems to respond to an a priori decision on whether asylum seekers are recognized as refugees depending on their nationality, which favors Venezuelan citizens. He identifies a premeditation not to analyze any Salvadoran and Honduran asylum cases based on the Cartagena refugee definition, even though it is likely that "generalized violence" or "other circumstances which have seriously disturbed public order" (Cartagena Declaration: 3rd Conclusion) should apply to some scenarios in these countries of origin. Also, although Mexico's law presents an exception, with its legislation establishing a period of forty-five days to resolve an asylum claim,[60] this period has not been respected since a 2017 earthquake destroyed part of the infrastructure of the Mexican Commission for Refugee Assistance in Mexico City. Further studies are needed to explain existing implementation gaps of refugee legislation across Latin America.

The shift toward progressive domestic refugee legislation in the region might be threatened by the coming to power of conservative or far-right governments that, in some cases, have suggested a punitive turnaround regarding migration (Domenech 2017). On the other hand, and as mentioned in the introduction of this volume, there is concern that the region's displacement crises might lead to more electoral success of extremist parties and politicians with xenophobic discourses and agendas who could try to limit immigration, and reverse the legislative liberalization of refugee protection in their countries (see Lyra Jubilut, Vera Espinoza, and Mezzanotti in this volume).

In addition, concerns have been raised that the restrictions to human mobility, including to asylum seekers and refugees, which were implemented in the context of COVID-19, might be extended beyond the sanitary crisis (Freier, Castillo Jara, and Luzes 2020). In order to stem such developments, it is crucial that civil society actors, politicians, and international organizations across the region combat xenophobia and demand the application of existing legislation. At the same time, the international community needs to support the region in carrying the financial burden that a coherent application of the Cartagena refugee definition, as well as the scope of protection and the de facto granting of the socioeconomic rights discussed in this chapter, would imply in the current Venezuelan displacement context and beyond.

Luisa Feline Freier is Associate Professor of Political Science at the Universidad del Pacífico (UP) in Lima. She holds a PhD in Political Science from the London School of Economics and Political Science (LSE), and a Master's degree in Latin American and Caribbean Studies from the University of Wisconsin at Madison. Feline's research focuses on Latin American immigration and refugee policies and inter-continental South-South migration, and the Venezuelan displacement crisis. Her work has been published in edited volumes and leading peer-reviewed journals.

Nieves Fernández Rodríguez is a Research Fellow at the Berlin Social Science Center (WZB) and a PhD candidate at the Berlin Graduate School for Transregional Studies (BGTS, Free University of Berlin). She holds an M.A in Human Rights Studies, a B.A. in Political Science, and a B.A in Law from Carlos III University of Madrid. Nieves's research focuses on the process of *othering* toward migrants in contexts of both South-North and South-South migration and on the recent rise of contestations to Liberal Democracies.

Notes

1. Nicaragua (Act 156-1993); Belize (Immigration Act, 2000); Argentina (Act 25,871-2004); Honduras (Decree 208-2003); Venezuela (Act 37,944-2004); the Dominican Republic (Act 285-2004); Uruguay (Act 18,250-2008); Panama (Decree-Law 3-2008); Costa Rica (Act 8,764-2009); Mexico (Migration Act, 2011); Bolivia (Act 370-2013); Colombia (Decree 834-2013); Guatemala (Decree 44-2016); Brazil (Act 13,445-2017); Ecuador (Human Mobility Law, 2017); Peru (Leg. Decree 1,350-2017).
2. Brazil (Act 9,474-1997); Belize (Refugees Act, 2000); Venezuela (Refugees and Asylees Act, 2001); Guatemala (Government Agreement 382-2001); El Salvador (Leg. Decree 918-2002); Paraguay (Act 1,938-2002); Peru (Act 27,891-2002); Argentina (Act 26,165-2006); Uruguay (Act 18,076-2006); Nicaragua (Act 655-2008); Chile (Act 20,430-2010); Costa Rica (Regulation 36,831-2009); Mexico (Refugees Act, 2011); Bolivia (Act 251-2012); Colombia (Decree 2,840-2013); Panama (Ex. Decree 5-2018).
3. Argentina (art. 4, Act 26,165-2006); Bolivia (art. 15, Act 251-2012); Brazil (art. 1. III, Law 9,474, 21 July 1997); Chile (art. 2, Act 20,430-2010); Colombia (art. 1,

Decree 2,840-2013); Ecuador (art. 98 of Human Mobility Law); El Salvador (art. 1, Leg. Decree 918-2002); Guatemala (art. 11, Gov. Agr. 382-2001); Mexico (art. 13, Refugees Act, 2011); Nicaragua (art. 1, Act 655-2008); Paraguay (art. 1, Act 1,938-2002); Peru (art. 3, Act 27,891-2002); Uruguay (art. 2, Act 18,076-2006).
4. Decree 1,182-2012 of Regulation for the Application of the Right to Refuge.
5. Decree 111-2017 of Regulation to the Human Mobility Law.
6. Haiti in 1984 and Honduras in 1992, with reservations to Articles 7, 17, 24, 26, 31, and 34.
7. The Decree 2,330-1984 establishes the regulations of the National Refugee Commission. According to the UNHCR, this commission was inactive between 2004 and 2012.
8. Freier and Gauci (2020) use numerical codes to describe to what extent Latin America domestic laws have incorporated legislative good practices for the protection of Human Rights identified by the UNHCR. This allows them to rank Latin American refugee laws from most liberal to most restrictive.
9. Bolivia (Decree 1,440-2012); Chile (Decree 837-2010); Peru (Decree 1,119-2003).
10. Argentina (art. 4, Act 26,165-2006); Bolivia (art. 15, Act 251-2012); Brazil (art. 1, Act 9,474-1997); Chile (art. 2, Act 20,430-2010); Colombia (art. 1, Decree 2,840-2013); Costa Rica (art. 12, Decree 36,831G-2011); El Salvador (art. 4, Decree 918-2002); Guatemala (art. 11, Gov. Agr. 383-2001); Mexico (art. 13, Refugee Act -2011); Nicaragua (art. 1, Act 655-2008); Panama (art. 5, Decree 5-2018); Paraguay (art. 1, Act 1,938-2002); Peru (art. 3, Act 27,891-2002); the Dominican Republic (art. 6, Decree 2,330-1984); Uruguay (art. 2, Act 18,076-2006); Venezuela (art. 7, Refugees Basic Law).
11. Argentina (art. 2, arts. 5–8, Act 26,165-2006); Bolivia (arts. 4–12, Act 251-2012); Brazil (arts. 33–37, Act 9,474-1997); Chile (arts. 3–12, art. 48, Act 20,430-2010); Colombia (arts. 25, 28, 31, 32, Decree 2,840-2013); Costa Rica (arts. 6, 7, 9–11, 39, 40, 51, 52, 63–65, 8, 136, 143, 137, Refugees Regulation 36,831G-2011); El Salvador (arts. 2, 46, Decree 918-2002); Guatemala (art. 52, Gov. Agr. 383-2001); Mexico (arts. 5–10, Refugees Act -2011); Nicaragua (arts. 2, 3, 8, 9, 10, 18, 19, Act 655-2008); Panama (arts. 6–15, Decree 5-2018); Paraguay (arts. 5–7, 32, Act 1,938-2002); Peru (arts. 5, 31, 32, Act 27,891-2002); Uruguay (arts. 10–18, Ley 18,076-2006); Venezuela (arts. 2–4, 6–8, Refugees Basic Law -2011).
12. Argentina (arts. 18–31, Act 26,165-2006); Bolivia (arts. 21–27, Act 251-2012); Brazil (arts. 14–17, Ley 9,474-1997); Chile (arts. 29–24, Act 20,430-2010); Colombia (arts. 2–6, Decree 2,840-2013); El Salvador (arts. 5–13, Decree 918-2002); Guatemala (arts. 1–3, 59, Gov. Agr. 383-2001); Mexico (arts. 15–17, Refugee Act -2011); Nicaragua (arts. 14–17, Act 655-2008); Panama (arts. 16–27, Decree 5-2018); Paraguay (arts. 13–20, Act 1,938-2002); Peru (arts. 6–11, Act 27,891-2002); Dominican Republic (arts. 1–5, Decree 2,330-1984); Uruguay (arts. 23–26, Act 18,076-2006); Venezuela (arts. 12, 13, Refugees Basic Law).
13. Argentina (arts. 32–56, Act 26,165-2006); Bolivia (arts. 28–45, Act 251-2012); Brazil (arts. 17–32, Act 9474-1997); Chile (arts. 25–44, Act 20430-2010); Colombia (arts. 7, 8, 11, 12, 13-33, Decree 2840-2013); El Salvador (arts. 14–31, Decree 918-2002); Guatemala (arts. 22–41, Gov. Agr. 383-2001); Mexico (arts. 18–27, Refugee Act -2011); Nicaragua (arts. 18–27, Act 655-2008); Panama (arts. 28–67, Decree 5-2018); Paraguay (arts. 21, 22, 30, 31, Act 1,938-2002); Peru (arts. 9–19,

Act 27,891); Dominican Republic (arts. 7–10, 14-16, Decree 2,330-1984); Uruguay (arts. 32–40, Act 18,076-2006); Venezuela (arts. 14–21, Refugees Basic Law -2001).

14. Argentina (arts. 9, 11–13, Act 26,165-2006); Bolivia (arts. 17–19, Act 251-2012); Brazil (arts. 3, 38–41, Act 9,474-1997); Chile (arts. 16–18, Act 20,430-2010); Colombia (arts. 34–36, Decree 2,840 -2013); Costa Rica (arts. 24–38, Regulation 36,831G-2011); Dominican Republic (art. 11, Decree 2,330-1984); El Salvador (arts. 3–40, Decree 918-2002); Guatemala (art. 4, Gov. Agr. 383-2001); Mexico (arts. 34–43, Refugee Act -2011); Nicaragua (arts. 4–7, Act 655-2008); Panama (arts. 3, 95–98, Decree 5-2018); Paraguay (arts. 8–12, Act 1,938-2002); Peru (arts. 4, 33 and 34, Act 27,891-2002); Uruguay (arts. 3–6, Act 18,076-2006); Venezuela (arts. 9, 11, Refugees Basic Law, 2001).
15. Article 1F of the 1951 Refugee Convention states that the provisions of that Convention "shall not apply to any person with respect to whom there are serious reasons for considering that (a) he [or she] has committed a crime against peace, a war crime, or a crime against humanity, as defined in the international instruments drawn up to make provision in respect of such crimes; (b) he [or she] has committed a serious non-political crime outside the country of refuge prior to his [or her] admission to that country as a refugee; or (c) he [or she] has been guilty of acts contrary to the purposes and principles of the United Nations."
16. Chile (arts. 13–15, Act 20,430-2010); El Salvador (arts. 35–39, Decree 918-2002); Guatemala (arts. 12–18, Gov. Agr. 383-2001); Mexico (arts. 44, 45, Refugee Act -2011); Nicaragua (arts. 11, 12, Act 655-2008); Panama (arts. 81–84, Decree 5-2018); Peru (arts. 20–29, Act 27,891-2002); Venezuela (arts. 22–26, Refugees Basic Law -2001).
17. Chile (arts. 34–47, Act 20,430-2010); Mexico (arts. 48–53, Refugee Act -2011); Paraguay (art. 26, Act 1,938-2002).
18. Bolivia (arts. 51, 52, Act 251-2012); Brazil (arts. 42, 43, Act 9,474-1997); Guatemala (arts. 42–47, Gov. Agr. 383-2001); Panama (arts. 92–94, Decree 5-2018).
19. Argentina (art. 52, Act 26,165-2006); Brazil (art. 6, Act 9,474-1997); Bolivia (arts. 46, 47, 50, Act 251-2012); Chile (arts. 46, 47, Act 20,430-2010); Colombia (art. 24, Decree 2,840-2013); El Salvador (arts. 33, 34, Decree 918-2002); Nicaragua (arts. 29, 31, Act 655-2008); Panama (arts. 75, 76, Decree 5-2018); Paraguay (arts. 25, 28, Act 1,938-2002); Peru (arts. 23, 34, Act 27,891-2002); Uruguay (art. 42, Act 18,076-2006).
20. This is the case of Mexico (Refugees Act 2011: arts. 25, 28).
21. The only exceptions are Brazil (art. 3, Decree 9,277-2018) and Costa Rica (arts. 54–55, Decree 36,831-2011). Travel outside the country is almost always explicitly excluded.
22. After the 2017 earthquake, the government tried to eliminate this deadline, and in February 2018 the National Human Rights Commission indicated the existence of 2016 requests still to be resolved (National Human Rights Commission [CNDH] 2018). In April 2018 a judge declared that elimination unconstitutional (Mexican Commission for the Defense and Promotion of Human Rights [CMPDH] 2018).
23. Guatemala (art. 11.c, Gov. Agr. 383-2001); El Salvador (art. 4.c, Decree 918-2002); Colombia (art. 1.b, Decree 4,503-2009). Paraguay (art. 1.b, Act 1,938-

2002); Peru (art. 3, Act 27,891-2002); Honduras (art. 42.3, Decree 208-2003); Bolivia (art. 12, Supreme Decree 28,329-2005); Argentina (art. 4.b, Act 26,165-2006); Uruguay (art. 2.b, Act 18,076-2006); Nicaragua (art. 1.c, Act 655-2008); Chile (art. 2.2, Act 20,430-2010); Mexico (art. 13, Refugees Act 2011); Ecuador (art. 98, Human Mobility Law-2017).
24. Sentence of the Administrative Dispute Tribunal, Section Four, at fourteen hundred hours on 28 November 2014 (vote number 0103-2014 IV) regarding the extended refugee definition in Costa Rica.
25. Argentina (arts. 2, 3, 39, Act 26,165-2006); Bolivia (arts. 4, 30, Act 251-2012); Brazil (art. 8, Act 9,474-1997); Chile (art. 3, 26, 27, Act 20,430-2010); Costa Rica (art. 134, Regulation 36,831G-2011); Ecuador (art. 41, 2008 Constitution); Guatemala (art. 13, Gov. Agr. 383-2001), Mexico (arts. 6, 21, Refugees Act 2011); Panama (art. 7, Ex. Decree 5-2018); Uruguay (arts. 10, 12, 32, Act 18,076-2006).
26. Argentina (arts. 2, 40, Act 26,165-2006); Brazil (arts. 8–10, Act 9,474-1997); Chile (art. 8, Act 20,430-2010); Costa Rica (art. 137, Regulation 36,831G-2011); Uruguay (arts. 12, 15, Act 18,076-2006).
27. Argentina (art. 25, Act 26,165-2006); Bolivia (art. 24, Act 251-2012); Brazil (art. 2, Act 9,474-1997); Costa Rica (arts. 66–74, Regulation 36,831G-2011); El Salvador (art. 37, Decree 918-2002); Guatemala (arts. 15, 47, Governmental Agreement 383-2001); Mexico (art. 44, Refugees Act 2011); Panama (arts. 77–80, Ex. Decree 5-2018); Paraguay (art. 14, Act 1,938-2012); Peru (art. 25, Act 27,891-2002); Uruguay (art. 21, Act 18,076-2006).
28. Argentina (arts. 5, 6, Act 26,165-2006); Bolivia (art. 29 II, Political Constitution); Chile (art. 9, Act 20,430-2010); Costa Rica (art. 106, Act 8,764-2009); Ecuador (art. 77, Ex. Decree 111-2018); Mexico (arts. 12, 58, 38, Refugees Act 2018); Nicaragua (art. 3, Act 655-2008); Paraguay (art. 2, Act 1,938-2002); Peru (arts. 5, 7, 64, Leg. Decree 1,350-2017); Uruguay (art. 21, Act 18,076-2006).
29. Article 9, Act 251-2012.
30. Article 6 Act 26,165-2006.
31. Costa Rica (arts. 106–123, Act 8,764-2010); Ecuador (arts. 98–109, Human Mobility Law, 2017); Honduras (arts. 42–51, Decree 208-2003); Peru (arts. 39–44, Leg. Decree 1,350-2017).
32. Brazil (art. 2, Act 13,445-2017); Costa Rica (art. 7, 31, Act 8,764-2009); Uruguay (art. 83, Act 18,250-2008)
33. Argentina (art. 1, Decree 616-2010); Brazil (art. 2, Act 13,445-2017); Peru (art. 5, Decree 007-2017).
34. Argentina (art. 23, Act 25,781-2004); Colombia (art. 7, Decree 0834-2013); Costa Rica (art. 94, Act 8,764-2009); Cuba (art. 3, Decree Act 1,312-1976); the Dominican Republic (art. 35, Act 285-2004); Ecuador (art. 60, Human Mobility Law, 2017); El Salvador (art. 8, Leg. Decree 2,772-1958); Honduras (art. 3, Decree 208-2003); Nicaragua (art. 29, Act 153-1993); Panama (art. 24, Decree Act 3-2008); Paraguay (art. 25, Act 978-1996); Peru (art. 29.2, Leg. Decree 1,350-2017).
35. Article 24, Decree Act 3-2008.
36. Decree 0834-2013.
37. Mexico (art. 54, Migration Act 2011); Uruguay (art. 9 Decree 394-2009).
38. Costa Rica (arts. 33, 105, Act 8,764-2009).

39. Bolivia (art. 26, Act 370-2013); the Dominican Republic (art. 48, Act 285-2004); Mexico (art. 42, Migration Act -2011); Peru (art. 130, Decree 007-2017); Uruguay (art. 48, Act 285-2004).
40. Article 62, Decree 61-62010.
41. Article 47, Act 18,250-2008.
42. Bolivia (art. 13, Act 251-2012); Nicaragua (art. 12, Act 655-2009).
43. Guatemala (art. 18 Gov. Agr. 383-2001); Mexico (art. 44 Refugees Act 2011).
44. Article 13, Act 20,430-2010.
45. Argentina (art. 52, Act 26,165-2006); Brazil (art. 6 Act 9,474-1997); Costa Rica (art. 56, Regulation 36,831G-2011); Nicaragua (art.26, Act 655-2009); Paraguay (art. 25, Act 1,938-2002); Venezuela (art. 19, Refugees Basic Law, 2001).
46. Argentina (art. 6, Act 25,871-2004); Brazil (art. 3, Act 13,445-2017); Uruguay (art. 8, Act 18,250-2008).
47. Article 12, Act 370-2013.
48. Argentina (art. 51, Act 26,165-2006); Ecuador (art. 51, Human Mobility Law, 2017); Panama (art. 26, Decree-Law 3-2008).
49. Article 60, Leg. Decree 670-1993.
50. Article 9, Leg. Decree 1,350-2017.
51. Article 15, Leg. Decree 110-1966.
52. See https://immigrationvisa247.com/es/residencia-permanente-como-profesional-extranjero-en-panama/
53. Bolivia (art. 13, Act 251-2012); El Salvador (art. 35, Leg. Decree 918-2002); Nicaragua (art. 12, Act 655-2008); Venezuela (art. 20, Refugees and Asylees Act, 2001)
54. Article 19 Refugees and Asylees Act, 2001.
55. Chile (art. 4, Act 20,430-2010); Mexico (art. 44, Refugees Act, 2011); Panama (art. 83, Ex. Decree 5-2018).
56. Argentina (art. 52, Act 26,165-2006); Nicaragua (art. 29, Act 655-2008); Paraguay (art. 25, Act 1,938-2002).
57. Argentina (art. 6, Act 25,871-2004); Brazil (art. 4, Act 13,445-2017); Guatemala (art. 2, 7, Decree 44-2016); Uruguay (art. 9, Act 18,250-2008).
58. Costa Rica (art. 31, Act 8,764-2009); Peru (art. 9, Leg. Decree 1,350-2017); Venezuela (art. 13, Act 37,944-2004).
59. Article 52, Human Mobility Law, 2017.
60. After the 2017 earthquake, the government tried to eliminate this deadline and in February 2018, the National Human Rights Commission indicated that there were requests from 2016 still to be resolved (CNDH 2018). In April 2018 a judge declared the elimination of the deadline unconstitutional (CMPDH 2018).

References

Acosta, Diego, and Luisa Feline Freier. 2015. "Turning the Immigration Policy Paradox Upside Down? Populist Liberalism and Discursive Gaps in South America." *International Migration Review*, 49 (3): 659–96. doi: 10.1111/imre.12146.

Aleinikoff, Thomas Alexander. 1992. "State-centered refugee law: From resettlement to containment." *Michigan Journal of International Law*, 14 (1): 120–138. https://repository.law.umich.edu/mjil/vol14/iss1/3.

Berganza, Isabel, Cécile Blouin, and Luisa Feline Freier. 2018. *La aplicación de la definición de Cartagena a las personas venezolanas en el Perú*. Documento de Discusión CIUP, DD1805, Agosto, 2018, Universidad del Pacífico.

———. 2020. "The Situational Element of Massive Violation of Human Rights of the Extended Definition of Cartagena: an Application in the Venezuelan Case." *Revista Chilena de Derecho*, 47 (2): 385–410.

Betts, Alexander, ed. 2011. *Global migration governance*. New York: Oxford University Press.

Cantor, David James. 2015. "Bucking the trend? Liberalism and illiberalism in Latin American refugee bloglaw and policy." In *A Liberal Tide? Immigration and Asylum Law and Policy in Latin America*, edited by David James Cantor, Luisa Feline Freier and Jean-Pierre Gauci : 185-212. London: School of Advanced Study, University of London. https://sas-space.sas.ac.uk/6159/1/12.%20ALT_Ch8_Cantor.pdf

Ceriani Cernadas, Pablo. 2011. "Luces y sombras en la legislación migratoria latinoamericana." *Nueva Sociedad*: 233: 68–86. http://nuso.org/media/articles/downloads/3775_1.pdf

Chimni, Bhupinder S. 2000. "Globalization, humanitarianism and the erosion of refugee protection." *Journal of Refugee Studies*, 13 (3): 243–63. doi: https://doi.org/10.1093/jrs/13.3.243.

Domenech, Eduardo Enrique. 2017. "Las políticas de migración en Sudamérica: elementos para el análisis crítico del control migratorio y fronterizo." *Terceiro Milênio*, 8 (1): 19-48. http://hdl.handle.net/11336/58156.

Fernández, Nieves, Luisa Feline Freier, and Omar Hammoud-Gallego. Forthcoming. "Importancia y limitaciones de las normas jurídicas para el estudio de la política migratoria en América Latina." In *Perspectivas jurídicas de las migraciones internacionales: abordajes teóricos y metodológicos contemporáneos*, edited by Elisa Ortega-Velazquez and Luciana Gandini. Mexico: UNAM.

Freier, Luisa Feline. 2015. "A liberal paradigm shift? A Critical Appraisal of Recent Trends in Latin American Asylum Legislation." In *Exploring the boundaries of refugee law: current protection challenges*, edited by Jean-Pierre Gauci, Mariagiulia Giuffré, and Evangelia Lilian Tsourdi: 118–145. Boston: Brill/ Nijhoff. https://doi.org/10.1163/9789004265585.

Freier, Luisa Feline, Isabel Berganza, and Cécile Blouin. Forthcoming. "The Cartagena Refugee Definition and Venezuelan Displacement in Latin America." *International Migration*.

Freier, Luisa Feline, Soledad Castillo Jara, and Marta Luzes. Forthcoming. "Forced Migrants, Refugees, and COVID-19." *Current History*.

Freier, Luisa Feline, and Jean-Pierre Gauci. Forthcoming. "Refugees Rights' Across Region: A Comparative Overview of Legislative Good Practices in Latin America and the EU." *Refugee Survey Quarterly*.

García, Lila. 2016. "Migraciones, Estado y una política del derecho humano a migrar: ¿hacia una nueva era en América Latina?" *Colombia Internacional*, 88: 107–133. doi: http://dx.doi.org/10.7440/colombiaint88.2016.05.

International Labour Organization (ILO). 1997. "Migración laboral en América Latina y el Caribe - Países: Brasil - Refugiados (ACNUR)." libguides.ilo.org/migracionlaboralALCpaises/Brasil-refugiados.

Long, Katy. 2012. "In search of sanctuary: Border closures, "safe" zones and refugee protection." *Journal of Refugee Studies*, 26 (3): 458–76. https://doi.org/10.1093/jrs/fes050.

Mármora, Lelio. 2010. "Modelos de gobernabilidad migratoria. La perspectiva política en América del Sur." *REMHU-Revista Interdisciplinar da Mobilidade Humana*, 18 (35): 71-92. https://www.redalyc.org/pdf/4070/407042012004.pdf.

Martínez Pizarro, Jorge, ed. 2011. *Migración internacional en América Latina y el Caribe. Nuevas tendencias, nuevos enfoques.* Santiago, Chile: CEPAL. https://repositorio.cepal.org/handle/11362/35288.

Mejía Ochoa, William. 2015. "Espacios intergubernamentales para la discusión de políticas migratorias en Latinoamérica." *OASIS: Observatorio de Análisis de los Sistemas Internacionales* 22: 7–21. doi: https://doi.org/10.18601/16577558.n22.02.

Mexican Commission for the Defense and Promotion of Human Rights [CMPDH]. 2018.

National Human Rights Commission [CNDH]. 2018.

Sánchez, Felipe. 2018. "Situación de solicitantes de asilo de origen venezolano." Observatorio de Protección Internacional. Universidad Iberoamericana, Ciudad de Mexico.

Scalettaris, Giulia. 2009. "Refugees and mobility." *Forced Migration Review*, 33: 58–59. http://www.ciaconlus.org/ciaconlus/wp-content/uploads/2016/12/Refugees_and_mobility.pdf.

Shaknove, Andrew. 1993. "From Asylum to Containment." *International Journal of Refugee Law*, 5(4): 516–33.

United Nations High Commissioner for Refugees (UNHCR). 2001. *States parties to the Refugee 1951 Convention relating to the Status of Refugees and the 1967 Protocol.* https://www.unhcr.org/protection/basic/3b73b0d63/states-parties-1951-convention-its-1967-protocol.html.

———. 2012. *Displacement: The New 21st Century Challenge-UNHCR Global Trends 2012.* http://www.unhcr.org/statistics/country/51bacb0f9/unhcr-global-trends-2012.html.

11

How Humanitarian Are Humanitarian Visas?

An Analysis of Theory and Practice in Latin America

Luisa Feline Freier and Marta Luzes

Introduction

Both academic and policy analyses have hailed humanitarian visas as a pragmatic complementary form of protection in the context of mixed migration flows (Freier 2019; Jubilut 2017). In the context of Latin America, many states have incorporated humanitarian visas in their immigration laws (Freier and Gauci 2020; Kvalvaag in this volume). They have seldom been used to grant temporary residence to vulnerable migrant populations, however, countries, such as Ecuador and Peru, have recently used humanitarian visas to limit the access of vulnerable Venezuelan migrants to their territory. In this chapter we analyze the use of humanitarian visas in Latin America, in theory and practice, from an interdisciplinary approach at the cross-section of legal and political studies.

The existing international regime of refugee protection, which consists of the 1951 Convention Relating to the Status of Refugees (1951 Refugee Convention), and its Protocol Relating to the Status of Refugees (1967 Protocol), is ill suited to provide protection to an increasing number of forcibly displaced people (International Organization for Migration [IOM] 2017a; United Nations High Commissioner for Refugees [UNHCR] 2019a). This regime originated in the aftermath of World War II, and emphasizes the need for international protection in cases of individualized persecution. However, sources of displacement are increasingly more complex and routed in humanitarian crises linked to internal conflict, violence, severe poverty, and human rights violations (see Jubilut, Vera Espinoza, and Mezzanotti in this volume). In this context, the conventional classification of population movements into voluntary (economically motivated) and involuntary/forced (coerced) migration, which continues at the base of the current regime, is obsolete because these boundaries are blurred (Horwood and Reitano 2016; Van Hear 2009).

As recently summarized by Zapata and Tapia (2020), scholars have increasingly proposed new concepts such as migration in the context of (humanitarian) crises, which occurs when "there is a widespread threat to life, physical safety, health or basic subsistence that is beyond the coping capacity of individuals and the communities in which they reside" (Martin, Weerasinghe, and Taylor 2013: 123). In the same vein, McAdam (2014: 10) defines "crisis migration" as "a response to a complex combination of social, political, economic and environmental factors, which may be triggered by an extreme event but not [necessarily] caused by it." Thus, in this context, migration and displacement should be understood as resulting from the cumulative effects of socioeconomic or political collapse, or systemic inequalities, all of which disproportionately affect marginalized and vulnerable populations.

Similarly, Betts (2010: 362) proposes the concept of "survival migration" to refer to "persons outside their country of origin because of an existential threat to which they have no access to a domestic remedy or resolution." These threats may arise from "serious human rights deprivations that fall outside the dominant interpretation of persecution" (Betts 2014: 77), namely conflict, generalized violence, and human rights violations; environmental degradation and livelihood collapse; and others. Hathaway (2014) argues that the "serious harm" clause of international human rights may apply to a range of situations, from fleeing from risks to essential socioeconomic rights, and that food deprivation, or famine, may constitute persecution, and may be potentially considered as a basis for claiming refugee status in its own right.

These reflections on forced migration are also mirrored in the international policy arena. Africa, Europe, and Latin America have developed expanded regional refugee definitions to address the shortcomings of the one laid out by the 1951 Refugee Convention (Freier, Berganza, and Blouin 2020; see also Fischel de Andrade in this volume). Worth mentioning here are the 1969 Organization of African Unity's (OAU) Convention Governing the Specific Aspects of Refugee Problems in Africa, the refugee definition of the 1984 Cartagena Declaration on Refugees (Cartagena Declaration), and the 2004 European Council Qualification Directive (2011/95/EC) on minimum standards for the qualification and status of third country nationals or stateless persons as refugees or as persons who otherwise need international protection (McAdam 2007). Even in Latin America, however, where fifteen states have incorporated the Cartagena Declaration refugee definition into their national legislation (Freier 2015), its actual application—especially in the context of Venezuelan forced displacement to which it clearly applies—remains unsatisfactory (Berganza, Blouin, and Freier 2018; Freier, Berganza, and Blouin 2020; see also Brumat, and Freier and Fernández in this volume).

In this context, some consider humanitarian visas as a politically more feasible alternative to protection measures, and there have been calls for researching how these have been, or should be, implemented (Freier 2019; Jubilut 2017). Latin America can be considered a regional leader in developing new pathways to legal territorial access and residence from a humanitarian lens, such as resettlement programs, humanitarian entry visas, humanitarian residence permits, regional residence permits, and regional citizenship (Jubilut 2017; see also Jubilut, Vera Espinoza, and Mezzanotti in this volume). Regarding the Venezuelan displacement crisis, however, countries such as Ecuador and Peru have used humanitarian visas to limit the access of vulnerable migrants to their territory. As such, humanitarian visas can offer additional protection, but can also be used to impose entry requirements and further jeopardize migrants in need of international protection.

In this chapter we first discuss the legislative context of humanitarian visas, as complementary forms of protection in Latin America, and then turn to an empirical discussion of their application in the context of Venezuelan forced displacement, including the problematic development of the so-called humanitarian entry visas. Focusing on the Peruvian case, we adopt a mixed-methods approach to legal analysis and empirical research, based on findings from interviews conducted at the official border crossing between Ecuador and Peru (Centro Binacional de Atención Fronterizo [CEBAF]) between April and August 2019. Before the introduction of the humanitarian entry visa on 15 June 2019, the majority of Venezuelan migrants entered Peru through CEBAF. We visited the border twice: from 8 to 16 April, when the humanitarian visa restrictions were not in place; and from 12 to 24 August 2019, after the visa introduction. In total we collected quantitative data on 1,600 Venezuelan migrants and conducted twenty-nine in-depth interviews with migrants entering Peru between April and August 2019.

Complementary Forms of Protection and Humanitarian Visas

Complementary forms of protection open up avenues to grant legal status to people who are not recognized as refugees under the 1951 Refugee Convention or the Cartagena Declaration, but whose return is contrary to the obligations of *non-refoulement*. According to the UNHCR, complementary forms of protection are "safe and regulated avenues for refugees that complement resettlement by providing lawful stay in a third country where their international protection needs are met. They are additional to resettlement and do not substitute the protection afforded to refugees under the international protection regime" (UNHCR 2019b: 5).

Complementary protection pathways include humanitarian visas, humanitarian admission, community sponsorship, family reunification, and education and employment opportunities. These forms of protection are meant to ease the pressure on receiving countries in protracted refugee situations, enhance refugees' self-reliance, and help build capacities to attain durable solutions (ibid). It has been argued that beneficiaries of complementary forms of protection should be entitled to the same legal status as refugees and should be protected by human rights law (McAdam 2007).

Significant ambiguity exists with regards to the terminology around humanitarian visas. According to the UNHCR, humanitarian admission is understood as a tool of burden and responsibility sharing, and a means to provide individuals in need of international protection with effective protection in a third country. Although humanitarian admission programs resemble resettlement, they offer slightly lower protection standards for two main reasons. First, these programs may use eligibility criteria in addition to the established UNHCR Resettlement Submission Categories. Second, individuals may be granted only temporary or other protection status and, as a consequence, might not have immediate access to a fully effective durable solution (UNHCR 2019b). Thus, in agreement with Jubilut (2017), a more unequivocal label for this legal category is humanitarian residence or residence permit.

Humanitarian visas, on the other hand, are defined as a pathway to legal access to a third country, where individuals in need of international protection are sometimes subsequently given the opportunity to apply for asylum, including through expedited procedures. Humanitarian visas thus differ from humanitarian admission programs, since, in the latter case, individual legal status is often determined prior to arrival in the third country. They have also been used to facilitate the admission of family members who would not otherwise qualify for family reunification under existing legislation. This legal category thus corresponds to humanitarian entry visas (Jubilut 2017).

Humanitarian Visas in Latin America

In the past twenty years, many Latin American countries have adopted exceptionally liberal immigration and refugee laws with a focus on the human rights and protection of vulnerable migrants and refugees (Acosta and

Freier 2015; Cantor, Freier and Gauci 2015; Freier and Gauci 2020; see also Freier and Fernández in this volume). At the same time, countries have worked toward achieving greater freedom of movement within the region, loosening up on visa restrictions and creating regional migration initiatives, such as the Mercado Común del Sur (MERCOSUR; Southern Common Market) (Acosta and Freier 2018; see also Brumat in this volume). In this context of legislative liberalization, several Latin American countries have included provisions for complementary forms of protection in their legislation. Chile, Ecuador, and Mexico included complementary protection specifically to ensure *non-refoulement*.[1] For example, the Mexican Refugee Law and Complementary Protection Act of 2011, in Article 2.IV, defines complementary protection as "Protection granted by the Ministry of the Interior to a foreigner who has not been recognized as a refugee under the terms of this law, consisting of not returning him to the territory of another country where his life would be threatened or where he would be at danger of being subjected to torture or other cruel, inhuman or degrading treatment or punishment."

The 2011 Mexican Migration Law also stipulates that individuals that are beneficiaries of complementary protection are granted permanent residence in the country. In Nicaragua, in contrast, complementary protection is stipulated more loosely in Article 220 of the Migration and Foreign Law of 2011: "In accordance with international human rights instruments, humanitarian visas may be granted to those who suffer violations of their human rights and to victims of trafficking in particular women, girls and boys."[2]

Regarding humanitarian visas, Argentina, Bolivia, Brazil, Costa Rica, Ecuador, Guatemala, Honduras, Mexico, Panama, Peru, Venezuela and Uruguay explicitly mention these in their legislation.[3] It is important to point out that Latin American legislation invokes the categories of both humanitarian residence permits and humanitarian entry visas, sometimes within the same law. For example, in the case of the Argentine Migration Law, Article 23 refers to humanitarian residence, whereas Article 34 invokes the concept of a humanitarian entry visa: "Temporary residence shall be granted to all foreigners who invoke humanitarian reasons that justify a special treatment in the opinion of the National Directorate of Migration (art. 23 of Law 25,871). Foreigners who do not meet the requirements established by law and its regulations may be authorized to enter the country, when there are exceptional reasons of humanitarian nature, public interest or fulfillment of commitments made by Argentina" (art. 34 of Law 25,871).

Similarly, Brazil and Uruguay's laws provide both temporary residence and the possibility to extend travel visas for humanitarian reasons.[4] Guatemala provides legal entry for humanitarian reasons, such as natural disasters or medical emergencies.[5] Panama, on the other hand, provides temporary residence for humanitarian reasons for six years,[6] Honduras for five,[7] Bolivia (conditioned to legal entry) for one,[8] and Ecuador for two.[9] In Article 66.5 of the 2017 Human Mobility Law, Ecuador defines a humanitarian visa as a humanitarian residence permit, and states, "The authorization granted by the highest authority of human mobility to remain in Ecuador to applicants of international protection until their application is resolved, or to persons in need of protection for humanitarian reasons for a period of up to two years in accordance with this law. This visa will have no cost."

On the other hand, humanitarian entry visas were used in 2010 in Brazil to facilitate the arrival of Haitians following the earthquake that left thousands displaced, as an alternative to tourist visas that demanded more entry requirements (Jubilut 2017). Argentina and Brazil applied the same type of humanitarian entry visa to victims affected by the Syrian conflict in 2013. In both of these cases, humanitarian visas were used as an instrument that facilitated legal entry, and not necessarily as an instrument to grant legal residence. As such, there is ambiguity as to what humanitarian visas in the region should encompass.

Humanitarian Visas and the Venezuelan Displacement Crisis

In the past three years, more than 5 million Venezuelans have fled their country's severe political, economic, and humanitarian crises (IOM 2020). Insecurity and crime, shortages of food, and systematic violations of human rights by public authorities have been repeatedly reported by the international media (BBC 2016, 2017), and have triggered large out-migration flows of Venezuelans. The Venezuelan displacement thus clearly falls within the realm of crisis or survival migration.

The majority of Venezuelans have moved within Latin America, a region that had never before seen such significant numbers of forced migrants. Governments have responded to the need of implementing (or adapting) legal pathways for entry and residence of Venezuelan migrants differently, with some of the most important receiving states—Colombia, Ecuador, and Peru—reacting in a rather ad hoc fashion (Acosta, Blouin, and Freier 2019; Jarochinski Silva, Castro Franco, and Sampaio in this volume). The initial response to the Venezuelan displacement crisis in the region was open and welcoming, in comparison to other international responses to forced migration, and applied a de facto free movement approach (Freier and Parent 2019; Selee et al. 2019).[10] Instead of applying existing legal pathways, however, such as the MERCOSUR Residence Agreement and the Cartagena Declaration refugee definition, the most important receiving states—Chile, Colombia, Ecuador, and Peru—developed ad hoc policy responses, such as special temporary work visas, residence permits, and, most recently, entry visas (Acosta, Blouin, and Freier 2019; Berganza, Blouin, and Freier 2020).

The two most important destination countries, Colombia and Peru, have implemented various types of residence permits for Venezuelan citizens since 2017. Colombia first created a Tarjeta de Movilidad Fronteriza (border mobility card). Dating back to February 2017, the card allowed Venezuelans to travel freely between the two countries; it was reactivated in December 2019 (Proyecto Migración Venezolana 2020a). The Permiso Especial de Permanencia (PEP; special permit of permanence)[11] was passed in two phases– July 2017 and January 2020–and authorized Venezuelan nationals to stay in Colombian territory for up to two years, allowing them to work in nonregulated occupations, and granting them access to education and health care. On 5 July 2019, the ministry of foreign affairs created the Permiso Especial Complementario de Permanencia (complementary special permit for permanence), a special permit for Venezuelans asylum seekers who filed and whose claim had been denied or not decided. Since January 2020, the Permiso Especial de Permanencia para el Fomento de la Formalización (special permanence permit for the promotion of formalization) allows employers to hire Venezuelan migrants who do not have a cédula de Extranjería (immigration card), work visa, or PEP. Migrants may also opt for one of the three general visas–visitor visa, migrant visa, or resident visa–or request asylum (Proyecto Migración Venezolana 2020b).

In Peru, the Permiso Temporal de Permanencia (PTP; Temporary Permanence Permit)[12] was introduced in January 2017; it granted Venezuelans a residence permit for one year, the right to work, and limited access to education and health care. It was possible to apply for the PTP only until 31 December 2018, however, and provided that the applicant had entered the country before 31 October. Since the end of 2018, Peru has not created new residence permits for Venezuelan citizens, although it has allowed Venezuelans to change their status to another temporary, preexisting special residence category after their PTP expired. As part of their ongoing compilation of legislative good practices in Latin America, the UNHCR has classified both the PEP and the PTP as humanitarian visas (Freier and Gauci 2020).[13] We disagree with this categorization for two reasons. First, although the legislation that implemented these special residence permits mentions both constitutional and migrants' rights, it fails to mention any humanitarian reasons for granting the residence permits, and instead focuses on safe and orderly migration and the competencies of the migration authorities.[14] Second, both the PEP and the PTP were implemented as retroactive regularization mechanisms and did not tie the length of residence granted to the crisis or any improvement of the situation in Venezuela.

With rising numbers of migrants and increasing levels of xenophobic public sentiment, the Venezuelan displacement has become increasingly politicized, which materialized into restrictive policies in Chile, Ecuador, and Peru (Aron and Castillo 2020; Doña and Gouveia 2020; Freier and Pérez 2020; Malo 2020). First, Chile, Ecuador, and Peru implemented new entry requirements, joining Panama in demanding passports for Venezuelan migrants (Selee et al. 2019). Second, all three countries implemented access restrictions through the introduction of the so-called humanitarian visas: the Visa de Responsabilidad Democrática (visa of democratic responsibility) in April 2018 in the case of Chile,[15] and humanitarian visas in June and August 2019 in the case of Peru[16] and Ecuador.[17] It is important to mention that, in the case of Chile and Ecuador, in addition to passport requirements, these visas cost US$30 and US$50, respectively. In Ecuador, the visa itself does not have a cost, but the form needed to apply for the visa costs US$50, which violates Article 66.5 of Ecuador's 2017 Human Mobility Law (see above).

Ecuador simultaneously implemented the humanitarian residence permit as an amnesty and a humanitarian entry visa. Although counterintuitive, migrant regularizations can be part of restrictive immigration policies when they are used in order to "wipe the slate clean and begin afresh" (Massey 2007: 312), possibly using more restrictive measures. This has been the case in Ecuador, where no entry visa was previously required for Venezuelan citizens. The introduction of such visa is especially remarkable since Ecuador has been promoting the principles of free human mobility, universal citizenship, and the rejection of calling migrants illegal based on their migratory condition, as reflected in its 2008 Constitution of Ecuador and the 2017 Human Mobility Law (Acosta and Freier 2015; Malo 2020), as well as in the guiding principles of Decree 826 of 2019, which implemented the humanitarian visa. These principles were translated into an open doors policy and the abolishment of all entry visa requirements in 2008 (Freier and Holloway 2019). Today, aside from Venezuela, only ten other nationalities are required to have an entry visa.[18]

The Case of Peru

In this section we analyze the case of Peru to exemplify the restrictive application of the humanitarian visa. After Colombia, Peru has become the second-largest host of the Venezuelan displaced diaspora, with more than 860,000 Venezuelan migrants and refugees officially registered as of March 2020 (UNHCR 2020a). In early December, almost 570,000 had regular residence status—mostly through PTPs. And, as of December 2019, more than 480,000 were asylum seekers, which is the highest number of Venezuelan asylum seekers in the world, making up more than half of all asylum applications made by Venezuelan nationals worldwide (ibid). The imposition of passports as an entry requirement in Peru, at the end of 2018, led many Venezuelan nationals to apply for asylum.

Regarding its legislative framework, Peru adopted the Cartagena Declaration refugee definition in its 2002 Refugee Law.[19] Very few asylum applications filed by Venezuelan citizens have been resolved, however, mostly due to the overburden of the asylum system and an increase in the backlog of applications (Freier, Berganza, and Blouin 2020; Selee et al. 2019). Furthermore, Peru has far refrained from applying the Cartagena Declaration refugee definition to Venezuelan forced migration (Berganza, Blouin, and Freier 2018; Selee et al. 2019; see also Freier and Fernández in this volume). At the end of 2019, Peru hosted only 1,230 recognized Venezuelan refugees, having decided 3,390 cases and recognized 578 refugees in the same year (UNHCR 2020b). Under the Peruvian refugee law, asylum seekers have the right to work and do not require any additional migratory status or visa to stay in the country. Nevertheless, in practice, the status of asylum seeker in Peru provides no judicial security and has hindered the socioeconomic integration of Venezuelans (Blouin and Freier 2019). Furthermore, the vast majority of applicants have not received their identification document—fewer than 100,000 had received it by mid-2020. Instead of giving adequate protection, the large number of pending claims leaves refugees with no durable solution and in vulnerable conditions (Freier and Parent 2019).

Peru's immigration law of 2017 provides for a humanitarian residence category:

> For the foreigner who, being in national territory and without meeting the requirements to access the condition of asylum or refugee, is in a situation of great vulnerability or danger of life in case of abandonment of the Peruvian territory or for him *who requires protection due to a serious threat or act of violation or affectation of his fundamental rights. In the same way, it will be applicable for asylum seekers* or for those who have migrated due to natural and environmental disasters; or for victims of people smuggling and human trafficking; or for unaccompanied children and adolescents; or for stateless persons. It also applies to people who are outside the national territory in exceptional situations of internationally recognized humanitarian crisis, who request to come to Peru and obtain protection. It allows both dependent and independent employment. It is granted by the Ministry of Foreign Affairs. The length of stay is one hundred eighty-three (183) days, with the possible extension as long as the conditions of vulnerability persist for which migratory quality was granted. [emphasis added].[20]

Despite the applicability of the Cartagena refugee definition to Venezuelan citizens (Berganza, Blouin, and Freier 2020; Freier, Berganza, and Blouin 2020), Peru could have also applied this humanitarian residence category to Venezuelans in the spirit of humanitarian admission. Instead, on 6 June 2019, the Peruvian government announced the humanitarian visa as a requirement for Venezuelan migrants to access its territory as of 15 June

2019.[21] Similar to the Ecuadorian case, the Peruvian policy combined a humanitarian entry visa with a humanitarian residence permit. Since there was no visa requirement in place before, the humanitarian visa represented a new barrier to legal access and residence in Peru.

This humanitarian visa was implemented through a resolution of the Superintendencia Nacional de Migraciones (Superintendencia Nacional; national superintendence of migration), which is adjunct to the ministry of the interior. Peru's migration governance is characterized by tension between the more security-centered outlook of the Superintendencia Nacional, which is in charge of migration policy within the country, and the more rights-focused perspective of the ministry of foreign affairs, which is in charge of vulnerable migrant groups (Berganza and Freier 2020; Freier and Aron 2020). It is thus telling that the official communication by the ministry of foreign affairs, on the humanitarian visa, at least acknowledged the humanitarian crisis in Venezuela: "Given the serious political and humanitarian crisis experienced by the Bolivarian Republic of Venezuela, and with a view to ensuring an orderly, regular and safe migration of their nationals, the Peruvian immigration control authorities, in compliance with current regulations, will only admit the entry of passport holders who have a valid visa."[22]

The implementing resolution of the humanitarian visa itself, however, which was passed by the Superintendencia Nacional, stressed the responsibility of the state security apparatus to "prevent or address any threat that endangers national security, public order or internal order," and the competencies of the Superintendencia Nacional regarding internal migration and border security policies. President Martín Vizcarra endorsed the humanitarian visa as a response to rising xenophobic sentiment (Aron and Castillo 2020; Freier and Pérez 2020). More specifically, President Vizcarra announced the new visa while personally accompanying the deportation of "bad elements . . . to ensure orderly and safe migration" at Lima's Jorge Chávez International Airport on 7 June 2019.

The ministry of foreign affairs informed that the procedure to obtain the visa would be free due to the humanitarian nature of the document, and that each Peruvian consulate would have up to seventy-two hours to evaluate each visa requirement. Requirements included (1) a valid or expired passport, and (2) an apostilled criminal record certificate. It was pointed out that the objectives of the requirements were to verify that migrant's identity, and to prevent the entry of Venezuelans with a criminal record. Additionally, the humanitarian visa contemplated special exemptions[23]:

i) Minors in transit to Peru to reunite with their parents, who do not have an identity card or passport and only a birth certificate;
ii) Adults in transit to Peru to reunite with their family nucleus residing in Peru;
iii) Adults in a situation of extreme vulnerability;

iv) Pregnant women in a situation of extreme vulnerability in transit to Peru; and,

v) Persons over 60 years of age, in transit to Peru.

The fact that the resolution for the implementation of these visas contemplated humanitarian exceptions clearly questions its humanitarian character. The requirements for the humanitarian visa further represented obstacles to the legal entry of vulnerable Venezuelan migrants to Peru. Obtaining a new passport had long become unfeasible for most in the country, where the real minimum monthly salary had ranged between approximately US$5 and US$20 in previous years. The official cost of a passport in November 2019 was more than US$200–making it the fourth-most-expensive passport in the world (El Pitazo 2019). Widespread corruption in the country had led to the appearance of illegal networks in the black market that offered express passports, but already in 2018 these were valued at US$800 (Washington Office on Latin America 2018).

Similar elevated costs due to corruption have been reported for attaining an apostilled criminal record. This explains why, according to the IOM, already in March 2019, only 23 percent of migrants crossing into Peru carried a passport (IOM 2019a). Even with passports, the process of obtaining the visa remained challenging; in August 2019, Peruvian consulates in Colombia, Ecuador, and Venezuela had month-long waiting times for appointments (Crónica Uno 2019). As a result, from 15 July to 23 December 2019, Peru issued only 8,386 humanitarian visas and 4,555 tourist visas to Venezuelan citizens.[24]

The imposition of the humanitarian visa increased the vulnerability of Venezuelan forced migrants, who were already arriving under more precarious conditions. According to Round One of the IOM's Displacement Monitoring Matrix, which took place in Peru in September 2017, the majority of Venezuelan migrants were male (63 percent), single (76 percent), traveling without their children (75 percent) and had high levels of education (68 percent had a university or technical degree) (IOM 2017b). Most of these migrants (98 percent) entered Peru with a passport.

Round Six of the Displacement Monitoring Matrix, which took place in August 2019, shows a much more vulnerable profile: more women (58 percent), higher prevalence of families (59 percent traveling in family groups), and more children (51 percent of groups traveling with one or more minor) (IOM 2019b). Venezuelan migrants who arrived in Peru in mid-2019 also had less education (35 percent had a university or technical degree), and only 35 percent held a passport. This profile is consistent with findings from our study at CEBAF in August 2019. Even more worrying, individuals reported limited or no access to food (52 percent in August compared to 20 percent in April, according to our data) and overall well-being and mental health indicators had deteriorated (Bolívar, Freier, and Luzes 2019a).

Furthermore, those who arrived at the Peruvian border in August often lacked information on legal requirements. Out of the eight hundred Venezuelan migrants we surveyed at the Ecuador-Peru border, 37 percent did not know about the visa requirements imposed by the Peruvian government. Confirming the above-mentioned, Renata (pseudonym, twenty years old), who traveled from Venezuela with her older sister and two infants to come and meet her mother in Peru, stated, "We only knew that Ecuador was going to ask for a visa, we didn't know Peru was asking for one. . . . We have been here for 3 days and we don't know what is going to happen. We thought that because our mum was here, we could be reunited with her. . . . There comes a time in the day that I feel defeated."

Once at the Peru-Ecuador border, Venezuelan migrants with a passport had to wait for an appointment to apply for the humanitarian visa in the Peruvian Consulate in Ecuador. Stranded at the border, without access to basic services or food, their vulnerability increased. During our study at CEBAF, Estella (pseudonym, sixty-six years old), who was waiting for her whole family to get their visas, mentioned that they had an appointment in the nearest consulate, but it was scheduled for sixteen days after their arrival: "[We] came all together, me my husband my daughter and my two grandchildren. We all have passports, but we couldn't take care of the visa in Venezuela. We have been here for nine days, waiting. The consulate only had appointments available for the 31st of August. I already got mine [passport] stamped because of my age, but I can't move on without them." Regarding the humanitarian exceptions for this particular visa, their vague formulation allowed for varying interpretations by officials at the border. More often than not, these exceptions were not applied, or took days until they were recognized, adding new restrictions and rules that were not initially contemplated in the decree. For example, during our study at CEBAF, we witnessed the rejection of Venezuelan medical reports of serious diseases, such as that of a minor who arrived at CEBAF with brain cancer: migration officials demanded the absurd entry requirement of a medical report signed by a Peruvian doctor. Similarly, Yosvely (pseudonym, thirty-one years old), who was seven months pregnant at the time of the study, traveled with her two-year-old daughter without a passport. With no access to financial resources and nothing to eat, they slept on the floor for four days until one migration officer agreed to grant her regular entry under a special exemption for pregnant women "I thought that they were letting pregnant women in, that was what I was told in Venezuela. I get here and they tell me that no, that law ended in August first. I had to wait four days and finally someone let me in to Peru."

Furthermore, in parallel to the introduction of the humanitarian visa, Peru has significantly limited the possibility of being protected as an asylum seeker and refugee, since most Venezuelan applicants at the border are rejected without due process (Amnesty International 2020). Joaquin (pseudonym, twenty-three years old) worked for the armed force in Caracas, and left the country after he deserted in February 2019. Having stayed in Colombia for months, he decided to move on to Chile where he has friends: "I consider myself a refugee.... My head has a price in Venezuela, but I was denied asylum here."

The imposition of the humanitarian visa has caused a significant increase in illegal people smuggling and human trafficking at the northern border (Amnesty International 2020; Bolívar, Freier, and Luzes 2019a). The Peruvian humanitarian visa, as well as its ineffective implementation, not only violated the country's immigration law, but it also contravened constitutional rights, prevented free transit, and violated the right to nondiscrimination and family reunification. This led the Peruvian Coordinadora Nacional de Derechos Humanos (national human rights coordinator) to immediately file a habeas corpus against the ministry of foreign affairs, the ministry of interior, and the Superintendencia Nacional on 17 June 2019 because, "They are violating and threatening the right of forced Venezuelan migrants who need to enter the national territory in search of refuge from the political, social and economic crisis in this country. More seriously, they are undermining the rights of children and adolescents fleeing Venezuela."[25]

Thus, instead of serving as a complementary form of protection, the implementation of the humanitarian visa posed a serious barrier to the protection of vulnerable migrants and refugees.

Conclusion

Humanitarian visas are a good practice when they grant protection, or legal residence, to people who do not qualify as refugees or those who are beneficiaries of complementary protection but who have humanitarian needs worthy of attention. On paper, Latin America can be considered a global leader in legislative provisions for complementary protection and humanitarian visas (Freier and Gauci 2020). When explicitly based on humanitarian concerns, the application of humanitarian visas can help untangle the migration narrative from security and economy concerns (Jubilut 2017). In practice, some initiatives have benefitted forced migrants both from within and outside the region, as well as people fleeing from multiple causes, such as was the case of Haitian displacement post-2010 earthquake.

Our analysis also suggests some caution, however, since we found that humanitarian visas can also be used as a euphemism to implement restrictive policies. Such restrictive policy implementation takes place in the context of the broader reconfiguration of global migration governance in ways that, instead of supporting the protection of vulnerable migrants in need of international protection, gravitate toward militarization, securitization, and the internationalization of border control and migration management (Pallister-Wilkins 2018; Tazzioli and Garelli 2018).

In the case of the Venezuelan displacement crisis, the implementation of humanitarian visas in Chile, Ecuador, and Peru created new barriers to legal entry and to the protection mechanisms that were previously in place, instead of presenting additional protection. In the case of Peru, the measure increased the vulnerability of displaced Venezuelans, as well as irregular routes and correlated dangers. Amidst the current COVID-19 pandemic and beyond, Peru should reopen feasible legal pathways for the entry and legal residence of Venezuelan migrants and refugees in order to guarantee their protection. Peru should also offer medical screenings and access to health-care services.

Luisa Feline Freier is Associate Professor of Political Science at the Universidad del Pacífico (UP) in Lima. She holds a PhD in Political Science from the London School of Economics and Political Science (LSE), and a Master's degree in Latin American and Caribbean Studies from the University of Wisconsin at Madison. Feline's research focuses on Latin American immigration and refugee policies, intercontinental South-South migration, and the Venezuelan displacement crisis. Her work has been published in edited volumes and leading peer-reviewed journals.

Marta Luzes is a Research Associate at the Centro de Investigación de la Universidad del Pacífico (CIUP). Marta holds a BA in economics from the University NOVA (Lisbon, Portugal) and a Master's degree in international development from the University of Warwick (United Kingdom). She has worked extensively in project evaluation of public policies in Latin America. Currently, her research at CIUP focuses on the Venezuelan displacement crisis. She is conducting research on topics such as the socioeconomic integration of migrants, and the local response to this phenomenon.

Notes

1. Chile (art. 4 of Law 20.430 of 2010); Ecuador (art. 2 of the Organic Law on Human Mobility of 2017); Mexico (art. 2.IV, arts. 6, 3, 7, 15, 16, 17, 48 of the Refugee Law and Complementary Protection Act of 2011).
2. Nicaragua (art. 220 of Law 761, General Migration Aliens of 2011).
3. Argentina (arts. 23, 29, 34 of Law 25.871 of 2004); Bolivia (art. 30 of the Migration Law of 2013); Brazil (art. 14 of Migration Law of 2017); Costa Rica (arts. 6.6, 94.12 of Law 8764); Ecuador (arts. 58, 57, 66.5 of the Organic Law on Human Mobility of 2017); Guatemala (art. Decree 44 of 2016); Honduras (art. 39 of Migration Law 208 of 2003); Mexico (arts. 52, 53, 74 of Migration Law of 2011);

Panama (arts. 6, 9, 18 of Law 3 of 2008); Peru (art. 29.k of Legislative Decree 1350 of 2017), Uruguay (arts. 34, 43, 44 of Law 18.250); and Venezuela (for the case of nationals from Haiti humanitarian visas (so-called social visas) were issued after the earthquake of 2010).
4. Brazil (art. 14 of Migration Law of 2017); Uruguay (arts. 34, 44 of Law 18.250).
5. Guatemala (art. Decree 44 of 2016).
6. Panama (art. 18 of Law 3 of 2008).
7. Honduras (art. 39 of Migration Law 208 of 2003).
8. Bolivia (art. 30 of the Migration Law of 2013).
9. Ecuador (art. 66.5 of the Organic Law on Human Mobility of 2017).
10. Freier and Parent (2019) argue that this initial response needs to be understood in the context of foreign policy considerations and the desire by right-of-center governments to discredit the Maduro regime in Venezuela by extending protection to Venezuelan citizens.
11. The ministry of foreign affairs, through Resolution 5797 of 25 July 2017, created the PEP as a mechanism of migratory facilitation for Venezuelan nationals. This card allows Colombia to preserve the internal and social order and to prevent exploitation of Venezuelan citizens; it will ensure their permanence in decent conditions in the country.
12. Supreme Decree 023-2017-IN.
13. CUADRO 32. VISAS HUMANITARIAS. https://acnur.org/fileadmin/Docu mentos/Proteccion/Buenas_Practicas/9234.pdf#_ga=2.4341627.975849778 .1596889588-2084176735.1568761786.
14. Peru (Decree 002 of 2017-IN); Ecuador (Resolution 1272 of 2017).
15. Circular Letter 96 of the ministry of foreign affairs.
16. Decree 1350 Migration, 2017 (art. 91.1(a)).
17. Decree 826 of 2019.
18. Afghanistan, Bangladesh, Eritrea, Ethiopia, Kenya, Nepal, Nigeria, Pakistan, Somalia, and Senegal.
19. Art. 3 of Refugee Law, Law 27.891 of 2002.
20. Art. 29.k of Legislative Decree 1350 of 2017.
21. Resolution of the Superintendencia Nacional 000177-2019.
22. https://www.gob.pe/institucion/rree/noticias/29204-aplicacion-de-visa-a-nacio nales-venezolanos.
23. Resolution of the Superintendencia Nacional 000177-2019.
24. Personal communication with María Antonia Masana García, president of Peru's Intersectoral Working Group on Migration (MTIGM). 23 December 2019.
25. http://derechoshumanos.pe/2019/06/presentan-habeas-corpus-ante-amena za-del-derecho-al-libre-transito-de-migrantes-venezolanos/.

References

Aron, Valeria, Soledad Castillo Jara. Forthcoming. "Reacting to Change within Change: Adaptive Leadership and the Peruvian Response to Venezuelan Immigration." *International Migration*.

Acosta, Diego, Cécile Blouin, and Luisa Feline Freier. 2019. "La emigración venezolana: respuestas latinoamericanas." Documento de Trabajo, 3 (2ª época). Madrid: Fundación Carolina.
Acosta, Diego, and Luisa Feline Freier. 2015. "Turning the Immigration Policy Paradox Upside Down? Populist Liberalism and Discursive Gaps in South America." *International Migration Review*, 49 (3): 659–96.
———. 2018. "Regional Migration Management in South America." In *Handbook of Migration and Globalisation*, edited by Anna Triandafyllidou, 69–87, Cheltenham, UK: Edward Elgar Publishing.
Amnesty International. 2020. "Perú: Buscando refugio: Perú da la espalda a quienes huyen de Venezuela." https://www.amnesty.org/es/documents/amr46/1675/2020/es/.
BBC. 2016. "Una pena de muerte disimulada: La Polemica Operación de Liberación del Pueblo, la Mano Dura del Gobierno de Venezuela Contra el Crimen." http://www.bbc.com/mundo/noticias-america-latina-38126651.
———. 2017. "Venezuela profile–Timeline." http://www.bbc.com/news/world-latin-america-19652436.
Berganza, Isabel, Cécile Blouin, and Luisa Feline Freier. 2018. La aplicación de la definición de Cartagena a las personas venezolanas en el Perú." Documento de Discusión CIUP, DD1805, Agosto, 2018, Universidad del Pacífico.
———. 2020. "The Situational Element of Massive Violation of Human Rights of the Extended Definition of Cartagena: Towards an Application in the Venezuelan Case." *Revista Chilena de Derecho*, 47(2): 385–410.
Berganza, Isabel, and Luisa Feline Freier. 2020. "Política Migratoria y de Refugio: Hacia una Política de Integración para un País de Acogida." *Proyecto Bicentenario: Contribuciones al Perú en Camino a su Desarrollo*. Lima: Fondo Editorial, Universidad del Pacífico.
Betts, Alexander. 2010. "Survival Migration: A New Protection Framework." *International Migration*, 16 (3): 361–82.
———. 2014. "The global governance of crisis migration." *Forced Migration Review*, 45: 76–79.
Blouin, Cécile, and Luisa Feline Freier. 2019. "Población venezolana en Lima: entre la regularización y la precariedad." In *Migración de Población Venezolana en Contextos de Crisis y las Respuestas de los países Latinoamericanos*, edited by Luciana Gandini, Fernando Lozano Ascencio and Victoria Prieto: 157–184. Mexico City: UNAM.
Bolívar, Ligia, Luisa Feline Freier, and Marta Luzes. 2019a. "Hacia Fronteras Humanas: Los impactos adversos de las visas humanitarias." Propuesta de Política Pública. CIUP. https://ciup.up.edu.pe/media/1583/ciup-ppp-no2.pdf.
———. 2019b. "Los Impactos Adversos de las Visas Humanitarias." CIUP. Propuesta de Política Pública. http://sisisemail.up.edu.pe/sisisemail/_data/2019/19350/CIUP-PPP-No2.pdf
Cantor, David James, Luisa Feline Freier, and Jean-Pierre Gauci, eds. 2015. *A Liberal Tide? Immigration and Asylum Law and Policy in Latin America*. Titles in the Studies of the Americas Series. London: Institute of Latin American Studies, School of Advanced Study, University of London.

Crónica Uno. 2019. "La carrera consular de los venezolanos por la estampa de una visa humanitarian." https://cronica.uno/la-carrera-consular-de-los-venezolanos-por-la-estampa-de-una-visa-humanitaria/.

Doña, Cristián, and Lourdes Gouveia. Forthcoming. "What do Immigrants make of Immigration Policies? The Case of Venezuelan Immigrants in Chile." *International Migration*.

El Pitazo. 2019. "*El pasaporte venezolano es el cuarto más caro del mundo.*" https://elpitazo.net/migracion/el-pasaporte-venezolano-es-el-cuarto-mas-caro-del-mundo/.

Freier, Luisa Feline. 2015. "A Liberal Paradigm Shift? A Critical Appraisal of Recent Trends in Latin American Asylum Legislation." In *Exploring the Boundaries of Refugee Law: Current Protection Challenges*, edited by Jean-Pierre Gauci, Mariagiulia Giuffré and Evangelia (Lilian) Tsourdi: 118–145. Leiden, Boston: Brill Publishers.

———. 2019. "Summary Report: Providing regular pathways from crisis to safety." GFMD/MIUEX. https://gfmd.org/docs/ecuador-2019#gfmd_2019_thematic_workshops.

Freier, Luisa Feline, and Valeria Aron. 2020. "La legislación migratoria en Perú: entre la promoción de los Derechos Humanos y la seguridad nacional." In *Tendencias y Retos de las Políticas y Reformas Migratorias en América Latina. Un Estudio Comparad*, edited by Natalia Caicedo Camacho: 267–96. Lima: Fondo Editorial, Universidad del Pacífico.

Freier, Luisa Feline, Isabel Berganza, and Cécile Blouin. Forthcoming. "The Cartagena Refugee Definition and Venezuelan Displacement in Latin America." *International Migration*.

Freier, Luisa Feline, and Jean-Pierre Gauci. Forthcoming. "Refugees Rights' Across Region: A Comparative Overview of Legislative Good Practices in Latin America and the EU." *Refugee Survey Quarterly*.

Freier, Luisa Feline, and Kyle Holloway. 2019. "The Impact of Tourist Visas on Intercontinental South-South Migration: Ecuador's Policy of 'Open Doors' as a Quasi-Experiment." *International Migration Review*, 53 (4): 1–38.

Freier, Luisa Feline, and Nicolas Parent. 2019. "The Regional Response to the Venezuelan Exodus." *Current History*, 118: 56–61.

Freier, Luisa Feline, and Leda Pérez. Forthcoming. "Criminalisation of South-South Migration: Venezuelan Immigrants in Peru." *European Journal on Criminal Policy and Research*.

Hathaway, James. 2014. "Food Deprivation: A Basis for Refugee Status?." *Social Research: An International Quarterly*, 81 (2), 327–39.

Horwood, Chris, and Tuesday Reitano. 2016. "A Perfect Storm? Forces Shaping modern Migration." *RMMS*.

International Organization for Migration (IOM). 2017a. *World Migration Report 2018*. Geneva: IOM. https://www.iom.int/sites/default/files/country/docs/china/r5_world_migration_report_2018_en.pdf.

———. 2017b. *Displacement Tracking Matrix Peru, Round 1: Migration Flow of Venezuelan Population*. https://www.globaldtm.info/es/peru/.

———. 2019a. *Displacement Tracking Matrix Peru, Round 5: Migration Flow of Venezuelan Population*. https://www.globaldtm.info/es/peru/.

———. 2019b. *Displacement Tracking Matrix Peru, Round 6: Migration Flow of Venezuelan Population*. https://www.globaldtm.info/es/peru/.

———. 2020. Venezuelan Refugee and Migrant Crisis–Overview. https://www.iom.int/venezuela-refugee-and-migrant-crisis.
Jubilut, Liliana Lyra. 2017. "Humanitarian Alternative Pathways for Protection for Forced Migrants in Latin America?" In *Ideas to Inform International Cooperation on Safe, Orderly and Regular Migration*, ed. Marie McAuliffe, and Michele Klein-Solomon (Conveners): 117–122. International Organization for Migration: Geneva.
Martin, Susan, Sanjula Weerasinghe, and Abbie Taylor. 2013. "Crisis Migration." *Brown Journal of World Affairs* 20 (1): 123–137.
Malo, María G. Forthcoming. "Between Liberal Legislation and Preventive Political Practice: Ecuador's Political Reactions to Venezuelan Immigration." *International Migration*.
Massey, Douglas S. 2007. "Understanding America's Immigration 'Crisis.'" *Proceedings of the American Philosophical Society*, 151: 309–27.
McAdam, Jane. 2007. *Complementary Protection in International Refugee Law*. Oxford: Oxford University Press.
———. 2014. "The concept of crisis migration." *Forced Migration Review*, 45: 10–11.
Pallister-Wilkins, Polly. 2018. "Hotspots and the geographies of humanitarianism." *Environment and Planning D: Society and Space*. https://doi.org/10.1177/0263775818754884.
Proyecto Migración Venezolana. 2020a. "Cómo va la política migratoria en Colombia." https://migravenezuela.com/web/articulo/politica-migratoria-en-colombia/860.
———. 2020b. "¿Qué papeles necesito en Colombia?." https://migravenezuela.com/web/articulo/que-papeles-necesito-en-colombia/745.
Selee, Andrew, Jessica Bolter, Betilde Muñoz-Pogossian, and Miryam Hazán. 2019. *Creativity amid Crisis: Legal Pathways for Venezuelan Migrants in Latin America*." Migration Policy Institute. https://www.migrationpolicy.org/research/legal-pathways-venezuelan-migrants-latin-america.
Tazzioli, Martine, and Glenda Garelli. 2018. "Containment beyond detention: The hotspot system and disrupted migration movements across Europe." *Environment and Planning D: Society and Space*. https://doi.org/10.1177/0263775818759335.
United Nations High Commissioner for Refugees (UNHCR). 2019a. *Global Trends: Forced Displacement in 2018*. Geneva: United Nations High Commissioner for Refugees. https://www.unhcr.org/globaltrends2018/.
———. 2019b. "Complementary Pathways for Admission of Refugees to Third Countries." Geneva: United Nations High Commissioner for Refugees. https://www.refworld.org/pdfid/5cebf3fc4.pdf.
———. 2020a. Operational Portal–Refugees Situations–Venezuela Situation. https://data2.unhcr.org/en/situations/vensit.
———. 2020b. Refugee Data Finder. https://www.unhcr.org/refugee-statistics/download/?url=6cNl.
Van Hear, Nicholas. 2009. "The Rise of Refugee Diasporas." *Current History*, 108: 180–86.
Washington Office on Latin America. 2018. *Adding to the Stress of Emigration from Venezuela: Passports hard to come by*. https://venezuelablog.org/migration-venezuela-passport-inefficiencies/.
Zapata, Gisela, and Vicente Tapia. Forthcoming. "Treating survival migration as a migration crisis: the Brazilian political-institutional response to the influx of Venezuelan migrants and refugees." *International Migration*.

PART IV COMMENTARY

Other Forms of Protection Beyond the Regional Refugee Regime in Latin America

Pablo Ceriani Cernadas

Part III of the book includes three interesting chapters that, by exploring different policy and legal tools that have been developed by Latin American countries, discuss how refugee protection could be strengthened within national and regional responses to human mobility in a global era depicted by restricted and securitized policies built on narrow and stereotyped narratives on migration. All the chapters promote timely discussions, since the region is coping not only with unprecedented challenges in terms of the dimensions and complexity of human mobility, but also with worrying and regressive trends that could undermine some of the progressive instruments that Latin America has developed in the field of migration governance policy.

Leiza Brumat, in the context of Venezuela's current migration crisis, examines what could be called the main regional migration policy instrument implemented in South America, the 2002 Acuerdo Sobre Residencia Para Nacionales de Los Estados Partes Del Mercosur, Bolivia y Chile (MERCOSUR Residence Agreement). Luisa Feline Freier and Nieves Fernández Rodríguez analyze Refugee Law trends and scope in Latin American countries, and also the extent to which a refugee's legal protection is complemented by provisions of migration laws and other pieces of legislation. Freier and Marta Luzes's chapter focuses on the incorporation of humanitarian visas in some Latin America countries, as well as on some recent challenges regarding the misuse of such instruments in countries such as Ecuador and Peru.

In chapter 9 Brumat studies the rationale and negotiation of this regional treaty in order to highlight the outcomes envisaged by the countries that boosted and approved this innovative tool in 2002. By underlining goals such as reducing and preventing irregular migration, ensuring a set of rights that are equal to those of nationals, and promoting regional integration, Brumat argues that the MERCOSUR Residence Agreement could be widely used in the region as a key means for addressing one of the major human mobility challenges in the region–the migration crisis for Venezuelans.

In this scenario, Brumat reminds that the MERCOSUR Residence Agreement "could be a legislative tool that countries are already familiar with and whose implementation they already know well." Moreover, she stresses the effectiveness of the MERCOSUR Residence Agreement, especially in the field of regularization to improve rights' fulfilment, as well as in the development of a regional migration governance policy. Therefore, taking into consideration the unprecedented numbers of Venezuelans' mobility in a short period of time, and the political context in the region with regard to the situation in Venezuela, Leiza points out that the MERCOSUR Residence Agreement would be critical for facilitating mobility, residence, and integration of Venezuelans as an alternative to refugee protection.

In chapter 10 Luisa Feline Freier and Nieves Fernández Rodríguez explore the refugee laws that have been adopted by Latin American countries. The authors highlight that the region has the higher standard in terms of refugee legislative protection, with regard to the refugee definition, to procedures for refugee determination, and to refugees' rights incorporation in the legislative framework. Nevertheless, they evidence not only the common trends, but also the different scope among the refugee laws in the region, as well as the contradictions of some of the laws with regional standards based on the 1984 Cartagena Declaration on Refugees (Cartagena Declaration), including the lack of a refugee law in few countries. Limited refugee laws' implementation is singled out as a critical and extended challenge in the region.

This chapter, when describing the progressive trends of refugee laws in the region, draw attention to the fact that several aspects that directly or indirectly apply to asylum seekers and refugees–residence permits, access to economic and social rights–are regulated in migration laws or other laws, including those related to specific themes, such as labor, health care, and education. The authors stress that, whereas refugees' rights recognition is superficial in many refugee laws, it can be evidenced in the "supplementary nature of migration laws." A timely and important discussion could be promoted on this issue, as will be mentioned below.

In chapter 11 Luisa Feline Freier and Marta Luzes evaluate the development and implementation–by some countries of the region–of one of the tools recognized as complementary protection: humanitarian visas. They describe the different meaning and scope that each country has given to this instrument. The examples provide evidence that it has been used both as a complement to refugee protection and as a residence category meant to facilitate regular status–and then, protection–to different people in vulnerable circumstances that would not be recognized as refugees.

Specifically, the chapter examines, with a critical approach, the recent use of the humanitarian visa in the context of Venezuela's migration crisis. They stress how euphemistically humanitarian visas were implemented as regressive measures directed to restrict access to safe territories by Venezuela's migrants and asylum seekers. Focusing on the case of Peru, Feline and Marta describe the particular situation of a humanitarian visa presented with a public security concern discourse, and correctly state, "The fact that the resolution for the implementation of these visas contemplated humanitarian exceptions clearly questions its humanitarian character." Contrary to the positive outcomes of the MERCOSUR Residence Agreement examined by Brumat, the authors here explain how this visa could increase migrants' precarious conditions, smuggling, and trafficking, and affect other policies–such as vaccination programs.

The three chapters of part III, although with a critical and well-founded analysis, evidence that Latin American countries, and in particular the South American ones, have been developing progressive and innovative policies and tools at both national and regional level directed to facilitate mobility, strengthening refugee protection, and fulfilling the rights of all migrants–that is, refugees and other migrants. Literature on this progressive era of migration governance in the region is vast (Acosta Arcarazo 2015 2018; Ceriani Cernadas 2017; Ceriani Cernadas and Freier 2015; Ceriani Cernadas and Jaramillo 2020; Domenech and Boito 2019; Gandini, Prieto, and Lozano-Asencio 2020; Ramírez 2017) and some of the main scholars on this field are included in the references of the three chapters.

In addition, these chapters address–from different angles and focusing on different tools–how the region and its countries have been responding to Venezuela's migration crisis, in a context where xenophobia is on the rise, as they all point out. They describe some of the policies and decisions adopted, the good practices but also their limitations and contradictions, especially in relation to refugee status determination and protection. Although implicitly, the chapters evidence the lack of a comprehensive and common approach of those policies and practices, differently from the regional standards that had been developed by the same countries since, at least, the Cartagena Declaration onwards.

These responses include some very positive notes in comparison to other regions—such as the facts that there are no massive detention and deportation practices, and millions have entered another country with a regular status. Nevertheless, as Freier and Luzes explain, many are still in an irregular migration situation, and recent regressive measures, such as so-called humanitarian visas, are increasing vulnerability and risks that migrants and asylum seekers face. The contradictions and the back and forth of some regional responses could be considered a continuity of the diverse legislative standards in the region explored by Freier and Fernández. Likewise, the partial application by many states of the MERCOSUR Residence Agreement, described by Brumat, also illustrates the lack of regional consensus, as well as the regressive trends in some countries.

On a separate note, all the chapters in this part IV, either directly or indirectly, lead to a paramount discussion in the field of migration governance at national, regional, and global level—namely, the need of comprehensive, rights-based human mobility policies that are directed to protect every person on the move under the complementarity of all the international instruments developed for the protection of the rights of all human beings, including their right to asylum. This holistic approach should address the adverse effects of the building of the concepts of migrants and refugees as rigid and disconnected categories that should have separate and different treatment, including in terms of the scope of respect, protection, and fulfilment of their human rights.

In another paper (Ceriani Cernadas 2016), I stressed the negative consequences of the efforts and strategies aimed at strictly separating—in narrative, and, more importantly, in policies and practices—refugees from the narrow and inaccurate concept of economic migrants. This narrative has contributed to legitimating migration control policies based on externalization, detention, and deportation with such a low set of basic rights and guarantees that in many cases they have led to what can be named as a permanent state of exception from equal protection principles under the rule of law.

Those policies have not only violated fundamental rights and contributed to the increasing of different forms of risks and abuses against migrants and asylum seekers, but they have also evidenced that they are ineffective and dangerous tools for preventing irregular migration. Moreover, the legitimization of those migration policy enforcement mechanisms have gone so far that it led to the current global crisis of the right of asylum and the protection of refugees. There are plenty of examples on how those measures negatively impact the right of asylum and refugees' rights of protection.[1]

The discussion on what actually means a holistic approach to human mobility can benefit from this section on "other forms of protection," as it could lead to a critical and needed starting point for such discussion: the existing international instruments for protecting individuals. International Human Rights Law (IHRL) is the universal and comprehensive umbrella of this framework, where Refugee and Humanitarian Law ensure additional and specific protection for people under certain circumstances. The 1989 Convention on the Rights of the Child, the 1990 Convention for the Protection of the Rights of All Migrant Workers and Members of Their Families, the 2006 Convention on the Rights of Persons with Disabilities, and the 1979 Convention on All Forms of Discrimination against Women are meant to serve the same purposes for each group of people according to different conditions.

The key of this complex system, and how it should be applied in policies on human mobility, is the complementarity of all those pieces, as well as how each of them, such as the 1951 Convention Relating to the Status of Refugees, becomes stronger in its effective application every time they are needed and used. All the cases examined by the authors are on persons that need international protection, whether under Refugee Law and/or other international instruments. They are all meant to protect the rights of persons in vulnerable circumstances. Complementary and intersectional interpretation and implementation of this protection is also paramount. Therefore, human mobility policies have to coherently and effectively include all those tools.

The discussion on holistic human mobility policies is linked to the analysis of Freier and Fernández on whether refugees' rights should be included in a separate piece of legislation from migrants. It is worth noting that, although not all migrants are refugees, all refugees fall within the international definition of migrant, despite the additional legal protection status based on (international and national) refugee laws. Beyond refugee status determination and the explicit, formal, and individualized protection against *refoulement*–although this jus cogens principle applies to all individuals– refugees are migrants in every other aspect. Therefore, including a set of human rights in different domestic laws might lead to a discussion that could affect the principles of no discrimination and universality.

An interesting discussion that could follow up this analysis is whether refugees and other migrants rights should or should not be incorporated in the common, thematic laws that recognize the same rights to every individual under the jurisdiction of the same state (e.g., education laws, healthcare laws, etc.). Whereas explicit recognition of refugees and other migrants' rights is critical, doing it in separate legal tools–e.g. immigration or refugee law-, instead of in thematic and general laws–may lead to different set of rights to nationals, migrants, migrants with irregular status, asylum seekers, refugees, and other categories. Legislative frameworks at global level evidence this issue nowadays.

The chapters of part IV evidence that comprehensive and complementary approaches of regional and national instruments actually work. Since the implementation of the MERCOSUR agreement has contributed to prevent irregular migration and protect people in vulnerable circumstances, it also has led to positive outcomes in fields such as labor, social protection, public security, and other policies (Brumat in this volume). At the national level, complementarity of pieces of legislation have led to the more protective and effective refugee policies (Freier and Fernández in this volume). Humanitarian visas, until recently (Freier and Luzes in this volume), helped to provide residence and protection to certain people that restricted migration and refuge policies would have rejected otherwise.

All these examples, once more, call for more and more-meaningful discussions on comprehensive and rights-centered human mobility policies as the key path for actually achieving regular, safe, and orderly migration governance. Otherwise, a narrow, classificatory, and restrictive approach could lead, as the chapters evidence, to the opposite outcomes: irregularity, lack of safety, and uncontrolled human mobility.

In sum, all the chapters of part IV are accessible and evidenced-based texts that clearly reflect the main trends, policies, and challenges in the region. More importantly, they invite the reader to continue paramount discussions on human mobility policies, and on how ensuring refugee protection could be achieved within a broader framework directed to fulfill the right of asylum along with all other human rights to every person that migrates in need of protection of these rights.

Pablo Ceriani Cernadas is Professor of Law and Coordinator of the Migration and Asylum Program at the Institute of Justice and Human Rights at the National University of Lanús (UNLa), Argentina, and Director of the Specialization on Migration, Asylum and Human Rights at the same university. Former Vice-Chair of the Committee on the Protection of the Rights of All Migrant Workers and Members of their Families of the United Nations. He has served as a consultant for the United Nations Children's Fund (UNICEF) and the United Nations Population Fund (UNFPA) on the rights of child, adolescent, and women migrants, and has consulted for the International Labour Organization (ILO) on migrant workers' rights and labor migration policies. With a Law degree from the University of Buenos Aires, he has a Master's degree from the European University in Madrid and a PhD from the University of Valencia, Spain.

Note

1. The Bilateral Agreement between the European Union and Turkey is formal evidence of this process and its impact on the right of asylum. Freier and Luzes's reflections on the responses to Venezuela's migration crisis by some countries,

as well as Brumat's, also evidence both the crisis of asylum and the need of integrated responses to human mobility.

References

Acosta Arcarazo, Diego. 2015. "Discursos y políticas de inmigración en Sudamérica: ¿Hacia un nuevo paradigma o la confirmación de una retórica sin contenido?." *REMHU. Revista Interdisciplinar da Mobilidade Humana.* 23 (44):171–189.

———. 2018. *The National versus the Foreigner in South America. 200 Years of Migration and Citizenship Law.* Cambridge University Press.

Acuerdo Sobre Residencia Para Nacionales de Los Estados Partes Del Mercosur, Bolivia y Chile. 2002. https://www.mercosur.int/documento/acuerdo-residencia-nacionales-estados-partes-mercosur-bolivia-chile/.

Cartagena Declaration on Refugees. 1984. https://www.oas.org/dil/1984_cartagena_declaration_on_refugees.pdf.

Ceriani Cernadas, Pablo. 2016. "Language as a Migration Policy Tool. Critical remarks on the concept of "economic migrant" and how it leads to human rights violations." *Sur International Journal on Human Rights*, 13(23): 97–111.

———. 2017. "Back to Basics? The limited use of immigration detention in South America: an interpretation based in human rights treaties and principles." In *Challenging Immigration Detention. Academics, Activists and Policy Makers*, ed. Michael J. Flynn and Matthew B. Flynn: 239-264. Cheltenham, UK: Edward Elgar Publishing.

Ceriani Cernadas, P., and Luisa Feline Freirer. 2015. "Migration policies and policymaking in Latin America and the Caribbean: lights and shadows in a region in transition." In *A Liberal Tide: Towards A Paradigm Shift in Latin American Migration and Asylum Policy-Making?*, ed. David Cantor, Luisa Freier and Jean Pierre Gauci: 11–32. London: ILAS.

Ceriani Cernadas, Pablo, and Verónica Jaramillo Fonnegra. 2021. "Políticas migratorias y Derechos Humanos en América Latina: Prácticas progresivas, viejos desafíos, preocupantes retrocesos y nuevos retos." In *Abordajes sociojurídicos contemporáneos para el estudio de las migraciones internacionales*, coord. Luciana Gandini, Universidad Nacional Autónoma de Mexico.

Domenech, Eduardo, and María Eugenia Boito. 2019. "Luchas migrantes en Sudamérica: reflexiones críticas desde la mirada de la autonomía de las migraciones." In *América Latina en movimiento. Autonomía de la migración, fronteras y nuevas geografías de lucha*, ed. Blanca Cordero, Sandrio Mezzadra, and Amarela Varela: 158–188. Madrid: Traficantes de Sueños/Tinta Limón.

Gandini, Luciana, Victoria Prieto, and Fernando Lozano-Asencio. 2020. "Nuevas movilidades en América Latina: la migración venezolana en contextos de crisis y las respuestas en la región." *Cuadernos Geográficos.* 59(3): 103–121.

Ramírez, Jacques, ed. 2017. *Migración, Estado y Políticas. Cambios y continuidades en América del Sur.* La Paz: Vicepresidencia del Estado Plurinacional de Bolivia.

Part V

Current Regional Refugees "Crisis"

12

Responding to Forced Displacement in the North of Central America

Progress and Challenges

Suzanna Nelson-Pollard

Introduction

In 2014 the sudden increase of unaccompanied minors apprehended at the US-Mexican border[1] brought the plight of displaced people from El Salvador, Guatemala, and Honduras (together known as the North of Central America,[2] or NCA) into the global spotlight (Cantor 2014a; Internal Displacement Monitoring Centre [IDMC] 2015; Stinchcomb and Hershberg 2014). Around the same time, agencies of the United Nations (UN) called attention to the needs of displaced people and researched their motives for fleeing (United Nations High Commissioner for Refugees [UNHCR] 2014, 2015), and academic studies explored the root causes, patterns, and characteristics of displacement in the region (such as Cantor 2014b; IDMC 2015). The rising criminal violence, and the humanitarian needs of those affected by the violence, started to attract international attention.

Six years on, what has changed? States, both those within and those beyond the region, have signed commitments agreeing to cooperate and tackle the phenomenon.[3] Several humanitarian organizations have devised programs to complement state responses, and the panorama of services on offer for displaced people in the region has grown (Cue and Núñez-Flores 2017; Muggah 2017). Yet despite these efforts, needs are arguably rising.

The number of people seeking asylum from the region has grown: by 2018 there were five times more refugees and asylum seekers from the NCA than in 2014 (UNHCR 2019b), and by 2019 new asylum claims had gone up by 53 percent in comparison to the previous year (UNHCR 2020).

Although much has been written by both policymakers and academics about the growing humanitarian needs in the NCA and the need for a stronger humanitarian response (e.g., Cue and Núñez-Flores 2017; Forced Migration Review 2017; Humanitarian Practice Network 2017), there is scarce literature evaluating the existing response provided by both states and humanitarian actors. This chapter attempts to provide a stocktaking of the recent response to the humanitarian needs of displaced people and affected communities in the NCA.

The chapter is divided into four main parts, starting with a brief overview of the situation: violence perpetrated by criminal groups and state actors, the resulting displacement (both internal and cross-border), and the humanitarian needs. The second section looks at the response from the humanitarian sector, including its geographical presence and the services provided, as well as the challenges humanitarian actors face in terms of access, funding, and capacity. The chapter then turns to states as the primary responsibility holders for responding to displacement, and looks at the commitments made to collectively respond to displacement in the NCA. Finally, the chapter focuses on the Marco Integral Regional de Protección y Soluciones (MIRPS; Comprehensive Regional Protection and Solutions Framework), as the most recent and comprehensive set of commitments made by states to address forced displacement in the region. After a brief overview of the origins of the MIRPS, the consultative process, and the commitments themselves, the section assesses the implementation and the impact of the MIRPS two years after signing, and provides a brief evaluation of the success of the process, or lack thereof. Piecing together the context, the humanitarian response and the state responses therefore provides a comprehensive overview of the situation for displaced people in the NCA, and sets the scene for outlining recommendations and the main priorities ahead. This research is based on the approach of a practitioner in the humanitarian sector, producing analysis on protection needs for both advocacy purposes and to improve operational decision-making in the humanitarian sector.

The methodology for this research had two phases. First, an overview of the humanitarian needs and the response of non-state actors was done based on five snapshot reports researched and published in 2018 and 2019 by the Regional Protection Group of the Risk, Emergency and Disaster Working Group for Latin America and the Caribbean (REDLAC)[4] (of which the author was the primary researcher). These snapshot reports collected publicly available secondary data (analysis and reports by UN and nongovernmental organizations [NGOs], academic articles, press releases, and official statistics), which were then analyzed in a secondary data review (an analysis tool used for protection assessments in the humanitarian sector[5]). Primary data were also collected through semi-structured interviews with a network of more than fifty international NGOs, local organizations, and UN agencies operating in El Salvador, Guatemala, and Honduras. These interviews were based on topics related to protection (displacement, sexual- and gender-based violence, adequate housing rights, education, and humanitarian access). Each report was peer-reviewed by the Regional Protection Group prior to publication. The second phase of the methodology focused on state commitments and actions to respond to displacement, in particular the MIRPS commitments as the main and most recent demonstration of an intent to respond to the situation. In order to establish the relevance and the novelty of the commitments, the MIRPS commitments and action plans document were comparatively analyzed against existing commitments made before 2017 (such as the San José Action Statement) and the recommendations established by civil society actors in the consultation process in the lead-up to the MIRPS process. Subsequently, the implementation of the MIRPS was evaluated by comparing each commitment with ongoing state practices, found in relevant publicly available documents (such as the UNHCR eighteen-month MIRPS evaluation report, an independent monitoring report on the MIRPS implementation by civil society organizations, as well as the REDLAC snapshot reports and other gray literature). This stocktaking exercise provides an assessment of the impact of the MIRPS, and highlights where states are falling short in terms of securing a comprehensive response to needs. Understanding the challenges and gaps in both state and humanitarian sector responses should provide guidance for the road ahead in ensuring protection for displaced people in the region.

Violence and Displacement in the NCA

Violence perpetrated by both criminal groups and state authorities has generated and continues to generate widespread human rights violations in the NCA. The underlying structural issues behind this violence are many, starting with a background of recent civil wars and militarization, as well as weak state structures, impunity, corruption, poverty, combined with the NCA's geographical location in the international drug trade (Cantor 2014b; Hallock, Ruiz Soto, and Fix 2018; IDMC 2015). All three countries are classified as middle income, yet they face high levels of inequality, with few opportunities for young people and high levels of poverty (Washington Office on Latin America [WOLA] 2018; World Bank 2019).

In recent years, gangs have grown in both territorial control and power over the mostly urban communities in which they operate (Cue and Núñez-

Flores 2017). Homicide levels hit an all-time high between 2011 and 2016, and have since decreased, but they remain at some of the highest in the world, and surpass the qualification of an epidemic.[6] Yet homicide rates are only part of the picture when it comes to assessing the impacts of criminal violence. Constantly looking to expand their territories, gangs and organized criminal groups maintain control over communities, prescribing who can enter and move within neighborhoods, and creating invisible borders between territories that residents cannot cross (Norwegian Refugee Council [NRC] 2016). Social control imposed by gangs ranges from regular extortion to death threats, sexual violence, homicides, feminicides, torture, kidnappings, and child recruitment. Children often have to drop out of school once they hit puberty and stay confined indoors for their safety. In Honduras a recent study found that 60 percent of students were scared to walk to school, and that twenty-six pupils abandon education every day (Córdova 2018). Women and girls are particularly affected by the high levels of violence, especially since criminal groups force them into sexual relationships, and they face rape and death should they refuse (Hallock, Ruiz Soto, and Fix 2018).

Political violence goes hand in hand with criminal violence in the three countries, where state authorities have often used militarized strategies to respond to gangs and narcotrafficking groups (Bullock 2017; IDMC 2015). In El Salvador in 2018, the UN special rapporteur on extrajudicial executions reported on the disproportionate use of force by the national police (Office of the United Nations High Commissioner for Human Rights 2018). Human rights groups also report the high levels of infiltration of criminals within authority structures, resulting in high levels of corruption and impunity. In Honduras, in late 2017, twenty-two civilians were killed during protests that erupted after irregularities in the national elections were reported (Human Rights Watch [HRW] 2019a). In Guatemala, political repression has particularly affected social movements of individuals working to defend environmental and land rights, and twenty-one indigenous leaders and environmental activists were assassinated in 2018 alone (Organización de los Estados Americanos [OEA] 2018).

With weak or nonexistent government responses to crimes, violence often goes underreported and unpunished. Humanitarian needs remain therefore largely invisible, and displacement is often the only coping mechanism available when the conditions for individuals or families become too dangerous to tolerate (NRC 2016). Generalized violence is a daily reality for many communities and families, but often a direct threat related to extortion, child recruitment, or sexual violence is the final trigger forcing people to flee, sometimes having to move several times in an attempt to find safety (NRC 2016; REDLAC 2019a, 2019b). With a scarce amount of state shelters or protection services on offer, internally displaced people (IDPs) often try to remain undetected by the persecutors that they fled from, and seek shelter through family networks or friends. This often means that they move to neighborhoods that are equally controlled by other armed groups as the one they left (NRC 2016). As a result, they are often highly vulnerable and lack access to basic needs such as food, housing, health care, education, and employment.

High levels of internal displacement have been reported by humanitarian organizations in the three countries, although severe data gaps remain. It is estimated that there were 247,000 IDPs in Honduras as of 2019, and 454,000 IDPs in El Salvador (IDMC 2020). In Guatemala, internal displacement due to violence has not been systematically quantified, nor has the phenomenon been recognized. A recent study suggests that, based on surveys from 2011 to 2014, there were at least 43,000 IDPs due to violence (Hernández Bonilla 2018). Departments with higher rates of reports of extortion and higher rates of school desertion correlated with departments registering internal displacement (ibid.).

Yet such internal displacements are often not enough to guarantee safety, and many have to take the dangerous route north to try to seek protection in the United States, or increasingly in Mexico. While the crisis of unaccompanied minors might have grabbed media attention in 2014, the number of Honduran children and adolescents who traveled to the United States was higher in 2018 than in any of the previous four years (Osorto 2018). In El Salvador one in three minors deported back to their country of origin in 2018 stated that they left because of violence (International Organization for Migration [IOM] 2019a). Yet international protection is routinely denied and many are deported back to their countries of origin. In 2018 there was a 56 percent greater increase of Hondurans being deported from the United States and Mexico in comparison to 2017 (IOM 2019b). Unable to return to their communities of origin or abandoned houses, people often try to remain undetected by the gangs that they fled, and are subsequently forcibly displaced internally, in a vicious circle of inexistent durable solutions (IDMC 2018; NRC 2016).

Prolonged mobility restrictions and obligatory quarantines imposed due to the COVID-19 pandemic have only exacerbated the protection crisis in the NCA. As food insecurity and poverty increases, people needing to flee violent situations are unable to do so, and those seeking international protection are faced with closed borders (REDLAC 2020b). In parallel, deportations from the United States and Mexico to the region have continued, including of deportees testing positive for the virus. Obligatory quarantine shelters have been set up for arrivals, but often lack adequate and hygienic conditions for the reception of thousands of people, as well as the necessary mechanisms to identify people with international protection needs (REDLAC 2020a).

Response from the Humanitarian Sector

Despite the growing recognition of the impact of violence and the phenomenon of displacement in the NCA, a significant amount of people remain unprotected and unassisted (REDLAC 2018a, 2018b). Certain zones are so heavily controlled that governments are unable and/or unwilling to provide basic services, and as a result humanitarian needs are widespread (REDLAC 2018b). Local organizations, including religious networks and human rights defenders, had been witnessing, and responding to, the growing humanitarian needs for years, but it has only been in the past few years that international humanitarian organizations and the UN have started to take notice (Cue and Núñez-Flores 2017; Muggah 2017). Several NGOs and UN agencies focused on both humanitarian and development work were already present in the three countries, addressing poverty reduction or education, or responding to natural disasters (REDLAC 2018b). Transitioning to programming in urban areas to respond to the specific needs of people displaced by criminal violence has not been straightforward. (The International Committee of the Red Cross defines "criminal violence" as other situations of violence.)

A recent evaluation of the humanitarian sector in the NCA showed the limited coverage that international NGOs and UN agencies have in the region (REDLAC 2018a). In Honduras and El Salvador the majority of these organizations work in capital cities and urban areas, despite the needs present in other cities and regions. This lack of national coverage limits the potential for case follow-up and management. In Guatemala poverty reduction in rural areas remains the main focus of humanitarian organizations (United Nations Office of Coordination of Humanitarian Affairs [OCHA] ROLAC 2018). Religious and local organizations do provide a response to violence (in particular to gender-based violence and violence against children), and work together in networks across the migration route. A handful of local organizations work in urban areas on health care, education, and employment. Across Guatemala, however, there are very few local or international organizations working in urban areas responding to violence, and fewer than five actors in the whole country for which responding to internal displacement is a priority (REDLAC 2018a).

In all three countries there are hard-to-reach communities, particularly in places with a lack of state presence and high levels of violence. For the organizations that do provide a humanitarian response to criminal violence—including the UNHCR, the International Committee of the Red Cross, Doctors Without Borders, the Norwegian Refugee Council, Cristosal, among others—many tend to provide services in their offices, outside of affected communities, or to enter affected urban areas no more than once a week or month to run capacity-building events or workshops (REDLAC 2018b). Few organizations have a permanent or semi-permanent presence in communities affected by violence, and are able to identify and monitor needs and provide a direct response. As a result, the majority of affected people have to come forward to seek support. This is particularly difficult in situations where people need to stay hidden to avoid further persecution, and where there is little trust in authorities (Bullock 2017; Nelson-Pollard 2017; REDLAC 2018b).

In a recent study on access involving a range of humanitarian actors in the region, 95 percent of the organizations interviewed stated that there are areas where they cannot work (REDLAC 2018b). Some of the main challenges in obtaining access are down to the invisible borders between territories controlled by armed groups, dividing communities, roads, and even neighbors. Most organizations, just like the many members of the community, are unable to cross these borders, making operations extremely complex (REDLAC 2018a). Violence and insecurity often affect the daily operations of humanitarian organizations, who are forced to suspend or shut down activities whenever there is a violent event within the community (NRC 2019a; REDLAC 2018a, 2018b). Organizations have reported surveillance and attacks by criminal groups (REDLAC 2018a). A range of security measures are usually used, from reduced working hours to comply with curfews, to the use of visibility items (such as branded clothing with official organizational logos) at all times. A high degree of flexibility is necessary for organizations to minimize disruptions in service provision, yet this often comes at the expense of scaling up programs (REDLAC 2018a, 2018b).

In part due to these challenges, so far the response of the humanitarian sector has been primarily concentrated on the prevention of violence through education, community work with youth, and peace culture promotion (REDLAC 2018a). Capacity to provide response to human rights violations, to provide humanitarian assistance, and to offer durable solutions is very limited, nor is it sufficient for the rising needs. In response to internal displacement, humanitarian organizations and UN agencies, often in partnership with local authorities, have set up referral pathways for IDPs to access a range of services, yet the identification of needs remains weak due to the issues around accessing communities. The same applies to services for deportees arriving back to their countries and who are unable to return to their former homes or communities. Over recent years, states have improved the reception conditions for deportees, yet the services on offer have been limited to a small amount of food, a hygiene kit, first aid, and an employment counseling session (Nelson-Pollard 2017). Protection has fallen on the shoulders of civil society, and so several humanitarian organizations have set up referral structures for people with protection needs, providing them with cash or temporary shelter. The issue remains with the identification of protection needs, since not all reception centers have permanent staff dedicated to identifying cases, whether those cases are people who were refused international protection or those who cannot return to their place of origin due to fear. Furthermore, conditions in the reception centers are often specifically set up to rapidly process people; there is neither privacy nor the secure appropriate conditions needed for building trust and enabling people to seek support and tell their often-traumatic stories (Nelson-Pollard 2017).

This is not to say that there has been no progress in the humanitarian response in the NCA. In both El Salvador and Honduras there are growing initiatives led by Cristosal, IDMC, and the Honduran Human Rights Commission to monitor displacement and establish more-reliable data for designing programs.[7] Protection Working Groups have been established in the three countries, led by the UNHCR and including UN agencies, international NGOs, and members of civil society. These groups are relatively new, but they are an important first step in identifying needs, strengthening coordination, and supporting the humanitarian response (REDLAC 2018a). Many organizations fill the gaps in state responses with innovative and flexible programming. A few examples of these include (1) the use of cash transfers to ensure a dignified and efficient response to displacement, (2) the use of networks that activate early warning alerts when people are at risk of displacement, and (3) the referral of cases between specialized organizations (REDLAC 2018a). Yet one of the main challenges for the humanitarians in the NCA remains the issue of funding for programs for responding to violence and displacement. The region has received various income streams for work on violence prevention and development, but few donors back work on humanitarian response (NRC et al. 2019).

State Responses to Displacement in the NCA

In response to the increasing levels of forced displacement across the region over the past six years, states from across the region have come together several times to adopt commitments to coordinate their response. As part of the continuous follow-up to the Cartagena process (see Fischel de Andrade in this volume) and the most recent Brazil Plan of Action (Arnold-Fernández, Sarmiento Torres, and Kallas in this volume) in 2016, a high-level roundtable was convened in San José, hosted by Costa Rica with the support of the UNHCR. Building on the regional framework on displacement, the Brazil Plan of Action, states stated their shared commitment to strengthen protection for those forcibly displaced in Central America, and voluntary pledges were made on tacking displacement and improving asylum systems. Although lacking in concrete action plans, binding commitments, and the necessary budgets to implement the agreement, it was a first step in getting states across Latin America to recognize the extent of the humanitarian needs (UNHCR 2018b).

A year later, during the ongoing negotiations on the Global Compact on Refugees, Honduras signed up to be a pilot country for the Comprehensive Refugee Response Framework (CRRF), an effort that was looking to tap into new financial and technical support for countries responding to displacement crises; after Honduras signed, there was a positive wave of countries in the region joining the process. As the CRRF process started to take shape in the region, it seemed like there was a growing movement for more-concrete commitments and action plans (Nelson-Pollard 2017).

A conference in October 2017 was organized to launch the regional CRRF process—now renamed the Marco Integral Regional de Protección y Soluciones (MIRPS; the Comprehensive Regional Protection and Solutions Framework). The conference was designed for states in and outside of the region to pledge their support to the situation through concrete commitments. In the build-up to the event, multi-stakeholder consultations were held in each pilot country, gathering the demands and expectations from civil society organizations, UN country teams, persons of concern to the UNHCR, the private sector, and academia (UNHCR 2017a). Participating countries developed national action plans, with actions under the four pillars of the CRRF, with targets for 2018 to 2020.

Yet despite the wide consultation and momentum, the meeting failed to represent a seismic shift in the regional response to displacement, nor did it ensure concrete responsibility sharing. A comparative analysis of the San José Action Statement, alongside the MIRPS action plans, civil society consultation documents, and relevant publicly available documents on the follow-up to the MIRPS declaration, permits an examination of the commitments made against those needed. Six countries signed up to the MIRPS document: Belize, Costa Rica, Guatemala, Honduras, Mexico, and Panama. El Salvador dropped out of the event in October 2017 at the last minute, refusing to use the term "internal displacement" to characterize the situation within its borders; the country subsequently rejoined the process under a new government in 2019. Although the format of the MIRPS document makes it difficult to establish which commitments were truly new and which were descriptions of activities already underway, it can be observed that many of the commitments made by the countries of origin, Guatemala and Honduras, were in line with existing national plans and efforts under the San José Action Statement.

Guatemala's commitments focused on its role as a country of destination and country of transit, despite receiving only 130 asylum applications in 2017 (UNHCR 2019a). Nineteen out of thirty commitments made by Guatemala were related to strengthening the asylum system, and five were focused on protecting people in transit (UNHCR 2017a). In comparison, its role as a country of origin—with 36,546 asylum requests made by Guatemalans in 2017 (UNHCR 2019a)—and as a country facing internal displacement was barely acknowledged. Five commitments out of thirty were related to improving conditions for deportees arriving back in Guatemala, and were based on the plans already made under the San José Action Statement (UNHCR 2017a). Only one commitment, related to Guatemala's participation in the nascent regional resettlement scheme–the Protection Transfer Agreement–could be interpreted as a recognition of the Guatemalans who were in need of international protection or who were experiencing internal displacement.

The commitments made by Honduras were more comprehensive, including a recognition of its role as a country of origin, transit, and return, with actions planned for responding to different population groups (UNHCR 2017a). Again, however, the commitments were repetitive of those laid out under the San José Action Statement. In both 2016 and 2017 Honduras committed to (1) finalizing the bill for a law on the protection, prevention, and care for IDPs; (2) creating a protection referral pathway managed by the state; (3) designing an information system tracking internal displacement; and (4) ensuring greater capacity and resources for the relevant authorities in charge of responding to displacement. Although most of these commitments were planned for or already underway, what was missing from the Honduran commitments was explicit financial commitments or indicators of success.

Of note also was the discrepancy between civil society demands and state commitments. Civil society consultations were held in Honduras and El Salvador prior to the conference, with thirty-nine local and international organizations and forty displaced people (NRC 2017). The key message was that financial commitments and increased public spending must be secured to prevent and respond to forced displacement, yet the lack of these resources pledged remained a notable gap. The report also called for several key priorities to be addressed with urgency, including improved access to education for IDPs, the protection of abandoned houses and land, the registration and tracking of cases of internal displacement, and the provision of legal services. The Honduran commitments did mention some of these issues, but the lack of concrete targets and increased funding failed to address the demands.

According to the UNHCR, "The MIRPS goes beyond addressing the issue nationally, and presents a plan for a regional comprehensive displacement response, responsibility-sharing, solidarity and mutual accountability between countries of origin, countries of transit and countries of asylum and return." (UNHCR 2018a). Indeed, under the framework of the Global Compact on Refugees, the initial focus of the CRRF and the MIRPS process was to improve responsibility sharing. Yet this is where the process fell short to the greatest extent. The responsibility sharing aspect of the agreement was focused on the Protection Transfer Arrangement, a program operational since 2016, and resettling very small numbers of cases that were in extreme need of protection (UNHCR 2017b). Several countries, including Brazil and Uruguay, committed to receive families for resettlement under the scheme, albeit in small numbers. With the focus on this limited program, the conference failed to ensure significant resettlement commitments, regular migration pathways, and financial assistance.

The MIRPS: A Framework for Tracking Incremental Changes

Although the commitments may have fallen short of the expectations, this is not to say that no progress has been made since October 2017. The MIRPS commitments are being tracked by a regional monitoring mechanism through the Organization of American States. One year on, the UNHCR released a stocktaking report listing the progress made under the framework (UNHCR 2018a, 2018b, 2018e). In both Guatemala and Honduras, public officials received training on international protection and migration. Guatemala took steps toward strengthening its asylum system and adopted a new migration protocol. In Honduras, government institutions had advanced on various policies and projects related to internal displacement, including the launch of a new department for the protection of displaced persons, progress on assistance, and protection referral pathways in several municipalities; and the construction of a pilot project for tracking abandoned houses and properties. Outside of the NCA in the other MIRPS states, asylum systems were strengthened in Belize, Costa Rica, Mexico, and Panama, with the support of the UNHCR and other UN agencies.

What was notable about these advances however, is that although many of the initiatives were planned for before the MIRPS process started, not all deadlines for 2018 under the MIRPS framework were met (UNHCR 2018b), suggesting that the process neither secured firm state commitments nor sped up projects that were already underway. As such, the MIRPS might provide a framework for monitoring their advancement, but it is nevertheless difficult to attribute an increase in efficiency in their implementation to the process. Deeper structural changes were also missing from the picture. According to recent research on the humanitarian response in the NCA, humanitarian organizations working in Guatemala said that the relationship between the government and civil society is extremely weak, especially since the former cancels appointments frequently and sends different civil servants to meetings—making a constructive working relationship difficult— and still fails to acknowledge its responsibilities on internal displacement (REDLAC 2018a: 8). In Honduras the legal framework on internal displacement, which the Comisión Interinstitucional para la Protección de las Personas Desplazadas por la Violencia (CIPPDV; Inter-institutional Commission for the Protection of Persons Internally Displaced by Violence) had been working on for more than five years, was yet to be adopted (CIPPDV 2019).

Furthermore, it is difficult to establish how much the advancements that have been made are down to the MIRPS process and how much is down to constant pressure from civil society and technical support from the UN system. Particularly telling is the case of El Salvador, which was not an original member of the MIRPS process, and yet saw a fundamental change in its response to displacement, in part due to civil society pressure (REDLAC 2018a). In July 2018 the Supreme Court of Justice of El Salvador ordered the government to recognize internal displacement and to enact public policies to protect its victims. In parallel to legal recognition, the government opened local victims assistance offices across the country. In the first six months of 2018, the offices attended more than four thousand people (Alas 2018). Although these offices lack in skilled personnel so far, and although they cannot support families in finding durable solutions, they remain an important initiative for providing specialized attention to victims (Instituto de Derechos Humanos de la UCA 2018).

As to the wider regional response, the MIRPS has failed to ensure responsibility sharing from other states. Civil society consultations prior to the San Pedro Sula conference showed that many people were desperate to leave the region, and did not see seeking asylum in a neighboring country as a viable option, particularly because gangs have extensive networks and can persecute people across the region (NRC 2017). According to the UNHCR, the Protection Transfer Agreement, the resettlement mechanism included in the MIRPS, "represents an innovative life-saving mechanism that provides individuals who are exposed to extreme risks in those three countries" (UNHCR 2018c). Yet only 288 people were resettled to Australia, Canada, the United States, and Uruguay from 2016 to 2018 out of a total of 2,443 people needing international protection identified by UNHCR partners (ibid.). This remains an important pilot project, demonstrating that resettlement from the region works, and is invaluable for those that have benefited from the program. The project's impact remains a drop in the ocean, however, compared to the 470,000 refugees and asylum seekers from the NCA countries in 2019 (UNHCR 2020).

Beyond resettlement, there are few safe places for people fleeing the NCA region. The response to displacement from the United States over the past two years has been characterized by an increasing criminalization, strengthened borders, and a series of policies that eroded the protection system for Central Americans (Capps et al. 2019; HRW 2019b; REDLAC 2018b). In June 2018 the US attorney general declared that gang violence and domestic violence would no longer be considered as grounds for asylum (Benner and Dickerson 2018). Over the span of six weeks in 2018, close to two thousand children were separated from their families at the US-Mexican border, in a zero tolerance deterrence policy (Foley and Planas 2018). By October 2018, although the policy had been changed, 13,200 children were still being held in detention in the United States, and unaccompanied minors were spending an average of seventy-four days in detention, double the average time spent in 2016 (HRW 2018). In early 2019 the United States started returning asylum seekers back to Mexico during the resolution of their refugee status determination processes (Gonzales 2019). These measures were implemented in addition to years of policies and practices that make it extremely difficult for people to regularly enter the United States and obtain international protection.

The recent collective displacements from the NCA, known in the media as the migrant caravans, provided the clearest example of the cracks in regional solidarity and state commitments to prevent displacement and protect displaced people. While up to 16,000 people left the NCA, traveling by foot in large groups over the space of several weeks in late 2018 (UNHCR 2018d), the state responses were an increase in efforts to criminalize migration (REDLAC 2018c). Violent clashes between members of the caravan and border police happened both at the Guatemalan-Mexican border (Agence France-Presse [AFP] 2018), and the US-Mexican border (Lind 2018). Asylum seekers remained blocked at the US border in precarious conditions while the US authorities used a variety of different methods to block entry (REDLAC 2018c). Across the region, a Safe Return program was swiftly set up, yet reports from organizations receiving returnees in countries of origin highlighted that these returns had taken place in involuntary conditions that failed to meet minimum standards of protection (REDLAC 2018c). Mexico temporarily offered work visas for Central Americans that agreed to remain in the south of the country (Ernst and Semple 2019), but missing from that offer were the countries stepping up to take responsibility for displaced people, offer resettlement places, or provide funding for the crisis.

The UNHCR acknowledged the challenges due to lack of adequate financing for the MIRPS process in its update report in 2018, and mentioned that financial requirements would be established in 2019 (UNHCR 2018b). A year later, however, in 2019, sixty-one civil society organizations from the region carried out an independent evaluation of the MIRPS, through national and regional consultations and a systematic revision of the impact of each commitment (NRC 2019b). Their analysis was clear on the shortcomings of the process, finding that "the implementation of the commitments have had a limited impact on the lives of hundreds of thousands of people forcibly displaced in countries of origin, transit and arrival in Central America and Mexico." (ibid.).

Conclusion

As evidenced in this chapter, over the past few years some clear progress has been made both by states and by the humanitarian sector on responding to displacement in the NCA. States have, to varying degrees, committed to take responsibility for those affected by violence and to work toward providing a comprehensive response. Humanitarian actors have scaled up their work and collaborated to create protection and assistance networks in the three countries. Yet, as demonstrated by the rising numbers of people seeking asylum in neighboring countries, needs continue to surpass the response capacity. Keeping track of both the challenges faced by humanitarian actors and the commitments made by states is key to ensuring accountability toward affected people.

For the situation for displaced people in the NCA to improve, greater state responsibility over the next few years will be key. In line with its commitments under the MIRPS framework, Honduras must approve the long-awaited legal framework to respond to internal displacement, as pledged several times since 2013, and start implementing the existing draft legislation, policies, and protocols that have been designed to respond to internal displacement. Now that El Salvador has passed legislation to protect IDPs, it must effectively finance its implementation. Guatemala must recognize the reality of internal displacement due to violence within its borders, and take responsibility for its consequences.

As the numbers of people being deported back to the region rise, states must ensure the identification of deportees arriving with protection needs, and establish procedures and responsibilities for their protection. Outside of the NCA, states must take responsibility, as espoused in the Global Compact on Refugees and CRRF processes, sign on to the Protection Transfer Agreement, and significantly increase the offer of resettlement places for those in need. The right to seek asylum and the principle of *non-refoulement* must be respected across the region; displaced people must be able to seek protection.

The humanitarian community must go beyond working on violence prevention and strengthen protection work that responds to human rights violations and supports access to durable solutions. Good practices on prioritizing the most affected communities and securing sustainable access to work in these areas must be shared and used. Protection groups should work together to establish clearer guidelines on how to work in the particular conditions related to gang violence, in order to widen the humanitarian space and defend the humanitarian principles.

Finally, for state commitments to be implemented, they must be matched with the necessary budgets. For humanitarian actors to increase their presence and reach those most vulnerable, an increasing number of donors must allocate funding for a humanitarian response to violence in the NCA. A solid foundation has been established for future work to respond to humanitarian needs in the NCA, but, as needs rise, the humanitarian response must scale up without delay.

Suzanna Nelson-Pollard holds a Master's degree in refugee protection and forced migration from the Refugee Law Initiative at the University of London. From 2018 to 2020, she worked as a researcher and advocacy coordinator with the Norwegian Refugee Council in Panama, leading a research project on the humanitarian needs of displaced people in the North of Central America, providing bimonthly situation and response reports to the Regional Protection Group. She previously worked in humanitarian policy in Geneva.

Notes

1. There were 10,622 unaccompanied minors in the month of June 2014 alone (Stinchcomb and Hershberg 2014: 5).
2. Also known as the Northern Triangle of Central America. Over the past three years there has been a shift from the term "Northern Triangle" to "North of Central America." Both the REDLAC Regional Protection Group and the UNHCR use the term.
3. These commitments include the San José Action Statement (as part of a follow-up to the 2014 Brazil Declaration and Plan of Action: A Framework for Cooperation and Regional Solidarity to Strengthen the International Protection of Refugees, Displaced and Stateless Persons in Latin America and the Caribbean [Brazil Declaration and Plan of Action, or BPA] under the 1984 Cartagena Declaration on Refugees process [Cartagena Declaration]). That statement brought states from across the region for the first time to discuss and commit toward responding to displacement in Central America. Other commitments are the Comprehensive Regional Protection and Solutions Framework (MIRPS), which is a list of concrete actions and commitments toward strengthening state responses to displacement in the region; and the Global Compact on Refugees a global level.
4. A sub-working group of the REDLAC coordination structure, based in Panama and covering coordination and advocacy for Central America. The group is co-led by the UNHCR and NRC and comprises UN agencies and international NGOs with operational presence in the region.
5. Guidance materials on conducting secondary data reviews can be found here: Child Protection Working Group Area of Responsibility http://cpaor.net/starter-kit/11-secondary-data-review-generic; ACAPS https://www.acaps.org/sites/acaps/files/resources/files/secondary_data_review-sudden_onset_natural_disasters_may_2014.pdf.
6. In 2018 the homicide rate per 100,000 inhabitants was forty in Honduras, fifty-one in El Salvador, and twenty-two in Guatemala (Insight Crime 2019). Rates of violent death above ten per 100,000 are considered an epidemic.

7. For further details see IDMC's research project on crime and displacement in Central America: http://www.internal-displacement.org/research-areas/crime-and-displacement-in-central-america; and Cristosal's Regional Forced Displacement Monitoring and Analysis System: https://enfoca.org/web/wp-content/uploads/2019/06/Señales-de-una-Crisis.-Desplazamiento-forzado-2018.pdf

References

Agence France-Presse (AFP). 2018. "Nuevo grupo de hondureños rompen cerco policial en intento de unirse a caravana." *La Prensa*, 28 October. https://www.prensa.com/mundo/Hondurenos-policial-Guatemala-intento-caravana_0_5155734427.html.
Alas, Saraí. 2018. "Inauguran oficina de atención a víctimas en el hospital Rosales." *Diario El Mundo*, 24 July. http://elmundo.sv/inauguran-oficina-de-atencion-a-victimas-en-el-hospital-rosales/.
Benner, Katie, and Caitlin Dickerson. 2018. "Sessions says Domestic and Gang Violence are Not Grounds for Asylum." *New York Times*, 11 June. https://www.nytimes.com/2018/06/11/us/politics/sessions-domestic-violence-asylum.html.
Bullock, Noah, 2017. "Towards a response: addressing forced displacement by violence in El Salvador." *Humanitarian Exchange*, 69: 9–12.
Capps, Randy, Doris Meissner, Ariel G. Ruiz Soto, Jessica Bolter, and Sarah Pierce. 2019. "From Control to Crisis: Changing Trends and Policies Reshaping U.S.-Mexico Border Enforcement." *Migration Policy Institute*. https://www.migrationpolicy.org/research/changing-trends-policies-reshaping-us-mexico-border-enforcement.
Cantor, David James. 2014a. "Gangs: the real 'humanitarian crisis' driving Central American children to the US." *The Conversation*, 22 August. https://theconversation.com/gangs-the-real-humanitarian-crisis-driving-central-american-children-to-the-us-30672.
———. 2014b. "The new wave: Forced displacement caused by organized crime in Central America and Mexico." *Refugee Survey Quarterly*, 33 (3): 34–68.
Comisión interinstitucional para la protección de las personas desplazadas por la violencia (CIPPDV). 2019. *Comisión Interinstitucional para la Protección de la Personas Desplazadas por la Violencia*. Accessed 1 March 2019. http://www.cippd.gob.hn/la-comision-interinstitucional-para-la-proteccion-de-las-personas-desplazadas-por-la-violencia-cippdv/.
Córdova, Yanitza. 2018. "En Honduras, 26 niños al día dejan la escuela por migrar a Estados Unidos." *El Heraldo*, 2 August. https://www.elheraldo.hn/minisitios/hondurenosenelmundo/1203342-471/en-honduras-26-ni%C3%B1os-al-d%C3%ADa-dejan-la-escuela-por-migrar-a.
Cue, Wendy, and Vicente Raimundo Núñez-Flores. 2017. "According to need? Humanitarian responses to violence in Central America." *Humanitarian Exchange*, 69: 6–9.
Ernst, Jeff, and Kirk Semple. 2019. "Mexico Moves to Encourage Caravan Migrants to Stay and Work." *New York Times*, 25 January 2019. https://www.nytimes.com/2019/01/25/world/americas/migrant-caravan-honduras-mexico.html.

Foley, Elise, and Roque Planas. 2018. "2,000 Kids Separated from Parents Under Trump Border Crackdown." *Huffington Post*, 15 June. https://www.huffingtonpost.com/entry/kids-separated-from-parents-under-trump-border-crackdown_us_5b240a7fe4b056b22639d9d2.

Forced Migration Review. 2017. *Latin America and the Caribbean*, 56. https://www.fmreview.org/latinamerica-caribbean.

Gonzales, Richard. 2019. "Trump Administration Begins "Remain in Mexico" Policy, Sending Asylum-Seekers Back." *NPR*, 29 January. https://www.npr.org/2019/01/29/689819928/trump-administration-begins-remain-in-mexico-policy-sending-asylum-seekers-back.

Hallock, Jeffrey, Ariel G. Ruiz Soto, and Michael Fix. 2018. "In Search of Safety, Growing Numbers of Women Flee Central America." *Migration Policy*. https://www.migrationpolicy.org/article/search-safety-growing-numbers-women-flee-central-america.

Hernández Bonilla, Sindy. 2018. "Desplazamiento forzado interno en Guatemala: Diagnóstico 2010–2016." *Universidad Rafael Landívar*. Editorial Kamar. http://rjmcentroamerica.org/wp-content/uploads/2018/10/Cuaderno-3.pdf.

Human Rights Watch (HRW). 2018. *Immigrant Children Still Being Locked Up in the US*. 22 October. https://www.hrw.org/news/2018/10/22/immigrant-children-still-being-locked-us.

——. 2019a. *Honduras*. https://www.hrw.org/world-report/2019/country-chapters/honduras.

——. 2019b. *We Can't Help You Here" US Returns of Asylum Seekers to Mexico*. 2 July. https://www.hrw.org/report/2019/07/02/we-cant-help-you-here/us-returns-asylum-seekers-mexico.

Humanitarian Practice Network. 2017. *The humanitarian consequences of violence in Central America*. The Humanitarian Exchange Special Feature, 69.

Instituto de Derechos Humanos de la UCA (IDHUCA). 2018. *Balance anual sobre la situación de los Derechos Humanos 2017*. http://www.uca.edu.sv/wp-content/uploads/2018/02/informe-de-derechos-humanos-2017.pdf.

Internal Displacement Monitoring Centre (IDMC). 2015. *New humanitarian frontiers: Addressing criminal violence in Mexico and Central America*. http://www.internal-displacement.org/publications/new-humanitarian-frontiers-addressing-criminal-violence-in-mexico-and-central-america.

——. 2018. *Thematic Series: The Invisible Majority, Returning to El Salvador*. http://www.internal-displacement.org/sites/default/files/inline-files/201809-idmc-el-salvador-case-study_3.pdf.

——. 2020. Countries. http://www.internal-displacement.org/countries.

Insight Crime. 2019. *InSight Crime's 2018 Homicide Round-Up*. 22 January. https://www.insightcrime.org/news/analysis/insight-crime-2018-homicide-roundup/.

International Organization for Migration (IOM). 2019a. "El Salvador: Cifras Oficiales de Retornos—Enero—Diciembre 2018." *IOM NTMI*. http://mic.iom.int/webntmi/descargas/sv/2018/12/ESdic2018.pdf.

——. 2019b. "Honduras: Cifras Oficiales de Retornos—Enero—Diciembre 2018." *IOM NTMI*. http://mic.iom.int/webntmi/descargas/hn/2018/12/HNdic2018.pdf.

Idhuca, 2018 "Balance anual sobre la situación de los Derechos Humanos," *Instituto de Derechos Humanos de la UCA*, 2017. http://www.uca.edu.sv/wp-content/uploads/2018/02/informe-de-derechos-humanos-2017.pdf.

Lind, Dara. 2018. "How a march at the US-Mexico border descended into tear gas and chaos." *Vox*, 26 November. https://www.vox.com/policy-and-politics/2018/11/26/18112474/tear-gas-border-patrol-caravan-rocks.

Muggah, Robert. 2017. "A humanitarian response to Central America's fragile cities." *Humanitarian Exchange*, 69: 17–20.

Nelson-Pollard, Suzanna. 2017. "Criminal violence in Honduras as a driver of displacement." *Forced Migration Review*, 56: 14–17.

Norwegian Refugee Council (NRC). 2016. *Extreme violence, treacherous journeys and invisible borders*. December 8. https://www.nrc.no/resources/reports/extreme-violence-treacherous-journeys-and-invisible-borders.

———. 2017. *Comprehensive Refugee Response Framework–Honduras and El Salvador, Less promises, more solutions*. https://www.nrc.no/globalassets/pdf/reports/honduras/24.11.2017-less-promises-more-solutions--crrf-ntca.pdf.

———. 2019a. *Una Generación Fuera de la Escuela, Resultados de Censo de Educación de Honduras 2015–2018*. https://www.nrc.no/globalassets/pdf/reports/hondurasel-salvador/una-generacion-fuera-de-la-escuela-honduras-nrc-web.pdf.

———. 2019b. *"De la Teoría a la Práctica": Un informe de 61 organizaciones de sociedad civil de Belice, Guatemala, Honduras, México y Panamá sobre el Marco Integral Regional de Protección y Soluciones (MIRPS)*. https://www.refworld.org.es/docid/5dcf17f94.html.

Norwegian Refugee Council, RET Americas, ChildFund International, Save the Children, Médicos del Mundo, Médecins du Monde, CARE, Plan International, OXFAM, and World Vision. 2019. *A Regional Humanitarian Response Plan for an Intensifying Humanitarian Crisis in the North of Central America*. https://www.nrc.no/globalassets/pdf/position-papers/north-of-central-america/a-regional-humanitarian-response-plan-for-the-nca.pdf.

United Nations Office of Coordination of Humanitarian Affairs ROLAC. 2018. *3W Guatemala*. https://data.humdata.org/visualization/ocha-rolac-guatemala-3w/.

Organización de los Estados Americanos (OEA). 2018. *CIDH y OACNUDH condenan asesinatos de defensores indígenas y campesinos en Guatemala*. 27 June. http://www.oas.org/es/cidh/prensa/comunicados/2018/137.asp.

Office of the United Nations High Commissioner for Human Rights (OHCHR). 2018. "Declaración final de misión en El Salvador." *Relatora Especial de la de sobre las ejecuciones extrajudiciales*, 5 February. https://www.ohchr.org/SP/NewsEvents/Pages/DisplayNews.aspx?NewsID=22634&LangID=S.

Osorto, Marcel. 2018. "Honduras, a un paso de la crisis migratoria de 2014." *El Heraldo*, 25 October 2018. https://www.elheraldo.hn/pais/1227767-466/honduras-a-un-paso-de-la-crisis-migratoria-de-2014.

Risk, Emergency and Disaster Working Group for Latin America and the Caribbean (REDLAC). Regional Protection Group). 2018a. *Protection in the North of Central America, Snapshot June–July 2018*. September 2018. http://www.nrc.org.co/wp-content/uploads/2018/11/Protection-Snapshot-ENG.pdf.

———. 2018b. *Protection in the North of Central America, Snapshot November 2018, Humanitarian access to needs in other situations of violence*. December. http://www.nrc.org.co/wp-content/uploads/2019/02/INFORME-REDLAC-NOVIEMBRE-2018-INGLES.pdf.

———. 2018c. *Protection in the North of Central America, Snapshot December 2018, The Humanitarian Response to the "Migrant Caravans."* December 2018. https://reliefweb

.int/report/mexico/redlac-violence-and-protection-north-central-america-snap shot-n3-december-2018.

———. 2019a. *Protection in the North of Central America, Snapshot April 2019, Access to Education in "Other Situations of Violence."* April 2019. https://reliefweb.int/report/ honduras/access-education-other-situations-violence-snapshot-n4-april-2019.

———. 2019b. *Protection in the North of Central America, Snapshot April 2019, Access to Adequate Housing.* September 2019. https://reliefweb.int/report/honduras/vio lence-and-protection-north-central-america-snapshot-5-impact-violence-right.

———. 2020a. *Los riesgos de las deportaciones y expulsiones a los países del Norte de Centroamérica en el marco de la pandemia de Covid-19.* May 2020. https://reliefweb.int/sites/re liefweb.int/files/resources/Los%20riesgos%20de%20las%20deportaciones%20 y%20expulsiones%20a%20los%20pa%C3%ADses%20del%20Norte%20de%20 Centroam%C3%A9rica%20en%20el%20marco%20de%20la%20pandemia%20 de%20Covid-19.pdf.

———. 2020b. *Riesgos de protección asociados a la violencia en el marco de la pandemia de Covid-19.* June 2020. https://www.humanitarianresponse.info/en/operations/ latin-america-and-caribbean/document/centroam%C3%A9rica-riesgos-de-pro tecci%C3%B3n-asociados-la.

Stinchcomb, Dennis, and Eric Hershberg. 2014. "*Unaccompanied Migrant Children from Central America: Context, Causes, and Responses.*" CLALS Working Paper Series, 7. http://dx.doi.org/10.2139/ssrn.2524001.

United Nations High Commissioner for Refugees (UNHCR). 2014. *Children on the Run.* https://www.unhcr.org/children-on-the-run.html.

———. 2015. *Women on the Run.* https://www.acnur.org/fileadmin/Documentos/Publi caciones/2015/10228.pdf.

———. 2016. *San José Action Statement.* 7 July. https://www.refworld.org/docid/57a8a 4854.html.

———. 2017a. *Marco Integral Regional para la Protección y Soluciones.* https://www.acnur .org/fileadmin/Documentos/BDL/2017/11335.pdf.

———. 2017b. "*Update on UNHCR's operations in the Americas.*" Standing Committee, 68th Meeting, 23 March. https://www.unhcr.org/58ca4ab87.pdf.

———. 2018a. *Comprehensive Response Case Study. The MIRPS: A regional integrative response to forced displacement.* http://www.globalcrrf.org/wp-content/uploads/2018/12/ UNHCR-CS-MIRPS-screen.pdf.

———. 2018b. *Marco Integral Regional Para la Protección y Soluciones–Informe Regional de Seguimiento 2017-2018.* https://www.acnur.org/publications/pub_mirps/5be 46de64/marco-integral-regional-para-la-proteccion-y-soluciones-informe-regio nal.html.

———. 2018c. *MIRPS, Pillar 4: Opportunities for Durable Solutions, Protection Transfer Agreement.* http://www.globalcrrf.org/wp-content/uploads/2018/10/6.-PTA-oct18 .pdf.

———. 2018d. *Respuesta "Caravanas' de Refugiados y Migrantes en Centro América.* http:// observatoriocolef.org/articulos/respuesta-regional-a-las-caravanas-de-refugiad os-y-migrantes-en-centroamerica/.

———. 2018e. *Two Year Progress Assessment of the CRRF Approach–September 2016–September 2018.* Evaluation Report, December. https://reliefweb.int/sites/reliefweb.int/ files/resources/5c63ff144.pdf.

——. 2019a. *Population Statistics–Asylum seekers.* http://popstats.unhcr.org/en/asylum_seekers.

——. 2019b. *Expanding Operations in Central America 2019.* https://reliefweb.int/sites/reliefweb.int/files/resources/2019%20Expanding%20Operations%20in%20Central%20America%20%28February%202019%29.pdf.

——. 2020. Global Trends, Forced Displacement in 2019. https://www.unhcr.org/5ee200e37.pdf.

Washington Office on Latin America (WOLA). 2018. *9 Questions (and Answers) About the Central American Migrant Caravan.* 22 October. https://www.wola.org/analysis/9-questions-answers-central-american-migrant-caravan/.

World Bank. 2019. *World Bank Country and Lending Groups.* https://datahelpdesk.worldbank.org/knowledgebase/articles/906519-world-bank-country-and-lending-groups.

13

Displacement in Colombia

IDPs, Refugees, and Human Rights in
the Legal Framework of the 2016 Peace Process

Wellington Pereira Carneiro

Introduction

In the masterpiece *Cien Años de Soledad* (*One Hundred Years of Solitude*), the Nobel laureate Colombian novelist Gabriel García Márquez (1967/2010) reproduces with the enchantment of magic realism some of the events of the tragic history of his country: the landmark Thousand Days' War,[1] the Banana Plantation workers' massacre,[2] and the armed conflicts between the conservative and liberal parties[3] that had shed blood and displaced thousands of Colombians for more than a century.

Colombia has been besotted by several waves of violence throughout its history, with the last civil conflict lasting for fifty years. Such long history of conflict has been commonly referenced during the peace process negotiations that took place between 2012 and 2016. However, a continuous wave of violence and displacement has been ongoing for about a hundred years.[4] Notwithstanding, after the adoption of the 1991 Constitution, Colombia started to develop a ground-breaking and sound body of law addressing the armed conflict–related internal displacement and later human rights violations (victimizing factors) with the support of the international community. That body of law constituted the foundation of the Victim's chapter of the 2016 Peace Agreement, covering Internally Displaced Persons (IDPs), refugees, and victims of serious human rights violations.

This chapter examines the main legal instruments, which tackle issues pertaining to the victims of the armed conflict; namely, Law 387/97, the Judgment T25/04 of the Constitutional Court of Colombia, Law 1448/2011 and its ethnic decrees as incorporated in chapter 5 of the Peace Agreements of 2016.[5] Hence, this chapter aims to briefly analyze the forced displaced protection development over twenty years and its impact on the peace agreement.

Background

The pattern of displacement and violence in Colombia[6] may be considered one of the most complex in history, as it has evolved from civil unrest with self-defense groups, to a Marxist guerrilla warfare, to an illicit drug dealing-related conflict (Centro Nacional de Memoria Histórica [CNMH; National Center for Historical Memory] 2013)[7] with an armed branch. Such complexity resulted in a highly politicized peace process underscored by historical grievances.[8] (Manetto 2019). Some historians (Zolberg 1983) place the creation of new States, others the anticolonial struggle (Ferro 2006) or the proxy conflicts of the Cold War[9] as the main sources of mass displacement in contemporary times. Nonetheless, the endemic violence and displacement in Colombia predates the Cold War, since it stems from the Thousand Days' War at the turn of the 20th Century, and, thus, precedes the context of the great political exterminations and mass displacements caused by the policies of containment of the (supposed or actual) advancement of communism and its Cold War proxy conflicts (Lewis Gaddis 2008). The last wave of systematic violence was unleashed when Colombia hosted the Pan-American Conference that formed the Organization of American States (OAS) in early 1948, while presidential elections were being held. A liberal populist politician, Jorge Eliezer Gaitan, the front runner, was assassinated in central Bogotá on the 9th of April. The date went down in history as the Bogotazo,[10] the day enraged liberals destroyed downtown Bogotá. Riots, murders, and arson committed against conservatives' and liberals' houses spread throughout Colombia (Bushnell, 2007). The government's response was one of the largest political exterminations in Latin American history. In the 1960s, the armed forces and paramilitary groups, attacked liberal activists in towns and villages who, in turn, responded with reprisals and counterattacks. Hundreds of self-defense groups and armed bands emerged throughout the country. In total, around two hundred thousand Colombians were killed in the ten years of bloody frenzy known as La Violencia (Bushnell 2007).

In 1958, impacted by the Cuban Revolution, the two main parties, Liberal and Conservative, agreed to a power-sharing arrangement aiming to deter the violence and pacify the country. But it was too late. By 1960, there were more than a hundred peasant self-defense armed groups active in Colombia, too suspicious of their leaders to disarm. In 1961, the Fuerzas Armadas Revolucionarias de Colombia (FARC; Revolutionary Armed Forces of Colombia) was founded in the southern part of the department of Tolima. Endemic violence entered a new cycle, now marked by the ideological dichotomy of the Cold War. The origin of the conflict, however, is completely autochthonous, a legitimate and unequivocal by-product of the internal contradictions of Colombian society. The moment, back in 1948, when the crisis unfolds is also quite graphic. It happened at the outset of the Pan-American Conference, which adopted the first regional Human Rights Declaration in the world, evidence that high-level diplomacy may fail to address the real dilemmas of the countries involved. Conversely, the metamorphosis of peasant self-defense groups and their conversion to Marxism, led by left-wing city intellectuals, demonstrates how the Cold War context transformed internal political phenomena and shaped them into typical local conflicts integrated within the global context. The FARC were not initially Marxist–they were peasant groups that embraced Marxism in the middle of the 1960s, inspired by urban middle-class militants who joined in (Silva Lujan 1989).

The end of the Cold War, thus, had its impact. In the mid-1980s, during the last decade of the Cold War, taking the El Salvador Agreements as an example, the Unidad Popular (UP), a leftist party, emerged in an attempt to disarm the FARC guerrillas and incorporate them into the democratic political process through a multilateral agreement pursued during the Belisario Betancourt government (González 2014). The FARC kept an armed branch throughout a gradual disarmament process in one of the most serious attempts to reach peace through political negotiations in recent Colombian history.

Another group, the notorious 19th of April Movement (M19) was responsible for one of the greatest tragedies of the troubled history of Colombia when it stormed the Supreme Court in 1984. M19 chose to lay down their arms completely and convert to a political organization. For both the UP and M19, it was also too late, or too early. The drug mafias were already entrenched in the State apparatus while the Colombian elites and private armies and paramilitary groups continued to pursue their alliances and existing political interests. Another frenzy of targeted assassinations was undertaken against M19 members, including its presidential candidate Carlos Pizarro. His murder during the 1990 presidential campaign, on board an Avianca (the State airline) flight, spelled the end of M19 as a leftist political party.

The UP, in turn, elected candidates to fourteen seats in parliament and more than three hundred city councilors countrywide. In just a few years, however, 3,500 of its members were murdered by paramilitary and military personnel and a thousand members survived direct attacks. Presidential candidate Bernardo Jaramillo was assassinated in March 1990 during the campaign that year. At the end of the 1980s the UP was eradicated, and its surviving members went into exile. The chance for peace at that moment in history had been destroyed by a corrupt, criminal State and an elite held hostage to the drug business. The same drug mafias that served to destroy opposition also turned against the State, demanding full freedom to conduct their business, since they were already wealthier and more powerful than the Army, the Office of the President, and Parliament. In the early 1990s, the drug cartels raged a direct war against the State, with terrorist attacks, bombs, and high-profile murders, including the presidential candidate, Luis Carlos Galan, in August 1989. The Medellín Cartel was disbanded with the death of its boss, Pablo Escobar, in December 1993, and the Cali Cartel sometime later with the arrest of its leaders in the late 1990s.

The Changing, Adapting Nature of the Conflict: The 1990s

The private armies of the disbanded drug cartels gave birth to the paramilitary groups that sprouted during the Colombian conflict from the mid-1990s onwards. The control of the production, distribution, and sale of coca paste and refined cocaine was contested by two main armed actors: the FARC guerrilla group and the Autodefensas Unidas de Colombia (AUC), a centralized collection of once-independent right-wing paramilitary groups which came to be organized under a unified command in 1995.

During the 1990s, internal displacement broke the veil of invisibility as it caught the attention of the international community. Simultaneously, another unrelated fact determined the fate of IDP protection in Colombia when, in 1992, Francis Deng was appointed Special Representative of the Secretary General of the United Nations for internal displacement. In 1998, the United Nations (UN) adopted the Guiding Principles on Internal Displacement, a landmark document that guided the whole framework on internal displacement (Deng and Cohen 1998).

The Law 387 of 1997

The trend toward displacement had already been observed in Colombia despite the attempt by authorities to deny it. Thousands of peasants and indigenous communities began moving to the cities, compelling the government to overhaul the denial policy and prompting Parliament to adopt the trailblazer Law 387 of 1997 on internal displacement.[11]

Law 387 was not only ground-breaking in regard to IDP protection in the world, it was also a landmark instrument that set the tone for others to follow in the domestic arena. It led to other IDP protection legal tools.[12] Law 387 contained the most important elements of IDP protection, which were later adopted in the Guiding Principles of the United Nations and in other IDP guidelines and methodologies used by the humanitarian community among whom IDP protection was still an emerging topic in the agenda of humanitarian actors worldwide.

Law 387 provided for prevention, response, assistance and socioeconomic stabilization with both an emergency and a development focus. The definition of displaced person was crafted within the Organization of African Unity (OAU) broad definition of refugee, replicated in the Americas by the 1984 Cartagena Declaration on Refugees (Cartagena Declaration) (see Fischel de Andrade in this volume). The wording of the IDP definition reflected the context of conflict: "generalized violence," "violations of International Humanitarian Law," "mass violation of human rights," "internal conflict" or "circumstances . . . that may have seriously altered public order."[13] The broad character of the definition allowed for the population to be identified as IDPs and, consequently, to receive assistance, since Article 1 contained seven broad definitions of situations that may cause forced displacement: (1) internal armed conflict, (2) disturbances, (3) internal tensions, (4) generalized violence, (5) mass violations of human rights, (6) breaches of International Humanitarian Law, and (7) other circumstances stemming from such situations that may drastically alter public order. Law 387 also established the institutional framework in which it operated and created a network of social solidarity to make the assistance mechanisms operational through decisions taken by national, provincial, and municipal councils in charge of managing the displacement policy. The importance of Law 387 rests on the fact that it established the doctrinal concepts on internal displacement; for instance, the right not to be forcibly displaced, which later came to encompass the concept of prevention, the protection against forced displacement, the right of a displaced person to seek asylum, the right to return, and the rights of restitution, through emergency assistance and socioeconomic stabilization. Therefore, Law 387contained several provisions that later became key rules for IDP management policies, not just in Colombia but in other countries, as reflected in international instruments.

The T25 Judgement

In the late 1990s, the conflict in Colombia was sinking into its worst years and Law 387 was very ambitious. With the formation and strengthening of the FARC and other guerrilla groups,[14] internal displacement figures skyrocketed between 1997 and 2002,[15] as the IDP statistics show:

Table 13.1 Displaced Population in Colombia

Year	Uprooted Population	Relocated Population	Persons Declared Internally Displaced
before 1985	19,294	5,487	2,746
1985	14,549	11,435	2
1986	16,195	13,164	2
1987	19,952	15,828	2
1988	34,233	26,453	8
1989	30,578	2,376	25
1990	39,173	3,211	281
1991	34,447	28,551	4
1992	45,565	37,886	25
1993	51,193	43,063	4
1994	5,569	92,964	361
1995	108,536	92,964	361
1996	141,222	113,719	3,467
1997	252,777	217,911	16,214
1998	245,904	221,750	61,514
1999	279,690	234,148	50,808
2000	605,110	582,813	331,076
2001	664,701	645,989	442,954
2002	769,777	742,918	528,274
2003	464,616	447,224	276,982
2004	424,474	417,183	258,033
2005	484,166	476,478	317,205
2006	463,526	470,752	382,245
2007	283,685	493,207	465,860
2008	426,848	452,520	523,076
2009	256,302	281,788	446,560
2010	199,641	218,161	391,742
2011	237,883	248,787	449,605
2012	239,550	222,242	534,515
2013	259,241	250,387	737,520
2014	250,387	251,188	780,399
2015	187,749	176,277	686,481

2016	103,500	93,273	141,347
2017	96,898	81,565	134,890
2018	129,496	107,537	157,353
2019	32,908	27,579	48,475
Cut-off date: 1 August 2019			

Source: Data from Victims Unit.[16] Created by Wellington Carneiro.

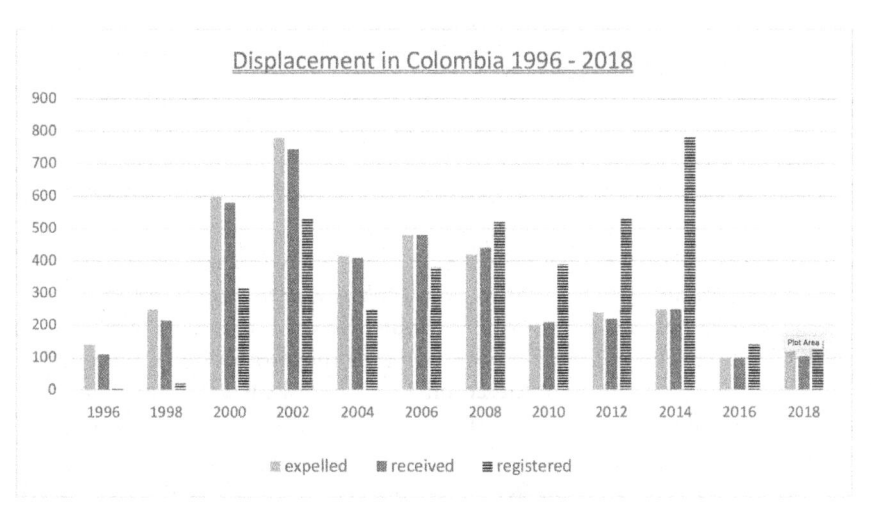

Figure 13.1. Displacement in Colombia 1996–2018
Source: Data from Victims Unit. Created by Wellington Carneiro.

In 1998, the number of displaced persons was 244,000, jumping to 607,000 only two years later. Nevertheless, the one-half million IDP population recorded in the year 2000 was overshadowed by the catastrophic, all-time-high figure of 767,000 people forcibly displaced in 2002.

Those numbers of IDPs capped a failed peace process conducted between 1998 and 2002, which projected a huge demilitarized zone the size of Switzerland (San Vicente del Caguán) (Sarmiento Santander 2011). The process presented the participants as two groups cynically negotiating for peace while simultaneously arming for war. This period was marked by a paramilitary offensives that resulted in the expansion of their territories all over Colombia, the tightening of their grip into the drug trafficking routes, invariably leaving a blood trail wherever they passed. The Army covertly cooperated with them as the paramilitaries penetrated regions to prepare for offensives. The Army remained at the margins as the AUC committed heinous massacres and terrorized the population with attacks that targeted certain civilian profiles (United Nations High Commissioner for Refugees [UNHCR] 2005)[17] and attacks in regions perceived as guerrilla sympathizers (ibid.).[18]

The Colombian Constitutional Court hit hard on the failure of the State institutions to tackle internal displacement caused by violence that spiraled out of control in Sentence T25 of 2004.[19] This judgement contains the famous statement describing the displacement of populations "an unconstitutional state of affairs." The judgement established follow-up mechanisms requiring the executive power to implement several measures to achieve the gradual elimination of each aspect of the aforementioned "unconstitutional state of affairs" (Duran García et al. 2007). The Court pronounced seventeen judgements concerning elements of IDP assistance and protection in similar cases,[20] refining the scope and extent of IDPs' rights under the Colombian legal system.

The Victims Law 1448 of 2011

The next ground-breaking step for Colombia was the adoption of a comprehensive law on the victims of the conflict. Law 1448 of 2011 (also known as the Victims Law)[21] amplified the scope of the protection of the civilian population in the context of the conflict and established the most complex victims' protection law in the world. The definition of victim in Article 3 is very broad, including spouses, family members, or those who intervened attempting to prevent damage or the attack itself. It extended unified victims' registration and improved the institutions to implement its own objectives on prevention, assistance, and protection of victims.

Law 1448 enshrined these humanitarian principles, giving them a legal formulation, and thereby made humanitarian assistance a legal obligation of the State. It defined 7 categories of victimizing factors, applying a broader human rights focus as its operational principle. Decree 4800, which regulates the law, mentions the following categories of victimizing factors related to the conflict situation: (1) homicide, forced disappearance, and abduction; (2) bodily harm with permanent impairment; (3) bodily harm with no permanent impairment; (4) torture and other inhuman or degrading treatment; (5) crimes against sexual liberty or integrity; (6) forced recruitment of minors; (7) forced displacement. All these factors entail a set of emergency or stabilization measures including reparations. The law established the principles of prevention, assistance, reparation, and guarantees of non-recurrence regarding the victimizing factors, in a situation of armed confrontation, reflecting the idiosyncrasy of the Colombian legal system: aiming high despite limited capacity for implementation.

An institutional framework to tackle the different aspects of the conflict was established within this legal arrangement, as follows:[22]

1. The Unidad Nacional de Protección (protection unit) as a department of the ministry of interior, was tasked with protecting persons at risk, such as threatened leaders, journalists, and activists, among others. Colombia became a country where hundreds of people had the right to a bodyguard, cell phones, or armored cars provided by the State as protective measures.[23]
2. The Unidad de Restitución de Tierras (unit of land restitution) was tasked with following up to obtain the property restitution of displaced persons through judicial channels, including collective land and abandoned property due to displacement.[24]
3. The Unidad para la Atención y Reparación Integral a las Víctimas (UARIV; care and integral reparation for victim's unit), was tasked with oversight of the unified registry of victims, having operational capacity to provide emergency humanitarian assistance, process compensations, and follow up on procedures regarding victims' rights.[25]

The law also addressed the subjective part of victimization caused by the conflict and its subjective reparation. It created the Centro Nacional de Memória Histórica CNMH, (a national centre of historic memory) as an institution in charge of recollecting and recovering the memory of the victims, with the aim of restoring their dignity and disseminating actual information about their experiences to counter the narratives of the actors in the conflict. The CNMH organizes commemorations, public debates, and undertakes research regarding the historical truth about several aspects of the armed struggle, the regions where it took place, and the victim's experience in the armed conflict. CNMH publications became the most authoritative sources of historical truth in Colombia.

For example, the port city of Buenaventura on the Pacific has registered, according to the CNMH report (CNMH 2015), published in 2015: 4,799 homicides between 1990 and 2012, 475 forced disappearances (1990–2013), 26 massacres between 1995 and 2013, 20 of which took place between 2000 and 2003 only, and the striking statistic that 153,000 persons were forcibly displaced in a population of around 370,000, meaning that one in every three inhabitants of the city was a victim of the conflict.

All over Colombia, the Victims Law included several other categories of victimizing factors, however, up to 90 percent of victims were included in the Unified Victims' Registry due to forced displacement, which continued to be the most striking humanitarian consequence of the conflict and the most frequent human rights violation in that context.[26]

Law 1448 brought about further effectiveness and leadership to the Defensoria del Pueblo (ombudsman's office),[27] a government body created by the 1991 Constitution, as a general human rights monitoring institution. The Defensoria del Pueblo managed to issue early warnings on situations of risk of displacement and accelerated the provision of UARIV's humanitarian aid, while also monitoring compliance with the law, for instance, in the protection and assistance to ethnic communities, women and children.

Some key elements of the Victims Law architecture are the Territorial Committees of Transitional Justice. These committees could be applied at the municipal, district, and provincial levels with the mandate to operationalize the IDP protection system within their jurisdiction. Depending on the gravity of the situation, the committees could be applied at a higher territorial level, gathering state entities to offer protection and assistance to the victims. For example, the local public works department would offer to rebuild or repair houses damaged by a mortar attack, the UARIV would provide food assistance, the social assistance department would provide psycho-social support, and so on, operating similarly to a crisis committee with a mandate to immediately address the humanitarian needs of those affected by the conflict, including situations involving recruitment of minors, threats of violence, and other protection needs.[28] One of the most audacious provisions of Law 1448, however, were the land restitution articles contained in chapter III.

The considerable land concentration and conflict regarding land distribution since colonial times are at the root of the Colombian conflict. Land grabbing has been a constant issue in several cycles of violence endured by the country in the past hundred years. The law created a registry of divested land in conflict areas to enable restitution of property and possession to remove from the equation the possibility of resorting to violence by paramilitary and guerrilla groups. Further, in 2015 a court in the southwestern Colombian city of Popayan issued the first judgement on collective land restitution to an afro-descendent community. The beneficiary was the community council of "Renacer Negro." The judgement determined the collective restitution of territorial rights to an ethnic community and included several measures to ensure their full enjoyment of territory, its wealth, and usufruct. The judgement also determined the state institutions to ensure the right of non-recurrence of the dispossession.[29]

The astonishing determination of a guarantee of non-recurrence is borderline utopian in the context of a country sunk into a pattern of uninterrupted violence for more than fifty years. Nonetheless, the audacious avant-garde spirit of the Colombian legislation attained its rewards when a feasible ideal was managed, in a historic reversal. A peace deal was reached in 2016 after more than fifty years of endemic violence.

The Ethnic Decrees 4633, 4634, and 4635

Law 1448 established the criteria, mechanisms, and assistance measures to address the armed conflict's victims in a general and universal way. Article

205, however, establishes that the attention, assistance, and reparation to indigenous and Afro-Colombian communities should be specifically established and should include previous consultation as well as factor in their customs, traditions, and collective rights. These measures have as their focus adapting and recognizing the specific impact that the violations of human rights have in these communities, attempting to redress the long process of exclusion and otherness faced by these communities since colonial times (Todorov, 2010). These obligations are aimed as the protection of individuals and the community, their ethnic diversity, language, and culture, in addition to the fulfillment of obligations regarding indigenous rights (UN Commission on Human Rights 2004)[30] including the 1989 Indigenous Convention (ILO Convention number 169) concerning previous consultation on all aspects affecting the communities (SR on indigenous people 2005). The same approach was taken in relation to Afro-Colombian communities for a particular reason. Colombia has a large territory divided into three Andean mountain chains, with striking heights cut through by two long valleys, the Cauca and the Magdalena. In colonial times enslaved Africans escaped from the fertile valleys where sugar, coffee, and other plantations that were at the core of the economy to climb the western mountains and establish free settlements in the remote and scarcely-populated Pacific Coast. There they reproduced the ways of life, customs, and community structures they had back in Africa (Morel 2006), except their language, Spanish, was adopted as the communities were made up of different tribal groups. The UN Committee on the Elimination of Racial Discrimination established that afro-descendant communities are entitled to preserve their traditions and ways of life as much as indigenous communities, particularly those who developed in isolation (Committee on the Elimination of Racial Discrimination 2011: General Recommendation 34).

As a result of such distinctive features of its territory, three decrees were adopted by the Colombian State: 4633/11 on a differentiated approach for the indigenous communities, 4634/11 on the Rom or Gypsy, and finally, 4635/11 regarding afro-descendant victims.[31] The decrees outlined assistance and protection, individually and collectively, for ethnic communities with a differentiated focus, a duty to consult, and linguistic rights protection. These principles were meant to ensure cultural and physical survival of the ethnically-distinct peoples ensuring security, autonomy, and freedom, adjusting to international standards on reparation, respecting their world vision, customs, and ancestral practices (Decree 4634/11 xxx: art. 93), and seeking the elimination of vulnerabilities. Due to their ethnic character, the communities were given special protection encompassing three different kinds of humanitarian assistance: (1) immediate humanitarian assistance for ethnic communities displaced in acute vulnerability, (2) emergency assistance due to registered victims in urgent need of subsistence, and lastly, (3) transition humanitarian assistance to stabilize communities' minimum subsistence when the urgency of assistance has ceased. Dietary restrictions and culture were addressed in the ethnic decrees combined with actions to attain physical and nutrition security. The effective implementation of the provisions contained in the decrees in a country of enormous ethnic, climate, and regional diversity pose obvious challenges.

These advances contained in the decrees, in terms of rights and guarantees, encouraged ethnic communities to lobby in La Habana for their inclusion in the Peace Process[32], in the chapter on the victims. Therefore, the ethnic communities and their needs, perhaps for the first time, were included in a Peace Agreement.

The Peace Agreements 2016

In August 2012 the FARC guerrillas and the government announced that after long confidential consultations they had decided to launch a public peace process. The long process of negotiations was concluded in 2016. The first draft of the Peace Agreement[33] was put to a popular vote through a referendum and was narrowly rejected. Consequently, for several months, contributions were received from civil society and many other stakeholders and were consolidated in a new agreement, signed on 24 November 2016 and endorsed by the Constitutional Court.

Not by chance, the first chapter of the peace agreement contains rural reform in an attempt to eradicate one of the most important underlying causes of all cycles of civil unrest in Colombian history. The first chapter aims to attain a fairer land distribution without recourse to expropriations or any radical solution. A land fund was created with, for instance, property expropriated from drug mafias, paramilitary groups or other criminals, and lands with expropriated titles due to lack of compliance with the social and environmental constitutional requirements for their use. Moreover, it seeks to boost the land market, thus making it accessible to the population as a whole, taking into account that farming and livestock are still a major sector in Colombia's economy.

The second chapter of the Peace Agreement is about political participation. The FARC and the government recognized that for the consolidation of peace it was necessary to ensure access to political participation and security. In other words, this meant access to power structures without any monopoly of certain political and economic elites, which has been the pattern in Colombia's history. To that end, the peace agreement established a series of safeguards based on prevention, evaluation, and monitoring the security of the opposition. Basically, it recognizes the obligation of the State to ensure that opposition politicians are not targets of assassination or persecution. The safeguards also apply to social movements, community or grassroots leadership, ensuring citizen participation, the right to pacific protest, and monitoring of citizens' rights by public institutions.

The third chapter regulates the end of the conflict, cease-fire, demobilization, disarmament and former combatants' reintegration and security. It also regulates the armed forces' role post conflict (Pulido, Castillo, and Gómez 2016c: 99). Chapter 4 contains the agreements on the solution to the illicit drugs issue. Taking into consideration that even after a decade under the Colombia Plan, which consumed hundreds of millions of dollars on the eradication of illicit drugs, the cultivated area dedicated to coca plantations was the biggest in history.[34] Therefore, the approach adopted in the Peace Agreement was of an economic and social nature by proposing the replacement of illicit crops (United Nations Office on Drugs and Crime [UNODC, 2018) with legal crops with market value, to avoid repression and criminalization of rural poverty.

The sixth chapter sets out the implementation, vetting, and endorsement of the Peace Agreement. This chapter was crucial to disarmament, demobilization, and re-integration of thousands of former combatants addressing considerable logistic, political, and military challenges. Therefore, all details regarding the collection and disarmament of different types of weapons, both light and heavy, the location of mines, and the security of former combatants, were critical and all approaches had to be planned in detail and executed scrupulously. The UN created a peace-vetting mission to supervise disarmament, which oversaw, among other actions, the establishment of demobilization zones, gathering of combatants, disposal and destruction of weaponry, the movement of former combatants to their final destination and their security.

The Victims' Chapter of the Peace Agreement 2016

The innovative fifth chapter contains the Integral System of Truth and Justice, Reparation and Non-recurrence, including the Special Jurisdiction for Peace and Commitments to Human Rights. Ranging from pages 124 to 193 of the agreement, this chapter states that the reparation of victims is central to the peace process.[35] It contains two subchapters on the victims' human rights and ascertainment of truth, practically reproducing the principles of reparations enshrined in Law 1448 and other victims'-related legislation. The reparation systems, which had been in place for five years before the agreement, reaffirms the principles that constitute the axis of the chapter, focusing on victims' rights, victims' recognition, recognition of accountability, victims' participation, truth-seeking, reparation, assurances of security and protection, assurances of non-recurrence, reconciliation, thus, reflecting the victims' deep influence on the peace process.

Otherwise, the institutionalization of the system of truth, justice, reparation, reconciliation, and non-recurrence (Pulido, Castillo, and Gómez

2016d: 29) is composed of the Truth, Coexistence and Non-Recurrence Commission, the National Search Commission for the Disappeared, and the Special Jurisdiction for Peace. It is noteworthy that the whole structure for prevention, assistance, reparation, and land restitution for victims (the majority of whom were forcibly displaced) was already created given that Law 1448 was fully incorporated into the peace agreement and thus became an integral part of the peace architecture. In fact, the Peace Agreement amplifies the scope of Law 1448 to incorporate also the victims of all violations of international humanitarian law according to Article 6.1.10 paragraph (h). The Peace Agreement safeguards the effects of Law 1448 against all effects of the amnesty given to perpetrators or if the state refrains from criminal prosecution as a result of cooperation with the Truth Commission and Reconciliation (Pulido, Castillo, and Gómez 2016a: 182). In any case the reparation and assurances of non-recurrence, as well as property and land restitution contained in Law 1448, continue to be binding on the State and the actors in the conflict.

By recognizing the victims, 90 percent of whom were victims of forced displacement, the Peace Agreement puts prevention and reparation at the forefront, in contrast to the common practice in most of the countries where the only hope of IDPs was to be able to return, without any compensation, any recognition as a victim, or any reparation or assurances that they would not be attacked again.

Refugees and Returnees

The Colombian conflict generated more than four hundred thousand refugees scattered all over the Americas and beyond. Chapter five of the Peace Agreement ensures that all refugees are entitled to their rights as victims no matter whether they have been recognized as refugees in other countries or not. The only requirement is that refugees and returnees are to be included in the general registry and go through the procedures for reparation as any other victim previously recognized. Residence in Colombia is not a requirement for refugees to be to be considered for the reparations system and they may also return anytime and have their rights claims preserved since the system is not subject to any statute of limitations or deadline for victims to claim their rights.

The aim of the legal approach established by Law 1448 and endorsed by the peace process was that forced displacement, both internal and external, forcing people to become refugees, is considered a serious crime and must entail a whole system of prevention, assistance, reparation, and assurances of non-recurrence. No national system has ever attained that systematic approach to the phenomenon of forced displacement. Although Colombia is far from achieving full implementation of the Peace Agreement, it clearly indicates the way forward to the international community and to countries attempting to establish a comprehensive system of transitional justice to overcome the consequences of conflict-related forced displacement.

Developments since 2016

Shortly after the Peace Agreement was endorsed in November 2016, the assassinations of social leaders multiplied, while the figures for forced displacement in 2017 where the lowest in history[36] as an immediate effect of peace. The figures on attacks against civil population and also on forced displacement dropped continuously between 2012 and 2018 during the peace process negotiations as a consequence of partial cease fires and good will gestures (United Nations Office of Coordination of Humanitarian Affairs Colombia 2018).

In 2018, two years after the Peace Agreement, the figures on forced displacement of individuals reached their lowest number ever, with a total of 18,158 individuals, given that the Ejército de Liberación Nacional was engaged in a separate peace process and that neo-paramilitary groups, and small groups of FARC dissidents who refrained to join the peace agreement and did not demobilize were still active.[37] Considering the figures usually encountered in Colombia, such low levels of displacement were an undeniable achievement. Nevertheless, the figure then jumped to 33,403 in 112 massive displacements[38] across the country, mostly involving areas in the Pacific, Putumayo, Cauca, and areas bordering Venezuela, areas with traditional armed activity. Moreover, a worse situation was reported in 2018 as more than a million people were affected by mobility restrictions due to the resurgence of the conflict in many areas, which meant a rise in displacements of 708 percent in relation to 2017. In 2018 172 social leaders were assassinated. The International Committee of the Red Cross informed that every four days, a new case of forced disappearance was being recorded. Therefore, this regression in the peace process was observed due to political trends, in which the new leadership was not willing or was incapable of managing the peace.

In 2018 the peace negotiations with the Ejército de Liberación Nacional were suspended, generating new armed actions (Moloney 2018). At the same time, the Special Jurisdiction for Peace suffered restrictions imposed by the new government, and consequently, peace is fading at local level, something that is clearly reflected in the figures for displacement. The FARC, converted into a political party, made assurances that it would not take up arms again, however, albeit not yet alarming, the number of party members assassinated started to rise. Until 20 May 2019, 137 former FARC combatants had lost their lives mainly in targeted killings.[39]

Nevertheless, in August 2019, Ivan Marquez, who had been one of the chief negotiators in La Habana, accused the government of betraying the peace process and took up arms again, followed by well-known leaders Santrich and El Paisa and a group of former combatants.[40] However, 90 percent of all FARC former combatants chose not to rearm, which is a standard success rate in disarmament, demobilization, and reintegration processes.[41]

This serious setback, brought about by the assassination of social activists and community leaders and the authorities' lenience, shed considerable doubt on the future of the peace process in Colombia. Since the signing of the peace agreement in November 2016 until 15 July 2020, 971 social leaders were murdered[42] with impunity and some regions plunged into threatening situations with the reported presence of new paramilitary groups and dissident guerrillas. The protection mechanisms for the victims established in the peace process are showing worrisome gaps and shortcomings. The 2020 COVID-19 pandemic further complicated the situation as armed groups started to impose their own disciplinary measures and restrictions and took advantage of lockdown measures to assassinate social leaders. Since the beginning of the pandemic, nine leaders have been murdered in different locations.[43]

Conclusion

Some conflict specialists consider that the first five years[44] following the time peace is established are the most critical for the possibility that conflict will recur (Collier and Sambanis 2002)[45] with new outbreaks of violence (Paris 2004).

Many factors are related to this sad but realistic conclusion. Many actors are still hostages of the conflict mind-set, the reintegration in civil life is a considerable challenge for former combatants, the social fabric is still damaged, reconciliation measures take time to implement, resources are scarce, and so on (Walter 2010).[46]

Transitional Justice per se means a series of processes towards normalization from a past of mass abuses to the achievement of reconciliation (Pulido, Castillo and Gómez 2016b: 26.). The victims chapter is a seminal tool to prevent the resurgence of conflict and mass violations of human rights as it is considered a key factor in post-conflict societies as a deterrence mechanism (Sikking 2011). The lasting sentiment of relative deprivation, as many conflicts may be considered deprivation-based conflicts (Håvard and Håvard 2012) is not the only factor, as peacebuilding is a complex process, which also involves, to a great extent, decisive peace governance, which basically means political will.

In war-torn societies, democratization is a form of legitimizing the new order and ensuring that a society in peace with itself will prevail over the previous one. Nonetheless, elections alone cannot ensure this outcome. In Colombia, the 2018 elections were the apex of a series of polarized events in a society already divided. The conflict was isolated in marginal regions torn away from the urban, middle-income regions of Colombia. For this reason, the effects of the conflict were not felt the same way in urban centers, divorcing them from the actual countryside where 7.9 million people were victims of violence. The anti-peace discourse could well gain a foothold in the context of such partial alienation.

It is undeniable, however, that the anti-peace forces started to act well before the Peace Agreement. Many high-ranking officials, high-profile members of the business community, and political groups were deeply involved in the conflict and feared the Special Justice for Peace. If Colombia manages to break the cycle of impunity, it shall eventually clear the way for a sustainable peace avoiding a repetition of its war-torn history.

Thus, sustained peace does not only depend on an advanced set of norms regarding victims. Peace is always a political process, and the lack of political will of the incumbent government to implement the peace deal is proving to be the most serious threat of relapse into conflict. This is particularly the case when, after fifty years, the whole political spectrum is marred by a conflict-related narrative. During the electoral campaign, opposition to the peace process was a main discourse. There was a massive spread of fake news about privileges for former guerrillas, amnesty for heinous crimes, FARC's wealth, the domination of the country by guerrillas, and so on. It is striking to acknowledge that one of the best peace deals ever drafted was rejected in a referendum by popular vote in a campaign marred by clear false statements and the considerable use of hate speech. This sad tendency often leads to surprising results. Brexit and certain similar electoral processes around the world, for instance, are not entirely foreign to Colombia, where, tragically, hate speech and fake news costs many lives.[47]

Excluding the considerable surge of victims in the political arena, from a Colombian perspective, the peace agreement empowered the victims to an unprecedented scale. Three thousand victims participated in the peace process in regional and national roundtables, drafted 27,000 proposals and were present in direct conversations with negotiating parties. This may be the key component in the resurgence of the social fabric that sustained the peace process and that may reverse the political will in a polarized society and lead the country toward a sustainable peace, justice, and reconciliation.

Therefore, it is not all bad or fake news. The great majority of Colombians are convinced that there is no turning back. Nevertheless, peace as a political process needs the right timing and the right leadership, conditions that have not yet been found. The main achievement that the peace process in Colombia established, and a hallmark of its own success, was to ensure the participation of the victims in all phases of its implementation as they are the driving force that will ensure non-recurrence. Peace may take more time but will eventually come.

Wellington Pereira Carneiro obtained his PhD in International Relations from the University of Brasilia, his master's degree in International Human Rights Law from the University of Oxford, and LLM from the University Drujby Narodov in Moscow. He has lectured at the University Center of Brasilia (Uniceub) and Univap. He joined the United Nations in 2004 and served in Africa, Latin America, and Central Asia. He has authored several articles and the book, *Crimes against Humanity*, published in 2015. He was head of the UNHCR field office in Buenaventura on the Colombian Pacific Coast between 2015 and 2017 during the conclusion of the peace agreements.

Notes

* The statements, analysis or assessments expressed in the article are those exclusively of the author and do not reflect the institutions where he works or worked in the past.

1. The Thousand Days War was an armed conflict between conservatives and liberals between 1899 and 1902 that cost a hundred thousand lives, representing 3.5 percent of the population at the time.
2. The Banana Plantation massacre refers to the shooting by the Colombian Army of peaceful demonstrators during the strike of United Fruit Co. workers' in Aracataca (the city where García Márquez was born) in 1928.
3. Between 1812 and 1902 Colombia underwent nine civil wars of national significance, in addition to regional conflicts. With the exception of the Federalist and Centralist War (1812–15) all other conflicts involved conservatives and liberals.
4. In the twentieth century, apart from the Thousand Days' War from 1899 to 1902, the conflict called the La Violencia started in 1948 and lasted until 1961; the last conflict involving several armed actors started with the FARC in 1964 and lasted until 2016.
5. Colombia has adopted three ethnic decrees, 4633, 4634 and 4635, to complement the Victims Law and regulate the assistance, reparation and land restitution of territorial rights for victims of the conflict pertaining to the three main ethnic groups: indigenous peoples and communities, Roma/Gipsy, and Afro-Colombian communities.
6. Most of historical references were extracted from Bushnell (2007), CNMH (2013), and other material from the collection of the CNMH in Bogotá, as well as from González 2014. To assist the reader, short explanations of historical events are included in footnotes but these do not replace an attentive reading of the history of Colombia. The author worked with Colombian refugees (1999–2010) and IDPs in the Pacific coast (2015–16) during the negotiations leading to the peace agreement.
7. After fifty years of conflict the CNMH defines it as follows: : "Se trata de una guerra difícil de explicar no solo por su carácter prolongado y por los diversos motivos y razones que la asisten, sino por la participación cambiante de múltiples actores legales e ilegales, por su extensión geográfica y por las particulari-

dades que asume en cada región del campo y en las ciudades, así como por su imbricación con las otras violencias que azotan al país" (Unofficial translation from the author: It's a war difficult to explain, not just due to its lasting character and for the diverse reasons and motivations underlying it but also to the everchanging participation of different legal and illegal actors, for its geographic extension and the particularities that shaped the conflict in each region of the countryside and cities in which it took place, as well as for its interconnection with other types of violence that affect the country.)

8. The peace process in Colombia was highly politicized due to an unprecedented political confrontation around the peace. The first version of the peace process was narrowly rejected in a referendum. Since the signing in 2016 xxx it continues to be at the center of political debate in Colombia, with controversies around reparations, truth, reconciliation, political participation of former combatants, and the suspected involvement of high-ranking politicians in the planning or abetting of violence and serious crimes during the conflict. Chapter III attempts to enable the political participation thought nonviolent means in Colombia. Please consult http://www.altocomisionadoparalapaz.gov.co/Documents/biblioteca-proceso-paz-farc/tomo-3-proceso-paz-farc-participacion-politica.pdf, and the El Pais series of reports on the politics of peace and war in Colombia: https://elpais.com/tag/proceso_paz_colombia/a.

9. Colombia had nine civil conflicts in the nineteenth century and two long conflicts in the twentieth century leading up to 2016.

10. The Bogotazo was a popular revolt unleashed by the assassination of Jorge Eliecer Gaitan in Bogotá.

11. Law 387/97: https://www.unidadvictimas.gov.co/es/ley-387-de-1997/13661 access in 22.08.2019

12. Law 387 was followed by numerous laws and decrees on IDP protection, and was followed by Law 487/1998 that created the peace investment fund; Law 975/2005 created a legal framework for the reincorporation of deserting members, and authorized humanitarian agreements, Law 1474/2011, the Victims Law; Decree 4800 on the definition of victimizing factors; Decrees 4633, 4634, and 4635 regulate the humanitarian assistance for minority ethnic groups.

13. See Article 1 of Law 387/97: Artículo 1°.-Del desplazado. "Es desplazado toda persona que se ha visto forzada a migrar dentro del territorio nacional abandonando su localidad de residencia o actividades económicas habituales, porque su vida, su integridad física, su seguridad o libertad personales han sido vulneradas o se encuentran directamente amenazadas con ocasión de cualquiera de las siguientes situaciones: Conflicto armado interno; disturbios y tensiones interiores, violencia generalizada, violaciones masivas de los Derechos Humanos, infracciones al Derecho Internacional humanitario u otras circunstancias emanadas de las situaciones anteriores que puedan alterar drásticamente el orden público."

14. There were nine armed actors in Colombia by 1999.

15. http://cifras.unidadvictimas.gov.co/Home/Desplazamiento. The source of displacement figures used in this table are from the Unidad de Victimas, the official government body responsible for displacement statistics in Colombia. These data are in public domain.

16. See http://cifras.unidadvictimas.gov.co/Home/Desplazamiento.
17. Paragraph 110 mentions, "Union leaders have often been viewed as sympathizers of the political left and, therefore, it is not a coincidence that the paramilitary groups are believed to be responsible for 80 percent of murders of union leaders in which the perpetrator is known."
18. Paragraph 21 states, "The paramilitary groups attack what they call the 'social roots' of the guerrillas. Their methods of combat have completely disregarded the principle of distinction between combatants and civilians and they have targeted social and community leaders, local public employees, human rights defenders and trade unionists, among others. Attempts to terrorize the population through torture, selective homicide, and massacres have been their principal means of combat. Due to the heinous nature of these tactics, the paramilitaries have been one of the main causes of massive population displacement."
19. See http://www.corteconstitucional.gov.co/relatoria/2004/t-025-04.html.
20. Judgements T-227/97; SU-1150/00; T-1635/00; T-258/01; T-327/01; T-1343/01; T-098/02; T-215/02; T-268/03; T-339/03; T-419/03; T-602/03; T-645/03; T-669/03; T-721/03; T-790/03; T-795/05.
21. http://www.centrodememoriahistorica.gov.co/micrositios/caminosParaLaMemoria/descargables/ley1448.pdf.
22. Law 1448. *Título II. Del Sistema Nacional de Atención Integrada a la Población Desplazada por la Violencia.*
23. Created by Law-Decree 4065 of 31 October 2011.
24. Law 1448, Victims and Land Restitution Law, in title IV chapter II, returns property lost since 1 January 1991.
25. Created by Article 166 of Law 1448.
26. In the Victims Day of 2017 according to UARIV, Colombia had 8,074,272 victims, 7,134,646 of which are persons forcibly displaced, 983,036 are victims of homicide, 165,927 of forced disappearances, there are 10,237 cases of torture and 34,814 abductions among other events, https://m.portafolio.co/economia/gobierno/el-numero-de-victimas-del-conflicto-armado-en-colombia-504833, press release, access in 23.08.2019.
27. See http://www.defensoria.gov.co/.
28. In Popayan, Cauca region, in 2015, the governor conveyed a Comité Territoriales de Justicia Transicional (territorial committee of transitional justice) to discuss the threat of recruitment of indigenous youth by the FARC. The community was awarded a considerable amount of resources to organize traditional ceremonies and ludic activities to protect them. The result was that from 103 youth at risk only 3 joined the guerrilla. (Report from the author, who attended the meeting.)
29. Judgement 071, from the 1st Civil Court of Popayan, Cauca, specialized in land restitution, from 1/07/2015. (Sentencia 071 del juzgado primero civil del circuito especializado en restitución de tierras de Popayán, Cauca 1/07/2015, referente al Consejo Comunitario Renacer Negro, Timbiquí, Cauca). Available at URT website archives at https://www.restituciondetierras.gov.co/documents/10184/1262129/SENTENCIA+2014-00104_RENACER+NEGRO.pdf/f983b8ee-30ff-470d-ba7b-1d8db4053cee?version=1.0. The author was head of a UN office covering this area.

30. According to Special Rapporteur Rodolfo Stavanhagen, "The situation of indigenous communities in the context of the Colombian conflict was very serious and some faced threats of extinction."
31. http://www.centrodememoriahistorica.gov.co/descargas/registroEspecialArchivos/Decreto4633-2011-ley-de-victimas.pdf.
32. The differentiated (ethnic) and gender approach is found throughout the agreement on a myriad of issues such as rural development, education, water, sanitation, security, individual and collective protection, political participation, and eradication of illicit drugs.
33. See http://www.altocomisionadoparalapaz.gov.co/procesos-y-conversaciones/Documentos%20compartidos/24-11-2016NuevoAcuerdoFinal.pdf.
34. See Coca Crops in Colombia at all-time high, UNODC Report finds; https://www.unodc.org/unodc/en/frontpage/2018/September/coca-crops-in-colombia-at-all-time-high--unodc-report-finds.html access in 03/29/2019.
35. See http://www.altocomisionadoparalapaz.gov.co/Prensa/Paginas/2016/junio/Conoce-el-Acuerdo-sobre-las-Victimas-en-video-y-en-cartilla.aspx.
36. Table in page 8. Source UARIV http://cifras.unidadvictimas.gov.co/Home/Desplazamiento, this table considers when the registry started to capture an approximate number of IDPs by state institutions, since the late 1990s.
37. Since the peace process, the first front based in Guaviare refused to demobilize and were expelled, becoming the FARC-dissident 1st front. They had 150 guerrilla combatants. They were joined by other individual dissidents and ex-rival paramilitary group "*Los urabeños.*" With the shifting political direction and growing violence against demobilized militants, the dissident movement tends to grow according to Insight Crime, an organization that studied the dissident phenomenon. https://www.insightcrime.org/colombia-organized-crime-news/first-front-dissidence/.
38. Mass displacement in Colombian law is defined as fifty people or more in one single event.
39. According the Instituto de estudios para el desarollo y la paz-Indepaz, 138 former combatants, and 971 social leaders were murdered until 15 July 2020; http://www.indepaz.org.co/wp-content/uploads/2020/07/Informe-Especial-Asesinato-lideres-sociales-Nov2016-Jul2020-Indepaz.pdf.
40. See https://www.bbc.com/mundo/noticias-america-latina-49509911.
41. See https://peacekeeping.un.org/en/disarmament-demobilization-and-reintegration.
42. Ibid.
43. https://www.hrw.org/news/2020/04/13/armed-groups-colombia-threaten-civilians-over-covid-19-measures.
44. George Frederick Willcoxon, in the *Washington Post* on 29 March 2017, titled "Why do countries relapse into war? Here are three good predictors," referencing the five-year trend of relapse into conflict as researched by Paul Collins from studies on conflicts between 1960–1999 and reproduced further in UN reports and other research.
45. Their research showed that 44% of countries relapse into conflict within the five-year period after a peace deal.

46. Barbara F. Walter (2010) expanded Collins statistical research and concluded that 57 percent of countries leaving conflict from 1945 to 2009 relapsed into conflict.
47. According to INDEPAZ, since the year of the signing of the Peace Agreements in 2016, 556 social leaders had been assassinated in a new wave of targeted violence 116 in 2016, 191 in 2017, 252 in 2018. From 7 August 2018, in the first 100 days of the new presidency of Ivan Duque, 120 social leaders were assassinated, according to INDEPAZ. Through 15 July 2020, 971 leaders were killed. See http://www.indepaz.org.co/wp-content/uploads/2020/07/Informe-Especial-Asesinato-lideres-sociales-Nov2016-Jul2020-Indepaz.pdf.

References

Bushnell, David. 2007. *Colombia: Una Nación a pesar de Sí Misma, Nuestra Historia desde los tiempos precolombinos.* Bogotá: Editorial Planeta.
Cassese, Antônio. 1994. *International Law in a Divided World.* Oxford: Clarendon Press.
Centro Nacional de Memoria Histórica (CNMH; National Center for Historical Memory). 2013. ¡*Basta Ya! Memorias de Guerra y Dignidad.* http://www.centrodememoriahistorica.gov.co/descargas/informes2013/bastaYa/basta-ya-memorias-guerra-dignidad-new-9-agosto.pdf
———. 2015. *Buenaventura, Un Puerto sin Comunidad.* http://www.centrodememoriahistorica.gov.co/descargas/informes2015/buenaventuraPuebloSinComunidad/buenaventura-un-puerto-sin-comunidad.pdf.
Collier, Paul, and Nicholas Sambanis. 2002. "Understanding Civil War: A New Agenda." *The Journal of Conflict Resolution,* 46 (1): 3–12.
Committee on the Elimination of Racial Discrimination. 2011. General Recommendation 34.
Deng, Francis M., and Roberta Cohen. 1998. *Masses in Flight.* Washington, D.C.: Brooking Institution Press.
Aguirre Román, Javier, ed. 2007. *Desplazamiento Forzado en Colombia, derechos, acceso a la justicia y reparaciones.* Bogotá: ACNUR, CEDHUL, Generalitat Valenciana.
Ferro, Marc. 2006. *História das Colonizações: das conquistas* às *independências, séculos XIII a XX.* 2006. São Paulo: Cia das Letras.
García Márquez, Gabriel. 1967/2010. *Cien años de Soledad.* Madrid: Ed Alfaguara.
González, Fernán E. 2014. *Poder y Violencia en Colombia.* Bogotá: Ed Odecofi-Cinep.
Håvard, Hegre, and Mokleiv Nygård Håvard. 2012. *Governance and Conflict Relapse.* Oslo: Folk.
Manetto, Francisco. 2019. El Gobierno reaviva la división sobre la paz en Colombia. *El País.* https://elpais.com/internacional/2019/03/23/colombia/1553380159_664970.html.
Moloney, Anastasia. 2018. Colombians flee homes amid fresh violence. *Reuters News Story.* https://www.reuters.com/article/us-colombia-conflict-lockdown/colombians-flee-homes-amid-fresh-violence-forced-lockdown-by-rebels-idUSKBN1HP33N.

Morel, Cynthia. 2006. Invisibility in the Americas: minorities, peoples and the Inter-American Convention against All Forms of Discrimination and Intolerance. *CEJIL Journal*, 1 (2): 124–135.

Paris, Roland. 2004. *At War's End, Building Peace After Civil Conflict*. Cambridge University Press.

Pulido, Carlos B., Gerardo B. Castillo, and Andrés R. C. Gómez, eds. 2016a. Justicia Transicional: retos teóricos, vol. 1. Bogotá: Ed Universidad Externado de Colombia.

——, eds. 2016b. El caso de Colombia vol.2 Bogotá: Ed UEC.

——, eds. 2016c. *Justicia Transicional: El papel de las Fuerzas Armadas*. vol. 3. Bogotá: Ed UEC.

——, eds. 2016d. *Justicia Transicional, Verdad y Responsabilidad*. vol.4. Bogotá: Ed UEC.

Sarmiento Santander, Fernando. 2011. *Lecciones para la Paz Negociada*. Bogotá: CINEP/Trocaire.

Sikking, Kathryn. 2011. *The Justice Cascade*. New York: W.W. Norton Co.

Silva Lujan, Gabriel. 1989. "El Origen del frente Nacional y el Gobierno de la Junta Militar." In Nueva Historia de Colombia, edited by Alvaro Tirado Mejía, Jaime Jaramillo Uribe and Jorge Orlando Melo. vol. II: Historia Política 1946–1986. Bogotá: Planeta.

Todorov, Tzvetan. 2010. *A Conquista da América*. São Paulo: Martins Fontes.

United Nations High Commissioner for Refugees (UNHCR). 2005. *Report of the Special Rapporteur on the Situation of Human Rights and Fundamental Freedoms of Indigenous People: Mission to Colombia*, E/CN.4/2005/88/Add.2.

——. 2005. *International Protection Considerations regarding Colombian Asylum-Seekers and Refugees*. Geneva: United Nations High Commissioner for Refugees.

United Nations Office of Coordination of Humanitarian Affairs Colombia. 2018. *Boletín Humanitario*, 74, 12/2018.

United Nations Office on Drugs and Crime (UNODC). 2018. Sistema integrado de monitoreo de cultivos ilícitos (SMCI). 2018. *Informe de Territorios Afectados por Cultivos Ilícitos 2017*. Bogotá: SMCI-UNODC.

Walter, Barbara F. 2010. *Conflict Relapse and the Sustainability of Post-Conflict Peace*, World Bank background paper.

Willcoxon, George Frederick. 2017. "Why do countries relapse into war? Here are three good predictors." *Washington Post*, March 29, 2017. https://www.washingtonpost.com/news/monkey-cage/wp/2017/03/29/why-do-countries-relapse-into-war-here-are-three-good-predictors/.

Zolberg, Aristide R. 1983. "The Formation of New States as a Refugee-Generating Process." *The ANNALS of the American Academy of Political and Social Science*, 467(1), pp. 24–38.

14

How the Venezuelan Exodus Challenges a Regional Protection Response

"Creative" Solutions to an Unprecedented Phenomenon in Colombia and Brazil

João Carlos Jarochinski Silva, Alexandra Castro Franco, and Cyntia Sampaio

Introduction

This chapter will analyze the current migratory movement originating in Venezuela that has reached several countries of South America and represents the largest ever exodus in Latin America (United Nations High Commissioner for Refugees [UNHCR] 2019a).

According to the R4V Platform (Plataforma de Coordinación para Refugiados y Migrantes de Venezuela), as of July 2020 refugees and migrants from Venezuela topped 5.2 million, with around 1.8 million migrants in Colombia, followed by 830,000 in Peru, 371,000 in Chile, 360,000 in Ecuador, and 264,000 in Brazil (R4V 2020). A special focus will be given to the special measures adopted by Colombia and Brazil to this unprecedented movement.

Despite the significant difference in the number of arrivals to Colombia, both countries have some interesting similarities. They both share a dry border with Venezuela, are key players within the regional protection system inaugurated by the 1984 Cartagena Declaration on Refugees (Cartagena

Declaration), and have developed practices that are appreciated in the international approaches to migration and refugees (Cabrera Serrano, Cano Salazar, and Castro Franco 2019). Besides the legal and political emergency responses that Colombia and Brazil have been putting in place, both countries are challenged with the promotion of the local integration of Venezuelans on the move, whether they are refugees or migrants. Timely durable solutions need to be designed based on policies that create welcoming and responsible environments in which these vulnerable people are supported to become additional agents of social, cultural, and economic development in both countries.

The content of this chapter is based on the perspective of the authors, who are connected to the subject not only academically, but also in practice, since they have been directly dealing with the daily challenges of these flows of people in their professional and/or personal lives. Thus, the argumentative construction of the text is generated through participatory observation, with an interdisciplinary approach (International Relations, Law, Political Science, Social Science, Social Work) that strives to go beyond the strict academic view, to allow the insertion of personal impressions and experiences. With this approach, we aim to convey the difficulties and tensions of this situation, and introduce readers to a reality in which decisions are made to face the emerging challenges, not only in the migratory scenarios under discussion but also in the political contexts of these two countries.

The chapter starts by highlighting some relevant aspects of the relations between Venezuela and its neighboring countries by briefly introducing four key general topics: (1) historical and cultural nexuses, (2) Venezuela as a former destination country, (3) natural and artificial borders, and (4) the great vulnerability of Venezuelans who are fleeing. Subsequently, the chapter outlines key aspects of the current Venezuelan crisis, then focuses on the different national responses, starting with the special condition of Colombia as the main destination country for Venezuelan migrants and refugees, followed by a thorough description of the situation of Brazil.

Particular Features of the Migratory Relations between Venezuela and Its Neighboring Countries

The political, economic, and social crises in Venezuela have forced millions of citizens to flee to neighboring countries to escape from starvation, violence, systematic shortage of medical care, and, ultimately, from the absence of opportunities. With a hyperinflation of 10 million percent (IMF 2018), more than 14 percent of the local population has decided to leave, sometimes putting their lives at risk by taking dangerous paths, boarding small boats, or walking thousands of miles (UNHCR 2019a).

The situation in Venezuela is dramatic. According to the available information, the child death toll has risen by 30 percent and maternal death has risen by 65 percent, while 88 percent of the hospitals lack medicine and 79 percent face shortages of medical equipment (Organization of American States [OAS] 2019). According to Singer (2018), malnutrition has also been increasing, since more than half of the population has been shown to have lost more than twenty-four pounds. A woman in Cucuta (Colombia) declared, "This is the first time I come to this side of the border [to the Colombian side] to buy some food, as we don't find anything in Venezuela. All this time we have been eating mangos or rice and beans; sometimes we only eat rice with salt" (OAS 2019: 27).

The political situation is not any better. The government retains all the political power by jailing political opponents without fair trials, and serious accusations of tortures and other cruel treatment have been reported. More than 12,500 people have been arrested for protesting since 2014 (OAS 2018).

In such conditions, it is not inexplicable that people, sometimes in despair, have been leaving Venezuela in order to search for better life conditions for them and their families.

Even if many research studies have focused on the characteristics of the outmigration from Venezuela, only a few have considered the historical and background information that is fundamental in understanding the full dimension and implications of this phenomenon. Therefore, this chapter will briefly introduce four key general topics, as follows.

Historical and Cultural Nexuses

Certain South American countries share more than borders. They also share a common history, culture, and traditions. These nexuses are particularly strong between Colombia, Ecuador, and Venezuela, since the latter two were part of the first for ten years (the Great Colombia). The three countries were freed from the Spanish crown by the same person (Simon Bolivar) and still share part of the Andean and Caribbean traditions, languages, and cultures.

There is also the existence of indigenous communities in these bordering territories, such as the Wayuus, Bari, and Yukpas, who live in both Venezuela and Colombia, and the Pemones, Yanomamis, and Piroas, who live in both Venezuela and Brazil. This shared background serves as a attraction for migrants, since Venezuelans find it easier to travel to places where they would be able to live according to their culture and traditions.

Venezuela as a Former Destination Country

Venezuela was, until not long ago, an important destination country for migration in the region. Thanks to its oil bonanza, it attracted millions of migrants coming not only from the neighboring countries but also from Europe and Central America. Venezuela was the third-most-important destination country for Colombians (IOM 2013) and also an important destination country for citizens from Ecuador and Peru, who are now returning home due to the harsh living conditions in the country. This appears to be an important fact reflected not only in the returning migratory flows, but also in the barriers that have been created through such processes (Paéz 2015).

Several migratory flows of Brazilians also settled in the mining regions in the south of Venezuela, usually a very sparsely populated region (Jarochinski Silva 2017). They created their own dynamics on the border between the two countries and are still relevant today. Venezuelans have been leaving their country in large numbers over recent years, and these localities near the Venezuelan border have also seen an increase in their population (UNHCR 2019a).

Natural and Artificial Borders

South American geography is known to be rough and diverse, full of mountains, rivers, forests, and deserts. When the international borders known today were established, many territories were delimited without considering such natural conditions (Alvarez de Flores 2004).The territory that separates Colombia and Venezuela includes rivers, deserts, forests, and mountains, and the border that separates Venezuela and Brazil includes a forest.

These geographical characteristics pose an additional challenge for the installation of border control checkpoints and police stations, especially since the presence of the local authorities in such remote places has been traditionally weak, which encourages the operation of trafficking smugglers and all sorts of delinquent actors, including guerillas and criminal gangs from the Colombian side (Centro Nacional de Memoria Histórica [CNMH] 2014). This reality facilitates the irregular migration of Venezuelans, but also makes migrants more vulnerable when they have to cross rivers, deserts, and forests, resulting in occasional encounters with criminal networks along their trajectory. (In sight Crime 2017).

Great Vulnerability of Venezuelans Who Are Fleeing

Venezuelans, as well as people from other nationalities, have been leaving the country since the beginning of Hugo Chavez's regime (Paéz 2015). At first, this migratory flow was characterized mostly by the presence of highly skilled business and industry people who were leaving as a consequence of the implementation of Chavist policies (LaboUR 2017). The recent flow of people coming from Venezuela appears to bring other kinds of people

(ACNUR 2018). Nowadays, the people who are leaving Venezuela are those suffering from malnutrition, from diseases that require proper care, pregnant women who cannot get prenatal care in their hometown, among other reasons (OAS 2019). This exodus has been called a migration of hopelessness (Paéz and Vivas Peñalver 2017). In addition, many are unable to pay the fee to get a passport in order to cross the border through a regular migratory checkpoint. The cost of a passport in Venezuela has made its acquisition highly prohibitive (El espectador 2018, El pitazo 2018). As a result, many people resort to crossing the border on foot, walking thousands of kilometers in order to reach the main cities of Colombia or Brazil while carrying their children and all their belongings (CODHES 2018). These are human beings in extremely vulnerable situations who are in dire need of humanitarian assistance (CIDH 2018).

The Venezuelan Crisis

Since 1920 oil has been the main Venezuelan product and the country's entire economy has been centered on its production (Maringoni 2009). The various power groups who have had control of the country since the beginning of the twentieth century have never been able to change the enormous economic dependence on this product, nor have they been able to develop and grow other types of manufacturing in the country. The Venezuelan economy had moments of strength when oil reached substantial price levels, such as in the 1970s (Maringoni 2009) and also during some periods of the Chavez government, when even with a drop in production, the high value of oil in the international market allowed the maintenance of welfare policies. Oil is so crucial to the country that in 2014 it accounted for 95 percent of its exports (Societe Generale 2019).

That same year, with a substantial drop in the price of oil, the economy of the country suffered greatly since there were no other products to sustain it. This aligned with the power vacuum caused by the Chavez's death and Maduro government historic difficulty to import products opened space for more vigorous manifestations from the political opposition (Jarochinski Silva 2017).

With the economic crisis of 2014, implementation of Chavez's previous welfare policies collapsed and inflation began to rise uncontrollably. The disruption of the Socialist-Bolivarian model (Vaz 2017), when unsuccessful attempts were made to artificially control inflation, then accelerated.

With the economic crisis and the subsequent reduction in welfare benefits, a political crisis arose characterized by the graduate emergence of government instability. During this period, marked by widespread food shortages and chaos in the country, the *Maduro Diet* (Krygier 2018) was installed, with serious struggles in the employment, health-care, and education sectors, as well as an upsurge in violence. This scenario led to a series of migratory movements of Venezuelans (3.7 million) to various parts of the globe, predominantly to other countries in South America (IOM 2019), which continues with intensity to this day.

The Regional Responses of South American States

The impact of this massive exodus has been stronger on neighboring countries such as Brazil and Colombia, but also Ecuador and Peru, who have publicly declared their unpreparedness to face this phenomenon (Briceno 2018).

As a matter of fact, the recent arrival of migrants has had an impact especially on the informal sectors of these countries' economies, since many migrants try to earn their living by selling goods and food on the streets, washing cars (this is especially true in countries such as Ecuador and Panama), or working as delivery persons (Organización Internacional para las Migraciones [OIM], Organización Internacional del Trabajo [OIT], and Universidad Antonio Ruiz de Montoya [UARM] 2019). This has created and encouraged a hostile environment for migrants, since many local citizens were already working in such informal economic activities (ibid.).

As a result, some countries, such as Colombia and Peru, have established special systems and regulations to cope with the arrival of Venezuelans (special residence permits), while others, such as Brazil and Ecuador, have used their existing norms and adapted them in order to address this specific situation (Gandini, Lozano, and Prieto 2019).

Some researchers, including Acosta, Blouin, and Freier (2019), describe the regional response to the Venezuelan migratory influx by classifying these countries' practices according to six different criteria: (1) countries that have used their own norms to respond to the situation of Venezuelan displacement; (2) those that have created a specific regimen; (3) those that have not made any decision; (4) those that have granted refugee status to migrants according to the Cartagena definition; (5) those that have used special or existing measures to document migrants; and (6) those that have criminalized the Venezuelan migration through expulsions or detentions.

Some states fall into more than one of these groups and the most common trend has been the promotion of actions that seek to regulate Venezuelans who have already entered the national territories in an *ad hoc* and temporary manner. All these countries, with the exception of Colombia and Brazil, are developing controversial mechanisms to prevent or hinder the entry of new migrants.

Chile, Ecuador, Panama, and Peru have established a visa requirement for Venezuelan citizens, creating a bottleneck in Colombia, or a barrier to transit from Colombia to neighboring states in the region (Prada 2019), since many migrants passed through the country on their way to other destinations in the continent and now find themselves stuck in Colombia (Cabrera Serrano, Cano Salazar, and Castro 2019).

While such responses hope to relieve the pressure on the national migration management systems, they prevent a unified regional response from being constructed or enforced. The severe and widespread violation of human rights, which is embedded in the Cartagena Declaration as a principled basis for the recognition of refugees, has been applied in a very timid manner, by a couple of countries in very specific cases and in scattershot fashion, even after the following appeal made by the Working Group to Address the Regional Crisis Caused by Venezuela's Migrant and Refugee Flows of the Organization of American States: "Considering that the Cartagena Declaration establishes that a refugee is a person who flees from his country because his life, security or freedom have been threatened by widespread violence, foreign aggression, internal conflicts, massive violation of Human Rights or other circumstances that have disturbed public order, the Working Group proposes that the above-mentioned Declaration be implemented so that Venezuelans are granted refugee status throughout the region" (OAS 2019).

To a greater or lesser extent, the countries of South America justify their failure to offer effective government responses to this flow—based strictly on their domestic legislations or international documents—claiming that it is a massive and uncontrollable flow, which makes some scholars wonder if the Cartagena Declaration consists only of a "decorative paper without a practical sense" (Acosta, Blouin, and Freier 2019). Nevertheless, we must remember that the Inter-American Court of Human Rights (IACtHR) has outlined the importance of this Cartagena Declaration as a consistent regional practice (IACtHR Consultative Opinion 23) (see Botero in this volume; and Casagrande in this volume).

Faced with this position adopted by some countries of the region, it is essential to question the function of such existing norms: when a situation requires the application of these measures, countries seek to establish practices that, although valid in some cases, attempt to create nonbinding mechanisms, especially regarding rules that may be more favorable and protective to migrants. Therefore, despite the advances in South America, in some countries more than others, the applicability of overarching protection and agreed-upon standards promoted through international instruments on migration and refugees still face a number of challenges for full implementation.

Regional organizations—to which multiple South American countries belong, such as Mercado Común del Sur (MERCOSUR; Southern Common Market), CAN (Andean Community of Nations), Unión de Naciones Suramericanas (UNASUR; Union of South American Nations) and the OAS–praise the common respect for some principles, including the protection of human rights and, in some cases, the free movement of citizens and residents of member states (Castro and Milkes Irit 2018). The Venezuelan migratory crisis, however, has revealed existing weaknesses in these regional organizations, which have failed to provide a common response to this mass movement of people (see Brumat in this volume).

The governments of Argentina, Brazil, Chile, Colombia, Costa Rica, Ecuador, Mexico, Panama, Paraguay, Peru, and Uruguay have held several technical meetings aiming to find a joint solution to the migratory crisis (known as the Quito Process).[1] In spite of this, such meetings do not consider the existing regional mechanisms and its conclusions are limited to political statements. A Regional Refugee and Migrant Response Plan was launched by the UNHCR and IOM in December 2018 in order to fund the host countries and communities. The interventions targeted 2.7 million people in sixteen countries: 2.2 million Venezuelans, and 500,000 non-Venezuelans in host communities. As reported by the UNHCR, however, the Regional Refugee and Migrant Response Plan is only 21 percent funded (UNHCR 2019b).[2]

Despite these precarious regional responses, there has been praise for Colombia's and Brazil's response as providing examples of best practices, which is why we will focus on the measures adopted by these two countries.

The Special Measures Taken by Colombia to Cope with the Arrival of More Than 1 Million Venezuelans

Colombia had never been a major destination country for international migration. On the contrary, it has historically been an origin country, with a diaspora of more than 4 million people (Castro 2016). As previously stated, Venezuela used to be the second-most-important destination country for Colombians. The welfare and prosperity of the neighbor contrasted with the poverty, the lack of opportunities, and the violence seen on the Colombian side of the border. Only recently has this trend begun to reverse and the number of Venezuelans entering Colombia has grown to reach more than 1.7 million in December 2020.[3]

The general inexperience of Colombian society dealing with massive migratory flows as a destination country has forced local authorities to adopt extraordinary measures in order to address the current situation. Many of the responses involve the regularization of migrants, their access to medical services and schools, as well as the granting of Colombian citizenship to the children of Venezuelans born in the territory.

Even if the number of Venezuelans arriving in Colombia is very large and the impact of the flow is heavy, local authorities continue to praise the positive impact of migration as a driver of development, and the promote the need to fight discrimination and xenophobia directed at migrants (Cancillería 2019). This position clearly differs from that adopted by the other neighboring states. Having said this, there are still a number of issues that need to be faced in order to fulfill the challenges of this migration crisis.

Colombian migratory regulation lacks established, permanent procedures, and establishes a visa system that can be expensive for Venezuelan migrants. It costs around 5,250,000 bolivares (US$2,625), while the Venezuelan minimum wage per hour is 40,000 bolivares (US$2).[4] This is why *ad hoc* procedures for regulating incoming migrants were created in order to cope with the massive arrival of Venezuelans.

Even if Venezuelans do not need a tourist visa to enter the country, the tourist status does not allow them to work legally in the country and authorizes only a ninety-day stay.[5] As a result, many of them have entered the country through regular channels but then remain without any type of legal status.

Also, the border between the two countries extends more than 1,373 miles, which makes implementation of any border control difficult. In some cases, Colombian authorities have made public declarations about closing the border between the two countries, which is unrealistic since there are many ways to cross from one country to the other informally. As a matter of fact, many so-called pendular migrants come and go easily through this international border on a daily basis in order to get their supplies, go to the doctor, or to school (Reina, 2018).

Aware of this reality, border control authorities have adopted several measures in order to cope with the arrival of Venezuelans. The first exceptional measure adopted to address the arrival of Venezuelans was the creation of a special permit in order to allow them to remain in the country without having to apply for a visa. This was named the Permiso Especial de Permanencia (PEP; special permit of permanence). This permit allows migrants to work and live in the country for no more than two years, while having access to medical care and to the public education system. To access this permit applicants must have a passport (which, as noted above, is not usually the case for most of the people leaving Venezuela), must not have a criminal record, and must have entered Colombia through an official checkpoint.

Until now, enrollment in PEP has been made available seven times, with a very limited window of time when Venezuelans were able to apply. The first one was set for those who were in Colombia by July 2017 (Unidad Administrativa Especial Migración Colombia 2017: Res. 5.797 of 2017)[6]; the second for those who were present in the country in February 2018 (Unidad Administrativa Especial Migración Colombia 2018: Res. 0740); the third for those who registered between April and June 2018[7] (Ministry of Foreign

Affairs 2018: Decree 542); the fourth PEP was offered for those who were in Colombia on 17 December 2018 (Migración Colombia 2018: Res. 1.0677). A fifth was created for Asylum seekers (Migración Colombia: 2019. Res.3548), while the sixth was for those who entered the country between 21st december 2019 and the 6th June 2020 (Migración Colombia 2020: Res.0740). The most recent one is for those who arrived between October 15th 2020 and February 2021 (Migración Colombia 2020: Res 240).

In 2020 a new PEP was offered called PEPFF which aimed to encourage labor recruitment in the formal sector (Migración Colombia 2020: Res 117).

Another special permit was issued addressing pendular migration. The Tarjeta de Mobilidad Fronteriza (border mobility card) allows Venezuelans to enter the country and circulate through the border towns, attend school, or get medical care (DNP 2018). This permit does not allow its holders to work, however. The permit was first issued in July 2017, was then temporarily suspended, and finally readopted through Policy Document 3.950 in 2018 (through the Departamento Nacional de Planeación).[8] Data from July 2020 (R4V 2020) show that approximately 763,000 Venezuelans have a residence or regular stay permit in Colombia.

These two kinds of permit present several challenges. First, as previously suggested, few migrants can access the PEP, which forces most Venezuelans living in Colombia to remain as undocumented migrants, to work in informal activities and sometimes even to engage in criminal activities (OAS 2019). Some of them are victims of labor and sexual exploitation (CIDH 2018). Second, the informality rate of the labor market in Colombia is very high[9] and, as a result, many migrants, even those who carry a PEP, end up working in the informal sector (OIM, OIT, and UARM 2019). Third, these measures focus only on migratory status, and allow them to stay in the country and to work without considering the situation of persons with special needs who cannot work and, ultimately, who need special care, including the case of unaccompanied children (Castro 2019; Van Praag 2019). For those persons, assistance has initially been offered by nongovernmental organizations (NGOs) and, as donations and new funds have been granted, local authorities have also started to provide such assistance.

Concerning access to nationality, neither the PEP nor the refugee status determination process allows children of migrants born in Colombia access to citizenship. Colombian citizenship is not granted merely by being born in the local territory. It also requires one of the parents to be Colombian or a foreigner holding a permanent residency status. As a result, there were many children being born in Colombia who did not have access either to Colombian or to Venezuelan citizenship, since Venezuelan consulates are not working properly in Colombia. Therefore, in 2019 there were more than 23,000 stateless children in Colombia, in violation of the international human rights standards (Castro 2019). To deal with this situation, Resolution

8.470 was adopted in order to grant Colombian nationality to children born in Colombia, from Venezuelan parents, beginning 19 August 2015. This resolution was valid for two years, and could have been suspended before if the situation of the neighboring country allowed the newborns access to Venezuelan citizenship. More recently, a law was adopted by Congress with the same purpose (Law 1.997 of 2019).

Another adjustment was recently added with regard to the refugee status determination process. As has previously been stated, the special measures taken by the Colombian state focused on granting Venezuelan migrants a regular status to remain in the territory. The measures do not provide special dispositions for those who were forced to leave the neighboring country and who need special assistance, such as asylum seekers and refugees, however.

In terms of refugee status determination, the number of refugees recognized under the scope of the Cartagena Declaration is insignificant in the region. Out of the 460,000 Venezuelans who have applied for asylum, only 21,000 had been granted this status worldwide by 2019 according to the OAS (2019). In this sense, Colombia has not been an exception: as of April 2019, 1,687 Venezuelans had applied for refugee status, but only three had been granted refugee permits (Mayorquin 2019).

Colombia has embraced the Cartagena Declaration and participated in all the follow-up summits, reinforcing its engagement with it. Decree 2.840 of 2013 incorporates the refugee definition included in the 1951 Convention Relating to the Status of Refugees (1951 Refugee Convention), and the commitments expressed in the Cartagena Declaration and in the 1984 Convention Against Torture and Other Cruel, Inhuman or Degrading Treatment or Punishment, into the Colombian asylum procedure. The local Comisión Nacional para los Refugiados [CONARE] (Commission for the Recognition of Refugee Status) has systematically denied the claims of Venezuelans who fail to prove individual persecution, under the scope of the 1951 Refugee Convention.[10]

This represents an important paradox since Colombia has openly considered the situation of Venezuela a humanitarian crisis (Welsh 2019) and has deployed many efforts to end the Nicolas Maduro regime (Sen 2019). Nevertheless, the national authorities deny that migrants coming from Venezuela meet the requirements of the Cartagena Declaration, even when it literally states that refugees are "persons who have fled their country because their lives, security or freedom have been threatened by generalized violence, foreign aggression, internal conflicts, massive violation of human rights or other circumstances which have seriously disturbed public order" (Cartagena Declaration: 3rd Conclusion 1984).

Another inconvenience regarding asylum procedures in Colombia is the fact that asylum seekers are granted a safe passage document that allows them to remain in the territory regularly while a decision is made concerning their refugee claim. It does not grant them permission to work nor allow their children born in the Colombian territory to acquire citizenship. Moreover, the refugee status determination procedure can take as long as three years. To overcome this situation, Resolution 3,548 was issued in order to grant asylum seekers a *Permiso Especial Complementario* (special complementary permit), allowing them to work while their eligibility process occurs.

Finally, the Colombian migratory regulation does not include subsidiary visas or other permits for those whose asylum claims have been rejected but nonetheless need international protection according to international human rights standards. As a result, those who are in the country but are not recognized as refugees, or who do not meet the requirements for a PEP, are forced to remain with an irregular status in the Colombian territory.

The Brazilian Response to an Unprecedented Cross-Border Movement

Usually seen as an important leader in the Americas, Brazil is facing a moment of political transition where the newly elected president, Jair Bolsonaro, might jeopardize the country's traditional welcoming legacy when it comes to migration- and refugee-related issues. The recent immigration of Venezuelans to the South American country increased dramatically in 2015 (Jarochinski Silva 2017). This was a result of frequent pendular movement already observed on the northern border for the acquisition of food, medicine, and temporary work. Because the situation of deprivation was aggravated due to a major inflationary process in the country of origin, the initial movement became permanent, resulting in thousands of Venezuelan nationals settling in the Brazilian cities of Pacaraima and Boa Vista, both located in the state of Roraima (ibid.).

The proximity of these bordering cities to Venezuela allows migrants to maintain links with their place of origin, especially by easily sending remittances in kind, and this resource proves to be a lifesaving necessity for those who remain on the other side of the border (ibid.). The fact that the northern state of Roraima is geographically isolated from the rest of Brazilian territory, with prohibitive transportation costs, also contributed to the permanence of migrants in the region at the beginning of the migratory movement (ibid.).

As a phenomenon resulting from economic and social crisis, the Venezuelan migration does not initially fit the traditional refugee definition, which refers to situations involving displacement of citizens from their countries influenced by wars and conflicts (see Brumat in this volume; Freier and Fernández in this volume). The traditional concept, based on the 1951 Refugee Convention and embedded in Brazilian law,[11] is that refugees are individuals who are forced to leave their countries of origin because they experienced situations of violence that threaten their well-being and violate human rights.

Emergency measures were adopted, but many were characterized by a discriminatory rhetoric from the government of the state of Roraima. Given this scenario, subnational authorities filed Original Civil Action 3121,[12] requesting the temporary closure of the border. This measure was seen as a way of drawing the federal government's attention to immigration issues, and also as an appeal to the prerogatives adopted by Brazil in international agreements (Mauat 2018). Besides this counterproductive and controversial administrative measure, additional obstacles were created with the intention of declaring migrants were not welcome. Passports were required for migrants to access public services, despite the fact that such requirement violates the Brazilian Constitution as well as a number of other federal laws (Jornal Nacional 2018).

These measures were justified by state authorities in order to publicly blame the migrants for the socioeconomic problems seen in the region, mainly relating to the public health system and the increase of criminality (Milesi, Coury, and Rovery 2018). This posture goes against the Brazilian tradition expressed in its laws and the international commitments adopted by the country. With such restrictive measures in effect, it became imperative for Venezuelans to search for regularization alternatives in order to be able to fit into the local dynamic and to be protected by the existing laws.

Given this situation and also due to the previous migration law in Brazil, which was very restrictive and based on security concerns,[13] the asylum regimen became an alternative strategy for temporary migratory regularization. To some extent, this option provided easy access and legal security to foreigners who enter Brazilian territory. Besides being less bureaucratic, this legal pathway also counts on the UNHCR to monitor and provide assistance to the displaced (Abrahão 2019).

It should be noted that migration experts advocated for the determination of refugee status to Venezuelans based on "grave and widespread human rights violation in his/her country of origin" as established in the Brazilian legislation inspired by the Cartagena Declaration, since the government of Brazil usually referred to the Maduro Regime as a dictatorship. Such recognition took time to be adopted by Comitê Nacional para os Refugiados ([CONARE], its acronym in Portuguese) and, when it occurred, it neither was from a prima facie perspective nor retroactive effects (Vidigal 2019). By mid-2020, 38,000 Venezuelans were recognized as refugees as a result of this change of position by the Brazilian government. This measure transformed Venezuelans into the national group representing the largest number of refugees in Brazil (Jarochinski Silva and Jubilut 2020).

From a different perspective, the new Brazilian immigration legislation has mechanisms capable of ensuring the humanitarian reception for this flow of migrants. As of this writing, however, there has been no regular application of this principle. That principle has represented an advance in other cases, such as for environmental migrations, but not in this case, where it represents a setback (Jarochinski Silva 2017; see also Freier and Luzes in this volume).

The new migration law (Law 13.445 of 2017)[14] embodies mechanisms to ensure a humanitarian reception to this migratory flow. Its application would have been extremely helpful, if the law had been already initiated. Nevertheless, this advanced hypothesis has not yet been applied to this flow of migrants.

Brazil then opted to adopt other measures and to offer temporary permanent residence permits. Such a measure can be seen as a way of reducing the number of asylum claims, since the country has long used its refugee protection system as a foreign policy asset. In this sense, having a large backlog of refugee claims could affect the credibility of the Brazilian asylum system. Based on this, Resolution 126 was issued in 2017 by the Conselho Nacional de Imigração [CNIg] (National Immigration Council), creating the possibility for Venezuelan nationals to apply for temporary residence, which was reaffirmed in the new law with the Interministerial Ordinance 9 of 2018.[15] These measures were designed for the specific situation of Venezuelans but ended up contemplating other citizens of countries bordering Brazil that were not contemplated by other visa policies (Abrahão 2019).

Resolution 126 does not address the lessons learned from previous national responses (Haitian and Syrian cases), and also lacks alignment with the advanced discussions held in international forums. The legal protection of these individuals could be ensured by the 1990 International Convention on the Protection of the Rights of All Migrant Workers and Members of Their Families, which was not ratified by Brazil (Jarochinski Silva 2017), as well as by the Global Compact for Safe, Orderly and Regular Migration, which Brazil abandoned.

The new migration law revoked the former foreign statute and facilitated the regularization of immigrants in the country, recognizing rights and providing more residence and protection opportunities. The law changed the treatment toward migrants in the country, expanding rights while reducing bureaucracy. It innovated by treating migration as a right, respecting the fundamental principles of human rights (Brasil 2018). Nevertheless, the application of the law was on a case-by-case basis, which is unsustainable especially at a time of great crisis aggravated by the COVID-19 pandemic.

Even with this important advance in terms of the recognition of Venezuelans as refugees, with the emergence of the coronavirus pandemic Brazil closed its borders especially to Venezuelans who, even with Brazilian documentation or children, wife, and/or other Brazilian relatives, do not have permission to enter the country under any circumstances. Venezuelan nationals deal with a more severe and restrictive legal approach than all the others and are prevented from accessing the Brazilian territory (Jarochinski Silva and Jubilut 2020).

At the federal level, Brazil was slow to adopt direct measures for the migration movement of Venezuelans. The first actions took place at the state level, aided by the international organizations of humanitarian aid and civil society organizations. Later, the federal government effectively positioned itself to address the migratory issue in Roraima and the rest of the country. For example, it launched Provisional Measure 820 of 15 February 2018, establishing the Federal Emergency Assistance Committee for the social emergency reception of Venezuelans.

This measure was implemented in response to the demands of subnational authorities that were looking for solutions or resources to contain situations aggravated by massive migration, including social vulnerability, xenophobia, and discrimination. Such problems caused violence and the marginalization of Venezuelan migrants (Jarochinski Silva and Sampaio 2018).

Goals were set for the creation of shelters and the transfer of immigrants to other states with higher potential of employment under the program for the reception and management of the Venezuelan migratory movement. The program was named Operation Acolhida and was led by the Brazilian armed forces, more specifically the army, which was in charge of coordinating the shelters and food distribution with the support of the UNHCR and IOM. The army also monitors the border, controls any illicit acts, and guides migrants in settlement and reception procedures. In this case, the army has been designated as the institution representing the state in the migratory issue and collaborates with other organizations, stakeholders, and authorities.

With the intensification of this migratory movement that generated a net migration of almost ten thousand people in 2016 (Jarochinski Silva 2017), and more than triple this number in 2017 (Brasil 2019), it is worth noting that the proportion of Venezuelans in relation to Brazilians is actually a small though visible group in this region, which has a low population density. The migration has also had a significant impact from a social, financial, and political perspective, having forced the state of Roraima to request aid from federal agencies and, in some periods, even forced it to declare a state of emergency to cope with the situation (Jarochinski Silva 2017).

The absence of a governing mechanism involving the various actors of the Brazilian state–the federal and subnational bodies in charge of migration management, plus those responsible for the provision of basic social services, such as health care, education, employment, and housing–has led to a slow and limited response. In addition, xenophobic narratives have, in a few isolated circumstances, led to physical violence at the border (Félix and Costa 2018).

It followed that a somewhat questionable general understanding was being consolidated over 2018, where the Brazilian state border and its municipalities would not be able to properly absorb the Venezuelan migration. Thus, the federal government started to promote the assisted displacement of Venezuelan migrants to other regions of the country, preceded by their temporary reception in emergency shelters at the border, known as the *interiorização* (interiorization) strategy, under the framework of Provisional Measure 820. This measure provides for "emergency assistance measures to accommodate people in situations of vulnerability due to migratory flows caused by a humanitarian crisis."

Launched in April 2018, the assisted displacement initially implemented by the Brazilian government actually achieved more impressive numbers one month before the elections (1,234 persons alone). This increase was directly associated with the violent episodes that occurred in the previous month motivated by the October elections for president, state governors, congressional representatives, and senators. In December 2019 more than 27,000 persons had been relocated to four hundred and fifty cities throughout the country since implementation of the strategy in April to 2018 (Alto Comissariado das Nações Unidas para Refugiados [ACNUR] 2020).

The narrative built around the *interiorização* strategy as the only possible solution led to the creation of additional modalities run by various actors. In total, five modalities have already been identified: (1) shelter to shelter, facilitated by the ministry of social development in partnership with the Brazilian Army, four United Nations agencies, and their implementing partners; (2) family reunification, run by the IOM and the Brazilian Army; (3) Social meeting, in which non-family members play a similar role to family members in the previous hypothesis (4) employment mobility, facilitated by the Brazilian Army; and (5) unspecified formats, promoted by a number of civil society organizations funded by different sources (Sampaio and Jarochinski Silva 2018).

Although each modality may have its own particular features, they do have a common element: they lack transparency and fail to provide proper information about what they entail, the requirements needed for enrollment, roles and responsibilities of each actor, and the models of assistance, if any, offered to Venezuelan migrants and refugees upon their arrival in the new cities of destination. Caution has to be used in order to avoid this special measure being used as the only solution possible. Its implementation might create misinformation and false expectations that might undermine the real possibilities of a smooth local integration process in the new Brazilian cities. In a context where the newly elected conservative president has made tough declarations against the Venezuelan migration to Brazil during his campaign, the *interiorização* strategy has to be faultless in order to survive.

Some of the lessons learned in the management of the Haitian migratory movement and in the implementation of the Brazilian Resettlement Program—both from the good results obtained as well as from the difficulties they faced—could be used and adapted in the *interiorização* strategy (Jarochinski Silva and Sampaio 2018). The experience and knowledge acquired by Brazilian society in recent years, concerning humanitarian reception and local integration of migrants and refugees, should lay the foundations for any current initiative in order to maximize positive outcomes and to ensure the protection of the most vulnerable persons to better address the complexity of the Venezuelan migration.

Furthermore, it should be emphasized that *interiorização* is but one of the measures necessary to respond to the unexpected, continuous, and growing flow of Venezuelan people to Brazil. Therefore, all the efforts undertaken to develop this strategy must be aligned with local and national initiatives that improve the good governance of this movement of persons and promote the best possible interaction between Venezuelans and Brazilian society.

Conclusion

To conclude, the practical, political, and temporal dimensions of the situation do not allow the responses to the Venezuelan displacement to be conceived under a single magical solution nor with answers that foresee normative creations that do not contemplate what already exists in legal terms. This is especially true if such strategies do not incorporate an understanding of the opportunities that this migratory movement can bring to the migrants and refugees, as well as to Colombia and Brazil and their populations. Public policies, infrastructure, and services can be strengthened and even created in the bordering cities—usually underdeveloped and forgotten by national authorities—in the wake of such migratory movements. In the case of Brazil, the presence of the army, with its competent logistics apparatus, still promotes a security framework that limits the actions of civil and local authorities that could be developing more-sustainable and longer-lasting solutions aimed at the integration of Venezuelans into the country.

The emergency and temporary responses given in both countries unfortunately do not necessarily comport with the purposes and commitments of a regional protection system, inspired by the 2004 Mexico Declaration and Plan of Action to Strengthen the International Protection of Refugees in Latin America (see Vera Espinoza this volume)—falling particularly short in the Cities of Solidarity component in the case of Colombia, and the Borders Solidarity component in the case of Brazil. In this regard, it is imperative to develop multiple and complementary responses that engage with the complexities and temporalities of this phenomenon, and that can be built in a strategic and respectful manner through the social participation of various actors and by putting the Venezuelan migrants and refugees at the center of this process.

João Carlos Jarochinski Silva is Professor at Universidade Federal de Roraima. He is a Post-doctoral Researcher at the Núcleo de Estudos de População "Elza Berquó" (NEPO)–Unicamp. He holds a PhD in Social Sciences from Pontifícia Universidade Católica de São Paulo and a Master's degree in International Law from Universidade Católica de Santos. He has been working with migration issues since his Master's degree and is actively involved in the assistance to and research on Venezuelans in Boa Vista (Roraima). His coedited book *Migrações Venezuelanas* (with Dr Rosana Baeninger) was published in 2018.

Alexandra Castro Franco is a Colombian lawyer with a PhD in International Law from the University Paris 2 Panthéon Assas and a Master's degree in Human Rights and Humanitarian Law from the same university. She works as Professor Researcher at the University Externado de Colombia where she is the Head of the Observatory on International Migrations.

Cyntia Sampaio is a social worker with a Master's degree in migration and intercultural relations from the University of Oldenburg, Germany. Starting her career with civil society organizations, she was mostly involved in protection, settlement, and integration of migrants and refugees. She also has experience in technically supporting the strengthening of migration governance, largely relying on social participatory processes both at the national and local level. Besides working for the leading UN agencies on migration-related issues, she also worked as a consultant for the United Nations Economic Commission for Latin America and the Caribbean, the Higher School of the Public Prosecution in Brazil, and as a member of the Working Group on Crisis of Venezuelan Migrants and Refugees of the OAS.

Notes

1. More information about the Quito Process at: https://www.comminit.com/la/content/proceso-de-quito.
2. unhcr.org/sites/default/files/2019%20RMRP%20Venezuela%20%28December%202018%29.pdf.
3. See https://r Full RMRP at: http://reporting 4v.info/en/situations/platform/location/7511.

4. The estimate of around US$293 for the whole procedure is based on the information provided by the local authority Migración Colombia (https://www.can cilleria.gov.co/tramites_servicios/visa/costos-medios-pago-oficinas-atencion).
5. According to Decree 1067 from 2015, available at: https://www.cancilleria.gov.co/sites/default/files/tramites_servicios/pasaportes/archivos/decreto_unico_re_.pdf.
6. All the norms concerning the Venezuelan migration are available at: https://www.migracioncolombia.gov.co/normativa/.
7. In this special opportunity only regularization was opened for those who registered themselves even if they did not have a passport.
8. Available at: https://www.cancilleria.gov.co/documento-conpes-estrategia-aten cion-migracion-venezuela.
9. Official statistics report more than 45.9 percent of informal labor in the main thirteen cities of the country. Information available in https://www.dane.gov.co/index.php/estadisticas-por-tema/mercado-laboral/empleo-informal-y-seguridad-social.
10. Such is the case of the ruling from the Constitutional Court T 250 from 2018, where the court disclaims the demand of a Venezuelan family because the family failed to prove a direct persecution.
11. Brazil Refugee Law (Law 9474 of 1997): http://www.planalto.gov.br/ccivil_03/leis/l9474.htm.
12. More information about the Original Civil Action at: https://portal.stf.jus.br/processos/detalhe.asp?incidente=5437155.
13. The new Migration Law (Law 13.445) was promulgated on 24 May 2017 and entered into force on 21 November 2017, 180 days after its publication.
14. Brazil Migration Law (Law 13,445 of 2017): https://www2.camara.leg.br/legin/fed/lei/2017/lei-13445-24-maio-2017-784925-publicacaooriginal-152812-pl.html.
15. Interministerial Ordinance 9: http://www.in.gov.br/materia/-/asset_publisher/Kujrw0TZC2Mb/content/id/6653698/do1-2018-03-15-portaria-interministeri al-n-9-de-14-de-marco-de-2018-6653694.

References

Acosta, Diego, Cècile Blouin, and Luisa Feline Freirer. 2019. *La Emigración Venezolana: respuestas latino-americanas*. Documento de Trabajo, n° 3 (2ª época). Madrid: Fundación Carolina. https://www.fundacioncarolina.es/wp-content/up loads/2019/04/DT_FC_03.pdf.

Abrahão, Bernardo Adame. 2019. *Solicitação de refúgio como estratégia migratória dos venezuelanos em Roraima nos anos de 2014 a 2017*. Dissertação apresentada ao Mestrado em Sociedades e Fronteiras da Universidade Federal de Roraima.

Alto Comisionado de las Naciones Unidas para los Refugiados (ACNUR). 2018. *Proyecto de caracterización de población proveniente de Venezuela en Colombia*. http://www.refworld.org.es/pdfid/5ac7f0534.pdf.

Alto Comissariado das Nações Unidas para Refugiados [ACNUR] 2020. *Venezuelanos no brasil: integração no mercado de trabalho e acesso a redes de proteção social.* https://

www.acnur.org/portugues/wp-content/uploads/2020/07/Estudo-sobre-Inte gra%C3%A7%C3%A3o-de-Refugiados-e-Migrantes-da-Venezuela-no-Brasil.pdf.

Álvarez de Flores, Raquel. 2004. "La dinámica migratoria colombo-venezolana: evolución y perspectiva actual." *Geoenseñanza*, 9 (2), 191–202. http://www.redalyc.org/pdf/360/36090205.pdf.

Brasil. 2018. Casa Civil. Operação Acolhida. Documentos. *Palestra comitê–apresentação General Pazuello coordenador operacional.* http://www.casacivil.gov.br/operacao-acolhida/documentos/palestra-comite-general-pazuello.pdf/view.

——. 2019. Polícia Federal. *Imigração Venezuela/Brasil.* http://www.pf.gov.br/servicos-pf/imigracao/apresentcao-policia-federal-ate-abril-de-2019.pdf.

Briceno, Franklin. 2018. Peru, Ecuador tighten requirements for Venezuela migrants. *AP News.* https://apnews.com/b875399c8d904d43977d20a77b674a65/Peru,-Ecuador-tighten-requirements-for-Venezuela-migrants.

Centro Nacional de Memoria Histórica (CNMH). 2014. *Cruzando la frontera: memorias del éxodo hacia Venezuela. El caso del río Arauca.* Bogotá: Centro Nacional de Memoria Histórica. http://www.centrodememoriahistorica.gov.co/descargas/informes2015/nacion-desplazada/cruzando-la-frontera.pdf.

Cabrera Serrano, Donna, Gabriela M. Cano Salazar, and Alexandra Castro. 2019. "Procesos recientes de movilidad humana entre Venezuela y Colombia 2016-2018." In *Crisis y migración de población venezolana. Entre la desprotección y la seguridade jurídica em Latinoamérica,* edited by Luciana Gandini, Fernando Lozano-Ascencio, and Victoria Prieto Rosas. Mexico: National Autonomous University of Mexico.

Castro, Alexandra. 2016. *La Gobernanza internacional de las migraciones: de la gestión migratoria a la protección de migrantes.* Bogotá: Univesidad Externado de Colombia.

——, ed. 2019. *Venezuela migra: aspectos sensibles del éxodo hacia Colombia.* Bogotá: Univesidad Externado de Colombia.

Castro, Alexandra, and Milkes Irit. 2018. "Potestad sancionatoria y Politica migratoria Colombiana." *Jornadas derecho administrativo.* Bogotá: Univesidad Externado de Colombia.

Cancillería. 2019. Cancillería, Migración Colombia y la OIM, lanzan la tercera semana Internacional de las migraciones: oportunidades para el desarrollo. https://www.cancilleria.gov.co/en/newsroom/news/cancilleria-migracion-colombia-oim-lanzan-tercera-semana-internacional-migraciones.

Cartagena Declaration on Refugees. 1984. https://www.oas.org/dil/1984_cartagena_declaration_on_refugees.pdf.

Comisión Interamericana de Derechos Humanos (CIDH). 2018. *Informe sobre la situación de Derechos Humanos en Venezuela.* http://www.oas.org/es/cidh/informes/pdfs/Venezuela2018-es.pdf.

Convention Against Torture and Other Cruel, Inhuman or Degrading Treatment or Punishment. 1984. https://www.ohchr.org/en/professionalinterest/pages/cat.aspx.

Convention Relating to the Status of Refugees. 1951. https://www.refworld.org/docid/3be01b964.html.

Consultancy for Human Rights and Displacement (CODHES). 2018. *Necesidades de protección de las personas venezolanas forzadas a migrar, refugiadas y en riesgo de apa-*

tridia en Colombia. Bogotá. https://codhes.files.wordpress.com/2018/07/informe-migrantes-y-refugiados-vz-en-col.pdf.
DNP. 2018. *CONPES 3950*. Bogotá.
El Espectador. 2018. ¿*Por qué es tan difícil sacar el pasaporte en Venezuela?* https://www.elespectador.com/noticias/el-mundo/por-que-es-tan-dificil-sacar-el-pasaporte-en-venezuela-articulo-738727.
El Pitazo. 2018. *Pasaportes y cédulas: El largo camino hacia la identidad en Venezuela*. https://elpitazo.com/reportajes/pasaportes-y-cedulas-el-largo-camino-hacia-la-identidad-en-venezuela/.
Félix, Jackson, and Emily Costa. 2018. Após ataques de brasileiros, 1,2 mil venezuelanos deixaram o país, diz Exército. *G1*. https://g1.globo.com/rr/roraima/noticia/2018/08/19/pacaraima-tem-ruas-desertas-apos-confronto-entre-brasileiros-e-venezuelanos.ghtml.
Gandini, Luciana, Fernando Lozano-Ascencio, and Victoria Prieto Rosas. 2019. *Crisis y Migración de la población venezolana. Entre la desprotección y la seguridad jurídica en Latinoamérica*. Mexico: National Autonomous University of Mexico.
Gobierno de Colombia. Defensoría del Pueblo, Fenalper and UNGRD. 2018. *Informe Final. Registro Administrativo de Migrantes Venezolanos en Colombia, 2018*. http://www.refworld.org.es/pdfid/5b2957524.pdf.
International Convention on the Protection of the Rights of All Migrant Workers and Members of Their Families. 1990. https://www.ohchr.org/EN/ProfessionalInterest/Pages/CMW.aspx.
International Monetary Fund (IMF). 2018. *World Economic Outlook, Cyclical Upswing, Structural Change*.
International Organization for Migration (IOM). 2019. *Venezuelan Refugee and Migrant Crisis*. https://www.iom.int/venezuela-refugee-and-migrant-crisis.
Insight Crime. 2017. *2017 Homicide rates in Latin America and the Caribbean*.
Jarochinski Silva, João Carlos. 2017. *Migração forçada de Venezuelanos pela fronteira norte do Brasil*. 41° encontro anual de ANPOCS. http://www.anpocs.com/.
Jarochinski Silva, João Carlos, and Liliana Lyra Jubilut. 2020. "Venezuelanos no Brasil e a COVID-19." In *Migrações Internacionais e a pandemia de Covid 19*, edited by Rosana Baeninger, Luís Renato Vedovato and Shailen Nandy: 417–425. Campinas: NEPO/Unicamp.
Jarochinski Silva, João Carlos, and Cyntia Sampaio. 2018. "As ações decorrentes da Migração de Venezuelanos para o Brasil–da acolhida humanitária para a interiorização." In *Direito Internacional dos Refugiados e o Brasil*, edited by Danielle Annoni: 734–746. Curitiba: Gedai, UFPR.
Jornal Nacional. 2018. *STF derruba exigência de passaporte para venezuelanos em Roraima*. https://g1.globo.com/jornal-nacional/noticia/2018/08/09/stf-derruba-exigencia-de-passaporte-para-venezuelanos-em-roraima.ghtml.
Krygier, Rachelle. 2018. "'The Maduro Diet': A Photo Essay from Venezuela." *Americas Quarterly*. https://www.americasquarterly.org/content/maduro-diet-photo-essay-venezuela.
LabOUR. 2017. "Características de los migrantes de Venezuela a Colombia." *Universidad El Rosario*, Informe 3, 9. https://docs.wixstatic.com/ugd/c80f3a_d2e0a0b4821e4238ae021904026a4459.pdf.
Maringoni, Gilberto. 2009. *A revolução venezuelana*. Unesp: São Paulo.

Mauat 2018
Mayorquin, Daniela. 2019. "El refugio como alternativa a la migración forzada de venezolanos en Colombia." In *Venezuela migra: aspectos sensibles del éxodo hacia Colombia*, edited by Alexandra Castro. Bogotá: Univesidad Externado de Colombia.
Mexico Declaration and Plan of Action to Strengthen the International Protection of Refugees in Latin America. 2004. https://www.refworld.org/docid/424bf6914.html.
Milesi, Rosita, Paula Coury, and Julia Rovery Julia. 2018. "Migração Venezuelana ao Brasil: discurso político e xenofobia no contexto atual." *AEDOS*, 10 (22): 53–70. https://seer.ufrgs.br/aedos/article/view/83376.
Organização Internacional para as Migrações (OIM). 2013. *Perfil migratorio de Colombia 2012*. Colombia.
Organização Internacional para as Migrações (OIM) and IPPDH. 2017. "Migración, derechos humanos y política migratoria." *Migración y Derechos Humanos*: 1–44. http://www.ippdh.mercosur.int/wp-content/uploads/2017/02/Migración-derechos-humanos-y-política-migratoria.pdf.
Organización Internacional para las Migraciones (OIM), Organización Internacional del Trabajo (OIT) y Universidad Antonio Ruiz de Montoya (UARM). 2019. *Impacto de la migración venezolana en el mercado laboral de tres ciudades: Lima, Arequipa y Piura*. Lima: OIM. https://www.ilo.org/wcmsp5/groups/public/---americas/---ro-lima/documents/publication/wcms_714888.pdf.
Organization of American States (OAS). 2018. *Informe de la Secretaria general de la organización de los Estados Americanos y del Panel de Expertos internacionales independientes sobre la posible comisión de crimes de lesa humanidad en Venezuela*.
———. 2019. *Final Report of the OAS Working Group to Address the Venezuelan Migrant and Refugee Crisis in the Region*. Working Group to Address the Regional Crisis Caused by Venezuelan Migrant and Refugee Flows.
Paéz, Tomás. 2015. *La voz de la diáspora venezolana*. Madrid: Catarata.
Paéz, Tomás, and Leonardo Vivas Peñalver. 2017. *The Venezuelan Diaspora—Another impending crisis*. Washington, D. C.: Freedom House.
Prada, Sara. 2019. *Cerco a la migración: cada vez más países exigen visa a los venezolanos*. https://migravenezuela.com/web/articulo/cuales-son-los-paises-que-exigen-visa-a-los-venezolanos/1531.
R4V, Plataforma de coordinación para refugiados y migrantes de Venezuela. https://r4v.info/es/situations/platform.
Reina, Mauricio, Carlos Antonio Mesa, and Tomás Ramírez Tobón. 2018. *Elementos para una política pública frente a la crisis de Venezuela*. Bogotá: Fedesarrollo. https://www.repository.fedesarrollo.org.co/bitstream/handle/11445/3716/CDF_No_69_Noviembre_2018.pdf?sequence=1&isAllowed=y.
Sampaio, Cyntia, and João Carlos Jarochinski Silva. 2018. "Complexidade X Singularidade—A Necessidade de outras soluções duradouras." In *Migrações Venezuelanas*, edited by Rosana Baeninger and João Carlos Jarochinski Silva: 391–394, Campinas: Nepo/Unicamp.
Sen, Ashish K. 2019. Maduro's Days Are Over, Says Colombian President Duque. *Atlantic Council*. https://www.atlanticcouncil.org/blogs/new-atlanticist/maduro-s-days-are-over-says-colombian-president-duque/.

Singer, Florantonia. 2018. Los venezolanos se acuestan con hambre. *El país*. https://elpais.com/internacional/2018/02/22/america/1519277784_904681.html.
SJR et. al. 2018. *Informe sobre la movilidad humana venezolana. Realidades y perspectivas de quienes emigran.*
Societe Generale. 2019. *Venezuela: Risque Pays.* https://import-export.societegenerale.fr/fr/fiche-pays/venezuela/risque-pays-commerce.
United Nations High Commissioner for Refugees (UNHCR). 2019a. *Venezuela: the largest exodus of Latin America.* https://www.unhcr.org/ph/15558-april-e-newsletter-venezuela.html.
———. 2019b. *Refugees and migrants from Venezuela, top 4 million.* https://www.unhcr.org/news/press/2019/6/5cfa2a4a4/refugees-migrants-venezuela-top-4-million-unhcr-iom.html#_ga=2.30516924.2029642107.1568998169-1255745267.1341612212.
Migración Colombia. 2017. *Boletín anual de estadísticas. Enero-diciembre 2017.* http://www.migracioncolombia.gov.co/index.php/estudios-migratorios/estadisticas.
———. 2018. *Radiografía migratoria Colombia–Venezuela 2017.* http://www.migracioncolombia.gov.co/index.php/es/prensa/multimedia/6308-radiografia-de-venezolanos-en-colombia-31-12-2017.
Universidad del Rosario 2018.
Van Praag, Oriana. 2019. *Understanding the Venezuelan Refugee Crisis.* Wilson Center. https://www.wilsoncenter.org/article/understanding-the-venezuelan-refugee-crisis.
Vaz, Alcides Costa. 2017. "A crise venezuelana como fator de instabilidade regional." *Centro de Estudos Estratégicos do Exército: Análise Estratégica*, 3 (3): 1–7.
Vidigal, Lucas. 2019. Conare reconhece "generalizada violação aos direitos humanos' na Venezuela para agilizar análise de pedidos de refúgio. *G1*. https://g1.globo.com/mundo/noticia/2019/06/19/conare-reconhece-grave-e-generalizada-ameaca-aos-direitos-humanos-na-venezuela-para-agilizar-analise-de-pedidos-de-refugio.ghtml.
Welsh, Teresa. 2019. Colombia preparing for prolonged response to Venezuela crisis. *Devex*. https://www.devex.com/news/colombia-preparing-for-prolonged-response-to-venezuela-crisis-95716.

15

No Place for Refugees?

The Haitian Flow within Latin America and the Challenge of International Protection in Disaster Situations

Beatriz Eugenia Sánchez-Mojica

Introduction

If there is just one word capable of describing Latin America, it is "diversity." Its 20 million square kilometers comprise more than twenty states, each with unique economic, social, political, and environmental traits. Despite their heterogeneity, however, all these countries share one feature; they are all seriously exposed to the risk of disasters (United Nations International Strategy for Disaster Reduction [UNISDR] 2013). Earthquakes, hurricanes, floods, and droughts have hit the region from north to south throughout history (Khamis and Osorio 2013: 28–43).

Despite their obvious differences, these disasters have the common capacity to modify the patterns of population mobility in the affected regions, provoking migration and displacement, both internally and transnationally (ibid.: 231). According to the Internal Displacement Monitoring Centre (IDMC), in the period 2008–14, almost 3 million people were displaced in the region due to sudden onset disasters (IDMC 2015: 31). The figures for 2019 reveal an even worse scenario, with around 1.1 million people forced to leave their homes (IDMC 2020: 152).

Despite the magnitude of these figures, human mobility related to disasters has not traditionally been a matter for concern in the region. Displacement and migration have been conceived as mere consequences of the catastrophe, and not even the most significant ones (Sánchez-Mojica 2018). Only exceptionally–the transnational exodus triggered by Hurricane Mitch in 1998, for example–has displacement caused by disasters been addressed as an issue in itself, and legal action been taken to protect the affected population (Nansen Initiative 2013: 16).

Recently, however, there has been a significant shift in the region. States have started to include specific categories into their migration laws, to accept and offer temporary shelter to people expelled from their countries due to disasters.[1] Although there has yet to be a regional response, some multilateral regional forums–the Regional Conference on Migration or the South American Conference on Migration, among others–have approved certain soft-law initiatives, providing states with guidelines to assist and protect both external environmentally displaced people and migrants unable to return to their home countries due to disasters. This shift can be traced back a decade to the Haitian exodus, a process linked to the massive earthquake that destroyed Port-au-Prince in January 2010. It put an end to the region's neglect of transnational displacement rooted in "natural disasters"[2] and forced states into enacting legal measures to address the matter.

Ad hoc mechanisms created by some states to cope with this exodus set the scene for legal measures being currently used to address transnational movements due to natural causes. Moreover, these initial measures established the key premise that underpins current national policies on the matter, namely the fact that people crossing national boundaries due to disasters cannot be considered refugees. On the other hand, they cannot be treated as mere economic migrants either, given their acute vulnerability and the threats to their lives, integrity, and security involved in a forced return to their own countries. States have therefore developed a special regime, based on humanitarian considerations, to grant temporary protection to this category of migrants.

This chapter questions the above premises, arguing that Refugee Law in Latin America does indeed provide states with a mechanism for protecting people forced to flee their countries due to disasters. The very complexity of the causes that lead to these flows of humanity means that these people should be included within the refugee definition set forth in the 1984 Cartagena Declaration on Refugees (Cartagena Declaration), which enlarges the concept of the 1951 Convention Relating to the Status of Refugees (1951 Refugee Convention) to include "persons who have fled their country because their lives, safety or freedom have been threatened by generalized violence, foreign aggression, internal conflicts, massive violation of human rights or other circumstances which have seriously disturbed public order" (Cartagena Declaration: Conclusion 3; see Fischel de Andrade in this volume).

Until now, this regional refugee definition[3] has been interpreted in such a way as to exclude people who have been forced to flee their countries due to natural events (López 2007). Nevertheless, a careful study of the Haitian exodus will inevitably lead to the conclusion that these people could have been included within this definition, since they were not just expelled due to a natural phenomenon. Human activity and, particularly, the profound alteration of public order following the natural events had a direct and powerful bearing on the forced displacement process that took place from 2010 to 2014. Therefore, Latin American states were mistaken when they assumed that Haitians could not be included in the regional refugee definition. This misconception has also impacted the more general measures enacted in ensuing years by some of countries in the region, precluding proper international protection for people externally displaced because of natural disasters.

As the study of the Haitian case will show, it is high time we reconsidered the Cartagena Declaration's traditional interpretation.

An Overview of Haitians' Motivations for Fleeing Their Country

On 12 January 2010, a magnitude 7.0 earthquake struck Port-au-Prince, the capital city of the poorest country in the Western Hemisphere. As a result, the city was completely devastated and its destruction led to the total collapse of the state (Feldmann 2013: 32; Weiss Faguen 2013: 5). At least 230,000 people were killed and more than half a million injured (Weiss Faguen 2013: 6). The lack of infrastructure and resources prevented authorities from providing the most elementary relief and protection for the affected population, leaving the victims to their own devices. In addition, armed gangs attacked the provisional camps where the now homeless people tried to find some shelter; the gangs sowed terror among the population and sexually assaulted women and girls (Bolton 2011).

The crumbling and collapse of most of the buildings and essential infrastructure of Port-au-Prince and the brutal activities of the armed groups were not the only outcomes of the natural event. Despite its magnitude, the massive destruction caused by the quake was possible only because of the almost absolute absence of enforcement of building codes for decades (Bolton 2011: 4). The incapacity–or unwillingness–of national and local authorities to apply the rule of law had a major role in the city's devastation. The historical fragility of the state had only served to increase the presence of criminal gangs and private militias (Becker 2011). The almost total absence of a police force after the catastrophe allowed these groups to freely wield their power through violence. Sexual violence, in particular against women and girls, has been traditionally tolerated both by authorities and society (Amnesty International 2008; Feldmann 2013).

In their attempt to escape from such a dangerous scenario, more than 1.5 million people fled the city during the days following the quake (International Organization for Migration [IOM] 2011: 84). Most of them sought relief in the Haitian countryside, but a not insignificant minority flocked to neighboring countries. An estimated 160,000 people crossed the border of the Dominican Republic, where they found a degree of succour and protection (Weiss Faguen 2013: 11). Several thousand more followed the traditional migration routes, looking for protection in Canada, France, the United States, and the neighboring islands. Finally, smaller groups decided to go where few Haitian had been before: Argentina, Chile, Ecuador, Mexico, Panama, Venezuela, and above all, Brazil (Thomaz 2013; Weiss Faguen 2013).

Despite the magnitude of the movement, not many of the displaced persons got very far. The Haitian countryside, impoverished after decades of inadequate agrarian policies and hit by multiple disasters, was incapable of offering a proper response to their needs. Besides, international relief agencies had focused their activities on the capital city, so these people gradually came back looking for some help (Weiss Faguen 2013: 6). But it was not a proper return. They remained as internally displaced persons for a long time. In fact, there were still more than 1.3 million of them a year later, most of them living in provisional camps, facing misery and being exposed to high levels of violence (Eves 2011: 18). What is more, the solidarity of the Dominican authorities evaporated after just a few months and most of the earthquake victims were forced to leave the country (Weiss Faguen 2013: 13).

The initial exodus did not end here, however. Throughout 2011 and early 2012 it continued, in a much more discreet way. By now the traditional destinations had raised their drawbridges, on the grounds that Haitians did not legally qualify as refugees under the 1951 Refugee Convention. Individuals and small groups thus turned to South America (Thomaz 2013: 35).

The stories of the Haitian exodus continued. From late 2012 to late 2014 a second wave departed. This time the goal was Brazil and, to a much lesser degree, Argentina and Chile. This flow was driven by three main causes. First, two years after the earthquake the country was still devastated and thousands of people remained uprooted as well as vulnerable. Second, in October 2012 Hurricane Sandy struck the south of the country, causing a massive flood and worsening the already hard living conditions (Miura 2014: 152). Finally, there was a third factor, perhaps less evident than the former two. The collapse of Haitian institutions, the massive destruction of livelihoods, and the reality of living in constant fear led to a number of social and psychological consequences. The widespread and profound damage to the mental health of the victims and survivors, together with the protracted chaos, drove citizens to simply lose hope in the country. Haiti came to be perceived by its inhabitants as a cursed place, where no future was possible. In this scenario, fleeing was conceived not just as a coping strategy, but as the only way to survive (Bernal 2014a: 39–44).

Since 2016 new waves of abandonment have been occurring, triggered by the political, economic, and social crises faced by the country. The devastating effects of hurricanes such as Mathew and Dorian have compounded the misery, and have had significant impacts as expelling factors (IDMC 2020: 54). There are also reports of the first waves of Haitians wandering around Latin America looking for job opportunities or even trying to reach the United States (IOM–Instituto de Políticas Públicas en Derechos Humanos del MERCOSUR [IPPDH] 2017: 45; Weerasinghe 2018: 74). These last flows of migrants will not be taken into consideration in this chapter, however, since it was the responses to the two previous waves that shaped the national mechanisms for dealing with transnational displacement caused by disasters.

Haitians' Pursuit of Safety and a Better Life

Haiti has a long tradition of migration, both forced and voluntary. Throughout its history, and particularly since the 1920s, migration has been a last resort strategy used by its population to deal with the multiple political, economic, and social crises faced by the country (Bernal 2014a: 38). The Bahamas, Canada, France, Turks and Caicos, and the United States, as well as the Dominic Republican and Cuba have traditionally been the main destinations (Audebert 2017: 59; Weiss Faguen 2013: 9–12).

This deep-rooted migratory tradition explains in part why, after the earthquake, thousands of Haitians abandoned the country. Since the traditional routes were closed to them, Latin America became their main destination. Mexico was considered, from the outset, as an attractive option; although only a minor number traveled there (Weiss Faguen 2013: 19–20). Most of the people turned their eyes to South America, particularly to Argentina, Brazil, and Chile; three countries that, back then, had no significant historical or cultural ties with Haiti, but that offered work and educational opportunities (Audebert 2017: 64; IOM-IPPDH 2017: 113; Miura 2014: 152–53; Weiss Faguen 2013: 17). By choosing these countries Haitian people were not only fleeing from chaos and despair but also pursuing the opportunity to build a bright new life for themselves and their families.

The price these people paid for the dream of a better future was usually high, since the journey to reach their final destination in South America was extremely arduous, particularly for those who chose Brazil. There were two possible paths for them to take. Between 2010 and 2012, most of them traveled without visas by a long, dangerous, and costly route designed by the human smuggling networks. It usually began by air to Ecuador and then by land to Peru, or less often to Bolivia, and onward through the Amazon rainforest to reach Brazil. The accompaniment of local paid guides or coyotes was absolutely essential to follow this convoluted route and these coyotes took advantage, demanding high fees for their services and exposing the travellers to extremely harsh living conditions. Selling them to human traffickers was not unusual, either (Bernal 2014b: 72–74; IOM-IPPDH 2017: 16).

The considerable number of Haitians moving into Brazil, their poor state of health on arrival, as well as the increasing evidence of people smuggling and trafficking involved in their journey, pushed Brazilian authorities into intervening. In 2012 a second pathway was opened, this time legal and much safer. Haitians still in Port-au-Prince were allowed to apply for a humanitarian visa at the Brazilian Embassy, an authorization that was later extended to all embassies along this route (Miura 2014: 154; Pacífico et al. 2015: 144).

Despite the existence of this second legal path, the first route continued to be actively used. The bureaucratic issues faced by those applying for humanitarian visas (particularly during the first year) coupled with Haitians' deep distrust of official institutions, led many to continue placing their trust and lives in the hands of the smugglers (Metzer 2014: 30; see also Freier and Luzes in this volume).

In sharp contrast, those who chose Argentina or Chile had a much shorter and safer trip. Most of them were students, were supported by their families, or were young professionals and skilled workers. Not needing a visa to get into these countries, and having sufficient resources, they arrived at their destination by air (IOM-IPPDH 2017: 34).

The Responses of the Latin American States

The flow of Haitians to South America was inevitable and predictable. Their country was devastated, unable to bounce back, and their traditional migratory routes had been blocked. Therefore, they could only go south. Foreseeing the influx, some regional organizations approved resolutions requesting member states to consider the temporary suspension of involuntary returns of Haitians already in their territories and to adopt special immigration measures on humanitarian grounds (Alianza Bolivariana de los Pueblos de Nuestra América 2010). Nevertheless, the arrival of thousands of Haitians took almost all countries by surprise.

National authorities' reactions to the influx varied. During the first years, some countries adopted ad hoc measures that later developed into laws to cope with transnational migrations brought on by natural disasters. Others implemented provisional measures to deal with the first wave but refused to take any more steps. Finally, there were some that failed to craft any new measures, applying preexistent legal immigration categories to the newcomers. Whatever the measures taken, they shared a common element: none of them considered the flow of Haitians to be a refugee issue.

The Mexican Response

Mexico, the only country in Mesoamerica to receive a significant number of Haitian people after the earthquake, put together a response founded on humanitarian and temporary grounds. The National Institute for Migrations prepared a three-tiered ad hoc program, which was in force between February and May 2010 (National Institute for Migrations [INM] 2010). First, students already in the country received work permits. Second, legal residents and refugees with family members affected by the earthquake were authorized to travel to Haiti, rescue them, and bring them back. Finally, the newcomers–both the resident relatives and those who arrived unofficially–received a document that legalized their presence for a year, allowing them to work. In principle, this document could be renewed, but not all of the beneficiaries were able to do this due to the different criteria applied by local authorities. When the program came to an end, those who had not arrived in time to benefit from it, and those who had not renewed their documents, became subject to deportation (Weerasinghe 2018: 77; Weiss Faguen 2013: 19–20).

The asylum option remained open through this period, but only a small percentage of Haitians claimed international protection. From 2011 to 2016 just twenty-three people were recognized as refugees (Weerasinghe 2018: 81). In most of these cases this decision was taken subject to the Cartagena Declaration's definition included in the Mexican Refugee Law.[4] Not on the grounds that they had suffered the consequences of a natural disaster, but taking into consideration the lack of protection and increased insecurity they faced back home in Haiti (Cantor 2015: 18).

Influenced to a point by the ad hoc program, Mexico has now developed a legal system to better cope with the exodus caused by disasters,[5] in the form of a humanitarian visa for those fleeing such catastrophes or other life-threatening circumstances, which grants temporary residence but does not allow people to work.[6]

The Andean Countries' Responses

The Andean countries were not thought of as final destinations, but rather stopovers on the journey down to Brazil, the first of these being Ecuador (Vásquez, Busse, and Izaguirre 2014: 85–88). The fact that this country had suspended visa requirements back in 2008 for all wouldbe entrants was highly influential in choosing Ecuador as the main port-of-entry (Weiss Faguen 2013: 14). Moreover, during the first months after the earthquake Rafael Correa's government implemented certain provisions to protect Haitian migrants already in its territory. Such measures may well have been wrongly interpreted as a welcoming sign held out for them.

Indeed, in February 2010 the regularization of Haitian immigrants and their families was approved.[7] This legal decision, based on humanitarian and solidarity grounds, granted a five-year residence and work permit. Although it seems like quite a protective measure, its impact was extremely low since it benefited only people who had arrived in the country prior to 1 February. Most of the Haitians arrived later, and only those living in the country *prior* to the disaster—around three hundred—were actually able to obtain the permit (Bernal 2014b: 68).

This regularization process was the sole measure adopted by Ecuador to deal with the inflow, and despite the growing numbers, there was no shift in the immigration policy. Haitians were allowed to enter without a visa and stay for a three-month period as tourists. Once the term ended, they had to leave or they became illegal aliens (Bernal 2014b: 76). Asylum played a very marginal role in the state response to this influx, but a small number of claims were recognized subject to the Cartagena Declaration's refugee definition. Applying the same rationale used by the Mexican authorities, chaos and insecurity in Haiti were deemed "circumstances that have seriously disrupted public order." (Cantor 2015: 18).

Peru was the next stopover on the Haitians' journey to Brazil. The government assumed the transitory nature of their presence in the country by allowing them to pass through. After the first years, however, it became evident that human smuggling and trafficking networks were victimizing them. In an attempt to protect them, a special visa was established in 2012.[8] In spite of all the good intentions, this measure did not diminish the influx and worsened the already acute vulnerability, since many of the Haitians did not meet the visa requirements and became illegal aliens (Vásquez, Busse, and Izaguirre 2014: 99).

As in Ecuador, asylum played a minor role. But in this case the refugee convention definition was applied. From 2011 to 2016, Peruvian authorities granted international protection in thirty-nine cases, acknowledging a well-founded fear of persecution by non-state actors that arose from the vacuum of governmental authority after the earthquake (Cantor 2015: 17; Weerasinghe 2018: 91).

Notwithstanding the paucity of activity shown by Peruvian authorities regarding the inflow of Haitians, the experience did lead to a debate regarding the need for proper measures to generally manage the influx of people following natural disasters. The outcome was a humanitarian visa, approved in 2015, that provides a short-term residence period, as well as a work permit.[9]

Finally, Bolivia did not implement any measures to deal with the influx, despite the fact that a small number of Haitians crossed through its territory to reach Brazil (Peraza-Breedy 2014: 12). In 2013 the law on immigration was, however, reformed, authorizing the granting of a humanitarian visa for people affected by disasters.[10] Unfortunately, this is only a theoretical possibility since the decree that implements the law makes no mention whatsoever of the humanitarian visa.[11]

The Venezuelan Response

The response of Venezuela deserves particular analysis, since Haitians did not conceive this country as a stopover but rather as a destination in itself. Right after the earthquake, President Hugo Chávez's government adopted measures to regularize the status of Haitian immigrants already in the country, around twenty thousand people (Weiss Faguen 2013: 21). A humanitarian visa program was also created. This latter measure, combined with the geographical proximity of the two countries, pushed tens of thousands of people to look for a haven in Venezuela. In fact, in 2013 around forty thousand Haitians were living in various locations of this country, more than half of them undocumented (Cantor 2015: 46).

It is likely that some of those people were considering settling down there, at least on a temporary basis. Nevertheless, the complex economic and political crisis that Venezuela has been experiencing since 2013 has deeply affected this already vulnerable population (Weiss Faguen 2013: 21). Information regarding the fate of these people is scarce, but it seems reasonable to assume that most of them have by now left the country.

The Brazilian Response

Brazil received a significant influx in a short period of time. According to the International Traffic System Database, 72,406 Haitians crossed the Brazilian border between 2010 and 2015 (Cavalcanti et al. 2017: 193). This was completely unexpected and at the time there were no adequate legal mechanisms to cope with it (Pacífico et al. 2015: 142). As a consequence, certain ad hoc measures were approved over a short period, some of which proved not to be as effective as was hoped. Adjustments were therefore needed.

At first, the possibility of recognizing Haitians as refugees was considered. After an intense debate among Brazilian immigration and refugee authorities, however, it was decided that environmental crises were not a valid reason for recognition of the refugee status. Haitians' refugee applications were thus referred to the National Immigration Council (CNIg), which has the jurisdiction to rule on those cases considered "special or not regulated" (Jubilut, Andrade, and Madureira 2016: 77). In 2011 CNIg granted permanent residency for humanitarian reasons to Haitians through a five-year permit, including the right to work.[12] Not only asylum seekers but also any Haitian fleeing from the earthquake who were already in the country could benefit from this measure. A year later this measure was reconsidered and in May 2012 the Brazilian government approved a humanitarian visa requirement for Haitians. The Brazilian Embassy in Port-au-Prince was authorized to issue a maximum of 1,200 visas per year[13] (Miura 2014: 153). Only people who had obtained such visa could claim a humanitarian residence permit upon arrival in Brazil (see Freier and Luzes in this volume).

The aim of this humanitarian visa was to provide migrants with a legal and safe way to reach the country; in spite of its good intentions, though, this mechanism soon had to be amended, since the fixed quota proved insufficient to meet the high demand in Haiti. Thus, in April 2013 the quota was withdrawn and any Brazilian consulate was authorized to issue humanitarian visas, including to those who were in the transit countries.[14] The decision to provide residence permits exclusively to humanitarian visa holders was also reconsidered. As has already been mentioned, the ad hoc visa program did not prevent many Haitians from continuing to travel along the illegal routes. Their increasing presence in the Brazilian border cities and towns demanded an effective response; therefore, they were allowed to regularize their legal status by applying for the humanitarian residence permit (Miura 2014: 157; Pacífico et al. 2015: 144).

These two mechanisms–the humanitarian visa and the humanitarian residence permit–benefited tens of thousands of people (Weerasinghe 2018: 65). Both have been harshly criticized, however, due to the lack of a proper human rights approach (Pacífico et al. 2015: 148). This criticism had some bearing on the debate involving academics, activists, and policymakers that had been taking place in the country since the early 2010s, regarding the need to shape a new migratory policy (Muñoz 2019). As a result of this process, in 2017 the national parliament approved a new immigration law, including a temporary humanitarian visa that could be issued to migrants fleeing from natural disasters, no matter where they came from. This visa– that can also be issued to people escaping from armed conflict or massive human rights violations–grants residence but also a work authorization.[15] It should be mentioned, however, that the fate of people uprooted by natural disasters was definitely a secondary concern in the complex debate that led to the birth of the new migratory system in Brazil.

The Chilean Response

Despite the almost six thousand kilometres that separate Haiti and Chile, the latter was perceived as a desirable destination since it seemed to offer job opportunities and safety; moreover, there was no visa requirement for

Haitians. Only a relatively small number—around three thousand—managed to reach this country during the first years following the earthquake, however (Weiss Faguen 2013: 21). Throughout this period the Chilean government did not take any specific measure to cope with their arrival. According to the provisions of the national immigration law, Haitians were allowed to enter the country as tourists for a ninety-day period. During such term they could find employment and lodging for their temporary residence. Most of them succeeded in this endeavor, legalizing their status (IOM-IPPDH 2017: 90–94).

This scenario soon shifted dramatically. From 2013 to 2016 the Haitian population grew by 731 percent, and more than 41,000 people crossed the Chilean border aiming to settle in the country (Sánchez 2018: 280). Arguing the need to set the house in order, the government of Sebastián Piñera adopted three measures that were to severely restrict Haitians' options to arrive in Chile and settle there. In 2018 two new visas were approved for this population. The first is a tourism visa that can be issued only by the Chilean consulate in Haiti and strictly forbids its holders from changing their migratory status once they are in Chile.[16] The second is a humanitarian visa for family reunification that, again, can be issued only in Port-au-Prince. The fact that both measures came into force as soon as they were approved—affecting people who were already on their way to Chile—was harshly criticized by human rights associations and certain academic sectors. Accusations of racial discrimination underlying both measures have also been made (Trabalón 2018: 170). A voluntary repatriation program was crafted for Haitians in October 2018.[17] All these legal dispositions made it clear to Haitians that they were no longer welcome in Chile.

The Argentinian Response

Unlike the other South American countries, in 2010 Argentina did have in place a legal disposition granting a humanitarian visa to people uprooted due to natural disasters.[18] This mechanism played a very limited role in the response to the inflow of Haitians, however. In fact, from 2011 to 2015 only three hundred and fifty humanitarian visas were issued (IOM-IPPDH 2017: 117).

The low number of humanitarian visas granted to Haitians has been attributed to the fact that most of those arriving in Argentina were college students, young professionals, or highly skilled workers. They had the resources and skills needed to fit into the Argentinian immigration regime and managed to obtain a student or a residence permit in a relatively short period of time. Their particular conditions, as well as the regularization opportunities offered by national law, rendered the humanitarian visa redundant. Nevertheless, there was a minority who were unable to obtain a residence permit and who stayed on as illegal migrants. In order to regularize their situation, the national government approved an ad hoc mechanism, benefiting Haitians who had arrived in the country before 1 March 2017 (IOM-IPPDH 2017: 114–20).[19]

As in the rest of the region, asylum played a minor role in the Argentinian response to this influx. Between 2010 and 2014 only thirty-two Haitians were recognized as refugees. It should be noted that in eight of these cases such recognition was based on the Cartagena Declaration's refugee definition, which is enshrined in national law[20] (Weerasinghe 2018: 87).

No Place for Refugees?

The states' responses that have been explained in the above section reveal that, although asylum was granted in a few exceptional cases, no Latin American country considered the influx of Haitians as a refugee issue. Instead, while recognizing the extreme vulnerability of these people and the perils of forcing them to return to their devastated country, most of these states drafted ad hoc measures based on humanitarian considerations to allow their entry and legalize their status. These legal provisions could be labeled complementary protection measures, since they all grant temporary protection to forced migrants who have well-founded reasons for not wishing to return to their home country, while being outside the Refugee Law framework (Jubilut, Madureira, and Levy 2018; Sánchez-Mojica 2020).

On several occasions the adoption of these legal provisions has led to lengthy public debate regarding the need for mechanisms to cope with transnational environmental influxes, resulting in new and permanent measures regulating the matter. Every one of these recent legal provisions grants a different kind of protection to environmental migrants, but all share certain common features, in particular that they have been framed within the scope of national immigration laws, and that they involve a humanitarian visa and a temporary residence permit.

This eclectic mix of new mechanisms is witness to the way that Latin American countries have decided to cope with transnational exoduses linked to disasters. Two soft law instruments, approved by the main regional forums on migration, confirm such trend. The first of them is the *Guide to Effective Practices for RCM* [Regional Conference on Migration] *Member Countries: protection for persons moving across borders in the context of disasters*, approved in November 2016 by the Regional Conference on Migration.[21] The second is the *Regional Guidelines on protection and assistance for people displaced across borders and migrants in countries affected by nature disasters* approved in November 2018 by the South American Conference on Migration.[22] Both guides have been inspired by the *Agenda for the Protection of Cross-Border Dis-*

placed Persons in the Context of Disasters and Climate Change, launched by the Nansen Initiative in 2015, but each has adopted a different interpretation of the agenda.

In spite of their differences, both instruments do share some common ground. People moving across international borders due to disasters are perceived, essentially, as immigrants facing acute vulnerability. Although both guides highlight the states' obligation to grant these people access to asylum procedures, it is somehow assumed that most of them do not meet the refugee definition. As a result, the assistance and protection measures that states are recommended to implement are founded on humanitarian considerations.

At this point, one has to wonder whether the path followed by the states of the region to manage the influx of people displaced by disasters has been the right one. At first glance, it would seem a good choice since it provides a temporary haven for a group of people who would otherwise be left to their own devices. Moreover, it is a response that follows the international guidelines on the matter, so one could hardly demand anything more from a region that has proven to be particularly open and generous on migration issues (Acosta 2018). Nevertheless, a query arises: What if the main premise that underpins the whole humanitarian response were wrong? What if people fleeing from disasters could be termed refugees pursuant to the provisions of the Cartagena Declaration?

In order to answer this question, two tasks must be performed. First, the refugee concept embedded in the national legislation of the countries that received Haitian migrants must be reviewed to analyze whether it leaves room for people displaced due to natural causes. Second, the circumstances that led to the Haitian exodus have to be revisited. The following sections will develop both issues

The Refugee Concept in Latin American Host Countries

Every country in the region that received Haitians migrants–whether they are transit or destination countries–is a party to the 1951 Refugee Convention and its 1967 Protocol Relating to the Status of Refugees (1967 Protocol; UNHCR 2015). All of them have also adopted the Cartagena Declaration's expanded refugee definition.[23] This does not mean that each national law on asylum and international protection has reproduced the Declaration in its exact terms, however. Most of them have added or excluded certain elements, an issue that will have a direct impact on the treatment given to Haitians, as will shortly be seen (Cantor and Trimiño 2015: 178).

Now, as a general rule, people fleeing their home country due to a disaster do not meet the 1951 Refugee Convention's definition, due to a lack of well-founded fear of persecution. This does not mean that the international agreement excludes every situation related to the effects of a natural disaster, however: it only means that the persecution element must be present. A scenario such as a catastrophe intentionally caused by a government that is trying to expel a group of population due to one or more of the five 1951 Refugee Convention grounds certainly meets the conventional definition. Discrimination in the distribution of post-disaster assistance could also be included, if it is based on the aforementioned grounds (McAdam 2012: 44–48; Stavropoulou 2008: 12).

Regarding the Cartagena Declaration's expanded definition, and despite the fact that its terms are broad enough to consider people uprooted by disasters as refugees, an early interpretation precluded such possibility. In 1989, the Conferencia Internacional sobre Refugiados Centroamericanos (CIREFCA; International Conference on Central American Refugees) decided that only human-induced causes can be included in the refugee concept, expressly excluding natural disasters.[24] Although no reasons were provided, this interpretation has aroused little debate (López 2007: 390); being adopted by several regional declarations and soft law agreements during the next years. The 1994 San José Declaration on Refugees and Displaced Persons (see Rushing and Lizcano Rodriguez in this volume) and the Mexico Declaration and Plan of Action to Strengthen the International Protection of Refugees in Latin America of 2004 (see Vera Espinoza in this volume) do not even mention the issue. On the other hand, the Brazil Declaration and Plan of Action: a Framework for Cooperation and Regional Solidarity to Strengthen the International Protection of Refugees, Displaced and Stateless Persons in Latin America and the Caribbean of 2014 does recognize the displacement of people across borders due to climate change and natural disasters as challenges that must be faced by the region, and highlights the importance of enhancing knowledge on this matter by conducting new studies (see Arnold-Fernández, Sarmiento Torres, and Kallas in this volume), but these people are by no means considered refugees.[25]

At first glance, it would seem that Haitians forced to leave their country do not meet either the refugee concept provided in the 1951 Refugee Convention—since persecution has not been mentioned as a key reason for the exodus—or the expanded definition set forth in the Cartagena Declaration. A detailed examination of the circumstances involved in their being expelled from their country might, however, leads to a different conclusion.

Revisiting the Causes of the Haitian Exodus

The causes of the first two waves of the Haitian exodus have been analyzed throughout this chapter. Although the 2010 earthquake and the 2012 hurricane had significant roles as pushing factors, the ultimate expelling factor was the violent and chaotic situation following both disasters. The two natural events exacerbated preexisting vulnerabilities caused by fragility of the state, poverty, corruption, environmental degradation, and a patriarchal culture that normalizes sexual violence. Therefore, the exodus was the outcome of a complex process in which human factors were way more significant than the natural events.

People fled driven by a combination of fear and hope: fear due to the state's inability to fulfill the basic functions of a modern state, including control of public order in the country and protection of its citizens' most essential rights; and hope regarding the vision of a safe haven but also job and education opportunities, impossible to find in the rubble of their home country.

This scenario can be framed within the terms of the Cartagena Declaration's refugee definition, specifically, within the terms of "other circumstances which have seriously disturbed public order"; the last of the five objective situations contemplated in the soft law instrument. These other circumstances refer to situations in which the normal functioning of the institutions of the state—based on the rule of law and respect for human dignity—has been interrupted, severely affecting peace, security, and stability of both the state and society itself (UNHCR 2016: 17). That was, precisely, the Haitian context in the early 2010s. As a consequence, people leaving this country should be considered, first and foremost, as refugees.

Indeed, a studied interpretation of Cartagena's expanded concept in this particular context, following the teleological method recommended by the UNHCR and the *pro homine* principle demanded by the Inter-American Court of Human Rights (IACtHR),[26] leads one to the indisputable conclusion that Haitians were refugees deserving of full international protection (Acosta 2018: 115; UNHCR 2016: 13).

Second Thoughts on the Response of Latin American States

Despite all the considerations detailed in the previous section, asylum and Refugee Law occupied a very secondary place in the thoughts behind the responses given by Latin American states to the influx of Haitians. The reasons that explain this phenomenon are diverse and relate to the particular circumstances of each state.

The Brazilian government's decision not to recognize Haitians as refugees was reached due to the definition enshrined in the 1997 National Refugee Act. Despite being inspired by the Cartagena Declaration, it includes only one of the five possible circumstances that force flight referred to in the soft law instrument—namely, the massive violations of human rights[27]—which in practice has served only as grounds for claims in situations of conflict and violence (Weerasinghe 2018: 98). Framing the Haitian scenario in the terms of this legal provision was particularly questionable at that point, since the causes of the exodus were more related to state fragility. According to some experts, however, the national definition could have been applied to many of the Haitians, but was discarded for fear of creating a precedent for similar situations that might arise in the future (Pacífico et al. 2015: 144).

On the other hand, in the rest of the countries, from Mexico to Argentina, national laws on asylum and protection of refugees do indeed include the other circumstances clause in their definition of refugees. Thus, the exceptional recognition of Haitians as refugees was not related to the lack of an adequate legal category. There were other factors explaining this situation. First, this sudden inflow of migrants took national authorities by surprise; it was the first time they had had to cope with a massive movement of people caused by natural events. The lack of previous experience led them to underestimate asylum and refugee laws as ways to tackle this issue. Second, most Haitians did not consider themselves as refugees. In fact, the number of claims of asylum in these countries remained quite low throughout the first and second waves. It is likely that the existence of immigration measures specifically designed for this population actually functioned as a deterrent (Weerasinghe 2018). Moreover, one must bear in mind that Bolivia, Ecuador, and Peru were transit countries. Since there was no intention to settle down there, there was no incentive to apply for asylum. Third, the fact that one of the main motives for the influx was that they were pursuing opportunities for work and education—as much as an escape from violence and chaos—led national authorities to perceive Haitians as economic immigrants. Finally, as in the case of Brazil, the government probably wanted to avoid creating a precedent by crafting a response that was founded on international protection for people fleeing a disaster.

The array of reasons behind Latin American countries' decision to avoid applying the Cartagena Declaration's definition to Haitians should not distract from the main point. Almost all of the states in the region could have framed these people within the terms of the refugee definition enshrined in their own national laws and grant them the corresponding international protection. Instead, they decided to draft new measures to cope with this influx, offering a lesser degree of protection than the refugee status would have provided. The only exception in this regard was the Brazilian five-year residence permit, which almost fulfilled the set of rights granted to refugees (Weerasinghe 2018: 101). Even in this case, however, the complementary protection measures were temporary and failed to pursue the durable solutions provided for those with the official status of refugees. Even in the most favorable scenario, therefore, Haitians received a protection that was inferior to the one they deserved.

Conclusion

The statement that Haitians could–and should–have been recognized as refugees provides a new perspective of the responses drafted in the region to cope with future transnational movements that are related to disasters. As has been mentioned, the mechanisms and measures approved since 2010 have been underscored by the premise that, as a general rule, people fleeing from disasters are not refugees, but the Haitian case severely questions this conclusion.

The fulfilment of international and domestic obligations under Refugee Law demands that Latin American conduct a careful study of the causes of a material exodus, in order to determine whether international protection is mandatory. At this point, it should be noted that the complex circumstances surrounding the Haitian influx are by no means exceptional. Several studies have analyzed the relationship between human mobility and disasters around the world, concluding that it is anything but simple. The occurrence of a catastrophic event does not, per se, cause either displacement or migration. The confluence of several factors is necessary, and it is not unusual that the consequences of the natural event exacerbate preexisting vulnerabilities–whether they be state fragility, armed conflict, or generalized violence–that lead to scenarios where fleeing is the only option to protect life, integrity, or freedom. Although most of these people will not cross an international border, a significant minority will (Aghazarm and Laczko 2009; Sánchez-Mojica and Rubiano 2018), and those who do will meet the Cartagena Declaration's refugee definition.

Therefore, Refugee Law cannot be relegated to a secondary role in the responses developed by Latin American states to cope with transnational movements of people brought about by natural disasters. The humanitarian visa option should not be the only solution; it should not even be the preeminent one.

Beatriz Eugenia Sánchez-Mojica is a lawyer and has a PhD in Human Rights. She is an expert in International Human Rights and forced migration issues. She has taught law in various universities both in Colombia and Spain and has been a consultant on forced migration issues for IOM, United Nations Development Programme (UNDP) and–throughout IECAH– the Spanish Agency for International Cooperation (AECID). Currently, she teaches at IE University and at Universidad Internacional de la Rioja, both in Spain. She also coordinates the Latin American Network on Internally Displaced Persons (LANID).

Notes

1. In 2010, Argentina was the first Latin American country to create a humanitarian visa for people uprooted by natural disasters. Since then, other countries have followed suit: Mexico approved a similar measure in 2013, Peru did so in 2015, and Brazil in 2017.
2. Disasters are not natural but rather are the combined result of exposure to a natural hazard with an affected community's adaptive capacity based on their pre-existing vulnerabilities. Nonetheless, at times the term "natural disaster" is used in this chapter to reflect the way in which this phenomenon is commonly included in national law.
3. In spite of its non-binding nature, the Cartagena Declaration's refugee definition has been incorporated into the national laws of Argentina, Belize, Bolivia, Brazil, Chile, Colombia, Ecuador, El Salvador, Guatemala, Honduras, Mexico, Nicaragua, Paraguay, Peru and Uruguay. (UNHCR 2016: 13).
4. United States of Mexico, Law on Refugees, Political Asylum and Complementary Protection, 27 January 2011, Article 13. II.
5. United States of Mexico, Migration Act. 25 May 2011, Article 52. V.
6. United States of Mexico, General guidelines for issuing visas (Lineamientos generales para la expedición de visas. Trámite 9), 10 October 2014.
7. Republic of Ecuador, Decree 248, 23 February 2010.
8. Republic of Peru, Supreme Decree No.001-2012-RE, 10 January 2012.
9. Republic of Peru, Legislative Decree 1.236, 2015, Article 59.
10. Plurinational state of Bolivia, Law on Immigration 370, 2013, Article 65.
11. Plurinational state of Bolivia, Regulation on immigration law, DS 1923, 13 March 2014.
12. Brazil, National Immigration Council, Resolution 08/2011.
13. Brazil, National Immigration Council, Resolution 97/2012.
14. Brazil, National Immigration Council, Resolution 102/2013.
15. Brazil, Law 13.445, 24 May 2017.
16. Republic of Chile, Ministry of Internal Affairs and Public Security, Decree 776, 2018.
17. Republic of Chile, Ministry of Internal Affairs and Public Security, Resolution 5.744, 2018.
18. Republic of Argentina, Decree 616, 2012, Article 24(h).
19. Republic of Argentina: National Government, Disposition DNM 1143/2017, 15 March 2017.
20. Republic of Argentina, General Law for Recognizing and Protecting Refugees 26.165, 8 November 2006.
21. The Regional Conference on Migration, also known as the Puebla Process, was established in February 1996. It is a multilateral mechanism for coordinating policies and actions relating to migration in the eleven member states from Central and North America. Its primary objectives are to exchange information, experiences, and best practices, and to promote regional cooperation on migration.
22. The South American Conference on Migration (SACM), or Lima Process, is a multilateral mechanism with twelve member states from South America. It aims to provide a platform for consultations regarding human mobility issues.

23. In spite of its nonbinding nature, the Cartagena Declaration's refugee definition has been incorporated into the national laws of Argentina, Belize, Bolivia, Brazil, Chile, Colombia, Ecuador, El Salvador, Guatemala, Honduras, Mexico, Nicaragua, Paraguay, Peru, and Uruguay (UNHCR 2016: 13).
24. International Conference on Central American Refugees, Document CIREFCA/89/9, para. 33.
25. "In light of the new challenges posed by climate change and natural disasters, as well as by displacement of persons across borders that these phenomena may generate, UNHCR is requested to prepare a study on the subject for the purpose of supporting the adoption of appropriate national and regional measures, tools and guidelines, including response strategies for countries in the region, contingency plans, integrated responses for disaster risk management and humanitarian visa programmes, within the framework of its mandate." (Brazil Declaration and Plan of Action: 18).
26. The IACtHR has included the expanded definition of a refugee in the content of the right of asylum. As a consequence, the IACtHR demands that its interpretation be guided by the same principles and methods as the rest of the rights enshrined in the American Convention of Human Rights. See Case *Pacheco Tineo Family v. Plurinational State of Bolivia*, Judgement of November, as well as Advisory Opinion CO-21/14, *Rights and guarantees of children in the context of migration and/or in need of international protection* (Arlettaz 2016).
27. Brasil, National Refugee Act 1997, Article 1, III.

References

Acosta, Diego. 2018 *The National versus the Foreigner in South America 200 Years of Migration and Citizenship Law*. Cambridge: Cambridge University Press.

Agenda for the Protection of Cross-Border Displaced Persons in the Context of Disasters and Climate Change.

Aghazarm, Christine, and Frank Laczko, eds. 2009 *Migration, Environment and Climate Change. Assesing the Evidence*. Geneva: International Organization for Migration.

Alianza Bolivariana de los Pueblos de Nuestra América. 2010. *Plan para la contribución solidaria de los países del ALBA al esfuerzo de la reconstrucción de Haití*, reunión de emergencia del Consejo Político del ALBA-TCP, Caracas, Venezuela, 25 January 2010. Unión de Naciones Suramericanas. *Solidaridad de UNASUR con Haití: Decisión de Quito*, Otavalo, Ecuador, 9 February 2010.

Amnesty International. 2008. *Don't turn your back on girls—Sexual violence in Haiti*. http://www.ijdh.org/2008/11/topics/womens-issues/dont-turn-your-back-on-girls-sexual-violence-in-haiti/

Arlettaz, Fernando. 2016. "Naturaleza y alcance del asilo en el sistema interamericano de Derechos Humanos." *Revista Ius et Praxis*, 22 (1): 187–226.

Audebert, Cedric. 2017. "The recent geodynamics of Haitian migration in the Americas: refugees or economic migrants?." *Revista Brasilera de Estudos de População*, 34 (1): 55–71.

Becker, David. 2011. "Gangs, Netwar, and "Community Counterinsurgency" in Haiti." *PRISM*, 2 (3): 67–98.

Bernal, Gabriela. 2014a. "¿Por qué migrar? Algunos apuntes sobre las viejas y nuevas heridas de Haití." In *La migración haitiana hacia Brasil: Características, oportunidades y desafíos*, edited by Organización Internacional para las Migraciones: 33–50. Buenos Aires: International Organization for Migration

———. 2014b. "La migración haitiana hacia Brasil: Ecuador, país de tránsito." In *La migración haitiana hacia Brasil: Características, oportunidades y desafíos*, edited by Organización Internacional para las Migraciones: 67–82. Buenos Aires: International Organization for Migration.

Bolton, Michael. 2011. *Human Security after State collapse: global governance in post-earthquake Haiti*. London School of Economics Global Governance Research Papers (RP 01/2011).

Brazil Declaration and Plan of Action: a Framework for Cooperation and Regional Solidarity to Strengthen the International Protection of Refugees, Displaced and Stateless Persons in Latin America and the Caribbean. 2014. http://www.refworld.org/docid/5487065b4.html.

Cartagena Declaration on Refugees. 1984. https://www.refworld.org/docid/3ae6b36ec.html.

Cavalcanti, Leonardo, Tânia Tonhati, Dina Araújo, and Emmanuel Brasil. 2017. "Haitian Immigrants in the Brazilian Labor Market." *Revista de Estudos e Pesquisas Sobre as Américas*, 11 (1): 192–203.

Cantor, David. 2015. *Law, Policy and Practice Concerning the Humanitarian Protection of Aliens on a Temporary Basis in the Context of Disasters, Climate Change and Dispalcement. Evidence for Action. Background paper*. Geneva: Nansen Initiative, 2015

Cantor, David, and Diana Trimiño Mora. 2015. "¿Una solución simple para los refugiados que huyen de la guerra? La definición ampliada de América Latina y su relación con el derecho internacional humanitario." *Anuario Mexicano de Derecho Internacional*, XV: 165–194.

Cartagena Declaration on Refugees, 1984. http://www.oas.org/dil/1984_cartagena_declaration_on_refugees.pdf.

Colloquium on the International Protection of Refugees in Central America 1984.

Convention Relating to the Status of Refugees. 1951. https://www.refworld.org/docid/3be01b964.htm.

Decisión de Quito: Solidaridad de UNASUR con Haití, 2010. http://s017.sela.org/es/cumbres-regionales/unasur/decisiones/.

Eves, Chris. 2011. "Haiti's IDP Camp Policy: The Management of Vulnerability." *Advocate's Forum*: 18–24.

Feldmann, Andreas. 2013. "The "phantom state" of Haiti." *Forced Migration Review*, 43: 32–34.

Guide to Effective Practices for RCM [Regional Conference on Migration] *Member Countries: protection for persons moving across borders in the context of disasters.*

Internal Displacement Monitoring Centre (IDMC). 2015. *Estimates 2015: People displaced by disasters*, Geneva: IDCM-Norwegian Refugee Council.

———. 2020. *Global Report on Internal Displacement*, Geneva: IDCM-Norwegian Refugee Council, 2020

International Organization for Migration–Instituto de Políticas Públicas en Derechos Humanos del MERCOSUR (IOM-IPPDH). 2017. *Diagnóstico regional sobre*

migración haitiana, Buenos Aires: International Organization for Migration–Instituto de Políticas Públicas en Derechos Humanos del MERCOSUR.
Jubilut, Liliana L., Camila M. S. de Andrade, and André de L. Madureira. 2016. "Humanitarian Visas: Brazil's experience as a starting point for discussion." *Forced Migration Review*, 53: 76–78.
Jubilut, Liliana L., André de L. Madureira, and Rafael V. Levy. 2018. "Proteção Complementar e Deslocados Ambientais: Itinerários, Limites e Possibilidades." In *"Refugiados Ambientais."* edited by Liliana Lyra Jubilut et al.: 292–321, Boa Vista: Editora da Universidade Federal de Roraima.
Khamis, Marion, and Claudio Osorio. 2013. *América del Sur: Una visión regional de la situación de riesgo de desastres*. UE-Ayuda Humanitaria y Protección Civil y Oficina de las Naciones Unidas para la Reducción de Riesgo por Desastres; UNISDR. http://dipecholac.net/docs/files/735-vision-regional-de-la-situacion-de-riesgo-de-desastres-america-del-sur-final.pdf.
López, Aurelie. 2007. "The Protection of Environmentally Displaced Persons in International Law." *Environmental Law Review*, 37 (2): 365–410.
McAdam, Jane. 2012. *Climate Change, Forced Migration and International Law*. Oxford and New York: Oxford University Press.
Metzer, Tobías. 2014. "La migración haitiana hacia Brasil: estudio en el país de origen." In *La migración haitiana hacia Brasil: Características, oportunidades y desafíos*, edited by Organización Internacional para las Migraciones: 15–32. Buenos Aires: International Organization for Migration.
Mexico Declaration and Plan of Action to Strengthen the International Protection of Refugees in Latin America. 2004. https://www.refworld.org/docid/424bf6914.html.
Miura, Heloisa. 2014. "The Haitian Migration Flow to Brazil: Aftermath of the 2010 Earthquake." In *The State of Environmental Migration 2014. A Review of 2013*, edited by François Gemmene et al.: 149–165. Paris: Institut du développement durable et des relations internationals-IOM.
Muñoz, Tomás. 2019. "El camino hacia la formulación de una nueva política migratoria en Brasil. De la visión militar restrictiva a la apertura." *Desafíos*: 1–45.
Nansen Initiative. 2013. *Disasters and Cross-Border displacement in Central America: Emerging Needs, New Responses. Outcome report*. https://environmentalmigration.iom.int/disasters-and-cross-border-displacement-central-america-emerging-needs-new-responses-conclusions.
National Institute for Migrations (Instituto Nacional para las Migraciones [INM]). 2020. "Oficio Instrucción INM/045/10, Asunto: Medidas Temporales Aplicables para la Internación y Estancia en el País de Extranjeros de Nacionalidad Haitiana," 8 February 2010.
Pacífico, Andrea, Ramos, Erika Pires, Abreu Bastista Claro, Carolina de and Cavalcante de Farias, and Nara Braga. 2015. "The migration of Haitians within Latin America: significance for Brazilian law and policy on asylum and migration" In *A Liberal Tide? Immigration and asylum law and policy in Latin America*, edited by David J. Cantor et al.: 139–152. London: Institute of Latin American Studies, School of Advanced Studies, University of London.
Plan para la contribución solidaria de los países del ALBA al esfuerzo de la reconstrucción de Haití. 2010. http://www.somossur.net/index.php/sur-america-latina/

el-abc-del-alba/216-plan-para-la-contribucion-solidaria-del-alba-para-recon-struccion-de-haiti.
Peraza-Breedy, Jorge. 2014. "Introducción." In *La migración haitiana hacia Brasil: Características, oportunidades y desafíos*, edited by Organización Internacional para las Migraciones: 11–14. Buenos Aires: International Organization for Migration.
Protocol Relating to the Status of Refugees. 1967. https://www.refworld.org/do cid/3ae6b3ae4.html.
Regional Conference on Migration. 1999. Agenda de la IV Conferencia Regional sobre Migración, San Salvador, El Salvador, 26–29 de enero de 1999.
Regional Guidelines on protection and assistance for people displaced across borders and migrants in countries affected by nature disasters.
San José Declaration on Refugees and Displaced Persons. 1994. https://www.ref world.org/docid/4a54bc3fd.html.
Sánchez, Katherin, Jaime Valderas, Karen Messenger, Carolina Sánchez, and Francisco Barrera. 2018. "Haití, la nueva comunidad inmigrante en Chile." *Revista chilena de pediatría*, 89 (2).
Sánchez-Mojica, Beatriz Eugenia. 2018. "Pájaros a punto de volar? La respuesta a la movilidad humana vinculada a desastres ambientales en América Latina." In "*Refugiados" Ambientais*, edited by Liliana Lyra Jubilut et. Al: 230–291. Boa Vista: Universidade Federal de Roraima.
———. 2020. "Refugiados ambientales. Una propuesta de protección a los desplazados trasnacionales por motivos ambientales en América Latina." *Latin American Law Review*, 5: 71–92.
Sánchez-Mojica, Beatriz Eugenia, and Sebastián Rubiano. 2018. *Territorios en transformación, derechos en movimiento. Cambio ambiental y movilidad humana en Colombia*, Bogotá: Universidad de los Andes.
Stavropoulou, Maria. 2008. "Drowned in Definitions?" *Forced Migration Review*, 31:11–12.
Thomaz Diana. 2013. "Post-disaster Haitian migration" *Forced Migration Review*, 43:35–36.
Trabalón, Carina. 2018. "Política de visado y regulación de las fronteras. Un análisis desde la movilidad de haitianos en Sudamérica." *Polis. Revista Latinoamericana*, 51: 163–186.
United Nations High Commissioner for Refugees (UNHCR). 2015 *States Parties to the 1951 Convention relating to the Status of Refugees and the 1967 Protocol*, 2015, available at: http://www.unhcr.org/protection/basic/3b73b0d63/states-parties-1951-convention-its-1967-protocol.html.
———. 2016. *Guidelines on International Protection N° 12. Claims for refugee status related to situations of armed conflict and violence under Article 1A(2) of the 1951 Convention and/or 1967 Protocol relating to the Status of Refugees and the regional refugee definitions.* Doc. HCR/GIP/16/12 02
United Nations International Strategy for Disaster Reduction (UNISDR). 2013. *Impacto de los desastres en América Latina y el Caribe 1990–2011*. Geneva: UNISDR.
Vásquez, Tania, Erika Busse, and Lorena Izaguirre. 2014. "La migración haitiana en Perú y su tránsito hacia Brasil." In *La migración haitiana hacia Brasil: Características, oportunidades y desafíos*, edited by Organización Internacional para las Migraciones: 83–106. Buenos Aires: International Organization for Migration.

Weerasinghe, Sanjula. 2018. *In Harm's Way. International protection in the context of nexus dynamics between conflict or violence and disaster or climate change.* Legal and Protection Policy Research Series, UNHCR PPLA/2018/05.

Weiss Faguen, Patricia. 2013. *Receiving Haitian migrants in the context of the 2010 earthquake.* Geneva: The Nansen Initiative.

PART V COMMENTARY

Current Regional Refugees "Crisis"

Leticia Calderón Chelius

The chapters in Part V show us the current complex migration landscape in Latin America, through an in-depth theoretical and empirical review and analysis that draws on the experience of the authors of each of the chapters, who are mostly academics but also activists.

These chapters take us on a journey through the most recent migratory flows in the region. The case of the North of Central America (NCA; El Salvador, Guatemala, and Honduras, and formerly referred to as the Northern Central America Triangle) is analyzed emphasizing that each country in the NCA must be understood according to its own dynamics as a nation, and, at the same time, as a region of high expulsion and transit migration, as Nelson-Pollard puts it. On the other hand, the Venezuelan displacement, the greatest exodus that the region has faced in its history, is discussed by Jarochinski, Castro, and Sampaio who focus on two of the main reception countries, Colombia and Brazil (Gandini, Lozano, and Prieto 2019).

As part of this section, the Haitian exodus is presented and detailed by Sánchez-Mojica, who, in addition to discussing the vicissitudes of the Haitian migrants throughout the Latin American region, uses this case to open the debate on a fundamental issue: the need to discuss environmental causes as a source of recognition of refugee status, which implies an in-depth review of the normative framework and a description of the causes that justify this international protection. Finally, this section of the book also includes a debate on the legal framework of displacement in Colombia, through a detailed legal historical journey in the context of the peace process. In this chapter, Carneiro adds elements to the understanding of the complexity of the current immigration and refugee process, emphasizing that violence is the main factor in explaining the forced displacement crisis in the Latin American region.

Some of the findings presented in the chapters of this section contribute to an understanding that both governmental and different societies' progress impact on efficient and lasting responses to the problems that result from forced migration. Jarochinski, Castro, and Sampaio draw attention to an important point as they argue that although there are specific events that trigger a mass exodus–which is perceived in public opinion as chaotic and with several consequences to the destination localities, as shown in the case of the arrival of Venezuelans to Roraima in the northern border of Brazil–the reality is that all migratory flows are the result of long-term processes. In the case of Central America, the conditions of poverty and structural violence are exacerbated by the control that local criminal gangs have over their own states (or in complicity with them), so the lack of protection of people's lives and associated insecurity are fundamental factors in explaining that exodus, as Nelson-Pollard shows. As discussed in one of many examples explored by the author, 60 percent of the students express fear of walking to their school; also, by 2017 190,000 people in Honduras and 296,000 in El Salvador were internally displaced. Another relevant fact raised by the author is that in Guatemala, although it is estimated that there are 43,000 people internally displaced, the state has yet to recognize this displacement. A constant in this region, as shown by Nelson-Pollard, is that there are multiple commitments signed by the three countries to alleviate this situation, but there are no indicators to assess the progress in areas that can be used to evaluate specific opportunities and challenges that allow them to address the magnitude of the problem (Basok, Rojas, Candiz 2015).

In the case of Venezuelans, a fundamental issue is the change to national regulations to allow the entry and settlement of this population in the different countries of the region, in light of the increased migration from Venezuela in the past years. A key aspect to explore is the permanent tension between the regional agreements that most countries have signed (which, depending on the government, have changed, as in Brazil or Chile) and the national and even local regulations themselves. Countries like Chile, Ecuador, Panama, and Peru have established visas that previously either did not exist or had other requirements, imposing a bottleneck for Venezuelan migration. In the case of other countries in the region, emergency meetings have been held to generate agreements and solutions to the Venezuelan migration crisis; however, according to Jarochinski, Castro, and Sampaio, these agreements seem to remain only as political declarations, as there is no effective and comprehensive financing to advance these agendas.

Added to this are the national laws that make recognition and subsequent settlement of refugees difficult. A constant across the countries of the region is data showing the low number of asylum seekers recognized as refugees, either because the migrants themselves do not follow this path of humanitarian legal accreditation due to the length of the procedure, or due to the low approval of recognitions. As of October 2019, only 21,000 Venezuelans had obtained refugee status out of 460,000 seeking asylum. In Colombia, the country with the highest number of Venezuelans in its territory, only 3 percent out of 1,687 asylum applications had been approved by April 2019, according to the data presented by Jarochinski, Castro, and Sampaio. Bureaucratic pitfalls are a legal impediment to the facilitation of the next stage of displacement, which is integration. Examples include the nationality laws of each country that create barriers for people trying to solve their legal situation in the long term and, therefore, to generate truly lasting solutions. Jarochinski, Castro, and Sampaio report issues such as the recognition of the nationality of babies born to foreign parents in a territory or the difficulties obtaining a work permit.

An experience that has provided an important lesson in the case of the Venezuelan exodus is Operation Acolhida, a program directed and implemented by the Brazilian army to deal with the massive arrival of people to a small community such as Roraima, at the border of Brazil with Venezuela. Subsequently, a new phase was implemented to relocate this population to different locations throughout the Brazilian territory. The experience left important lessons that are worth highlighting here. First, the pressure received by a host community is often complicated and sometimes unmanageable by local authorities, and requires a federal effort to lighten the burden of a sudden and massive immigration flux. Second, much of the immigration policy depends on the vision that the government in place has, which was seen in the case of Brazil with the arrival of Jair Bolsonaro to the presidency (the same happened in Chile with Sebastián Piñera), who changed the rules and agreements, including international ones, such as leaving the Global Compact on Migration. This lesson is essential to accomplish lasting solutions that seek to generate reception frameworks that go beyond changes in governments.

Among these agreements that could go beyond political situations is the urgent debate that Sánchez-Mojica raises: the need to review the international legal framework of refuge protection to include environmental conditions as trigger for such forced migration. The author points out that an environmental catastrophe by itself might not be an isolated displacement factor; in this type of situation, however, preexisting vulnerabilities, such as the fragility of the state and generalized violence, create scenarios that provoke displacement, not only as an option but also the only possibility for protecting life, integrity, and freedom (Coraza and Gatica 2019).

It is relevant that the entry point to the discussion on environmental displacement is the Haitian exodus, of which a deep analysis is made through the lens of its own history, with a particular emphasis on the 2010 earthquake that devastated the island. The response of the Latin American region was varied and is revised by Sánchez-Mojica country by country. The author subsequently assesses the consequences that this had on the integration experience of the Haitian communities across the region. In the case of Chile, for example, this country went from a generous opening to a practically prohibitive policy given the limitations that were introduced. The latter implied that the procedures for requesting shelter, humanitarian visa, or family reunification should be done exclusively from the capital of Haiti, effectively closing the doors to those who had literally fled their country.

Taking this case as a guiding thread, the author shows how an experience like the Haitian flow radically modified the migration landscape in Latin America, highlighting the urgency of opening up to the international debate and legislating on factors that were not previously considered as drivers of forced migration. The reality of climate change and its consequences are not elements automatically associated with forced displacement, but represents a catastrophe that exposes with all its harshness the limited capabilities of a state to safeguard its own population in extreme circumstances.

The conclusion offered in this section is that the fragility of the state, poverty, corruption, environmental degradation, and the culture of patriarchy that naturalizes sexual violence, are all factors that can result in an exodus that should be considered from a humanitarian perspective. This can be seen through internal displacement (as in the Colombia case, analyzed by Carneiro), or transnational cases that are reviewed in detail in the chapters of this section.

The new migration scenarios of the Latin American region open up many more questions than those that were thought to have been resolved, at least at the legal and conceptual level, but also, as demonstrated in each chapter, there are many lessons learned that force international efforts to be strengthened while facing these humanitarian crises.

Leticia Calderón Chelius has a PhD in Political Science from FLACSO-Mexico and she is member of the Mexican Academy of Sciences. She coordinates the Xenophobia Research Group within the INTEGRA/Conacyt Network and the website www.migrantologos.mx. She is a member of the board of trustees of the Mexican civil association Without Borders, is advisor to Organization of Mexicans in Exile, and is member of the board of directors of Other Dreamers in Action. She has taught in institutions in Mexico and abroad, and has several publications on the political sociology of migration. She currently works at Instituto Mora.

References

Basok, Belanger D. Tanya, Martha Luz Rojas, and Guillermo Candiz, eds. 2015. *Thinking transit migration: Precarity, mobility and self-making in Mexico.* Canada: Palgrave.

Coraza de los Santos, Enrique, and Monica Gatica. 2019. "Reflexionando sobre el carácter forzado en las movilidades humanas." *Revista de Historia Social y de las Mentalidades,* 23(2): 111–131.

Gandini, Luciana, Fernardo Lozano, and Victoria Prieto, eds. 2019. *Crisis y migración de población venezolan: Entre la desproteciόny la seguridad jurídica en Latinoamérica.* Mexico: UNAM.

AFTERWORD

Driving with the Rearview Mirror?

Latin America and Refugee Protection

Carolina Moulin

It seems fair to conclude that Latin American experiences with asylum are rather ambivalent in terms of its framework, its effectiveness, and its ability to respond and build long-lasting trends toward robust protection of refugees and prevention of forced displacement. Contributions in this volume highlight the mixed results of two centuries of evolution and the difficulty in translating multi-scalar and multilevel governance into enduring protection and integration policies at the national and subnational levels (see Vera Espinoza, Sanchez-Mojica, and Jarochinski Silva et al. in this volume).

Despite considerable gains in relation to the normative dimension of the refugee regimes, particularly at the regional level, evidenced in the Cartagena Declaration on Refugees (Cartagena Declaration) process and its subsequent updates (and commitments), Latin American countries have faced ongoing dynamics of displacement caused by multiple and overlapping causes that range from institutional and political instability, staggering levels of violence in both urban and rural areas, and environmental collapse due to natural and human-induced processes (see Jubilut, Vera Espinoza, and Mezzanotti in this volume).

Responses to such phenomena have created the conditions for experimenting with ad hoc solutions, sometimes enabling alternative policies that have enlarged the scope and depth of protection, as was the case with the Conferencia Internacional sobre Refugiados Centroamericanos (International Conference on Central American Refugees) process back in the 1980s, and, other times, consolidating structural patterns of inequality or discrimination, and/or reinforcing displacement and humanitarian needs.

In this short conclusion, I focus, based on the contributions to this volume, on two major aspects of Latin America's approach to thinking and devising solutions to refugee and displacement issues. The first, and perhaps most salient aspect of the regional response, lies in its flexible, yet sustained, legal and institutional innovations in relation to who are the displaced and to what counts as displacement, thus enabling a stronger role for courts, administrative processes, and increased multilateral cooperation between national, regional, and international actors. We can speak of a rising normative assemblage that has consolidated what has been framed as a regional approach to refugee protection.

In this assemblage, Latin America has been at the forefront of a robust political mobilization of civil society and refugee and migrant's organizations as a productive and somewhat autonomous force that has systematically pressed national and regional systems toward more inclusive and participatory mechanisms and procedures.

A second and more deleterious aspect of the regional experience lies in its reactive approach, oriented toward responding to crises and events, with little attention paid to the social and political environment required not only to prevent displacement, but also to think seriously and hard about integration and life after and during displacement. These two processes are, obviously, connected, and have produced a trend toward understanding protection increasingly in terms of regularization and humanitarian response, and therefore, in emergency and provisional terms.

Fischel de Andrade and Rushing and Lizcano Rodriguez (in this volume) provide a comprehensive overview of how Latin American countries have developed innovative ways of dealing and translating forced displacement definitions to specific and contextual demands in the region. From the expanded definition of refugees adopted in Cartagena in 1984 to the recognition of internal displacement as a major protection issue in San José in 1994, Latin American countries have repeatedly reinforced an expansive and inclusive categorization of displacement that has enabled the enlargement of the refugee system and the development of situated practices of status determination. Expansive definitions have been systematically incorporated into national legislation and procedures, thus evincing a regional approach that has been more open and flexible than the restrictive and securitized trends in northern, richer countries.

The role of the Inter-American Human Rights System, as well as of regional courts, has been pivotal in calling states on their role as providers of rights and security for populations in need of international protection (Botero and Casagrande in this volume). Good practices are particularly salient in issues related to statelessness, sponsored by strong commitments in Brazil Declaration and Plan of Action: a Framework for Cooperation and Regional Solidarity to Strengthen the International Protection of Refugees, Displaced and Stateless Persons in Latin America and the Caribbean (Brazil Declaration and Plan of Action).[1] (2014) and the subsequent adherence (or pledging to accede) of several Latin American countries to the 1954 Convention relating to the Status of Stateless Persons and 1961 Convention on the Reduction of Statelessness.

Another important aspect, developed in the contributions by Freier and Luzes and Brumat in this volume, relates to the rise of subsidiary protection mechanisms in the region, enacted through legal solutions that now compose the humanitarian assemblage of protection. Residency permits and humanitarian visas have become central traits in the management of regional circulations and have provided an alternate route for regularization for important groups of displaced persons, including Haitians and Venezuelans.

On the positive side of regional protection, one has to highlight the central role played by civil society and refugees' and migrants' movements in many of the most progressive developments, both legal and institutional, that have imprinted the regional approach to asylum and migration. From the 1980s onwards, not only legal protection but also, and importantly, integration and resettlement policies have been produced (or induced) by strong and durable articulation and mobilization of nongovernmental organizations, of many inklings and designs. Religious-based institutions with a transnational base, such as Caritas and the Jesuit Service, have historically provided a sociopolitical base in many countries and have acted as a central hub for thinking and enacting public policies for refugee and migrant populations. At the local level, the history of solidary cities in Latin America has been constituted by and for migrants and refugees. Experiences such as those in the city of São Paulo might be regarded as one of the success cases of protection in urban spaces in the region. São Paulo has developed local legislation and institutions devoted exclusively to implement access to rights and to establish direct participation of refugees and migrants in public policy. Though governmental initiatives have played a pivotal role, the historical process that resulted in a pro-rights agenda for migrants and refugees in such a complex and unequal urban setting was consequential to the robust and systematic mobilization of a myriad of migrant communities that pressed and demanded voice and resources. Advocacy groups, especially those operating through the legal system, have been crucial in litigating strategically in national and regional courts, thus forcing for more transparency and coordination between different governmental agencies and bureaucracies.

That said, a general trait observed in the evolution of the regional system lies in its reactive and, often times, improvised policies and arrangements to respond to sudden and protracted displacements. From the Central American crisis in the 1980s to the recent Venezuelan exodus, solutions have been devised on the go, with governmental cooperation and legal responses designed accordingly.

Far from a proactive and sustained response to structural dynamics in the region, subsidiary protection mechanisms have served the ebb and flow of political tides, produced ephemeral alignments between governmental and social actors and, not unsurprisingly, reduced our understanding of protection to issues of regularization and legal status. There is little discussion in political circles about how the fragmentation of categories (Zetter 2007) has created a confusing bureaucratic meander for migrants and refugees to navigate and produced a complex network of humanitarian governance, increasingly illegible and unaccountable in terms of its mandate and functions.

Brazil, hailed for its legal response to Haitians and Venezuelans, is a case in point. For almost four years the country waited to see the impact of the influx of Venezuelans at its borders. Only in 2017 was a temporary residency enabled with so many administrative demands that the number of asylum seekers exponentially grew. Faced with a clog in its refugee status determination procedures, the reactive decision was to reduce the threshold for residency permits and, at last in 2019, adopt the Cartagena Declaration refugee definition to expedite processing of Venezuelan asylum seekers. Similar moves have been observed, for example in Ecuador in 2009, with its open door policy, that recognized more than fifty thousand Colombians as refugees (White 2011). The granting of refugee status becomes a solution to an administrative and logistical "problem" created by a reactive and ad hoc humanitarian policy.

It is also important to mention the increasing role played by technology and digital procedures in this regional assemblage. A growing number of borders, reception centers, camps, shelters, and migration authorities now use biometrics and forms of digitalization to recognize, process, and control migrant and refugee bodies. Fingerprints, online systems, iris scanning, and digital documents now compose the material network of regional modes of assessing and monitoring circulations. Countries like Brazil are moving toward completely digital asylum application systems, thus posing a new and important trend in the possibilities of access to procedures and also in migrant and refugees' capacity to respond to and to react to, if necessary, politics of care and control (Moulin and Magalhães 2020). As Stierl remarks, looking at the European case and in a premonition to a transition we might be witnessing in Latin America: "Current border regimes increasingly infiltrate mobile subjects themselves, not merely by harvesting bodily information, but also by creating border obstacles that inscribe themselves as lingering feelings of anxiety, fear, unrest, precariousness and trauma onto these contemporary subjects" (Stierl 2017: 224) .

The current political scene in Latin America has also highlighted the importance of geopolitical alignments and the need for making refugees' and migrants' rights and protection a matter of states and not of governments. Recent changes toward right-wing and conservative governments in several countries of the region, growing political and social unrest marked by large demonstrations, and protests against austerity policies and social inequalities have reinforced structural challenges to the regional regimes. In a continent marked by outrageous levels of violence, including state-sponsored lethality, and by one of the largest discrepancies between rich and poor, how can we think of refugee and migrant citizenships (Nyers 2015)? If citizenship is, in most countries of the region, a far-fetched and largely incomplete promise, how do we bridge the divide between those that arrive in conditions of vulnerability and precarity and those who are already there yet almost permanently excluded? Gender, racial, and socioeconomic disparities produce a deleterious context for integration and durable solutions. It is no surprise, then, that little has been done in terms of long-term public policies that tackle intercultural dialogue and life after refuge.

This is a particularly worrisome aspect, since it forces us to rethink asylum and migration in tandem with development and equality. Though these aspects have been highlighted in several of the commitments produced after the 1984 Cartagena Declaration (as stated, for example, in the 2004 Mexico Declaration and Plan of Action to Strengthen the International Protection of Refugees in Latin America), the region, as a whole, has been less effective in fostering integrated solutions to refugees, migrants, and their local communities.

The political scenario has also been marked by a rise in emergency response and a growing participation of military and security agencies in both border control and humanitarian assistance. Militarization of Latin American societies has come hand in hand with the militarization of several aspects of refugee and migrant care and control. This can be viewed in the central participation of security professionals in processes of refugee status determination (both formally and informally) and in the increasingly visible presence of such actors in emergency contexts. In some cases, military personnel have been responsible for producing safe areas for humanitarian provision, but in others they have subsumed almost entirely national policies for refugee and migrant populations. In a region marked by a tragic history with the penal and military arms of the state, this is a trend that must be monitored and watched with, at a minimum, a grain of salt.

Driving with the rearview mirror, Latin American countries and societies would do well to remember the historical processes that have created an expansive and somewhat inclusive legal and institutional framework for the displaced through its regional regimes, as this book aptly demonstrates. But they also must see how such guarantees can melt into thin air without strong social and political commitments to development and security and less reactive strategies toward displacement. The past is important, but the road ahead is indispensable and there is little evidence that our displacements' crises will not become permanent.

Carolina Moulin Aguiar is Professor at the Center for Regional Planning and Development, Federal University of Minas Gerais, Brazil (CEDEPLAR/ UFMG). She holds a PhD in Political Science from McMaster University, Canada. She is Executive-Secretary of the Brazilian International Relations Association and Associate Editor of Review of International Studies. She currently coordinates the UNHCR Sergio Vieira de Mello Chair and the Center for Latin American and Caribbean Studies at UFMG. She researches and writes on borders, human mobility, citizenship and international relations.

Note

1. Available at https://www.refworld.org/docid/5487065b4.html.

References

Moulin Aguiar, Carolina and Bruno Magalhães. 2020. "Operation shelter as humanitarian infrastructure: material and normative renderings of Venezuelan migration in Brazil." *Citizenship Studies*, 24(5): 642–662.
Nyers, Peter. 2015. "Migrant Citizenships and Autonomous Mobilities." *Migration, Mobility and Displacement*, 1 (1): 23–39.
Stierl, Maurice. 2017. "Excessive Migration, Excessive Governance–Border Entanglements in Greek EUrope." In *The Borders of "Europe': Autonomy of Migration, Tactics of Bordering*, edited by Nicholas De Genova: 210:232. Durham, NC.: Duke University Press.
White, Ana G. 2011. In the shoes of refugees: providing protection and solutions for displaced Colombians in Ecuador. *New Issues in Refugee Research*, 217. https://www.unhcr.org/4e4bd6c19.pdf.
Zetter, Roger. 2007. More Labels, Fewer Refugees: Remaking the Refugee Label in an Era of Globalization. *Journal of Refugee Studies*, 20 (2) : 172–192. https://doi.org/10.1093/jrs/fem011.

ANNEX

Legal Frameworks for Refugee Protection in Latin America

Alyssa Marie Kvalvaag

Introduction

This annex was designed to provide a structured overview of legal frameworks for refugee protection in Latin America and is composed of three sections listing protection information in the regional and national levels. Section 1 provides information on the regime of the Cartagena Declaration on Refugees (Cartagena Declaration). Section 2 lists the regime of the Inter-American Human Rights System's (IAHRS) main documents for migrants in general and refugees in particular. Section 3 profiles refugee protection in the region, describing legislation at the national level based on seven categories: (1) right of asylum in the constitution, (2) law on refugees, (3) humanitarian visas, (4) adoption of the regional definition of refugees, (5) no deadline for applying for refugee status, (6) noncriminalization of entry, and (7) the right to work. These practices were selected for being connected to protection and because they are practices that set Latin America as a region apart. For this purpose, Latin America will encompass seventeen countries: Argentina, Bolivia, Brazil, Chile, Colombia, Costa Rica, Ecuador, El Salvador, Guatemala, Honduras, Mexico, Nicaragua, Panama, Paraguay, Peru, Uruguay, and Venezuela.

Information for this annex on issues of policy largely use the United Nations Commission for Refugees' (UNHCR) Refworld, the UNHCR's website for Latin America (ACNUR), and the OAS Database of Migration Legislation in the Americas (MILEX) and have been supplemented by the third cycle of UNHCR country compilation reports submitted for the

Universal Periodic Review. Documents and decisions of the Inter-American Human Rights System, can also largely be found at Refworld.[1] The information provided in this annex (extended version available online) is intended to be a tool for further research, and therefore is not exhaustive.[2]

1. The Cartagena Declaration Regime

Cartagena Declaration

Date   22 November 1984

Adopted By   Belize, Colombia, Costa Rica, El Salvador, Guatemala, Honduras, Mexico, Nicaragua, Panama, and Venezuela. Although the declaration was originally adopted by ten countries, it is now additionally embraced by Argentina, Bolivia, Brazil, Chile, Ecuador, Paraguay, Peru, and Uruguay.

San José Declaration

Date   07 December 1994

Adopted By   Argentina, Bahamas, Belize, Bolivia, Brazil, Chile, Colombia, Costa Rica, Dominican Republic, Ecuador, El Salvador, Guatemala, Honduras, Nicaragua, Panama, Peru, and Uruguay.

Mexico Declaration and Plan of Action

Date   16 November 2004

Adopted By   Argentina, Belize, Bolivia, Brazil, Chile, Colombia, Costa Rica, Ecuador, El Salvador, Guatemala, Guyana, Honduras, Mexico, Nicaragua, Panama, Paraguay, Peru, Suriname, Uruguay, and Venezuela.

Brazil Declaration and Plan of Action

Date   03 December 2014

Adopted By   Antigua and Barbuda, Argentina, Bahamas, Barbados, Belize, Bolivia, Brazil, Cayman Islands, Chile, Colombia, Costa Rica, Cuba, Curacao, El Salvador, Ecuador, Guatemala, Guyana, Haiti, Honduras, Jamaica, Mexico, Nicaragua, Panama, Paraguay, Peru, Saint Lucia, Suriname, Trinidad and Tobago, Turks and Caicos, Uruguay, and Venezuela.

2. The IAHRS Regime
Inter-American Court of Human Rights

Advisory Opinions

Case	Advisory Opinion OC-25/18
Parties Involved	Ecuador
Date	30 May 2018
Topics Debated	Institution of asylum

Case	Advisory Opinion OC-21/14
Parties Involved	Argentina, Brazil, Paraguay, and Uruguay
Date	19 August 2014
Topics Debated	Rights and guarantees of children in the context of migration and/or international protection

Case	Advisory Opinion OC-18/03
Parties Involved	Mexico
Date	17 September 2003
Topics Debated	Principle of equality and nondiscrimination

Case	Advisory Opinion OC-16/99
Parties Involved	Mexico
Date	01 October 1999
Topics Debated	Principle of due process, minimum judicial guarantees

Contentious Cases

Case	Case of Roche Azaña et al. v. Nicaragua (Case 403)
Date	03 June 2020
Topics Debated	Right to life and personal integrity, judicial guarantees and protection

Case	Expelled Dominicans and Haitians v. Dominican Republic (Case 282)
Date	28 August 2014
Topics Debated	Discrimination, migrant rights, the right to nationality

Case	Pacheco Tineo Family v. Plurinational State of Bolivia (Case 272)
Date	25 November 2013
Topics Debated	International protection, *non-refoulement*, refugee status determination, asylum procedures, procedural fairness, voluntary repatriation

Case	Nadege Dorzema et al. v. Dominican Republic (Case 251)
Date	24 October 2012
Topics Debated	Nondiscrimination due to immigration status, migrant rights, access to legal procedures

Case	Vélez Loor v. Panama (Case 218)
Date	23 November 2010
Topics Debated	Nondiscrimination due to immigration status, immigration detention, migrant rights, the right to liberty and security[3]

Inter-American Commission on Human Rights

Resolutions

Case	Resolution 41/2020
Date	27 July 2020
Topics Debated	Rights to life, personal integrity, and health of migrants detained in detention centers considering the threat of COVID-19

Case	Resolution 02/18
Date	14 March 2018
Topics Debated	Cartagena Declaration, asylum seekers, complementary forms of protection

Case	Resolution 03/08
Date	25 July 2008
Topics Debated	Migrant rights, *non-refoulement*, return conditions

Merits Reports

Case	Report N. 78/11 (Case 12.586)
Parties Involved	John Doe et al v. Canada
Date	21 July 2011
Topics Debated	Access to procedures, asylum policy, *refoulement*, right to seek asylum, due process

Case	Report N. 51/96 (Case 10.675)
Parties Involved	The Haitian Centre for Human Rights et al. v. United States of America
Date	13 March 1997
Topics Debated	Denial of refugee status, involuntary repatriation, *refoulement*, rescue at sea/interception at sea

3. Good Practices in Refugee Protection

Argentina

- Right of asylum indirectly established in 1994 Constitution (art. 75).
- Specific refugee law (Law 26.165, 2006) and general migration law (Law 25.871, 2003).
- Humanitarian visas (Law 25.871, 2003, arts. 23(m)-(n), 29, 34).
- Has adopted the regional definition of refugee.
- No deadline for applying for refugee status.
- Noncriminalization of irregular entry.
- Grants asylum seekers the right to work.

Bolivia

- Right of asylum in the 2009 Constitution (art. 29).
- Specific refugee law (Law 251, 2012) and general migration law (Law 370, 2013).
- Humanitarian visas (Law 370, 2013 art. 30(4)).
- Has adopted the regional definition of refugee.
- Ninety-day deadline for applying for refugee status.
- Noncriminalization of irregular entry.
- Grants asylum seekers the right to work.

Brazil

- Right of asylum in the 1988 Constitution (art. 4).
- Specific refugee law (Law 9.474, 1997) and general migration law (Law 13.445, 2017).
- Humanitarian visas (Law 13.445, 2017, art. 14 §3).
- Has adopted the regional definition of refugee.
- No deadline for applying for refugee status.
- Criminal procedures pertaining to irregular entry are suspended until end of refugee status determination.
- Grants asylum seekers the right to work.

Chile

- Specific refugee law (Law 20.430, 2010) and general migration law (Decree 1.094, 1975).
- Has adopted the regional definition of refugee.
- Ten-day deadline for applying for refugee status.
- Noncriminalization of irregular entry, provided those who wish to apply for refugee status present themselves to the authorities within ten days.
- Grants asylum seekers the right to work.

Colombia

- Right of asylum in the 1991 Constitution (art. 36).
- Specific refugee law (Decree 2.840, 2013; Decree 1.067, 2015) and general migration law (Decree 0.834, 2013).
- Has adopted the regional definition of refugee.
- Two-month deadline for applying for refugee status.

Costa Rica

- Right of asylum in the 1949 Constitution (art. 31).
- Specific refugee law (Decree 36.831-G, 2011) and general migration law (Law 8.764, 2010).
- Humanitarian visas (Law 8.764, 2010, arts. 93, 94(12)).
- Administrative Dispute Tribunal, 2014 (vote number 0103-2014 IV) concluded the Cartagena Declaration should be interpreted as a part of the national system.
- No deadline for applying for refugee status.
- Noncriminalization of irregular entry.
- Can grant asylum seekers right to work if request for refugee status determination is not resolved within three months.

Ecuador

- Right of asylum in the 2008 Constitution (art. 41).
- General migration law (Law 938, 2017).
- Humanitarian visas (Law 938, 2017, arts. 58, 66).
- Has adopted the regional definition of refugee.
- Ninety-day deadline for applying for refugee status.
- Noncriminalization of irregular entry.
- Indirectly grants asylum seekers the right to work.

El Salvador

- Right of asylum in the 1983 Constitution (art. 28).
- Specific refugee law (Decree 918, 2002) and general migration law (Decree 286, 2019).
- Humanitarian visas (Decree 286, 2019).
- Has adopted the regional definition of refugee.
- Five-business-day deadline for applying for refugee status.
- Noncriminalization of entry for those who present before the authorities without delay.
- Grants asylum seekers the right to work.

Guatemala

- Right of asylum in the 1985 Constitution (art. 27).
- Specific refugee law (National Migratory Authority Agreement 2-2019, 2019) and general migration law (Decree 44, 2016).
- Humanitarian visas (Decree 44, 2016, art. 68).
- Has adopted the regional definition of refugee.
- No deadline for applying for refugee status.
- Noncriminalization of irregular entry.
- Grants asylum seekers the right to work.

Honduras

- Right of asylum in the 1982 Constitution (art. 101).
- Specific refugee law (Executive Decree PCM-053, 2013) and general migration law (Decree 208-2003, 2004).
- Humanitarian visas (Decree 208-2003, 2004, art. 39).
- Has adopted the regional definition of refugees.
- No deadline for applying for refugee status.
- Noncriminalization of irregular entry.
- Indirectly grants foreigners, and thereby asylum seekers, restrictive access to paid employment.

Mexico

- Right of asylum in the 2011 Constitution (art. 11).
- Specific refugee law (Law on Refugees, Complementary Protection, and Political Asylum, 2011) and general migration law (Migration Act, 2011).
- Humanitarian visas (Law on Refugees, Complementary Protection, and Political Asylum, 2011, art. 52(V)).
- Has adopted the regional definition of refugee.
- Thirty-business-day deadline for applying for refugee status.
- Noncriminalization of irregular entry.
- Opens possibility of granting asylum seekers the right to work.

Nicaragua

- Right of asylum in 1987 Constitution (art. 5).
- Specific refugee law (Law 655, 2008) and general migration law (Law 761, 2011).
- Humanitarian visas (Law 761, 2011, art. 220).
- Has adopted the regional definition of refugee.
- One-year deadline for applying for refugee status.
- Noncriminalization of irregular entry.
- Grants asylum seekers the right to work.

Panama

- Specific refugee law (Decree 5, 2018; Law 74, 2013) and general migration law (Decree 3, 2008).
- Humanitarian visas (Decree 3, 2008, art. 6(9)).
- Six-month deadline for applying for refugee status.
- Noncriminalization of irregular entry.

Paraguay

- Right of asylum in the 1992 Constitution (art. 43).
- Specific refugee law (Law 1.938, 2002) and general migration law (Law 978, 1996).
- Has adopted the regional definition of refugee.
- No deadline for applying for refugee status.
- Grants asylum seekers the right to work.

Peru

- Right of asylum in the 1993 Constitution (art. 36).
- Specific refugee law (Law 27.891, 2002; Law 27.840, 2002) and general migration law (Decree 1.350, 2017).
- Humanitarian visas (Decree 1.350, 2017, art. 29.2(k)).
- Has adopted the regional definition of refugee.
- Thirty-day deadline for applying for refugee status.
- Noncriminalization of irregular entry.
- Grants asylum seekers the right to work.

Uruguay

- Specific refugee law (Law 18.076, 2006; Law 18.382, 2007) and general migration law (Law 18.250, 2008).
- Humanitarian visas (Decree 356/018, 2018 Regulations to Law 18.250, 2008, art. 1(f)).
- Has adopted the regional definition of refugee.
- No deadline for applying for refugee status.
- Noncriminalization of irregular entry.
- Indirectly grants asylum seekers the right to work.

Venezuela

- Right of asylum in the 1999 Constitution (art. 69).
- Specific refugee law (Law 37.296, 2001) and general migration law (Law 37.944, 2004).
- No explicit established deadline for applying for refugee status.
- Noncriminalization of irregular entry.

Alyssa Marie Kvalvaag currently works as a PhD Research Fellow in Sociology at the Faculty of Social Sciences, Nord University, Bodø, Norway, where she is researching the integration of immigrants in the north of Norway. Her scholarly research focuses on international migration, immigrant integration, and human rights, using qualitative methods. She holds a Master of Science degree in human rights and multiculturalism from the University of South-Eastern Norway, Drammen, Norway. Kvalvaag has previously worked at Women at Risk, International, an anti-human trafficking organization, and Bethany Christian Services offices in the United States and Ethiopia.

Notes

1. More information about good practices in national legislation may be found at the UNHCR's website for Latin America (see https://www.acnur.org/buenas-practicas.html) and more in-depth detailing of the right to work for refugees and asylum seekers in Latin America is available in the report (Grupo Articulador 2018).
2. An extended version of the annex—which includes more in-depth profiling of each section as well as further references—is available at the publisher website (see https://www.berghahnbooks.com/title/JubilutLatin).
3. Provisional measures have adopted by the Inter-American Court of Human Rights on 26 May 2020 and 29 July 2020, indicating the right to health, life, and personal integrity of individuals found in migrant detention centers. Requires Panama to ensure access to essential health-care services, including early detection and treatment of COVID-19.

References

ACNUR. n.d. Accessed August 14, 2020. https://www.acnur.org/.
Grupo Articulador Regional del Plan de Acción Brasil 2017. 2018. *El derecho al trabajo de las personas solicitantes de asilo y refugiadas en américa Latina y el Caribe.*
MILEX. n.d. "Database on Migration Legislation in the Americas." Accessed August 14, 2020. http://www.migracionoea.org/index.php/en/milex-en.html.
Refworld. n.d. Accessed August 14, 2020. https://www.refworld.org/.

Index

access to documentation, 214, 218
accountability, 101, 104, 312, 316, 335
acquisition of nationality, 140–41, 186, 195
adjudicatory jurisdiction, 130, 153, 160, 170
admission, 206, 212, 215, 216, 219, 243, 279, 284
advisory jurisdiction, 130, 139, 151, 153, 160, 189
advisory body, 129, 130
Africa, 13, 31, 38, 40, 98, 109, 277, 333, 340; African descent, 4, 126; African Refugee Regime, 11, 208; enslaved, 333; North Africa, 230; Organization of African Unity (OAU), 32, 108, 229, 277, 327
African Charter and Court of Human and Peoples' Rights, 109
afro-descendant, 105, 183; communities, 333; peoples, 127; victims, 333
age, 101, 163, 183, 192, 213, 215, 219, 286–87. *See also* vulnerability
agencies, 55–57, 62, 132, 185, 248, 303, 305, 308–10, 313, 360–61, 363, 372, 399, 401
agency, 54, 62, 82, 85, 88
inter-agency, 61
Agenda for Protection, 81, 119
alternative pathways, 218
amnesty, 243–44, 283, 336, 339
analysis, 12, 53, 59, 78, 90, 96–97, 99, 116, 142, 151–53, 156, 172, 215, 257, 264–65, 277, 288, 298, 304–5, 315, 377, 392, 395; comparative, 311; double level of, 84, 120; dual, 5; interdisciplinary, 16; legal, 97, 230, 257, 267, 278; multilevel, 6; objective, 136; qualitative, 240; rhetorical, 85; thematic, 81; well-founded, 296
Antigua and Barbuda, 19n11, 198n2, 199n19, 404
architecture of refugee protection, 3, 7, 11, 13–17, 203; multilevel, 2; of the GCR, 228; of the Victims Law, 332; of the peace, 336
Argentina, 4, 54, 86, 88–89, 133, 157, 206–7, 217, 404–5, 407; asylum claims, 213; asylum protection, 384; gender identity law, 213; Haitian refugees, 373–74; humanitarian visas, 206, 212, 280–81, 379; immigrant law, 143, 263–64; migration routes, 372; migratory crisis, 353; political situation, 33; RAM, 238–40, 242–45, 246, 248; refugee children, 214; refugee law, 257–58, 260–63, 265–67; RSD, 207, 211; Statelessness, 186, 191; voluntary pledges, 185
armed conflict, 43–44, 58, 323–24, 327, 331–32, 378, 385
internal tensions, 327
armed confrontation, 34, 330
Asia, 13, 31, 98, 109, 116, 228, 230
assessments, 86, 89, 90, 204, 305
asylum, 14, 88, 90, 103–4, 107–8, 143, 145, 156, 170, 256, 376, 380, 383;

application, 134, 136–37, 206, 247, 261, 268, 279, 311, 394; concepts, 37; gender, 173; human right, 158; in Africa, 31; international protection, 381; legal framework, 407–11; legislation, 86, 118, 257, 260; national laws, 384; *non-refoulement,* 262; Peru, 283–84, 287; policies, 171; political, 2; principle, 117; procedure, 138, 219, 356; protection, 152, 169; quality, 218, 229; receive, 133–34, 136, 155; regime, 34, 358; regional approach, 399; returning, 172; right to, 1, 6–7, 151, 159, 161, 164, 299, 403; seekers, 32–33, 35, 38–39, 79, 85, 117, 126–33, 135, 139, 161, 171, 191, 231, 297, 314–16, 356, 394; solutions, 118; system, 313, 359; temporary, 40; tradition, 33, 44, 97, 145, 154; treaties, 156; Venezuela, 282, 400; vulnerable, 206
austerity policies, 401
authority, 135–36, 138, 170, 196, 260, 262, 267, 281, 306, 376
autonomy, 246, 333

Bahamas, 207, 373, 404
Barbados, 19n11, 404
Barichello, Stefania, 99, 145, 169
barriers, 89, 106, 190, 195, 285, 288–89, 349, 352, 394
basic rights, 85, 99, 211, 238, 264, 297
Belize, 38, 45n2, 133, 206, 258, 263, 311, 313, 404
belonging to a social group, 154
biometrics, 191, 400
birth registration, 183, 187, 190–91, 214
Bolivia, 4, 12, 33, 38; domestic immigration law, 263–67; domestic refugee law, 260–63; humanitarian visas, 280; legislation, 86; migration, 374, 377, 384; migration and refugee law, 258; Pacheco Tineo Family v. Plurinational State of Bolivia, 151, 159–60; RAM, 241, 245; recognition of refugee status, 9; refugee protection, 404, 406–7; regional definition, 133; right to asylum, 210; RSD, 211; violence, 58
border control, 128, 289, 349, 354, 360, 401
borders, 56, 60, 64–65, 79–80, 101–2, 105, 119, 136–37, 162, 172, 217, 243, 306, 309, 311, 314, 316, 347, 400; closed, 126, 307, 359; militarization, 127; natural and artificial, 348–49; nature disasters, 380–82
Borders of Solidarity program, 80, 83, 85, 87, 90, 229
Brazil, 4, 8–9, 154; asylum tradition, 154; Global Compact on Refugees, 207, 210–12; Haitians, 373–78; humanitarian visas, 280–81; legal frameworks, 403–5, 408; New York Declaration, 206; RAM, 244–46; reception, 392–94, 400; refugee and immigration legislation, 257–58, 260–63, 265–66, 358–59; refugee definition, 133; Regional Resettlement Program, 78, 80, 86–89; SJD, 54; statelessness, 191; Venezuelans, 238–40, 346–51, 353, 357–62; voluntary pledges, 185; *See also* BPA (Brazilian Plan of Action), the 100 Points of Brasilia
Brazilian Constitution, 358
Brazilian Refugee Act in 1997 (Law 9.474/97), 262, 383
bureaucracy, 212, 359

Canada, 88, 154, 169–72, 314, 372–73, 407; *See also* John Doe v. Canada
Caribbean subregion, 104
Cartagena +30, 101, 186, 229
Cartagena +30 Initiative, 101
Cartagena Declaration, 2, 7, 11, 13, 17, 31–32, 35, 39, 40–44, 53, 55, 58–59, 68–69, 77, 79, 81, 84, 86, 96, 98–99, 108–9, 116–20, 131–33, 152, 155–56, 161, 163–64, 182–86, 197, 207–8, 210, 229, 247–48, 256, 261–62, 268, 277–79, 281, 284, 295–96, 327, 346, 352, 356, 358, 370, 371, 375–76, 380–85, 397, 400–401, 403–4, 406, 408

Cartagena process, 98–99, 102, 105–6, 109–10, 161, 310,
categorization of displacement, 398
Cayman Islands, 404
Central America, 4, 13, 32, 34–5, 38–41, 44, 54, 56, 125–26, 206, 260, 310, 314–15, 349, 393, 400
challenges, 2–4, 7, 11–15, 33, 53, 59–60, 62–63, 68, 85–86, 90, 100, 103–4, 107, 110, 129, 133, 145, 155–56, 183, 185–86, 204, 207, 211, 217–20, 237,40, 267, 294–95, 299, 304–5, 309–10, 315–16, 334–35, 347, 352, 354–55, 382, 393, 401
child migration, 213
children, 14, 66, 101, 105–6, 127–27, 133–34, 136, 160, 162, 190, 215, 263, 286, 306–7, 353; documentation, 360; migratory status, 140, 192; nationality, 189, 356–57; protection, 158, 195, 213–14, 332, 350, 405; recruitment, 65; rights, 242, 288; separated, 12, 315; unaccompanied, 86, 118, 164, 183, 355; violence, 213, 308
Chile, 4, 9, 13, 54; Haitian exodus, 372–74, 378–79, 395; humanitarian visa, 107, 281, 283, 289; immigration and refugee legislation, 133, 154, 258, 261–63, 265–67, 280; legal frameworks, 403–4, 408; MPA implementation, 78, 80, 85–89; *Pacheco Tineo family v. Plurinational State of Bolivia*, 159; political situation, 33; RAM implementation, 238, 240–41, 245; RSD, 211; Venezuelan citizens, 352–53, 393; visa of democratic responsibility, 248;
citizenship, 241, 278, 283, 353, 355–57, 401
civil society organizations, 64, 100–101, 104–5, 145, 173, 182, 187, 215, 305, 311, 315, 360–61
civil society participants, 101
civil war, 34, 55, 65, 132, 305, 340n3
climate change, 52, 66–67, 126, 382, 395
closings of borders, 126, 354, 395

coexistence, 1, 2, 6, 9–11, 210, 212, 215, 336
Cold War, 41, 55, 229–30, 325
collective expulsions, 136, 143
colloquium on the International Protection of Refugees in Latin America, Mexico and Panama, 6–7, 38, 53
colloquim in Asylum and International Protection of Refugees in Latin America, 35, 37
Colombia, 4; Afro-Colombian communities, 333; asylum, 213; conflict, 78, 86, 325–27, 332, 335–36; displacement, 2, 13, 79–80, 83, 141, 323, 328–30, 392; humanitarian visas, 281, 283, 286; migration and refugee legislation, 258–60, 263–64, 266, 324, 330, 332, 403–4, 408; national legislation, 54, 58; peace agreement, 334; peace process, 338–39; protection, 79, 154, 331; refugee, 38, 86, 133, 210; resettlement, 87; SJD, 54; statelessness, 188–90; temporary stay permits, 248; Venezuelan, 282, 346–362, 394, 400; violence, 58, 63, 68, 89, 324, 330; voluntary pledges, 185
colonialism, 229
common trends, 257, 260, 263, 295
complexity, 5–6, 10–11, 15, 204, 294, 324, 362, 370, 393; complexities, 6, 90, 362
compliance, 64, 103, 157, 160, 172, 285, 332, 334
Comprehensive Refugee Response Framework (CRRF), 66, 206, 230, 311
Comprehensive Regional Protection and Solutions Framework, 12, 62, 66, 68, 206, 304, 311
confidential, 214, 334; confidentiality, 138, 262
control, 68, 83, 127–28, 135, 143, 189, 213, 243, 285, 289, 297, 305–9, 326, 330, 349–50, 354, 360, 383, 393, 400–401

control of conventionality (conventionality control), 143, 189
cooperation, 1, 3, 5–7, 9–10, 35, 77–85, 87–88, 90, 98, 111, 117, 150, 152, 204, 208, 215, 217–18, 220, 230, 242, 248, 336, 398, 400
corruption, 63, 65, 67, 286, 305–6, 383, 395
Costa Rica, 4, 12, 16, 33–34, 38, 53–54, 56, 58, 84, 86, 130, 133, 144, 185, 191, 206–7, 210–11, 214, 257–58, 260, 262–67, 280, 310–11, 313, 353, 403–4, 408
coronavirus pandemic, 359; COVID-19, 2, 15, 174, 268, 406, 412n3; COVID-19 pandemic, 13–14, 126, 145, 211, 260, 289, 307, 338, 359
credibility, 32, 359
crimes against humanity, 144
criminal groups, 304–6, 309
criminal investigations, 144
Cristosal, 308, 310
cross-application of human rights, 218
cross-border 304; dimension, 64; initiative, 108; movement, 125, 357
Cuban Revolution, 324
cultural 4–5, 98, 153, 208, 229, 263, 333, 347–48, 373; intercultural, 401; multiculturalism, 411; multiculturality, 210; sociocultural, 212
culture of impunity, 63
Curacao, 19n11, 404
current crisis of displacement, 11–12
Current Regional Refugees Crisis, 392

democracy, 4, 152
dependence, 216, 350
deportation, 131, 136–37, 144, 285, 297, 375
deprivation of nationality, 142, 184, 196
detention, 14–15, 101, 103, 127, 138–39, 142–43, 169, 171, 174, 211, 214, 231, 297, 315, 351, 406; non-detention, 134, 158
development, 3, 7, 15, 31–32, 34, 39–40, 42–43, 52, 56–58, 63, 65–67, 78–83, 90, 97, 101, 103, 107, 109–10, 128–30, 135, 139, 143, 145, 152, 170, 173, 205, 212, 214–15, 217–18, 245, 249, 278, 295–96, 308, 310, 324, 327, 347, 354, 361, 398, 401, 402
dictatorships, 211; military, 254
diplomatic channels, 32; efforts, 34; language, 37; protection, 139
disappearance, 65; forced disappearance, 130, 331, 342n26
disarmament, 335, 338; process, 325
disaster, 53, 63, 66, 369–70, 372–73, 375–77 381–85; natural disasters, 126, 280, 284, 308, 370–71, 374–76, 378–80, 382, 385
discretionary, 6, 87, 154, 261, 268
discrimination 4, 8, 65, 127, 140–41, 143, 194, 212, 298, 354, 360, 405; gender, 186, 188; nondiscrimination, 106, 157–58, 161, 190, 213–14, 262, 288, 405–6; racial, 379, 398; *See also* racism, xenophobia
discriminatory reasons, 190; rhetoric, 358; treatment, 157
displaced persons, 12, 55, 57–59, 83, 106, 118, 156, 219–20, 231, 329, 331, 372, 399; environmentally, 13; forced, 204, 210, 219; in need of protection, 80; internally, 55, 57–58, 78, 81, 118–19, 126, 129, 151, 229, 372; protection of, 313
displacement, 2–3, 8, 11–14, 17, 84, 104, 107–8, 110, 118, 213, 217, 219, 220, 229, 267–68, 277, 303–6, 310–11, 315, 332, 369–70, 382, 385, 393–94, 397–98, 400, 402; crises, 13, 58, 68, 110, 267–68, 311, 402; environmental, 395; forced, 79, 96, 102, 106, 108, 133, 184, 206–7, 210–11, 218–19, 231, 246, 260, 278, 304, 312, 327, 330, 336–37, 371, 395, 397; internal, 52–56, 58–69, 118–19, 307–9, 311–14, 316, 395; nondisplacement, 265; transnational, 373; *See also* displacement in Colombia; Venezuelan displacement

diversity, 101, 213–15, 219, 369; ethnic, 333; gender-age-diversity, 183, 192, 210; regional, 334 *See also* cultural and discrimination
Doctors Without Borders, 308
domestic law, 40, 131, 142, 185, 189, 190, 192, 194, 262, 298
Dominican Republic, 33, 54, 86, 133, 139, 141–42, 210, 216, 259–60, 262–66, 372, 404–6
drug trafficking, 58, 329
dual jurisdictional role, 153, 160
due process, 102, 104, 131, 134, 137, 141, 143, 151, 157–58, 169, 193, 218, 288, 405, 407
durable solutions, 53, 60, 63, 64–5, 77, 79, 80, 82–83, 85, 87–88, 90, 106, 117–18, 208, 212, 214–16, 218–19, 229, 279, 284, 307, 309, 314, 316, 347, 384, 401

economic, 5, 15–16, 33, 58, 64–67, 80, 107, 110, 127, 153, 158, 204, 208, 210, 212–13, 216–17, 229, 238, 241–43, 249, 263, 277, 281, 295, 335, 347, 369, 373; cooperation, 248; crisis, 246, 288, 350, 357, 377; dependence, 350; elites, 334; socioeconomic, 65, 67, 82, 212, 257, 267, 269, 277, 284, 327, 358, 401
Ecuador, 4, 13, 16, 54, 79, 80, 86, 133, 143, 158, 185, 191, 207, 210, 210–11, 240, 247, 257, 258, 260, 262–63, 265, 267, 276, 280, 285–86, 295, 346, 348–49, 351–53, 372, 374–76, 384, 393, 400, 403–5, 409; humanitarian visas, 278, 281, 283; immigration law, 266; Venezuelan migrants, 287, 289, 346
education, 98, 153, 214–15, 230, 242, 247, 257, 264, 266–67, 279, 282, 286, 295, 298, 305–9, 312, 351, 354, 360, 373, 383–84
effectiveness, 145, 260, 295, 331, 397
efficient, 192, 393; procedure for determining statelessness, 192; procedure for the determination of refugee status, 134; response to displacement, 310
El Salvador, 2, 4, 12, 34, 38, 54, 56, 61, 62, 63, 89, 133, 206–7, 210, 214, 258, 261–63, 266–67, 305, 308, 310, 403–4, 409; agreements, 325; civil society, 312, 314; displacement, 64, 303, 311, 393; extrajudicial executions, 306; IDPs, 66, 307, 316; immigration law, 265; national peace agreements, 58
elimination, 330; of the irregular status of the citizens, 239, 241; of irregularity and illegal employment, 242; of vulnerabilities, 333
emergency, 55–56, 66, 135, 266, 327, 330–31, 333, 347, 358, 360, 361–62, 393, 398, 401
emigration, 67, 238, 244, 248–49
employment, 80, 307–9, 351, 360, 379, 409; illegal, 242; mobility, 361; opportunities, 279; unemployment, 67; wage-earning, 265–65
encompass, 12, 35–36, 40, 44, 80, 151, 154–55, 211, 261–62, 281, 327, 333, 403
environment, 14, 41, 53, 66–67, 104, 126, 277, 284, 306, 334, 347, 351, 359, 370, 377, 380, 383, 393–5, 397–98
environmentally displaced persons, 13
equality, 105, 157, 190, 242, 401, 405; inequality, 65–66, 126, 305, 398
equitable responsibility, 204
ethnically-distinct peoples, 333
EU (European Union), 237, 257, 299n1
Europe, 40, 108, 165n1, 257, 277, 349
European Court of Human Rights, 161
ExCom: UNHCR Executive Committee, 35, 37, 39, 40–41, 47n15, 47n20
executive power, 248, 330
exile, 1, 326
exodus, 393; caused by disasters, 375; of Cubans, 33; of Haitians, 370–72, 381–85, 395; of Venezuelans, 237, 239–40, 246, 346, 350–51, 392, 394, 400; transnational, 370, 380

expanded definition, 118, 120, 156, 211, 382, 387n26, 398
expectations, 89, 103, 245, 311, 313, 361
exposing human rights abuse, 172-73
expulsion, 131, 134, 136-38, 264, 392
extradition, 159, 262
extrajudicial executions, 130, 306
extraregional Palestinian program, 88
extraterritorial, 137; application, 134; control, 128
extreme, 309, 314, 395; events, 277; need of protection, 313; vulnerability, 285-86, 350, 380; weather events, 66

family, 132, 159-60, 162, 195, 242, 262, 267, 287, 307, 330, 375; break down, 67; protection, 14; reunification, 63-64, 230, 242, 262, 263, 279, 288, 361, 379, 395; right to, 158; separated from, 190; unity, 164, 214, 262
Federal Emergency Assistance Committee for the social emergency reception of Venezuelans, 360
feminicide, 306
forced immobility, 2
forced migration, 32, 34, 59, 103, 126, 129, 151, 210, 277, 393; governance, 208; legal framework, 394-95; movements, 32, 40, 43, 45; of women and girls, 213; recognition, 65; responses, 151, 281; Venezuelan people, 133, 284; *See also* migration
forced recruitment, 67; of children, 65; of minors, 330
forced transfer of population, 144
foreign aggression, 7, 38, 98, 132, 155, 262, 352, 356, 370
foreign policy, 186, 242, 246, 248, 359
freedom of movement, 60, 110, 131, 159, 238, 260, 280; restrictions on, 67, 126
French Guyana, 4, 19n9, 45n1
funding, 57, 88-89, 204, 206, 212, 215, 217-18, 231, 304, 310, 312, 315-16

gender, 14, 86, 101, 118, 138, 173, 183, 186, 192, 213, 215, 219, 401; gender-based-violence, 12, 63, 105-6, 213, 305, 308; transgender and intersex, 14, 105, 126, 213
General Assembly (OAS), 36-37, 39, 55, 58, 153, 181, 184-85, 187
generalized insecurity, 63
generalized violations of human rights, 208
generalized violence, 7, 38, 98, 144, 155, 158, 262, 268, 277, 306, 327, 356, 370, 385, 394; generalized, 127
geographical limitations, 87
geography of protection, 230
Global Compact for Safe, Orderly and Regular Migration, 18, 150, 205, 220, 221, 228, 359, 394
Global Compact on Refugees, 2-3, 17-18, 82, 101, 106, 108, 150-51, 197, 203, 221, 228, 311-12, 316
global migration governance, 288
Global Refugee Forum, 215, 219
global scale, 204, 229
goals, 83, 101, 109, 182, 197, 204, 206, 219, 295, 360
good practices in refugee protection, 2, 17, 82, 91, 101, 203, 211, 217, 219, 407-11
Group of Latin America and Caribbean Countries, 187
guarantees of non-repetition, 142
Guatemala, 2, 4; children, 214; displacement, 12, 61, 63, 65-66, 303, 307-8, 311-13, 316, 393; humanitarian visas, 280; legislation, 58, 259-64, 266-67, 403-4, 409; peace agreement, 54, 58; political repression, 306; protection, 207; refugee, 133, 206, 210; reintegration, 57; SJD, 54; violence, 65, 315; women's right, 213
Guatemalan-Mexican border, 315
guerrilla, 58, 324, 330, 332; FARC guerrillas, 325-27, 334, 338-39
guidelines (UNHCR), 192
Guyana, 4, 14, 207, 210, 246, 404

Haiti, 372; asylum, 33; brutality, 136; displacement, 2, 13, 210, 232,

288, 373–85, 399; exodus, 370–72, 392, 395; humanitarian visa, 281; interdiction, 171–72; migratory movement, 362; military repression, 58; refugee and migration legislation, 259–60, 267, 404–5, 407; responses, 359, 373–85; statelessness, 141–42; voluntary pledges, 185
Hathaway, 135, 277
health care, 85, 98, 127, 247, 257, 264, 266–67, 282, 295, 307–8, 351, 360
homicide, 63, 306, 330–31
Honduran Human Rights Commission, 310
Honduras, 4, 33, 38, 54, 56, 65, 206–7, 306, 308, 311; asylum, 210; commitments, 312; humanitarian response, 310; humanitarian visas, 280; internal displacement, 63, 307; migratory flows, 392–93; protection, 305–6, 313; refugee and migration legislation, 259–60, 263, 265–67, 313, 316, 403–4, 409; refugee camps, 56; refugee children, 214; refugee definition, 133; voluntary pledges, 185
host States, 163, 212, 229, 242, 245
human mobility, 103, 150, 219, 239–40, 247, 268, 281, 283, 294–95, 297–99, 369, 385
human rights, 2, 4, 10, 37, 58, 60, 62–63, 65, 97, 100, 102–11, 117, 120, 126, 130, 150, 152–53, 161, 169–70, 172, 174, 181, 190–92, 197, 205, 210–11, 218, 229–31, 242, 245, 249, 263, 298–99, 308, 330, 355, 357, 359; approach, 17, 198, 378; law, 61, 69, 119, 129, 131, 134–35, 139, 143, 279; protection, 77, 160, 173, 194, 257, 279, 353; violation, 7, 12, 15, 34, 36, 38, 57, 67, 82, 98, 118, 132–34, 142–45, 155, 158, 171, 208, 262, 268, 277, 280–81, 305, 309, 316, 323, 327, 331, 333, 338, 352, 356, 358, 370, 378, 383
human trafficking, 212, 284, 288, 374
humanism, 82

humanitarian, 32, 41, 51, 56–57, 59, 83, 182, 217, 376; action, 90; actors, 304, 316, 327; admission programs, 279, 284; agenda, 53, 68, 119; assistance, 55, 66, 69, 98, 206, 330–31, 333–34, 350, 401; crisis, 63, 79, 155, 356, 361, 395; emergency, 55; governance, 400; help, 247; initiatives, 13; migration, 212; needs, 37, 80, 287, 304, 306, 310, 332, 398; organizations, 215, 307–9, 313; policy, 400; principles, 60; problem, 184, 197; protection, 14, 131, 191, 218, 228; reasons, 280; reception, 359, 362; residency permits, 212, 279, 281, 284, 378; responses, 232, 308, 310, 381, 398; solutions, 204; spirit, 208; support, 229; visas, 8, 127, 206, 276–89, 294, 296–97, 299, 374–80, 385, 395, 399, 403, 407–11
humanitarianism, 10

IACHtHR Advisory Opinion 16/99 (OC 16), 157, 405
IACHtHR Advisory Opinion 18/03 (OC 18), 157, 405
IACHtHR Advisory Opinion 21/14 (OC 21), 133, 157, 163, 191–92, 405
IACHtHR Advisory Opinion 25/18 (OC 25), 133, 158, 405
IASC: Inter-Agency Standing Committee, 56, 62
identity, 84, 191, 195, 211, 239, 241, 246, 249, 285; documents, 106, 143, 193, 195, 261, 264, 266, 285; gender law, 213
ideological dichotomy, 325; orientation, 243
ILO (International Labor Organization), 262, 299
immigration, 357, 374, 393–94; categories, 375; control, 127, 285; detention, 127, 143; issues, 358; legislation, 143, 256–61, 263–68, 276, 279, 284, 288, 298, 359, 377–80, 384, 406; policies, 171, 283, 376
imperialism, 229

impunity, 63, 65, 67, 143–45, 305–6, 338–39
inclusion, 4, 10, 53, 60, 68, 81, 86–87, 99, 100–103, 105, 108, 110, 119–20, 185–86, 212, 215, 334
independence, 230; process, 1
indigenous population, 86; communities, 326, 333, 348; leaders, 306; people, 105, 126–27, 183, 333; right, 333
indiscriminate bombing, 34
individual identity, 195
individuals in need of international protection, 279
information, 57, 69, 81, 89, 91, 103, 138, 141, 157, 215, 247, 287, 312, 331, 348, 361, 377, 400, 403
innovative actions, 2
insecurity, 63–64, 66–7, 281, 309, 375–76, 393; food, 66–67, 126, 307; health, 246; *See also* security
institutional innovations, 68, 398
institutions, 9, 10, 33, 44, 56, 66, 69, 81, 100, 104, 107, 117, 172–73, 206, 216, 240, 313, 330, 332, 335, 372, 374, 383, 395, 399
integration, 2–4, 8, 12, 15, 57, 80, 85, 87, 97, 99, 102, 104, 106–7, 117, 212, 216, 218–20, 238–40, 242–46, 248–49, 257, 264, 267, 284, 295, 335, 347, 361–62, 394–95, 397–99, 401
Inter-American Commission on Human Rights (IACmHR), 11, 17, 33, 36–37, 54, 56–58, 61, 64, 69, 126–27, 129–37, 139–45, 151, 153, 155–56, 163, 170–73, 181, 197–98
Inter-American Convention to Prevent and Punish Torture, 135
Inter-American Court of Human Rights (IACtHR), 11, 41, 108, 129–45, 150–64, 170, 172–74, 181, 189–96, 198, 352, 383
Inter-American Human Rights System (IAHRS), 128–31, 133–35, 139–45, 151–52, 154, 161, 169–73, 403, 405
Inter-American Institute of Human Rights, 57–59

Inter-American Judicial Committee, 185
Inter-American Principles on the Human Rights of All Migrants, Refugees, Stateless Persons and Victims of Human Trafficking, 145
interdisciplinary analysis, 16; approach, 3, 15, 276, 347
intergovernmental, 57, 96, 108, 111, 173, 182
interiorization, 8, 361; interiorização, 361–62
internalization of border control, 289
Internally Displaced Persons (IDPs), 2, 52–64, 66, 69, 81, 118, 306–7, 309, 312, 316, 324, 327, 329–30, 336
International Committee of the Red Cross, 55, 57, 69, 308, 337
International Conference on Central American Refugees (CIREFCA), 206, 382, 55
international cooperation, 10, 111, 150, 215
international criminal law, 143–45
International Human Rights Law, 2, 33, 59, 61, 69, 103, 129, 131, 134–35, 139, 143, 145, 152, 155, 157, 160–61, 205, 210, 298
International Humanitarian Law, 2, 6, 59, 61, 103, 119–20, 131, 155, 161, 210, 231, 327, 336
international law, 33, 42, 58–60, 79, 117, 119, 125, 131, 133–34, 136, 138, 145, 171, 187–89, 194, 196, 204, 210, 230
International Monetary Fund, 59, 246
International Refugee Law, 2, 31–32, 42, 59, 61, 79, 103, 119, 131–32, 134, 143, 145, 152, 155, 161, 203–4, 210, 213, 217, 230
international refugee protection, 79, 116–17, 214
international regimes on refugee protection, 11, 17, 118, 228, 276
International Relations, 44, 78, 118, 140, 204, 239, 347
interrelationship within international law, 143, 145

intersectional interpretation, 298; phenomenon, 126, 144
intra-regional mobility, 241; movement, 240
IOM (International Organization for Migration), 10, 57, 62, 231, 245, 247, 286, 353, 360-61
irregular entry, 134, 407-11
irregularity, 242-43, 248-49, 299

Jamaica, 19n11, 198n1, 404
job, 85, 215, 217, 265, 373, 378, 383; *See also* employment
John Doe v. Canada, 131, 135, 137, 407
judicial function, 143
judicial guarantees, 136-37, 159, 162, 405
jurisprudence, 53-54, 58, 61, 68, 103, 108-9, 119, 129, 132, 137, 139, 142-44, 151-52, 154-57, 161, 181, 189, 193-95
jus cogens, 102, 151, 161, 163-64, 298

kidnappings, 65, 306
knowledge, 78-79, 81, 97, 232, 243, 248, 362, 382

labor, 67, 106, 157, 240, 260, 265, 267, 295, 299, 355; market, 244, 247, 264, 355
language, 37, 59, 82-83, 102, 158, 182, 218, 333, 348
Latin American tradition of asylum, 7, 44, 143
Latin Americanist rhetoric, 246, 248
leftist party, 325
legal clinics, 173; framework, 187, 192-93, 204, 313, 316, 323, 392, 394, 403; recognition, 102, 314; residence, 157, 281, 288-89; status, 33-34, 39-40, 55, 102, 238-39, 244, 278-79, 354, 378, 400; systems, 330, 375, 399
legalization, 213
legislative gaps, 140; good practices, 257, 282; liberalization, 257, 280; liberalization of refugee protection, 268; reforms, 256

legitimacy, 39, 99, 110; of the BPA, 101-2; of the IAHRS, 171; of UNHCR, 32
LGBTI+ (lesbian, gay, bisexual, transgender and intersex, plus other sexual and gender orientations and identities), 14, 66, 105, 126, 213-14
limitations, 8, 78, 83, 87, 91, 97, 99, 107, 169-70, 173, 245, 256, 265-66, 296, 336, 395
local integration, 80, 85, 106, 212, 216, 218-19, 347, 361-62
lockdown, 126, 338

mainstreaming of international displacement issues, 59
management, 308, 360, 362, 399; of migration, 8, 81, 289; of natural resources, 215; of policies, 327; of registration systems, 219; of special needs, 208, 213, 229; of systems, 352
manifestation, 80, 87, 246, 350
Marco Integral Regional de Protección y Soluciones (MIRPS; Comprehensive Regional Protection and Solutions Framework), 12, 304-5, 311-16
marginalized groups, 104-6; persons, 102; population, 277
Marxism, 325
mass violation of human rights, 327, 338
massive violation of human rights, 7, 38, 98, 155, 262, 268, 352, 356, 370
MERCOSUR (Southern Common Market), 9, 17, 80, 108, 186, 212, 237-38, 241-45, 280-81, 294-97, 299, 352
MERCOSUR Residence Agreement, 281, 294-97
methods, 104, 156, 278, 315
Mexico, 4, 7, 12; asylum tradition, 33, 313, 315; disasters, 63; humanitarian assistance, 206-7, 212; migrant caravans, 125; migrant children, 214; migratory crisis, 353, 373, 375, 382; policy, 173; protection, 280, 307, 372; refugee, 41, 107, 133, 157, 210;

refugee and immigration legislation, 257, 259, 261–64, 266–68, 384, 403–5, 410; refugee camps, 56; RSD, 211; SJD, 54; statelessness, 186; *See also* Mexico Plan of Action

Mexico Declaration and Plan of Action (MPA [2004]), 7, 43, 62, 77–91, 99–111, 116–20, 183, 207–18, 362, 382, 401, 404

Middle East, 109, 228, 230

middle-class militants, 325

migrant caravans, 125, 315

migration, 2, 8, 10, 13, 31, 67, 136, 142, 144, 158, 205, 208, 210, 212, 230, 239–40, 245, 247–49, 287–88, 294, 308, 369–70, 373, 385, 399, 401; control, 127, 285, 297; criminalize, 315; crisis, 125, 127; detention, 15, 127, 143; governance, 78, 87, 203–4, 220, 238–41, 282, 285, 295–97, 299; human rights, 103, 110; humanitarian, 212; in the context of humanitarian crisis, 277, 348–62; irregular, 60, 127, 150, 295, 297, 349; law, 239, 245–46, 258–60, 263–68, 280, 288, 295, 370, 405, 407–11; legal, 218; management, 81, 289; mixed, 183, 219, 278; policy, 142, 239, 248, 283, 285, 297, 299; politicization, 14; regular, 183, 297, 313; regulation, 145; response, 104; rights, 246; status, 106; subregional, 103; transnational, 374; Venezuelan, 133, 238, 249, 281, 284, 296, 348–62, 393–95

Migration and Refugee Laws, 257, 279; in Latin America, 258–59

migration governance, 78, 87, 203–4, 208, 220, 237–41, 249, 285, 288, 294–97, 299

migratory status, 140, 190, 238, 242–43, 284, 355

militarization, 67, 127, 289, 305, 401

Ministerial Intergovernmental Event on Refugees and Stateless Persons, 185

most favorable treatment, 262, 266

motivations, 88, 371

multiaxial integration, 248

multicausal and intersectional phenomenon, 144

multiculturality, 210

multidisciplinary, 53

multilateral, 9, 240, 247, 325, 370; cooperation, 398; negotiations, 241

multilevel architecture, 2; governance, 397

narco-trafficking, 306

narratives, 288, 296–97, 331, 339, 361

National Committee for Refugees (CONARE), 356, 358

national regimes, 11, 17; regulations, 242, 393; resettlement program, 89; responses, 11, 17, 347, 359

nationality principle, 241

nationalization process for refugees, 261

natural disasters, 126, 280, 308, 370–71, 374, 376, 378–79, 382, 385

naturalization, 87, 89, 106, 139, 185, 187, 193–96, 219

necessity, 139, 171, 357

negotiation, 5, 152, 182, 186, 205, 216–17, 220, 238–44, 295, 311, 323, 325, 334, 337

network, 54, 79, 215, 231, 286, 305, 307–8, 310, 314, 316, 327, 349, 374, 376, 400

2016 New York Declaration on Refugees and Migrants, 150, 203, 228, 230

NGOs (nongovernmental organizations), 57, 62, 66, 78, 170–74, 304–5, 308, 310, 355

Nicaragua, 4; armed conflicts, 58; asylum, 33–34; displacement, 12, 58; legislation, 86, 259, 261–63, 265–67, 280, 403–5, 410; refugee; 38, 56, 133, 210, 257; statelessness, 186; violence, 144; vulnerability, 67

1988 International Conference on the Plight of Refugees, Returnees, and Displaced Persons in Southern Africa, 55

1985 OAS General Assembly resolution on "Legal Status of Asylees,

Refugees, and Displaced Persons in the American Hemisphere", 39, 55
1989 Convention on the Rights of the Child, 190, 195, 298
1981 Mexico Colloquium (colloquium on "Asylum and International Protection of Refugees in Latin America"), 36–39, 41
1983 La Paz Seminar (seminar "Political Asylum and the Refugee Situation"), 38
1954 Caracas Conventions on Territorial and Diplomatic Asylum, 33
1954 Convention on Diplomatic Asylum, 154, 185, 188, 191, 193–94, 399
1954 Convention on Territorial Asylum, 154
1951 Convention Relating to the Status of Refugees (1951 Refugee Convention), 2, 7, 10, 38, 54, 96, 117, 132, 134–35, 151, 170, 182, 205, 210, 228–30, 260, 276, 298, 356, 370
1948 American Declaration on the Rights and Duties of Man (American Declaration), 54, 130–31, 133–34, 136–39, 152, 154–56, 159, 161–62, 164, 170–71, 191
1990 Convention for the Protection of the Rights of All Migrant Workers and Members of Their Families, 205, 298, 359
1995 *Report on the Situation of Human Rights in Haiti*, 173
1994 San Jose Declaration on Refugees and Displaced Persons, 7, 43, 52–54, 58, 105, 116, 183, 207, 382, 404
1979 Convention on the Elimination of All Forms of Discrimination Against Women (CEDAW), 188, 298
1969 American Convention on Human Rights (ACHR), 33, 54, 130, 151, 170, 188
1969 Inter-American Specialized Conference on Human Rights, 130, 153
1969 Organization of African Unity Refugee Convention (1969 OAU Refugee Convention), 32, 108, 118, 229, 277
1967 Protocol Relating to the Status of Refugees (1967 Protocol), 205, 210, 228–30, 260, 276, 381
1966 Draft Convention on Refugees proposed by the Comité Jurídico Interamericano, 33
1939 Montevideo Convention on Asylum and Political Refuge, 154
1933 Montevideo Convention on Political Asylum, 154
1928 Havana Convention on Asylum, 154
non criminalization, 403, 407–11
non-refoulement, 14, 34, 102–3, 118, 131–32, 134–37, 151, 155–56, 158–59, 161, 163–64, 171, 210–11, 218–19, 231, 262, 264, 279–80, 316, 406
non-refugee, 110, 192
non-state actors, 6, 102, 126, 304, 376
norm development, 7, 83
North America, 232
North America expansionist endeavor, 4
North of Central America (NCA), 2, 63, 104, 206, 267, 303, 394
Norwegian Refugee Council, 100, 308

OAS Member States, 130, 132, 160, 170
OAU (Organization of African Unity), 32, 108–9, 229, 277, 327
obstacles, 63, 120, 155, 286, 358, 400
omissions, 55, 140
Operation Acolhida, 360, 394
Organization of American States (OAS), 36–37, 39, 55, 58, 61, 69, 129–30, 132, 145, 152–53, 160, 170–71, 198, 324, 348, 353, 355
orientialism, 229–30, 232
overdependence, 77

Pacheco Tineo Family v. Plurinational State of Bolivia (2013), 132, 137, 151, 159, 162–64, 406
Palestinian refugees, 89

Panama, 4, 7; asylum, 313; displacement, 206, 311; humanitarian visas, 280, 283, 393; legislation, 259–63, 265–66, 403–4, 406, 410; migratory crisis, 353; protection, 372; refugee regime, 34, 38, 79, 86, 133; RSD, 211; statelessness, 186, 191; Venezuelan, 352; work, 351; *See also* Velez Loor v. Panama

Panama renewable residence permit, 263

Pan-American Conference, 324–25

pandemic, 3, 15

pandemic-related border closures, 172

Paraguay, 4; legislation, 259, 261–63, 265–66, 403–5, 410; migratory crisis, 353; policy, 240; protection, 33; refugee regime, 86, 88–89, 133, 210; statelessness, 191; voluntary pledges, 185

Participation, 37, 53, 59, 68, 86, 100–102, 105, 110, 119, 204, 217, 220, 312, 334–35, 339, 363, 399, 401

peace agreement, 2, 13, 54, 323–24, 334–39; culture, 309; process, 323–24, 329, 334–39, 392

peaceful coexistence, 215

Permanent Consultation on Internal Displacement in the Americas (CPDIA), 57

Permanent Consultative Group on Internally Displaced in the Americas, 60

permanent residence, 242, 264, 280, 359

persecution, 6–7, 12, 34, 63–64, 126, 133, 135, 137, 144, 154, 158–59, 163–64, 173, 184, 213, 229, 277, 309, 334, 356, 376, 381–82

personal liberty, 138, 158

persons in need of international protection, 80–81, 84, 125–31, 138, 143–44, 170, 211, 281

persons with disabilities, 14, 126–27, 183, 214

Peru, 4; conventionality control, 189; displacement, 61; Haitian, 374, 376, 384; humanitarian visa, 107, 276, 278, 280–89, 393; legislation, 58, 189, 259, 261–67, 403–4, 411; policy, 240; political asylum, 154; refugee protection, 9, 133, 207, 210; RSD, 211; statelessness, 139; temporary stay permit, 248; Venezuelan, 247, 283–89, 296, 346, 349, 351–53; Violence, 58, 159; voluntary pledges, 185

physical and social distancing measures, 126

planning, 57, 100

policies, 4, 8, 16, 32–33, 53–54, 62, 64, 66–68, 79, 81–82, 84–85, 87, 98, 106, 145, 170–71, 173, 183, 195, 205, 240–41, 245, 248, 283, 285, 288, 294, 296–99, 313–16, 324, 327, 347, 350, 359, 362, 370, 372, 395, 399, 401

policy instruments, 239, 248, 294

policymaking actors / processes, 239–40

political and economic elites, 334

political manifestation, 246; mobilization, 398; opinion, 6, 154, 159, 213; repression, 67–68, 306; science, 347

politicization of migration, 8, 14

politics of extraction, 229

postcolonial, 228, 230

post-hegemonic/post-neoliberal regionalism, 242, 245

poverty, 63, 65–67, 87, 126–27, 277, 305, 307–8, 335, 353, 383, 393, 395

power, 4–5, 8–9, 33, 65, 68, 101, 116, 129–30, 138–39, 153, 169, 208, 216, 220, 239, 241–42, 244, 248–49, 268, 305, 324, 326, 330, 334, 339, 348, 350, 371

priorities, 62, 205, 245–46, 304, 312

privatization, 217

pro persona principle, 152, 160–61

procedural remedies and guarantees, 142

procedures, 14–15, 86, 102–5, 131, 134, 137–38, 141–42, 158, 164, 185, 187, 191–94, 197, 207–8, 211, 214–15, 219, 245, 247, 262, 279, 295, 316, 331,

336, 354, 356, 360, 381, 395, 398, 400, 406–8
proportionality, 139
Prospects for International Migration Governance (MIGPROSP), 240
Protection Transfer Agreement, 312, 314, 316
Protection Transfer Arrangement, 206, 312
public policies, 79, 84–85, 145, 170, 289, 314, 362, 399, 401

qualitative analysis, 240; methods, 411
quantitative data, 278
quarantines, 126, 307

R4V Platform, 348
Racism, 14, 236; *See also* xenophobia
rape, 65, 173, 213, 306
Rapporteurship on Migrant Workers and Members of their Families, 69, 129, 132, 145
reasonableness, 139
recognition, 7, 34, 53, 60, 63, 65, 69, 81–83, 86, 102, 104, 111, 126, 132–33, 142, 163, 172, 184, 193, 217, 238, 261, 295, 298, 308, 312, 314, 335–36, 352, 356, 358–59, 377, 380, 384, 392, 394, 398
Red Crescent Societies, 55
REDLAC: Risk, Emergency and Disaster Working Group for Latin America and the Caribbean, 304–8, 310
refoulement, 102, 104, 131, 134–35, 298, 407
refugee camps, 56, 215; refugee crisis, 127; refugee legislation, 40, 86, 256, 260–62, 268; refugee movements, 15; refugee regime, 10, 13, 15–17, 32, 34, 81–82, 107, 117–19, 206, 210–11, 216, 229, 294, 397; refugee resettlement, 78; refugee status determination, 7, 79, 81, 84, 86, 98, 102, 119, 136–37, 151, 155, 162, 207, 260, 262, 296, 298, 315, 355–57, 400–401, 406, 408; refugee sub-regime, 34, 39

refugee-hosting countries, 99; refugee-hosting region, 96, 109
region's contrasts, 4
regional identity, 84, 241, 246, 249; integration, 237, 239–40, 242, 245–46, 248–49, 295; leadership, 88; policy, 237–38, 241; refugee protection regime, 5, 116–17, 231, 257; solidarity, 83, 87, 96, 99, 208, 212, 315
Regional Working Group of the Brazil Plan of Action (GAR-PAB), 101–2
regionalism, 5, 78, 81, 84, 98, 116, 239–40, 242, 245
regionalization, 5
regularization of the citizens, 241
relationship between the government and civil society, 100, 313
religion, 6, 154, 158–59, 213
repatriation, 215, 217–18, 379; involuntary, 407; voluntary, 118, 159, 184, 216, 236, 379, 406
requesting shelter, 395
resettlement, 34, 78–80, 83, 85–90, 118–20, 204, 212, 216, 231, 278–79, 312–16, 362, 399
residence permits, 142, 219, 241, 245–46, 249, 278, 280–83, 295, 351, 359, 378
responsibility, 54, 60, 63–65, 67–69, 97, 117, 119–20, 132, 144, 157, 191, 205–6, 211, 217, 248, 285, 304, 315–16; sharing, 1, 3, 5, 7, 12, 77–79, 82–83, 88, 90–91, 108, 117, 120, 150, 204, 207, 212, 215–16, 218, 279, 311–12, 314; to protect, 220
right; of asylum, 1, 6–7, 210, 297, 399, 403, 407–11; to a hearing, 172, 193; to ask and receive support, 63; to asylum, 137, 151, 154–55, 158–59, 164, 210, 297; to consular assistance, 143; to education, 266; to family protection, 14; to family reunification, 262, 288; to freedom, 135, 152; to fundamental due process, 169; to grant asylum, 117, 133–38, 151, 158–64, 192, 210; to healthcare, 266; to information, 157; to integrity,

134, 160, 405; to life, 134–35, 152, 405–6; to nationality, 139–42, 184, 187, 190–91, 194–98, 405; to non-discrimination, 288; to not to be subject to torture or detention, 14; to pacific protest, 335; to return, 327; to security, 136; to seek asylum, 86, 132, 137, 154, 161-62, 171, 316, 407; to work, 211, 264–65, 282, 284, 378, 403, 407–11
rights; access to, 2, 15, 89; as a refugee, 104; collective, 333; cultural, 80; economic, 80; for people on the move, 103, 109; labor, 106; of IDP's, 56, 61, 64; of persons in need of protection, 128–32, 143; of refugees, 2, 97, 107–8, 118, 261; principles, 60; social, 80; social benefits, 85; to judicial guarantee, 159; to refugees, 237; violations, 38; *See also* human rights
iolations, 38; *See also* human rights
risk, 56, 67, 85, 98, 103–6, 137, 158, 163, 190, 195, 213, 277, 297, 310, 314, 331, 347, 370
RSD (refugee status determination), 7, 14–15, 98, 101–7, 162–64, 207, 211, 219

safe country, 171
San José Action Statement, 305, 311–12
secondary, 78, 80, 97, 242, 267, 304–5, 378, 383, 385
security, 12, 60, 63–64, 67, 83, 134, 136, 152, 158, 208, 211, 215, 243–44, 262, 284–85, 288, 296, 299, 309, 333–35, 352, 356, 358, 362, 370, 383, 398, 401–2, 406
self-identification, 213
seriously disturbed public order, 7, 38, 98, 155, 262, 268, 356, 370, 383
service provision, 309
settlement, 143, 153, 333, 360, 393, 394, 399
social constructions, 208; hierarchies, 4; inclusion, 87; inequalities, 401

Social Science, 347
Social Work, 347
socioeconomic, 65, 67, 80, 82, 212, 257, 267, 277, 284, 327, 358, 401
soft law, 7, 54, 78, 90, 120, 171, 205, 216, 370, 380, 382–83
solidarity, 1, 7–8, 60, 77–80, 82–91, 99, 107, 117, 119–20, 126, 150, 208, 211–12, 216–18, 229, 231, 312, 315, 327, 372, 376
Solidarity Cities, 80, 85–86, 90
solution to irregularity, 243, 248
South America, 1, 4, 88–90, 228, 231, 238–41, 244–46, 248–49, 256, 294, 296, 346, 348–49, 351–53, 357, 372–74, 379–80
Southern Cone, 88
South-South, 7, 77, 80, 83, 208
specific obligations on states (IACtHR), 134, 137–38
spirit of Cartagena, 43, 45
sponsorship, 279
stakeholders, 78, 81, 88, 97, 99, 100, 103, 109, 119, 155–56, 182, 334, 360
standards, 5, 103–4, 130–31, 139, 144–45, 150–51, 153, 158, 160, 170–71, 187–89, 191, 196, 203, 210–11, 215, 257, 278–79, 295–97, 315, 333, 352, 355, 357
state-centric, 229
statelessness, 131, 139–41, 145, 170, 181–88, 190–98, 207, 210, 214–15, 227–29, 399
Statelessness Eradication Program, 182, 186
stereotyped narratives on migration, 294
strategic framework, 181, 185
structural barriers, 89; challenges, 401; changes, 313; dynamics, 400; factors, 65, 67; issues, 88, 305; measures, 142; patterns, 398; services, 80; shortcomings, 170; violence, 63, 67–68, 393
strategic use of resettlement, 86
Suriname, 4, 19n10, 91n3, 404

"survival migration", 277, 281
sustainable, 207, 212, 215, 218, 316, 339, 359, 362
Syrian refugee crisis, 127
systemic, 14–15, 67, 277
technology and digital procedures, 400
temporary; basis, 377; migratory regularization, 358; protection, 127, 279, 370, 380; reception, 361; refuge, 35, 40, 309, 381, 384; residence, 265, 276, 280, 375, 379, 400; residence permit, 242, 359, 380; residence status, 261, 263; stay, 248; suspension of involuntary returns, 374; visa, 264, 281, 378; work, 357
Territorial Committees of Transitional Justice, 332
territory, 36, 39, 131, 133, 135, 137, 140–41, 143, 154–55, 157, 159, 163, 190–91, 237, 241, 243, 247, 262, 276, 278, 280, 282, 284, 288, 332–33, 349, 353, 355–58, 360, 376–77, 394
terrorism, 159
terrorist, 34, 326
the 100 Points of Brasilia, 182, 196–98, 203–20, 228, 232
The Regional Conference on Migration or The South American Conference on Migration, 370, 380
theoretical, 10, 16, 204, 240, 377, 392
torture, 14, 135, 158, 173, 280, 306, 330, 348
transit countries, 3, 378, 384
transitional justice, 144, 337–38
transnational cases, 395
transsystemic approach, 156
trauma, 400
traumatic stories, 310
Trinidad and Tobago, 19n11, 198n1, 199n19, 404
Turks and Caicos, 19n11, 198n1, 373, 404
2014 Brazil Declaration and Plan of Action (BPA), 7, 62, 87, 96, 116, 181–82, 206, 382, 399, 404

2006 Convention on the Rights of Persons with Disabilities, 298
2010 Brasilia Declaration, 43, 182, 228

UN (United Nations), 54, 82, 133, 150, 204, 230, 326, 340
UN agencies, 85, 303, 361
UN Committee on the Elimination of Racial Discrimination, 333
UN Sustainable Development Goals, 231
uncertainty, 217
unconstitutional, 8, 141, 330
unemployment, 67; *See also* employment
UNGA (United Nations General Assembly), 31, 34, 55–56, 68, 108, 150–52, 204
UNHCR (United Nations High Commissioner for Refugees), 10, 32, 34–39, 41–45, 55, 57–59, 62, 77–78, 81–82, 84–86, 88–90, 96–98, 100–101, 110, 116–19, 126, 132, 137, 182–83, 186–87, 192, 196, 198, 205, 207, 216–17, 247–48, 256–57, 260, 279, 282, 305, 308, 310–15, 353, 358, 360, 383, 403
UNHCR Executive Committee (ExCom), 35, 37, 39–41
UNHCR Global Action Plan to End Statelessness, 187
UNHCR Resettlement Submission Categories, 279
uniaxial integration, 248
UNICEF (United Nations International Children's Emergency Fund), 55, 57, 246
Unión de Naciones Suramericanas (UNASUR; Union of South American Nations), 353
United Nations Office of Coordination of Humanitarian Affairs, 62, 308, 337
United States, 2, 4, 8, 12, 16, 65, 88, 125, 127, 136, 154, 170–74, 185–86, 267, 307, 314–15, 372–73, 407, 411
Universal Declaration of Human Rights, 154

universal system of refugee protection, 204, 220–21
urban, 339; areas, 229, 308, 397; centers, 79–80; communities, 305; context, 80; spaces, 399
urgent, 69, 79, 129, 174, 333, 394
Uruguay, 4; gender protection, 213; humanitarian assistance, 206–7; legislation, 86, 259, 261–66, 280, 403–5, 411; migratory crisis, 353; refugee protection, 133; resettlement, 8, 88–89, 237, 313–14; SJD, 54; statelessness, 191; Venezuelan, 238–40, 244, 246; voluntary pledges, 185
US-Mexican border, 303, 315

Velez Loor v. Panama, 138, 142, 406
Venezuela, 4; armed activity, 337; asylum tradition, 154, 296; Borders of Solidarity, 80; children, 189; displacement, 12, 79, 87, 91, 210, 265–69, 278–88, 399; exodus, 237, 239, 246, 346–63, 400; forced migration, 133, 210, 278, 393; humanitarian crisis, 155, 294–96, 346–63; humanitarian visas, 276, 286; legislation, 259–63, 265–69, 404, 411; refugee flows, 2, 9, 68, 86, 107, 125, 210, 232, 238–40, 247–49, 265–69, 278–88, 295–98, 346–63, 394; response, 377; SJD, 54; social crisis, 127, 238
victims, 45, 64, 82, 129, 142, 144, 172, 183, 212, 228, 280–81, 314, 323–24, 330–36, 338–39, 355, 371–73
violation complaints of, 153; danger of, 33; of existing norms, 14; of human rights, 7, 12, 34, 36, 38, 67, 82, 98, 118, 130, 132–33, 142–44, 155, 170–72, 208, 262, 268, 277, 280–81, 305, 309, 316, 323, 327, 331, 333, 338, 352, 356, 358, 370, 378, 383; of international human rights standards, 355; of international humanitarian law, 336; of multiple rights, 141; of the human right to a nationality, 184; of the right to security, 136; of the right to seek and receive asylum, 159
violence, 43–44, 52, 63, 65–69, 132, 144, 277, 307–10, 316, 324, 332, 347, 353, 358, 360, 371, 384, 401; against children, 213; against women and LGBTI+ persons, 213; Colombia, 324–39; criminal, 64, 67, 303–6, 308; domestic, 314; drug trafficking-related, 58, 105; gang, 107, 314, 316; gender-based, 12, 63, 105–6, 213, 305, 308; generalized, 7, 38, 98, 144, 155, 158, 262, 268, 277, 327, 356, 370, 385, 394; perpetrated by the security forces, 64; persecution, 12; physical, 361; political, 132, 306; sexual, 105, 306, 371, 383, 395; structural, 67–68, 393; wide spread, 352
voluntary, 61, 67, 237; act, 188; commitments, 188, 198; migration, 277, 373; nature of return, 60; pledges, 181, 185–86, 197, 310; *See also* repatriation
vulnerability, 297, 333, 347, 370, 376, 381, 401; age, 213; of displaced populations, 2; of migrants deprived of their liberty, 138; of statelessness persons, 140; overlapping vulnerabilities, 158, 163; preexisting, 383, 385; situations of, 126; to environmental factors, 67
vulnerable, 296, 298–99, 316, 347, 349–50, 372; asylum, 206; conditions, 284; groups, 105; migrants, 219, 276, 278–79, 285, 288; of Venezuelan forced migrants, 286, 289, 349–50, 360–61, 362, 377; pregnant women, 286; refugees, 214, 279, 288; to becoming involved in criminal activities as a survival strategy, 67; to displacement, 66; to forced recruitment, 67; to the deterioration of political will, 110

waiting, 136, 286–87
welfare, 98, 193, 350, 353

well-founded analysis, 296; fear for not wishing to return, 380; fear of being expelled from the country or separated from family, 190; fear of persecution, 6–7, 34, 133, 135, 154, 159, 164, 381

Western, 229, 230; countries, 31; Hemisphere, 172, 371; regimes, 229

women, 14, 66, 85, 106, 126–27, 140, 183, 188, 213–15, 280, 286, 306, 332, 371–72; Haitian, 173; migrants, 299; pregnant, 286–87, 350; refugees, 105

work, 34, 37, 43, 56, 60, 62, 66–67, 69, 82, 108, 174, 231–32, 308–10, 316, 332, 354–55, 375, 384; assistance, 33; authorization, 378; contract, 238; migrant workers, 157; opportunities, 245; permits, 375–76, 394; policy, 54; right to, 211, 257, 264–66, 282, 284, 378, 407–11; temporary, 357; visas, 281, 282, 315; workers, 157, 378; workers massacre, 323

Working Group to Address the Regional Crisis Caused by Venezuela's Migrant and Refugee Flows, 352

World Bank, 59

World Council of Churches and the Refugee Policy Group, 57

World Food Programme (WFP), 55, 57

World War II, 3, 9, 54, 229–30, 276

xenophobia, 8–9, 14, 97, 216, 269, 354, 360; *See also* discrimination, racism

xenophobic acts, 87; discourses, 248, 268; narratives, 361; sentiment, 282, 285

Yean and Bosico children v. Dominican Republic, 139, 140, 194

CPSIA information can be obtained
at www.ICGtesting.com
Printed in the USA
BVHW012043200921
617142BV00002B/18